# Growing Up America

# Growing Up American

Edited by

**Peter Nagourney**
**Susan Steiner**

Wadsworth Publishing Company, Inc.
Belmont, California

ISBN: 0–534–00087–8

L. C. Cat. Card No.: 70–178180

Printed in the United States of America

1  2  3  4  5  6  7  8  9  10—76  75  74  73  72

# Acknowledgments

Selections and excerpts in this book are reprinted from the following sources:

United States Declaration of Independence.

The Boy Scouts of America, from *Handbook for Boys,* published by the Boy Scouts of America. Reprinted by permission.

Elbridge S. Brooks, from *The True Story of George Washington,* Lothrop, Lee, and Shephard Co., 1895, pp. 11–38.

Benjamin Franklin, "Arriving at Moral Perfection," from *The Autobiography of Benjamin Franklin,* Houghton Mifflin Company, 1906, pp. 80–97.

Booker T. Washington, from *Up from Slavery,* Doubleday & Co., Inc., 1928.

Henry A. Shute, from *The Real Diary of a Real Boy,* Everett Press, 1902.

"Horatio Alger's Books," from Publisher's Preface.

Horatio Alger, Jr., "How Johnny Bought a Sewing Machine," from *Our Young Folks,* Vol. II, No. viii, pp. 482–487.

Alfred Kazin, from *A Walker in the City*. Copyright 1951 by Alfred Kazin. Reprinted by permission of Harcourt Brace Jovanovich, Inc.

Claude M. Fuess, "The Schoolboy's Code," from *The Atlantic,* September 1952, pp. 46–50. Reprinted by permission of John Fuess.

John F. Kennedy, "Inaugural Address."

Frederick Douglass, from *Narrative of the Life of Frederick Douglass,* 1845.

Jacob Riis, "The Problem of the Children," from *How the Other Half Lives* by Jacob Riis, Charles Scribner's Sons, 1890, pp. 134–140.

Millen Brand, "When You Spend a Dollar," from *New Masses,* October 25, 1938. Reprinted by permission of the publisher.

Jean Shepherd, "The Counterfeit Secret Circle Member Gets the Message, Or The Asp Strikes Again," from *In God We Trust All Others Pay Cash* by Jean Shepherd. Copyright © 1966 by Jean Shepherd. Reprinted by permission of Doubleday & Company, Inc.

Sherwood Anderson, "The Egg," from *The Triumph of the Egg* by Sherwood Anderson. Copyright 1921 by B. W. Heubsch, Inc. Copyright renewed 1948 by Eleanor C. Anderson. Reprinted by permission of Harold Ober Associates Incorporated.

Norman Podhoretz, "My Negro Problem—And Ours," from *Doings and Undoings* by Norman Podhoretz. Copyright © 1963 by Norman Podhoretz. Reprinted by permission of Farrar, Straus & Giroux, Inc.

Malcolm X, "Mascot," excerpt from *The Autobiography of Malcolm X,* pp. 23–38. Copyright © 1964 by Alex Haley and Malcolm X. Copyright © 1965 by Alex Haley and Betty Shabazz. Reprinted by permission of Grove Press, Inc.

M. Carl Holman, "The Afternoon of a Young Poet," from *Anger, And Beyond* edited by Herbert Hill. Copyright © 1966 by Herbert Hill. Reprinted by permission of Harper & Row, Publishers.

Jack London, "How I Became a Socialist," from *War of the Classes* by Jack London, The Macmillan Co., 1905.

Amado Muro, "Cecilia Rosas," from *New Mexico Quarterly,* Vol. XXXIV: 4. Copyright 1965 by the University of New Mexico Press. Reprinted by permission of the publisher and author.

Beatrice Griffith, from *American Me.* Copyright 1947 and 1948 by Beatrice Winston Griffith. Reprinted by permission of the publisher, Houghton Mifflin Company.

John Fante, "The Odyssey of a Wop," from *American Mercury,* Vol. XXX, September 1933, pp. 89–97. Reprinted by permission of the publisher.

F. Scott Fitzgerald, "Winter Dreams," (copyright 1922 Francis Scott Fitzgerald Lanahan; renewal copyright 1950) is reprinted by permission of Charles Scribner's Sons from *All the Sad Young Men* by F. Scott Fitzgerald.

James T. Farrell, "The Benefits of American Life," from *The Short Stories of James T. Farrell,* pp. 215–230. Copyright 1935, 1937, 1962, 1964 by James T. Farrell. Reprinted by permission of the publisher, The Vanguard Press.

Carey McWilliams, "Life in a Relocation Center," from *Prejudice: Japanese-Americans: Symbol of Racial Intolerance* by Carey McWilliams, Little, Brown & Co., 1944, pp. 206–215. Reprinted by permission of the author.

Rocky Marciano (with W. C. Heinz), "How It Feels to Be Champ," from *Collier's Magazine,* May 13, 1955. Copyright © 1955 by W. C. Heinz. Reprinted by permission of William Morris Agency, Inc.

Bill Libby, "A Different Kind of Hell," from *West* Magazine, in *Los Angeles Times,* July 18, 1971. Reprinted by permission of the author.

Debbie D'Amico, "To My White Working-Class Sisters," from *Up from Under,* August/September 1970, Vol. 1, No. 2. Reprinted by permission of the publisher and author.

Jay Neugeboren, "Luther," from *Corky's Brother* by Jay Neugeboren. Copyright © 1966, 1969 by Jay Neugeboren. Reprinted by permission of Farrar, Straus & Giroux, Inc.

Minnijean Brown (and J. Robert Moskin), "What They Did to Me in Little Rock," from *Look,* June 24, 1958. Reprinted by permission of the publisher.

Piri Thomas, "If You Ain't Got Heart, You Ain't Got Nada," from *Down These Mean Streets* by Piri Thomas. Copyright © 1967 by Piri Thomas. Reprinted by permission of Alfred A. Knopf, Inc.

Harvey Swados, "Joe, The Vanishing American," from *On the Line* by Harvey Swados, Little, Brown & Co., 1957. Reprinted by permission of the author.

A Princeton student, "So Here I Am," from *The Unsilent Generation* compiled and edited by Otto Butz. Copyright © 1958 by Otto Butz. Reprinted by permission of Holt, Rinehart and Winston, Inc.

Malcolm Wood, "What Really Matters," from *The Saturday Evening Post,* May 16, 1964. Copyright © 1964 by The Curtis Publishing Co. Reprinted by permission of John Schaffner, Literary Agent.

Leo Skir, "Other Chanukahs," from *Commentary,* March 1965. Copyright © 1965 by the American Jewish Committee. "Other Chanukahs" is part of the novel *Boychick,* which was published by Winter House, New York, in 1970. Reprinted by permission of *Commentary* and the author.

William Melvin Kelley, "The Ivy League Negro," from *Esquire,* August 1963. Copyright © 1963 by Esquire, Inc. Reprinted by permission of William Morris Agency, Inc.

John Clellon Holmes, "This Is the Beat Generation," from *Nothing More To Declare* by John Clellon Holmes. Copyright © 1967, 1966, 1965, 1964, 1963 by John Clellon Holmes. Published by E. P. Dutton & Co., Inc. and re-printed with permission. This article appeared originally in a somewhat different form in *The New York Times.*

Paul Goodman, "Patriotism," from *Growing Up Absurd* by Paul Goodman. Copyright © 1960 by Paul Goodman. Reprinted by permission of Random House, Inc.

Renata Adler, "Radicalism and the Skipped Generation," from *Toward a Radical Middle* by Renata Adler. Copyright © 1969 by Renata Adler. Reprinted by permission of Random House, Inc.

Roderick Thorp, "Chris," from pp. 1, 5, 6, 14–16, 36, 44–47, 58, 62 in *The Music of Their Laughter* by Roderick Thorp and Robert Blake. Copyright © 1970 by Roderick Thorp and Robert Blake. Reprinted by permission of Harper & Row, Publishers, Inc.

Ralph J. Gleason, "The Power of Non-Politics or the Death of the Square Left," from *Evergreen Review,* September 1967. Reprinted by permission of the author.

Jim Gardiner, "Growing Up Radical," from *The High School Revolutionaries* edited by Marc Libarle and Tom Seligson. Copyright © 1970 by Marc Libarle and Tom Seligson. Reprinted by permission of Random House, Inc.

Flannery O'Connor, from *Everything That Rises Must Converge.* Copyright © 1961, 1965, by The Estate of Mary Flannery O'Connor. Reprinted by permission of Farrar, Straus & Giroux, Inc.

Peter Collier, "The Red Man's Burden," from *Ramparts,* February 1970, Vol. 8, No. 8, pp. 27–35. Copyright 1970 by Ramparts Magazine, Inc. Reprinted by permission of the author.

Jean Smith, "I Learned to Feel Black," from *Redbook,* August 1967. Reprinted by permission of the author.

Connell Persicó, "Live and Let Live," from *To Make a Difference* by Otto Butz. Copyright © 1967 by Otto Butz. Reprinted by permission of Harper & Row, Publishers, Inc.

John Clayton, "I Am Staying Where I Am," from *The Antioch Review,* Spring 1970, Vol. XXX, No. 1, pp. 7–20. Reprinted by permission of the publisher.

Barry N. Schwartz, "Youth in the Technological Era," from *Midwest Quarterly,* April 1969, Vol. X, No. 3, pp. 215–225. Reprinted by permission of the publisher.

Russell Kirk, "You Can't Trust Perpetual Adolescents," from *Enemies of the Permanent Things* by Russell Kirk. Copyright © 1969 by Arlington House, New Rochelle, New York. All rights reserved.

President's Commission on Campus Unrest, "To the American People," September 26, 1970.

The epigraphs to Parts One, Two, Three, and Four are reprinted from the following sources:

Emma Lazarus, "The New Colossus."

Genevieve Taggard, "Ode in Time of Crisis" from *New Masses,* October 29, 1940. Reprinted by permission of the publisher.

Louis Simpson, "The Inner Part," Copyright © 1963 by Louis Simpson. Reprinted from *At the End of the Open Road* by Louis Simpson, by permission of Wesleyan University Press.

Gregory Corso, from "America Politica Historia, In Spontaniety" from *Elegiac Feelings American* by Gregory Corso. Copyright © 1970 by Gregory Corso. Reprinted by permission of New Directions Publishing Corporation.

# Preface

This collection of autobiography, fiction, essay, and primary material, deals in diverse ways with the unique and varied experiences of growing up in America. From whatever economic, social, and cultural background he may come, whatever geographical area and historical era, each writer makes his personal comment on the underlying themes of the book: the American myth of equal opportunity for all and the American dream of success.

The experiences in the first section are ultimately positive; the writers represented here have faced difficulties but remained faithful to their beliefs in America's opportunities. The material in the second section, extending from the nineteenth century to the 1950s, represents more practical, realistic, and often more pessimistic accounts of growing up in this country. The writers represented in the third section continue to question the dream and qualify their personal expectations, but they often mollify their disappointment by an acceptance and conformity peculiar to the 1950s. The final section of the book focuses on the youth of today and the multiplicity of their experiences, visions, and responses to all that America has promised.

The editors have chosen the selections on the basis of literary excellence and stylistic originality. The pieces do not conform to any single notion of "good writing"; they convey great stylistic variety, ranging from the formal rhetoric of a Presidential inaugural speech to the contemporary vernacular of a revolutionary youth. Each article, however, is an effective literary presentation of an important aspect of American experience.

The introductions to each section provide an historical context and a cultural overview, placing in perspective the individual experiences of each author. The arrangement of the selections is more or less chronological; however, the appendix offers other ways to organize and approach the same material.

# Contents

## Part Three: The Silent Generation: Growing Up in the 1950s    227

### Careful Dreamers: The 1950s Generation    228

## Part Four: Reclaiming the Myth: Growing Up Now    337

### Waking Struggles: Reclaiming America    338

# Part One

## Myths and Dreams of Growing Up American

Not like the brazen giant of Greek fame,
With conquering limbs astride from land to land;
Here at our sea-washed, sunset gates shall stand
A mighty woman with a torch, whose flame
Is the imprisoned lightning, and her name
Mother of Exiles. From her beacon-hand
Glows world-wide welcome; her mild eyes command
The air-bridged harbor that twin cities frame.
"Keep, ancient lands, your storied pomp!" cries she
With silent lips. "Give me your tired, your poor,
Your huddled masses yearning to breathe free,
The wretched refuse of your teeming shore.
Send these, the homeless, tempest-tost to me,
I lift my lamp beside the golden door!"

Emma Lazarus (1849–1887)

*The New Colossus*
(Selected to be inscribed at base of Statue of Liberty
in New York Harbor, 1886.)

## Glorious Dreams: America's Myth of Success

Before America was even known to the Western world there were dreams of Utopia: dreams of lands with political opportunities or religious freedoms, lands that would provide magnificent stores of food and wealth, lands in which to build ideal social structures, flawless systems of education, lands where the human soul and the human mind might be perfected. The discovery of America allowed any man to transfer his visions to the real new land; and since then adventurers, travelers, fugitives, entrepreneurs, idealists, opportunists and practical politicians have continued to dream their individual dreams in terms of America. The American Dream itself is both a sum of all these particulars and a sort of Platonic Ideal from which they emanate. It existed before individual dreams because the utopian longing existed before them; and it continues because America has proved to be a land where many of these dreams can come true.

The American Dream guarantees success to any man—whoever his parents are, however poor, however limited—if that man is virtuous, hardworking and industrious. He will become rich and happy because of the endless opportunities available to him. It must be remembered, however, that the Dream was never inherent in the land and never was America without poverty and social inequality or without critics to publicize these failings. But in the early years of the country's development intellectuals and politicians wanted to believe that a collective utopia was possible. The Founding Fathers, although hesitant about the workability of a pure democracy and distrusting the naked will of the majority, set up the only form of government under which the American Dream might in fact be realized. The Constitution they wrote guarded the rights of every man, not only in their basically agrarian society but, prophetically, for the more complex industrialized society to come.

The expanding economy provided occasion for almost unlimited development, attracting men who were eager to create their own business opportunities for financial rewards. Consequently, the basis for advancement changed from inherited wealth and status to individual talent and aggressiveness. By the time of Andrew Jackson the American Dream as we know it today had become the property and right of every man, and the common belief in it helped to unite the rapidly expanding nation. At this time also, adolescence became thought of as a unique stage in life, not merely the preparatory state before adult responsibilities. It was now possible for a young man to find his own place in society, unrestricted by the social and occupational position of his father; growing up could mean growing successful within the Dream.

For those who had not yet experienced America or whose experience had not yet been tarnished, the Dream remained pure. Even awareness that the myth might be superimposed upon the land could not destroy the reality and

2

potentials of the country's vast resources. Implicit in this magnificence, as Henry Steele Commager points out in *The American Mind,* are the land's defects but also its greatness.

> Nothing in history had ever succeeded like America, and every American knew it. Nowhere else on the globe had nature been at once so rich and so generous, and her riches were available to all who had the enterprise to take them and the good fortune to be white.

The psychic and physical resources developed by the American were shaped by the wealth and size of the land. He could move constantly because there was always more territory and newer opportunities; he cherished the freedom that enabled him to improve his well-being. His heroes were big, expansive men like Paul Bunyan and Sam Houston, inhabitants of wide open spaces where everything was done largely. Many of his pastimes were competitive sports which required great strength, skill and training. By the twentieth century outstanding athletes replaced frontier heroes in the popular imagination, and as athletics became more professional, enjoyment came to depend almost as much on the spectator's tabulation of statistics and new records as on the games themselves. All areas of American culture, moreover, were geared to the measurable: values were mainly materialistic; education, mainly practical; philosophy, mainly pragmatic. The Boy Scout Oath, *The True Story of George Washington,* and Benjamin Franklin's *Autobiography* exemplify this dedication to practicality, hard work and common sense. Even when the rural ambience of America had passed, and country heroes gave way to Horatio Alger's popular city successes or Andrew Carnegie's model rise as a business mogul, the modes for achievement remained the same. Determination and practicality persisted, although the innocence of the pastoral world was gone.

For a while, Americans seemed able to repress what was unattractive in themselves and to ignore those groups whose actions would destroy the public image of America or discredit the Dream. If there were shady dealings on the frontiers or corruption in the cities, for the most part social deviance was considered a sign of individual pathology, not social disease; and so much of everything remained for everyone that such behavior seemed not to matter. No television kept the people in mind of their evils; both the Dream and the dreaming could continue.

By the time of the Civil War, however, it was no longer possible to believe that America had fulfilled all the promises of her Dream. Whether one chooses to understand the Civil War as caused and continued by men with political motives or by men fighting for human rights and liberties, it certified the equality of the Negro and made it necessary for all Americans to extend to him at least the myth of the Dream, if not the Dream itself. For years after the war, *Up from Slavery,* Booker T. Washington's autobiography, served as a model for the Negro; although he was born into slavery, Washington was able to go to college and later to become president of the first Negro university in the South. Like an Horatio Alger hero he rose from nothing, and like his fellow white countrymen his moral precepts were traditionally American: he was honest, thrifty and hardworking.

For the young child, whose optimism recreates the faith of the founders, the Dream is always self-evident and true. The child is the most perfect of all utopian thinkers, for in his eyes all things are possible. There is a safe truth to fantasy, and anyone can do or become anything he chooses, from president of the country to heavyweight champion of the world. Like the early Americans, the child is free from responsibilities to the future. In the selection from Henry Shute's *The Real Diary of a Real Boy,* the real dangers of a fight, the real immorality of a lie, the real imminence of adulthood and death do not impinge on the child's daily life. There is here a freedom from anxiety as well as from the past and the future.

Young America attracted groups and individuals from the old world because of the freedoms we have already mentioned. Once men were here, the additional freedom from economic and geographical limitations, the lack of past cultural and social restraints, and the absence of future fears contributed to the possibility of grown men also pursuing dreams as reality rather than watching them fade before the obligations and restrictions of maturity. It is, therefore, not surprising to find American authors devoting long chapters in autobiographies to the formative years of childhood, and writers of fiction and nonfiction talking of growing up. Alfred Kazin's piece is set against a background of ghettos, racial discrimination, economic snobbishness and economic deprivation. His criticism of America, however, is only implicit. There are no recommendations for social change, no violent hostilities against outmoded forms of education, no disgust at prejudice; the answer to his background is personal and individual achievement. Kazin became a college teacher, writer and editor, proud of his middle-class family and their virtues, conscious of his role and success as the first-born American in his family.

Growing up American is a growing up of both the country and the people, a growing into problems but also into a realization of those problems in the hope of solving them. For some the earlier dream of a land of endless opportunity still exists. They have not yet understood the disenchantment of the young; they have not yet felt the cities closing in or envisioned problems for which there may be no solutions. They believe in all that was set forth in the Inaugural Address of John F. Kennedy—in the unity of men and nations, in the effectiveness of negotiation, and in the creative power of faith and devotion. And like Claude M. Fuess, in "The Schoolboy's Code," they believe in the integrity and constructive energy of youth.

Today, however, the great American Dream has spawned a great American Irony. Fewer and fewer young people believe any more in the dream of opportunity and success, and many adults who continue to believe in the dream have lost trust and faith in the young. The optimism and the riches which allowed imaginative development but also careless exploitation of natural resources, and the spirit which created American democracy but limited its benefits to whites only, have produced the ecological, political, social and moral problems we face today.

# United States Declaration of Independence

*In Congress, July 4, 1776*
*The unanimous Declaration of the thirteen*
*United States of America*

When in the course of human events, it becomes necessary for one people to dissolve the political bands which have connected them with another, and to assume among the powers of the earth, the separate and equal station to which the Laws of Nature and of Nature's God entitle them, a decent respect to the opinions of mankind requires that they should declare the causes which impel them to the separation.

We hold these truths to be self-evident, that all men are created equal, that they are endowed by their Creator with certain unalienable rights, that among these are life, liberty and the pursuit of happiness. That to secure these rights, governments are instituted among men, deriving their just powers from the consent of the governed. That whenever any form of government becomes destructive of these ends, it is the right of the people to alter or to abolish it, and to institute new government, laying its foundation on such principles and organizing its powers in such form, as to them shall seem most likely to effect their safety and happiness. Prudence, indeed, will dictate that governments long established should not be changed for light and transient causes; and accordingly all experience hath shown, that mankind are more disposed to suffer, while evils are sufferable, than to right themselves by abolishing the forms to which they are accustomed. But when a long train of abuses and usurpations, pursuing invariably the same object evinces a design to reduce them under absolute despotism, it is their right, it is their duty, to throw off such government, and to provide new guards for their future security. Such has been the patient sufferance of these Colonies; and such is now the necessity which constrains them to alter their former systems of government. The history of the present King of Great Britain is a history of repeated injuries and usurpations, all having in direct object the establishment of an absolute tyranny over these States. To prove this, let facts be submitted to a candid world.

He had refused his assent to laws, the most wholesome and necessary for the public good.

He has forbidden his Governors to pass laws of immediate and pressing importance, unless suspended in their operation till his assent should be obtained; and when so suspended, he has utterly neglected to attend to them.

He has refused to pass other laws for the accommodation of large districts of people, unless those people would relinquish the right of representation in the Legislature, a right inestimable to them and formidable to tyrants only.

He has called together legislative bodies at places unusual, uncomfortable, and distant from the depository of their public records, for the sole purpose of fatiguing them into compliance with his measures.

He has dissolved representative houses repeatedly, for opposing with manly firmness his invasions on the rights of the people.

He has refused for a long time, after such dissolutions, to cause others to be elected; whereby the legislative powers, incapable of annihilation, have returned to the people at large for their exercise; the State remaining in the meantime exposed to all the dangers of invasion from without and convulsions within.

He has endeavoured to prevent the population of these states; for that purpose obstructing the laws of naturalization of foreigners; refusing to pass others to encourage their migration hither, and raising the conditions of new appropriations of lands.

He has obstructed the administration of justice, by refusing his assent to laws for establishing judiciary powers.

He has made judges dependent on his will alone, for the tenure of their offices, and the amount and payment of their salaries.

He has erected a multitude of new offices, and sent hither swarms of officers to harass our people, and eat out their substance.

He has kept among us, in times of peace, standing armies without the consent of our legislatures.

He has affected to render the military independent of and superior to the civil power.

He has combined with others to subject us to a jurisdiction foreign to our constitution, and unacknowledged by our laws; giving his assent to their acts of pretended legislation:

For quartering large bodies of armed troops among us:

For protecting them, by a mock trial, from punishment for any murders which they should commit on the inhabitants of these States:

For cutting off our trade with all parts of the world:

For imposing taxes on us without our consent:

For depriving us in many cases, of the benefits of trial by jury:

For transporting us beyond seas to be tried for pretended offences:

For abolishing the free system of English laws in a neighbouring Province, establishing therein an arbitrary government, and enlarging its boundaries so as to render it at once an example and fit instrument for introducing the same absolute rule into these Colonies:

For taking away our Charters, abolishing our most valuable laws, and altering fundamentally the forms of our governments:

For suspending our own Legislatures, and declaring themselves invested with power to legislate for us in all cases whatsoever.

He has abdicated government here, by declaring us out of his protection and waging war against us.

He has plundered our seas, ravaged our coasts, burnt our towns, and destroyed the lives of our people.

He is at this time transporting large armies of foreign mercenaries to complete the works of death, desolation and tyranny, already begun with circumstances of cruelty and perfidy scarcely paralleled in the most barbarous ages, and totally unworthy the head of a civilized nation.

He has constrained our fellow citizens taken captive on the high seas to bear arms against their country, to become the executioners of their friends and brethren, or to fall themselves by their hands.

He has excited domestic insurrections amongst us, and has endeavoured to bring on the inhabitants of our frontiers, the merciless Indian savages, whose known rule of warfare, is an undistinguished destruction of all ages, sexes, and conditions.

In every stage of these oppressions we have petitioned for redress in the most humble terms: our repeated petitions have been answered only by repeated injury. A prince whose character is thus marked by every act which may define a tyrant is unfit to be the ruler of a free people.

Nor have we been wanting in attention to our British brethren. We have warned them from time to time of attempts by their legislature to extend an unwarrantable jurisdiction over us. We have reminded them of the circumstances of our emigration and settlement here. We have appealed to their native justice and magnanimity, and we have conjured them by the ties of our common kindred to disavow these usurpations, which would inevitably interrupt our connections and correspondence. They too have been deaf to the voice of justice and of consanguinity. We must, therefore, acquiesce in the necessity, which denounces our separation, and hold them, as we hold the rest of mankind, enemies in war, in peace friends.

We, therefore, the Representatives of the United States of America, in General Congress assembled, appealing to the Supreme Judge of the world for the rectitude of our intentions, do, in the name, and by authority of the good people of these Colonies, solemnly publish and declare, That these United Colonies are, and of right ought to be Free and Independent States; that they are absolved from all allegiance to the British Crown, and that all political connection between them and the State of Great Britain, is and ought to be totally dissolved; and that as Free and Independent States, they have full power to levy war, conclude peace, contract alliances, establish commerce, and to do all other acts and things which Independent States may of right do. And for the support of this declaration, with a firm reliance on the protection of Divine Providence, we mutually pledge to each other our lives, our fortunes, and our sacred honor.

## Handbook for Boys
## 1948

## The Boy Scouts of America

### The Scout Oath or Promise

ON MY HONOR I WILL DO MY BEST:
TO DO MY DUTY TO GOD AND MY COUNTRY, AND TO OBEY
THE SCOUT LAW;
TO HELP OTHER PEOPLE AT ALL TIMES;
TO KEEP MYSELF PHYSICALLY STRONG, MENTALLY AWAKE,
AND MORALLY STRAIGHT.

### The Scout Law

1. *A Scout Is Trustworthy:* A Scout's honor is to be trusted. If he were to violate his honor by telling a lie, or by cheating, or by not doing exactly a given task, when trusted on his honor, he may be directed to hand over his Scout Badge.

2. *A Scout Is Loyal:* He is loyal to all to whom loyalty is due, his Scout leader, his home, and parents and country.

3. *A Scout Is Helpful*: He must be prepared at any time to save life, help injured persons, and share the home duties. He must do at least one "Good Turn" to somebody every day.

4. *A Scout Is Friendly:* He is a friend to all and a brother to every other Scout.

5. *A Scout Is Courteous:* He is polite to all, especially to women, children, old people and the weak and helpless. He must not take pay for being helpful or courteous.

6. *A Scout Is Kind:* He is a friend to animals. He will not kill nor hurt any living creature needlessly, but will strive to save and protect all harmless life.

8

7. *A Scout Is Obedient:* He obeys his parents, Scoutmaster, Patrol Leader, and all other duly constituted authorities.

8. *A Scout Is Cheerful:* He smiles whenever he can. His obedience to orders is prompt and cheery. He never shirks nor grumbles at hardships.

9. *A Scout Is Thrifty:* He does not wantonly destroy property. He works faithfully, wastes nothing, and makes the best use of his opportunities. He saves his money so that he may pay his own way, be generous to those in need, and helpful to worthy objects. He may work for pay, but must not receive tips for courtesies or Good Turns.

10. *A Scout Is Brave:* He has the courage to face danger in spite of fear, and to stand up for the right against the coaxings of friends or the jeers or threats of enemies, and defeat does not down him.

11. *A Scout Is Clean*: He keeps clean in body and thought, stands for clean speech, clean sport, clean habits, and travels with a clean crowd.

12. *A Scout Is Reverent:* He is reverent toward God. He is faithful in his religious duties, and respects the convictions of others in matters of custom and religion.

## The True Story of
## George Washington
## Called the Father of His Country
## 1895

### Elbridge S. Brooks

#### Chapter I: A Boy of Virginia, and
#### How He Grew Up

I wish to write for young Americans the story of their noblest man. His name was George Washington. One hundred and sixty years and more ago he was a helpless baby in a pleasant Virginia home. That home was a low-roofed, big-beamed, comfortable-looking old farmhouse on a hill that sloped down to the Potomac, the beautiful river that separates the present States of Virginia and Maryland. One hundred and sixty years ago there were no States in America. All the land, from Maine to Georgia, belonged to England. King George the Second was its owner and master, and the thirteen colonies into which it was divided were ruled by men sent over from England by King George, and called royal governors.

The people who lived in these colonies were mostly Englishmen or the sons and daughters of Englishmen, except a few thousand Dutchmen in the colony of New York, who had been conquered by the English many years before, and were gradually becoming English in manners and speech.

The old farmhouse of which I speak overlooked the Potomac River, and the plantation to which it belonged was called Bridge's Creek, because, there, a little stream of that name flowed into the Potomac. All about it was farm-land or forest. There were then but few cities in America. New York and Boston and Philadelphia were the largest and almost the only real cities, and they were small enough when compared with the cities of to-day.

The colony of Virginia, however, was the richest and most populous of all the thirteen English colonies along the Atlantic. Its people were farmers; the richer ones owned great farms or plantations upon which they raised tobacco for the English market. The plantation of Augustine Washington at Bridge's Creek on the Potomac, was one of the large ones; it was in Westmoreland County, on the Virginia side of the Potomac, and not many miles from where the river empties into the Chesapeake Bay; the Washington plantation contained

10

a thousand acres, and stretched along the Potomac for fully a mile. The old house in which Augustine Washington and his wife Mary lived was built years before by his grandfather, the first of the Washingtons who came to America. It is said that the Washingtons came originally from a thatch-roofed sandstone house in the English village of Little Brington; but this is not clearly proved. It is enough to know that Grandfather John Washington came to Virginia in 1657 and built the house on Bridge's Creek. It was not a mansion. It was a plain, old-style Southern farmhouse, with steep, sloping roof and projecting eaves, with a broad piazza in front, a great chimney at either end, and just such a big, delightful attic as boys and girls love to play in, on days when the wind blows and whistles without, or the rain pours and patters on the roof.

It was to this old Virginia farm-house that Augustine Washington, in the year 1730, brought home his second wife, Mary Ball, of Lancaster County, Virginia; but whom, so it is said, he met and married in England. In the old house were two boys of seven and nine years; they were Lawrence and Augustine; their mother, their father's first wife, had been dead nearly two years, but their new mother became almost like an own mother to them.

In this old farmhouse at Bridge's Creek, the eldest son of Augustine and Mary Washington was born on the twenty-second of February, 1732. They named him George. What with his two half-brothers, Lawrence and Augustine, and his own brothers and sisters who were born after him, George Washington had plenty of company in his home. He never remembered the house in which he was born, however; for in 1735 some sparks from a bonfire set it in flames and it was burned to the ground.

Not a stick nor a stone of that old house remains to-day; but it has been a famous spot for many a year. In 1815, a memorial stone was placed on the spot where the house once stood, and on the stone were these words:

*Here, on the eleventh of February, 1732, George Washington was born.*

What is called the "old style" of reckoning time was used in those days, and the eleventh of February was in 1732, the same as the twenty-second of February to us; therefore, under our modern way of reckoning time the birthday of George Washington was the twenty-second of February—the day that we celebrate as a National holiday.

When his house at Bridge's Creek was thus destroyed, Augustine Washington moved into another farmhouse that belonged to him on another plantation, further up the Potomac. This plantation was in Stafford County, and did not border on the Potomac River, but was on the banks of the Rappahannock, nearly opposite the little town of Fredericksburg.

This house was very much like the one that was burned. It stood back from the river, on a ridge or bluff that overlooked the Rappahannock, and between the house and the river was a stretch of meadow that was the playground of the Washington children. For in this pleasant old Virginia country home George Washington lived until he was sixteen years old. As with the birthplace of Washington, so it was with the home of his boyhood. It was long since destroyed, and nothing marks the spot where, as a boy, he who was to be the "Father of his Country" lived and played and dreamed and thought and grew. It would be pleasant to know more about his boyhood days, for it is always interesting to know what sort of a "bringing up" a great man had when a boy. But there is, really, very little known about the boyhood of George Washington.

His father was what we should call a "well-to-do" farmer. He owned several large farms, or plantations, as they were then called, in the colony of Virginia, along the Potomac River. He never had much money, for money was not plentiful in those "old colony days." Planters and farmers were rich in land and in the crops they raised, but these crops were not always sold for money; they were exchanged for the things that were needed on the farm or in the home. The Virginia farmers, as I have told you, raised more tobacco than anything else; for a great many folks in Europe had learned to smoke tobacco since the time when Sir Walter Raleigh (who introduced into England the practice of smoking tobacco) was drenched from head to foot by his terrified servant who, seeing the tobacco smoke, thought his master was on fire. So the rich Virginia farmlands were planted with tobacco, and the ships that came from England took away the tobacco, and left in exchange things to eat and things to wear, and things to make home comfortable.

And a very comfortable home the son of this Virginia planter had. It was not a great nor a grand house, as were a few of the houses of the very richest Virginians; it was not, perhaps, what the boys and girls of to-day, with to-day's idea of comfort, would call comfortable. It was a story and a half house, with a low sloping roof, with great chimneys and fireplaces at either end, and with half a dozen "roomy" rooms, one of which had its fireplace bordered with the funny Dutch tiles and was called the "best room." There were no carpets on the floors, no gas, nor oil, nor coal, nor stoves for light and heat; the furniture was neither elaborate nor plenty; the books were but few, and the household games and toys made for girls and boys to-day were then unknown. No bicycles, no postage stamp albums, no tennis nor croquet, nor baseball—what could the "sons of gentlemen" find to do when Washington was a boy?

Well—they had plenty to eat and drink; there were horses to ride and guns to shoot with and dogs to hunt with; there were fish to be caught and out-of-door games to be played, and the boys were just as full of fun and just as ready to play as they are to-day.

The Washingtons, as I have told you, were considered "well off," although they had not much money to spend and did not live in a grand house; so the sons of the smaller planters, the boy who belonged to what was known as the "poor white families," and the little black and white servant-boys—for there were both kinds in Virginia then—looked upon George Washington as a good deal of a boy, and followed him as their leader in their out-of-door sports and games.

When he was a little fellow, eight or nine years old, he had a pony named

Hero, that "Uncle Ben," one of his father's slaves, taught him to ride; and he owned a "whip-top," something rare in those days. And this he considered so fine a possession that he wrote about it to his friend Dickey Lee (afterwards a famous American), and generously told him, "You may see it and whip it." But, best of all, he liked the free life out of doors, the rough-and-ready boy play that gives health and strength and vigor and muscle to boys, and fits them to become robust and active men.

When he was eleven years old, in April, 1743, his father died suddenly, and Mary Washington had the management of the great plantation and the houseful of children. How well she succeeded we all know; for, to-day, George Washington's mother is almost as famous as her son. One of the older boys— George's half-brother Lawrence—had been sent to England to school; but, when his father died, there was scarcely money enough to do this for the other boys; so George got what small schooling he obtained in the simple country schools about his home, where he learned little more than what was called "the three R's"—reading, 'riting and 'rithmetic.

So he grew up at home a brave, generous, quiet, manly boy. He loved to roam the fields and row and swim in the rivers, and talk with the other boys as to what he should like to do or be when he grew up. For the Virginia boy of one hundred and fifty years ago, there were great attractions—dangers are always attractive—the sea and the forest. George Washington, going down to the tobacco sheds on the wharf which was a part of every plantation, would talk with the men who had sailed across the sea from England, and listen to their hair-breadth escapes from wreck and pirates (for there were fierce pirates sailing the seas in those days) and he would think he would like to be a sailor; then at other times he would talk with the hunters who came in with the "peltry," about the great forests that stretched away, no one knew how far to the westward, and that were believed by the boys to be full of all kinds of dangers and all sorts of ferocious monsters, and then he would think he would like to be a hunter.

But after all I imagine he was ready, just then, to agree that it was not a bad thing to be a boy on a big Virginia plantation with plenty of servants and horses and dogs and boy comrades, and with a watchful mother whom, if he had to obey strictly, he loved dearly.

He was strong, he was active, he was healthy, he was happy—big for his years, strong, for a boy, the best wrestler ("rassler," they all called it then), the best runner, the best rider among all the boys of his section. He grew to be what are called in these days an athlete. Not a boy could "stump him" successfully or unsuccessfully, or "dare him" to any feat of boyish strength or skill. He studied faithfully—he always did everything thoroughly—but he did not really enjoy his schools. What he did enjoy when he went to the little log school-house (called a "field school") near his home, was his corn-stalk brigade. For William Bustle and some of the schoolboys played they were French while George Washington and other of the schoolboys played they were Americans, and with cornstalks for guns and gourds for drums, the rival soldiers played at charge and skirmish and furious battle, and the Americans, led by Captain Washington, were always victorious.

With such a father and mother George Washington could not have been other than a good boy. And he was. He was big and strong, and sometimes mischievous and careless—fearing nothing and daring much, as such big, good-natured, quiet and determined boys are apt to; but he hated a lie; he was never mean, nor low; he never did an underhand action; and he knew that the first lesson a boy needs to learn is obedience to parents, respect toward older people, and kindness to all.

Some folks will tell you that Washington had no boyhood; that is to say, he was not one of those fun-loving, fun-making boys we all like to know. But I wish you to believe otherwise. I wish you to feel that George Washington, as a boy, though quiet and thoughtful, was just as fond of fun and of sport, just as careless, reckless, and boisterous, just as high-strung and as boyish a boy as are any of you who read his story, and who, in the schools and homes of America to-day are, because of this Virginia boy of long ago, learning, hoping and meaning to be loyal, true and helpful American men and women when you grow up.

### Chapter II: Why the Boy Who Wished to Be a Sailor Became a Surveyor

Everybody likes a boy who is strong and manly, and that was what George Washington was. The boy who, while in his early teens, could tame an unbroken colt, firmly keeping his seat until he had mastered the wild and plunging thoroughbred, the boy who could "down" the best wrestlers in the county, who could throw a stone clear across the Rappahannock, toss bars and pitch quoits better than any man or boy about him, and sight and fire a rifle held with one hand only; the boy who could always be trusted to keep his promises, tell the truth, and do as he was bid without asking why, was a boy who could be at once bold and brave, good and gentle, sturdy and strong, wise and cautious.

If he tamed the unbroken colt, killing it rather than let it master him, he did not excuse himself nor lie about it to his mother when the trial of will was past. And, if he mastered the thoroughbred, (as he once did in a wager of his head against the horse) he would not take an unfair advantage, nor accept the horse as his because he had neither kept his seat nor fully kept his claim of ability.

He would get dreadfully "mad" with other boys sometimes, and he was so strong that if he had been at all bad, he might have been what is called a bully. But, even when he was a small boy, he had learned to control his temper; and this he always did throughout his useful life, losing it so seldom and only when there was every excuse for his getting "mad," that we can set this splendid habit of self-control as one of the things that made him great and noble. . . .

Even as a boy, you see, George Washington had what we call the qualities of mind and brain, the courage, the caution and the determination to succeed that made him, in after years, a leader of men and the chieftain of America.

---

## Arriving at Moral Perfection

---

## Benjamin Franklin

---

It was about this time that I conceiv'd the bold and arduous Project of arriving at moral Perfection. I wish'd to live without committing any Fault at any time; I would conquer all that either Natural Inclination, Custom, or Company might lead me into. As I knew, or thought I knew, what was right and wrong, I did not see why I might not *always* do the one and avoid the other. But I soon found I had undertaken a Task of more Difficulty than I had imagined. While my *Attention was taken up* in guarding against one Fault, I was often surpriz'd by another. Habit took the Advantage of Inattention. Inclination was sometimes too strong for Reason. I concluded at length, that the mere speculative Conviction that it was our Interest to be compleatly virtuous, was not sufficient to prevent our Slipping, and that the contrary Habits must be broken and good ones acquired and established, before we can have any Dependance on a steady uniform Rectitude of Conduct. For this purpose I therefore contriv'd the following Method.

In the various Enumerations of the moral Virtues I had met with in my Reading, I found the Catalogue more or less numerous, as different Writers included more or fewer Ideas under the same Name. Temperance, for Example, was by some confin'd to Eating and Drinking, while by others it was extended to mean the moderating every other Pleasure, Appetite, Inclination or Passion, bodily or mental, even to our Avarice and Ambition. I propos'd to myself, for the sake of Clearness, to use rather more Names with fewer Ideas annex'd to each, than a few Names with more Ideas; and I included under Thirteen Names of Virtues all that at that time occurr'd to me as necessary or desirable, and annex'd to each a short Precept, which fully express'd the Extent I gave to its Meaning.

These Names of Virtues with their Precepts were

1. TEMPERANCE. Eat not to Dulness. Drink not to Elevation.

2. SILENCE. Speak not but what may benefit others or yourself. Avoid trifling Conversation.

3. ORDER. Let all your Things have their Places. Let each Part of your Business have its Time.

4. RESOLUTION. Resolve to perform what you ought. Perform without fail what you resolve.

5. FRUGALITY. Make no Expence but to do good to others or yourself: i.e. Waste nothing.

6. INDUSTRY. Lose no Time. Be always employ'd in something useful. Cut off all unnecessary Actions.

7. SINCERITY. Use no hurtful Deceit. Think innocently and justly; and, if you speak, speak accordingly.

8. JUSTICE. Wrong none, by doing Injuries or omitting the Benefits that are your Duty.

9. MODERATION. Avoid Extreams. Forbear resenting Injuries so much as you think they deserve.

10. CLEANLINESS. Tolerate no Uncleanness in Body, Cloaths or Habitation.

11. TRANQUILITY. Be not disturbed at Trifles, or at Accidents common or unavoidable.

12. CHASTITY. Rarely use Venery but for Health or Offspring; Never to Dulness, Weakness, or the Injury of your own or another's Peace or Reputation.

13. HUMILITY. Imitate Jesus and Socrates.

My Intention being to acquire the *Habitude* of all these Virtues, I judg'd it would be well not to distract my Attention by attempting the whole at once, but to fix it on one of them at a time, and when I should be Master of that, then to proceed to another, and so on till I should have gone thro' the thirteen. And as the previous Acquisition of some might facilitate the Acquisition of certain others, I arrang'd them with that View as they stand above. *Temperance* first, as it tends to procure that Coolness and Clearness of Head, which is so necessary where constant Vigilance was to be kept up, and Guard maintained, against the unremitting Attraction of ancient Habits, and the Force of perpetual Temptations. This being acquir'd and establish'd, *Silence* would be more easy, and my Desire being to gain Knowledge at the same time that

I improv'd in Virtue, and considering that in Conversation it was obtain'd rather by the use of the Ears than of the Tongue, and therefore wishing to break a Habit I was getting into of Prattling, Punning and Joking, which only made me acceptable to trifling Company, I gave *Silence* the second Place. This, and the next, *Order,* I expected would allow me more Time for attending to my Project and my Studies; RESOLUTION, once become habitual, would keep me firm in my Endeavours to obtain all the subsequent Virtues; *Frugality* and *Industry,* by freeing me from my remaining Debt, and producing Affluence and Independance, would make more easy the Practice of *Sincerity* and *Justice,* &c. &c. Conceiving then that agreable to the Advice of Pythagoras in his Golden Verses daily Examination would be necessary, I contriv'd the following Method for conducting that Examination.

I made a little Book in which I allotted a Page for each of the Virtues. I rul'd each Page with red Ink, so as to have seven Columns, one for each Day of the Week, marking each Column with a Letter for the Day. I cross'd these Columns with thirteen red Lines, marking the Beginning of each Line with the first Letter of one of the Virtues, on which Line and in its proper Column I might mark by a little black Spot every Fault I found upon Examination to have been committed respecting that Virtue upon that Day.

I determined to give a Week's strict Attention to each of the Virtues successively. Thus in the first Week my great Guard was to avoid every the least Offence against Temperance, leaving the other Virtues to their ordinary Chance, only marking every Evening the Faults of the Day. Thus if in the first Week I could keep my first Line marked T clear of Spots, I suppos'd the Habit of that Virtue so much strengthen'd and its opposite weaken'd, that I might venture extending my Attention to include the next, and for the following Week keep both Lines clear of Spots. Proceeding thus to the last, I could go thro' a Course compleat in Thirteen Weeks, and four Courses in a Year. And like him who having a Garden to weed, does not attempt to eradicate all the bad Herbs at once, which would exceed his Reach and his Strength, but works on one of the Beds at a time, and having accomplish'd the first proceeds to a Second; so I should have (I hoped) the encouraging Pleasure of seeing on my Pages the Progress I made in Virtue, by clearing successively my Lines of their Spots, till in the End by a Number of Courses, I should be happy in viewing a clean Book after a thirteen Weeks daily Examination.

## Up from Slavery

## 1928

## Booker T. Washington

### Chapter I: A Slave among Slaves

I was born a slave on a plantation in Franklin County, Virginia. I am not quite sure of the exact place or exact date of my birth, but at any rate I suspect I must have been born somewhere and at some time. As nearly as I have been able to learn, I was born near a cross-roads post-office called Hale's Ford, and the year was 1858 or 1859. I do not know the month or the day. The earliest impressions I can now recall are of the plantation and the slave quarters—the latter being the part of the plantation where the slaves had their cabins.

My life had its beginning in the midst of the most miserable, desolate, and discouraging surroundings. This was so, however, not because my owners were especially cruel, for they were not, as compared with many others. I was born in a typical log cabin, about fourteen by sixteen feet square. In this cabin I lived with my mother and a brother and sister till after the Civil War, when we were all declared free.

Of my ancestry I know almost nothing. In the slave quarters, and even later, I heard whispered conversations among the coloured people of the tortures which the slaves, including, no doubt, my ancestors on my mother's side, suffered in the middle passage of the slave ship while being conveyed from Africa to America. I have been unsuccessful in securing any information that would throw any accurate light upon the history of my family beyond my mother. She, I remember, had a half-brother and a half-sister. In the days of slavery not very much attention was given to family history and family records—that is, black family records. My mother, I suppose, attracted the attention of a purchaser who was afterward my owner and hers. Her addition to the slave family attracted about as much attention as the purchase of a new horse or cow. Of my father I know even less than of my mother. I do not even know his name. I have heard reports to the effect that he was a white man who lived on one of the near-by plantations. Whoever he was, I never heard of his taking the least interest in me or providing in any way for my rearing. But I do not find especial fault with him. He was simply another unfortunate victim of the institution which the Nation unhappily had engrafted upon it at that time.

The cabin was not only our living-place, but was also used as the kitchen for the plantation. My mother was the plantation cook. The cabin was without glass windows; it had only openings in the side which let in the light, and also the cold, chilly air of winter. There was a door to the cabin—that is, something that was called a door—but the uncertain hinges by which it was hung, and the large cracks in it, to say nothing of the fact that it was too small, made the room a very uncomfortable one. In addition to these openings there was, in the lower right-hand corner of the room, the "cat-hole,"—a contrivance which almost every mansion or cabin in Virginia possessed during the ante-bellum period. The "cat-hole" was a square opening, about seven by eight inches, provided for the purpose of letting the cat pass in and out of the house at will during the night. In the case of our particular cabin I could never understand the necessity for this convenience, since there were at least a half-dozen other places in the cabin that would have accommodated the cats. There was no wooden floor in our cabin, the naked earth being used as a floor. In the centre of the earthen floor there was a large, deep opening covered with boards, which was used as a place in which to store sweet potatoes during the winter. An impression of this potato-hole is very distinctly engraved upon my memory, because I recall that during the process of putting the potatoes in or taking them out I would often come into possession of one or two, which I roasted and thoroughly enjoyed. There was no cooking-stove on our plantation, and all the cooking for the whites and slaves my mother had to do over an open fireplace, mostly in pots and "skillets." While the poorly built cabin caused us to suffer with cold in the winter, the heat from the open fireplace in summer was equally trying.

The early years of my life, which were spent in the little cabin, were not very different from those of thousands of other slaves. My mother, of course, had little time in which to give attention to the training of her children during the day. She snatched a few moments for our care in the early morning before her work began, and at night after the day's work was done. One of my earliest recollections is that of my mother cooking a chicken late at night, and awakening her children for the purpose of feeding them. How or where she got it I do not know. I presume, however, it was procured from our owner's farm. Some people may call this theft. If such a thing were to happen now, I should condemn it as theft myself. But taking place at the time it did, and for the reason that it did, no one could ever make me believe that my mother was guilty of thieving. She was simply a victim of the system of slavery. I cannot remember having slept in a bed until after our family was declared free by the Emancipation Proclamation. Three children—John, my older brother, Amanda, my sister, and myself—had a pallet on the dirt floor, or, to be more correct, we slept in and on a bundle of filthy rags laid upon the dirt floor.

I was asked not long ago to tell something about the sports and pastimes that I engaged in during my youth. Until that question was asked it had never occurred to me that there was no period of my life that was devoted to play. From the time that I can remember anything, almost every day of my life has been occupied in some kind of labour; though I think I would now be a more useful man if I had had time for sports. During the period that I spent in slavery I was not large enough to be of much service, still I was occupied most of the time in cleaning the yards, carrying water to the men in the fields, or going to the mill, to which I used to take the corn, once a week, to be ground. The mill was about three miles from the plantation. This work I always dreaded. The heavy bag of corn would be thrown across the back of the horse, and the corn divided about evenly on each side; but in some way, almost without exception, on these trips, the corn would so shift as to become unbalanced and would fall off the horse, and often I would fall with it. As I was not strong enough to reload the corn upon the horse, I would have to wait, sometimes for many hours, till a chance passer-by came along who would help me out of my trouble. The hours while waiting for some one were usually spent in crying. The time consumed in this way made me late in reaching the mill, and by the time I got my corn ground and reached home it would be far into the night. The road was a lonely one, and often led through dense forests. I was always frightened. The woods were said to be full of soldiers who had deserted from the army, and I had been told that the first thing a deserter did to a Negro boy when he found him alone was to cut off his ears. Besides, when I was late in getting home I knew I would always get a severe scolding or a flogging.

I had no schooling whatever while I was a slave, though I remember on several occasions I went as far as the schoolhouse door with one of my young mistresses to carry her books. The picture of several dozen boys and girls in a schoolroom engaged in study made a deep impression upon me, and I had the feeling that to get into a schoolhouse and study in this way would be about the same as getting into paradise.

So far as I can now recall, the first knowledge that I got of the fact that we were slaves, and that freedom of the slaves was being discussed, was early one morning before day, when I was awakened by my mother kneeling over her children and fervently praying that Lincoln and his armies might be successful, and that one day she and her children might be free. In this connection I have never been able to understand how the slaves throughout the South, completely ignorant as were the masses so far as books or newspapers were concerned, were able to keep themselves so accurately and completely informed about the great National questions that were agitating the country. From the time that Garrison, Lovejoy, and others began to agitate for freedom, the slaves throughout the South kept in close touch with the progress of the movement. Though I was a mere child during the preparation for the Civil War and during the war itself, I now recall the many late-at-night whispered discussions that I heard my mother and the other slaves on the plantation indulge in. These discussions showed that they understood the situation, and that they kept themselves informed of events by what was termed the "grape-vine" telegraph.

During the campaign when Lincoln was first a candidate for the Presidency, the slaves on our far-off plantation, miles from any railroad or large city or daily newspaper, knew what the issues involved were. When war was begun between the North and the South, every slave on our plantation felt and knew that, though other issues were discussed, the primal one was that of slavery. Even the most ignorant members of my race on the remote plantations felt in their hearts, with a certainty that admitted of no doubt, that the freedom of the slaves would be the one great result of the war, if the Northern armies conquered. Every success of the Federal armies and every defeat of the Confederate forces was watched with the keenest and most intense interest. Often the slaves got knowledge of the results of great battles before the white people received it. This news was usually gotten from the coloured man who was sent to the post-office for the mail. In our case the post-office was about three miles from the plantation and the mail came once or twice a week. The man who was sent to the office would linger about the place long enough to get the drift of the conversation from the group of white people who naturally congregated there, after receiving their mail, to discuss the latest news. The mail-carrier on his way back to our master's house would as naturally retail the news that he had secured among the slaves, and in this way they often heard of important events before the white people at the "big house," as the master's house was called.

I cannot remember a single instance during my childhood or early boyhood when our entire family sat down to the table together, and God's blessing was asked, and the family ate a meal in a civilized manner. On the plantation in Virginia, and even later, meals were gotten by the children very much as dumb animals get theirs. It was a piece of bread here and a scrap of meat there. It was a cup of milk at one time and some potatoes at another. Sometimes a portion of our family would eat out of the skillet or pot, while some one else would eat from a tin plate held on the knees, and often using nothing but the hands with which to hold the food. When I had grown to sufficient size, I was required to go to the "big house" at meal-times to fan the flies from the table by means of a large set of paper fans operated by a pulley. Naturally much of the conversation of the white people turned upon the subject of freedom and the war, and I absorbed a good deal of it. I remember that at one time I saw two of my young mistresses and some lady visitors eating ginger-cakes, in the yard. At that time those cakes seemed to me to be absolutely the most tempting and desirable things that I had ever seen; and I then and there resolved that, if I ever got free, the height of my ambition would be reached if I could get to the point where I could secure and eat ginger-cakes in the way that I saw those ladies doing.

Of course as the war was prolonged the white people, in many cases, often found it difficult to secure food for themselves. I think the slaves felt the deprivation less than the whites, because the usual diet for the slaves was corn bread and pork, and these could be raised on the plantation; but coffee, tea, sugar, and other articles which the whites had been accustomed to use could not be raised on the plantation, and the conditions brought about by the war frequently made it impossible to secure these things. The whites were often in great straits. Parched corn was used for coffee, and a kind of black molasses was used instead of sugar. Many times nothing was used to sweeten the so-called tea and coffee. . . .

One may get the idea from what I have said, that there was bitter feeling toward the white people on the part of my race, because of the fact that most of the white population was away fighting in a war which would result in keeping the Negro in slavery if the South was successful. In the case of the slaves on our place this was not true, and it was not true of any large portion of the slave population in the South where the Negro was treated with anything like decency. During the Civil War one of my young masters was killed, and two were severely wounded. I recall the feeling of sorrow which existed among the slaves when they heard of the death of "Mars' Billy." It was no sham sorrow but real. Some of the slaves had nursed "Mars' Billy"; others had played with him when he was a child. "Mars' Billy" had begged for mercy in the case of others when the overseer or master was thrashing them. The sorrow in the slave quarter was only second to that in the "big house." When the two young masters were brought home wounded, the sympathy of the slaves was shown in many ways. They were just as anxious to assist in the nursing as the family relatives of the wounded. Some of the slaves would even beg for the privilege of sitting up at night to nurse their wounded masters. This tenderness and sympathy on the part of those held in bondage was a result of their kindly and generous nature. In order to defend and protect the women and children who were left on the plantations when the white males went to war, the slaves would have laid down their lives. The slave who was selected to sleep in the "big house" during the absence of the males was considered to have the place of honour. Any one attempting to harm "young Mistress" or "old Mistress" during the night would have had to cross the dead body of the slave to do so. I do not know how many have noticed it, but I think that it will be found to be true that there are few instances, either in slavery or freedom, in which a member of my race has been known to betray a specific trust.

As a rule, not only did the members of my race entertain no feelings of bitterness against the whites before and during the war, but there are many instances of Negroes tenderly caring for their former masters and mistresses who for some reason have become poor and dependent since the war. I know of instances where the former masters of slaves have for years been supplied with money by their former slaves to keep them from suffering. I have known of still other cases in which the former slaves have assisted in the education of the descendants of their former owners. I know of a case on a large plantation in the South in which a young white man, the son of the former owner of the estate, has become so reduced in purse and self-control by reason of drink that he is a pitiable creature; and yet, notwithstanding the poverty of the coloured people themselves on this plantation, they have for years supplied this young white man with the necessities of life. One sends him a little coffee or sugar, another a little meat, and so on. Nothing that the coloured people possess is too good for the son of "old Mars' Tom," who will perhaps never be permitted to suffer while any remain on the place who knew directly or indirectly of "old Mars' Tom.". . .

From some things that I have said one may get the idea that some of the slaves did not want freedom. This is not true. I have never seen one who did not want to be free, or one who would return to slavery.

I pity from the bottom of my heart any nation or body of people that is so unfortunate as to get entangled in the net of slavery. I have long since ceased to cherish any spirit of bitterness against the Southern white people on account of the enslavement of my race. No one section of our country was wholly responsible for its introduction, and, besides, it was recognized and protected for years by the General Government. Having once got its tentacles fastened on to the economic and social life of the Republic, it was no easy matter for the country to relieve itself of the institution. Then, when we rid ourselves of prejudice, or racial feeling, and look facts in the face, we must acknowledge that, not withstanding the cruelty and moral wrong of slavery, the ten million Negroes inhabiting this country, who themselves or whose ancestors went through the school of American slavery, are in a stronger and more hopeful condition, materially, intellectually, morally, and religiously, than is true of an equal number of black people in any other portion of the globe. This is so to such an extent that Negroes in this country, who themselves or whose forefathers went through the school of slavery, are constantly returning to Africa as missionaries to enlighten those who remained in the fatherland. This I say, not to justify slavery—on the other hand, I condemn it as an institution, as we all know that in America it was established for selfish and financial reasons, and not from a missionary motive—but to call attention to a fact, and to show how Providence so often uses men and institutions to accomplish a purpose. When persons ask me in these days how, in the midst of what sometimes seem hopelessly discouraging conditions, I can have such faith in the future of my race in this country, I remind them of the wilderness through which and out of which, a good Providence has already led us. . . .

Finally the war closed, and the day of freedom came. It was a momentous and eventful day to all upon our plantation. We had been expecting it. Freedom was in the air, and had been for months. Deserting soldiers returning to their homes were to be seen every day. Others who had been discharged, or whose regiments had been paroled, were constantly passing near our place. The "grape-vine telegraph" was kept busy night and day. The news and mutterings of great events were swiftly carried from one plantation to another. In the fear of "Yankee" invasions, the silverware and other valuables were taken from the "big house," buried in the woods, and guarded by trusted slaves. Woe be to any one who would have attempted to disturb the buried treasure. The slaves would give the Yankee soldiers food, drink, clothing—anything but that which had been specifically intrusted to their care and honour. As the great day grew nearer, there was more singing in the slave quarters than usual. It was bolder, had more ring, and lasted later into the night. Most of the verses of the plantation songs had some reference to freedom. True, they had sung those same verses before, but they had been careful to explain that the "freedom" in these songs referred to the next world, and had no connection with life in this world. Now they gradually threw off the mask, and were not afraid to let it be known that the "freedom" in their songs meant freedom of the body in this world. The night before the eventful day, word was sent to the slave quarters to the effect that something unusual was going to take place at the "big house" the next morning. There was little, if any, sleep that night. All was excitement and expectancy. Early the next morning word was sent to all the slaves, old and young, to gather at the house. In company with my mother, brother, and sister, and a large number of other slaves, I went to the master's house. All of our master's family were either standing or seated on the veranda of the house, where they could see what was to take place and hear what was said. There was a feeling of deep interest, or perhaps sadness, on their faces, but not bitterness. As I now recall the impression they made upon me, they did not at the moment seem to be sad because of the loss of property, but rather because of parting with those whom they had reared and who were in many ways very close to them. The most distinct thing that I now recall in connection with the scene was that some man who seemed to be a stranger (a United States officer, I presume) made a little speech and then read a rather long paper—the Emancipation Proclamation, I think. After the reading we were told that we were all free, and could go when and where we pleased. My mother, who was standing by my side, leaned over and kissed her children, while tears of joy ran down her cheeks. She explained to us what it all meant, that this was the day for which she had been so long praying, but fearing that she would never live to see.

For some minutes there was great rejoicing, and thanksgiving, and wild scenes of ecstasy. But there was no feeling of bitterness. In fact, there was pity among the slaves for our former owners. The wild rejoicing on the part of the emancipated coloured people lasted but for a brief period, for I noticed that by the time they returned to their cabins there was a change in their feelings. The great responsibility of being free, of having charge of themselves, of having to think and plan for themselves and their children, seemed to take possession of them. It was very much like suddenly turning a youth of ten or twelve years out into the world to provide for himself. In a few hours the great questions with which the Anglo-Saxon race had been grappling for centuries had been thrown upon these people to be solved. These were the questions of a home, a living, the rearing of children, education, citizenship, and the establishment and support of churches. Was it any wonder that within a few hours the wild rejoicing ceased and a feeling of deep gloom seemed to pervade the slave quarters? To some it seemed that, now that they were in actual possession of it, freedom was a more serious thing than they had expected to find it. Some of the slaves were seventy or eighty years old; their best days were gone. They had no strength with which to earn a living in a strange place and among strange people, even if they had been sure where to find a new place of abode. To this class the problem seemed especially hard. Besides, deep down in their hearts there was a strange and peculiar attachment to "old Marster" and "old Missus," and to their children, which they found it hard to think of breaking off. With these they had spent in some cases nearly a half-century, and it was no light thing to think of parting. Gradually, one by one, stealthily at first, the older slaves began to wander from the slave quarters back to the "big house" to have a whispered conversation with their former owners as to the future.

### Chapter II: Boyhood Days

After the coming of freedom there were two points upon which practically all the people on our place were agreed, and I find that this was generally true throughout the South: that they must change their names, and that they must leave the old plantation for at least a few days or weeks in order that they might really feel sure that they were free.

In some ways a feeling got among the coloured people that it was far from proper for them to bear the surname of their former owners, and a great many of them took other surnames. This was one of the first signs of freedom. When they were slaves, a coloured person was simply called "John" or "Susan." There was seldom occasion for more than the use of the one name. If "John" or "Susan" belonged to a white man by the name of "Hatcher," sometimes he was called "John Hatcher," or as often "Hatcher's John." But there was a feeling that "John Hatcher" or "Hatcher's John" was not the proper title by which to denote a freeman; and so in many cases "John Hatcher" was changed to "John S. Lincoln" or "John S. Sherman," the initial "S" standing for no name, it being simply a part of what the coloured man proudly called his "entitles."

As I have stated, most of the coloured people left the old plantation for a short while at least, so as to be sure, it seemed, that they could leave and try their freedom on to see how it felt. After they had remained away for a time, many of the older slaves, especially, returned to their old homes and made some kind of contract with their former owners by which they remained on the estate.

My mother's husband, who was the stepfather of my brother John and myself, did not belong to the same owners as did my mother. In fact, he seldom came to our plantation. I remember seeing him there perhaps once a year, that being about Christmas time. In some way, during the war, by running away and following the Federal soldiers, it seems, he found his way into the new state of West Virginia. As soon as freedom was declared, he sent for my mother to come to the Kanawha Valley, in West Virginia. At that time a journey from Virginia over the mountains to West Virginia was rather a tedious and in some cases a painful undertaking. What little clothing and few household goods we had were placed in a cart, but the children walked the greater portion of the distance, which was several hundred miles.

I do not think any of us ever had been very far from the plantation, and the taking of a long journey into another state was quite an event. The parting from our former owners and the members of our own race on the plantation was a serious occasion. From the time of our parting till their death we kept up a correspondence with the older members of the family, and in later years we have kept in touch with those who were the younger members. We were several weeks making the trip, and most of the time we slept in the open air and did our cooking over a log fire out of doors. One night I recall that we camped near an abandoned log cabin, and my mother decided to build a fire in that for cooking, and afterward to make a "pallet" on the floor for our sleeping. Just as the fire had gotten well started a large black snake fully a yard and a half long dropped down the chimney and ran out on the floor. Of course we at once abandoned that cabin. Finally we reached our destination—a little town called Malden, which is about five miles from Charleston, the present capital of the state.

At that time salt-mining was the great industry in that part of West Virginia, and the little town of Malden was right in the midst of the salt-furnaces. My stepfather had already secured a job at a salt-furnace, and he had also secured a little cabin for us to live in. Our new house was no better than the one we had left on the old plantation in Virginia. In fact, in one respect it was worse. Notwithstanding the poor condition of our plantation cabin, we were at all times sure of pure air. Our new home was in the midst of a cluster of cabins crowded closely together, and as there were no sanitary regulations, the filth about the cabins was often intolerable. Some of our neighbours were coloured people, and some were the poorest and most ignorant and degraded white people. It was a motley mixture. Drinking, gambling, quarrels, fights, and shockingly immoral practices were frequent. All who lived in the little town were in one way or another connected with the salt business. Though I was a mere child, my stepfather put me and my brother at work in one of the furnaces. Often I began work as early as four o'clock in the morning.

The first thing I ever learned in the way of book knowledge was while working in this salt-furnace. Each salt-packer had his barrels marked with a certain number. The number allotted to my stepfather was "18." At the close of the day's work the boss of the packers would come around and put "18" on each of our barrels, and I soon learned to recognize that figure wherever I saw it, and after a while got to the point where I could make that figure, though I knew nothing about any other figures or letters.

From the time that I can remember having any thoughts about anything, I recall that I had an intense longing to learn to read. I determined, when quite a small child, that, if I accomplished nothing else in life, I would in some way get enough education to enable me to read common books and news-papers. Soon after we got settled in some manner in our new cabin in West

Virginia, I induced my mother to get hold of a book for me. How or where she got it I do not know, but in some way she procured an old copy of Webster's "blue-back" spelling-book, which contained the alphabet, followed by such meaningless words as "ab," "ba," "ca," "da." I began at once to devour this book, and I think that it was the first one I ever had in my hands. I had learned from somebody that the way to begin to read was to learn the alphabet, so I tried in all the ways I could think of to learn it,—all of course without a teacher, for I could find no one to teach me. At that time there was not a single member of my race anywhere near us who could read, and I was too timid to approach any of the white people. In some way, within a few weeks, I mastered the greater portion of the alphabet. In all my efforts to learn to read my mother shared fully my ambition, and sympathized with me and aided me in every way that she could. . . .

In the midst of my struggles and longing for an education, a young coloured boy who had learned to read in the state of Ohio came to Malden. As soon as the coloured people found out that he could read, a newspaper was secured, and at the close of nearly every day's work this young man would be surrounded by a group of men and women who were anxious to hear him read the news contained in the papers. How I used to envy this man! He seemed to me to be the one young man in all the world who ought to be satisfied with his attainments.

About this time the question of having some kind of a school opened for the coloured children in the village began to be discussed by members of the race. As it would be the first school for Negro children that had ever been opened in that part of Virginia, it was, of course, to be a great event, and the discussion excited the widest interest. The most perplexing question was where to find a teacher. The young man from Ohio who had learned to read the papers was considered, but his age was against him. In the midst of the discussion about a teacher, another young coloured man from Ohio, who had been a soldier, in some way found his way into town. It was soon learned that he possessed considerable education, and he was engaged by the coloured people to teach their first school. As yet no free schools had been started for coloured people in that section, hence each family agreed to pay a certain amount per month, with the understanding that the teacher was to "board 'round"—that is, spend a day with each family. This was not bad for the teacher, for each family tried to provide the very best on the day the teacher was to be its guest. I recall that I looked forward with an anxious appetite to the "teacher's day" at our little cabin.

This experience of a whole race beginning to go to school for the first time, presents one of the most interesting studies that has ever occurred in connection with the development of any race. Few people who were not right in the midst of the scenes can form any exact idea of the intense desire which the people of my race showed for an education. As I have stated, it was a whole race trying to go to school. Few were too young, and none too old, to make the attempt to learn. As fast as any kind of teachers could be secured, not only were day-schools filled, but night-schools as well. The great ambition of the older people was to try to learn to read the Bible before they died. With this end in view, men and women who were fifty or seventy-five years old would often be found in the night-school. Sunday-schools were formed soon after freedom, but the principal book studied in the Sunday-school was the spelling-book. Day-school, night-school, Sunday-school, were always crowded, and often many had to be turned away for want of room.

The opening of the school in the Kanawha Valley, however, brought to me one of the keenest disappointments that I ever experienced. I had been working in a salt-furnace for several months, and my stepfather had discovered that I had a financial value, and so, when the school opened, he decided that he could not spare me from my work. This decision seemed to cloud my every ambition. The disappointment was made all the more severe by reason of the fact that my place of work was where I could see the happy children passing to and from school, mornings and afternoons. Despite this disappointment, however, I determined that I would learn something, anyway. I applied myself with greater earnestness than ever to the mastering of what was in the "blue-back" speller.

My mother sympathized with me in my disappointment, and sought to comfort me in all the ways she could, and to help me find a way to learn. After a while I succeeded in making arrangements with the teacher to give me some lessons at night, after the day's work was done. These night lessons were so welcome that I think I learned more at night than the other children did during the day. My own experiences in the night-school gave me faith in the night-school idea, with which, in after years, I had to do both at Hampton and Tuskegee. But my boyish heart was still set upon going to the day-school, and I let no opportunity slip to push my case. Finally I won, and was permitted to go to the school in the day for a few months, with the under-standing that I was to rise early in the morning and work in the furnace till nine o'clock, and return immediately after school closed in the afternoon for at least two more hours of work.

The schoolhouse was some distance from the furnace, and as I had to work till nine o'clock, and the school opened at nine, I found myself in a difficulty. School would always be begun before I reached it, and sometimes my class had recited. To get around this difficulty I yielded to a temptation for which most people, I suppose, will condemn me; but since it is a fact, I might as well state it. I have great faith in the power and influence of facts. It is seldom that anything is permanently gained by holding back a fact. There was a large clock in a little office in the furnace. This clock, of course, all the hundred or more workmen depended upon to regulate their hours of be-ginning and ending the day's work. I got the idea that the way for me to reach school on time was to move the clock hands from half-past eight up to the nine o'clock mark. This I found myself doing morning after morning, till the furnace "boss" discovered that something was wrong, and locked the clock in a case. I did not mean to inconvenience any body. I simply meant to reach that schoolhouse in time.

When, however, I found myself at the school for the first time, I also found myself confronted with two other difficulties. In the first place, I found that all of the other children wore hats or caps on their heads, and I had neither hat nor cap. In fact, I do not remember that up to the time of going to school I had ever worn any kind of covering upon my head, nor do I recall that either I or anybody else had even thought anything about the need of covering for my head. But, of course when I saw how all the other boys were dressed, I began to feel quite uncomfortable. As usual, I put the case before my mother, and she explained to me that she had no money with which to buy a "store hat," which was a rather new institution at that time among the members of my race and was considered quite the thing for young and old to own, but that she would find a way to help me out of the difficulty. She accordingly got two pieces of "homespun" (jeans) and sewed them together, and I was soon the proud possessor of my first cap. . . .

My second difficulty was with regard to my name, or rather *a* name. From the time when I could remember anything, I had been called simply "Booker." Before going to school it had never occurred to me that it was needful or appropriate to have an additional name. When I heard the school-roll called, I noticed that all of the children had at least two names, and some of them indulged in what seemed to me the extravagance of having three. I was in deep perplexity, because I knew that the teacher would demand of me at least two names, and I had only one. By the time the occasion came for the enrolling of my name, an idea occurred to me which I thought would make me equal to the situation; and so, when the teacher asked me what my full name was, I calmly told him "Booker Washington," as if I had been called by that name all my life; and by that name I have since been known. Later in my life I found that my mother had given me the name of "Booker Taliaferro" soon after I was born, but in some way that part of my name seemed to disappear, and for a long while was forgotten, but as soon as I found out about it I revived it, and made my full name "Booker Taliaferro Washington." I think there are not many men in our country who have had the privilege of naming themselves in the way that I have.

More than once I have tried to picture myself in the position of a boy or man with an honoured and distinguished ancestry which I could trace back through a period of hundreds of years, and who had not only inherited a name, but fortune and a proud family homestead; and yet I have sometimes had the feeling that if I had inherited these, and had been a member of a more popular race, I should have been inclined to yield to the temptation of depending upon my ancestry and my colour to do that for me which I should do for myself. Years ago I resolved that because I had no ancestry myself I would leave a record of which my children would be proud, and which might encourage them to still higher effort.

The world should not pass judgment upon the Negro, and especially the Negro youth, too quickly or too harshly. The Negro boy has obstacles, discouragements, and temptations to battle with that are little known to those not situated as he is. When a white boy undertakes a task, it is taken for granted that he will succeed. On the other hand, people are usually surprised if the Negro boy does not fail. In a word, the Negro youth starts out with the pre-sumption against him.

The influence of ancestry, however, is important in helping forward any individual or race, if too much reliance is not placed upon it. Those who constantly direct attention to the Negro youth's moral weaknesses, and com-pare his advancement with that of white youths, do not consider the influence of the memories which cling about the old family homesteads. I have no idea, as I have stated elsewhere, who my grandmother was. I have, or have had, uncles and aunts and cousins, but I have no knowledge as to where most of them are. My case will illustrate that of hundreds of thousands of black people in every part of our country. The very fact that the white boy is conscious that, if he fails in life, he will disgrace the whole family record, extending back through many generations, is of tremendous value in helping him to resist temptations. The fact that the individual has behind and surrounding him proud family history and connection serves as a stimulus to help him to over-come obstacles when striving for success. . . .

In those days, and later as a young man, I used to try to picture in my imagination the feelings and ambitions of a white boy with absolutely no limit placed upon his aspirations and activities. I used to envy the white boy who had no obstacles placed in the way of his becoming a Congressman, Governor, Bishop, or President by reason of the accident of his birth or race. I used to picture the way that I would act under such circumstances; how I would begin at the bottom and keep rising until I reached the highest round of success.

In later years, I confess that I do not envy the white boy as I once did. I have learned that success is to be measured not so much by the position that one has reached in life as by the obstacles which he has overcome while trying to succeed. Looked at from this standpoint, I almost reach the conclusion that often the Negro boy's birth and connection with an unpopular race is an advantage, so far as real life is concerned. With few exceptions, the Negro youth must work harder and must perform his task even better than a white youth in order to secure recognition. But out of the hard and unusual struggle through which he is compelled to pass, he gets a strength, a confidence, that one misses whose pathway is comparatively smooth by reason of birth and race.

From any point of view, I had rather be what I am, a member of the Negro race, than be able to claim membership with the most favoured of any other race. I have always been made sad when I have heard members of any race claiming rights and privileges, or certain badges of distinction, on the ground simply that they were members of this or that race, regardless of their own individual worth or attainments. I have been made to feel sad for such persons because I am conscious of the fact that mere connection with what is known as a superior race will not permanently carry an individual forward unless he has individual worth, and mere connection with what is regarded as an inferior race will not finally hold an individual back if he possesses intrinsic, individual merit. Every persecuted individual and race should get much consolation out of the great human law, which is universal and eternal, that merit, no matter under what skin found, is in the long run, recognized and rewarded. This I have said here, not to call attention to myself as an individual, but to the race to which I am proud to belong.

## The Real Diary of a Real Boy

### 1860s

### Henry A. Shute

Father thot i aught to keep a diry, but i sed i dident want to, because i coodent wright well enuf, but he sed he wood give $1000 dolars if he had kept a diry when he was a boy.

Mother said she gessed nobody wood dass to read it, but father said everybody would tumble over each other to read it, anyhow he would give $1000 dolars if he had kept it. I told him i would keep one regular if he would give me a quarter of a dolar a week, but he said i had got to keep it anyhow and i woodent get no quarter for it neither, but he woodent ask to read it for a year, and i know he will forget it before that, so i am going to wright just what i want to in it. Father always forgets everything but my lickins. he remembers them every time you bet.

So i have got to keep it, but it seems to me that my diry is worth a quarter of a dolar a week if fathers is worth $1000 dolars, everybody says father was a buster when he was a boy and went round with Gim Melcher and Charles Talor. my grandmother says i am the best boy she ever see, if i didn't go with Beany Watson and Pewter Purinton, it was Beany and Pewt made me tuf.

there dos'nt seem to be much to put into a diry only fites and who got licked at school and if it ranes or snows, so i will begin to-day.

December 1, 186–   brite and fair, late to brekfast, but mother dident say nothing. father goes to boston and works in the custum house so i can get up as late as i want to. father says he works like time, but i went to boston once and father dident do anything but tell stories about what he and Gim Melcher usted to do when he was a boy. once or twice when a man came in they would all be wrighting fast, when the man came in again i sed why do you all wright so fast when he comes in and stop when he goes out, and the man sort of laffed and went out laffing, and the men were mad and told father not to bring that dam little fool again.

December 2.   Skinny Bruce got licked in school today. I told my granmother about it and she said she was glad i dident do enything to get punnished for and she felt sure i never wood. i dident tell her i had to stay in the wood box all the morning with the cover down. i dident tell father either you bet.

December 2.   rany. i forgot to say it raned yesterday too. i got cold and have a red rag round my gozzle.

December 2.   pretty near had a fite in schol today. Skinny Bruce and Frank Elliot got rite up with there fists up when the bell rung. it was two bad, it wood have been a buly fite. i bet on Skinny. . . .

December 15.   Fite at recess today, Gran Miller and Ben Rundlet. Ben licked him easy. the fellers got to stumping each other to fite. Micky Gould said he cood lick me and i said he want man enuf and he said if i wood come out behind the school house after school he wood show me and i said i wood and all the fellers hollered and said they wood be there. But after school i thaught i aught to go home and split my kindlings and so i went home. a feller aught to do something for his family ennyway. i cood have licked him if i had wanted to. . . .

December 25.   Crismas. got a new nife, a red and white scarf and a bag of Si Smiths goozeberies. pretty good for me.

December 26.   Crismas tree at the town hall. had supper and got a bag of candy and a long string of pop corn. Mr. Lovel took off the presents and his whiskers caught fire, and he hollered o hell right out. that was pretty good for a sunday school teacher, wasent it. Jimmy Gad et too much and was sick. . . .

Jan. 3.   brite and fair. Went down to Pewts tonite to make hayseed cigars. We made 5 kinds, hayseed, sweet firn, cornsilk, mullin leeves, and grape vine. my mouth taisted aufuly all nite.

Jan. 4.   brite and fair. Pewt dident come to school today. i gess he. was sick. my mouth taisted aufuly all day.

Jan. 5.   clowdy and aufuly cold. Pewt came to school today and got a licking for puting gum on Nigger Bells seat. Nig set in it til it dride and then tride to get up and coodent. then old Francis come down the ile and snaiked Nigger out and when he see the gum he asked us who put it there. we all said we dident, but he licked Pewt becaus he had seen Pewt chooing gum. . . .

Jan. 10.   rany. Nipper Brown is the best scholar in my class. i am the wirst. i can lick Nipper easy. . . .

Jan. 15.   i am all spekled over. mother says she is afrade i have got chicken pocks. i gess i have been in the hen koop to mutch.

Jan. 16.   the speckels have all gone of. doctor Perry says i et to many donuts. . . .

Jan. 20.   father is sick becaus he et to mutch salt fish and potato and pork. he is auful cross and hit me a bat today becaus i left the door open. i guess he will be sorry when i am ded. . . .

Jan. 29.   Nothing puticular today. it always seams harder to go to school mundays, more fellers gets licked mundays than enny day in the weak. i got stood on the platform with my head in the corner for looking of my book today. . . .

Feb. 3.   Snowed like time all the forenoon. in the afternoon me and Pewt and Beany rolled up some big snowballs. then tonite we put all the balls together and made a big snowman rite in front of Mrs. Lewises front door. then we put a old hat on it and hung a peace of paper on it and wrote man wanted on the paper. tomorrow all the people who go to church will see it and laff because Mister Lewis got a devorse. they will be some fun tomorrow.

Feb. 5.   i coodent wright ennything last nite becaus i got sent to bed and got a licking. i tell you we got in a auful scrape. sunday morning me and Pewt and Beany went out erly to see our snowman. he was there and when people began to go by they began to laff, and most of the people said it was the funniest thing they ever see and who ever put it there was a pretty smart feller. so we said we did it and Pewt said he thought of it ferst and Beany said he did, and i said i did most of the werk.

Well, pretty soon some people came along and looked at it and said it was a shame and they went over to pull of the paper and she came out and see it, and she took a broom and nocked it over and broke it all up. and then she went rite down to my house to tell father. then she went over to Beanys house and then up to Pewts. well after church father took me over to her house, and Beany was there with his father and Pewt with his father. she said she wood have us arested for it. but they talked a long time and after a while she said if our fathers wood lick us and make us saw and split a cord of wood she woodent say no more about it. when we went out father said, i never see such dam boys did you Brad, did you Wats, and they said they never did. so we have got to saw and split that wood and we got licked two. . . .

Mar. 4.   Brite and fair. Went to church to-day, the fernace smoked so the people had to come home. They say they will have it fixed before next sunday. i hope not. . . .

Mar. 10.   plesent day. old Si Smiths big white dog and a bull dog had an awful fite today. neether licked and they had to squert water on them to seperate them. they dident make no noise, only jest hung write on to each others gozzles. my aunt Sarah said it was dredful, and she staid to the window to see how dredful it was.

Mar. 11, 186–   Went to church in the morning. the fernace was all write. Mister Lennard preeched about loving our ennymies, and told every one if he had any angry feelings towards ennyone to go to him and shake hands and see how much better you wood feel. i know how it is becaus when me and Beany are mad we dont have eny fun and when we make up the one who is to blam always wants to treet. why when Beany was mad with me becaus i went home from Gil Steels surprise party with Lizzie Towle, Ed Towles sister, he woodent speak to me for 2 days, and when we made up he treated me to ice cream with 2 spoons and he let me dip twice to his once. he took pretty big dips to make up. Beany is mad if enny of the fellers go with Lizzie Towle. she likes Beany better than she does enny of the fellers and Beany ought to be satisfied, but sometimes he acks mad when i go down there to fite roosters with Ed. i gess he needent worry much, no feller isnt going to leave of fiting roosters to go with no girls. well i most forgot what i was going to say, but after church i went up to Micky Gould who was going to fite me behind the school house, and said Micky lets be friends and Micky said, huh old Skinny, i can lick you in 2 minits and i said you aint man enuf and he called me a nockneed puke, and i called him a wall eyed lummix and he give me a paist in the eye and i gave him a good one in the mouth, and then we rassled and Micky threw me and i turned him, and he got hold of my new false bosom and i got hold of his hair, and the fellers all hollered hit him Micky, paist him Skinny, and Mister Purington, Pewts father pulled us apart and i had Mickys paper collar and necktie and some of his hair and he had my false bosom and when i got home father made me go to bed and stay there all the afternoon for fiting, but i gess he dident like my losing my false bosom. ennyway he asked me how many times i hit Micky and which licked. he let me get up at supper time. next time i try to love my ennymy i am a going to lick him first.

Went to a sunday school concert in the evening. Keene and Cele sung now i lay me down to sleep. they was a lot of people sung together and Mister Gale beat time. Charlie Gerish played the violin and Miss Packerd sung. i was scart when Keene and Cele sung for i was afraid they would break down, but they dident, and people said they sung like night horks. i gess if they knowed how night horks sung they woodent say much. father felt pretty big and to hear him talk you wood think he did the singing. he give them ten cents apeace. i dident get none. you gest wait, old man till i get my cornet.

Went to a corcus last night. me and Beany were in the hall in the after-noon helping Bob Carter sprinkle the floor and put on the sordust. the floor was all shiny with wax and aufully slipery. so Bob got us to put on some water to take off the shiny wax. well write in front of the platform there is a low platform where they get up to put in their votes and then step down and Beany said, dont put any water there only jest dry sordust. so i dident. well that night we went erly to see the fun. Gim Luverin got up and said there was one man which was the oldest voter in town and he ought to vote the first, the name of this destinkuished sitizen was John Quincy Ann Pollard. then old mister Pollard got up and put in his vote and when he stepped down his heels flew up and he went down whak on the back of his head and 2 men lifted him up and lugged him to a seat, and then Ed Derborn, him that rings the town bell, stepped up pretty lively and went flat and swore terrible, and me and Beany nearly died we laffed so. well it kept on, people dident know what made them fall, and Gim Odlin sat write down in his new umbrella and then they sent me down stairs for a pail of wet sordust and when i was coming up i heard an awful whang, and when i got up in the hall they were lugging old mister Stickney off to die and they put water on his head and lugged him home in a hack. they say Bob Carter will lose his place. me and Beany dont know what to do. if we dont tell, Bob will lose his place and if we do we will get licked.

Mar. 12.  Mister Stickney is all write today. gosh you bet me and Beany are glad. . . .

Mar. 23.  school today. went down to Pewts to draw pictures. Charlie Woodbury can draw the best, then Pewt. and then me. Beany dont like to draw. we was talking about what we was going to be when we grew up. Charlie Woodbury is going to be a picture painter, Pewt is going to be a lawyer, Potter Gorham and Chick Chickering are going to stuff birds for a living, Beany is going to be a hack driver, Gim Wingit is going to run a newspaper, Cawcaw Harding is going to be a piscopal minister becaus he says they only have to read their speaches out of a book, Nipper Brown is going to be a professor, Priscilla Hobbs is going to play a organ in the baptist church. Prisil can play 3 tunes now on a little organ. i am going to be a cornet player like Bruce Briggam. cornet players can go to all the dances and fairs and prosessions and are invited in and treated when people are married and they serrinade them at night, and they don't have to work either. . . .

Mar. 29, 186–  The toads has come out. fine warm day. me and Potter Gorham have been ketching toads this afternoon. they sit in the puddles and peep. folks think it is frogs but most of it is toads. Potter got 23 and i got 18. tonite i put my toads in a box in the kitchen after the folks went to bed. in the night they all got out of the box and began to hop round and peep mother heard it and waked father and they lissened. when i waked up father was coming threw my room with a big cane and a little tin lamp. he had put on his britches and was in his shirt tale, and i said, what are you going to lick me for now i havent done nothing and he said, keep still there is some one down stairs and mother said dont go down George and father said, lissen i can hear him giving a whistle for his confedrit, i will jump in and give him a whack on the cokonut. i had forgot all about the toads and you bet i was scart. well father he crep down easy and blowed out his lite and opened the door quick and jest lammed round with his club. then i heard him say what in hell have i stepped on, bring a lite here. then i thought of the toads and you bet i was scarter than before, mother went down with a lite and then i heard him say, i will be cussed the whole place is full of toads. then mother said did you ever, and father said he never did, and it was some more of that dam boys works and he yelled upstairs for me to come down and ketch them. so i went down and caught them and put them out all but 2 that father had stepped on and they had to be swep up. then all the folks came down in their nitegounds and i went up stairs lively and got into bed and pulled the clothes round me tite, but it dident do enny good for father came up and licked me. he dident lick me very hard becaus i gess he was glad it wasent a berglar and if it hadent been for me it might have been berglars insted of toads.

Mar. 30.   brite and fair. went out with Potter Gorham. saw some toads 2 robins and a blewbird. gosh it makes a feller feel good to see birds and toads and live things. . . .

April 15.   Brite and fair. we all went to church today to see the Lanes. they come from New York and when they go to church everybody goes to see them. there was a boy with them named Willie. i bet i cood lick him. . . .

June 12.   brite and fair. Me and Chick Chickering went bullfroging today. we got 3 dozen hind legs and sold them to Mr. Hirvey for 30 cents and took our pay in icecream. . . .

June 14.   Rashe Belnap and Horris Cobbs go in swimming every morning at six o'clock. i got a licking today that beat the one Beany got. last summer me and Tomtit Tomson and Cawcaw Harding and Whack and Poz and Boog Chadwick went in swimming in May and all thru the summer until October. one day i went in 10 times. well i dident say anything about it to father so as not to scare him. well today he dident go to Boston and he said i am going to teech you to swim. when i was as old as you i cood swim said he, and you must lern, i said i have been wanting to lern to swim, for all the other boys can swim. so we went down to the gravil and i peeled off my close and got ready, now said he, you jest wade in up to your waste and squat down and duck you head under. i said the water will get in my nose. he said no it wont jest squat rite down. i cood see him laffin when he thought i wood snort and sputter.

so i waded out a little ways and then div in and swam under water most across, and when i came up i looked to see if father was supprised. gosh you aught to have seen him. he had pulled off his coat and vest and there he stood up to his waste in the water with his eyes jest bugging rite out as big as hens eggs, and he was jest a going to dive for my dead body. then i turned over on my back and waved my hand at him. he dident say anything for a minute, only he drawed in a long breth. then he began to look foolish, and then mad, and then he turned and started to slosh back to the bank where he slipped and went in all over. When he got to the bank he was pretty mad and yelled for me to come out. when i came out he cut a stick and whaled me, and as soon as i got home he sent me to bed for lying, but i gess he was mad becaus i about scart the life out of him. but that nite i heard him telling mother about it and he said that he dive 3 times for me in about thirty feet of water. but he braged about my swiming and said i cood swim like a striped frog. i shall never forget how his boots went kerslosh kerslosh kerslosh when we were skinning home thru croslots. i shall never forget how that old stick hurt either. ennyhow he dident say ennything about not going in again, so i gess i am all rite. . . .

June 16.   Dennis Cokely and Tomtit Tomson had a fite behind Hirvey's resterent today. Hirvey stopped them jest as they were having a good one. Thats jest the way. i dont see why they always want to stop a fite. All fellers fite for is to see which can lick, and how can they tell unless they fite it out. . . .

June 21.   brite and fair. went fishing today with Potter Gorham. i cought 5 pirch and 4 pickeril. i cleaned them and we had them for supper.

father said they was the best fish he ever et. i also cought the biggest roach i ever saw, almost as big as a sucker, and i cant tell what i did with him. i thought Potter had hooked him for fun, but he said he dident, and we hunted everwhere for him. i dont know where i put that roach. . . .

June 23.   there is a dead rat in the wall in my room. it smells auful.

June 24.   Rany. most time for vacation. the smell in my room is fearful.

June 25.   more trouble today. it seems as if there wasent any use in living. nothing but trouble all the time. mother said i coodent sleep in that room until the rat was taken out. well father he came into my room and sniffed once and said, whew, what a almity smell. then he held his nose and went out and came back with mister Staples the father of the feller that called me Polelegs. well he came in and put his nose up to the wall and sniffed round until he came to where my old close hung. then he said, thunder George, this is the place, rite behind this jacket, it is the wirst smell i ever smelt. then he threw my close in a corner and took out his tools and began to dig a hole in the wall, while father and mother and aunt Sarah stood looking at him and holding their nose. after he dug the hole he reached in but dident find ennything, then he stuck in his nose and said, it dont smell enny in there. then they all let go of their nose and took a sniff and said murder it is wirse than ever it must be rite in the room somewhere. then father said to me, look in those close and see if there is ennything there. so i looked and found in the poket of my old jaket that big roach that i lost, when i went fishing with Potter Gorham. it was all squashy and smelt auful. father was mad and made me throw the jaket out of the window and wont let me go fishing for a week. ennyway i know now what became of my roach. . . .

June 28.   clowdy but no rane. 4th of July pretty soon. father says when he was a boy all they had for fireworks was balls of wool soked in tirpentine whitch they lit an fired round. i am glad i did not live then. . . .

July 3.   Nite before 4th. Pewt and Beany can stay out all nite. father took my snapcrackers into his room and said if i get up before 5 i cant have enny.

July 4.   i am to tired to wright ennything. i never had so much fun in my life. i only got burned 5 times. 1 snapcracker went off rite in my face and i coodent see ennything til mother washed my eyes out. Zee Smith fired a torpedo and a peace of it flew rite in the corner of my eye and made a blew spot there. i fired every one of my snapcrackers. it took me all day.

July 5.   brite and fair. i dident wake up today til 10 o'clock. i was pretty sore and my eyes felt as if they was sawdust in them. . . .

July 7.   father told me i cood go fishing and stay all day. i dont know what had come over him becaus most always he raises time when i go fishing and dont come home erly. so i went and cought 3 pickerels and 4 pirch and 2 hogbacks and went in swiming 2 times. well as i was a coming home 2 or 3 people met me and said they was company at my house, so when i got home i skined in the back way so as not to see the company til i got on my best britches, but i met father in the door and he told me to go rite up to mothers room and see the company. so i skined up to her room holding my hand behind me becaus i had tore my britches auful getting over a fence and i dident want the company to see. well what do you think the company was. it was the homliest baby you ever see, it looked jest like a munky and made feerful faces and kinder squeaked like. Mother was sick and they was a old fat woman who told me to go out, but mother said she wanted to see me and she kissed me and asked me to kiss the baby. i dident want to but i did it becaus mother was sick. mother asked me how many fish i caught and what kind and i told her and said she shood have some for her supper, but she said she gessed she woodent have enny jest then.

then i went down stairs and father said did i like the baby and i said it was homly, and he said it was 10 times as good looking as i was and he said he was glad that when the baby grode up it woodent have Beany and Pewt to play with and woodent be tuff like me, and then Aunt Sarah said she guessed me and Beany and Pewt wasent enny tuffer than father and Gim Melcher were when they was boys, and then father laffed and told me to go to bed and i went. that was a auful homly baby ennyway.

July 8.   nothing particular today. you bet that baby can howl. went to church.

July 9.   brite and fair. most every morning we go up in mothers room to see the old fat woman wash the baby and hear it howl. it turns black in the face. i bet it will be a fiter. . . .

Aug. 8, 186–   brite and fair. the fellers played a pretty mean trick on me tonite. they played it on Nibby Hartwel last nite. Nibby is visiting his aunt and comes from the city and is pretty green like most folks from the city. you see if i hadent got sent to bed because Cele told on me i wood have been there and seen them play it on Nibby. well last nite all the fellers was out. Whack and Boog and Pozzy and Pewt and Beany and Nipper and Cawcaw and Pile and Chick and Micky and Pricilla and Fatty. Nibby he was there too. they wanted to play lead the old blind horse to water and i was to be the blind horse. they said they had some fun playing it the nite before, that was when they played it on Nibby but i dident know that. Well you blindfole a feller and give him a rope and a swich and the other fellers get on the other end of the rope and the feller nearest you has a bell and rings it and you pull and if you can pull him up to you, you can paist time out of him with your swich, only if you pull off your blindfole all the fellers can paist time out of you. Well they blindfolded me and hollered ready and i began to yank and pull and the feller rung his bell and he came pretty hard at first but i kept yanking and bimeby he come so quick that i nearly fell over back wards and i felt him and grabed him and began to paist time out of him when he grabed away my swich and began to paist me, and that wasent fair and i pulled off my blindfole and who do you suppose it was, well it was Wiliam Perry Molton and he was mad. they had tied me to his door bell and i had yanked out almost ten feet of wire. when i saw who it was gosh i began to holler and he stoped licking me. i gess he never licked anyone before becaus he dident know jest how to lay

it on. well when he found out how it was he let me go but he said he shood have
to do something about the boys distirbing him so. it was a pretty mean trick
to play on a feller. we are going to try and play it on Pop Clark tomorrow
nite. . . .

    Sept. 1.   school commences monday. father hasent asked once about my
diry, so i aint going to wright enny more.

## Horatio Alger's Books

    There is a warm spot in the heart of every boy for Horatio Alger,
because he understood boys so well that his stories please them thoroughly.

    The spirit that he tried to infuse into the minds and hearts of American
boys is just as desirable to-day as when Mr. Alger first penned his books.
Love of home, country, parents; honesty, kindness, justice, valor, patriotism—
all these the author dealt with in his stories, but in such a manner that the boy
reader inbibes them unconsciously. Nevertheless, they become a part of him,
and he really lives as Mr. Alger's heroes do—upright and God-fearing.

    These are not "Sunday-school" books, but they well deserve to be, if the
good influence they exert over the boy may be taken into consideration.

    From the publisher's preface to *Tom Temple's Career, or, A Struggle for Fame
and Fortune,* published by Street and Street in 1888, for a price of ten cents.

## How Johnny Bought a
## Sewing Machine
### 1866

### Horatio Alger, Jr.

Just across the street from the Methodist Church, in the principal street of Benton, is a small one-story house, consisting of three rooms only. This is occupied by Mrs. Cooper, a widow, and her only son Johnny, with whom it is our purpose to become further acquainted. When the great Rebellion broke out, Johnny's father was one of the first to enlist. It was a great trial to him to leave behind his wife and son, but he felt it his duty to go. For more than a year he wrote cheerful letters home; but one dark day there came over the wires tidings of the disastrous battle of Fredericksburg, and in the list of killed was the name of James Cooper.

It was a sad day for Mrs. Cooper; but she had little time to mourn. The death of her husband threw the burden of maintaining herself and Johnny upon her shoulders. After a while she obtained a pension of eight dollars a month, which helped her considerably. One half of it paid her rent, and the other half paid for her fuel and lights. But it costs a good deal to buy food and clothes for two persons, and she was obliged to toil early and late with her needle to make up the requisite sum. Johnny was now eleven years old, and might have obtained a chance to peg shoes in some of the shoe-shops in the village, as indeed he wanted to do; but Mrs. Cooper felt that he ought to be kept at school. As she would not be able to leave him money, she was resolved at least to give him as good an education as the village schools would allow.

One evening, just after tea, Mrs. Cooper laid down her work, with a little sigh. "Johnny," said she, "I will get you to run over to Squire Baker's, and say that I shall not be able to finish his shirts to-night, but I will try to send them over in the morning before he goes."

"You don't feel well, mother, do you?"

"No, I have a bad headache. I think I shall go to bed early, and see if I can't sleep it off."

"I don't believe it agrees with you to sew so much," said Johnny.

"I sometimes wish I had a sewing-machine," said his mother. "That would enable me to do three times as much work with less fatigue."

"How much does a sewing-machine cost?"

"I suppose a good one would cost not far from a hundred dollars."

"A hundred dollars! That is a good deal of money," said Johnny.

"Yes, quite too much for our means. Of course there is no chance of my being able to purchase one."

As Johnny went across the field to Squire Baker's, he could not help thinking of what his mother had said. He had hoped the cost of a machine would not exceed twenty dollars, for in that case there might be some chance of his earning the amount in time. Occasionally the neighbors called upon him to do odd jobs, and paid him small sums. These in time might amount to twenty dollars. But a hundred seemed quite too large for him to think of accumulating.

"Still," thought Johnny, "I've a good mind to try. I won't wait for jobs to come to me; I'll look out for them. I have a good deal of time out of school when I might be doing something. If I don't get enough to buy a sewing-machine, I may get something else that mother will like."

The next day was Saturday, and school did not keep. It was about the first of October. In the town where Johnny lived there were many swamps planted with cranberries, which were now ripe and ready for gathering. It was necessary to pick them before a frost, since this fruit, if touched with the frost, will decay rapidly. As Johnny was coming home from the store, he met a school companion, who seemed to be in a hurry.

"Where are you going, Frank?" he inquired.

"I'm going to pick cranberries for Squire Baker."

"How much does he pay?"

"Two cents a quart."

"Do you think he would hire me?" asked Johnny, with a sudden thought.

"Yes, and be glad to get you. He's got a good many cranberries on the vines, and he's afraid there will be a frost to-night."

"Then I'll go and ask mother if I can go. Just hold on a minute."

"All right."

Having obtained permission, Johnny rejoined his companion, and proceeded at once to the swamp. The fruit was abundant; for the crop this year was unusually good, and Johnny found that he could pick quite rapidly. When noon came, he found that he had picked twenty quarts.

"Can you come again this afternoon?" asked the Squire.

"Yes, sir," said Johnny, promptly.

"I shall be very glad to have you, for hands are scarce."

Johnny had already earned forty cents, and hoped to earn as much more in the afternoon. He was so excited by his success that he hurried through his dinner with great rapidity, and was off once more to the swamp. He worked till late, and found at the end of the day that he had gathered fifty quarts. He felt very rich when the Squire handed him a one-dollar greenback in return for his services. He felt pretty tired in consequence of stooping so much, but the thought that he had earned a whole dollar in one day fully repaid him.

"Mother," said Johnny when he got home, "if you are willing, I will keep this money. There is something very particular I want it for."

"Certainly," said his mother. "You shall keep this, and all you earn. I am very sure you will not wish to spend it unwisely."

"No, mother you may be sure of that."

On Monday it so happened that the teacher was sick, and school was suspended. Johnny found no difficulty in obtaining a chance to pick cranberries for another neighbor. He was determined to do a little better than on Saturday. When evening came, he was paid for fifty-three quarts,—one dollar and six cents.

"I wish there were cranberries to be picked all the year round," thought Johnny. "I should soon get a hundred dollars."

But this was about the last of his picking. School kept the next day, and though he got a little time after school, he could only pick a few quarts. When the cranberry season was over, Johnny found himself the possessor of four dollars. After that his gains were small. Occasionally he ran on an errand for a neighbor. Once he turned the grindstone for about half an hour, and received the small compensation of one cent from a rather parsimonious farmer. Johnny was about to throw it away, when the thought came to him, that, small as it was, it would help a little.

So the autumn slipped away, and winter came and went. In the spring Johnny found more to do. On the first day of June he counted his money, and found he had fifteen dollars.

"It'll take a long time to get a hundred dollars," sighed Johnny. "If mother would only let me go to work in a shoe-shop! But she thinks I had better go to school. But by and by there'll be a chance to pick cranberries again. I wish there'd be a vacation then."

One morning Johnny had occasion to cross the fields near a small pond about half a mile from his mother's house. He was busily thinking about his little fund, and what he could do to increase it, when his attention was all at once attracted by a sharp cry of distress. Looking up, he saw a gentleman in a row-boat on the pond, who appeared to be in the greatest trouble.

"Boy," he called out, "can you swim?"

"Yes, sir," said Johnny.

"Then save my little daughter, if you can. She has just fallen out of the boat. There she is."

The little girl just appeared above the surface of the water. Luckily it was very near the shore, yet too deep for any one to venture who was unable to swim. Our young hero had plenty of courage. Moreover, he was an expert swimmer, having been taught by his father before he went to the war. Without a minute's hesitation he stripped off his jacket and plunged in. A few vigorous strokes brought him to the little girl. He seized her, just as she was about sinking for the third time. He held her till her father could receive her from his arms into the boat.

"Let me lift you in, too," he said.

"No, sir; I'll swim to shore," said Johnny.

"Come up to the hotel this afternoon. I want to see you."

The father applied himself to the restoration of his daughter, and Johnny went home and changed his wet clothes. He had recognized the gentleman as a merchant from the city who had been boarding at the hotel for a week or two. He felt a glow of satisfaction in the thought that he had been instrumental in saving a human life; for it was very evident that, her father being unable to swim, the little girl would but for him have been drowned.

In the afternoon he went to the hotel, and inquired for Mr. Barclay, for he had heard the gentleman's name. He was conducted up stairs into a private parlor.

Mr. Barclay advanced towards him with a smile of welcome. "I am glad to see you, my brave boy," he said.

"Is your little girl quite recovered?" asked Johnny, modestly.

"Yes, nearly so. I thought it best to let her lie in bed the remainder of the day, as she might have got chilled. And now, my dear boy, how shall I express my gratitude to you for your noble conduct? Under God, you have been the means of saving my dear child's life. I am quite unable to swim, and I shudder to think what would have happened but for your timly presence and courage."

"I am very glad I was able to be of service," said Johnny.

"I cannot allow such a service to go unrewarded," said Mr. Barclay. "Adequate compensation I cannot offer, for money will not pay for the saving of life; but you will allow me to give you this as a first instalment of my gratitude." He pressed into the hands of the astonished boy a one-hundred-dollar bill.

"One hundred dollars!" exclaimed Johnny in bewilderment. "Do you really mean to give me so much?"

"It is little enough, I am sure."

"O, I am so glad!" said Johnny, delighted. "Now I can buy mother a sewing-machine."

"But don't you want to buy something for yourself?" asked Mr. Barclay, with interest.

"No, sir; I would rather have a sewing-machine than anything."

Then Johnny, encouraged by Mr. Barclay's evident interest, proceeded to tell him how for nearly a year he had been saving up money, without his mother's knowledge, to buy her a machine, in order that she need not work so hard in future. But thus far he had only succeeded in saving up fifteen dollars. Now, thanks to this unexpected gift, he would be able to buy it at once. "And it'll come just right, too," he said, with sparkling eyes; "for it will be mother's birthday in a week from to-day, and I can give it to her then. Only," he said doubtfully, "I don't know whom I can get to buy it."

"I can help you there," said Mr. Barclay. "I am going to the city in a day or two. I will select the machine, and arrange to have it sent down by express on your mother's birthday."

"That'll be just the thing," said Johnny. "Won't she be astonished? I sha'n't say anything to her about it beforehand. Here's the money, sir; I thank you very much for that, and for your kind offer."

"I ought to be kind to you, my dear boy, when I think how much you have done for me."

"Good afternoon, sir."

"Good afternoon. Call again to-morrow, and you shall see the little girl you have saved."

Johnny did call the next day, and made acquaintance with little Annie Barclay, whom he found a sprightly little girl of four years of age. She took quite a fancy to our young hero, with whom she had a fine game of romps.

Mrs. Cooper knew that Johnny had saved a little girl from drowning, but never inquired what reward he had received, feeling sure that he would tell her some time. As for Johnny, he had his reasons for keeping silent, as we know.

At length Mrs. Cooper's birthday came. Johnny was full of impatience for evening, for then the express-wagon would arrive from Boston with the present for his mother. As soon as he heard the rumble of the wheels, he ran to the door. To his delight, the wagon stopped at the gate.

"Come here, youngster, and give us a lift," called the express-man. "I've got something heavy for you."

It was a large article, looking something like a table; but what it was Mrs. Cooper could not tell, on account of its many wrappings. "There must be some mistake," she said, going to the door. "I am not expecting anything."

"No, there isn't," said Johnny; "it's all right, directed in large letters to Mrs. Mary Cooper, Benton."

"I shall want fifty cents," said the express-man.

"I've got it here," said Johnny, seeing that his mother was searching for her pocket-book.

"O, by the way, here's something else,—a letter directed to you. That will be fifteen cents more."

"Indeed!" said Johnny surprised. "Well, here's the money." He took the letter, but did not open it at once. He wanted to enjoy his mother's surprise.

Mrs. Cooper was unwrapping the machine. "What is this?" she exclaimed, in delighted surprise. "A sewing-machine! Who could have sent it? Do you know anything about it, Johnny?"

"Yes, mother. It's a birthday present for you from me."

"My dear boy! How could you ever have earned money enough to pay for it?"

Then Johnny told his mother all about it. And her eyes glistened with pride and joy as she heard, for the first time, how he had worked for months with this end in view, and she could not help giving him a grateful kiss, which I am sure paid Johnny for all he had done.

It was really a beautiful machine, and, though Johnny did not know it, cost considerably more than the hundred dollars he had sent. Mrs. Cooper found that it worked admirably, and would lighten her labors more even than she had hoped.

"But you haven't opened your letter," she said with a sudden recollection.

"So I haven't," said Johnny.

What was his surprise on opening it to discover the same hundred-dollar bill which Mr. Barclay had originally given him, accompanied by the following note.

"My DEAR YOUNG FRIEND:—I have bought your mother a sewing-machine, which I send by express to-day. I hope it will please you both, and prove very useful. I also send you a hundred dollars, which I wish you to use for yourself. The sewing-machine will be none the less your present to your mother, since both that and the money are a very insufficient recompense for the service you have rendered me. Continue to love and help your mother, and when you are old enough to go into a store I will receive you into mine.

"Your friend,

"HENRY BARCLAY."

There was great joy in the little cottage that evening. Johnny felt as rich as a millionaire, and could not take his eyes from the corner where the handsome new sewing-machine had been placed. And his mother, happy as she was in her present, was happier in the thought that it had come to her through the good conduct of her son.

# A Walker in the City

## 1951

## Alfred Kazin

When I was a child I thought we lived at the end of the world. It was the eternity of the subway ride into the city that first gave me this idea. It took a long time getting to "New York"; it seemed longer getting back. Even the I.R.T. got tired by the time it came to us, and ran up into the open for a breath of air before it got locked into its terminus at New Lots. As the train left the tunnel to rattle along the elevated tracks, I felt I was being jostled on a camel past the last way stations in the desert. Oh that ride from New York! Light came only at Sutter Avenue. First across the many stations of the Gentiles to the East River. Then clear across Brooklyn, almost to the brink of the ocean all our fathers crossed. All those first stations in Brooklyn—Clark, Borough Hall, Hoyt, Nevins, the junction of the East and West Side express lines—told me only that I was on the last leg home, though there was always a stirring of my heart at Hoyt, where the grimy subway platform was suddenly enlivened by Abraham and Straus's windows of ladies' wear. Atlantic Avenue was vaguely exciting, a crossroads, the Long Island railroad; I never saw a soul get in or out at Bergen Street; the Grand Army Plaza, with its great empty caverns smoky with dust and chewing-gum wrappers, meant Prospect Park and that stone path beside a meadow where as a child I ran off from my father one summer twilight just in time to see the lamplighter go up the path lighting from the end of his pole each gas mantle suddenly flaring within its corolla of pleated paper—then, that summer I first strayed off the block for myself, the steps leading up from the boathouse, the long stalks of grass wound between the steps thick with the dust and smell of summer—then, that great summer at sixteen, my discovery in the Brooklyn Museum of Albert Pinkham Ryder's cracked oily fishing boats drifting under the moon. Franklin Avenue was where the Jews began—but all middle-class Jews, *alrightniks,* making out "all right" in the New World, they were still Gentiles to me as they went out into the wide and tree-lined Eastern Parkway. For us the journey went on and on—past Nostrand, past Kingston, past Utica, and only then out

46

into the open at Sutter, overlooking Lincoln Terrace Park, "Tickle-Her" Park, the zoo of our adolescence, through which no girl could pass on a summer evening without its being understood forever after that she was "in"; past the rickety "two-family" private houses built in the fever of Brownsville's last real-estate boom; and then into Brownsville itself—Saratoga, Rockaway, and home. For those who lived still beyond, in East New York, there was Junius, there was Pennsylvania, there was Van Siclen, and so at last into New Lots, where the city goes back to the marsh, and even the subway ends.

Yet it was not just the long pent-up subway ride that led me to think of Brownsville as the margin of the city, the last place, the car barns where they locked up the subway and the trolley cars at night. There were always raw patches of unused city land all around us filled with "monument works" where they cut and stored tombstones, as there were still on our street farmhouses and the remains of old cobbled driveways down which chickens came squealing into our punchball games—but most of it dead land, neither country nor city, with that look of prairie waste I have so often seen on my walks along the fringes of American cities near the freight yards. We were nearer the ocean than the city, but our front on the ocean was Canarsie—in those days the great refuse dump through which I made my first and grimmest walks into the city—a place so celebrated in New York vaudeville houses for its squalor that the very sound of the word was always good for a laugh. CAN-NARR-SIE! They fell into the aisles. But that was the way to the ocean we always took summer evenings—through silent streets of old broken houses whose smoky red Victorian fronts looked as if the paint had clotted like blood and had then been mixed with soot—past infinite weedy lots, the smell of freshly cut boards in the lumber yards, the junk yards, the marshland eating the pavement, the truck farms, the bungalows that had lost a window or a door as they tottered on their poles against the damp and the ocean winds. The place as I have it in my mind still reeks of the fires burning in the refuse dumps. Farms that had once been the outposts of settlers in Revolutionary days had crumbled and sunk like wet sand. Canarsie was where they opened the sluice gates to let the city's muck out into the ocean. But at the end was the roar of the Atlantic and the summer house where we stood outside watching through lattices the sports being served with great pitchers of beer foaming onto the red-checked tablecloths. Summer, my summer! Summer!

We were of the city, but somehow not in it. Whenever I went off on my favorite walk to Highland Park in the "American" district to the north, on the border of Queens, and climbed the hill to the old reservoir from which I could look straight across to the skyscrapers of Manhattan, I saw New York as a foreign city. There, brilliant and unreal, the city had its life, as Brownsville was ours. That the two were joined in me I never knew then—not even on those glorious summer nights of my last weeks in high school when, with what an ache, I would come back into Brownsville along Liberty Avenue, and, as soon as I could see blocks ahead of me the Labor Lyceum, the malted milk and Fatima signs over the candy stores, the old women in their housedresses sitting in front of the tenements like priestesses of an ancient cult, knew I was home.

We were the end of the line. We were the children of the immigrants who had camped at the city's back door, in New York's rawest, remotest, cheapest ghetto, enclosed on one side by the Canarsie flats and on the other by the hallowed middle-class districts that showed the way to New York. "New York" was what we put last on our address, but first in thinking of the others around us. *They* were New York, the Gentiles, America; we were Brownsville— *Brunzvil,* as the old folks said—the dust of the earth to all Jews with money, and notoriously a place that measured all success by our skill in getting away from it. So that when poor Jews left, *even* Negroes, as we said, found it easy to settle on the margins of Brownsville, and with the coming of spring, bands of Gypsies, who would rent empty stores, hang their rugs around them like a desert tent, and bring a dusty and faintly sinister air of carnival into our neighborhood. . . .

All my early life lies open to my eye within five city blocks. When I passed the school, I went sick with all my old fear of it. With its standard New York public-school brown brick courtyard shut in on three sides of the square and the pretentious battlements overlooking that cockpit in which I can still smell the fiery sheen of the rubber ball, it looks like a factory over which has been imposed the façade of a castle. It gave me the shivers to stand up in that courtyard again; I felt as if I had been mustered back into the service of those Friday morning "tests" that were the terror of my childhood.

It was never learning I associated with that school: only the necessity to succeed, to get ahead of the others in the daily struggle to "make a good impression" on our teachers, who grimly, wearily, and often with ill-concealed distaste watched against our relapsing into the natural savagery they expected of Brownsville boys. The white, cool, thinly ruled record book sat over us from their desks all day long, and had remorselessly entered into it each day —in blue ink if we had passed, in red ink if we had not—our attendance, our conduct, our "effort," our merits and demerits; and to the last possible decimal point in calculation, our standing in an unending series of "tests"—surprise tests, daily tests, weekly tests, formal midterm tests, final tests. They never stopped trying to dig out of us whatever small morsel of fact we had managed to get down the night before. We had to prove that we were really alert, ready for anything, always in the race. That white thinly ruled record book figured in my mind as the judgment seat; the very thinness and remote blue lightness of its lines instantly showed its cold authority over me; so much space had been left on each page, columns and columns in which to note down everything about us, implacably and forever. As it lay there on a teacher's desk, I stared at it all day long with such fear and anxious propriety that I had no trouble believing that God, too, did nothing but keep such record books, and that on the final day He would face me with an account in Hebrew letters whose phonetic dots and dashes looked strangely like decimal points counting up my every sinful thought on earth.

All teachers were to be respected like gods, and God Himself was the greatest of all school superintendents. Long after I had ceased to believe that our teachers could see with the back of their heads, it was still understood, by me, that they knew everything. They were the delegates of all visible and invisible power on earth—of the mothers who waited on the stoops every day after three for us to bring home tales of our daily triumphs; of the glacially remote Anglo-Saxon principal, whose very name was King; of the incalculably important Superintendent of Schools who would someday rubberstamp his name to the bottom of our diplomas in grim acknowledgment that we had, at last, given satisfaction to him, to the Board of Superintendents, and to our benefactor the City of New York—and so up and up, to the government of the United States and to the great Lord Jehovah Himself. My belief in teachers' unlimited wisdom and power rested not so much on what I saw in them —how impatient most of them looked, how wary—but on our abysmal humility, at least in those of us who were "good" boys, who proved by our ready compliance and "manners" that we wanted to get on. The road to a professional future would be shown us only as we pleased *them. Make a good impression the first day of the term, and they'll help you out. Make a bad impression, and you might as well cut your throat.* This was the first article of school folkore, whispered around the classroom the opening day of each term. You made the "good impression" by sitting firmly at your wooden desk, hands clasped; by silence for the greatest part of the live-long day; by standing up obsequiously when it was so expected of you; by sitting down noiselessly when you had answered a question; by "speaking nicely," which meant reproducing their painfully exact enunciation; by "showing manners," or an ecstatic submissiveness in all things; by outrageous flattery; by bringing little gifts at Christmas, on their birthdays, and at the end of the term—the well-known significance of these gifts being that they came not from us, but from our parents, whose eagerness in this matter showed a high level of social consideration, and thus raised our standing in turn.

It was not just our quickness and memory that were always being tested. Above all, in that word I could never hear without automatically seeing it raised before me in gold-plated letters, it was our *character.* I always felt anxious when I heard the word pronounced. Satisfactory as my "character" was, on the whole, except when I stayed too long in the playground reading; outrageously satisfactory, as I can see now, the very sound of the word as our teachers coldly gave it out from the end of their teeth, with a solemn weight on each dark syllable, immediately struck my heart cold with fear—they could not believe I really had it. Character was never something you had; it had to be trained in you, like a technique. I was never very clear about it. On our side *character* meant demonstrative obedience; but teachers already had it— how else could they have become teachers? They had it; the aloof Anglo-Saxon principal whom we remotely saw only on ceremonial occasions in the assembly was positively encased in it; it glittered off his bald head in spokes of triumphant light; the President of the United States had the greatest conceivable amount of it. Character belonged to great adults. Yet we were constantly being driven onto it; it was the great threshold we had to cross. *Alfred Kazin, having shown proficiency in his course of studies and having displayed satisfactory marks of character* . . . Thus someday the hallowed diploma, passport to my further advancement in high school. But there—I could already feel it in my bones—they would put me through even more doubting tests of character; and after that, if I should be good enough and bright enough, there would be still more. *Character* was a bitter thing, racked with my endless striving to please. The school—from every last stone in the courtyard to the battlements frowning down at me from the walls—was only the stage for a trial. I felt that the very atmosphere of learning that surrounded us was fake—that every lesson, every book, every approving smile was only a pretext for the constant probing and watching of me, that there was not a secret in me that would not be decimally measured into that white record book. All week long I lived for the blessed sound of the dismissal gong at three o'clock on Friday afternoon.

I was awed by this system, I believed in it, I respected its force. The alternative was "going bad." The school was notoriously the toughest in our tough neighborhood, and the dangers of "going bad" were constantly impressed upon me at home and in school in dark whispers of the "reform school" and in examples of boys who had been picked up for petty thievery, rape, or flinging a heavy inkwell straight into a teacher's face. Behind any failure in school yawned the great abyss of a criminal career. Every refractory attitude doomed you with the sound "Sing Sing." Anything less than absolute perfection in school always suggested to my mind that I might fall out of the daily race, be kept back in the working class forever, or—dared I think of it? —fall into the criminal class itself.

I worked on a hairline between triumph and catastrophe. Why the odds should always have felt so narrow I understood only when I realized how little my parents thought of their own lives. It was not for myself alone that I was expected to shine, but for them—to redeem the constant anxiety of their existence. I was the first American child, their offering to the strange new God; I was to be the monument of their liberation from the shame of being— what they were. And that there was shame in this was a fact that everyone seemed to believe as a matter of course. It was in the gleeful discounting of themselves—what do we know?—with which our parents greeted every fresh victory in our savage competition for "high averages," for prizes, for a few condercending words of official praise from the principal at assembly. It was in the sickening invocation of "Americanism"—the word itself accusing us of everything we apparently were not. Our families and teachers seemed tacitly agreed that we were somehow to be a little ashamed of what we were. Yet it was always hard to say why this should be so. It was certainly not—in Brownsville!—because we were Jews, or simply because we spoke another language at home, or were absent on our holy days. It was rather that a "refined," "correct," "nice" English was required of us at school that we did not naturally speak, and that our teachers could never be quite sure we would keep. This English was peculiarly the ladder of advancement. Every future young lawyer was known by it. Even the Communists and Socialists on Pitkin Avenue spoke it. It was bright and clean and polished. We were expected to show it off like a new pair of shoes. When the teacher sharply called a question out, then your name, you were expected to leap up, face the class, and eject those new words fluently off the tongue. . . .

In the great cool assembly hall, dominated by the gold sign above the stage KNOWLEDGE IS POWER, the windowsills were lined with Dutch bulbs, each wedged into a mound of pebbles massed in a stone dish. Above them hung a giant photograph of Theodore Roosevelt. Whenever I walked in to see the empty assembly hall for myself, the shiny waxed floor of the stage dangled in the middle of the air like a crescent. On one side was a great silk American flag, the staff crowned by a gilt eagle. Across the dry rattling of varnish-smelling empty seats bowing to the American flag, I saw in the play of the sun on those pebbles wildly sudden images of peace. *There* was the other land, crowned by the severe and questioning face of Theodore Roosevelt, his eyes above the curiously endearing straw-dry mustache, behind the pince-nez glittering with light, staring and staring me through as if he were uncertain whether he fully approved of me.

The light pouring through window after window in that great empty varnished assembly hall seemed to me the most wonderful thing I had ever seen. It was that thorough varnished cleanness that was of the new land, that light dancing off the glasses of Theodore Roosevelt, those green and white roots of the still raw onion-brown bulbs delicately flaring up from the hill of pebbles into which they were wedged. The pebbles moved me in themselves, there were so many of them. They rose up around the bulbs in delicately strong masses of colored stone, and as the sun fell between them, each pebble shone in its own light. Looking across the great rows of empty seats to those pebbles lining the windowsills, I could still smell summer from some long veranda surrounded by trees. On that veranda sat the family and friends of Theodore Roosevelt. I knew the name: Oyster Bay. Because of that picture, I had read *The Boy's Life of Theodore Roosevelt;* knew he had walked New York streets night after night as Police Commissioner, unafraid of the Tenderloin gangsters; had looked into *Theodore Roosevelt's Letters to His Children*, pretending that those hilarious drawings on almost every page were for me. *There* was America, I thought, the real America, *his* America, where from behind the glass on the wall of our assembly hall he watched over us to make sure we did right, thought right, lived right.

"Up, boys! Up San Juan Hill!" I still hear our roguish old civics teacher, a little white-haired Irishman who was supposed to have been with Teddy in Cuba, driving us through our Friday morning tests with these shouts and cries.

He called them "Army Navy" tests, to make us feel big, and dividing the class between Army and Navy, got us to compete with each other for a coveted blue star. Civics was city government, state government, federal government; each government had functions; you had to get them out fast in order to win for the Army or the Navy. Sometimes this required filling in three or four words, line by line, down one side of the grimly official yellow foolscap that was brought out for tests. (In the tense silence just before the test began, he looked at us sharply, the watch in his hand ticking as violently as the sound of my heart, and on command, fifty boys simultaneously folded their yellow test paper and evened the fold with their thumbnails in a single dry sigh down the middle of the paper.) At other times it meant true-or-false tests; then he stood behind us to make sure we did not signal the right answers to each other in the usual way—for true, nodding your head; for false, holding your nose. You could hear his voice barking from the rear. *"Come on now, you Army boys! On your toes like West Point cadets! All ready now? Get set! Go! Three powers of the legislative branch? The judiciary? The executive? The subject of the fifteenth amendment? The capital of Wyoming? Come on, Navy! Shoot those landlubbers down! Give 'em a blast from your big guns right through the middle! The third article of the Bill of Rights? The thirteenth amendment? The sixteenth? True or false, Philadelphia is the capital of Pennsylvania. Up and at 'em, Navy! Mow them down! COME ON!!!"* Our "average" was calculated each week, and the boys who scored 90 per cent or over were rewarded by seeing *their own names* lettered on the great blue chart over the blackboard. Each time I entered that room for a test, I looked for my name on the blue chart as if the sight of it would decide my happiness for all time. . . .

On Belmont Avenue, Brownsville's great open street market, the pushcarts are still lined on each other for blocks, and the din is as deafening, marvelous, and appetizing as ever. They have tried to tone it down; the pushcarts are now confined to one side of the street. When I was a boy, they clogged both sides, reached halfway up the curb to the open stands of the stores; walking down the street was like being whirled around and around in a game of blind man's buff. But Belmont Avenue is still the merriest street in Brownsville. As soon as I walked into it from Rockaway, caught my first whiff of the herrings and pickles in their great black barrels, heard the familiarly harsh, mocking cries and shouts from the market women—*"Oh you darlings! Oh you sweet ones, oh you pretty ones! Storm us! Tear us apart! Devour us!"*—I laughed right out loud, it was so good to be back among *them*. Nowhere but on Belmont Avenue did I ever see in Brownsville such open, hearty people as those market women. Their shrewd open-weather eyes missed nothing. The street was their native element; they seemed to hold it together with their hands, mouths, fists, and knees; they stood up in it behind their stands all day long, and in every weather; they stood up for themselves. In winter they would bundle themselves into five or six sweaters, then putting long white aprons over their overcoats, would warm themselves at fires lit in black oil drums between the pushcarts, their figures bulging as if to meet the rain and cold head-on in defiance.

I could hear them laughing and mock-crying all the way to Stone Avenue, still imploring and pulling at every woman on the street—*"Vayber! Vayber! Sheyne gute vayber! Oh you lovelies! Oh you good ones! Oh you pretty ones! See how cheap and good! Just come over! Just taste! Just a little look! What will it cost you to taste? How can you walk on without looking? How can you resist us? Oh! Oh! Come over! Come over! Devour us! Storm us! Tear us apart! BARGAINS BARGAINS!!"* I especially loved watching them at dusk, an hour before supper, when the women would walk through to get the food at its freshest. Then, in those late winter afternoons, when there was that deep grayness on the streets and that spicy smell from the open stands at dusk I was later to connect with my first great walks inside the New York crowd at the rush hour—then there would arise from behind the great flaming oil drums and the pushcarts loaded with their separate mounds of shoelaces, corsets, pots and pans, stockings, kosher kitchen soap, memorial candles in their wax-filled tumblers and glassware, "chiney" oranges, beet roots and soup greens, that deep and good odor of lox, of salami, of herrings and half-sour pickles, that told me I was truly home.

As I went down Belmont Avenue, the copper-shining herrings in the tall black barrels made me think of the veneration of food in Brownsville families. I can still see the kids pinned down to the tenement stoops, their feet helplessly kicking at the pots and pans lined up before them, their mouths pressed open with a spoon while the great meals are rammed down their throats. *"Eat! Eat! May you be destroyed if you don't eat! What sin have I committed that God should punish me with you! Eat! What will become of you if you don't eat! Imp of darkness, may you sink ten fathoms into the earth if you don't eat! Eat!"*

We never had a chance to know what hunger meant. At home we nibbled all day long as a matter of course. On the block we gorged ourselves continually on "Nessels," Hersheys, gumdrops, polly seeds, nuts, chocolate-covered cherries, charlotte russe, and ice cream. A warm and sticky ooze of chocolate ran through everything we touched; the street always smelled faintly like the candy wholesaler's windows on the way back from school. The hunger for sweets, jellies, and soda water raged in us like a disease; during the grimmest punchball game, in the middle of a fist fight, we would dash to the candy store to get down two-cent blocks of chocolate and "small"—three-cent—glasses of cherry soda; or calling "upstairs" from the street, would have flung to us, or carefully hoisted down at the end of a clothesline, thick slices of rye bread smeared with chicken fat. No meal at home was complete without cream soda, root beer, ginger ale, "celery tonic." We poured jelly on bread; we poured it into the tea; we often ate chocolate marshmallows before breakfast. At school during the recess hour Syrian vendors who all looked alike in their alpaca jackets and black velour hats came after us with their white enameled trays, from which we took *Halvah*, Turkish Delight, and three different kinds of greasy nut-brown pastry sticks. From the Jewish vendors, who went around the streets in every season wheeling their little tin stoves, we bought roasted potatoes either in the quarter or the half—the skins were hard as bark and still smelled of the smoke pouring out of the stoves; apples you ate off a stick that were encrusted with a thick glaze of baked jelly you never entirely got down your throat or off your fingers, so that you seemed to be with it all day; *knishes;* paper spills of hot yellow chick peas. I still hear those peddlers crying up and down the street—*"Árbes! Árbes! Hayse gute árbes! Kinder! Kinder! Hayse gute árbes!"* From the "big" Italians, whom we saw only in summer, we bought watermelons as they drove their great horse-smelling wagons down the street calling up to every window—"Hey you ladies! *Hey ladies! Freschi* and good!"—and from the "small" ones, who pushed carts through the streets, paper cups of shaved ice sprinkled before our eyes with drops of lemon or orange or raspberry syrup from a narrow water bottle.

But our greatest delight in all seasons was "delicatessen"—hot spiced corned beef, pastrami, rolled beef, hard salami, soft salami, chicken salami, bologna, frankfurter "specials" and the thinner, wrinkled hot dogs always taken with mustard and relish and sauerkraut, and whenever possible, to make the treat fully real, with potato salad, baked beans, and french fries which had been bubbling in the black wire fryer deep in the iron pot. At Saturday twilight, as soon as the delicatessen store reopened after the Sabbath rest, we raced into it panting for the hot dogs sizzling on the gas plate just inside the window. The look of that blackened empty gas plate had driven us wild all through the wearisome Sabbath day. And now, as the electric sign blazed up again, lighting up the words JEWISH NATIONAL DELICATESSEN, it was as if we had entered into our rightful heritage. Yet *Wurst* carried associations with the forbidden, the adulterated, the excessive; with spices that teased and maddened the senses to demand more, still more. This was food that only on Saturday nights could be eaten with a good conscience. Generally, we bought it on the sly; it was supposed to be bad for us; I thought it was made in dark cellars. Still, our parents could not have disapproved of it altogether. Each new mouthful of food we took in was an advantage stolen in the battle. The favorite injunction was to *fix yourself,* by which I understood we needed to do a repair job on ourselves. In the swelling and thickening of a boy's body was the poor family's earliest success. "Fix yourself!" a mother cried indignantly to the child on the stoop. "Fix yourself!" The word for a fat boy was *solid.* . . .

In Brownsville tenements the kitchen is always the largest room and the center of the household. As a child I felt that we lived in a kitchen to which four other rooms were annexed. My mother, a "home" dressmaker, had her workshop in the kitchen. She told me once that she had begun dressmaking in Poland at thirteen; as far back as I can remember, she was always making dresses for the local women. She had an innate sense of design, a quick eye for all the subtleties in the latest fashion, even when she despised them, and great boldness. For three or four dollars she would study the fashion magazines with a customer, go with the customer to the remnants store on Belmont Avenue to pick out the material, argue the owner down—all remnants stores, for some reason, were supposed to be shady, as if the owners dealt in stolen goods—and then for days would patiently fit and baste and sew and fit again. Our apartment was always full of women in their housedresses sitting around the kitchen table waiting for a fitting. My little bedroom next to the kitchen was the fitting room. The sewing machine, an old nut-brown Singer with golden scrolls painted along the black arm and engraved along the two tiers of little drawers massed with needles and thread on each side of the treadle, stood next to the window and the great coalblack stove which up to my last year in college was our main source of heat. By December the two outer bedrooms were closed off, and used to chill bottles of milk and cream, cold borscht and jellied calves' feet.

The kitchen held our lives together. My mother worked in it all day long, we ate in it almost all meals except the Passover *seder,* I did my homework and first writing at the kitchen table, and in winter I often had a bed made up for me on three kitchen chairs near the stove. On the wall just over the table hung a long horizontal mirror that sloped to a ship's prow at each end and was lined in cherry wood. It took up the whole wall, and drew every object in the kitchen to itself. The walls were a fiercely stippled whitewash, so often rewhitened by my father in slack seasons that the paint looked as if it had been squeezed and cracked into the walls. A large electric bulb hung down the center of the kitchen at the end of a chain that had been hooked into the ceiling; the old gas ring and key still jutted out of the wall like antlers. In the corner next to the toilet was the sink at which we washed, and the square tub in which my mother did our clothes. Above it, tacked to the shelf on which were pleasantly ranged square, blue-bordered white sugar and spice jars, hung calendars from the Public National Bank on Pitkin Avenue and the Minsker Progressive Branch of the Workman's Circle; receipts for the payment of insurance premiums, and household bills on a spindle; two little boxes engraved with Hebrew letters. One of these was for the poor, the other to buy back the Land of Israel. Each spring a bearded little man would suddenly appear in our kitchen, salute us with a hurried Hebrew blessing, empty the boxes (sometimes with a sidelong look of disdain if they were not full), hurriedly bless us again for remembering our less fortunate Jewish brothers and sisters, and so take his departure until the next spring, after vainly trying to persuade my mother to take still another box. We did occasionally remember to drop coins in the boxes, but this was usually only on the dreaded morning of "midterms" and final examinations, because my mother thought it would bring me luck. She was extremely superstitious, but embarrassed about it, and always laughed at herself whenever, on the morning of an examination, she counseled me to leave the house on my right foot. "I know it's silly," her smile seemed to say, "but what harm can it do? It may calm God down."

The kitchen gave a special character to our lives; my mother's character. All my memories of that kitchen are dominated by the nearness of my mother sitting all day long at her sewing machine, by the clacking of the treadle against the linoleum floor, by the patient twist of her right shoulder as she automatically pushed at the wheel with one hand or lifted the foot to free the needle where it had got stuck in a thick piece of material. The kitchen was her life. Year by year, as I began to take in her fantastic capacity for labor and her anxious zeal, I realized it was ourselves she kept stitched together. I can never remember a time when she was not working. She worked because the law of her life was work, work and anxiety; she worked because she would have found life meaningless without work. She read almost no English; she could read the Yiddish paper, but never felt she had time to. We were always talking of a time when I would teach her how to read, but somehow there was never time. When I awoke in the morning she was already at her machine, or in the great morning crowd of housewives at the grocery getting fresh rolls for breakfast. When I returned from school she was at her machine, or conferring over *McCall's* with some neighborhood woman who had come in pointing hopefully to an illustration—"Mrs. Kazin! Mrs. Kazin! Make me a dress like it shows here in the picture!" When my father came home from work she had somehow mysteriously interrupted herself to make supper for us, and the dishes cleared and washed, was back at her machine. When I went to bed at night, often she was still there, pounding away at the treadle, hunched over the wheel, her hands steering a piece of gauze under the needle with a finesse that always contrasted sharply with her swollen hands and broken nails. Her left hand had been pierced through when as a girl she had worked in the infamous Triangle Shirtwaist Factory on the East Side. A needle had gone straight through the palm, severing a large vein. They had sewn it up for her so clumsily that a tuft of flesh always lay folded over the palm.

    The kitchen was the great machine that set our lives running; it whirred down a little only on Saturdays and holy days. From my mother's kitchen I gained my first picture of life as a white, overheated, starkly lit workshop redolent with Jewish cooking, crowded with women in housedresses, strewn with fashion magazines, patterns, dress material, spools of thread—and at whose center, so lashed to her machine that bolts of energy seemed to dance out of her hands and feet as she worked, my mother stamped the treadle hard against the floor, hard, hard, and silently, grimly at war beat out the first rhythm of the world for me.

    Every sound from the street roared and trembled at our windows—a mother feeding her child on the doorstep, the screech of the trolley cars on Rockaway Avenue, the eternal smash of a handball against the wall of our house, the clatter of *"der Italyéner"*'s cart packed with watermelons, the singsong of the old-clothes men walking Chester Street, the cries *"Árbes! Árbes! Kinder! Kinder! Heyse gute árbes!"* All day long people streamed into our apartment as a matter of course—"customers," upstairs neighbors, downstairs neighbors, women who would stop in for a half-hour's talk, salesmen, relatives, insurance agents. Usually they came in without ringing the bell— everyone knew my mother was always at home. I would hear the front door opening, the wind whistling through our front hall, and then some familiar face would appear in our kitchen with the same bland, matter-of-fact inquiring look: no need to stand on ceremony: my mother and her kitchen were available to everyone all day long.

At night the kitchen contracted around the blaze of light on the cloth, the patterns, the ironing board where the iron had burned a black border around the tear in the muslin cover, the finished dresses looked so frilly as they jostled on their wire hangers after all the work my mother had put into them. And then I would get that strangely ominous smell of tension from the dress fabrics and the burn in the cover of the ironing board—as if each piece of cloth and paper crushed with light under the naked bulb might suddenly go up in flames. Whenever I pass some small tailoring shop still lit up at night and see the owner hunched over his steam press; whenever in some poorer neighborhood of the city I see through a window some small crowded kitchen naked under the harsh light glittering in the ceiling, I still smell that fiery breath, that warning of imminent fire. I was always holding my breath. What I must have felt most about ourselves, I see now, was that we ourselves were like kindling—that all the hard-pressed pieces of ourselves and all the hard-used objects in that kitchen were like so many slivers of wood that might go up in flames if we came too near the white-blazing filaments in that naked bulb. Our tension itself was fire, we ourselves were forever burning—to live, to get down the foreboding in our souls, to make good.

## The Schoolboy's Code
## 1952

## Claude M. Fuess

1

At a conservative estimate I must have known during my four decades at Andover six thousand boys. They march before me on sleepless nights like a panorama of the generations, a procession of American life, with its brilliance and folly, its accomplishments and failures. I can see now the fledglings who later became Mayor of Denver, the Governor of Wisconsin, Bishop of Minnesota, author of *The White Tower,* the producer of *Oklahoma!,* the President of Oberlin College, the Director of the Detroit Symphony Orchestra, the Director of the Yale Art School, the president of Boston's largest bank, the Headmaster of Lawrenceville School, the Managing Editor of *Fortune,* the Sports Editor of *Newsweek,* a foreign correspondent of the New York *Times,* the Chairman of the New York Federal Reserve Board, two of the greatest of American surgeons, the toughest of motion picture actors and the most benign of clergymen, as well as heroes, alive and dead, on many a battlefield around the world.

In his delightful and authoritative book, *Understanding Your Son's Adolescence,* my former school physician, Dr. J. Roswell Gallagher, has a chapter headed "There Is No Average Boy." With this dictum I fully concur. Each boy, like each man or woman, is an individual, with his own personal traits, emotions, ambitions, hopes, and whimseys. Each is a male, with all which that implies, and likely to be in some moods rough, predatory, and obscene. Furthermore, boys have their mob movements, resembling hysteria, when they are swept as a group by uncontrollable impulses. But the variations among seven hundred youngsters from fourteen to eighteen are immense. They are usually coöperative but often unpredictable, sophisticated but also childish, idealistic but also vulgar, lovable but also exasperating, noble but also degraded —in short, just like children of a larger growth.

Andover was not at all an exclusive school, except in the sense that it was not easy to meet the scholastic requirements for admission. Nearly one third of the students were either being aided by financial grants or working their way, but they made no difference in the treatment which they received from the faculty and their mates. It seemed to me to be a completely democratic society, in which each member made his way on his own merits, regardless of the social position or financial status of his family. It was highly, sometimes ruthlessly, competitive, not only in studies but in athletics and all the other alluring phases of undergraduate activity; but in this respect it was like life. Indeed the school was a microcosm, a miniature world, with most of the problems of human relations to be found in its larger counterpart. Perhaps this is why the "type" was rugged, resourceful, and self-reliant.

As a corollary, we displayed a cross section of American life—the opulent and the indigent, boys from farms and from city apartments, representatives of almost every state in the Union. If there was any discrimination on the basis of race or color, I was not aware of it. In a school established by rather bigoted Calvinistic Congregationalists, we had nearly 10 per cent of Jews and about the same proportion of Roman Catholics, who attended assembly and sang the Protestant hymns without protest. We usually had two or three Negroes and would have accepted more if they could have met the stiff entrance requirements. They told me afterwards that they never felt themselves at any disadvantage.

Some boys are blessed by their ancestors or by the fickle gods with every attribute making for social success. With sound bodies, they are capable if not outstanding sportsmen; they have the mesmeric quality of making friends easily; they do their class assignments without strain and possess the precious knack of passing examinations; they are emotionally well-balanced, responding normally to the violent stimuli of adolescence; and they have an instinct for avoiding serious blunders. These are the "naturals," the delight of parents' hearts, who advance uninhibited and undismayed through the ordeals of school and college, captaining the teams and making the "right" fraternities, evading disaster and claiming leadership as their privilege. I have known many such, and have thanked God for them.

But side by side with these Olympians are the less conspicuous who are glad for modest honors and occasionally slip sadly into failure, who bear uncomplainingly the inevitable disappointments of group living, whose progress is often slow and painful, and who are content to serve in the ranks while others win letters and other decorations. One never knows, however, what the end will be. Often the campus favorites weaken early, perhaps because they are not toughened by adversity; while some lad relatively obscure on commencement morning turns up forty years later as an eminent surgeon or judge. I liked to feel that Phillips Academy was a good training ground for both types. I hope I was right.

2

The boys sorted themselves out with bewildering rapidity through a process seldom understood by their elders. As the new youngsters of fourteen and fifteen appeared each September at the headmaster's tea, they seemed superficially to be all equally well-mannered, shy, and undistinguished. By Thanksgiving, however, some were standing out above their mates for qualities which gave them prestige. Neither too aggressive nor too diffident, they had aroused the admiration of those around them. We on the faculty often deplored the choices, but they were the consequences of a pure democracy functioning freely. The boys would have resisted any attempt by the faculty to select their leaders. They wanted their own.

Allowing again for the inevitable exceptions, the students were basically well-intentioned and serious-minded. The reprobates won a good deal of publicity, just as hoodlums make the headlines in the newspapers; and the faculty knew them all. Indeed these offenders took up an inordinate amount of our time at meetings. But the large proportion of the undergraduates, day in and day out, worked reasonably hard, tried to obey the rules, and kept out of trouble. Like any other body of isolated males, on a battleship, in an army camp, or in prison, they had their gripes, especially over the food and the minor regulations. But I found them pleasant in manner, amenable to argument, and in an emergency very reliable. However they may have behaved on their vacations, their conduct in public places was as impeccable as that of the teaching staff.

Dr. Stearns, my predecessor, more than once quoted to me with approval the advice which he received from his predecessor, Dr. Bancroft: "Alfred, a lot of things go on all over the campus that a school principal ought never to see!" If a headmaster spends his time looking for little infractions of the rules, he will soon find himself with shattered nerves. Having been no angel myself in my childhood, I was often tempted to laugh when a frightened lad was brought before me for some offense like chewing gum in chapel or indulging in mild profanity. But I suppose that no teacher in a school can avoid occasional irritation. When I first went to live in Tucker House, I raked and seeded a neat bit of ground for my lawn and then put up signs: NO CROSSING! The land was on a corner, and the temptation to cut across was almost irresistible. One spring when I had been particularly vigorous in my denunciation of depraved young men who trampled down my grass, a diminutive offender squeaked, "Mr. Fuess, do you know who walked across there just before me?" "No," said I, "I guess I didn't see him." "It was Mr. Wilkins, the physics teacher— did you bawl him out?" The situation was a trifle difficult to explain, and I am sure that I was inconsistent in meeting it. In the following June the *Pot-pourri,* the Academy yearbook, devoted an entire page to a drawing of my house, with my face at each one of the twenty or more front windows, glaring with baleful eyes at my newly seeded lawn. After that, I tried to keep my irritation under control. I eventually concluded that the proper place to make paths on a campus is where boys—and men—naturally go.

Each boy is an individual, but collectively they have their lapses, when they are swept by uncontrollable impulses. Phillips Academy traditionally has no faculty supervision in the dining hall. Week after week everything would go smoothly as it does in the average restaurant. Then during the week before an Andover-Exeter game some excited lad would throw a bun, and soon there would be an outburst of bun throwing, with the accompanying clamor. The student headwaiters could do little to quell the riot. Inevitably the bachelor teachers sitting by themselves in their own dining room would be disturbed, some of the chief offenders would be reported to the Discipline Committee, and we would have penalties to inflict. Because some of the best boys in school were often involved, the problem of suitable punishments was difficult. The attitudes of faculty members would range from the savage to the gentle, with all the emotional variations in between. Some of the instructors whom I most respected felt that we should tolerate no nonsense, but should act promptly and severely. Others merely murmured, "Boys will be boys," and were inclined to forget the episode. The final votes usually reflected both the violence of the provocation and the weariness of the staff.

Through experience I learned that heavy penalties do not prevent violations of the rules. When we were "firing" boys for many offenses, we had much more disorder than we did later when we became more reasonable. Expelling undergraduates for smoking does not stop the use of tobacco any more than prohibition shut off drinking in the 1920s. A cigarette addict can always be tempted by a convenient grove or fireplace. Even when smoking is allowed under specified conditions, as it is at Andover, it is a perennial problem; but it should not be treated like drunkenness or stealing.

A few responsible school leaders with good instincts and a feeling for law and order can do more than any number of irate faculty members. If the students, guided by their elected officers, reach the conclusion that certain things just "aren't done," the headmaster can cease to worry. Here again boys are extraordinarily like sheep in their proneness to ape the Big Men on campus and to coöperate when coöperation becomes fashionable. Ian Hay was right when he wrote, "The god that schoolboys dread most is Public Opinion."

I made plenty of mistakes in administering discipline. Being temperamentally quick-tempered, I sometimes burst out angrily, thus losing whatever advantage I claimed over the offender. Occasionally I took matters into my own hands and exercised my constitutional right of pardon, only to learn that my soft-heartedness was regarded as weakness, even by the beneficiary. I never quite got over the sinking sensation when I had to announce to a mother that her son would have to withdraw. To such unfortunate incidents I attribute many sleepless nights.

The saddest sequence occurred when, after I had pleaded for an offender and he had been let off lightly, he was shortly detected in an even more heinous breach of regulations. Then my associates cried, "We told you so!" and I was left with the awareness that I was regarded as an "easy mark." I was obliged reluctantly to reach the conclusion that, in spite of what the psychologists maintain, there are some "incorrigibles," on whom kindness or sympathy is wasted and who insist on going wrong, no matter how decently they are treated. More times than I like to admit, my confidence in the essential goodness of human nature was shattered by a gross violation of my trust.

3

I soon came to perceive a kind of pulse beat or rhythm for the school year. The hubbub and adjustment of the opening days in September were followed by a period of relative quiet, when the correspondence was light and I could relax and play golf and pass untroubled evenings. After the first marks were given out in late October, the scholastic goats were separated from the sheep, letters of warning multiplied, and I had to meet with disappointed parents. During the two weeks before the Andover-Exeter football game, tension mounted, and the entire school was on edge. Then came the letdown of the Thanksgiving recess and the studious weeks before the Christmas vacation, when the boys were too busy preparing for examinations to engage in many illicit activities. As the holidays opened, I was busy for three or four days, dictating more than seven hundred personal letters to parents in an attempt to present a brief description of their sons' successes or failures. After that heavy pressure, Florida for a few days was always a welcome relief.

With the return at the opening of the winter term even the drones settled down to hard work, broken by the Winter Promenade, which stirred the boys who were susceptible to female charms. At the end of the term came another period of intense application to books.

Spring was a delightful season at Andover. Most farsighted teachers completed the hardest part of their assignments during the winter, when conditions were favorable for study. The dullards in the student body were by that time pretty well sorted out. Some of them had left, unable to stand the competition, and others had undergone enough of a reform to meet the minimum requirements. Hence the atmosphere in May and June was pleasant, except for those borderline seniors who were worried about getting into college. The tempo slowed down, the boys could lie around on the grass on warm afternoons, and life seemed again worth living after the New England winter. It is true that the faculty had to keep prodding the delinquents into action, and then more action, so that the lights in certain rooms burned far into the night. Moreover the first humid winds of spring stirred the blood and inspired some undergraduates with a desire for a little deviltry. But for most of us the days passed altogether too quickly, and commencement, with its absorbing busyness, was upon us before we knew it. After that came hurried faculty meetings, the good-by greetings, and then the almost oppressive calm which envelops school campuses when the life force has gone and "all that mighty heart is lying still."

Placing myself in the confessional, I must admit that I sometimes took terrifying chances. After one close football contest with Exeter, a gang of adventurous students tore down two Exeter banners from the dormitories where they had been hanging. When the news spread on Sunday morning, I was much concerned, for Bill Saltonstall and I had an informal understanding that no such high jinks would be permitted. On Monday morning, after spending a restless night, I rose in assembly and explained that while this in some respects was only a childish prank, it did involve me in an embarrassing situation with the Exeter authorities. "I should greatly appreciate it," I continued, "if the fellows who have those stolen banners would return them to my office this morning. I shall be out from eleven to twelve and would like to find them there when I come back. No questions will be asked."

This was one of those speeches which either succeed—or fail miserably! As I walked back to my office after assembly, not quite sure whether or not I had made a tactical blunder, two boys—members of the Student Council—asked to see me for a moment. One of them announced rather sheepishly, "Mr. Fuess, Bill and I have those banners, and we'll bring them in to you right away. To tell the truth we didn't realize that there would be so much fuss about the matter. We just wanted to pep things up a bit!" I could only thank them warmly, and before night the banners were on their way to Exeter, with my apologies. But suppose they hadn't been returned!

4

The schoolboy code of honor, no matter how absurd it may seem to an adult, can never be ignored in dealing with undergraduates. Only when one of their mates has become positively vicious will they testify against him. He may copy his neighbor's answers, he may have liquor in his room, he may filch magazines from the newsstand, he may sneak out of his dormitory on nefarious missions—but nobody will "squeal" on him. This is the chief reason why honor systems, however successful they may be in some colleges, seldom work in secondary schools.

On the other hand, the code is subject to strange interpretations. When I was busy with the alumni fund and with money-raising campaigns, I often had to desert my class to keep an engagement. I would then explain, "I'm sorry, but I am called away for the rest of the hour, and I'm leaving an examination for you to take. Please put your papers on the desk when you have finished and leave quietly." In after years several of my former pupils told me that on such occasions nobody did any cribbing. One of them remarked, "You did a smart thing in just going out and never warning us not to cheat. The way you left us completely to our own devices made it impossible for anybody to pull anything crooked!" That is one interesting aspect of boy psychology.

To "visiting firemen," boys are not only tolerant—they are courteously demonstrative. They may complain bitterly of the monotony of talks by the headmaster or the school minister, but when anybody from the outside speaks, no matter how platitudinously or tediously, they will applaud until their palms are sore. In church, they suffered patiently the dullest of sermons.

The patience of a schoolboy congregation is often sorely tried. One winter three successive clergymen took as their theme the parable of the Prodigal Son. Again three visiting clergymen in a row ended their sermons with a stereotyped quotation from Sir Henry Newbolt, beginning, "There's a breathless hush in the close tonight," and concluding dramatically, "Play up! play up! and play the game!" There was a hush all right as number three started on his peroration, and I could see the lips of many undergraduates forming the familiar words. Indeed I almost expected the whole congregation to burst out simultaneously, in accord with their leader, "Play up! play up! and play the game!" But some deep-seated respect for the church as an institution repressed any demonstration.

On one painful morning a clergyman of national reputation preached a sermon identical in text and argument with that used by an eminent divine the week before. A little Sherlock Holmes investigation disclosed the unfortunate fact that both were "canned" sermons, evidently from the same source. At another tense moment a Yale dean suddenly stopped in the middle of his remarks and said, "If the man who is moving about in the gallery will only keep still, I shall be grateful. I am speaking extemporaneously and can't keep my mind on my theme." The "man" thus admonished was one of the faculty proctors, who was moving cautiously about, checking the attendance below. A lady present in the congregation told me afterwards that she had heard the dean deliver precisely the same "extemporaneous" talk the week before at Vassar College. Such are some of the weaknesses of members of "the cloth."

Boys are diabolically clever at discerning, mimicking, and ridiculing the eccentricities of their teachers. Often at commencement the seniors would prepare and present a skit of some kind, "taking off" the peculiarities of the faculty. I was cured forever of rubbing the bare top of my bald head by an imitation of me given by a clever student. When in assembly I announced that most of the trouble in the school was caused by a disorderly "5 per cent" of the undergraduate body, I was haunted by ironic references to that unfortunate phrase. A boy caught in an indiscretion would grin and say, "Well, sir, I guess I'm one of the disreputable 5 per cent!" At first I laughed, but as time went on I smiled only as if I mocked myself, and I was soon sick of the expression.

During one recitation a young instructor talked for some time about a trip to the British Isles which he had taken the previous summer. After class a very small lad looking as innocent as one of Murillo's cherubs came up to the master's desk and asked, "You've been a good deal in England, haven't you, Mr. Odell?" "Well, yes, I think I might say I have." "I guess you know a lot about their customs, don't you?" "Yes, I probably do," was the reply. Then the tiny youngster looked up and, his eyes twinkling, said, "Well, cheerio, Old Top, cheerio!" What could be done about that?

Boys in these days have a genuine respect for rules, especially when the reason for them is explained. When a mother would plead for some exceptional privilege for her son, he would frequently come to me privately and say, "I knew perfectly well that I couldn't have my Christmas vacation extended, but Mom simply wouldn't listen to me." A youngster deprived of some of his precious weekends because of his poor scholastic record told me, "I got exactly what I deserved, and Dad should never have come up here to kick about it to you." Boys understand all the recognized conventions of the school much better than their parents do, and this is the chief reason why they don't like to have them too much around on the campus. Their elders simply do not comprehend the principles by which the lives of their sons are governed.

In dealing with boys it is imperative that a headmaster should have two important qualities— a sense of relative values and a sense of humor. He should perceive the difference between a sin and an indiscretion, between a calculated defiance of law and order and a careless neglect of a rule. He should understand that laughter is a great solvent of confusion, often clearing completely an atmosphere fraught with tragedy.

As I have suggested, differentiations in temperament and ambition appear very early and are readily recognizable. Some boys are visibly nervous; others are lethargic. Some are conscientious; others are excruciatingly careless. I once escorted a bishop through a senior dormitory where two rooms were side by side on the second floor. One was neat and orderly, with every necktie smoothed out and each article in its proper place. The other was strewn with shirts and shoes and crowded with miscellaneous and unattractive junk. Both boys were members of the Student Council, and each was a reliable citizen. But they were entirely opposite in personal habits and modes of living, and probably neither has changed to this day.

Living in my house at one period we had a most extraordinary aggregation of undergraduate types. Ned was shy, methodical, reserved, and studious. Pete was a muscular and gregarious extrovert, interested chiefly in games and regarding classes as a sideshow to the main tent. Horace wanted to spend all his time in the biological laboratory nursing snakes. Oscar had a passion for stage carpentry and could be found at almost any hour designing and constructing scenery. Bill was a born trader who made a profit on every financial transaction. Hank was constantly writing editorials for the school paper although he loathed his English class on general principles. Each had his own private interests; yet they dwelt together in amity.

I do not mean to imply that these boys were static. Their special interests sometimes shifted almost overnight, and after a summer vacation they came back physically bigger and intellectually more mature.

People often ask me what I think of the "younger generation." This is a difficult question to answer, for the boys of the 1950s are as varied as any group which preceded them, and no generalizations can be more than approximately accurate. Furthermore I have been in contact only with a rather carefully selected group, which included very few perverts or "hot-rods" or amateur holdup men. The teen-agers who set fire to school buildings, chop up grand pianos, and overturn tombstones do not often seek admission to a school like Andover.

The boys whom I know in this generation give the impression of competence and self-reliance. They are not communicative, even with their parents; consequently it is difficult to find out what their real reactions are. But they have an amazing capacity for meeting crises without quailing—and they have already had plenty of them to face. These youngsters born in the 1930s know little from personal knowledge of an orderly world. No one could blame them very much for crying simultaneously and with anguish:—

> The time is out of joint; O cursed spite
> That ever I was born to set it right!

This, however, they do not do. Although they do not relish the confusion in the midst of which they have been thrown, they make few complaints. They accept military service, even when it interrupts their cherished plans, as if it were as inevitable as birth or death. Because they wish to snatch what happiness they can before their universe dissolves, they plan to marry early. But they do not quit! It may be resignation which keeps them going, but it more closely resembles pride. Pity in any form is what they least desire.

Perhaps because of bitter family experience they care less about making money than their fathers and more about doing good. More and more they are choosing the missionary professions, such as teaching, medicine, the Christian ministry, and public service. They have a very real concept of what satisfactions are durable and what are transitory. They do plenty of thinking about such perennial and intrusive problems as labor relations, racial discrimination, censorship, poverty, disease, crime, and education. In many cases they have, as adolescents, evolved for themselves a pattern for living. They are aware that they have to fight for the freedoms which they enjoy, but they are ready— not enthusiastic or glory-seeking, but prepared to face whatever comes.

# Inaugural Address
## 1961

## John F. Kennedy

We observe today not a victory of party but a celebration of freedom, symbolizing an end as well as a beginning, signifying renewal as well as change. For I have sworn before you and Almighty God the same solemn oath our forebears prescribed nearly a century and three-quarters ago.

The world is very different now. For man holds in his mortal hands the power to abolish all forms of human poverty and all forms of human life. And yet the same revolutionary belief for which our forebears fought is still at issue around the globe, the belief that the rights of man come not from the generosity of the state but from the hand of God.

We dare not forget today that we are the heirs of that first revolution. Let the word go forth from this time and place, to friend and foe alike, that the torch has been passed to a new generation of Americans, born in this century, tempered by war, disciplined by a hard and bitter peace, proud of our ancient heritage, and unwilling to witness or permit the slow undoing of those human rights to which this nation has always been committed, and to which we are committed today at home and around the world.

Let every nation know, whether it wishes us well or ill, that we shall pay any price, bear any burden, meet any hardship, support any friend, oppose any foe to assure the survival and the success of liberty.

This much we pledge—and more.

To those old allies whose cultural and spiritual origins we share, we pledge the loyalty of faithful friends. United, there is little we cannot do in a host of cooperative ventures. Divided, there is little we can do, for we dare not meet a powerful challenge at odds and split asunder.

To those new states whom we welcome to the ranks of the free, we pledge our word that our form of colonial control shall not have passed away merely to be replaced by a far more iron tyranny. We shall not always expect to find them supporting our view. But we shall always hope to find them strongly supporting their own freedom, and to remember that, in the past, those who foolishly sought power by riding the back of the tiger ended up inside.

To those peoples in the huts and villages of half the globe struggling to break the bonds of mass misery, we pledge our best efforts to help them help themselves, for whatever period is required, not because the Communists may be doing it, not because we seek their votes, but because it is right. If a free society cannot help the many who are poor, it cannot save the few who are rich.

To our sister republics south of our border, we offer a special pledge: to convert our good words into good deeds, in a new alliance for progress, to assist free men and free governments in casting off the chains of poverty. But this peaceful revolution of hope cannot become the prey of hostile powers. Let all our neighbors know that we shall join with them to oppose aggression or subversion anywhere in the Americas. And let every other power know that this hemisphere intends to remain the master of its own house.

To that world assembly of sovereign states, the United Nations, our last best hope in an age where the instruments of war have far outpaced the instruments of peace, we renew our pledge of support: to prevent it from becoming merely a forum for invective, to strengthen its shield of the new and the weak, and to enlarge the area in which its writ may run.

Finally, to those nations who would make themselves our adversary, we offer not a pledge but a request: that both sides begin anew the quest for peace, before the dark powers of destruction unleashed by science engulf all humanity in planned or accidental self-destruction.

We dare not tempt them with weakness. For only when our arms are sufficient beyond doubt can we be certain beyond doubt that they will never be employed.

But neither can two great and powerful groups of nations take comfort from our present course—both sides overburdened by the cost of modern weapons, both rightly alarmed by the steady spread of the deadly atom, yet both racing to alter that uncertain balance of terror that stays the hand of mankind's final war.

So let us begin anew, remembering on both sides that civility is not a sign of weakness, and sincerity is always subject to proof. Let us never negotiate out of fear, but let us never fear to negotiate.

Let both sides explore what problems unite us instead of belaboring those problems which divide us.

Let both sides, for the first time, formulate serious and precise proposals for the inspection and control of arms, and bring the absolute power to destroy other nations under the absolute control of all nations.

Let both sides seek to invoke the wonders of science instead of its terrors. Together let us explore the stars, conquer the deserts, eradicate disease, tap the ocean depths and encourage the arts and commerce.

Let both sides unite to heed in all corners of the earth the command of Isaiah to "undo the heavy burdens . . . [and] let the oppressed go free."

And if a beachhead of cooperation may push back the jungle of suspicion, let both sides join in creating a new endeavor, not a new balance of power, but a new world of law, where the strong are just and the weak secure and the peace preserved.

All this will not be finished in the first one hundred days. Nor will it be finished in the first one thousand days, nor in the life of this Administration, nor even perhaps in our lifetime on this planet. But let us begin.

In your hands, my fellow citizens, more than mine, will rest the final success or failure of our course. Since this country was founded, each generation of Americans has been summoned to give testimony to its national loyalty. The graves of young Americans who answered the call to service surround the globe.

Now the trumpet summons us again—not as a call to bear arms, though arms we need; not as a call to battle, though embattled we are; but a call to bear the burden of a long twilight struggle, year in and year out, "rejoicing in hope, patient in tribulation," a struggle against the common enemies of man: tyranny, poverty, disease and war itself.

Can we forge against these enemies a grand and global alliance, North and South, East and West, that can assure a more fruitful life for all mankind? Will you join in that historic effort?

In the long history of the world, only a few generations have been granted the role of defending freedom in its hour of maximum danger. I do not shrink from this responsibility; I welcome it. I do not believe that any of us would exchange places with any other people or any other generation. The energy, the faith, the devotion which we bring to this endeavor will light our country and all who serve it, and the glow from that fire can truly light the world.

And so, my fellow Americans, ask not what your country can do for you; ask what you can do for your country.

My fellow citizens of the world, ask not what America will do for you, but what together we can do for the freedom of man.

Finally, whether you are citizens of America or citizens of the world, ask of us here the same high standards of strength and sacrifice which we ask of you. With a good conscience our only sure reward, with history the final judge of our deeds, let us go forth to lead the land we love, asking His blessing and His help, but knowing that here on earth God's work must truly be our own.

# Part Two

## Outside the Myth: Other Views of Growing Up American

Now in the fright of change when bombed towns vanish
In fountains of debris
We say to the stranger coming across the sea
Not here, not here, go elsewhere!
Here we keep
Bars up. Wall out the danger, tightly seal
The ports, the intake from the alien world we fear.

It is a time of many errors now.
And this the error of children when they feel
But cannot say their terror. To shut off the stream
In which we moved and still move, if we move.
The alien is the nation, *nothing more nor less.*
How set ourselves at variance to prove
The alien is not the nation. And so end the dream.
Forbid our deep resource from whence we came,
And the very seed of greatness.

This is to do
Something like suicide; to choose
Sterility—forget the secret of our past
Which like a magnet drew
A wealth of men and women hopeward. And now to lose
In ignorant blindness what we might hold fast.

The fright of change, not readiness. Instead
Inside our wall we will today pursue
The man we call the alien, take his print,
Give him a taste of the thing from which he fled,
Suspicion him. And again we fail.
How shall we release his virtue, his good-will
If by such pressure we hold his life in Jail?

*The alien is the nation. Nothing else.*
*And so we fail and so we jail ourselves.*
*Landlocked, the stagnant stream.*
*So ends the dream.*

*O countrymen, are we working to undo*
*Our lusty strength, our once proud victory?*
*Yes, if by this fright we break our strength in two.*
*If we make of every man we jail the enemy.*
*If we make ourselves the jailer locked in jail.*
*Our laboring wills, our brave, too brave to fail*
*Remember this nation by millions believed to be*
*Great and of mighty forces born, and resolve to be free,*
*To continue and renew.*


Genevieve Taggard

*Ode in Time of Crisis*
(Written for the New York City Conference for Protection
of Foreign Born.)

*October 29, 1940*

The variety of America is an important part of the American Dream. People of diverse national background and talents built America; people of different ethnic, religious, and occupational habits compose it and give America its unique texture. The very goals the country has set for itself and the course of its development have been based on and maintained in recognition of this variety. America could promise harmony, happiness and comfort for all men; on this promise the hopes of most were founded and the success of many was assured. Although some seemed to be especially favored by fortune or providence, others had no need to consider themselves losers. In a land as rich and various as America, there would be more than one kind of prize.

This is the ideal, and as an ideal it raised the aspirations of all. But the reality was usually different. Success has been measured mainly in the limited terms of financial achievement, and happiness was believed to come primarily with material gain. Although most citizens strove for this success, hoping that hard work and virtuous action would bring the rewards which fictive heroes always won, many who searched found only disappointment and failure. For the young, who—partly from innocence and partly from optimism—tend to view the world in ideals, any evidence contrary to the propaganda of the Dream was shattering; initiation into the real world could bring disillusionment and destruction, all the more bitter because the fantasies were so great.

Growing up, forced into an awareness of another kind of diversity—the diversity of failure in the midst of plenty—many Americans began to see the myths of success in a different light. The cherished dreams seemed available to just a few; moreover, when juxtaposed to the experiences and hardships of most people, the dreams lost their validity. Although a new society had been created in America, the traditional forms of human unhappiness remained. Men's bodies were still weakened by poverty, crime, violence and slavery; men's minds, distorted by ignorance and bigotry; men's ideals, destroyed through discouragement, cynicism and fear. Norman Podhoretz discusses the prejudices of one minority group against another; and Carey McWilliams, in his description of the 1942 relocation centers established for Japanese and Japanese-Americans, documents an even more shocking example of races and cultures in conflict. The official myths said nothing of these experiences; and when those brought up to believe in the American Dream met with failure in its pursuit, the awakening to these realities often produced disbelief and doubt about this land of unlimited opportunity.

During the nineteenth century, the dissatisfaction generated significant experimentation with utopian community living as an alternative to and an escape from the America of the myth. Jack London's conversion to socialism in the 1890s antedates that of many twentieth-century Americans, who created new utopias for America based on faith in work and the working man. But not all sought to remedy social ills by rearranging social structures. For some, re-evaluation meant personal rededication to labors needed to overcome failure. It became a strength, a key to a new world whose complexities still allowed personal assertion and creative development. But for others the defeat itself was too destructive and they resigned themselves to a life without hope, concentrating on physical survival. Why were these people excluded from the Dream? Why were their experiences so different from those portrayed in the readings of Part One?

In some cases, the circumstances of birth determined the difficulties. Frederick Douglass, born a slave, consequently considered only three-fifths a man by the Constitution, was almost automatically excluded from aspiring beyond slavehood. Although Malcolm X lived over one hundred years later, long after slavery had legally ended, he found his color almost as detrimental to his aspirations as Douglass' had been. Advised by his junior high school teacher about a career, he was told ". . . you've got to be realistic about being a nigger." The young boy in Beatrice Griffith's "American Me," likewise unaware that his race was a limitation, discovered early that not being white meant not being accepted. In other cases, such as the one Amado Muro describes in his short story, an individual's particular cultural and national characteristics, because they remained unassimilated, produced conflicts of belonging and loyalty in the self. It was one thing for John Fante in "The Odyssey of a Wop" to be called Wop by members of his family; but to be so named by outsiders was to be acknowledged as ethnically different and, therefore, in spite of his protestations, not American.

Not all the people unable to live out the American Dream were members of ethnic, racial or religious minorities. Many were white, Anglo-Saxon and Protestant; and many shared the same ancestry which in others yielded success. The young boys and girls described by Jacob Riis in "The Problem of the Children" were from families so overburdened by poverty that they lacked even a chance at the miraculous luck of an Horatio Alger hero. Failure of parental love and guidance can be more destructive to a child than lack of funds; but for the little girl in Millen Brand's "When You Spend a Dollar," the chaotic economic condition of the entire country made the Dream impossible. She was born at the wrong time and in the wrong place—in New York City in the 1930s when there were no jobs and no escape.

Knowledge of the unrealistic nature of America's greatest promises did not necessarily have to come from perceptions of massive economic and social discrepancies. Often a unique private experience, a particular psychological set or the natural process of maturation brought epiphanies. Jean Shepherd in "The Counterfeit Secret Circle Member Gets the Message, Or The Asp Strikes Again" cites one example from his youth when boyhood expectations and fantasies crumbled in a confrontation with American commercialism. M. Carl Holman's excitement as a young prize-winning poet is soon replaced by disillusionment when the hostess at his celebration recognizes him as a Negro.

It is understandable that a young man, surrounded by other people's luxury, constantly tempted by symbols of success, goaded by the pressures of status, is often himself responsible for distorting the Dream. The father in Sherwood Anderson's "The Egg" grows into a sad and pathetic figure in his thwarted desire to overcome anonymity, to "get up in the world"; he preserves chickens that are grotesque, like his dreams, hoping to exhibit them far and wide at fairs throughout the land. There are those, furthermore, either totally broken by their quest for the unattainable or left totally empty by the tremendous cost of achieving success. The cost for F. Scott Fitzgerald's hero is spiritual exhaustion from a waste of love and young dreams; the cost for James T. Farrell's hero in "The Benefits of American Life" is death from a disease acquired in the frenzied striving for fame.

Perhaps there is a closer connection between America's successes and America's failures than one would care to admit. The propagation of the myth of a material success accompanied inevitably by happiness has been the spur to America's great economic success. Every individual working to achieve his own dream has added his energy and labors to the fullest and most efficient development of the land. And so, because Americans have achieved one of the highest standards of living in the world today, even the poorest citizen is better off than the poor of most other countries, and even he still has a chance to succeed. But because the American Dream itself is a myth, a construction of utopian idealism, success according to that myth simply is not feasible for every man. Yet, it is precisely because the Dream exists, and so many have achieved according to its precepts, that the success of America is held responsible for its failures. Even among those who have had only partial success according to the Dream, but who still enjoy material comforts and sometimes even luxury, there has not been a corresponding level of satisfaction. To admit the existence of both failure and unhappiness would be to discredit the Dream. This is impossible for some, difficult for others, bitterly easy for still others; but however often discredited, the Dream persists. America is still called the land of unlimited opportunity, and deep within the American character remains an unresolvable conflict.

## Narrative of the Life of Frederick Douglass

## 1845

## Frederick Douglass

### Chapter 1

I was born in Tuckahoe, near Hillsborough, and about twelve miles from Easton, in Talbot county, Maryland. I have no accurate knowledge of my age, never having seen any authentic record containing it. By far the larger part of the slaves know as little of their age as horses know of theirs, and it is the wish of most masters within my knowledge to keep their slaves thus ignorant. I do not remember to have ever met a slave who could tell of his birthday. They seldom come nearer to it than planting-time, harvest-time, cherry-time, spring-time, or fall-time. A want of information concerning my own was a source of unhappiness to me even during childhood. The white children could tell their ages. I could not tell why I ought to be deprived of the same privilege. I was not allowed to make any inquiries of my master concerning it. He deemed all such inquiries on the part of a slave improper and impertinent, and evidence of a restless spirit. The nearest estimate I can give makes me now between twenty-seven and twenty-eight years of age. I come to this, from hearing my master say, some time during 1835, I was about seventeen years old.

My mother was named Harriet Bailey. She was the daughter of Isaac and Betsey Bailey, both colored, and quite dark. My mother was of a darker complexion than either my grandmother or grandfather.

My father was a white man. He was admitted to be such by all I ever heard speak of my parentage. The opinion was also whispered that my master was my father; but of the correctness of this opinion, I know nothing; the means of knowing was withheld from me. My mother and I were separated when I was but an infant—before I knew her as my mother. It is a common custom, in the part of Maryland from which I ran away, to part children from their mothers at a very early age. Frequently, before the child has reached its twelfth month, its mother is taken from it, and hired out on some farm a considerable distance off, and the child is placed under the care of an old woman, too old for field labor. For what this separation is done, I do not know, unless it be to hinder the development of the child's affection toward its mother, and to blunt and destroy the natural affection of the mother for the child. This is the inevitable result.

I never saw my mother, to know her as such, more than four or five times in my life; and each of these times was very short in duration, and at night. She was hired by a Mr. Stewart, who lived about twelve miles from my home. She made her journeys to see me in the night, travelling the whole distance on foot, after the performance of her day's work. She was a field hand, and a whipping is the penalty of not being in the field at sunrise, unless a slave has special permission from his or her master to the contrary—a permission which they seldom get, and one that gives to him that gives it the proud name of being a kind master. I do not recollect of ever seeing my mother by the light of day. She was with me in the night. She would lie down with me, and get me to sleep, but long before I waked she was gone. Very little communication ever took place between us. Death soon ended what little we could have while she lived, and with it her hardships and suffering. She died when I was about seven years old, on one of my master's farms, near Lee's Mill. I was not allowed to be present during her illness, at her death, or burial. She was gone long before I knew any thing about it. Never having enjoyed, to any considerable extent, her soothing presence, her tender and watchful care, I received the tidings of her death with much the same emotions I should have probably felt at the death of a stranger.

Called thus suddenly away, she left me without the slightest intimation of who my father was. The whisper that my master was my father, may or may not be true; and, true or false, it is of but little consequence to my purpose whilst the fact remains, in all its glaring odiousness, that slaveholders have ordained, and by law established, that the children of slave women shall in all cases follow the condition of their mothers; and this is done too obviously to administer to their own lusts, and make a gratification of their wicked desires profitable as well as pleasurable; for by this cunning arrangement, the slaveholder, in cases not a few, sustains to his slaves the double relation of master and father.

I know of such cases; and it is worthy of remark that such slaves invariably suffer greater hardships, and have more to contend with, than others. They are, in the first place, a constant offence to their mistress. She is ever disposed to find fault with them; they can seldom do any thing to please her; she is never better pleased than when she sees them under the lash, especially when she suspects her husband of showing to his mullato children favors which he withholds from his black slaves. The master is frequently compelled to sell this class of his slaves, out of deference to the feelings of his white wife; and, cruel as the deed may strike any one to be, for a man to sell his own children to human flesh-mongers, it is often the dictate of humanity for him to do so; for, unless he does this, he must not only whip them himself, but must stand by and see one white son tie up his brother, of but few shades darker complexion than himself, and ply the gory lash to his naked back; and if he lisp one word of disapproval, it is set down to his parental partiality, and only makes a bad matter worse, both for himself and the slave whom he would protect and defend.

Every year brings with it multitudes of this class of slaves. It was doubtless in consequence of a knowledge of this fact, that one great statesman of the south predicted the downfall of slavery by the inevitable laws of population. Whether this prophecy is ever fulfilled or not, it is nevertheless plain that a very different-looking class of people are springing up at the south, and are now held in slavery, from those originally brought to this country from Africa; and if their increase will do no other good, it will do away the force of the argument, that God cursed Ham, and therefore American slavery is right. If the lineal descendants of Ham are alone to be scripturally enslaved, it is certain that slavery at the south must soon become unscriptural; for thousands are ushered into the world, annually, who, like myself, owe their existence to white fathers, and those fathers most frequently their own masters.

I have had two masters. My first master's name was Anthony. I do not remember his first name. He was generally called Captain Anthony—a title which, I presume, he acquired by sailing a craft on the Chesapeake Bay. He was not considered a rich slaveholder. He owned two or three farms, and about thirty slaves. His farms and slaves were under the care of an overseer. The overseer's name was Plummer. Mr. Plummer was a miserable drunkard, a profane swearer, and a savage monster. He always went armed with a cowskin and a heavy crudgel. I have known him to cut and slash the women's heads so horribly, that even master could be enraged at his cruelty, and would threaten to whip him if he did not mind himself. Master, however, was not a humane slaveholder. It required extraordinary barbarity on the part of an overseer to affect him. He was a cruel man, hardened by a long life of slaveholding. He would at times seem to take great pleasure in whipping a slave. I have often been awakened at the dawn of day by the most heart-rending shrieks of an own aunt of mine, whom he used to tie up to a joist, and whip upon her naked back till she was literally covered with blood. No words, no tears, no prayers, from his gory victim, seemed to move his iron heart from its bloody purpose. The louder she screamed, the harder he whipped; and where the blood ran fastest, there he whipped longest. He would whip her to make her scream, and whip her to make her hush; and not until overcome by fatigue, would he cease to swing the blood-clotted cowskin. I remember the first time I ever witnessed this horrible exhibition. I was quite a child, but I will remember it. I never shall forget it whilst I remember any thing. It was the first of a long series of such outrages, of which I was doomed to be a witness and a participant. It struck me with awful force. It was the blood-stained gate, the entrance to the hell of slavery, through which I was about to pass. It was a most terrible spectacle. I wish I could commit to paper the feelings with which I beheld it.

This occurrence took place very soon after I went to live with my old master, and under the following circumstances. Aunt Hester went out one night, —where or for what I do not know,—and happened to be absent when my master desired her presence. He had ordered her not to go out evenings, and warned her that she must never let him catch her in company with a young man, who was paying attention to her belonging to Colonel Lloyd. The young man's name was Ned Roberts, generally called Lloyd's Ned. Why master was so careful of her, may be safely left to conjecture. She was a woman of noble form, and of graceful proportions, having very few equals, and fewer superiors, in personal appearance, among the colored or white women of our neighborhood.

Aunt Hester had not only disobeyed his orders in going out, but had been found in company with Lloyd's Ned; which circumstance, I found, from what he said while whipping her, was the chief offence. Had he been a man of pure morals himself, he might have been thought interested in protecting the innocence of my aunt; but those who knew him will not suspect him of any such virtue. Before he commenced whipping Aunt Hester, he took her into the kitchen, and stripped her from neck to waist, leaving her neck, shoulders, and back, entirely naked. He then told her to cross her hands, calling her at the same time a d—d b—h. After crossing her hands, he tied them with a strong rope, and led her to a stool under a large hook in the joist, put in for the purpose. He made her get upon the stool, and tied her hands to the hook. She now stood fair for his infernal purpose. Her arms were stretched up at their full length, so that she stood upon the ends of her toes. He then said to her, "Now, you d—d b—h, I'll learn you how to disobey my orders!" and after rolling up his sleeves, he commenced to lay on the heavy cowskin, and soon the warm, red blood (amid heart-rending shrieks from her, and horrid oaths from him) came dripping to the floor. I was so terrified and horror-stricken at the sight, that I hid myself in a closet, and dared not venture out till long after the bloody transaction was over. I expected it would be my turn next. It was all new to me. I had never seen any thing like it before. I had always lived with my grandmother on the outskirts of the plantation, where she was put to raise the children of the younger women. I had therefore been, until now, out of the way of the bloody scenes that often occurred on the plantation.

## Chapter 2

My master's family consisted of two sons, Andrew and Richard; one daughter, Lucretia, and her husband, Captain Thomas Auld. They lived in one house, upon the home plantation of Colonel Edward Lloyd. My master was Colonel Lloyd's clerk and superintendent. He was what might be called the overseer of the overseers. I spent two years of childhood on this plantation in my old master's family. It was here that I witnessed the bloody transaction recorded in the first chapter; and as I received my first impressions of slavery on this plantation, I will give some description ot it, and of slavery as it there existed. The plantation is about twelve miles north of Easton, in Talbot county, and is situated on the border of Miles River. The principal products raised upon it were tobacco, corn, and wheat. These were raised in great abundance; so that, with the products of this and the other farms belonging to him, he was able to keep in almost constant employment a large sloop, in carrying them to market at Baltimore. This sloop was named Sally Lloyd, in honor of one of the colonel's daughters. My master's son-in-law, Captain Auld, was master of the vessel; she was otherwise manned by the colonel's own slaves. Their names were Peter, Isaac, Rich, and Jake. These were esteemed very highly by the other slaves, and looked upon as the privileged ones of the plantation; for it was no small affair, in the eyes of the slaves, to be allowed to see Baltimore.

Colonel Lloyd kept from three to four hundred slaves on his home plantation, and owned a large number more on the neighboring farms belonging to him. The names of the farms nearest to the home plantation were Wye Town and New Design. "Wye Town" was under the overseership of a man named Noah Willis. New Design was under the overseership of a Mr. Townsend. The overseers of these, and all the rest of the farms, numbering over twenty, received advice and direction from the managers of the home plantation. This was the great business place. It was the seat of government for the whole twenty farms. All disputes among the overseers were settled here. If a slave was convicted of any high misdemeanor, became unmanageable, or evinced a determination to run away, he was brought immediately here, severely whipped, put on board the sloop, carried to Baltimore, and sold to Austin Woolfolk, or some other slave-trader, as a warning to the slaves remaining.

Here, too, the slaves of all the other farms received their monthly allowance of food, and their yearly clothing. The men and women slaves received, as their monthly allowance of food, eight pounds of pork, or its equivalent in fish, and one bushel of corn meal. Their yearly clothing consisted of two coarse linen shirts, one pair of linen trousers, like the shirts, one jacket, one pair of trousers for winter, made of coarse negro cloth, one pair of stockings, and one pair of shoes; the whole of which could not have cost more than seven dollars. The allowance of the slave children was given to their mothers, or the old women having the care of them. The children unable to work in the field had neither shoes, stockings, jackets, nor trousers, given to them; their clothing consisted of two coarse linen shirts per year. When these failed them, they went naked until the next allowance-day. Children from seven to ten years old, of both sexes, almost naked, might be seen at all seasons of the year.

There were no beds given the slaves, unless one coarse blanket be considered such, and none but the men and women had these. This, however, is not considered a very great privation. They find less difficulty from the want of beds, than from the want of time to sleep; for when their day's work in the field is done, the most of them having their washing, mending, and cooking to do, and having few or none of the ordinary facilities for doing either of these, very many of their sleeping hours are consumed in preparing for the field the coming day; and when this is done, old and young, male and female, married and single, drop down side by side, on one common bed,—the cold, damp floor, —each covering himself or herself with their miserable blankets; and here they sleep till they are summoned to the field by the driver's horn. At the sound of this, all must rise, and be off to the field. There must be no halting; every one must be at his or her post; and woe betides them who hear not this morning summons to the field; for if they are not awakened by the sense of hearing, they are by the sense of feeling: no age nor sex finds any favor. Mr. Severe, the overseer, used to stand by the door of the quarter, armed with a large hickory stick and heavy cowskin, ready to whip any one who was so unfortunate as not to hear, or, from any other cause, was prevented from being ready to start for the field at the sound of the horn.

Mr. Severe was rightly named: he was a cruel man. I have seen him whip a woman, causing the blood to run half an hour at the time; and this, too, in the midst of her crying children, pleading for their mother's release. He seemed to take pleasure in manifesting his fiendish barbarity. Added to his cruelty, he was a profane swearer. It was enough to chill the blood and stiffen the hair of an ordinary man to hear him talk. Scarce a sentence escaped him but that was commenced or concluded by some horrid oath. The field was the place to witness his cruelty and profanity. His presence made it both the field of blood and of blasphemy. From the rising till the going down of the sun, he was cursing, raving, cutting, and slashing among the slaves of the field, in the most frightful manner. His career was short. He died very soon after I went to Colonel Lloyd's; and he died as he lived, uttering, with his dying groans, bitter curses and horrid oaths. His death was regarded by the slaves as the result of a merciful providence.

Mr. Severe's place was filled by a Mr. Hopkins. He was a very different man. He was less cruel, less profane, and made less noise, than Mr. Severe. His course was characterized by no extraordinary demonstrations of cruelty. He whipped, but seemed to take no pleasure in it. He was called by the slaves a good overseer.

The home plantation of Colonel Lloyd wore the appearance of a country village. All the mechanical operations for all the farms were performed here. The shoemaking and mending, the blacksmithing, cartwrighting, coopering, weaving, and grain-grinding, were all performed by the slaves on the home plantation. The whole place wore a business-like aspect very unlike the neighboring farms. The number of houses, too, conspired to give it advantage over the neighboring farms. It was called by the slaves the *Great House Farm*. Few privileges were esteemed higher, by the slaves of the out-farms, than that of being selected to do errands at the Great House Farm. It was associated in their minds with greatness. A representative could not be prouder of his election to a seat in the American Congress, than a slave on one of the out-farms would be of his election to do errands at the Great House Farm. They regarded it as evidence of great confidence reposed in them by their overseers; and it was on this account, as well as a constant desire to be out of the field from under the driver's lash, that they esteemed it a high privilege, one worth careful living for. He was called the smartest and most trusty fellow, who had this honor conferred upon him the most frequently. The competitors for this office sought as diligently to please their overseers, as the office-seekers in the political parties seek to please and deceive the people. The same traits of character might be seen in Colonel Lloyd's slaves, as are seen in the slaves of the political parties.

The slaves selected to go to the Great House Farm, for the monthly allowance for themselves and their fellow-slaves, were peculiarly enthusiastic.
While on their way, they would make the dense old woods, for miles around,
reverberate with their wild songs, revealing at once the highest joy and the
deepest sadness. They would compose and sing as they went along, consulting
neither time nor tune. The thought that came up, came out—if not in the
word, in the sound;—and as frequently in the one as in the other. They would
sometimes sing the most pathetic sentiment in the most rapturous tone, and the
most rapturous sentiment in the most pathetic tone. Into all of their songs
they would manage to weave something of the Great House Farm. Especially
would they do this, when leaving home. They would then sing most exultingly
the following words:—

> "I am going away to the Great House Farm!
> O, yea! O, yea! O!"

This they would sing, as a chorus, to words which to many would seem un-
meaning jargon, but which, nevertheless, were full of meaning to themselves. I
have sometimes thought that the mere hearing of those songs would do more to
impress some minds with the horrible character of slavery, than the reading of
whole volumes of philosophy on the subject could do.

I did not, when a slave, understand the deep meaning of those rude and
apparently incoherent songs. I was myself within the circle; so that I neither
saw nor heard as those without might see and hear. They told a tale of woe
which was then altogether beyond my feeble comprehension; they were tones
loud, long, and deep; they breathed the prayer and complaint of souls boiling
over with the bitterest anguish. Every tone was a testimony against slavery, and
a prayer to God for deliverance from chains. The hearing of those wild notes
always depressed my spirit, and filled me with ineffable sadness. I have frequently found myself in tears while hearing them. The mere recurrence to those
songs, even now, afflicts me; and while I am writing these lines, an expression
of feeling has already found its way down my cheek. To those songs I trace my
first glimmering conception of the dehumanizing character of slavery. I can
never get rid of that conception. Those songs still follow me, to deepen my
hatred of slavery, and quicken my sympathies for my brethren in bonds. If any
one wishes to be impressed with the soul-killing effects of slavery, let him go to
Colonel Lloyd's plantation, and, on allowance-day, place himself in the deep
pine woods, and there let him, in silence, analyze the sounds that shall pass
through the chambers of his soul,—and if he is not thus impressed, it will only
be because "there is no flesh in his obdurate heart."

I have often been utterly astonished, since I came to the north, to find
persons who could speak of the singing, among slaves, as evidence of their contentment and happiness. It is impossible to conceive of a greater mistake.
Slaves sing most when they are most unhappy. The songs of the slave represent

the sorrows of his heart; and he is relieved by them, only as an aching heart is relieved by its tears. At least, such is my experience. I have often sung to drown my sorrow, but seldom to express my happiness. Crying for joy, and singing for joy, were alike uncommon to me while in the jaws of slavery. The singing of a man cast away upon a desolate island might be as appropriately considered as evidence of contentment and happiness, as the singing of a slave; the songs of the one and of the other are prompted by the same emotion.

## The Problem of the Children
## 1890

## Jacob Riis

The problem of the children becomes, in these swarms, to the last degree perplexing. Their very number make one stand aghast. I have already given instances of the packing of the child population in East Side tenements. They might be continued indefinitely until the array would be enough to startle any community. For, be it remembered, these children with the training they receive—or do not receive—with the instincts they inherit and absorb in their growing up, are to be our future rulers, if our theory of government is worth anything. More than a working majority of our voters now register from the tenements. I counted the other day the little ones, up to ten years or so, in a Bayard Street tenement that for a yard has a triangular space in the centre with sides fourteen or fifteen feet long, just room enough for a row of ill-smelling closets at the base of the triangle and a hydrant at the apex. There was about as much light in this "yard" as in the average cellar. I gave up my self-imposed task in despair when I had counted one hundred and twenty-eight in forty families. Thirteen I had missed, or not found in. Applying the average for the forty to the whole fifty-three, the house contained one hundred and seventy children. It is not the only time I have had to give up such census work. I have in mind an alley—an inlet rather to a row of rear tenements—that is either two or four feet wide according as the wall of the crazy old building that gives on it bulges out or in. I tried to count the children that swarmed there, but could not. Sometimes I have doubted that anybody knows just how many there are about. Bodies of drowned children turn up in the rivers right along in summer whom no one seems to know anything about. When last spring some workmen, while moving a pile of lumber on a North River pier, found under the last plank the body of a little lad crushed to death, no one had missed a boy, though his parents afterward turned up. The truant officer assuredly does not know, though he spends his life trying to find out, somewhat illogically, perhaps, since the department that employs him admits that thousands of poor children are crowded out of the schools year by year for want of room. There was a big tenement in the Sixth Ward, now happily appropriated by the beneficent spirit of business that blots out so many foul spots in New York—it figured not long ago in the official reports as "an out-and-out hog-pen"—that had a record of one hundred and two arrests in four years among its four hundred and seventy-eight tenants, fifty-seven of them for drunken and disorderly conduct. I do not know how many children there were in it, but the inspector reported that he found only seven in the whole house who owned that they went to school. The rest gathered all the instruction they received running for beer for their elders. Some of them claimed the "flat" as their home as a mere matter of form. They slept in the streets at night. The official came upon a little party of four drinking beer out of the cover of a milk-can in the hallway. They were of the seven good boys and proved their claim to the title by offering him some.

The old question, what to do with the boy, assumes a new and serious phase in the tenements. Under the best conditions found there, it is not easily answered. In nine cases out of ten he would make an excellent mechanic, if trained early to work at a trade, for he is neither dull nor slow, but the short-sighted despotism of the trades unions has practically closed that avenue to him. Trade-schools, however excellent, cannot supply the opportunity thus denied him, and at the outset the boy stands condemned by his own to low and ill-paid drudgery, held down by the hand that of all should labor to raise him. Home, the greatest factor of all in the training of the young, means nothing to him but a pigeonhole in a coop along with so many other human animals. Its influence is scarcely of the elevating kind, if it have any. The very games at which he takes a hand in the street become polluting in its atmosphere. With no steady hand to guide him, the boy takes naturally to idle ways. Caught in the street by the truant officer, or by the agents of the Children's Societies, peddling, perhaps, or begging, to help out the family resources, he runs the risk of being sent to a reformatory, where contact with vicious boys older than himself soon develop the latent possibilities for evil that lie hidden in him. The city has no Truant Home in which to keep him, and all efforts of the children's friends to enforce school attendance are paralyzed by this want. The risk of the reformatory is too great. What is done in the end is to let him take chances—with the chances all against him. The result is the rough young savage, familiar from the street. Rough as he is, if any one doubt that this child of common clay have in him the instinct of beauty, of love for the ideal of which his life has no embodiment, let him put the matter to the test. Let him take into a tenement block a handful of flowers from the fields and watch the brightened faces, the sudden abandonment of play and fight that go ever hand in hand where there is no elbow-room, the wild entreaty for "posies," the eager love with which the little messengers of peace are shielded, once possessed; then let him change his mind. I have seen an armful of daisies keep the peace of a block better than a policeman and his club, seen instincts awaken under their gentle appeal, whose very existence the soil in which they grew may seem a mockery. I have not forgotten the deputation of ragamuffins from a Mulberry Street alley that knocked at my office door one morning on a mysterious expedition for flowers, not for themselves, but for "a lady," and having obtained what they wanted, trooped off to bestow them, a ragged and dirty little band, with a solemnity that was quite unusual. It was not until an old man called the next day to thank me for the flowers that I found out they had decked the bier of a pauper, in the dark rear room where she lay waiting in her pine-board coffin for the city's hearse. Yet, as I knew, that dismal alley with its bare brick walls, between which no sun ever rose or set, was the world of those children. It filled their young lives. Probably not one of them had ever been out of the sight of it. They were too dirty, too ragged, and too generally disreputable, too well hidden in their slum besides, to come into line with the Fresh Air summer boarders.

With such human instincts and cravings, forever unsatisfied, turned into a haunting curse; with appetite ground to keenest edge by a hunger that is never fed, the children of the poor grow up in joyless homes to lives of wearisome toil that claims them at an age when the play of their happier fellows has but just begun. Has a yard of turf been laid and a vine been coaxed to grow within their reach, they are banished and barred out from it as from a heaven that is not for such as they. I came upon a couple of youngsters in a Mulberry Street yard a while ago that were chalking on the fence their first lesson in "writin'." And this is what they wrote: "Keeb of te Grass." They had it by heart, for there was not, I verily believe, a green sod within a quarter of a mile. Home to them is an empty name. Pleasure? A gentleman once catechized a ragged class in a down-town public school on this point, and recorded the result: Out of forty-eight boys twenty had never seen the Brooklyn Bridge that was scarcely five minutes' walk away, three only had been in Central Park, fifteen had known the joy of a ride in a horse-car. The street, with its ash-barrels and its dirt, the river that runs foul with mud, are their domain. What training they receive is picked up there. And they are apt pupils. If the mud and the dirt are easily reflected in their lives, what wonder? Scarce half-grown, such lads as these confront the world with the challenge to give them their due, too long withheld, or——. Our jails supply the answer to the alternative.

A little fellow who seemed clad in but a single rag was among the flotsam and jetsam stranded at Police Headquarters one day last summer. No one knew where he came from or where he belonged. The boy himself knew as little about it as anybody, and was the least anxious to have light shed on the subject after he had spent a night in the matron's nursery. The discovery that beds were provided for boys to sleep in there, and that he could have "a whole egg" and three slices of bread for breakfast put him on the best of terms with the world in general, and he decided that Headquarters was "a bully place." He sang "McGinty" all through, with Tenth Avenue variations, for the police, and then settled down to the serious business of giving an account of himself. The examination went on after this fashion:

"Where do you go to church, my boy?"

"We don't have no clothes to go to church." And indeed his appearance, as he was, in the door of any New York church would have caused a sensation.

"Well, where do you go to school, then?"

"I don't go to school," with a snort of contempt.

"Where do you buy your bread?"

"We don't buy no bread; we buy beer," said the boy, and it was eventually the saloon that led the police as a landmark to his "home." It was worthy of the boy. As he had said, his only bed was a heap of dirty straw on the floor, his daily diet a crust in the morning, nothing else.

Into the rooms of the Children's Aid Society were led two little girls whose father had "busted up the house" and put them on the street after their mother died. Another, who was turned out by her step-mother "because she had five of her own and could not afford to keep her," could not remember ever having been in church or Sunday-school, and only knew the name of Jesus through hearing people swear by it. She had no idea what they meant. These were specimens of the overflow from the tenements of our home-heathen that are growing up in New York's streets to-day, while tender-hearted men and women are busying themselves with the socks and the hereafter of well-fed little Hottentots thousands of miles away. According to Canon Taylor, of York, one hundred and nine missionaries in the four fields of Persia, Palestine, Arabia, and Egypt spent one year and sixty thousand dollars in converting one little heathen girl. If there is nothing the matter with those missionaries, they might come to New York with a good deal better prospect of success.

By those who lay flattering unction to their souls in the knowledge that to-day New York has, at all events, no brood of the gutters of tender years that can be homeless long unheeded, let it be remembered well through what effort this judgment has been averted. In thirty-seven years the Children's Aid Society, that came into existence as an emphatic protest against the tenement corruption of the young, has sheltered quite three hundred thousand outcast, homeless, and orphaned children in its lodging-houses, and has found homes in the West for seventy thousand that had none. Doubtless, as a mere stroke of finance, the five millions and a half thus spent were a wiser investment than to have let them grow up thieves and thugs. In the last fifteen years of this tireless battle for the safety of the State the intervention of the Society for the Prevention of Cruelty to Children has been invoked for 138,891 little ones; it has thrown its protection around more than twenty-five thousand helpless children, and has convicted nearly sixteen thousand wretches of child-beating and abuse. Add to this the standing army of fifteen thousand dependent children in New York's asylums and institutions, and some idea is gained of the crop that is garnered day by day in the tenements, of the enormous force employed to check their inroads on our social life, and of the cause for apprehension that would exist did their efforts flag for ever so brief a time.

Nothing is now better understood than that the rescue of the children is the key to the problem of city poverty, as presented for our solution to-day; that character may be formed where to reform it would be a hopeless task. The concurrent testimony of all who have to undertake it at a later stage: that the young are naturally neither vicious nor hardened, simply weak and undeveloped, except by the bad influences of the street, makes this duty all the more urgent as well as hopeful. Helping hands are held out on every side. To private charity the municipality leaves the entire care of its proletariat of tender years, lulling its conscience to sleep with liberal appropriations of money to foot the bills. Indeed, it is held by those whose opinions are entitled to weight that it is far too liberal a paymaster for its own best interests and those of its wards. It deals with the evil in the seed to a limited extent in gathering in the outcast babies from the streets. To the ripe fruit the gates of its prisons, its reformatories, and its workhouses are opened wide the year round. What the showing would be at this end of the line were it not for the barriers wise charity has thrown across the broad highway to ruin—is building day by day—may be measured by such results as those quoted above in the span of a single life.

# When You Spend a Dollar
## 1938

## Millen Brand

Coyle, his wife, and daughter, Katy, lived in a tenement. Coyle was Irish; at one time he had lived in a better neighborhood but he was now working two days a week—he had found this apartment in a big tenement which housed for the most part Italian and Greek families. It was cheaper; he was glad now to have anything. The apartment, as it was called, had two small rooms—one was a nine-by-twelve bedroom, the other a six-by-nine kitchen. They had a toilet in a closet in the bedroom; in order to sit on it they had to leave the door open to make room for their feet.

But that was better than a common toilet in the hallway.

The worst time to be in a tenement is summer. The Coyles were on the next to the top floor and the heat of the sun came down and the heat of the building rose up to them. Heat and noise. But always heat.

As the days became really unbearably hot, the Coyles got into the habit of sleeping late, exhausted by the heat of the night before; they did this except on Thursday and Friday, when Coyle worked.

One morning, a Wednesday, they woke up at about quarter to nine. The heat of the day was now, just as they woke, as terrible as it had been when they fell into a fatigued sleep the night before. It was even worse. On the floor below they heard Mrs. Andriolo, one of their friends in the building, walking back and forth with her baby; the baby was crying—it seemed to be protesting against the furnace-like heat that Coyle, his wife, everybody in the building felt.

"The baby won't drink the bottle," Mrs. Coyle said.

"Why don't she nurse it?"

"She can't. She tried. Her breasts bleed."

Coyle lay silent. His wife lay beside him on her back, her half-hidden breasts—which had richly nursed their own baby—with dark flattened nipples, like black roses on her skin. "Look at Katy," he said "still sleeping. Asleep, Katy?" he said softly. There was no answer.

A canary began to sing in the Paraskevopoulos' apartment down the hall.

After an hour, Mrs. Coyle put her feet into slippers and stood up, shaking her long dark hair down her back and twisting it. "Come on, get up," she said. "You're gettin' lazy, my man."

"Me lazy?" he said. "And I work ten hours a day?"

"Twenty hours a week."

"Ah, but I wish it was sixty for your sake, Mary," he said.

Katy woke up. The first thing she said was, "It's so hot."

"All right, it's hot," Coyle said. "So what?"

"I wish we could go to the beach."

He said nothing. He felt angry. Katy should have more sense.

Mary went into the kitchen and Katy got up and went in too. He heard the two of them talking in low voices.

Why should he be angry? Why not? It was twenty hours, as Mary had said. Just twenty hours. No work for a man—only enough to keep from starving. No life; this was not living.

Well, if they were badly off, the Andriolos were worse. He had been talking to Andriolo—it was a wonder how they existed.

He lay thinking until breakfast was ready, then went into the kitchen in his pajamas. The room was airless; as he drank the coffee set out for him, beads of sweat came out on his forehead. His wife served some warmed-over potatoes and some bacon.

"Warm stuff," he said.

"It's all we have."

He ate without appetite and helped his wife with the dishes. The work was done; then his wife made the beds; then the day was ahead of them. The day and its heat.

At about eleven o'clock they were all three sitting around the one window they had on the courtyard. No air seemed to come in at all. Being a flight down from the top of the building, if there was any breeze, it would not reach as far down into the narrow court as to reach them.

"It's so hot," Katy said again. She leaned across the sill of the window; her arms stretched out as of imploring pity from the heat. But the heat, from the crowded buildings, the streets, the sweating pores of thousands of human beings, could not have pity. From other windows people reached too, like Katy, for some impossible coolness—in one window a man sat naked to the waist, his wife in a damp slip.

Italianos, Coyle thought. Hellaynays. But human beings. He was sorry for Andriolo, with four kids, with a brother hurt in the steel strike. He gave him a quarter sometimes for the Red Fighting Fund.

The sun was rising; it struck down straight on the roofs; the heat was more than blood temperature. There was no escape. Heat, death. . . . He looked at Katy. Her eyes seemed dull; her continual goodness, he thought, was more than half passivity. He was afraid; it was no good to see children become so good, so quiet. His wife too. She was too resigned, was—

A flood of canary song poured out of the Paraskevopoulos' apartment, first a few straight notes, then the bird's full repertoire.

"Mary," he said. He hesitated. "Mary," he said again, his voice unsure but hard, "let's go to the beach."

His wife turned and looked at him with shocked eyes. He might have proposed holding up a bank.

"Jim—" she said.

"Yes," he said, "why can't we go, Mary? In the name of God don't we deserve some happiness? Must we think about money always?"

"We need money for food."

"We have enough till Friday."

"Hardly enough."

"Enough, come, Mary, a dollar for everything—carfare, bathhouse, everything."

"And the rent?"

"I don't think anybody'll come."

They were two months behind in the rent. They had saved just fourteen dollars to pay one month's rent—if the landlord or his agent came.

"No, if they ain't come yet, they won't come till Friday," he said. On Friday he would be paid again.

"They might come."

"They won't."

"They might. Oh Jim, how can y' talk like that?"

"How can I talk like that! But it's the happiness of you and Katy I'm thinking of. Can't I—"

"No, Jim, no."

Both of them heard a funny sound and looked at Katy. She was hunched over the window sill, making a funny sound—when he turned her head up, he saw she was crying. "Katy!" He and his wife knelt down and he took the girl into his arms. "Katy," Coyle said, "Katy, don't you know we're goin' to the beach?"

Ahead of them they smelled the sea, a salt fresh smell they never smelled in the city; already the trip was worthwhile, to get that smell. As they came nearer, they began to hear the continuous thrashing of the surf—they could hear it past the stands of the concessionaires, the voices of people. . . . A year, Coyle thought, since they had been here.

The steady sound of the surf seemed to draw them; Katy became excited, wanted to hurry.

They went to the city bathhouses. As it was a week day, they rented one for 20 cents. It was small and dark and there were only a few faint bars of light coming through a heavily latticed window at the back. Darkness was for the poor, he thought. He thought of the tenement with its interior rooms, its air-shafts, its narrow courtyard, dark—why could he not escape even here, feel really free?

As he hung up his pants, he heard the silver jingling in his pocket; that was the dollar. They had rented suits, rough cheap suits of blue. Katy's was small for her; when she wriggled into it, it hugged her buttocks in a tight line.

"Well, Mary," he said, "how's it feel?"

His wife looked at him and smiled.

They went out and down to the beach. At first they could not see it because they were in a corridor of the bathhouses, then it came in view. The sea; there it was, the large fathomless element, blue, glittering, living. For a moment Coyle saw it as "the sea"; then he saw it only as a place to swim in, to get cool in, "the beach" they had come to for a day's relief from heat and the airless tenement.

Katy ran forward and into a wave that was coming in. The wave spread out over the almost level sand; first it rushed up at her ankles, then going out, it dug cups at her heels. She was excited, feeling the fine sand escaping under her heels and her heels sinking down.

They went in. Their suits turned from light to dark blue, the water streamed from their limbs. Up and down the beach were hundreds of other hot, exhausted city dwellers getting some of the natural health of the sea. There were screams, arms and heads floating, bodies intermingled. Kay churned her arms; she remembered the swimming lessons her father had given her the summer before. "Mary," Coyle said to his wife, "look at Katy. She's gonna make a swimmer."

After a half-hour they came out. They lay down feeling pleasantly tired. Coyle put his cheek against his wife's shoulder; together he and his wife looked at Katy. A little body that had come out of their own, a child, something to live beyond them. Yes, but into what kind of a world, Coyle thought. Unemployment. Depression. Well, it could change. At least now he felt good. Katy looked better—tired but with color, there was some animation in her stretched-out limbs.

After they had sprawled out resting a few minutes, Katy said, "Pop, the tide coming in?"

"Yeah, it's comin' in."

He knew that she wanted it to be coming in, but she said, "How can y'tell, Pop?"

"Look a' that pier down there, see the posts under it?"

"Yeah."

"Well, there's five posts outa water now. When we came, there was seven or eight outa water."

Then she said what he expected her to say, "Let's build a fort."

Obligingly he got to his feet and they went down just out of reach of the water and started a fort. They made a big one—a trench or moat first in front of the fort, then walls a foot and a half or more thick, packed hard, leveled smooth, then some outworks and towers. He made some imitation cannon with wet sand; Katy copied him with others; all the cannon pointed towards the menacing sea.

"Look," Katy said, running to her mother. "It's a good one, look."

Coyle came up again and lay down by Mary.

"Y' like it, Mama?" Katy said.

"I like it. It's fine."

"Now watch—"

As the three of them waited, under the sun somehow burning and cool at the same time, the sea began to come in. Wave after wave came up, ebbed out. At times there would be a long one and then several short ones so that it almost seemed as if the tide was going out. "You're sure the tide's comin' in?" Katy said.

"Yeah, it's comin' in."

Katy sat at her parent's feet. She watched patiently. At last a long wave rolled up and broke through one point of the outworks of the fort and ran into the moat where, as the wave ebbed out again, it was absorbed into the sand. This one long wave was the signal to others; soon they were coming stronger and they poured into and filled the moat.

With the gentle motion of the water rolling back and forth in the moat, a sliver was dislodged from the front wall and slid down and disappeared. Still the waves came slowly, gradually; the fort looked strong and Katy said, "It's strong enough, ain't it, Pop? It won't break, will it?"

"I don't know," he said. "Wait and see."

Now a long wave, with unexpected force, rolled in, crossed the moat, and hit the fort in a jet of thrownup foaming water. "Oh," Katy said, as if she herself were hurt by this first mortal blow to the fort. Once the blow had been struck, there was no relaxing in the attack of the sea. More waves poured in, they hit and washed around the fort, huge slices of its walls—undermined—fell and crumbled away. The tide hurried on either side; the fort became a salient in the long line of the sea. Water in its mass was threatening, all the miles of the sea rose up. It now seemed unbelievable that the fort held at all. It held, then with a leap the sea was inside it; it pulled and thrust; everything went. The waves in a moment leveled and with steady suction erased the fallen walls, the sand, until nothing was left.

Sighing, Katy said, "I didn't think it could do it."

"You can't stop the sea," her father said.

They had to get up and sit further back. It was a defeat; he felt it. But man is not sand, something to be washed away. Man fights.

He looked out again over the sea; its mass was cool, calm, beautiful.

"Well, we're home," Coyle said to his wife as they stood outside the entrance to the tenement. It was only about seven-thirty; they came home early because Katy was tired—also they had no money to eat away from home. Still, it had been good, Coyle felt good. He had given his family a day at the beach as any family deserved—they had needed it and it had been good for them. Particularly it had been good for Katy. Weeks of being in this place, playing in the hallways and kitchens of neighbors—with Lily Andriolo—playing in the hot streets.

"Glad to get home?" he said to Katy.

She nodded.

Glad? he thought. They went into the building.

It was still far from sundown; the heat was almost as bad as at midday. In the papers on the way home he had seen that today was breaking records for heat. The heat closed like a furnace around them as they entered the building.

There was something else. Coming from the beach, with the clean smell of the ocean so late in his nostrils, Coyle particularly noticed, as he came in, the smell of the tenement. A peculiar unmistakable smell—rot, old paint, remnants of garbage falling from the pails left outside of doors, all the close packed human smell—from cooking, breathing, living in a space that was meant for half the number of people.

They started upstairs. Once they had gone up half a flight, although it was still full daylight outside, here it was almost pitch dark. No wonder he had noticed the darkness at the beach bathhouse—darkness, poverty. Instead of decent windows—airshafts, airshaft windows. Windows like the ones at each landing here, windows that out of the two-foot-wide airshaft dropped a spot of ghostly light on the landing platform. The light was invisible in the air, it could only be seen actually on the landing. Coyle was astonished—looking at it—to see that there could be light without illumination. The darkness of the stairway angered him. He had always hated to have Katy going up and down it. Even now, holding her mother's hand, she stumbled. It would be easy, by herself, to have a bad fall. But that was not the principal thing he feared. It was—

"You have the key?" his wife said.

They had reached the fifth floor, their floor, and Coyle got out his key and opened the apartment door for them. They were back. There were the same two rooms, the same stifling atmosphere, the same furniture, walls, life. Even the Andriolo baby was crying again; they could hear Mrs. Andriolo, who was still overweight from her pregnancy, walking back and forth with it. He turned and looked at his wife and Katy. In their eyes was no longer the happiness they had felt at the beach. They were oppressed; like him they knew their lives had little in them.

They ate supper, with a better appetite than they usually had. But Coyle noticed something. His wife was worrying. He knew what she was worrying about, whether anybody would come for the rent. Nobody would come; nobody would come before Friday. But he began to worry too.

When they had finished eating and cleaned up, they went to the window and sat down. It was just like the morning except that now there was not so long to wait for darkness, for possible coolness. He reached over and took his wife's hand; they sat without speaking. Katy leaned on the window sill and Coyle noticed that her arms were again outstretched; they seemed again to be imploring the heat as they had in the morning.

Other people sat at other windows; people came and went; voices called, changed, grew loud or soft.

When the sun finally set, it seemed to get dark quickly. They put Katy to bed and did not put on the light so that she would sleep. He knew now why tenement children stayed up late, why—

Yes, he knew plenty he had not known until the last two years.

He and Mary said nothing, but sat in silence by the window. The air had cooled a little, had to. A few lights came on around the courtyard, threw a faint radiance in their room. He heard a radio announce, faintly, "—nine o'clock." At almost the same moment he heard Andriolo.

Andriolo was talking in the hallway downstairs. He could tell his voice. There was another voice, under it—he knew that voice too. The two voices continued, one loud, the other less loud.

What was there to say?

After a few minutes it was quiet; steps sounded on the stairs, then there was the expected knock on the door. He answered it. In order not to wake up Katy, he opened the door quickly, stepped into the hall, and closed the door behind him.

"What's the matter, don't I come in?" Mr. Regan said.

"The kid's asleep."

"Okay—well, what I want don't take long. You got the rent?"

"No, I'll have it Friday." Fourteen dollars. He had never offered less than at least one month's full rent, would not now.

"You're two months behind, y' know? Wha' d' y' expect me to do, come every day for it?"

"I'm sorry, but—"

"You think all I got to do is collect rent?"

Coyle held himself in. "It's the best I can do. Two days' work a week—"

"And maybe that's my fault. Coyle, if you wanta live here, pay. If you don't—"

"Live here," he said explosively. "Live."

"It's better than the street—"

Coyle got the hidden threat; his anger flared up.

"This tenement's better than the street. Stairs like sewers—"

"All right, I didn't come here to argue, Coyle. I been renting this place to keep it going; it's about time I made some money. Fourteen a month with a toilet, two rooms—it's cheap. I oughta get sixteen, eighteen. You don't pay your rent, I'll get somebody who'll pay it and pay more."

"So that's it, hey? You're getting the place filled up so now you raise the rent."

"Why not? Rents have gone up—"

"Listen, maybe I'm short today but I'll have it Friday. Before you talk about raisin' rent, why don't you fix some of the violations?"

"What violations?"

"You think I don't know? You think because there's a lot of Greeks and Italians here they don't know a few things? Fire escapes—the front door—

does it lock? See that door over there? That's a dumbwaiter only it don't work an' it's filled up with paper an' garbage. Maybe you don't know about that—"

"All right, pay a couple more dollars and I'll put improvements in—"

"The house is lousy with violations. What you ever put into it? If it was to fall apart, you wouldn't buy a nail to hold it together. Now you wanta raise the rent. Raise the rent outa what—food for my kid? Outa Andriolo's baby—?"

Without realizing it, his voice had risen. In the room behind him he heard something; Katy was beginning to cry. He knew what it was, she had heard him and was frightened. Her crying was muffled with sleep; in a minute she would be crying loud.

"Okay," he said, turning, "you'll get your rent Friday."

"Coyle, I don't like people that talk—"

Coyle went back into the apartment and closed the door. After a while his wife quieted Katy; afterwards Katy tossed restlessly. They kept the light off so that she would go back to sleep again.

"Nice, ain't it?" he said to his wife.

He wondered if his wife would throw the dollar up to him, but she did not. She was intelligent.

They went to bed. In bed, neither of them slept. At ten—it was still early —the doorway of the Paraskevopoulos' apartment opened; they heard the trill of the canary, three sweet sucking gasps.

"Jim," Mary said.

"What?"

"Regan gonna put us out."

Coyle said nothing. He got up and, pulling on his pants, said, "I'm going down an' talk to Andriolo. He's got ideas."

## The Counterfeit Secret Circle
## Member Gets the Message,
## Or The Asp Strikes Again

### 1966

## Jean Shepherd

Every day when I was a kid I'd drop anything I was doing, no matter what it was—stealing wire, having a fistfight, siphoning gas—no matter what, and tear like a blue streak through the alleys, over fences, under porches, through secret short-cuts, to get home not a second too late for the magic time. My breath rattling in wheezy gasps, sweating profusely from my long cross-country run I'd sit glassy-eyed and expectant before our Crosley Notre Dame Cathedral model radio.

I was never disappointed. At exactly five-fifteen, just as dusk was gathering over the picturesque oil refineries and the faint glow of the muttering Open Hearths was beginning to show red against the gloom, the magic notes of an unforgettable theme song came rasping out of our Crosley:

> *"Who's that little chatterbox . . . ?*
> *The one with curly golden locks. . . .*
> *Who do I see . . . ?*
> *It's Little Orphan Annie."*

Ah, they don't write tunes like that any more. There was one particularly brilliant line that dealt with Sandy, Little Orphan Annie's airedale sidekick. Who can forget it?

> *Arf goes Sandy.*

I think it was Sandy more than anyone else that drew me to the Little Orphan Annie radio program. Dogs in our neighborhood never went "Arf." And they certainly were a lot of things, but never faithful.

Little Orphan Annie lived in this great place called Tompkins Corners. There were people called Joe Corntassle and Uncle. They never mentioned the

poolroom. There were no stockyards or fistfights. Or drunks sleeping in door-
ways in good old Tompkins Corners. Orphan Annie and Sandy and Joe Corntassle were always out chasing pirates or trapping smugglers, neither of which
we ever had in Indiana as far as I knew. We had plenty of hubcap stealers and
once even a guy who stole a lawn. But no pirates. At least they didn't call them
that.

She also had this friend named The Asp, who whenever she was really in
a tight spot would just show up and cut everybody's head off. I figured that if
there was anything a kid of seven needed it was somebody named The Asp.
Especially in our neighborhood. He wore a towel around his head.

Immediately after the nightly adventure, which usually took place near
the headwaters of the dreaded Orinoco, on would come a guy named Pierre
André, the *definitive* radio announcer.

"FELLAS AND GALS. GET SET FOR A MEETING OF THE LITTLE ORPHAN
ANNNIE SECRET CIRCLE!"

His voice boomed out of the Crosley like some monster, maniacal pipe
organ played by the Devil himself. Vibrant, urgent, dynamic, commanding.
Pierre André. I have long had a suspicion that an entire generation of Americans grew up feeling inferior to just the *names* of the guys on the radio. Pierre
André. Harlow Wilcox. Vincent Pelletier. Truman Bradley. Westbrook Van
Voorhees. André Baruch. Norman Brokenshire. There wasn't a Charlie Shmid-
lap in the lot. Poor little Charlie crouching next to his radio—a born Right
Fielder. Playing right field all of his life, knee-deep in weeds, waiting for a fly-
ball that never comes and more than half afraid that one day they *will* hit one
in his direction.

"OKAY, KIDS. TIME TO GET OUT YOUR SECRET DECODER PIN. TIME FOR
ANOTHER SECRET MESSAGE DIRECT FROM LITTLE ORPHAN ANNIE TO MEM-
BERS OF THE LITTLE ORPHAN ANNIE SECRET CIRCLE."

I got no pin. A member of an Out Group at the age of seven. And the
worst kind of an Out Group. I am living in a non-Ovaltine-drinking neighborhood.

"ALL RIGHT. SET YOUR PINS TO B-7. SEVEN . . . TWENTY-TWO . . .
NINETEEN . . . EIGHT . . . *FORTY-NINE* . . . SIX . . . THIRTEEN . . .
*THREE!* . . . TWENTY-TWO . . . ONE . . . FOUR . . . NINTEEN."

Pierre André could get more out of just numbers than Orson Welles was
able to squeeze out of *King Lear*.

"FOURTEEN . . . NINE . . . THIRTY-TWO. OKAY, FELLAS AND GALS,
OVER AND OUT."

Then—silence. The show was over and you had a sinister feeling that out
there in the darkness all over the country there were millions of kids—decod-
ing. All I could do was to go out into the kitchen where my mother was cooking
supper and knock together a salami sandwich. And plot. Somewhere kids were
getting the real truth from Orphan Annie. The message. And I had no pin. I
lived in an Oatmeal-eating family and listened to an Ovaltine radio show. To

get into the Little Orphan Annie Secret Circle you had to send in the silver inner seal from a can of what Pierre André called "that rich chocolate-flavored drink that all the kids love." I had never even *seen* an Ovaltine can in my life.

But as the old truism goes, every man has his chance, and when yours comes you had better grab it. They do not make appointments for the next day. One day while I am foraging my way home from school, coming down one of my favorite alleys, knee-deep in garbage and the thrown-out effluvia of kitchen life, there occurred an incident which forever changed my outlook on Existence itself, although of course at the time I was not aware of it, believing instead that I had struck the Jackpot and was at last on my way into the Big Time.

There was a standard game played solo by almost every male kid I ever heard of, at least in our neighborhood. It was simple, yet highly satisfying. There were no rules except those which the player improvised as he went along. The game had no name and is probably as old as creation itself. It consisted of kicking a tin can or tin cans all the way home. This game is not to be confused with a more formal athletic contest called Kick The Can, which *did* have rules and even teams. This kicking game was a solitary, dogged contest of kid against can, and is quite possibly the very earliest manifestation of the Golf Syndrome.

Anyway, I am kicking condensed milk cans, baked bean cans, sardine cans along the alley, occasionally changing cans at full gallop, when I suddenly found myself kicking a can of a totally unknown nature. I kicked it twice; good, solid, running belts, before I discovered that what I was kicking was an Ovaltine can, the first I had ever seen. Instantly I picked it up, astounded by the mere presence of an Ovaltine drinker in our neighborhood, and then discovered that they had not only thrown out the Ovaltine can but had left the silver inner seal inside. Some rich family had thrown it *all* away! Five minutes later I've got this inner seal in the mail and I start to wait. Every day I would rush home from school and ask:

"Is there any mail for me?"

Day after day, eon after eon. Waiting for three weeks for something to come in the mail to a kid is like being asked to build the Pyramids singlehanded, using the #3 Erector set, the one without the motor. We never did get much mail around our house anyway. Usually it was bad news when it *did* come. Once in a while a letter marked OCCUPANT arrived, offering my Old Man $300 on his signature only, no questions asked, "Even your employer will not be notified." They began with:

"Friend, are you in Money troubles?"

My Old Man could never figure out how they knew, especially since they only called him OCCUPANT. Day after day I watched our mailbox. On Saturdays when there was no school I would sit on the front porch waiting for the mailman and the sound of the yelping pack of dogs that chased him on his appointed rounds through our neighborhood, his muffled curses and thumping kicks mingling nicely with the steady uproar of snarling and yelping. One thing I knew. Trusty old Sandy never chased a mailman. And if he *had,* he would have caught him.

Everything comes to he who waits. I guess. At last, after at least 200 years of constant vigil, there was delivered to me a big, fat, lumpy letter. There are few things more thrilling in Life than lumpy letters. That rattle. Even to this day I feel a wild surge of exultation when I run my hands over an envelope that is thick, fat, and pregnant with mystery.

I ripped it open. And there it was! My simulated gold plastic Decoder pin. With knob. And my membership card.

It was an important moment. Here was a real milestone, and I knew it. I was taking my first step up that great ladder of becoming a real American. Nothing is as important to an American as a membership card with a seal. I know guys who have long strings of them, plastic-enclosed: credit cards, membership cards, identification cards, Blue Cross cards, driver's licenses, all strung together in a chain of Love. The longer the chain, the more they feel they belong. Here was my first card, I was on my way. And the best of all possible ways—I was making it as a Phony. A non-Ovaltine drinking Official Member.

BE IT KNOWN TO ALL AND SUNDRY THAT MR. RALPH WESLEY PARKER IS HEREBY AP-POINTED A MEMBER OF THE LITTLE ORPHAN ANNIE SECRET CIRCLE AND IS ENTITLED TO ALL THE HONORS AND BENEFITS ACCRUING THERETO.

Signed: Little Orphan Annie. Countersigned: Pierre André. In ink.

Honors and benefits. Already, at the age of seven, I am *Mister* Parker. They hardly ever even called my Old Man that.

That night I can hardly wait until the adventure is over. I want to get to the real thing, the message. That's what counts. I had spent the entire day sharpening pencils, practicing twirling the knob on my plastic simulated gold Decoder pin. I had lined up plenty of paper and was ready at the radio by three-thirty, sitting impatiently through the drone of the late afternoon Soap Operas and newscasts, waiting for my direct contact with Tompkins Corners, my first night as a full Member.

As five-fifteen neared, my excitement mounted. Running waves of goose pimples rippled up and down my spine as I hunched next to our hand-carved, seven-tube Cathedral in the living room. A pause, a station break. . . .

*"Who's that little chatterbox . . . ?*
*The one with curly golden locks. . . .*
*Who do I see . . . ?*
*It's Little Orphan Annie."*

Let's get on with it! I don't need all this jazz about smugglers and pirates. I sat through Sandy's arfing and Little Orphan Annie's perils hardly hearing a word. On comes, at long last, old Pierre. He's one of *my* friends now. I am In. My first secret meeting.

"OKAY, FELLAS AND GALS. GET OUT YOUR DECODER PINS. TIME FOR

THE SECRET MESSAGE FOR ALL THE REGULAR PALS OF LITTLE ORPHAN
ANNIE, MEMBERS OF THE LITTLE ORPHAN ANNIE SECRET CIRCLE. ALL SET?
HERE WE GO. SET YOUR PINS AT B-12."

My eyes narrowed to mere slits, my steely claws working with precision,
I set my simulated gold plastic Decoder pin at B-12.

"ALL READY? PENCILS SET?"

Old Pierre was in great voice tonight. I could tell that tonight's message
was really important.

"SEVEN . . . TWENTY-TWO . . . THIRTEEN . . . NINETEEN . . .
EIGHT!"

I struggled furiously to keep up with his booming voice dripping with
tension and excitement. Finally:

"OKAY, KIDS. THAT'S TONIGHT'S SECRET MESSAGE. LISTEN AGAIN TO-
MORROW NIGHT, WHEN YOU HEAR . . ."

> *"Who's that little chatterbox . . . ?*
> *The one with curly golden locks. . . ."*

Ninety seconds later I am in the only room in the house where a boy of
seven could sit in privacy and decode. My pin is on one knee, my Indian Chief
tablet on the other. I'm starting to decode.

7. . . .

I spun the dial, poring over the plastic scale of letters. Aha! B. I carefully
wrote down my first decoded number. I went to the next.

22. . . .

Again I spun the dial. E . . .

The first word is B-E.

13 . . . S . . .

It was coming easier now.

19 . . . U.

From somewhere out in the house I could hear my kid brother whimpering, his wail gathering steam, then the faint shriek of my mother:

"Hurry up! Randy's gotta go!"

Now what!

"I'LL BE RIGHT OUT, MA! GEE WHIZ!"

I shouted hoarsely, sweat dripping off my nose.

S . . . U . . . 15 . . . R . . . E. BE SURE! A message was coming
through!

Excitement gripped my gut. I was getting The Word. BE SURE . . .

14 . . . 8 . . . T . . . O . . . BE SURE TO what? What was Little
Orphan Annie trying to say?

17 . . 9 . . . DR . . . 16 . . 12 . . I . . . 9 . . . N . .
K . . . 32 . . . OVA . . 19 . . LT . . .

I sat for a long moment in that steamy room, staring down at my Indian
Chief notebook. A crummy commercial!

Again a high, rising note from my kid brother.

"I'LL BE RIGHT OUT, MA! FOR CRYING OUT LOUD."

I pulled up my corduroy knickers and went out to face the meat loaf and the red cabbage. The Asp had decapitated another victim.

---

## The Egg

## 1921

---

## Sherwood Anderson

---

My father was, I am sure, intended by nature to be a cheerful, kindly man. Until he was thirty-four years old he worked as a farmhand for a man named Thomas Butterworth whose place lay near the town of Bidwell, Ohio. He had then a horse of his own, and on Saturday evenings drove into town to spend a few hours in social intercourse with other farm-hands. In town he drank several glasses of beer and stood about in Ben Head's saloon—crowded on Saturday evenings with visiting farmhands. Songs were sung and glasses thumped on the bar. At ten o'clock father drove home along a lonely country road, made his horse comfortable for the night, and himself went to bed, quite happy in his position in life. He had at that time no notion of trying to rise in the world.

It was in the spring of his thirty-fifth year that father married my mother, then a country school-teacher, and in the following spring I came wriggling and crying into the world. Something happened to the two people. They became ambitious. The American passion for getting up in the world took possession of them.

It may have been that mother was responsible. Being a school-teacher she had no doubt read books and magazines. She had, I presume, read of how Garfield, Lincoln, and other Americans rose from poverty to fame and greatness, and as I lay beside her—in the days of her lying-in—she may have dreamed that I would some day rule men and cities. At any rate she induced father to give up his place as a farmhand, sell his horse, and embark on an independent enterprise of his own. She was a tall silent woman with a long nose and troubled gray eyes. For herself she wanted nothing. For father and myself she was incurably ambitious.

The first venture into which the two people went turned out badly. They rented ten acres of poor stony land on Grigg's Road, eight miles from Bidwell, and launched into chicken-raising. I grew into boyhood on the place and got my first impressions of life there. From the beginning they were impressions of disaster, and if, in my turn, I am a gloomy man inclined to see the darker side of life, I attribute it to the fact that what should have been for me the happy joyous days of childhood were spent on a chicken farm.

One unversed in such matters can have no notion of the many and tragic things that can happen to a chicken. It is born out of an egg, lives for a few weeks as a tiny fluffy thing such as you will see pictured on Easter cards, then becomes hideously naked, eats quantities of corn and meal bought by the sweat of your father's brow, gets diseases called pip, cholera, and other names, stands looking with stupid eyes at the sun, becomes sick and dies. A few hens and now and then a rooster, intended to serve God's mysterious ends, struggle through to maturity. The hens lay eggs out of which come other chickens and the dreadful cycle is thus made complete. It is all unbelievably complex. Most philosophers must have been raised on chicken farms. One hopes for so much from a chicken and is so dreadfully disillusioned. Small chickens, just setting out on the journey of life, look so bright and alert and they are in fact so dreadfully stupid. They are so much like people they mix one up in one's judgments of life. If disease does not kill them, they wait until your expectations are thoroughly aroused and then walk under the wheels of a wagon—to go squashed and dead back to their maker. Vermin infest their youth, and fortunes must be spent for curative powders. In later life I have seen how a literature has been built up on the subject of fortunes to be made out of the raising of chickens. It is intended to be read by the gods who have just eaten of the tree of the knowledge of good and evil. It is a hopeful literature and declares that much may be done by simple ambitious people who own a few hens. Do not be led astray by it. It was not written for you. Go hunt for gold on the frozen hills of Alaska, put your faith in the honesty of a politician, believe if you will that the world is daily growing better and that good will triumph over evil, but do not read and believe the literature that is written concerning the hen. It was not written for you.

I, however, digress. My tale does not primarily concern itself with the hen. If correctly told it will center on the egg. For ten years my father and mother struggled to make our chicken farm pay and then they gave up that struggle and began another. They moved into the town of Bidwell, Ohio, and embarked in the restaurant business. After ten years of worry with incubators that did not hatch, and with tiny—and in their own way lovely—balls of fluff that passed on into semi-naked pullethood and from that into dead henhood, we threw all aside and, packing our belongings on a wagon, drove down Grigg's Road toward Bidwell, a tiny caravan of hope looking for a new place from which to start on our upward journey through life.

We must have been a sad-looking lot, not, I fancy, unlike refugees fleeing from a battlefield. Mother and I walked in the road. The wagon that contained our goods had been borrowed for the day from Mr. Albert Griggs, a neighbor. Out of its sides stuck the legs of cheap chairs, and at the back of the pile of beds, tables, and boxes filled with kitchen utensils was a crate of live chickens, and on top of that the baby carriage in which I had been wheeled about in my infancy. Why we stuck to the baby carriage I don't know. It was unlikely other children would be born and the wheels were broken. People who have few possessions cling tightly to those they have. That is one of the facts that make life so discouraging.

Father rode on top of the wagon. He was then a bald-headed man of forty-five, a little fat, and from long association with mother and the chickens he had become habitually silent and discouraged. All during our ten years on the chicken farm he had worked as a laborer on neighboring farms and most of the money he had earned had been spent for remedies to cure chicken diseases, on Wilmer's White Wonder Cholera Cure or Professor Bidlow's Egg Producer or some other preparations that mother found advertised in the poultry papers. There were two little patches of hair on father's head just above his ears. I remember that as a child I used to sit looking at him when he had gone to sleep in a chair before the stove on Sunday afternoons in the winter. I had at that time already begun to read books and have notions of my own, and the bald path that led over the top of his head was, I fancied, something like a broad road, such a road as Caesar might have made on which to lead his legions out of Rome and into the wonders of an unknown world. The tufts of hair that grew above father's ears were, I thought, like forests. I fell into a half-sleeping, half-waking state and dreamed I was a tiny thing going along the road into a far beautiful place where there were no chicken farms and where life was a happy eggless affair.

One might write a book concerning our flight from the chicken farm into town. Mother and I walked the entire eight miles—she to be sure that nothing fell from the wagon and I to see the wonders of the world. On the seat of the wagon beside father was his greatest treasure. I will tell you of that.

On a chicken farm, where hundreds and even thousands of chickens come out of eggs, surprising things sometimes happen. Grotesques are born out of eggs as out of people. The accident does not often occur—perhaps once in a thousand births. A chicken is, you see, born that has four legs, two pairs of wings, two heads, or what not. The things do not live. They go quickly back to the hand of their maker that has for a moment trembled. The fact that the poor little things could not live was one of the tragedies of life to father. He had some sort of notion that if he could but bring into henhood or roosterhood a five-legged hen or a two-headed rooster his fortune would be made. He dreamed of taking the wonder about the county fairs and of growing rich by exhibiting it to other farmhands.

At any rate, he saved all the little monstrous things that had been born on our chicken farm. They were preserved in alcohol and put each in its own glass bottle. These he had carefully put into a box, and on our journey into town it was carried on the wagon seat beside him. He drove the horses with one hand and with the other clung to the box. When we got to our destination, the box was taken down at once and the bottles removed. All during our days as keepers of a restaurant in the town of Bidwell, Ohio, the grotesques in their little glass bottles sat on a shelf back of the counter. Mother sometimes protested, but father was a rock on the subject of his treasure. The grotesques were, he declared, valuable. People, he said, liked to look at strange and wonderful things.

Did I say that we embarked in the restaurant business in the town of Bidwell, Ohio? I exaggerated a little. The town itself lay at the foot of a low hill and on the shore of a small river. The railroad did not run through the town and the station was a mile away to the north at a place called Pickleville. There had been a cider mill and pickle factory at the station, but before the time of our coming they had both gone out of business. In the morning and in the evening busses came down to the station along a road called Turner's Pike from the hotel on the main street of Bidwell. Our going to that out-of-the-way place to embark in the restaurant business was mother's idea. She talked of it for a year and then one day went off and rented an empty store building opposite the railroad station. It was her idea that the restaurant would be profitable. Traveling men, she said, would be always waiting around to take trains out of town and town people would come to the station to await incoming trains. They would come to the restaurant to buy pieces of pie and drink coffee. Now that I am older I know that she had another motive in going. She was ambitious for me. She wanted me to rise in the world, to get into a town school and become a man of the towns.

At Pickleville father and mother worked hard, as they always had done. At first there was the necessity of putting our place into shape to be a restaurant. That took a month. Father built a shelf on which he put tins of vegetables. He painted a sign on which he put his name in large red letters. Below his name was the sharp command—"EAT HERE"—that was so seldom obeyed. A showcase was bought and filled with cigars and tobacco. Mother scrubbed the floor and the walls of the room. I went to school in the town and was glad to be away from the farm and from the presence of the discouraged, sad-looking chickens. Still I was not very joyous. In the evening I walked home from school along Turner's Pike and remembered the children I had seen playing in the town school yard. A troop of little girls had gone hopping about and singing. I tried that. Down along the frozen road I went hopping solemnly on one leg. "Hippity Hop To The Barber Shop," I sang shrilly. Then I stopped and looked doubtfully about. I was afraid of being seen in my gay mood. It must have seemed to me that I was doing a thing that should not be done by one who, like myself, had been raised on a chicken farm where death was a daily visitor.

Mother decided that our restaurant should remain open at night. At ten in the evening a passenger train went north past our door followed by a local freight. The freight crew had switching to do in Pickleville, and when the work was done they came to our restaurant for hot coffee and food. Sometimes one of them ordered a fried egg. In the morning at four they returned north-bound and again visited us. A little trade began to grow up. Mother slept at night and during the day tended the restaurant and fed our boarders while father slept. He slept in the same bed mother had occupied during the night and I went off to the town of Bidwell and to school. During the long nights, while mother and I slept, father cooked meats that were to go into sandwiches for the lunch baskets of our boarders. Then an idea in regard to getting up in the world came into his head. The American spirit took hold of him. He also became ambitious.

In the long nights when there was little to do, father had time to think. That was his undoing. He decided that he had in the past been an unsuccessful man because he had not been cheerful enough and that in the future he would adopt a cheerful outlook on life. In the early morning he came upstairs and got into bed with mother. She woke and the two talked. From my bed in the corner I listened.

It was father's idea that both he and mother should try to entertain the people who came to eat at our restaurant. I cannot now remember his words, but he gave the impression of one about to become in some obscure way a kind of public entertainer. When people, ·particularly young people from the town of Bidwell, came into our place, as on very rare occasions they did, bright entertaining conversation was to be made. From father's words I gathered that something of the jolly innkeeper effect was to be sought. Mother must have been doubtful from the first, but she said nothing discouraging. It was father's notion that a passion for the company of himself and mother would spring up in the breasts of the younger people of the town of Bidwell. In the evening bright happy groups would come singing down Turner's Pike. They would troop shouting with joy and laughter into our place. There would be song and festivity. I do not mean to give the impression that father spoke so elaborately of the matter. He was, as I have said, an uncommunicative man. "They want some place to go. I tell you they want some place to go," he said over and over. That was as far as he got. My own imagination has filled in the blanks.

For two or three weeks this notion of father's invaded our house. We did not talk much, but in our daily lives tried earnestly to make smiles take the place of glum looks. Mother smiled at the boarders and I, catching the in-fection, smiled at our cat. Father became a little feverish in his anxiety to please. There was, no doubt, lurking somewhere in him, a touch of the spirit of the showman. He did not waste much of his ammunition on the railroad men he served at night, but seemed to be waiting for a young man or woman from Bidwell to come in to show what he could do. On the counter in the restaurant there was a wire basket kept always filled with eggs, and it must have been before his eyes when the idea of being entertaining was born in his brain. There was something pre-natal about the way eggs kept themselves connected with the development of his idea. At any rate, an egg ruined his new impulse in life. Late one night I was awakened by a roar of anger coming from father's throat. Both mother and I sat upright in our beds. With trembling hands she lighted a lamp that stood on a table by her head. Downstairs the front door of our restaurant went shut with a bang and in a few minutes father tramped up the stairs. He held an egg in his hand and his hand trembled as though he were having a chill. There was a half-insane light in his eyes. As he stood glaring at us I was sure he intended throwing the egg at either mother or me. Then he laid it gently on the table beside the lamp and dropped on his knees beside mother's bed. He began to cry like a boy, and I, carried away by his grief, cried with him. The two of us filled the little upstairs room with our wailing voices. It is ridiculous, but of the picture we made I can remember only the fact that mother's hand continually stroked the bald path that ran across the top of his head. I have forgotten what mother said to him and how she induced him to tell her of what had happened downstairs. His explanation also has gone out of my mind. I remember only my own grief and fright and the shiny path over father's head glowing in the lamplight as he knelt by the bed.

As to what happened downstairs. For some unexplainable reason I know the story as well as though I had been a witness to my father's discomfiture. One in time gets to know many unexplainable things. On that evening young Joe Kane, son of a merchant of Bidwell, came to Pickleville to meet his father, who was expected on the ten-o'clock evening train from the South. The train was three hours late and Joe came into our place to loaf about and to wait for its arrival. The local freight train came in and the freight crew were fed. Joe was left alone in the restaurant with father.

From the moment he came into our place the Bidwell young man must have been puzzled by my father's actions. It was his notion that father was angry at him for hanging around. He noticed that the restaurant-keeper was apparently disturbed by his presence and he thought of going out. However, it began to rain and he did not fancy the long walk to town and back. He bought a five-cent cigar and ordered a cup of coffee. He had a newspaper in his pocket and took it out and began to read. "I'm waiting for the evening train. It's late," he said apologetically.

For a long time father, whom Joe Kane had never seen before, remained silently gazing at his visitor. He was no doubt suffering from an attack of stage fright. As so often happens in life he had thought so much and so often of the situation that now confronted him that he was somewhat nervous in its presence.

For one thing, he did not know what to do with his hands. He thrust one of them nervously over the counter and shook hands with Joe Kane. "How-de-do," he said. Joe Kane put his newspaper down and stared at him. Father's eyes lighted on the basket of eggs that sat on the counter and he began to talk. "Well," he began hesitatingly, "well, you have heard of Christopher Columbus, eh?" He seemed to be angry. "That Christopher Columbus was a cheat," he declared emphatically. "He talked of making an egg stand on its end. He talked, he did, and then he went and broke the end of the egg."

My father seemed to his visitor to be beside himself at the duplicity of Christopher Columbus. He muttered and swore. He declared it was wrong to teach children that Christopher Columbus was a great man when, after all, he cheated at the critical moment. He had declared he would make an egg stand on end and then, when his bluff had been called, he had done a trick. Still grumbling at Columbus, father took an egg from the basket on the counter and began to walk up and down. He rolled the egg between the palms of his hands. He smiled genially. He began to mumble words regarding the effect to be produced on an egg by the electricity that comes out of the human body. He declared that, without breaking its shell and by virtue of rolling it back and forth in his hands, he could stand the egg on its end. He explained that the warmth of his hands and the gentle rolling movement he gave the egg created a new center of gravity, and Joe Kane was mildly interested. "I have handled thousands of eggs," father said. "No one knows more about eggs than I do."

He stood the egg on the counter and it fell on its side. He tried the trick again and again, each time rolling the egg between the palms of his hands and saying the words regarding the wonders of electricity and the laws of gravity. When after a half-hour's effort he did succeed in making the egg stand for a moment, he looked up to find that his visitor was no longer watching. By the time he had succeeded in calling Joe Kane's attention to the success of his effort, the egg had again rolled over and lay on its side.

Afire with the showman's passion and at the same time a good deal disconcerted by the failure of his first effort, father now took the bottles containing the poultry monstrosities down from their place on the shelf and began to show them to his visitor. "How would you like to have seven legs and two heads like this fellow?" he asked, exhibiting the most remarkable of his treasures. A cheerful smile played over his face. He reached over the counter and tried to slap Joe Kane on the shoulder as he had seen men do in Ben Head's saloon when he was a young farmhand and drove to town on Saturday evenings. His visitor was made a little ill by the sight of the body of the terribly deformed bird floating in the alcohol in the bottle and got up to go. Coming from behind the counter, father took hold of the young man's arm and led him back to his seat. He grew a little angry and for a moment had to turn his face away and force himself to smile. Then he put the bottles back on the shelf. In an ouburst of generosity he fairly compelled Joe Kane to have a fresh cup of coffee and another cigar at his expense. Then he took a pan and filling it with vinegar, taken from a jug that sat beneath the counter, he declared himself about to do a new trick. "I will heat this egg in this pan of vinegar," he said. "Then I will put it through the neck of a bottle without breaking the shell. When the egg is inside the bottle it will resume its normal shape and the shell will become hard again. Then I will give the bottle with the egg in it to you. You can take it about with you wherever you go. People will want to know how you got the egg in the bottle. Don't tell them. Keep them guessing. That is the way to have fun with this trick."

Father grinned and winked at his visitor. Joe Kane decided that the man who confronted him was mildly insane but harmless. He drank the cup of coffee that had been given him and began to read his paper again. When the egg had been heated in vinegar, father carried it on a spoon to the counter and going into a back room got an empty bottle. He was angry because his visitor did not watch him as he began to do his trick, but nevertheless went cheerfully to work. For a long time he struggled, trying to get the egg to go through the neck of the bottle. He put the pan of vinegar back on the stove, intending to reheat the egg, then picked it up and burned his fingers. After a second bath in the hot vinegar, the shell of the egg had been softened a little, but not enough for his purpose. He worked and worked and a spirit of desperate determination took possession of him. When he thought that at last the trick was about to be consummated, the delayed train came in at the station and Joe Kane started to go nonchalantly out at the door. Father made a last desperate effort to conquer the egg and make it do the thing that would establish his reputation as one who knew how to entertain guests who came into his restaurant. He worried the egg. He attempted to be somewhat rough with it. He swore and the sweat stood out on his forehead. The egg broke under his hand. When the contents spurted over his clothes, Joe Kane, who had stopped at the door, turned and laughed.

A roar of anger rose from my father's throat. He danced and shouted a string of inarticulate words. Grabbing another egg from the basket on the counter, he threw it, just missing the head of the young man as he dodged through the door and escaped.

Father came upstairs to mother and me with an egg in his hand. I do not know what he intended to do. I imagine he had some idea of destroying it, of destroying all eggs, and that he intended to let mother and me see him begin. When, however, he got into the presence of mother, something happened to him. He laid the egg gently on the table and dropped on his knees by the bed as I have already explained. He later decided to close the restaurant for the night and to come upstairs and get into bed. When he did so, he blew out the light and after much muttered conversation both he and mother went to sleep. I suppose I went to sleep also, but my sleep was troubled. I awoke at dawn and for a long time looked at the egg that lay on the table. I wondered why eggs had to be and why from the egg came the hen who again laid the egg. The question got into my blood. It has stayed there, I imagine, because I am the son of my father. At any rate, the problem remains unsolved in my mind. And that, I conclude, is but another evidence of the complete and final triumph of the egg—at least as far as my family is concerned.

## My Negro Problem—and Ours
### 1963

### Norman Podhoretz

*If we—and . . . I mean the relatively conscious whites and the rela-
tively conscious blacks, who must, like lovers, insist on, or create, the
consciousness of the others—do not falter in our duty now, we may be
able, handful that we are, to end the racial nightmare, and achieve our
country, and change the history of the world.*—James Baldwin

Two ideas puzzled me deeply as a child growing up in Brooklyn during
the 1930's in what today would be called an integrated neighborhood. One of
them was that all Jews were rich; the other was that all Negroes were
persecuted. These ideas had appeared in print; therefore they must be true. My
own experience and the evidence of my senses told me they were not true,
but that only confirmed what a day-dreaming boy in the provinces—for the
lower-class neighborhoods of New York belong as surely to the provinces as
any rural town in North Dakota—discovers very early: *his* experience is
unreal and the evidence of his senses is not to be trusted. Yet even a boy with
a head full of fantasies incongruously synthesized out of Hollywood movies
and English novels cannot altogether deny the reality of his own experience—
especially when there is so much deprivation in that experience. Nor can he
altogether gainsay the evidence of his own senses—especially such evidence
of the senses as comes from being repeatedly beaten up, robbed, and in
general hated, terrorized, and humiliated.

And so for a long time I was puzzled to think that Jews were supposed
to be rich when the only Jews I knew were poor, and that Negroes were supposed to be persecuted when it was the Negroes who were doing the only
persecuting I knew about—and doing it, moreover, to *me*. During the early
years of the war, when my older sister joined a left-wing youth organization, I
remember my astonishment at hearing her passionately denounce my father
for thinking that Jews were worse off than Negroes. To me, at the age of
twelve, it seemed very clear that Negroes were better off than Jews—indeed,
than *all* whites. A city boy's world is contained within three or four square

109

blocks, and in my world it was the whites, the Italians and Jews, who feared the Negroes, not the other way around. The Negroes were tougher than we were, more ruthless, and on the whole they were better athletes. What could it mean, then, to say that they were badly off and that we were more fortunate? Yet my sister's opinions, like print, were sacred, and when she told me about exploitation and economic forces I believed her. I believed her, but I was still afraid of Negroes. And I still hated them with all my heart.

It had not always been so—that much I can recall from early childhood. When did it start, this fear and this hatred? There was a kindergarten in the local public school, and given the character of the neighborhood, at least half of the children in my class must have been Negroes. Yet I have no memory of being aware of color differences at that age, and I know from observing my own children that they attribute no significance to such differences even when they begin noticing them. I think there was a day—first grade? second grade?— when my best friend Carl hit me on the way home from school and announced that he wouldn't play with me any more because I had killed Jesus. When I ran home to my mother crying for an explanation, she told me not to pay any attention to such foolishness, and then in Yiddish she cursed the *goyim* and the *schwartzes,* the *schwartzes* and the *goyim.* Carl, it turned out, was a *schwartz,* and so was added a third to the categories into which people were mysteriously divided.

Sometimes I wonder whether this is a true memory at all. It is blazingly vivid, but perhaps it never happened: can anyone really remember back to the age of six? There is no uncertainty in my mind, however, about the years that followed. Carl and I hardly ever spoke, though we met in school every day up through the eighth or ninth grade. There would be embarrassed moments of catching his eye or of his catching mine—for whatever it was that had attracted us to one another as very small children remained alive in spite of the fantastic barrier of hostility that had grown up between us, suddenly and out of nowhere. Nevertheless, friendship would have been impossible, and even if it had been possible, it would have been unthinkable. About that, there was nothing anyone could do by the time we were eight years old.

*Item:* The orphanage across the street is torn down, a city housing project begins to rise in its place, and on the marvelous vacant lot next to the old orphanage they are building a playground. Much excitement and anticipation as Opening Day draws near. Mayor LaGuardia himself comes to dedicate this great gesture of public benevolence. He speaks of neighborliness and borrowing cups of sugar, and of the playground he says that children of all races, colors, and creeds will learn to live together in harmony. A week later, some of us are swatting flies on the playground's inadequate little ball field. A gang of Negro kids, pretty much our own age, enter from the other side and order us out of the park. We refuse, proudly and indignantly, with superb masculine fervor. There is a fight, they win, and we retreat, half whimpering, half with bravado. My first nauseating experience of cowardice. And my first appalled realization that there are people in the world who do not seem to be afraid of anything, who act as though they have nothing to lose. Thereafter the playground becomes a battleground, sometimes quiet, sometimes the scene of athletic competition between Them and Us. But rocks are thrown as often as baseballs. Gradually we abandon the place and use the streets instead. The streets are safer, though we do not admit this to ourselves. We are not, after all, sissies—that most dreaded epithet of an American boyhood.

*Item:* I am standing alone in front of the building in which I live. It is late afternoon and getting dark. That day in school the teacher had asked a surly Negro boy named Quentin a question he was unable to answer. As usual I had waved my arm eagerly ("Be a good boy, get good marks, be smart, go to college, become a doctor") and, the right answer bursting from my lips, I was held up lovingly by the teacher as an example to the class. I had seen Quentin's face—a very dark, very cruel, very Oriental-looking face—harden, and there had been enough threat in his eyes to make me run all the way home for fear that he might catch me outside.

Now, standing idly in front of my own house, I see him approaching from the project accompanied by his little brother who is carrying a baseball bat and wearing a grin of malicious anticipation. As in a nightmare, I am trapped. The surroundings are secure and familiar, but terror is suddenly present and there is no one around to help. I am locked to the spot. I will not cry out or run away like a sissy, and I stand there, my heart wild, my throat clogged. He walks up, hurls the familiar epithet ("Hey, mo'f——r"), and to my surprise only pushes me. It is a violent push, but not a punch. A push is not as serious as a punch. Maybe I can still back out without entirely losing my dignity. Maybe I can still say, "Hey, c'mon Quentin, whaddya wanna do *that* for? I dint do nothin' to *you*," and walk away, not too rapidly. Instead, before I can stop myself, I push him back—a token gesture—and I say, "Cut that out, I don't wanna fight, I ain't got nothin' to fight about." As I turn to walk back into the building, the corner of my eye catches the motion of the bat his little brother has handed him. I try to duck, but the bat crashes colored lights into my head.

The next thing I know, my mother and sister are standing over me, both of them hysterical. My sister—she who was later to join the "progressive" youth organization—is shouting for the police and screaming imprecations at those dirty little black bastards. They take me upstairs, the doctor comes, the police come. I tell them that the boy who did it was a stranger, that he had been trying to get money from me. They do not believe me, but I am too scared to give them Quentin's name. When I return to school a few days later, Quentin avoids my eyes. He knows that I have not squealed, and he is ashamed. I try to feel proud, but in my heart I know that it was fear of what his friends might do to me that had kept me silent, and not the code of the street.

*Item:* There is an athletic meet in which the whole of our junior high school is participating. I am in one of the seventh-grade rapid-advance classes, and "segregation" has now set in with a vengeance. In the last three or four years of the elementary school from which we have just graduated, each grade had been divided into three classes, according to "intelligence." (In the earlier grades the divisions had either been arbitrary or else unrecognized by us as having anything to do with brains.) These divisions by IQ, or however it was arranged, had resulted in a preponderance of Jews in the "1" classes and a corresponding preponderance of Negroes in the "3's," with the Italians split unevenly along the spectrum. At least a few Negroes had always made the "1's," just as there had always been a few Jewish kids among the "3's," and more among the "2's" (where Italians dominated). But the junior high's rapid-advance class of which I am now a member is overwhelmingly Jewish and entirely white—except for a shy lonely Negro girl with light skin and reddish hair.

The athletic meet takes place in a city-owned stadium far from the school. It is an important event to which a whole day is given over. The winners are to get those precious little medallions stamped with the New York City emblem that can be screwed into a belt and that prove the wearer to be a distinguished personage. I am a fast runner, and so I am assigned the position of anchor man on my class's team in the relay race. There are three other seventh-grade teams in the race, two of them all Negro, as ours is all white. One of the all-Negro teams is very tall—their anchor man waiting silently next to me on the line looks years older than I am, and I do not recognize him. He is the first to get the baton and crosses the finishing line in a walk. Our team comes in second, but a few minutes later we are declared the winners, for it has been discovered that the anchor man on the first-place team is not a member of the class. We are awarded the medallions, and the following day our home-room teacher makes a speech about how proud she is of us for being superior athletes as well as superior students. We want to believe that we deserve the praise, but we know that we could not have won even if the other class had not cheated.

That afternoon, walking home, I am waylaid and surrounded by five Negroes, among whom is the anchor man of the disqualified team. "Gimme my medal, mo'f——r," he grunts. I do not have it with me and I tell him so. "Anyway, it ain't yours," I say foolishly. He calls me a liar on both counts and pushes me up against the wall on which we sometimes play handball. "Gimme my mo'f——n' medal," he says again. I repeat that I have left it home. "Le's search the li'l mo'f——r," one of them suggests, "he prolly got it *hid* in his mo'f——n' *pants.*" My panic is now unmanageable. (How many times had I been surrounded like this and asked in soft tones, "Len' me a nickel, boy." How many times had I been called a liar for pleading poverty and pushed around, or searched, or beaten up, unless there happened to be someone in the marauding gang like Carl who liked me across that enormous divide of hatred and who would therefore say, "Aaah, c'mon, le's git someone else, *this* boy ain't got no money on 'im.") I scream at them through tears of rage and self-contempt, "Keep your f——n' filthy lousy black hands offa me! I swear I'll get the cops." This is all they need to hear, and the five of them set upon me. They bang me around, mostly in the stomach and on the arms and shoulders, and when several adults loitering near the candy store down the block notice what is going on and begin to shout, they run off and away.

I do not tell my parents about the incident. My team-mates, who have also been waylaid, each by a gang led by his opposite number from the disqualified team, have had their medallions taken from them, and they never squeal either. For days, I walk home in terror, expecting to be caught again, but nothing happens. The medallion is put away into a drawer, never to be worn by anyone.

Obviously experiences like these have always been a common feature of childhood life in working-class and immigrant neighborhoods, and Negroes do not necessarily figure in them. Wherever, and in whatever combination, they have lived together in the cities, kids of different groups have been at war, beating up and being beaten up: micks against kikes against wops against spicks against polacks. And even relatively homogeneous areas have not been spared the warring of the young: one block against another, one gang (called in my day, in a pathetic effort at gentility, an "S.A.C.," or social-athletic club) against another. But the Negro-white conflict had—and no doubt still has— a special intensity and was conducted with a ferocity unmatched by intramural white battling.

In my own neighborhood, a good deal of animosity existed between the Italian kids (most of whose parents were immigrants from Sicily) and the Jewish kids (who came largely from East European immigrant families). Yet everyone had friends, sometimes close friends, in the other "camp," and we often visited one another's strange-smelling houses, if not for meals, then for glasses of milk, and occasionally for some special event like a wedding or a wake. If it happened that we divided into warring factions and did battle, it would invariably be half-hearted and soon patched up. Our parents, to be sure, had nothing to do with one another and were mutually suspicious and hostile. But we, the kids, who all spoke Yiddish or Italian at home, were Americans, or New Yorkers, or Brooklyn boys: we shared a culture, the culture of the street, and at least for a while this culture proved to be more powerful than the opposing cultures of the home.

Why, *why* should it have been so different as between the Negroes and us? How was it borne in upon us so early, white and black alike, that we were enemies beyond any possibility of reconciliation? Why did we hate one another so?

I suppose if I tried, I could answer those questions more or less adequately from the perspective of what I have since learned. I could draw upon James Baldwin—what better witness is there?—to describe the sense of entrapment that poisons the soul of the Negro with hatred for the white man whom he knows to be his jailer. On the other side, if I wanted to understand how the white man comes to hate the Negro, I could call upon the psychologists who have spoken of the guilt that white Americans feel toward Negroes and that turns into hatred for lack of acknowledging itself as guilt. These are plausible answers and certainly there is truth in them. Yet when I think back upon my own experience of the Negro and his of me, I find myself troubled and puzzled, much as I was as a child when I heard that all Jews were rich and all Negroes persecuted. How could the Negroes in my neighborhood have regarded the whites across the street and around the corner as jailers? On the whole, the whites were not so poor as the Negroes, but they were quite poor enough, and the years were years of Depression. As for white hatred of the Negro, how could guilt have had anything to do with it? What share had these Italian and Jewish immigrants in the enslavement of the Negro? What share had they—downtrodden people themselves breaking their own necks to eke out a living—in the exploitation of the Negro?

No, I cannot believe that we hated each other back there in Brooklyn because they thought of us as jailers and we felt guilty toward them. But does it matter, given the fact that we all went through an unrepresentative confrontation? I think it matters profoundly, for if we managed the job of hating each other so well without benefit of the aids to hatred that are supposedly at the root of this madness everywhere else, it must mean that the madness is not yet properly understood. I am far from pretending that I understand it, but I would insist that no view of the problem will begin to approach the truth unless it can account for a case like the one I have been trying to describe. Are the elements of any such view available to us?

At least two, I would say, are. One of them is a point we frequently come upon in the work of James Baldwin, and the other is a related point always stressed by psychologists who have studied the mechanisms of prejudice. Baldwin tells us that one of the reasons Negroes hate the white man is that the white man refuses to *look* at him: the Negro knows that in white eyes all Negroes are alike; they are faceless and therefore not altogether human. The psychologists, in their turn, tell us that the white man hates the Negro because he tends to project those wild impulses that he fears in himself onto an alien group which he then punishes with his contempt. What Baldwin does *not* tell us, however, is that the principle of facelessness is a two-way street and can operate in both directions with no difficulty at all. Thus, in my neighborhood in Brooklyn, *I* was as faceless to the Negroes as they were to me, and if they hated me because I never looked at them, I must also have hated them for never looking at *me*. To the Negroes, my white skin was enough to define me as the enemy, and in a war it is only the uniform that counts and not the person.

So with the mechanism of protection that the psychologists talk about: it too works in both directions at once. There is no question that the psychologists are right about what the Negro represents symbolically to the white man. For me as a child the life lived on the other side of the playground and down the block on Ralph Avenue seemed the very embodiment of the values of the street—free, independent, reckless, brave, masculine, erotic. I put the word "erotic" last, though it is usually stressed above all others, because in fact it came last, in consciousness as in importance. What mainly counted for me about Negro kids of my own age was that they were "bad boys." There were plenty of bad boys among the whites—this was, after all, a neighborhood with a long tradition of crime as a career open to aspiring talents—but the Negroes were *really* bad, bad in a way that beckoned to one, and made one feel inadequate. *We* all went home every day for a lunch of spinach-and-potatoes; *they* roamed around during lunch hour, munching on candy bars. In winter *we* had to wear itchy woolen hats and mittens and cumbersome galoshes; *they* were bare-headed and loose as they pleased. *We* rarely played hookey, or got into serious trouble in school, for all our street-corner bravado; *they* were defiant, forever staying out (to do what delicious things?), forever making disturbances in class and in the halls, forever being sent to the principal and returning uncowed. But most important of all, they were *tough;* beautifully, enviably tough, not giving a damn for anyone or anything. To hell with the teacher, the truant officer, the cop; to hell with the whole of the adult world that held *us* in its grip and that we never had the courage to rebel against except sporadically and in petty ways.

This is what I saw and envied and feared in the Negro: this is what finally made him faceless to me, though some of it, of course, was actually there. (The psychologists also tell us that the alien group which becomes the object of a projection will tend to respond by trying to live up to what is expected of them.) But what, on his side, did the Negro see in me that made me faceless to *him?* Did he envy me my lunches of spinach-and-potatoes and my itchy woolen caps and my prudent behavior in the face of authority, as I envied him his noon-time candy bars and his bare head in winter and his magnificent rebelliousness? Did those lunches and caps spell for him the prospect of power and riches in the future? Did they mean that there were possibilities open to me that were denied to him? Very likely they did. But if so, one also supposes that he feared the impulses within himself toward sub-mission to authority no less powerfully than I feared the impulses in myself toward defiance. If I represented the jailer to him, it was not because I was oppressing him or keeping him down: it was because I symbolized for him the dangerous and probably pointless temptation toward greater repression, just as he symbolized for me the equally perilous tug toward greater freedom. I personally was to be rewarded for this repression with a new and better life in the future, but how many of my friends paid an even higher price and were given only gall in return.

We have it on the authority of James Baldwin that all Negroes hate whites. I am trying to suggest that on their side all whites—all American whites, that is—are sick in their feelings about Negroes. There are Negroes, no doubt, who would say that Baldwin is wrong, but I suspect them of being less honest than he is, just as I suspect whites of self-deception who tell me they have no special feeling toward Negroes. Special feelings about color are a contagion to which white Americans seem susceptible even when there is nothing in their background to account for the susceptibility. Thus everywhere we look today in the North, we find the curious phenomenon of white middle-class liberals with no previous personal experience of Negroes—people to whom Negroes have always been faceless in virtue rather than faceless in vice—discovering that their abstract commitment to the cause of Negro rights will not stand the test of a direct confrontation. We find such people fleeing in droves to the suburbs as the Negro population in the inner city grows; and when they stay in the city we find them sending their children to private school rather than to the "integrated" public school in the neighborhood. We find them resisting the demand that gerrymandered school districts be rezoned for the purpose of overcoming de facto segregation; we find them judiciously considering whether the Negroes (for their own good, of course) are not perhaps pushing too hard; we find them clucking their tongues over Negro militancy; we find them speculating on the question of whether there may not, after all, be something in the theory that the races are biologically different; we find them saying that it will take a very long time for Negroes to achieve full equality, no matter what anyone does; we find them deploring the rise of black nationalism and expressing the solemn hope that the leaders of the Negro community will discover ways of containing the impatience and incipient violence within the Negro ghettos.

But that is by no means the whole story; there is also the phenomenon of what Kenneth Rexroth once called "crow-jimism." There are the broken-down white boys like Vivaldo Moore in Baldwin's *Another Country* who go to Harlem in search of sex or simply to brush up against something that looks like primitive vitality, and who are so often punished by the Negroes they meet for crimes that they would have been the last ever to commit and of which they themselves have been as sorry victims as any of the Negroes who take it out on them. There are the writers and intellectuals and artists who romanticize Negroes and pander to them, assuming a guilt that is not properly theirs. And there are all the white liberals who permit Negroes to blackmail them into adopting a double standard of moral judgment, and who lend themselves—again assuming the responsibility for crimes they never committed—to cunning and contemptuous exploitation by Negroes they employ or try to befriend.

And what about me? What kind of feelings do I have about Negroes today? What happened to me, from Brooklyn, who grew up fearing and envying and hating Negroes? Now that Brooklyn is behind me, do I fear them and envy them and hate them still? The answer is yes, but not in the same proportions and certainly not in the same way. I now live in the upper west side of Manhattan, where there are many Negroes and many Puerto Ricans, and there are nights when I experience the old apprehensiveness again, and there are streets that I avoid when I am walking in the dark, as there were streets that I avoided when I was a child. I find that I am not afraid of Puerto Ricans, but I cannot restrain my nervousness whenever I pass a group of Negroes standing in front of a bar or sauntering down the street. I know now, as I did not know when I was a child, that power is on my side, that the police are working for me and not for them. And knowing this I feel ashamed and guilty, like the good liberal I have grown up to be. Yet the twinges of fear and the resentment they bring and the self-contempt they arouse are not to be gainsaid.

But envy? Why envy? And hatred? Why hatred? Here again the intensities have lessened and everything has been complicated and qualified by the guilts and the resulting over-compensations that are the heritage of the enlightened middle-class world of which I am now a member. Yet just as in childhood I envied Negroes for what seemed to me their superior masculinity, so I envy them today for what seems to me their superior physical grace and beauty. I have come to value physical grace very highly, and I am now capable of aching with all my being when I watch a Negro couple on the dance floor, or a Negro playing baseball or basketball. They are on the kind of terms with their own bodies that I should like to be on with mine, and for that precious quality they seem blessed to me.

The hatred I still feel for Negroes is the hardest of all the old feelings to face or admit, and it is the most hidden and the most overlarded by the conscious attitudes into which I have succeeded in willing myself. It no longer has, as for me it once did, any cause or justification (except, perhaps, that I am constantly being denied my right to an honest expression of the things I earned the right as a child to feel). How, then, do I know that this hatred has never entirely disappeared? I know it from the insane rage that can stir in me at the thought of Negro anti-Semitism; I know it from the disgusting prurience that can stir in me at the sight of a mixed couple; and I know it from the violence that can stir in me whenever I encounter that special brand of paranoid touchiness to which many Negroes are prone.

This, then, is where I am; it is not exactly where I think all other white liberals are, but it cannot be so very far away either. And it is because I am convinced that we white Americans are—for whatever reason, it no longer matters—so twisted and sick in our feelings about Negroes that I despair of the present push toward integration. If the pace of progress were not a factor here, there would perhaps be no cause for despair: time and the law and even the international political situation are on the side of the Negroes, and ultimately, therefore, victory—of a sort, anyway—must come. But from everything we have learned from observers who ought to know, pace has become as important to the Negroes as substance. They want equality and they want it *now,* and the white world is yielding to their demand only as much and as fast as it is absolutely being compelled to do. The Negroes know this in the most concrete terms imaginable, and it is thus becoming increasingly difficult to buy them off with rhetoric and promises and pious assurances of support. And so within the Negro community we find more and more people declaring that they want *out:* people who say that integration will never come, or that it will take a hundred or a thousand years to come, or that it will come at too high a price in suffering and struggle for the pallid and sodden life of the American middle class that at the very best it may bring.

The most numerous, influential, and dangerous movement that has grown out of Negro despair with the goal of integration is, of course, the Black Muslims. This movement, whatever else we may say about it, must be credited with one enduring achievement: it inspired James Baldwin to write an essay * which deserves to be placed among the classics of our language. Everything Baldwin has ever been trying to tell us is distilled here into a statement of overwhelming persuasiveness and prophetic magnificence. Baldwin's message is and always has been simple. It is this: "Color is not a human or personal reality; it is a political reality." And Baldwin's demand is correspondingly simple: color must be forgotten, lest we all be smited with a vengeance "that does not really depend on, and cannot really be executed by, any person or organization, and that cannot be prevented by any police force or army: historical vengeance, a cosmic vengeance based on the law that we recognize when we say, 'Whatever goes up must come down.' " The Black Muslims Baldwin portrays as a sign and a warning to the intransigent white world. They come to proclaim how deep is the Negro's disaffection with the white world and all its works, and Baldwin implies that no American Negro can fail to respond somewhere in his being to their message: that the white man is the devil, that Allah has doomed him to destruction, and that the black man is about to inherit the earth. Baldwin of course knows that this nightmare inversion of the racism from which the black man has suffered can neither win nor even point to the neighborhood in which victory might be located. For in his view the neighborhood of victory lies in exactly the opposite direction: the transcendence of color through love.

Yet the tragic fact is that love is not the answer to hate—not in the world of politics, at any rate. Color is indeed a political rather than a human or a personal reality and if politics (which is to say power) has made it into a human and a personal reality, then only politics (which is to say power) can unmake it once again. But the way of politics is slow and bitter, and as impatience on the one side is matched by a setting of the jaw on the other, we move closer and closer to an explosion and blood may yet run in the streets.

Will this madness in which we are all caught never find a resting-place? Is there never to be an end to it? In thinking about the Jews I have often wondered whether their survival as a distinct group was worth one hair on the head of a single infant. Did the Jews have to survive so that six million innocent people should one day be burned in the ovens of Auschwitz? It is a terrible question and no one, not God himself, could ever answer it to my satisfaction. And when I think about the Negroes in America and about the image of integration as a state in which the Negroes would take their rightful place as another of the protected minorities in a pluralistic society, I wonder whether they really believe in their hearts that such a state can actually be attained, and if so *why* they should wish to survive as a distinct group. I think I know why

---

* Originally published in the *New Yorker* under the title "Letter from a Region in My Mind," it has been reprinted (along with a new introduction) by Dial Press under the title *The Fire Next Time*.

the Jews once wished to survive (though I am less certain as to why we still do): they not only believed that God had given them no choice, but they were tied to a memory of past glory and a dream of imminent redemption. What does the American Negro have that might correspond to this? His past is a stigma, his color is a stigma, and his vision of the future is the hope of erasing the stigma by making color irrelevant, by making it disappear as a fact of consciousness.

I share this hope, but I cannot see how it will ever be realized unless color does *in fact* disappear: and that means not integration, it means assimilation, it means—let the brutal word come out—miscegenation. The Black Muslims, like their racist counterparts in the white world, accuse the "so-called Negro leaders" of secretly pursuing miscegenation as a goal. The racists are wrong, but I wish they were right, for I believe that the wholesale merging of the two races is the most desirable alternative for everyone concerned. I am not claiming that this alternative can be pursued programmatically or that it is immediately feasible as a solution; obviously there are even greater barriers to its achievement than to the achievement of integration. What I am saying, however, is that in my opinion the Negro problem can be solved in this country in no other way.

I have told the story of my own twisted feelings about Negroes here, and of how they conflict with the moral convictions I have since developed, in order to assert that such feelings must be acknowledged as honestly as possible so that they can be controlled and ultimately disregarded in favor of the convictions. It is *wrong* for a man to suffer because of the color of his skin. Beside that clichéd proposition of liberal thought, what argument can stand and be respected? If the arguments are the arguments of feeling, they must be made to yield; and one's own soul is not the worst place to begin working a huge social transformation. Not so long ago, it used to be asked of white liberals, "Would you like your sister to marry one?" When I was a boy and my sister was still unmarried, I would certainly have said no to that question. But now I am a man, my sister is already married, and I have daughters. If I were to be asked today whether I would like a daughter of mine "to marry one," I would have to answer: "No, I wouldn't *like* it at all. I would rail and rave and rant and tear my hair. And then I hope I would have the courage to curse myself for raving and ranting, and to give her my blessing. How dare I withhold it at the behest of the child I once was and against the man I now have a duty to be?"

# Mascot
## 1964

### Malcolm X

On June twenty-seventh of that year, nineteen thirty-seven, Joe Louis knocked out James J. Braddock to become the heavyweight champion of the world. And all the Negroes in Lansing, like Negroes everywhere, went wildly happy with the greatest celebration of race pride our generation had ever known. Every Negro boy old enough to walk wanted to be the next Brown Bomber. My brother Philbert, who had already become a pretty good boxer in school, was no exception. (I was trying to play basketball. I was gangling and tall, but I wasn't very good at it—too awkward.) In the fall of that year, Philbert entered the amateur bouts that were held in Lansing's Prudden Auditorium.

He did well, surviving the increasingly tough eliminations. I would go down to the gym and watch him train. It was very exciting. Perhaps without realizing it I became secretly envious; for one thing, I know I could not help seeing some of my younger brother Reginald's lifelong admiration for me getting siphoned off to Philbert.

People praised Philbert as a natural boxer. I figured that since we belonged to the same family, maybe I would become one, too. So I put myself in the ring. I think I was thirteen when I signed up for my first bout, but my height and raw-boned frame let me get away with claiming that I was sixteen, the minimum age—and my weight of about 128 pounds got me classified as a bantamweight.

They matched me with a white boy, a novice like myself, named Bill Peterson. I'll never forget him. When our turn in the next amateur bouts came up, all of my brothers and sisters were there watching, along with just about everyone else I knew in town. They were there not so much because of me but because of Philbert, who had begun to build up a pretty good following, and they wanted to see how his brother would do.

I walked down the aisle between the people thronging the rows of seats, and climbed in the ring. Bill Peterson and I were introduced, and then the

120

referee called us together and mumbled all of that stuff about fighting fair and breaking clean. Then the bell rang and we came out of our corners. I knew I was scared, but I didn't know, as Bill Peterson told me later on, that he was scared of me, too. He was so scared I was going to hurt him that he knocked me down fifty times if he did once.

He did such a job on my reputation in the Negro neighborhood that I practically went into hiding. A Negro just can't be whipped by somebody white and return with his head up to the neighborhood, especially in those days, when sports and, to a lesser extent show business, were the only fields open to Negroes, and when the ring was the only place a Negro could whip a white man and not be lynched. When I did show my face again, the Negroes I knew rode me so badly I knew I had to do something.

But the worst of my humiliations was my younger brother Reginald's attitude: he simply never mentioned the fight. It was the way he looked at me —and avoided looking at me. So I went back to the gym, and I trained— hard. I beat bags and skipped rope and grunted and sweated all over the place. And finally I signed up to fight Bill Peterson again. This time, the bouts were held in his hometown of Alma, Michigan.

The only thing better about the rematch was that hardly anyone I knew was there to see it; I was particularly grateful for Reginald's absence. The moment the bell rang, I saw a fist, then the canvas coming up, and ten seconds later the referee was saying *"Ten!"* over me. It was probably the shortest "fight" in history. I lay there listening to the full count, but I couldn't move. To tell the truth, I'm not sure I wanted to move.

That white boy was the beginning and the end of my fight career. A lot of times in these later years since I became a Muslim, I've thought back to that fight and reflected that it was Allah's work to stop me: I might have wound up punchy.

Not long after this, I came into a classroom with my hat on. I did it deliberately. The teacher, who was white, ordered me to keep the hat on, and to walk around and around the room until he told me to stop. "That way," he said, "everyone can see you. Meanwhile, we'll go on with class for those who are here to learn something."

I was still walking around when he got up from his desk and turned to the blackboard to write something on it. Everyone in the classroom was looking when, at this moment, I passed behind his desk, snatched up a thumbtack and deposited it in his chair. When he turned to sit back down, I was far from the scene of the crime, circling around the rear of the room. Then he hit the tack, and I heard him holler and caught a glimpse of him spraddling up as I disappeared through the door.

With my deportment record, I wasn't really shocked when the decision came that I had been expelled.

I guess I must have had some vague idea that if I didn't have to go to school, I'd be allowed to stay on with the Gohannas' and wander around town, or maybe get a job if I wanted one for pocket money. But I got rocked on my heels when a state man whom I hadn't seen before came and got me at the Gohannas' and took me down to court.

They told me I was going to go to a reform school. I was still thirteen years old.

But first I was going to the detention home. It was in Mason, Michigan, about twelve miles from Lansing. The detention home was where all the "bad" boys and girls from Ingham County were held, on their way to reform school—waiting for their hearings.

The white state man was a Mr. Maynard Allen. He was nicer to me than most of the state Welfare people had been. He even had consoling words for the Gohannas' and Mrs. Adcock and Big Boy; all of them were crying. But I wasn't. With the few clothes I owned stuffed into a box, we rode in his car to Mason. He talked as he drove along, saying that my school marks showed that if I would just straighten up, I could make something of myself. He said that reform school had the wrong reputation; he talked about what the word "reform" meant—to change and become better. He said the school was really a place where boys like me could have time to see their mistakes and start a new life and become somebody everyone would be proud of. And he told me that the lady in charge of the detention home, a Mrs. Swerlin, and her husband were very good people.

They were good people. Mrs. Swerlin was bigger than her husband, I remember, a big, buxom, robust, laughing woman, and Mr. Swerlin was thin, with black hair, and a black mustache and a red face, quiet and polite, even to me.

They liked me right away, too. Mrs. Swerlin showed me to my room, my own room—the first in my life. It was in one of those huge dormitory-like buildings where kids in detention were kept in those days—and still are in most places. I discovered next, with surprise, that I was allowed to eat with the Swerlins. It was the first time I'd eaten with white people—at least with grown white people—since the Seventh Day Adventist country meetings. It wasn't my own exclusive privilege, of course. Except for the very troublesome boys and girls at the detention home, who were kept locked up—those who had run away and been caught and brought back, or something like that—all of us ate with the Swerlins sitting at the head of the long tables.

They had a white cook-helper, I recall—Lucille Lathrop. (It amazes me how these names come back, from a time I haven't thought about for more than twenty years.) Lucille treated me well, too. Her husband's name was Duane Lathrop. He worked somewhere else, but he stayed there at the detention home on the weekends with Lucille.

I noticed again how white people smelled different from us, and how their food tasted different, not seasoned like Negro cooking. I began to sweep and mop and dust around in the Swerlins' house, as I had done with Big Boy at the Gohannas'.

They all liked my attitude, and it was out of their liking for me that I soon became accepted by them—as a mascot, I know now. They would talk about anything and everything with me standing right there hearing them, the same way people would talk freely in front of a pet canary. They would even talk about me, or about "niggers," as though I wasn't there, as if I wouldn't understand what the word meant. A hundred times a day, they used the word "nigger." I suppose that in their own minds, they meant no harm; in fact they probably meant well. It was the same with the cook, Lucille, and her husband, Duane. I remember one day when Mr. Swerlin, as nice as he was, came in from Lansing, where he had been through the Negro section, and said to Mrs. Swerlin right in front of me, "I just can't see how those niggers can be so happy and be so poor." He talked about how they lived in shacks, but had those big, shining cars out front.

And Mrs. Swerlin said, me standing right there, "Niggers are just that way. . . ." That scene always stayed with me.

It was the same with the other white people, most of them local politicians, when they would come visiting the Swerlins. One of their favorite parlor topics was "niggers." One of them was the judge who was in charge of me in Lansing. He was a close friend of the Swerlins. He would ask about me when he came, and they would call me in, and he would look me up and down, his expression approving, like he was examining a fine colt, or a pedigreed pup. I knew they must have told him how I acted and how I worked.

What I am trying to say is that it just never dawned upon them that I could understand, that I wasn't a pet, but a human being. They didn't give me credit for having the same sensitivity, intellect, and understanding that they would have been ready and willing to recognize in a white boy in my position. But it has historically been the case with white people, in their regard for black people, that even though we might be *with* them, we weren't considered *of* them. Even though they appeared to have opened the door, it was still closed. Thus they never did really see *me*.

This is the sort of kindly condescension which I try to clarify today, to these integration-hungry Negroes, about their "liberal" white friends, these so-called "good white people"—most of them anyway. I don't care how nice one is to you; the thing you must always remember is that almost never does he really see you as he sees himself, as he sees his own kind. He may stand with you through thin, but not thick; when the chips are down, you'll find that as fixed in him as his bone structure is his sometimes subconscious conviction that he's better than anybody black.

But I was no more than vaguely aware of anything like that in my detention-home years. I did my little chores around the house, and everything was fine. And each week-end, they didn't mind my catching a ride over to Lansing for the afternoon or evening. If I wasn't old enough, I sure was big enough by then, and nobody ever questioned my hanging out, even at night, in the streets of the Negro section.

I was growing up to be even bigger than Wilfred and Philbert, who had begun to meet girls at the school dances, and other places, and introduced me to a few. But the ones who seemed to like me, I didn't go for—and vice versa. I couldn't dance a lick, anyway, and I couldn't see squandering my few dimes on girls. So mostly I pleasured myself these Saturday nights by gawking around the Negro bars and restaurants. The jukeboxes were wailing Erskine Hawkins' "Tuxedo Junction," Slim and Slam's "Flatfoot Floogie," things like that. Sometimes, big bands from New York, out touring the one-night stands in the sticks, would play for big dances in Lansing. Everybody with legs would come out to see any performer who bore the magic name "New York." Which is how I first heard Lucky Thompson and Milt Jackson, both of whom I later got to know well in Harlem.

Many youngsters from the detention home, when their dates came up, went off to the reform school. But when mine came up—two or three times— it was always ignored. I saw new youngsters arrive and leave. I was glad and grateful. I knew it was Mrs. Swerlin's doing. I didn't want to leave.

She finally told me one day that I was going to be entered in Mason Junior High School. It was the only school in town. No ward of the detention home had ever gone to school there, at least while still a ward. So I entered their seventh grade. The only other Negroes there were some of the Lyons children, younger than I was, in the lower grades. The Lyons and I, as it happened, were the town's only Negroes. They were, as Negroes, very much respected. Mr. Lyons was a smart, hardworking man, and Mrs. Lyons was a very good woman. She and my mother, I had heard my mother say, were two of the four West Indians in that whole section of Michigan.

Some of the white kids at school, I found, were even friendlier than some of those in Lansing had been. Though some, including the teachers, called me "nigger," it was easy to see that they didn't mean any more harm by it than the Swerlins. As the "nigger" of my class, I was in fact extremely popular—I suppose partly because I was kind of a novelty. I was in demand, I had top priority. But I also benefited from the special prestige of having the seal of approval from that Very Important Woman about the town of Mason, Mrs. Swerlin. Nobody in Mason would have dreamed of getting on the wrong side of her. It became hard for me to get through a school day without someone after me to join this or head up that—the debating society, the Junior High basketball team, or some other extracurricular activity. I never turned them down.

And I hadn't been in the school long when Mrs. Swerlin, knowing I could use spending money of my own, got me a job after school washing the dishes in a local restaurant. My boss there was the father of a white classmate whom I spent a lot of time with. His family lived over the restaurant. It was fine working there. Every Friday night when I got paid, I'd feel at least ten feet tall. I forget how much I made, but it seemed like a lot. It was the first time I'd ever had any money to speak of, all my own, in my whole life. As soon as I could afford it, I bought a green suit and some shoes, and at school I'd buy treats for the others in my class—at least as much as any of them did for me.

English and history were the subjects I liked most. My English teacher, I recall—a Mr. Ostrowski—was always giving advice about how to become something in life. The one thing I didn't like about history class was that the teacher, Mr. Williams, was a great one for "nigger" jokes. One day during my first week at school, I walked into the room and he started singing to the class, as a joke, " 'Way down yonder in the cotton field, some folks say that a nigger won't steal." Very funny. I liked history, but I never thereafter had much liking for Mr. Williams. Later, I remember, we came to the textbook section on Negro history. It was exactly one paragraph long. Mr. Williams laughed through it practically in a single breath, reading aloud how the Negroes had been slaves and then were freed, and how they were usually lazy and dumb and shiftless. He added, I remember, an anthropological footnote on his own, telling us between laughs how Negroes' feet were "so big that when they walk, they don't leave tracks, they leave a hole in the ground."

I'm sorry to say that the subject I most disliked was mathematics. I have thought about it. I think the reason was that mathematics leaves no room for argument. If you made a mistake, that was all there was to it.

Basketball was a big thing in my life, though. I was on the team; we traveled to neighboring towns such as Howell and Charlotte, and wherever I showed my face, the audiences in the gymnasiums "niggered" and "cooned" me to death. Or called me "Rastus." It didn't bother my teammates or my coach at all, and to tell the truth, it bothered me only vaguely. Mine was the same psychology that makes Negroes even today, though it bothers them down inside, keep letting the white man tell them how much "progress" they are making. They've heard it so much they've almost gotten brainwashed into believing it—or at least accepting it.

After the basketball games, there would usually be a school dance. Whenever our team walked into another school's gym for the dance, with me among them, I could feel the freeze. It would start to ease as they saw that I didn't try to mix, but stuck close to someone on our team, or kept to myself. I think I developed ways to do it without making it obvious. Even at our own school, I could sense it almost as a physical barrier, that despite all the beaming and smiling, the mascot wasn't supposed to dance with any of the white girls.

It was some kind of psychic message—not just from them, but also from within myself. I am proud to be able to say that much for myself, at least. I would just stand around and smile and talk and drink punch and eat sandwiches, and then I would make some excuse and get away early.

They were typical small-town school dances. Sometimes a little white band from Lansing would be brought in to play. But most often, the music was a phonograph set up on a table, with the volume turned up high, and the records scratchy, blaring things like Glenn Miller's "Moonlight Serenade"—his band was riding high then—or the Ink Spots, who were also very popular, singing "If I Didn't Care."

I used to spend a lot of time thinking about a peculiar thing. Many of these Mason white boys, like the ones at the Lansing school—especially if they knew me well, and if we hung out a lot together—would get me off in a corner somewhere and push me to proposition certain white girls, sometimes their own sisters. They would tell me that they'd already had the girls themselves—including their sisters—or that they were trying to and couldn't. Later on, I came to understand what was going on: If they could get the girls into the position of having broken the terrible taboo by slipping off with me somewhere, they would have that hammer over the girls' heads, to make them give in to them.

It seemed that the white boys felt that I, being a Negro, just naturally knew more about "romance," or sex, than they did—that I instinctively knew more about what to do and say with their own girls. I never did tell anybody that I really went for some of the white girls, and some of them went for me, too. They let me know in many ways. But anytime we found ourselves in any close conversations or potentially intimate situations, always there would come up between us some kind of a wall. The girls I really wanted to have were a couple of Negro girls whom Wilfred or Philbert had introduced me to in Lansing. But with these girls, somehow, I lacked the nerve.

From what I heard and saw on the Saturday nights I spent hanging around in the Negro district I knew that race-mixing went on in Lansing. But strangely enough, this didn't have any kind of effect on me. Every Negro in Lansing, I guess, knew how white men would drive along certain streets in the black neighborhoods and pick up Negro streetwalkers who patrolled the area. And, on the other hand, there was a bridge that separated the Negro and Polish neighborhoods, where white women would drive or walk across and pick up Negro men, who would hang around in certain places close to the bridge, waiting for them. Lansing's white women, even in those days, were famous for chasing Negro men. I didn't yet appreciate how most whites accord to the Negro this reputation for prodigious sexual prowess. There in Lansing, I never heard of any trouble about this mixing, from either side. I imagine that everyone simply took it for granted, as I did.

Anyway, from my experience as a little boy at the Lansing school, I had become fairly adept at avoiding the white-girl issue—at least for a couple of years yet.

Then, in the second semester of the seventh grade, I was elected class president. It surprised me even more than other people. But I can see now why the class might have done it. My grades were among the highest in the school. I was unique in my class, like a pink poodle. And I was proud; I'm not going to say I wasn't. In fact, by then, I didn't really have much feeling about being a Negro, because I was trying so hard, in every way I could, to be white. Which is why I am spending much of my life today telling the American black man that he's wasting his time straining to "integrate." I know from personal experience. I tried hard enough.

"Malcolm, we're just so *proud* of you!" Mrs. Swerlin exclaimed when she heard about my election. It was all over the restaurant where I worked. Even the state man, Maynard Allen, who still dropped by to see me once in a while, had a word of praise. He said he never saw anybody prove better exactly what "reform" meant. I really liked him—except for one thing: he now and then would drop something that hinted my mother had let us down somehow.

Fairly often, I would go and visit the Lyons, and they acted as happy as though I was one of their children. And it was the same warm feeling when I went into Lansing to visit my brothers and sisters, and the Gohannas'.

I remember one thing that marred this time for me: the movie "Gone with the Wind." When it played in Mason, I was the only Negro in the theater, and when Butterfly McQueen went into her act, I felt like crawling under the rug.

Every Saturday, just about, I would go into Lansing. I was going on fourteen, now. Wilfred and Hilda still lived out by themselves at the old family home. Hilda kept the house very clean. It was easier than my mother's plight, with eight of us always under foot or running around. Wilfred worked wherever he could, and he still read every book he could get his hands on. Philbert was getting a reputation as one of the better amateur fighters in this part of the state; everyone really expected that he was going to become a professional.

Reginald and I, after my fighting fiasco, had finally gotten back on good terms. It made me feel great to visit him and Wesley over at Mrs. Williams'. I'd offhandedly give them each a couple of dollars to just stick in their pockets, to have something to spend. And little Yvonne and Robert were doing okay, too, over at the home of the West Indian lady, Mrs. McGuire. I'd give them about a quarter apiece; it made me feel good to see how they were coming along.

None of us talked much about our mother. And we never mentioned our father. I guess none of us knew what to say. We didn't want anybody else to mention our mother either, I think. From time to time, though, we would all go over to Kalamazoo to visit her. Most often we older ones went singly, for it was something you didn't want to have to experience with anyone else present, even your brother or sister.

During this period, the visit to my mother that I most remember was toward the end of that seventh-grade year, when our father's grown daughter by his first marriage, Ella, came from Boston to visit us. Wilfred and Hilda had exchanged some letters with Ella, and I, at Hilda's suggestion, had written to her from the Swerlins'. We were all excited and happy when her letter told us that she was coming to Lansing.

I think the major impact of Ella's arrival, at least upon me, was that she was the first really proud black woman I had ever seen in my life. She was plainly proud of her very dark skin. This was unheard of among Negroes in those days, especially in Lansing.

I hadn't been sure just what day she would come. And then one afternoon I got home from school and there she was. She hugged me, stood me away, looked me up and down. A commanding woman, maybe even bigger than Mrs. Swerlin, Ella wasn't just black, but like our father, she was jet black. The way she sat, moved, talked, did everything, bespoke somebody who did and got exactly what she wanted. This was the woman my father had boasted of so often for having brought so many of their family out of Georgia to Boston. She owned some property, he would say, and she was "in society." She had come North with nothing, and she had worked and saved and had invested in property that she built up in value, and then she started sending money to Georgia for another sister, brother, cousin, niece or nephew to come north to Boston. All that I had heard was reflected in Ella's appearance and bearing. I had never been so impressed with anybody. She was in her second marriage; her first husband had been a doctor.

Ella asked all kinds of questions about how I was doing; she had already heard from Wilfred and Hilda about my election as class president. She asked especially about my grades, and I ran and got my report cards. I was then one of the three highest in the class. Ella praised me. I asked her about her brother, Earl, and her sister, Mary. She had the exciting news that Earl was a singer with a band in Boston. He was singing under the name of Jimmy Carleton. Mary was also doing well.

Ella told me about other relatives from that branch of the family. A number of them I'd never heard of; she had helped them up from Georgia. They, in their turn, had helped up others. "We Littles have to stick together," Ella said. It thrilled me to hear her say that, and even more, the way she said it. I had become a mascot; our branch of the family was split to pieces; I had just about forgotten about being a Little in any family sense. She said that different members of the family were working in good jobs, and some even had small businesses going. Most of them were homeowners.

When Ella suggested that all of us Littles in Lansing accompany her on a visit to our mother, we all were grateful. We all felt that if anyone could do anything that could help our mother, that might help her get well and come back, it would be Ella. Anyway, all of us, for the first time together, went with Ella to Kalamazoo.

Our mother was smiling when they brought her out. She was extremely surprised when she saw Ella. They made a striking contrast, the thin near-white woman and the big black one hugging each other. I don't remember much about the rest of the visit, except that there was a lot of talking, and Ella had everything in hand, and we left with all of us feeling better than we ever had about the circumstances. I know that for the first time, I felt as though I had visited with someone who had some kind of physical illness that had just lingered on.

A few days later, after visiting the homes where each of us were staying, Ella left Lansing and returned to Boston. But before leaving, she told me to write to her regularly. And she had suggested that I might like to spend my summer holiday visiting her in Boston. I jumped at that chance.

That summer of 1940, in Lansing, I caught the Greyhound bus for Boston with my cardboard suitcase, and wearing my green suit. If someone had hung a sign, "HICK," around my neck, I couldn't have looked much more obvious. They didn't have the turnpikes then; the bus stopped at what seemed every

corner and cowpatch. From my seat in—you guessed it—the back of the bus,
I gawked out of the window at white man's America rolling past for what
seemed a month, but must have been only a day and a half.

When we finally arrived, Ella met me at the terminal and took me home.
The house was on Waumbeck Street in the Sugar Hill section of Roxbury, the
Harlem of Boston. I met Ella's second husband, Frank, who was now a soldier;
and her brother Earl, the singer who called himself Jimmy Carleton; and
Mary, who was very different from her older sister. It's funny how I seemed to
think of Mary as Ella's sister, instead of her being, just as Ella is, my own half-
sister. It's probably because Ella and I always were much closer as basic types;
we're dominant people, and Mary has always been mild and quiet, almost shy.

Ella was busily involved in dozens of things. She belonged to I don't know
how many different clubs; she was a leading light of local so-called "black
society." I saw and met a hundred black people there whose big-city talk and
ways left my mouth hanging open.

I couldn't have feigned indifference if I had tried to. People talked casually
about Chicago, Detroit, New York. I didn't know the world contained as many
Negroes as I saw thronging downtown Roxbury at night, especially on Saturdays.
Neon lights, nightclubs, poolhalls, bars, the cars they drove! Restaurants made
the streets smell—rich, greasy, down-home black cooking! Jukeboxes blared
Erskine Hawkins, Duke Ellington, Cootie Williams, dozens of others. If somebody had told me then that some day I'd know them all personally, I'd have
found it hard to believe. The biggest bands, like these, played at the Roseland
State Ballroom, on Boston's Massachusetts Avenue—one night for Negroes, the
next night for whites.

I saw for the first time occasional black-white couples strolling around arm
in arm. And on Sundays, when Ella, Mary, or somebody took me to church, I
saw churches for black people such as I had never seen. They were many times
finer than the white church I had attended back in Mason, Michigan. There,
the white people just sat and worshiped with words; but the Boston Negroes,
like all other Negroes I had ever seen at church, threw their souls and bodies
wholly into worship.

Two or three times, I wrote letters to Wilfred intended for everybody back
in Lansing. I said I'd try to describe it when I got back.

But I found I couldn't.

My restlessness with Mason—and for the first time in my life a restlessness
with being around white people—began as soon as I got back home and entered
eighth grade.

I continued to think constantly about all that I had seen in Boston, and
about the way I had felt there. I know now that it was the sense of being a real
part of a mass of my own kind, for the first time.

The white people—classmates, the Swerlins, the people at the restaurant
where I worked—noticed the change. They said, "You're acting so strange.
You don't seem like yourself, Malcolm. What's the matter?"

I kept close to the top of the class, though. The top-most scholastic standing, I remember, kept shifting between me, a girl named Audrey Slaugh, and a boy named Jimmy Cotton.

It went on that way, as I became increasingly restless and disturbed through the first semester. And then one day, just about when those of who had passed were about to move up to 8-A, from which we would enter high school the next year, something happened which was to become the first major turning point of my life.

Somehow, I happened to be alone in the classroom with Mr. Ostrowski, my English teacher. He was a tall, rather reddish white man and he had a thick mustache. I had gotten some of my best marks under him, and he had always made me feel that he liked me. He was, as I have mentioned, a natural-born "advisor," about what you ought to read, to do, or think—about any and everything. We used to make unkind jokes about him: why was he teaching in Mason instead of somewhere else, getting for himself some of the "success in life" that he kept telling us how to get?

I know that he probably meant well in what he happened to advise me that day. I doubt that he meant any harm. It was just in his nature as an American white man. I was one of his top students, one of the school's top students— but all he could see for me was the kind of future "in your place" that almost all white people see for black people.

He told me, "Malcolm, you ought to be thinking about a career. Have you been giving it thought?"

The truth is, I hadn't. I never have figured out why I told him, "Well, yes, sir, I've been thinking I'd like to be a lawyer." Lansing certainly had no Negro lawyers—or doctors either—in those days, to hold up an image I might have aspired to. All I really knew for certain was that a lawyer didn't wash dishes, as I was doing.

Mr. Ostrowski looked surprised, I remember, and leaned back in his chair and clasped his hands behind his head. He kind of half-smiled and said, "Malcolm, one of life's first needs is for us to be realistic. Don't misunderstand me, now. We all here like you, you know that. But you've got to be realistic about being a nigger. A lawyer—that's no realistic goal for a nigger. You need to think about something you *can* be. You're good with your hands—making things. Everybody admires your carpentry shop work. Why don't you plan on carpentry? People like you as a person—you'd get all kinds of work."

The more I thought afterwards about what he said, the more uneasy it made me. It just kept treading around in my mind.

What made it really begin to disturb me was Mr. Ostrowski's advice to others in my class—all of them white. Most of them had told him they were planning to become farmers. But those who wanted to strike out on their own, to try something new, he had encouraged. Some, mostly girls, wanted to be teachers. A few wanted other professions, such as one boy who wanted to become a county agent; another, a veterinarian; and one girl wanted to be a nurse. They all reported that **Mr.** Ostrowski had encouraged what they had wanted. Yet nearly none of them had earned marks equal to mine.

It was a surprising thing that I had never thought of it that way before, but I realized that whatever I wasn't, I *was* smarter than nearly all of those white kids. But apparently I was still not intelligent enough, in their eyes, to become whatever I wanted to be.

It was then that I began to change—inside.

I drew away from white people. I came to class, and I answered when called upon. It became a physical strain simply to sit in Mr. Ostowski's class.

Where "nigger" had slipped off my back before, wherever I heard it now, I stopped and looked at whoever said it. And they looked surprised that I did.

I quit hearing so much "nigger" and "What's wrong?"—which was the way I wanted it. Nobody, including the teachers, could decide what had come over me. I knew I was being discussed.

In a few more weeks, it was that way, too, at the restaurant where I worked washing dishes, and at the Swerlins'.

One day soon after, Mrs. Swerlin called me into the living room, and there was the state man, Maynard Allen. I knew from their faces that something was about to happen. She told me that none of them could understand why—after I had done so well in school, and on my job, and living with them, and after everyone in Mason had come to like me—I had lately begun to make them all feel that I wasn't happy there anymore.

She said she felt there was no need for me to stay at the detention home any longer, and that arrangements had been made for me to go and live with the Lyons family, who liked me so much.

She stood up and put out her hand. "I guess I've asked you a hundred times, Malcolm—do you want to tell me what's wrong?"

I shook her hand, and said, "Nothing, Mrs. Swerlin." Then I went and got my things, and came back down. At the living room door I saw her wiping her eyes. I felt very bad. I thanked her and went out in front to Mr. Allen, who took me over to the Lyons'.

Mr. and Mrs. Lyons, and their children, during the two months I lived with them—while finishing eighth grade—also tried to get me to tell them what was wrong. But somehow I couldn't tell them, either.

I went every Saturday to see my brothers and sisters in Lansing, and almost every other day I wrote to Ella in Boston. Not saying why, I told Ella that I wanted to come there and live.

I don't know how she did it, but she arranged for official custody of me to be transferred from Michigan to Massachusetts, and the very week I finished the eighth grade, I again boarded the Greyhound bus for Boston.

I've thought about that time a lot since then. No physical move in my life has been more pivotal or profound in its repercussions.

If I had stayed on in Michigan, I would probably have married one of those Negro girls I knew and liked in Lansing. I might have become one of those state capitol building shoeshine boys, or a Lansing Country Club waiter, or gotten one of the other menial jobs which, in those days, among Lansing Negroes, would have been considered "successful"—or even become a carpenter.

Whatever I have done since then, I have driven myself to become a success at it. I've often thought that if Mr. Ostowski had encouraged me to become a lawyer, I would today probably be among some city's professional black bourgeoisie, sipping cocktails and palming myself off as a community spokesman for and leader of the suffering black masses, while my primary concern would be to grab a few more crumbs from the groaning board of the two-faced whites with whom they're begging to "integrate."

All praise is due to Allah that I went to Boston when I did. If I hadn't, I'd probably still be a brainwashed black Christian.

---

## The Afternoon of a Young Poet
### 1966

---

### M. Carl Holman

---

In the late winter of my senior year in high school I entered a poem in an annual literary competition sponsored by the Arts Club of St. Louis. Because I was almost pathologically shy, and because I was not sure I actually intended to go through with it until I was picking my way back up the icy street from the corner mailbox, I told no one what I had done. Until that night I had submitted poems to Negro newspapers and magazines and had won one or two small prizes, but I had never before ventured to enter a "white" contest.

I had found the announcement of the Arts Club competition in the section of one of the white dailies where I read avidly about plays, concerts and ballets which might just as well have been taking place on the moon. During that period of my life I was strongly influenced by three or four university-trained teachers on our high school faculty who were still caught up in the afterglow of the Negro Renaissance. Mr. Watts, Miss Armstrong, Mr. Blanton and Miss

Lewis taught us from the "lily-white" textbooks prescribed by the St. Louis school system, but they also mounted on their bulletin boards the works and pictures of Langston Hughes, James Weldon Johnson, Claude McKay, Sterling Brown, Countee Cullen and Jean Toomer.

Entering the contest, however secretly, represented unusual daring for me, though it would have been as easy as breathing for Miss Armstrong, a vibrantly energetic mahogany-skinned woman whose voice flayed our budding manhood with contempt when she read McKay's poem "If We Must Die." (Her voice accused and disturbed me, conjuring up two confusing memories from my childhood downtown on Carroll Street—the first, that day in the depths of the Depression when half the fathers on the block straggled back from their protest march on City Hall, their heads broken and bleeding. Some of them weeping, but only one of them laughing. The potbellied little man next door who came stumbling up the alley apart from the others, tittering like a drunken woman, one eye puffed shut, his bloody rag of a shirt dragging in the dust. Giggling and whispering. *"Don't hit me no mo, Cap'n. You the boss. You sho God is the boss. . . ."* And less than five years later, Big Crew, standing in the middle of the yard, his lips drawn back from his blue gums in a wolfish grin, smashing his black fist like a hammer into the rent man's face, picking the man up like a sack of flour and knocking him down again. All time talking to him as quietly as one friend to another: *"Git up and fight, you peckerwood sonuva-bitch. Git up and fight for your country."*)

I yearned during those high school years to write something as defiantly bitter as McKay's "If We Must Die" or Sterling Brown's "Strong Men." My temper was capable of flaring up and consuming me so utterly that during a period of a few months I found myself in wildly hopeless fights with the older boys. Deep in hostile north St. Louis I had placed my life and those of two boys with me in jeopardy when, without thinking, I spat in the face of a young white boy seated on the stoop surrounded by at least seven members of his beefy family, because he called me a "skinny black nigger" as my friends and I were passing. My mother's long campaign to curb my temper had only taught me at last to swallow my feelings, hiding them so deep that I could not have dredged up my rages and despairs and found words for them even if I had wanted to. The long poem I finally mailed to the Arts Club was called "Nocturne on a Hill." Though it was probably honest enough in its way, it echoed more of the white writers I had been reading and told more about my reactions to the shapes and sounds of the city than it did about the people I loved and hated, or the things which delighted, hurt or confused me most.

We had moved from Carroll Street downtown three years earlier and we were living that year on Driscoll Avenue in midtown, halfway between the river on the east and that section of West End the whites had ceded to the Negro doctors, schoolteachers and postal workers. For a long time after the move to Driscoll Avenue I had continued to go back to the old neighborhood. In part this was because the customers to whom I sold Negro weekly newspapers lived there (ranging from an ancient self-ordained bishop, whose wife

was never permitted to expose anything more than a slender wax-yellow hand
and a black-clad sleeve as I handed the paper through the double-chained
door, to the heavily powdered ladies in the big house on Seymour Street who
had bought a dozen papers from me every Friday for a month before I learned
how they made their living). But even on days when I had no papers to sell,
Carroll Street for a long time continued to have the same love-fear magnetism
for me it had exercised when I lived there; racked by sweaty nightmares on
nights when the patrol wagons and ambulances pounded past our house, listening by the hour to the Italians singing from the backyards where they had
strung light bulbs for the parties that left the alley littered with snail shells and
the discarded bottles the winos fought over the next morning. On Carroll Street
we had lived closely, though not intimately, with whites: the Italians on Bouie
Avenue to the rear, the Jewish storekeepers, the Germans who worked in the
bakery and the bank, the Irish truck drivers and policemen (and one saloon
keeper who reconverted his storefront when Prohibition ended, returning to its
old place in the window the faded, flyspecked sign whose legend we chanted
up and down the street: "Coolidge Blew the Whistle, Mellon Rang the Bell,
Hoover Pulled the Throttle and the Country Went to Hell").

Driscoll Avenue was a less impoverished and more self-contained world
than Carroll Street. Except for the merchants and bill collectors, it was possible
to walk through midtown for blocks without seeing a white face. We lived on
the first floor of a three-story brick house set on a concrete terrace from which
three stone steps led down to the street. My chores during that long winter included keeping the steps salted down and making sure the heavy hall door was
kept tightly shut.

My mother was ill for a long time that winter, and the grown-ups came to
visit her, stamped into the house wrapped like mummies with only their eyes
showing, bringing pots of stew, pickled preserves and the latest tale of some
drunk who had been found frozen stiff in an alley or a neighbor who had been
taken to "Old Number Two" with double pneumonia. Number Two was the
nearest city hospital, and the neighborhood saying was that they did more
killing there than Mr. Swift did over at his packing house. Old people in the
neighborhood sometimes clung stubbornly to their beds at home, hiding the
seriousness of their ailments, for fear they would be sent to Number Two to
die. My mother was not old, but I lay awake many nights that winter, listening
to her rasping breathing and praying that she would not have to be taken to
Number Two. Sometimes, after her breathing had smoothed out and she had
fallen asleep, I would get out of bed and go over to the window, raising the
shade enough to let in the white winter moonlight. Fumbling for a pencil and
piece of paper, I would write lines and fragments which I could not see, then
fold the paper and stuff it into my hiding place back of the piano which nobody
in the house played.

My mother's conviction that both her children were going to finish high
school and college and "amount to something" had persisted in the face of the
bleakest realities her native Mississippi and a half-flat near the tracks in south

St. Louis could marshal against her. Even in her illness, hollow-eyed and feverish, she wanted to know what we had done in school daily, what the teachers
had said, whether our homework was done. A gifted seamstress and a careful
manager of small change for most of her life, she never doubted she would one
day find the proper use for the patterns, scraps of cloth, Eagle stamps, buttons
and pins she scrupulously put aside, each in its proper place. She cooked huge
pots of soup, with opulent aromas suggesting magnitudes of power and promise
out of all proportion to the amount of meat in the pot. She felt she had ample
reason to sing "He Leadeth Me," and when we had amazed ourselves and our
teachers by prodigies of nerve-straining effort she only said mildly, "Didn't He
promise He would make a way out of no way for those who believed in Him?"

Lacking her faith, I was so beset with premonitions and terrors during
those months of her illness that I lost all recollection of the poem I had mailed
to the Arts Club. The cousin I loved most had died in childbirth just two years
before, at the age of nineteen, and I had been tormented ever since by the
fragility of the web separating life and death. Though she met the slightest
ache or pain visited on her children as if it were an outrider of the Devil's
legions fully armed, my mother regarded her own illnesses as nuisances to be
gotten through with as little fuss as possible. By the time the snow had melted
in the gutters she was on her feet again, halfway through her spring cleaning
and fretting to have the last frost gone so that she could start planting the
narrow rectangle of earth out front she called her garden.

I came home from school one afternoon in early May to find a letter from
the Arts Club in our mailbox. I was afraid to open it until I had first made sure
it was not bulky enough to contain the rejected poem. There was only a single
sheet inside, a note typed on the most elegant stationery I had ever seen, congratulating me on the selection of my poem as one of the five best works submitted in that year's contest and inviting me to meet the other winners at the
club two weeks later.

The first surge of surprise and pleasure was followed almost at once by a
seizure of blind panic. How could I go out there to Westmoreland Place, a street
I had never seen, to meet a group of strangers, most if not all of them white—
when I stammered or fell silent whenever I had to talk to one of my teachers
without the supporting presence of the rest of the class? Reading the note again
I saw that the meeting had been scheduled for mid-afternoon of a school day.
For most of that next week I debated whether I should accept the club's invitation or prepare to be sick on that day. Finally, just forty-eight hours before
the date set in the letter, I went down to the principal and secured permission
to be excused from my afternoon classes to attend the Arts Club meeting.

That same afternoon I showed my mother the letter. She knew me well
enough to play down the pride she felt, complaining instead about people who
would miss Heaven one day because they always waited until the last minute.
She consulted with a friend who worked in the section where the club was
located and wrote down the directions for me, dryly reminding me to have the
conductor give me a transfer when I boarded the trolley outside the school. I

had once had to walk home a distance of some six miles away because I forgot to ask for a transfer. Actually, I was less concerned about the transfer than about the possibility that on the way out to the club I might develop motion sickness. This often happened when I rode the trolleys. Usually I got off the car as soon as the first queasy stirrings began in the pit of my stomach, and walked the rest of the way. But this time I would be in a part of town that I did not know at all. I resolved to ride standing up all the way, trusting that my mother's God would not let me be sick.

I left school on a hazily bright afternoon alive with the tarry tang of smoke and the green smell of growing things which I associate still with spring in St. Louis. It was good to be a privileged truant with the whole block in front of the school to myself, the typewriters clicking behind me in the principal's office and the unheeded voices of the teachers floating out of the classroom windows overhead. The first trolley was a long time coming. When I got on I remembered to ask for the transfer, and though over half the seats were empty on both trolleys, I stood up all the way. But when I got off the second car I found that I had managed to lose the directions my mother had given me. I could not remember whether I was to go north or south from the trolley stop. My palms promptly began sweating and I took out the letter from the Arts Club, reading the address again as if that would give me a clue. In my neighborhood most of the houses were row houses, or were separated from each other by nothing more than a narrow passageway. Even houses like the one we lived in, though not flush with the pavement, were close enough so that the addresses could be easily read from the sidewalk. But out here the houses were set back from wide lawns under shade trees and there was no way of making out the addresses without going up a long walk to the front door. No small children were playing outside, there were no stores into which a stranger might go and ask directions, and the whole neighborhood was wrapped in a fragrant but forbidding stillness. Remembering that my mother had said the club was only two blocks away from the trolley stop, I started walking south, deciding that if it turned out I was going the wrong way I could always come back and go two blocks in the other direction. I walked three blocks for good measure without finding Westmoreland Place, then turned and started back.

A red-faced old man with bushy military whiskers that reminded me of pictures I had seen of the Kaiser came down one of the walks with a bulldog on a leash. I braced myself to ask him where Westmoreland Place was, but before I could speak, his china blue eyes suddenly glared at me with such venomous hatred that I had the feeling he was about to set the dog on me. I averted my eyes and walked on, trembling suddenly with an answering hatred as senseless as his. Not noticing where I was going, I was about to cross into the next block when I looked up at the street sign and found that I was on Westmoreland Place. It was a street of thick hedges and houses which, if anything, were more inaccessible than those I had already passed. I walked up the street in one direction, then crossed and reversed my course. By now the letter was wilting in my hand. The trolley ride had taken longer than I had estimated and I was sure I was already late. One of the last things my mother had said to me that morning was, "Now try to be sure not to get out there on Colored People's Time." My mind groped for a plausible lie that would let me give up the whole business and go home. I thought of saying that the meeting had been called off, that the place was closed when I got there, that I had caught the wrong car and gone too far out of the way to get back in time. At one point, I almost convinced myself that I should go back to the trolley stop and catch a car that would take me downtown to my old refuge, the main public library. I could stay there reading for an hour or two, then claim I had actually attended the tea. But my spirit quailed at the prospect of inventing answers to all the questions that would follow. And what if in the meantime someone from the club had already called my home or the school? I hated myself for entering the competition and felt sick with envy when I thought of my schoolmates who by now were idling down the halls on free period or dreaming their way through the last classes before the liberating bell.

I was plodding down the same block for the second time when around the corner of a big stone house across the street came an unmistakably colored man in work clothes, uncoiling a garden hose. We might have been the only two living souls on a desert island. Almost faint with relief I angled across the street toward him. But the handyman, his high shiny forehead furrowed in elaborate concentration, adjusted the nozzle and began playing rainbow jets of spray across the grass. I halted at the edge of the lawn and waited for him to take note of my presence. In due time he worked himself close enough so that I was able to ask him if he knew where the Arts Club was. I held out the letter as I asked him, but he merely turned his rusty deepset eyes on me with a look that plainly said *I hope to God you ain't come out here to make trouble for the rest of us.* In later years I have seen that look in the eyes of Negro businessmen, schoolteachers, college presidents, reverend ministers—and a trio of cooks and dishwashers peering through the swinging doors of a restaurant kitchen at the dark-skinned students sitting at counters where no one of their color ever presumed to sit before.

But I was of another generation, another temperament and state of mind from those students. So when the handyman flicked one hand in the direction from which I had just come and said, "There 'tis, over there," I thanked him— rather thanked his back, which was already turned to me.

I would never have taken the two-story brick building at the end of the flagstone walk to be anything other than the residence of a comfortably well- off family. Just before I pushed the button beside the broad door it occurred to me that the handyman might be playing his notion of a joke on me. Then I looked down at the thick mat on which I was standing and saw the letters "A-C." I pressed the button, waited and was about to press it again when the door swung open. The rake-thin white maid standing there had composed for her plain freckled face a smile of deferential welcome. The smile faded and her body stiffened in the neat gray uniform. For an instant I thought she would close the door in my face, but she braked it so that it was barely ajar and said,

"Yes?" I mumbled something and held out the letter. She squinted at the envelope and said, "You wait here." The door closed and I stood there with my face burning, wanting to turn and go away but unwilling to confront the expression of sour satisfaction I expected to see on the face of the handyman across the street. After what seemed fifteen full minutes a gray-haired woman in a blue uniform with starched cuffs came to the door. "All right, what is it now?" she said, sounding like a very busy woman. I held out the letter and she took it, measured me up and down with her shrewd eyes and said to the younger woman hovering behind her, "I'll be right back." The freckle-faced thin one looked miles above my head toward the street but we shared the unspoken understanding that I was not to move from where I stood and that she was to watch me.

I stood rooted there, calling myself every kind of black fool for coming in the first place, my undershirt cleaving to my damp skin. It had become clear to me that I had received the invitation by mistake. And now that I had surrendered the letter, the only proof that I had been invited, my sole excuse for being there at all was gone. I pictured them huddled inside, talking in whispers, waiting for me to have the good sense to leave. Then I heard voices coming toward the door. My keeper faded back into the gloom of the hallway and an attractive woman in her forties held the door open and smiled at me. Everything about her, her fine-textured skin, the soft-colored dress and the necklace she was wearing, her candid gaze, defined an order of relationships which did away with any need for me to deal further with the other two women. "Hello," she said. "So you're the boy who came over to tell us Mr. Holman couldn't come?"

I stared dumbly at her, wondering how I could have been fooled into thinking she was one of those white women my mother would have described approvingly as "a real lady, as nice as they come."

"Please tell him we hope he'll be feeling better soon," the woman said. "We had so hoped to meet him."

"I'm—I got the letter saying to come out here," I blurted. We stood there for a minute staring at one another and then her pink skin flushed red. "Oh, you mean you—oh, I *am* so sorry," she said. "Please do come in. I didn't know." She glanced back at the maids. "I mean, we thought—"

It was finally clear to all of us what she had thought. That the white boy who wrote the poem had been unable to come so his family had thoughtfully sent their colored boy to tender his regrets.

"You come right on in," the woman said. "I'm your hostess. All the others are already here and we've been waiting for you." She drew me inside the cool, dim hallway and guided me up the stairs like an invalid. I could not remember ever walking on such thick carpets. I had a hazy impression of cut flowers in vases, and paintings hanging along the walls like those I had seen in the Art Museum in the park. As she went up she kept on talking, but I made very little of what she was saying because now I could hear the murmur of other voices and laughter coming from the floor above us. I had the feeling that an intimate and very pleasant family party was in progress which we were about to ruin and I wanted to ask my hostess if I might not be excused after all. Instead I let myself be piloted into a sunny high-ceilinged room which at one and the same time seemed as spacious as a playing field and so intimate that no one could move without touching the person beside him. A blur of white faces turned toward us, some of them young, some middle-aged, some older, but all of them clearly belonging to a different world from that of the uniformed women downstairs. A different world from mine. For a flickering moment there was a drop in energy like that sudden dimming of lights during a summer storm and then I was being introduced in a flurry of smiles, bobbing heads and a refrain seeming to consist of variations on "Delightful . . . delighted . . . so good you could come . . . a pleasure."

Whenever I have tried to recollect that afternoon since, the faces in that upstairs room elude me like objects seen through sunlit water. I remember that one of the girls was blonde and turned eagerly from one speaker to another as if anxious not to miss one word, that there was a boy there from a school out in the country who talked and moved with the casual, almost insulting assurance which for a long time afterward I automatically associated with private schools. All of the other students there who had won prizes or honorable mentions in the area-wide competition were either from private schools or from white high schools whose very names were new to me. One of the girls was from a Catholic school and one of the sisters from the faculty had come along with her. I discovered that other winners were accompanied by their teacher and I mentally kicked myself for not realizing that I might have been buttressed by the presence of Miss Armstrong or Mr. Blanton. Certainly they would have been much more at home in this company than I was. Gradually, as cookies, tea and punch were passed and the talk again swirled back and forth, I began to relax somewhat, content to be on the periphery of that closed circle. I kept stealing glances around the room, taking in the wide fireplace and the portrait above the mantel of some famous man whose identity kept eluding me, the rows of books in the recessed shelves along the wall, and the magazines scattered tantalizingly just out of reach on the long oaken table in the center of the room.

In school, except to recite, I had rarely ever talked even to my English teachers about poems, books and writers. But this group, comfortably seated or standing about the pleasant room with the haze of spring sunlight sifting through the windows, shared a community of language and interests which enabled them largely to ignore differences of age and individual preference and to move from one idea or work to another as effortlessly as fish in a pond. They talked of Shakespeare and Keats, Milton and Shelley, but there were other writers whose lines I had spoken aloud, sometimes in puzzlement, when I was alone. Now they were being argued over, attacked, defended, ridiculed: Eliot, Frost, Sandburg, Millay, Vachel Lindsay, Amy Lowell, Yeats. There were moments when someone touched on something I had read and I was tempted to speak out in agreement or disagreement. At other times I was overcome by the gloomy conviction that I could never in the years there were left to me read all the works some of them seemed to know by heart. I felt particularly lost as the talk shifted to novels only recently written, to concerts they had attended and plays seen at the American Theatre downtown or "on our last trip to New York." (I had been drunk for days on the free concert given for Negro high school students by the St. Louis Symphony the year before, shutting myself off in my room with an umbrella spoke for a baton, trying to be all the voices of the orchestra and graceful Mr. Golschmann conducting the *New World Symphony*. Later I was to go to the American as often as I could to see the road companies in performance and, during intermissions, to devour the posters advertising the plays I would not be able to see. Often my companion and I were among less than a dozen Negroes present. (Years afterward, on a trip back to St. Louis I was triumphantly informed that Negroes were no longer segregated in the second-balcony seats at the American. Second-balcony seats being all we could afford, my friend and I had never asked for anything else, a neat dovetailing of covert discrimination and economic necessity.)

Toward the end of the long afternoon, it was proposed that the young writers read their poems. Once again I was plunged into sweaty-palmed agony. My torment only increased as the first two readers read their poems like seasoned professionals, or so it seemed to me. When my turn came I tried to beg off, but the additional attention this focused upon me only increased my discomfort and I plunged in, at first reading too fast and almost inaudibly but finally recollecting some of the admonitions my teachers had dinned into my head in preparation for "recitations" before Negro school and church audiences as far back as the second grade. I had not realized how long a poem it was when I was writing it and I was squirmingly conscious of certain flaws and failures which had never before loomed so large. The applause and praise that followed when I finished, if anything, exceeded that given the others; a situation which, even then, aroused the fleeting suspicion that the dancing bear was being given higher marks than a man might get for the same performance. One of the older women murmured something about Paul Laurence Dunbar. Someone else asked me if I liked Pushkin. I could only look blank, since at that time I knew almost nothing about the great Russian's poetry and even less about his Negro lineage. Inevitably, there was a flattering and irrelevant comparison to Langston Hughes. A wavy-haired gentleman took his pipe out of his mouth to ask if I didn't think "The Negro Speaks of Rivers" was a marvelous poem. I said I certainly did. (But stopped short of trying to explain why the Mississippi always made me think not of Lincoln at New Orleans but of the playmate on Carroll Street drowned during an Easter baptism, the cold, feral grin of the garfish skeleton which two of us stumbled on as we moped along the riverfront toward the pickle factory and the high platform beyond where the city garbage trucks dumped their loads into the frothing stream, and the dimly remembered "high waters" sucking at the edge of the roadbed as the train brought my father and me back to St. Louis from our grandfather's funeral.)

Gradually, as the light faded outside the window, people began looking at their watches and saying good-by. One of the club members thanked all of us for coming and said she could not remember when the Arts Club had had such a fine and talented group. The blonde girl clapped her hands for attention, her eyes shining with the enthusiasm of the born organizer. Why, she wanted to know, did this year's group really have to scatter? It seemed to her that we should not let our companionship, our new friendships die. Some of us were going away for the summer, but there were still several weeks left yet before school would be out. Some might be going off to college in the fall, but others would not, and probably some of those who would be entering college would be going no farther away than the University of Missouri at Columbia, or St. Louis, Washington, or one of the other schools in the St. Louis area. I was silent as the others chimed in, suggesting that we meet at the various high schools or rotate meetings from one home to another before and after summer vacations. Such a point was made of including me in and I felt already so much the witch at the wedding party that I was not inclined to remind them that I would have a much harder time getting into a meeting at the schools they attended or the colleges in the area than I had had getting into the Arts Club that afternoon. To say nothing of what their parents and friends and mine would make of those meetings in the homes. I tried to picture those well-dressed and half-assured young white poets strolling past the cleaning and pressing shop to a meeting at my house. Nevertheless, my Driscoll Avenue cynicism began crumbling under the effervescent pressures of their youth and mine. We made our way down the thick-carpeted stairs, true poets and comrades, a verbal skyscraper of plans and projects rising as we descended. We would exchange our favorite original poems by phone and by mail. We would do a volume of poems together and a famous novelist who was a good friend of our hostess would get the book published for us. The Arts Club would serve as secretariat and haven, keeping track of addresses and phone numbers and providing a place where we could meet, read and write.

Good will, mutual admiration, flowering ambition united us as we parted in the gathering spring dusk. The air was scented with the watermelony smell of freshly cut grass. The lights were on in the stone house across the street, but the handyman was gone.

I did not hear from the young men and women I met that afternoon at the Arts Club the next week, the next month, or ever. But I had a great many more serious disappointments than that, along with a decent amount of good fortune, in the two remaining years I spent in my home town. Like many other young men similarly situated I was involved during those pre-war years in a quiet but no less desperate scramble simply to hold on to life and not go under. By the end of that period of twenty-odd months I had run an elevator, worked as a machine operator, delivered parcels, patrolled a lake stocked with fish nobody ever tried to steal, and stood in half a hundred job lines with white and black men who showed up every morning less out of hope than the need to put off as long as possible that time of day when they must once again face their families. For me and a good many others my age it was not a question really of having something to eat and a place to sleep. The battle was, rather, to find ways of withstanding the daily erosion, through tedium, through humiliation, through various short-term pleasures, of the sense of your own possibilities. Necessary, too, was some sensitivity to possibilities outside yourself. Here I do not exclude chance, the lucky break. For me it came with the opportunity to become a part-time student at a college I might have attended full time two years earlier.

On the night before I left for college my mother gave a party for me, inviting a dozen of my friends. Some of them brought gifts. As I was walking past the Catholic church on Garth Avenue, shortly after midnight, going home to the flat I shared with my father, a squad car pulled up and two officers jumped out. Night sticks at the ready, they flashed a light in my face and wanted to know where I was coming from and where I had picked up all that stuff. They pawed through the presents I was carrying until they came across an anthology of poetry autographed for me that night by my friends. The first officer grunted and snapped off his light. The second seemed tempted to take a swipe at me anyhow for wasting their time. They got back in the car and drove off, leaving me to walk the two blocks remaining between the church and home.

The next morning, on a cold, sooty, old-style St. Louis day, I left home. I got on a bus and headed for Jefferson City, Missouri. That trip away from home has been a much longer journey than I had anticipated and a very much different one. On certain occasions, as when my poetry was published or while lecturing at Atlanta University, I have remembered that afternoon. And I have thought that perhaps when I next visited St. Louis, I would try once again to find my way to the Arts Club. I never have and it is probably just as well. It may be that I got as much as could reasonably be expected on that first visit.

# How I Became a Socialist
## 1905

## Jack London

It is quite fair to say that I became a Socialist in a fashion somewhat similar to the way in which the Teutonic pagans became Christians—it was hammered into me. Not only was I not looking for Socialism at the time of my conversion, but I was fighting it. I was very young and callow, did not know much of anything, and though I had never even heard of a school called "Individualism," I sang the pæan of the strong with all my heart.

This was because I was strong myself. By strong I mean that I had good health and hard muscles, both of which possessions are easily accounted for. I had lived my childhood on California ranches, my boyhood hustling newspapers on the streets of a healthy Western city, and my youth on the ozone-laden waters of San Francisco Bay and the Pacific Ocean. I loved life in the open, and I toiled in the open, at the hardest kinds of work. Learning no trade, but drifting along from job to job, I looked on the world and called it good, every bit of it. Let me repeat, this optimism was because I was healthy and strong, bothered with neither aches nor weaknesses, never turned down by the boss because I did not look fit, able always to get a job at shovelling coal, sailorizing, or manual labor of some sort.

And because of all this, exulting in my young life, able to hold my own at work or fight, I was a rampant individualist. It was very natural. I was a winner. Wherefore I called the game, as I saw it played, or thought I saw it played, a very proper game for MEN. To be a MAN was to write man in large capitals on my heart. To adventure like a man, and fight like a man, and do a man's work (even for a boy's pay)—these were things that reached right in and gripped hold of me as no other thing could. And I looked ahead into long vistas of a hazy and interminable future, into which, playing what I conceived to be MAN'S game, I should continue to travel with unfailing health, without accidents, and with muscles ever vigorous. As I say, this future was interminable. I could see myself only raging through life without end like one of Nietzsche's *blond beasts,* lustfully roving and conquering by sheer superiority and strength.

As for the unfortunates, the sick, and ailing, and old, and maimed, I must confess I hardly thought of them at all, save that I vaguely felt that they, barring accidents, could be as good as I if they wanted to real hard, and could work just as well. Accidents? Well, they represented FATE, also spelled out in capitals, and there was no getting around FATE. Napoleon had had an accident at Waterloo, but that did not dampen my desire to be another and later Napoleon. Further, the optimism bred of a stomach which could digest scrap iron and a body which flourished on hardships did not permit me to consider accidents as even remotely related to my glorious personality.

I hope I have made it clear that I was proud to be one of Nature's strong-armed noblemen. The dignity of labor was to me the most impressive thing in the world. Without having read Carlyle, or Kipling, I formulated a gospel of work which put theirs in the shade. Work was everything. It was sanctification and salvation. The pride I took in a hard day's work well done would be inconceivable to you. It is almost inconceivable to me as I look back upon it. I was as faithful a wage slave as ever capitalist exploited. To shirk or malinger on the man who paid me my wages was a sin, first, against myself, and second, against him. I considered it a crime second only to treason and just about as bad.

In short, my joyous individualism was dominated by the orthodox bourgeois ethics. I read the bourgeois papers, listened to the bourgeois preachers, and shouted at the sonorous platitudes of the bourgeois politicians. And I doubt not, if other events had not changed my career, that I should have evolved into a professional strike-breaker, (one of President Eliot's American heroes), and had my head and my earning power irrevocably smashed by a club in the hands of some militant trades-unionist.

Just about this time, returning from a seven months' voyage before the mast, and just turned eighteen, I took it into my head to go tramping. On rods and blind baggages I fought my way from the open West, where men bucked big and the job hunted the man, to the congested labor centres of the East, where men were small potatoes and hunted the job for all they were worth. And on this new *blond-beast* adventure I found myself looking upon life from a new and totally different angle. I had dropped down from the proletariat into what sociologists love to call the "submerged tenth," and I was startled to discover the way in which that submerged tenth was recruited.

I found there all sorts of men, many of whom had once been as good as myself and just as *blond-beastly;* sailor-men, soldier-men, labor-men, all wrenched and distorted and twisted out of shape by toil and hardship and accident, and cast adrift by their masters like so many old horses. I battered on the drag and slammed back gates with them, or shivered with them in box cars and city parks, listening the while to life-histories which began under auspices as fair as mine, with digestions and bodies equal to and better than mine, and which ended there before my eyes in the shambles at the bottom of the Social Pit.

And as I listened my brain began to work. The woman of the streets and the man of the gutter drew very close to me. I saw the picture of the Social Pit as vividly as though it were a concrete thing, and at the bottom of the Pit I saw them, myself above them, not far, and hanging on to the slippery wall by main strength and sweat. And I confess a terror seized me. What when my strength failed? when I should be unable to work shoulder to shoulder with the strong men who were as yet babes unborn? And there and then I swore a great oath. It ran something like this: *All my days I have worked hard with my body, and according to the number of days I have worked, by just that much am I nearer the bottom of the Pit. I shall climb out of the Pit, but not by the muscles of my body shall I climb out. I shall do no more hard work, and may God strike me dead if I do another day's hard work with my body more than I absolutely have to do.* And I have been busy ever since running away from hard work.

Incidentally, while tramping some ten thousand miles through the United States and Canada, I strayed into Niagara Falls, was nabbed by a fee-hunting constable, denied the right to plead guilty or not guilty, sentenced out of hand to thirty days' imprisonment for having no fixed abode and no visible means of support, handcuffed and chained to a bunch of men similarly circumstanced, carted down country to Buffalo, registered at the Erie County Penitentiary, had my head clipped and my budding mustache shaved, was dressed in convict stripes, compulsorily vaccinated by a medical student who practised on such as we, made to march the lock-step, and put to work under the eyes of guards armed with Winchester rifles—all for adventuring in *blond-beastly* fashion. Concerning further details deponent sayeth not, though he may hint that some of his plethoric national patriotism simmered down and leaked out of the bottom of his soul somewhere—at least, since that experience he finds that he cares more for men and women and little children than for imaginary geographical lines.

To return to my conversion. I think it is apparent that my rampant individualism was pretty effectively hammered out of me, and something else as effectively hammered in. But, just as I had been an individualist without knowing it, I was now a Socialist without knowing it, withal, an unscientific one. I had been reborn, but not renamed, and I was running around to find out what manner of thing I was. I ran back to California and opened the books. I do not remember which ones I opened first. It is an unimportant detail anyway. I was already It, whatever It was, and by aid of the books I discovered that It was a Socialist. Since that day I have opened many books, but no economic argument, no lucid demonstration of the logic and inevitableness of Socialism affects me as profoundly and convincingly as I was affected on the day when I first saw the walls of the Social Pit rise around me and felt myself slipping down, down, into the shambles at the bottom.

# Cecilia Rosas
## 1965

## Amado Muro

When I was in the ninth grade at Bowie High School in El Paso, I got a job hanging up women's coats at La Feria Department Store on Saturdays. It wasn't the kind of a job that had much appeal for a Mexican boy or for boys of any other nationality either. But the work wasn't hard, only boring. Wearing a smock, I stood around the Ladies' Wear Department all day long waiting for women customers to finish trying on coats so I could hang them up.

Having to wear a smock was worse than the work itself. It was an agonizing ordeal. To me it was a loathsome stigma of unmanly toil that made an already degrading job even more so. The work itself I looked on as onerous and effeminate for a boy from a family of miners, shepherds, and ditchdiggers. But working in Ladies' Wear had two compensations: earning three dollars every Saturday was one; being close to the Señorita Cecilia Rosas was the other.

This alluring young woman, the most beautiful I had ever seen, more than made up for my mollycoddle labor and the smock that symbolized it. My chances of looking at her were almost limitless. And like a good Mexican, I made the most of them. But I was only too painfully aware that I wasn't the only one who thought this saleslady gorgeous.

La Feria had water fountains on every one of its eight floors. But men liked best the one on the floor where Miss Rosas worked. So they made special trips to Ladies' Wear all day long to drink water and look at her.

Since I was only fourteen and in love for the first time, I looked at her more chastely than most. The way her romantic lashes fringed her obsidian eyes was especially enthralling to me. Then, too, I never tired of admiring her shining raven hair, her Cupid's-bow lips, the warmth of her gleaming white smile. Her rich olive skin was almost as dark as mine. Sometimes she wore a San Juan rose in her hair. When she did, she looked so very lovely I forgot all about what La Feria was paying me to do and stood gaping at her instead. My admiration was decorous but complete. I admired her hourglass figure as well as her wonderfully radiant face.

Other men admired her too. They inspected her from the water fountain.

146

Some stared at her boldly, watching her trimly rhythmic hips sway. Others, less frank and open, gazed furtively at her swelling bosom or her shapely calves. Their effrontery made me indignant. I, too, looked at these details of Miss Rosas. But I prided myself on doing so more romantically, far more poetically than they did, with much more love than desire.

Then, too, Miss Rosas was the friendliest as well as the most beautiful saleslady in Ladies' Wear. But the other salesladies, Mexican girls all, didn't like her. She was so nice to them all they were hard put to justify their dislike. They couldn't very well admit they disliked her because she was pretty. So they all said she was haughty and imperious. Their claim was partly true. Her beauty was Miss Rosas' only obvious vanity. But she had still another. She prided herself on being more American than Mexican because she was born in El Paso. And she did her best to act, dress, and talk the way Americans do. She hated to speak Spanish, disliked her Mexican name. She called herself Cecile Roses instead of Cecilia Rosas. This made the other salesladies smile derisively. They called her La Americana or the Gringa from Xochimilco every time they mentioned her name.

Looking at this beautiful girl was more important than money to me. It was my greatest compensation for doing work that I hated. She was so lovely that a glance at her sweetly expressive face was enough to make me forget my shame at wearing a smock and my dislike for my job with its eternal waiting around.

Miss Rosas was an exemplary saleslady. She could be frivolous, serious or demure, primly efficient too, molding herself to each customer's personality. Her voice matched her exotically mysterious eyes. It was the richest, the softest I had ever heard. Her husky whisper, gentle as a rain breeze, was like a tender caress. Hearing it made me want to dream and I did. Romantic thoughts burgeoned up in my mind like rosy billows of hope scented with Miss Rosas' perfume. These thoughts made me so languid at my work that the floor manager, Joe Apple, warned me to show some enthusiasm for it or else suffer the consequences.

But my dreams sapped my will to struggle, making me oblivious to admonitions. I had neither the desire nor the energy to respond to Joe Apple's warnings. Looking at Miss Rosas used up so much of my energy that I had little left for my work. Miss Rosas was twenty, much too old for me, everyone said. But what everyone said didn't matter. So I soldiered on the job and watched her, entranced by her beauty, her grace. While I watched I dreamed of being a hero. It hurt me to have her see me doing such menial work. But there was no escape from it. I needed the job to stay in school. So more and more I took refuge in dreams.

When I had watched her as much, if not more, than I could safely do without attracting the attention of other alert Mexican salesladies, I slipped out of Ladies' Wear and walked up the stairs to the top floor. There I sat on a window ledge smoking Faro cigarettes, looking down at the city's canyons, and best of all, thinking about Miss Rosas and myself.

They say Chihuahua Mexicans are good at dreaming because the mountains are so gigantic and the horizons so vast in Mexico's biggest state that men don't think pygmy thoughts there. I was no exception. Lolling on the ledge, I became what I wanted to be. And what I wanted to be was a handsome American Miss Rosas could love and marry. The dreams I dreamed were imaginative masterpieces, or so I thought. They transcended the insipid realities of a casual relationship, making it vibrantly thrilling and infinitely more romantic. They transformed me from a colorless Mexican boy who put women's coats away in the debonair American, handsome, dashing and worldly, that I longed to be for her sake. For the first time in my life I revelled in the magic of fantasy. It brought happiness. Reality didn't.

But my window ledge reveries left me bewildered and shaken. They had a narcotic quality. The more thrillingly romantic fantasies I created, the more I needed to create. It got so I couldn't get enough dreaming time in Ladies' Wear. My kind of dreaming demanded disciplined concentration. And there was just too much hubbub, too much gossiping, too many coats to be put away there.

So I spent less time in Ladies' Wear. My flights to the window ledge became more recklessly frequent. Sometimes I got tired sitting there. When I did, I took the freight elevator down to the street floor and brazenly walked out of the store without so much as punching a time clock. Walking the streets quickened my imagination, gave form and color to my thoughts. It made my brain glow with impossible hopes that seemed incredibly easy to realize. So absorbed was I in thoughts of Miss Rosas and myself that I bumped into Americans, apologizing mechanically in Spanish instead of English, and wandered down South El Paso Street like a somnambulist, without really seeing its street vendors, cafes and arcades, tattoo shops, and shooting galleries at all.

But if there was confusion in these walks there was some serenity too. Something good did come from the dreams that prompted them. I found I could tramp the streets with a newly won tranquillity, no longer troubled by, or even aware of, girls in tight skirts, overflowing blouses, and drop-stitch stockings. My love for Miss Rosas was my shield against the furtive thoughts and indiscriminate desires that had made me so uneasy for a year or more before I met her.

Then, too, because of her, I no longer looked at the pictures of voluptuous women in the *Vea* and *Vodevil* magazines at Zamora's newsstand. The piquant thoughts Mexicans call *malos deseos* were gone from my mind. I no longer thought about women as I did before I fell in love with Miss Rosas. Instead, I thought about a woman, only one. This clear-cut objective and the serenity that went with it made me understand something of one of the nicest things about love.

I treasured the walks, the window-ledge sittings, and the dreams that I had then. I clung to them just as long as I could. Drab realities closed in on me chokingly just as soon as I gave them up. My future was a time clock with an American Mister telling me what to do and this I knew only too well. A career as an ice-dock laborer stretched ahead of me. Better said, it dangled over me like a Veracruz machete. My uncle, Rodolfo Avitia, a straw boss on the ice docks, was already training me for it. Every night he took me to the mile-long docks overhanging the Southern Pacific freight yards. There he handed me tongs and made me practice tripping three-hundred-pound ice blocks so I could learn how to unload an entire boxcar of ice blocks myself.

Thinking of this bleak future drove me back into my fantasies, made me want to prolong them forever. My imagination was taxed to the breaking point by the heavy strain I put on it.

I thought about every word Miss Rosas had ever said to me, making myself believe she looked at me with unmistakable tenderness when she said them. When she said: "Amado, please hang up this fur coat," I found special meaning in her tone. It was as though she had said: "Amadito, I love you."

When she gave these orders, I pushed into action like a man blazing with a desire to perform epically heroic feats. At such times I felt capable of putting away not one but a thousand fur coats, and would have done so joyously.

Sometimes on the street I caught myself murmuring: "Cecilia, *linda amorcita,* I love you." When these surges swept over me, I walked down empty streets so I could whisper: "Cecilia, *te quiero con toda mi alma*" as much as I wanted to and mumble everything else that I felt. And so I emptied my heart on the streets and window ledge while women's coats piled up in Ladies' Wear.

But my absences didn't go unnoticed. Once an executive-looking man, portly, gray, and efficiently brusque, confronted me while I sat on the window ledge with a Faro cigarette pasted to my lips, a cloud of tobacco smoke hanging over my head, and many perfumed dreams inside it. He had a no-nonsense approach that jibed with his austere mien. He asked me what my name was, jotted down my work number, and went off to make a report on what he called "sordid malingering."

Other reports followed his. Gruff warnings, stern admonitions, and blustery tirades developed from them. They came from both major and minor executives. These I was already inured to. They didn't matter anyway. My condition was far too advanced, already much too complex to be cleared up by mere lectures, fatherly or otherwise. All the threats and rebukes in the world couldn't have made me give up my window-ledge reveries or kept me from roaming city streets with Cecilia Rosas' name on my lips like a prayer.

The reports merely made me more cunning, more doggedly determined to city-slick La Feria out of work hours I owed it. The net result was that I timed my absences more precisely and contrived better lies to explain them. Sometimes I went to the men's room and looked at myself in the mirror for as long as ten minutes at a time. Such self-studies filled me with gloom. The mirror reflected an ordinary Mexican face, more homely than comely. Only my hair gave me hope. It was thick and wavy, deserving a better face to go with it. So I did the best I could with what I had, and combed it over my temples in ringlets just like the poets back in my hometown of Parral, Chihuahua, used to do.

My inefficiency, my dreams, my general lassitude could have gone on indefinitely, it seemed. My life at the store wavered between bright hope and leaden despair, unrelieved by Miss Rosas' acceptance or rejection of me. Then one day something happened that almost made my overstrained heart stop beating.

It happened on the day Miss Rosas stood behind me while I put a fur coat away. Her heady perfume, the fragrance of her warm healthy body, made me feel faint. She was so close to me I thought about putting my hands around her lissome waist and hugging her as hard as I could. But thoughts of subsequent disgrace deterred me, so instead of hugging her I smiled wanly and asked her in Spanish how she was feeling.

"Amado, speak English," she told me. "And pronounce the words slowly and carefully so you won't sound like a country Mexican."

Then she looked at me in a way that made me the happiest employee who ever punched La Feria's time clock.

"Amadito," she whispered the way I had always dreamed she would.

"Yes, Señorita Cecilia," I said expectantly.

Her smile was warmly intimate. "Amadito, when are you going to take me to the movies?" she asked.

Other salesladies watched us, all smiling. They made me so nervous I couldn't answer.

"Amadito, you haven't answered me," Miss Rosas said teasingly. "Either you're bashful as a village sweetheart or else you don't like me at all."

In voluble Spanish, I quickly assured her the latter wasn't the case. I was just getting ready to say "Señorita Cecilia, I more than like you, I love you" when she frowned and told me to speak English. So I slowed down and tried to smooth out my ruffled thoughts.

"Señorita Cecilia," I said. "I'd love to take you to the movies any time."

Miss Rosas smiled and patted my cheek. "Will you buy me candy and popcorn?" she said.

I nodded, putting my hand against the imprint her warm palm had left on my face.

"And hold my hand?"

I said "yes" so enthusiastically it made her laugh. Other salesladies laughed too. Dazed and numb with happiness, I watched Miss Rosas walk away. How proud and confident she was, how wholesomely clean and feminine. Other salesladies were looking at me and laughing.

Miss Sandoval came over to me. "*Ay papacito,*" she said. "With women you're the divine tortilla."

Miss de la Rosa came over too. "When you take the Americana to the movies, remember not to speak Christian," she said. "And be sure you wear the pants that don't have any patches on them."

What they said made me blush and wonder how they knew what we had been talking about. Miss Arroyo came over to join them. So did Miss Torres.

"Amado, remember women are weak and men aren't made of sweet bread," Miss Arroyo said.

This embarrassed me but it wasn't altogether unpleasant. Miss Sandoval winked at Miss de la Rosa, then looked back at me.

"Don't go too fast with the Americana, Amado," she said. "Remember the procession is long and the candles are small."

They laughed and slapped me on the back. They all wanted to know when I was going to take Miss Rosas to the movies. "She didn't say," I blurted out without thinking.

This brought another burst of laughter. It drove me back up to the window ledge where I got out my package of Faros and thought about the wonderful thing that had happened. But I was too nervous to stay there. So I went to the men's room and looked at myself in the mirror again, wondering why Miss Rosas liked me so well. The mirror made it brutally clear that my looks hadn't influenced her. So it must have been something else, perhaps character. But that didn't seem likely either. Joe Apple had told me I didn't have much of that. And other store officials had bulwarked his opinion. Still, I had seen homely men walking the streets of El Paso's Little Chihuahua quarter with beautiful Mexican women and no one could explain that either. Anyway it was time for another walk. So I took one.

This time I trudged through Little Chihuahua, where both Miss Rosas and I lived. Little Chihuahua looked different to me that day. It was a broken-down Mexican quarter honeycombed with tenements, Mom and Pop groceries, herb shops, cafes, and spindly salt-cedar trees; with howling children running its streets and old Mexican revolutionaries sunning themselves on its curbs like iguanas. But on that clear frosty day it was the world's most romantic place because Cecilia Rosas lived there.

While walking, I reasoned that Miss Rosas might want to go dancing after the movies. So I went to Professor Toribio Ortega's dance studio and made arrangements to take my first lesson. Some neighborhood boys saw me when I came out. They bawled "Mariquita" and made flutteringly effeminate motions, all vulgar if not obscene. It didn't matter. On my lunch hour I went back and took my first lesson anyway. Professor Ortega danced with me. Softened by weeks of dreaming, I went limp in his arms imagining he was Miss Rosas.

The rest of the day was the same as many others before it. As usual I spent most of it stealing glances at Miss Rosas and slipping up to the window ledge. She looked busy, efficient, not like a woman in love. Her many other admirers trooped to the water fountain to look at the way her black silk dress fitted her curves. Their profane admiration made me scowl even more than I usually did at such times.

When the day's work was done, I plodded home from the store just as dreamily as I had gone to it. Since I had no one else to confide in, I invited my oldest sister, Dulce Nombre de María, to go to the movies with me. They were showing Jorge Negrete and María Felix in *El Rapto* at the Colon Theater. It was a romantic movie, just the kind I wanted to see.

After it was over, I bought Dulce Nombre *churros* and hot *champurrado* at the Golden Taco Cafe. And I told my sister all about what had happened to me. She looked at me thoughtfully, then combed my hair back with her fingertips as though trying to soothe me. "Manito," she said, softly. "I wouldn't. . . ." Then she looked away and shrugged her shoulders.

On Monday I borrowed three dollars from my Uncle Rodolfo without telling him what it was for. Miss Rosas hadn't told me what night she wanted me to take her to the movies. But the way she had looked at me made me think that almost any night would do. So I decided on Friday. Waiting for it to come was hard. But I had to keep my mind occupied. So I went to Zamora's newsstand to get the Alma Norteña songbook. Poring through it for the most romantic song I could find, I decided on *La Cecilia.*

All week long I practiced singing it on my way to school and in the shower after basketball practice with the Little Chihuahua Tigers at the Sagrado Corazón gym. But, except for singing this song, I tried not to speak Spanish at all. At home I made my mother mad by saying in English. "Please pass the sugar."

My mother looked at me as though she couldn't believe what she had heard. Since my Uncle Rodolfo couldn't say anything more than "hello" and "goodbye" in English, he couldn't tell what I had said. So my sister Consuelo did.

"May the Dark Virgin with the benign look make this boy well enough to speak Christian again," my mother whispered.

This I refused to do. I went on speaking English even though my mother and uncle didn't understand it. This shocked my sisters as well. When they asked me to explain my behavior, I parroted Miss Rosas, saying "We're living in the United States now."

My rebellion against being a Mexican created an uproar. Such conduct was unorthodox, if not scandalous, in a neighborhood where names like Burciaga, Rodríguez, and Castillo predominated. But it wasn't only the Spanish language that I lashed out against.

"Mother, why do we always have to eat *sopa, frijoles refritos, mondongo,* and *pozole?*" I complained. "Can't we ever eat roast beef or ham and eggs like Americans do?"

My mother didn't speak to me for two days after that. My Uncle Rodolfo grimaced and mumbled something about renegade Mexicans who want to eat ham and eggs even though the Montes Packing Company turned out the best *chorizo* this side of Toluca. My sister Consuelo giggled and called me a Rio Grande Irishman, an American Mister, a gringo, and a *bolillo.* Dulce Nombre looked at me worriedly.

Life at home was almost intolerable. Cruel jokes and mocking laughter made it so. I moped around looking sad as a day without bread. My sister

Consuelo suggested I go to the courthouse and change my name to Beloved Wall which is English for Amado Muro. My mother didn't agree. "If Nuestro Señor had meant for Amadito to be an American he would have given him a name like Smeeth or Jonesy," she said. My family was unsympathetic. With a family like mine, how could I ever hope to become an American and win Miss Rosas?

Friday came at last. I put on my only suit, slicked my hair down with liquid vaseline, and doused myself with Dulce Nombre's perfume.

"Amado's going to serenade that pretty girl everyone calls La Americana," my sister Consuelo told my mother and uncle when I sat down to eat. "Then he's going to take her to the movies."

This made my uncle laugh and my mother scowl.

"Quépantalones tiene (what nerve that boy's got)," my uncle said, "to serenade a twenty-year-old woman."

"La Americana," my mother said derisively. "That one's Mexican as pulque cured with celery."

They made so nervous I forgot to take off my cap when I sat down to eat.

"Amado, take off your cap," my mother said. "You're not in La Lagunilla Market."

My uncle frowned. "All this boy thinks about is kissing girls," he said gruffly.

"But my boy's never kissed one," my mother said proudly.

My sister Consuelo laughed. "That's because they won't let him," she said.

This wasn't true. But I couldn't say so in front of my mother. I had already kissed Emalina Uribe from Porfirio Díaz Street not once but twice. Both times I'd kissed her in a darkened doorway less than a block from her home. But the kisses were over so soon we hardly had time to enjoy them. This was because Ema was afraid her big brother, the husky one nicknamed Toro, would see us. But if we'd had more time it would have been better, I knew.

Along about six o'clock the three musicians who called themselves the Mariachis of Tecalitlán came by and whistled for me, just as they had said they would do. They never looked better than they did on that night. They had on black and silver charro uniforms and big black, Zapata sombreros.

My mother shook her head when she saw them. "Son, who ever heard of serenading a girl at six o'clock in the evening," she said. "When your father had the mariachis sing for me it was always at two o'clock in the morning— the only proper time for a six-song gallo."

But I got out my Ramírez guitar anyway. I put on my cap and rushed out to give the mariachis the money without even kissing my mother's hand or waiting for her to bless me. Then we headed for Miss Rosas' home. Some boys and girls I knew were out in the street. This made me uncomfortable. They looked at me wonderingly as I led the mariachi band to Miss Rosas' home.

A block away from Miss Rosas' home I could see her father, a grizzled veteran who fought for Pancho Villa, sitting on the curb reading the Juárez newspaper, *El Fronterizo.*

The sight of him made me slow down for a moment. But I got back in stride when I saw Miss Rosas herself.

She smiled and waved at me. "Hello, Amadito," she said.

"Hello, Señorita Cecilia," I said.

She looked at the miriachis, then back at me.

"Ay, Amado, you're going to serenade your girl," she said. I didn't reply right away. Then when I was getting ready to say "Señorita Cecilia, I came to serenade you," I saw the American man sitting in the sports roadster at the curb.

Miss Rosas turned to him. "I'll be right there, Johnny," she said.

She patted my cheek. "I've got to run now, Amado," she said. "Have a real nice time, darling."

I looked at her silken legs as she got into the car. Everything had happened so fast I was dazed. Broken dreams made my head spin. The contrast between myself and the poised American in the sports roadster was so cruel it made me wince.

She was happy with him. That was obvious. She was smiling and laughing, looking forward to a good time. Why had she asked me to take her to the movies if she already had a boyfriend? Then I remembered how the other salesladies had laughed, how I had wondered why they were laughing when they couldn't even hear what we were saying. And I realized it had all been a joke, everyone had known it but me. Neither Miss Rosas nor the other salesladies had ever dreamed I would think she was serious about wanting me to take her to the movies.

The American and Miss Rosas drove off. Gloomy thoughts oppressed me. They made me want to cry. To get rid of them I thought of going to one of the "bad death" cantinas in Juárez where tequila starts fights and knives finish them—to one of the cantinas where the panders, whom Mexicans call *burros,* stand outside shouting "It's just like Paris, only not so many people" was where I wanted to go. There I could forget her in Jalisco-state style with mariachis, tequila, and night-life women. Then I remembered I was so young that night-life women would shun me and *cantineros* wouldn't serve me tequila.

So I thought some more. Emalina Uribe was the only other alternative. If we went over to Porfirio Díaz Street and serenaded her I could go back to being a Mexican again. She was just as Mexican as I was, Mexican as *chicharrones.* I thought about smiling, freckle-faced Ema.

Ema wasn't like the Americana at all. She wore wash dresses that fitted loosely and even ate the *melcocha* candies Mexicans like so well on the street. On Sundays she wore a Zamora shawl to church and her mother wouldn't let her use lipstick or let her put on high heels.

But with a brother like Toro who didn't like me anyway, such a serenade might be more dangerous than romantic. Besides that, my faith in my looks, my character, or whatever it was that made women fall in love with men, was so undermined I could already picture her getting into a car with a handsome American just like Miss Rosas had done.

The Mariachis of Tecalitlán were getting impatient. They had been paid to sing six songs and they wanted to sing them. But they were all sympathetic. None of them laughed at me.

"Amado, don't look sad as I did the day I learned I'd never be a millionaire," the mariachi captain said, putting his arm around me. "If not that girl, then another."

But without Miss Rosas there was no one we could sing *La Cecilia* to. The street seemed bleak and empty now that she was gone. And I didn't want to serenade Ema Uribe even though she hadn't been faithless as Miss Rosas had been. It was true she hadn't been faithless, but only lack of opportunity would keep her from getting into a car with an American, I reasoned cynically.

Just about then Miss Rosas' father looked up from his newspaper. He asked the mariachis if they knew how to sing *Cananea Jail*. They told him they did. Then they looked at me. I thought it over for a moment. Then I nodded and started strumming the bass strings of my guitar. What had happened made it only too plain I could never trust Miss Rosas again. So we serenaded her father instead.

## American Me
## 1948

### Beatrice Griffith

We go every July from Los Angeles to pick the fruits in the summer hills of Hanford. We lived in tents and would get up early in the grey morning when it was cold. Then we all ate outdoors over a little fire. Everybody getting up from their tents and talking and calling to each other and cooking the beans. Then we go to work and stand on our feet from seven in the morning until six at night. Gee, man, I would get so tired. You know, in the fruits you dream, sleep, walk, breathe, and talk apricots—yellow and big and soft all around

you. You pick 'em, you dump 'em, you squash 'em, you peel 'em, you cut
'em, you count 'em. Everything is apricots. How many you pick? How many
you peel? How much buckets or trays? Always it is to eat and smell apricots.
Cause apricots is pennies and sometimes they are silver dollars after you pick
them a long time. Now we get lots more money in the fruits cause there is a
war, and now we can go to the carnival with rich money like the boss of the
ranch.

This day I tell you the boss came and paid the checks. Man, it was great.
To all the working people and kids he paid them. My father and mother and me
and my brother gots a hundred dollars for working three weeks, would you
believe it? When I saw that check I told my mother she was fooling. The boss
was just playing a game. But she said it was real money, and when I heard
that I jumped up crazy I guess. I told her that check was a lot of school
dresses. She said that in that check was a couch that made a bed at night for
my father and brother who are tired to sleep on the little iron bed by the
washing machine. And it was clothes for my brother and my father, and in it
was a car. Would you believe it? A little broken car was in that check?
And sure it was. Oh I tell you all was happy that for getting money and lots
clothes and food and stuff in that check.

At this camp was my new boy friend, Mokey. He was clean and handsome, not too tall—just right for me with a big smile and a handsome nose.
He always looks like a movie actor in his Levis. And he walks with a swing
real sure, like the Negro baseball player at school who never hurries, just
reaches out and grabs the ball so slow he count the stitches on them. It was
Mokey who helped Freddie and my cousin Ramón fix a good shower for us
when we got to camp. They took some rubber hose and put it up high, then
spread branches to spray from the water. Then they made it private with
boards, and we had a shower. Sure, there was a little hole down by our legs
and the boys used to look in and sing and yell:

> Shakes like a Devil
> Waves like a frog
> When she makes love to me
> Oh hot dog!
> She's fine . . . she's fine,
> Fine and mellow.

That's what they sing. But we had a shower, the only ones.

This night of getting paid was excitement, *Jijola!* All the kids call from
the tents about going to the carnival near Fresno. My old aunt who remembers
the little jamaicas in Mexico, and who is with a young heart still, comes to our
fire to talk over the war, and her boy who is a prisoner in Bataan, and the
long fights and revolutions of the Mexicans, with my father. My aunt is a
very beautiful woman with smooth brown skin and a proud face. She knows
everything, all things in the heart of a girl. She had eight with five in the

grave behind the abode house on the hill. It is like all those dead girls were making her heart sweet with their wants of living in their dark graves. She brought my father a little bottle of her old old wine this night, and he goes with her and my mother to sit by the fire, where others from the fields are sitting and eating under the trees in the night.

My cousin Ramón from Hanford has a little truck that's green and cute named Benito, that will take us to town. To get to this truck and Ramón, Mokey and me walk through the fields to the long dusty road. In the fields was sometimes little rabbits and birds, and there was always haystacks all bunched to jump on real quick and run. With Mokey, he loved those rabbits and sometimes would catch one and rub it soft on his face. Always it was like that. Sometimes he look at a little black fly, so careful how his wings is made, and his head put on by God. And he looks so long at the plants to see their little veins and how is a leaf put on that his sister tell him, "What you see in that plant, a picture of a pretty girl, a blondie maybe?" Then Mokey tell her to go lay an egg—and a big one.

Walking across the fields into the dark hills far away with Mokey was keen. He took my hand and said, "I wish Felix and Frankie could see this sky. Man, they knew this country, they worked this country."

"Mokey, you know lots, what makes wars anyway? All my brothers too are gone to war and they weren't mad at anybody—except the cops." I looked at him but he only shake his head.

"Lucy, I don't know. Sister at church says wars is from all the people's sins. But my mother says it's the big heads make 'em, and the little people slave 'em. I tell her, wars just don't happen. It's from the people bumping and pushing and getting mad at each other, I guess. Maybe they're afraid." He stopped and cut two sunflowers, then he stuck each the one in my braids. "Now let's run, I'll race you to the truck," and so we did.

Inside the truck without much paint was lots kids already. Everybody was happy and singing and calling to everybody, pushing and laughing. All the kids sit tight in the truck cause it goes to pieces lots of times and the sides all fall down. You always hit hard when you drive cause the tires go flat sometimes. Then Ramón and the boys stuff rags into the tires when they go flat so we ride lots of hitting together. Manuel he's my cousin they call Jitterbug Sanchez, cause he's a good dancer and his picture is in the paper for the prize fight, well Manuel brings his good guitar to sing some ranchero songs and some songs for love. All sing "Soldatos Razos," and are happy for smiling and yelling, cause all are happy for living, I guess.

It used to be that when I wanted to make a boy run after me I would give him a pretty little smile, now I throw my head and give him a dirty look— and boy do they run, then I run! But with Mokey it is to sit down, and he puts his arm down and holds my hand tight for fun. I like Mokey lots. Adelita was there too, with ribbons and braids done up on her head like she was going for a dance. Adelita is always throwing looks at the boys, but man they like it, so she just toss her braids and look to see they not run for the flirty Chavella from

Fresno. Adelita and me wear cute little brassières with soft in them so they don't hurt, and the boys can't see so much, but we don't wear pillows in them to make them stick up. I wear my God skin and no cheating.

When we come onto the long highway that goes to Hanford this night I tell you about, two policemen in their white car stopped the truck because they see us Mexicans inside. But my cousin Ramón, who's been to high school and who is smart knowing all about maps and what means a filibuster and the United States Congress, says to that cop, "This is a free country ain't it? We can sing in this little truck if we want can't we? Who says Mexicans can't sing for breaking the law in this truck doesn't know his country."

So the cops, seeing my cousin was smart said, "Oh, wise guy, huh? Okay, let's see your draft cards. All of you."

But only my cousin had a card from the draft, only he was eighteen. The cops look hard at his draft card and then tells us, "Okay, cholos, go on."

And so we go down the long bright highway into the streets of the town. Lots of people and kids were holding hands and walking down the streets. Little cars from the ranches and fruit camps passed us, some fast with only one light, some honking horns, but everybody was laughing and calling. Mokey waves his arms and says some dirty words to the car in back of us that gives us a big bump. The boys all pile out to look, then pile in again when they see it was nothing.

Pretty soon we come to the carnival. You know it's the place before you get there cause the music comes right through the trees and houses and into our truck. And you can see high up in the pink sky the ferris wheel going swing around the stars. And the voice of the ticket man you can hear a little, just like the radio from the boss's house in the night on the ranch. Only sometimes you cannot hear it with the crickets, like it went around the posts and cars and barns to get to us who were listening.

At the carnival everything was excitement, and all the kids pile out. First thing I see is my cousin Danny. My cousin Danny, I tell you, was fun like Cantinflas in the Mexican movies. Gee, man, he is so dirty it's a ten-to-one shot the dirt grows from one week on his face, and his pants and shirt gots a big tore in them, and he never never take a bathe. But always he is laughing, and for giving money, and always I tell you he is singing. And Danny is the only kid I know who can make rich money out of poor money.

The popcorn man saw Danny and called him, "Peanuts, popcorn, five cents, only five cents . . . peanuts, popcorn . . . *piñones.*"

But what the popcorn man don't know is that Danny only had some poor money this night, five pennies he had. Danny called him with a smile and say, "How much fifteen bags of popcorn with butter coming through the sack?"

So the popcorn man get his pencil from under his apron and write the figures on a pink striped sack. "Seventy-five cents for fifteen sacks with the butter coming through," he tells Danny.

So my cousin tells him thanks he wasn't good for arithmetic in school, only he always wanted to know how much fifteen bags of popcorn was. Then he laugh and say, "Keep the bags. I'll be back and make you rich, old man."

But the man was mad and spilled the popcorn white from the sack on the ground.

The flying baskets with shirts and legs swinging in the sky stopped, and Mokey and me got in a gold basket. Adelita and Manuel sit in a red one, and soon the music begin and we are whizzing in the sky with all the stars falling around and down down to the ground. Then we jerked up high almost to a pink cloud, and Mokey held me tight, with the air whirring around us like a dive bomber. There was little screams coming from around like they was whistles that got stuck, but it was only the girls liking the hugging I think.

When we got out from the gold basket Mokey and me was still hugging like in the movies. All the peoples and tents and music and little screams was going around dancing in my head like a jitterbug. Up the streets some kids was riding on the merry-go-round and yelling and laughing to catch the gold ring from the horses and lions. Mokey and me watched Felix showing how strong he was from working and getting hard muscles in the hay fields that summer. He hit the wood block bang with the big hammer, and hit it so hard the little bell at the top in the dark would ring. The other guys was laughing and making fun of him showing off big for Theresa, him that didn't know she was going steady with two marines.

The tin woman in the next show was laughing too, but always she is laughing. Whenever you walk or ride in that carnival, or down the near streets, you hear her big laugh, in the night or day, you always hear it.

Across the carnival street, behind the wire fence, was the place where the little green and yellow and red automobiles go bump and crash around the big floor with music and fun. In one of the automobiles was an old man with red hair waving his arms and bumping the other autos like a borrachito. He had a white duck he won in the carnival and waved that duck over his head like a flag I think.

Pretty soon down the carnival street come all the kids singing and laughing and shouting. All their arms was around each other like a chain. In the middle was Danny with his arms full of Kewpie dolls. He had Kewpie feathers in his dirty green shirt and over his ears. His pants was falling down from the string that was a belt. There was some Kewpies in his belt too. Around his neck was a clock he won. Danny was happy like nobody I ever seen in my life. He was like Flip Corkin. Everybody loved him and wanted to be his friend. But he only laugh and say he was taking all the Kewpies home for the Virgin Mary who stands on the little wooden shelf by his bed. All the girls love him and he throws them a big look, but is not caring for nothing but to laugh and sing.

Danny was always like the miracle man in the circus. Always he could go to a carnival with nothing but poor money, some pennies and nickels, and come home with hams and ducks and alarm clocks and Kewpies. Only never before tonight was there so many Kewpies.

He gave a Kewpie to Mokey for some tickets to ride the little automobiles. Then he yelled us, "Come on, let's have a race!"

We all piled in the cars, red, green, yellow—all the cars that was empty gots full. Danny put all his Kewpie dolls around him and piled some more in the other cars. Then the race began. *Qué suave.* Man it was swell. My heart was pumping up and down like some jumping beans. I got scared bumping so many cars and my heart went black and my ears go clank . . . clank, but it was fun.

Danny banged my car, Mokey hit him, then Manuel and Adelita and Ramón and Rosie all was banging cars and yelling. Everybody got bumped, nobody got hurt and the music was loud like in the circus. The American kid bumped Mokey and laughed, and Mokey bumped him back. Then they was bumping, laughing and pushing, each car a little faster and a little harder. Pretty soon then the American guy looked away, and Mokey gave him a hard bump. Then they was getting mad for reals. The American kid called him, "Dirty Mexican, I'll fix you!"

Mokey tell him, "Who do you think you are, calling me dirty Mexican?"

The guy banged him hard and say, "Well, I'm me American me. That's who I am!"

So Mokey banged him hard on the head with a pink Kewpie and yell him, "Yeah? Well I'm American me too. American inside, but Mexican on top!"

Danny throws a Kewpie to Mokey who jumps high in his car to catch it. Then all the kids begin to make trouble for purpose, all bunching and popping out of the cars to fight and hit. Danny throws us all his Kewpies, and the fight was on hard. The Kewpies was going over the cars hitting kids, busting on the floor with broken pieces getting smashed and run over. Everybody was mad with anger falling down and busting like a bomb in that place. The Kewpies was going zoom like big bullets. The cars was driving hard and spinning and bumping. Adelita's car she whirled in a circle, round and round. The air was thick and hot with kids. Some stand up in their cars the better to hit. The cars all jammed up in bunches. Everybody was all mixed up and tangled, hitting hard, zam the next one to him.

The manager or somebody cut off the electricity. Ramón yells, "Cops coming!"

Then it was a fight to get out that door with everybody running and tripping and getting socked. The American kids beat it out first, running through all the carnival people to where their cars was parked. We got in our truck, but before Ramón got the engine started everything was all mixed up again, with the American kids and us all yelling and hitting and pulling hair and getting socked. But we finally got going and drove bumping down the street by the popcorn man and the carnival people. Some of those kids was hanging on the truck but we banged their hands and they let go.

Ramón drove fast going down that big road in our truck. Danny turned off the lights so the cops wouldn't see our truck and we rode into the very night across the fields to the highway. Like Danny, Mokey's hands was bloody and his clothes was torn, and his breath was breathing hard—but he put his arms tight around me in that little ride.

It was quiet in the dark with the trees and fields and hills. Only could we hear the kids whispering and the car going fast like the wind, and the loud crazy laughing of the tin woman at the carnival following us down the road into the mist to our tents across the black fields.

Soon we would be in bed in our tents by the camp in the fruits, and I would put my head from under the tent and Mokey put his from his tent in the dark and stars, and we would talk and talk so long, our heads by the dark ground. All swell, until our mothers say, "Quit your talking and long gossip." And then we would go to sleep in the warm tent for morning to wake us to move on to pick the prunes.

But now, this little minute, I was sitting tight close to Mokey. I ask him, "Mokey, knowing about pushing and bumping and hating and all that, doesn't keep people from getting mad, huh?"

Mokey hugs me tighter. Then he kissed me soft soft, the first kiss. For Mokey knows that to be a gentleman means always please the lady for what she wants.

## The Odyssey of a Wop
### 1933

### John Fante

I pick up little bits of information about my grandfather. My grandmother tells me of him. She tells me that when he lived he was a good fellow whose goodness evoked not admiration but pity. He was known as a good little Wop. Of an evening he liked to sit at a table in a saloon sipping a tumbler of anisette, all by himself. He sat there like a little girl nipping an ice-cream cone. The old boy loved that green stuff, that anisette. It was his passion, and when folks saw him sitting alone it tickled them, for he was a good little Wop.

One night, my grandmother tells me, my grandfather was sitting in the saloon, he and his anisette. A drunken teamster stumbled through the swinging doors, braced himself at the bar, and bellowed:

"All right, everybody! Come an' get 'em! They're on me!"

And there sat my grandfather, not moving, his old tongue coquetting with the anisette. Everyone but he stood at the bar and drank the teamster's liquor. The teamster swung round. He saw my grandfather. He was insulted.

"You too, Wop!" said he. "Come up and drink!"

Silence. My grandfather arose. He staggered across the floor, passed the teamster, and then what did he do but go through the swinging doors and down the snowy street! He heard laughter coming after him from the saloon and his chest burned. He went home to my father.

*"Mamma mia,"* he blubbered. "Tummy Murray, he calla me Wopa."

*"Sangue de la Madonna!"*

Bareheaded, my father rushed down the street to the saloon. Tommy Murray was not there. He was in another saloon half a block away, and there my father found him. He drew the teamster aside and spoke under his breath. A fight! Immediately blood and hair began to fly. Chairs were drawn back. The customers applauded. The two men fought for an hour. They rolled over the floor, kicking, cursing, biting. They were in a knot in the center of the floor, their bodies wrapped around each other. My father's head, chest and arms buried the teamster's face. The teamster screamed. My father growled. His neck was rigid and trembling. The teamster screamed again, and lay still. My father got to his feet and wiped blood from his open mouth with the back of his hand. On the floor the teamster lay with a loose ear hanging from his head. . . . This is the story my grandmother tells me.

I think about the two men, my father and the teamster, and I picture them struggling on the floor. Boy! *Can* my father fight!

I get an idea. My two brothers are playing in another room. I leave my grandmother and go to them. They are sprawled on the rug, bent over crayons and drawing-paper. They look up and see my face flaming with my idea.

"What's wrong?" one asks.

"I dare you to do something!"

"Do what?"

"I dare you to call me a Wop!"

My youngest brother, barely four, jumps to his feet, and dancing up and down, screams, "Wop! Wop! Wop! Wop!"

I look at him. Pooh! He's too small. It's that other brother, that bigger brother, I want. He's got ears too, he has.

"I bet *you're* afraid to call me Wop."

But he senses the devil in the woodpile.

"Nah," says he. "I don't wanna."

"Wop! Wop! Wop! Wop!" screams the little brother.

"Shut your mouth, you!"

"I won't neither. You're a Wop! Wop! Woppedy Wop!"

My older brother's box of crayons lies on the floor in front of his nose. I put my heel upon the box and grind it into the carpet. He yells, seizing my leg. I back away, and he begins to cry.

"Aw, that was sure dirty," he says.

"I dare you to call me a Wop!"

"Wop!"

I charged, seeking his ear. But my grandmother comes into the room flourishing a razor-strop.

## II

From the beginning, I hear my mother use the words Wop and Dago with such vigor as to denote violent disrepute. She spits them out. They leap from her lips. To her, they contain the essence of poverty, squalor, filth. If I don't wash my teeth, or hang up my cap, my mother says, "Don't be like that. Don't be a Wop." Thus, as I begin to acquire her values, Wop and Dago to me become synonymous with things evil. But she's consistent.

My father isn't. He's loose with his tongue. His moods create his judgments. I at once notice that to him Wop and Dago are without any distinct meaning, though if one not an Italian slaps them on to him, he's instantly insulted. Christopher Columbus was the greatest Wop who ever lived, says my father. So is Caruso. So is this fellow and that. But his very good friend Peter Ladonna is not only a drunken pig, but a Wop on top of it; and of course all his brothers-in-law are good-for-nothing Wops.

He pretends to hate the Irish. He really doesn't, but he likes to think so, and he warns us children against them. Our grocer's name is O'Neil. Frequently and inadvertently he makes errors when my mother is at his store. She tells my father about short weights in meats, and now and then of a stale egg.

Straightway, my father grows tense, his lower lip curling. "This is the last time that Irish bum robs me!" And he goes out, goes to the grocery-store, his heels booming.

Soon he returns. He's smiling. His fists bulge with cigars. "From now on," says he, "everything's gonna be all right."

I don't like the grocer. My mother sends me to his store every day, and instantly he chokes up my breathing with the greeting, "Hello, you little Dago! What'll you have?" So I detest him, and never enter his store if other customers are to be seen, for to be called a Dago before others is a ghastly, almost a physical humiliation. My stomach expands and recedes, and I feel naked.

I steal recklessly when the grocer's back is turned. I enjoy stealing from him: candy bars, cookies, fruit. When he goes into his refrigerator I lean on his meat scales, hoping to snap a spring; I press my toe into egg baskets. Sometimes I pilfer too much. Then, what a pleasure it is to stand on the curb, my appetite gorged, and heave *his* candy bars, *his* cookies, *his* apples into the high yellow weeds across the street. . . . "Damn you, O'Neil, you can't call me a Dago and get away with it!"

His daughter is of my age. She's cross-eyed. Twice a week she passes our house on her way to her music lesson. Above the street, and high in the branches of an elm tree, I watch her coming down the sidewalk, swinging her violin case. When she is under me, I jeer in sing-song:

Martha's crooooooss-eyed!
Martha's crooooooss-eyed!
Martha's crooooooss-eyed!

## III

As I grow older I find out that Italians use Wop and Dago much more than Americans. My grandmother, whose vocabulary of English is confined to the commonest of nouns, always employs them in discussing contemporary Italians. The words never come forth quietly, unobtrusively. No; they bolt forth. There is a blatant intonation, and then in the sense of someone being scathed, stunned.

I enter the parochial school with an awful fear that I will be called Wop. As soon as I find out why people have such things as surnames, I match my own against such typically Italian cognomens as Bianci, Borello, Pacelli—the names of other students. I am pleasantly relieved by the comparison. After all, I think, people will say I am French. Doesn't my name sound French? Sure! So thereafter, when people ask my nationality, I tell them I am French. A few boys begin calling me Frenchy. I like that. It feels fine.

Thus I begin to loathe my heritage. I avoid Italian boys and girls who try to be friendly. I thank God for my light skin and hair, and I choose my companions by the Anglo-Saxon ring of their names. If a boy's name is Whitney, Brown, or Smythe, then he's my pal; but I'm always a little breathless when I am with him; he may find me out. At the lunch hour I huddle over my lunch pail, for my mother doesn't wrap my sandwiches in wax paper, and she makes them too large, and the lettuce leaves protrude. Worse, the bread is homemade; not bakery bread, not "American" bread. I make a great fuss because I can't have mayonnaise and other "American" things.

The parish priest is a good friend of my father's. He comes strolling through the school grounds, watching the children at play. He calls to me and asks about my father, and then he tells me I should be proud to be studying about my great countrymen, Columbus, Vespucci, John Cabot. He speaks in a loud, humorous voice. Students gather around us, listening, and I bite my lips and wish to Jesus he'd shut up and move on.

Occasionally now I hear about a fellow named Dante. But when I find out that he was an Italian I hate him as if he were alive and walking through the classrooms, pointing a finger at me. One day I find his picture in a dictionary. I look at it and tell myself that never have I seen an uglier bastard.

We students are at the blackboard one day, and a soft-eyed Italian girl whom I hate but who insists that I am her beau stands beside me. She twitches and shuffles about uneasily, half on tiptoe, smiling queerly at me. I sneer and turn my back, moving as far away from her as I can. The nun sees the wide space separating us and tells me to move nearer the girl. I do so, and the girl draws away, nearer the student on her other side.

Then I look down at my feet, and there I stand in a wet, spreading spot.

I look quickly at the girl, and she hangs her head and looks at me in a way that begs me to take the blame for her. We attract the attention of others, and the classroom becomes alive with titters. Here comes the nun. I think I am in for it again, but she embraces me and murmurs that I should have raised two fingers and of course I would have been allowed to leave the room. But, says she, there's no need for that now; the thing for me to do is go out and get the mop. I do so, and amid the hysteria I nurse my conviction that only a Wop girl, right out of a Wop home, would ever do such a thing as this.

Oh, you Wop! Oh, you Dago! You bother me even when I sleep. I dream of defending myself against tormentors. One day I learn from my mother that my father went to the Argentine in his youth, and lived in Buenos Aires for two years. My mother tells me of his experiences there, and all day I think about them, even to the time I go to sleep. That night I come awake with a jerk. In the darkness I grope to my mother's room. My father sleeps at her side, and I awaken her gently, so that he won't be aroused.

I whisper, "Are you sure Papa wasn't *born* in Argentina?"

"No. Your father was born in Italy."

I go back to bed, disconsolate and disgusted.

## IV

During a ball game on the school grounds, a boy who plays on the opposing team begins to ridicule my playing. It is the ninth inning, and I ignore his taunts. We are losing the game, but if I can knock out a hit our chances of winning are pretty strong. I am determined to come through, and I face the pitcher confidently. The tormentor sees me at the plate.

"Ho! Ho!" he shouts. "Look who's up! The Wop's up. Let's get rid of the Wop!"

This is the first time anyone at school has ever flung that word at me, and I am so angry that I strike out foolishly. We fight after the game, this boy and I, and I make him take it back.

Now school days become fighting days. Nearly every afternoon at 3:15 a crowd gathers to watch me make some guy take it back. This is fun; I am getting somewhere now, so come on, you guys, I dare you to call me a Wop! When at length there are no more boys who challenge me, insults come to me by hearsay, and I seek out the culprits. I strut down the corridors. The smaller boys admire me. "Here he comes!" they say, and they gaze and gaze. My two younger brothers attend the same school, and the smallest, a little squirt, seven years old, brings his friends to me and asks me to roll up my sleeve and show them my muscles. Here you are, boys. Look me over.

My brother brings home furious accounts of my battles. My father listens voraciously, and I stand by, to clear up any doubtful details. Sadly happy days! My father gives me pointers; how to hold my fist, how to guard my head. My mother, too shocked to hear more, presses her temples and squeezes her eyes and leaves the room.

I am nervous when I bring friends to my house; the place looks so Italian. Here hangs a picture of Victor Emmanuel, and over there is one of the cathedral of Milan, and next to it, one of St. Peter's, and on the buffet stands a wine-pitcher of medieval design; it's forever brimming, forever red and brilliant with wine. These things are heirlooms belonging to my father, and no matter who may come to our house, he likes to stand under them and brag.

So I begin to shout at him. I tell him to cut out being a Wop and be an American once in a while. Immediately he gets his razor-strop and whales hell out of me, clouting me from room to room and finally out the back door. I go into the woodshed and pull down my pants and stretch my neck to examine the blue slices across my rump. A Wop! that's what my father is! Nowhere is there an American father who beats his son this way. Well, he's not going to get away with it; some day I'll get even with him.

I begin to think that my grandmother is hopelessly a Wop. She's a small, stocky peasant who walks with her wrists criss-crossed her belly, a simple old lady and fond of boys. She comes into the room and tries to talk to my friends. She speaks English with a bad accent, her vowels rolling out like hoops. When, in her simple way, she confronts a friend of mine and says, her old eyes smiling. "You lika go the Seester scola?" my heart roars. *Mannaggia!* I'm disgraced; now they all know that I'm an Italian.

My grandmother has taught me to speak her native tongue. By seven, I know it pretty well, and I always address her in it. But when friends are with me, when I am twelve and thirteen, I pretend to ignorance of what she says, and smirk stiffly; my friends daren't know that I can speak any language but English. Sometimes this infuriates her. She bristles, the loose skin at her throat knits hard, and she blasphemes with a mighty blasphemy.

## V

When I finish in the parochial school my people decide to send me to a Jesuit academy in another city. My father comes with me on the first day. Chiseled into the stone coping that skirts the roof of the main building of the academy is the Latin inscription: *Religioni et Bonis Artibus.* My father and I stand at a distance, and he reads it aloud and tells me what it means.

I look up at him in amazement. Is this man my father? Why, look at him! He reads with an Italian inflection! He's wearing an Italian mustache. I have never realized it until this moment, but he looks exactly like a Wop. His suit hangs carelessly in wrinkles upon him. Why the deuce doesn't he buy a new one? And look at his tie! It's crooked. And his shoes: they need a shine. And for the Lord's sake, will you look at his pants! They're not even buttoned in front. And oh, damn, damn, damn, you can see those dirty old suspenders that he won't throw away. Say, mister, are you really my father? you there, why, you're such a little guy, such a runt, such an old-looking fellow! You look exactly like one of those immigrants carrying a blanket. You can't be *my* father! Why, I thought, . . . I've always thought . . .

I'm crying now, the first time I've ever cried for any reason except a licking, and I'm glad he's not crying too. I'm glad he's as tough as he is, and we say goodbye quickly, and I go down the path quickly, and I do not turn to look back, for I know he's standing there and looking at me.

I enter the administration building and stand in line with strange boys who also wait to register for the Autumn term. Some Italian boys stand among them. I am away from home and I sense the Italians. We look at one another and our eyes meet in an irresistible amalgamation, a suffusive consanguinity; I look away.

A burly Jesuit rises from his chair behind the desk and introduces himself to me. Such a voice for a man! There are a dozen thunderstorms in his chest. He asks my name, and writes it down on a little card.

"Nationality?" he roars.

"American."

"Your father's name?"

I whisper it, "Luigi."

"How's that? Spell it out. Talk louder."

I cough. I touch my lips with the back of my hand and spell out the name.

"Ha!" shouts the registrar. "And still they come! Another Wop! Well, young man, you'll be at home here! Yes sir! Lots of Wops here! We've even got kikes! And, you know, this place reeks with shanty Irish!"

*Dio!* How I hate that priest!

He continues, "where was your father born?"

"Buenos Aires, Argentina."

"Your mother?"

At last I can shout with the gusto of truth.

"Chi-cag-oo!" Aye, just like a conductor.

Casually, by way of conversation, he asks, "You speak Italian?"

"Nah! Not a word."

"Too bad," he says.

"You're nuts," I think.

## VI

That semester I wait on table to defray my tuition fee. Trouble ahead; the chef and his assistants in the kitchen are all Italians. They know at once that I am of the breed. I ignore the chef's friendly overtures, loathing him from the first. He understands why, and we become enemies. Every word he uses has a knife in it. His remarks cut me to pieces. After two months I can stand it no longer in the kitchen, and so I write a long letter to my mother; I am losing weight, I write; if you don't let me quit this job, I'll get sick and flunk my tests. She telegraphs me some money and tells me to quit at once; oh, I feel so sorry for you, my boy; I didn't dream it would be so hard on you.

I decided to work just one more evening, to wait on table for just one more meal. That evening, after the meal, when the kitchen is deserted save for the cook and his assistants, I take off my apron and take my stand across the kitchen from him, staring at him. This is my moment. Two months I have waited for this moment. There is a knife stuck into the chopping block. I pick it up, still staring. I want to hurt the cook, square things up.

He sees me, and he says, "Get out of here, Wop!"

An assistant shouts, "Look out, he's got a knife!"

"You won't throw it, Wop," the cook says. I am not thinking of throwing it, but since he says I won't, I do. It goes over his head and strikes the wall and drops with a clatter to the floor. He picks it up and chases me out of the kitchen. I run, thanking God I didn't hit him.

That year the football team is made up of Irish and Italian boys. The linemen are Irish, and we in the backfield are four Italians. We have a good team and win a lot of games, and my team-mates are excellent players who are unselfish and work together as one man. But I hate my three fellow-players in the backfield; because of our nationality, we seem ridiculous. The team makes a captain of me, and I call signals and see to it my fellow-Italians in the backfield do as little scoring as possible. I hog the play.

The school journal and the town's sport pages begin to refer to us as the Wop Wonders. I think it an insult. Late one afternoon, at the close of an important game, a number of students leave the main grandstand and group themselves at one end of the field, to improvise some yells. They give three big ones for the Wop Wonders. It sickens me. I can feel my stomach move; and after that game I turn in my suit and quit the team.

I am a bad Latinist. Disliking the language, I do not study, and therefore I flunk my examinations regularly. Now a student comes to me and tells me that it is possible to drop Latin from my curriculum if I follow his suggestion, which is that I fail deliberately in the next few examinations, fail hopelessly. If I do this, the student says, the Jesuits will bow to my stupidity and allow me to abandon the language.

This is an agreeable suggestion. I follow it out. But it backtracks, for the Jesuits are wise fellows. They see what I'm doing, and they laugh and tell me that I am not clever enough to fool them, and that I must keep on studying Latin, even if it takes me twenty years to pass. Worse, they double my assignments and I spend my recreation time with Latin syntax. Before examinations in my junior year the Jesuit who instructs me calls me to his room and says:

"It is a mystery to me that a thoroughbred Italian like yourself should have any trouble with Latin. The language is in your blood, and believe me, you're a darned poor Wop."

*Abbastanzia!* I go upstairs and lock my door and sit down with my book in front of me, my Latin book, and I study like a wild man, tearing crazily into the stuff until, lo! What is this? What am I studying here? Sure enough, it's a lot like the Italian my grandmother taught me so long ago—this Latin, it isn't so hard, after all. I pass the examination. I pass it with such an incredibly fine grade that my instructor thinks there is knavery somewhere.

Two weeks before graduation I get sick and go to the infirmary and am quarantined there. I lie in bed and feed my grudges. I bite my thumbs and ponder old grievances. I am running a high fever, and I can't sleep. I think about the principal. He was my close friend during my first two years at the school, but in my third year, last year, he was transferred to another school in the Province. I lie in bed thinking of the day we met again in this, the last year. We met again on his return that September, in the principal's room. He said hello to the boys, this fellow and that, and then he turned to me, and said:

"And you, the Wop? So you're still with us."

Coming from the mouth of the priest, the word had a lumpish sound that shook me all over. I felt the eyes of everyone, and I heard a giggle. So that's how it is! I lie in bed thinking of the priest and now of the fellow who giggled.

All of a sudden I jump out of bed, tear the fly-leaf from a book, find a pencil and write a note to the priest. I write, "Dear Father: I haven't forgotten your insult. You called me a Wop last September. If you don't apologize right away there's going to be trouble." I call the brother in charge of the infirmary and tell him to deliver the note to the priest.

After a while I hear the priest's footsteps rising on the stairs. He comes to the door of my room, opens it, looks at me for a long time, not speaking, but only looking querulously. I wait for him to come in and apologize, for this is a grand moment for me. But he closes the door quietly and walks away. I am astonished. A double insult!

I am well again on the night of graduation. On the platform the principal makes a speech and then begins to distribute the diplomas. We're supposed to say, "Thank you," when he gives them to us. So thank you, and thank you, and thank you, everyone says in his turn. But when he gives me mine, I look squarely at him, just stand there and look, and I don't say anything, and from that day we never speak to each other again.

The following September I enroll at the university.

"Where was your father born?" asks the registrar.

"Buenos Aires, Argentina."

Sure, that's it. The same theme, with variations.


## VII

Time passes, and so do school days.

I am sitting on a wall along the plaza, watching a Mexican *fiesta* across the street. A man comes along and lifts himself to the wall beside me, and asks if I have a cigarette. I have, and lighting the cigarette, he makes conversation with me, and we talk of casual things until the *fiesta* is over. Then we get down from the wall, and still talking, go walking through the Los Angeles Tenderloin. This man needs a shave and his clothes do not fit him; it's plain that he's a bum. He tells one lie upon another, and not one is well told. But I am lonesome in this town, and a glad listener.

We step into a restaurant for coffee. Now he becomes intimate. He has bummed his way from Chicago to Los Angeles, and has come in search of his sister; he has her address, but she is not at it, and for two weeks he has been looking for her in vain. He talks on and on about this sister, seeming to gyrate like a buzzard over her, hinting to me that I should ask some questions about her. He wants me to touch off the fuse that will release his feelings.

So I ask, "Is she married?"

And then he rips into her, hammer and tongs. Even if he does find her, he will not live with her. What kind of a sister is she to let him walk these streets without a dime in his pocket, and she married to a man who has plenty of money and can give him a job? He thinks she has deliberately given him a false address so that he will not find her, and when he gets his hands on her he's going to wring her neck. In the end, after he has completely demolished her, he does exactly what I think he is going to do.

He asks, "Have *you* got a sister?"

I tell him yes, and he waits for my opinion of her; but he doesn't get it.

We meet again a week later.

He has found his sister. Now he begins to praise her. She had induced her husband to give him a job, and tomorrow he goes to work as a waiter in his brother-in-law's restaurant. He tells me the address, but I do not think more of it beyond the fact that it must be somewhere in the Italian Quarter.

And so it is, and by a strange coincidence I know his brother-in-law, Rocco Saccone, an old friend of my people and a *paesano* of my father's. I am in Rocco's place one night a fortnight later. Rocco and I are speaking in Italian when the man I have met on the plaza steps out of the kitchen, an apron over his legs. Rocco calls him and he comes over, and Rocco introduces him as his brother-in-law from Chicago. We shake hands.

"We've met before," I say, but the plaza man doesn't seem to want this known, for he lets go my hand quickly and goes behind the counter, pretending to be busy with something back there. Oh, he's bluffing; you can see that.

In a loud voice, Rocco says to me, "That man is a skunk. He's ashamed of his own flesh and blood." He turns to the plaza man.

"Ain't you?"

"Oh, yeah?" the plaza man sneers.

"How do you mean—he's ashamed? How do you mean?"

"Ashamed of being an Italian," Rocco says.

"Oh, yeah?" from the plaza man.

"That's all he knows," Rocco says. "Oh, yeah? That's all he knows. Oh, yeah? Oh, yeah? Oh, yeah? That's all he knows."

"Oh, yeah?" the plaza man says again.

"Yah," Rocco says, his face blue. *"Animale codardo!"*

The plaza man looks at me with peaked eyebrows, and he doesn't know it, he standing there with his black, liquid eyes, he doesn't know that he's as good as a god in his waiter's apron; for he is indeed a god, a miracle worker; no, he doesn't know; no one knows; just the same, he is that—he, of all people. Standing there and looking at him, I feel like my grandfather and my father and the Jesuit cook and Rocco; I seem to have come home, and I am surprised that this return, which I have somehow always expected, should come so quietly, without trumpets and thunder.

"If I were you, I'd get rid of him," I say to Rocco.

"Oh yeah?" the plaza man says again.

I'd like to paste him. But that won't do any good. There's no sense in hammering your own corpse.

---

## Winter Dreams

### 1922

---

### F. Scott Fitzgerald

---

Some of the caddies were poor as sin and lived in one-room houses with a neurasthenic cow in the front yard, but Dexter Green's father owned the second best grocery-story in Black Bear—the best one was "The Hub," patronized by the wealthy people from Sherry Island—and Dexter caddied only for pocket-money.

In the fall when the days became crisp and gray, and the long Minnesota winter shut down like the white lid of a box, Dexter's skis moved over the snow that hid the fairways of the golf course. At these times the country gave him a feeling of profound melancholy—it offended him that the links should lie in enforced fallowness, haunted by ragged sparrows for the long season. It was dreary, too, that on tees where the gay colors fluttered in summer there were now only the desolate sandboxes knee-deep in crusted ice. When he crossed the hills the wind blew cold as misery, and if the sun was out he tramped with his eyes squinted up against the hard dimensionless glare.

In April the winter ceased abruptly. The snow ran down into Black Bear Lake scarcely tarrying for the early golfers to brave the season with red and black balls. Without elation, without an interval of moist glory, the cold was gone.

Dexter knew that there was something dismal about this Northern spring, just as he knew there was something gorgeous about the fall. Fall made him clinch his hands and tremble and repeat idiotic sentences to himself, and make brisk abrupt gestures of command to imaginary audiences and armies. October filled him with hope which November raised to a sort of ecstatic triumph, and in this mood the fleeting brilliant impressions of the summer at Sherry Island were ready grist to his mill. He became a golf champion and defeated Mr. T. A. Hedrick in a marvellous match played a hundred times over the fairways of his imagination, a match each detail of which he changed about untiringly—sometimes won with almost laughable ease, sometimes he came up magnificently from behind. Again, stepping from a Pierce-Arrow automobile, like Mr. Mortimer Jones, he strolled frigidly into the lounge of the Sherry Island Golf Club—or perhaps, surrounded by an admiring crowd, he gave an exhibition of fancy diving from the spring-board of the club raft. . . . Among those who watched him in open-mouthed wonder was Mr. Mortimer Jones.

And one day it came to pass that Mr. Jones—himself and not his ghost —came up to Dexter with tears in his eyes and said that Dexter was the —— best caddy in the club, and wouldn't he decide not to quit if Mr. Jones made it worth his while, because every other —— caddy in the club lost one ball a hole for him—regularly——

"No, sir," said Dexter decisively, "I don't want to caddy any more." Then, after a pause: "I'm too old."

"You're not more than fourteen. Why the devil did you decide just this morning that you wanted to quit? You promised that next week you'd go over to the state tournament with me."

"I decided I was too old."

Dexter handed in his "A Class" badge, collected what money was due him from the caddy master, and walked home to Black Bear Village.

"The best —— caddy I ever saw," shouted Mr. Mortimer Jones over a drink that afternoon. "Never lost a ball! Willing! Intelligent! Quiet! Honest! Grateful!"

The little girl who had done this was eleven—beautifully ugly as little girls are apt to be who are destined after a few years to be inexpressibly lovely and bring no end of misery to a great number of men. The spark, however, was perceptible. There was a general ungodliness in the way her lips twisted down at the corners when she smiled, and in the—Heaven help us!—in the almost passionate quality of her eyes. Vitality is born early in such women. It was utterly in evidence now, shining through her thin frame in a sort of glow.

She had come eagerly out on to the course at nine o'clock with a white linen nurse and five small new golf-clubs in a white canvas bag which the nurse was carrying. When Dexter first saw her she was standing by the caddy house, rather ill at ease and trying to conceal the fact by engaging her nurse in an obviously unnatural conversation graced by startling and irrelevant grimaces from herself.

"Well, it's certainly a nice day, Hilda," Dexter heard her say. She drew down the corners of her mouth, smiled, and glanced furtively around, her eyes in transit falling for an instant on Dexter.

Then to the nurse:

"Well, I guess there aren't very many people out here this morning, are there?"

The smile again—radiant, blatantly artificial—convincing.

"I don't know what we're supposed to do now," said the nurse, looking nowhere in particular.

"Oh, that's all right. I'll fix it up."

Dexter stood perfectly still, his mouth slightly ajar. He knew that if he moved forward a step his stare would be in her line of vision—if he moved backward he would lose his full view of her face. For a moment he had not realized how young she was. Now he remembered having seen her several times the year before—in bloomers.

Suddenly, involuntarily, he laughed, a short abrupt laugh—then, startled by himself, he turned and began to walk quickly away.

"Boy!"

Dexter stopped.

"Boy——"

Beyond question he was addressed. Not only that, but he was treated to that absurd smile, that preposterous smile—the memory of which at least a dozen men were to carry into middle age.

"Boy, do you know where the golf teacher is?"

"He's giving a lesson."

"Well, do you know where the caddy-master is?"

"He isn't here yet this morning."

"Oh." For a moment this baffled her. She stood alternately on her right and left foot.

"We'd like to get a caddy," said the nurse. "Mrs. Mortimer Jones sent us out to play golf, and we don't know how without we get a caddy."

Here she was stopped by an ominous glance from Miss Jones, followed immediately by the smile.

"There aren't any caddies here except me," said Dexter to the nurse, "and I got to stay here in charge until the caddy-master gets here."

"Oh."

Miss Jones and her retinue now withdrew, and at a proper distance from Dexter became involved in a heated conversation, which was concluded by Miss Jones taking one of the clubs and hitting it on the ground with violence. For further emphasis she raised it again and was about to bring it down smartly upon the nurse's bosom, when the nurse seized the club and twisted it from her hands.

"You damn little mean old *thing!*" cried Miss Jones wildly.

Another argument ensued. Realizing that the elements of the comedy were implied in the scene, Dexter several times began to laugh, but each time restrained the laugh before it reached audibility. He could not resist the monstrous conviction that the little girl was justified in beating the nurse.

The situation was resolved by the fortuitous appearance of the caddy-master, who was appealed to immediately by the nurse.

"Miss Jones is to have a little caddy, and this one says he can't go."

"Mr. McKenna said I was to wait here till you came," said Dexter quickly.

"Well, he's here now." Miss Jones smiled cheerfully at the caddy-master. Then she dropped her bag and set off at a haughty mince toward the first tee.

"Well?" The caddy-master turned to Dexter. "What you standing there like a dummy for? Go pick up the young lady's clubs."

"I don't think I'll go out to-day," said Dexter.

"You don't——"

"I think I'll quit."

The enormity of his decision frightened him. He was a favorite caddy, and the thirty dollars a month he earned through the summer were not to be made elsewhere around the lake. But he had received a strong emotional shock, and his perturbation required a violent and immediate outlet.

It is not so simple as that, either. As so frequently would be the case in the future, Dexter was unconsciously dictated to by his winter dreams.

## II

Now, of course, the quality and the seasonability of these winter dreams varied, but the stuff of them remained. They persuaded Dexter several years later to pass up a business course at the State university—his father, prospering now, would have paid his way—for the precarious advantage of attending an older and more famous university in the East, where he was bothered by his scanty funds. But do not get the impression, because his winter dreams happened to be concerned at first with musings on the rich, that there was anything merely snobbish in the boy. He wanted not association with glittering things and glittering people—he wanted the glittering things themselves. Often he reached out for the best without knowing why he wanted it—and sometimes he ran up against the mysterious denials and prohibitions in which life indulges. It is with one of those denials and not with his career as a whole that this story deals.

He made money. It was rather amazing. After college he went to the city from which Black Bear Lake draws its wealthy patrons. When he was only twenty-three and had been there not quite two years, there were already people who liked to say: "Now *there's* a boy—." All about him rich men's sons were peddling bonds precariously, or investing patrimonies precariously, or plodding through the two dozen volumes of the "George Washington Commercial Course," but Dexter borrowed a thousand dollars on his college degree and his confident mouth, and bought a partnership in a laundry.

It was a small laundry when he went into it, but Dexter made a specialty of learning how the English washed fine woolen golf-stockings without shrinking them, and within a year he was catering to the trade that wore knicker-bockers. Men were insisting that their Shetland hose and sweaters go to his laundry, just as they had insisted on a caddy who could find golf-balls. A little later he was doing their wives' lingerie as well—and running five branches in different parts of the city. Before he was twenty-seven he owned the largest string of laundries in his section of the country. It was then that he sold out and went to New York. But the part of his story that concerns us goes back to the days when he was making his first big success.

When he was twenty-three Mr. Hart—one of the gray-haired men who like to say "Now there's a boy—" gave him a guest card to the Sherry Island Golf Club for a week-end. So he signed his name one day on the register, and that afternoon played golf in a foursome with Mr. Hart and Mr. Sandwood and Mr. T. A. Hedrick. He did not consider it necessary to remark that he had once carried Mr. Hart's bag over this same links, and that he knew every trap and gully with his eyes shut—but he found himself glancing at the four caddies who trailed them, trying to catch a gleam or gesture that would remind him of himself, that would lessen the gap which lay between his present and his past.

It was a curious day, slashed abruptly with fleeting, familiar impressions. One minute he had the sense of being a trespasser—in the next he was impressed by the tremendous superiority he felt toward Mr. T. A. Hedrick, who was a bore and not even a good golfer any more.

Then, because of a ball Mr. Hart lost near the fifteenth green, an enormous thing happened. While they were searching the stiff grasses of the rough there was a clear call of "Fore!" from behind a hill in their rear. And as they all turned abruptly from their search a bright new ball sliced abruptly over the hill and caught Mr. T. A. Hedrick in the abdomen.

"By Gad!" cried Mr. T. A. Hedrick, "they ought to put some of these crazy women off the course. It's getting to be outrageous."

A head and a voice came up together over the hill:

"Do you mind if we go through?"

"You hit me in the stomach!" declared Mr. Hedrick wildly.

"Did I?" The girl approached the group of men. "I'm sorry. I yelled 'Fore!' "

Her glance fell casually on each of the men—then scanned the fairway for her ball.

"Did I bounce into the rough?"

It was impossible to determine whether this question was ingenuous or malicious. In a moment, however, she left no doubt, for as her partner came up over the hill she called cheerfully:

"Here I am! I'd have gone on the green except that I hit something."

As she took her stance for a short mashie shot, Dexter looked at her closely. She wore a blue gingham dress, rimmed at throat and shoulders with a white edging that accentuated her tan. The quality of exaggeration, of thinness, which had made her passionate eyes and down-turning mouth absurd at eleven, was gone now. She was arrestingly beautiful. The color in her cheeks was centered like the color in a picture—it was not a "high" color, but a sort of fluctuating and feverish warmth, so shaded that it seemed at any moment it would recede and disappear. This color and the mobility of her mouth gave a continual impression of flux, of intense life, of passionate vitality —balanced only partially by the sad luxury of her eyes.

She swung her mashie impatiently and without interest, pitching the ball into a sand-pit on the other side of the green. With a quick, insincere smile and a careless "Thank you!" she went on after it.

"That Judy Jones!" remarked Mr. Hedrick on the next tee, as they waited —some moments—for her to play on ahead. "All she needs is to be turned up and spanked for six months and then to be married off to an old-fashioned cavalry captain."

"My God, she's good-looking!" said Mr. Sandwood, who was just over thirty.

"Good-looking!" cried Mr. Hedrick contemptuously, "she always looks as if she wanted to be kissed! Turning those big cow-eyes on every calf in town!"

It was doubtful if Mr. Hedrick intended a reference to the maternal instinct.

"She'd play pretty good golf if she'd try," said Mr. Sandwood.

"She has no form," said Mr. Hedrick solemnly.

"She has a nice figure," said Mr. Sandwood.

"Better thank the Lord she doesn't drive a swifter ball," said Mr. Hart, winking at Dexter.

Later in the afternoon the sun went down with a riotous swirl of gold and varying blues and scarlets, and left the dry, rustling night of Western summer. Dexter watched from the veranda of the Golf Club, watched the even overlap of the waters in the little wind, silver molasses under the harvest-moon. Then the moon held a finger to her lips and the lake became a clear pool, pale and quiet. Dexter put on his bathing-suit and swam out to the farthest raft, where he stretched dripping on the wet canvas of the spring-board.

There was a fish jumping and a star shining and the lights around the lake were gleaming. Over on a dark peninsula a piano was playing the songs of last summer and of summers before that—songs from "Chin-Chin" and "The Count of Luxemburg" and "The Chocolate Soldier"—and because the sound of a piano over a stretch of water had always seemed beautiful to Dexter he lay perfectly quiet and listened.

The tune the piano was playing at that moment had been gay and new five years before when Dexter was a sophomore at college. They had played it at a prom once when he could not afford the luxury of proms, and he had stood outside the gymnasium and listened. The sound of the tune precipitated in him a sort of ecstasy and it was with that ecstasy he viewed what happened to him now. It was a mood of intense appreciation, a sense that, for once, he was magnificently attune to life and that everything about him was radiating a brightness and glamour he might never know again.

A low, pale oblong detached itself suddenly from the darkness of the Island, spitting forth the reverberate sound of a racing motor-boat. Two white streamers of cleft water rolled themselves out behind it and almost immediately the boat was beside him, drowning out the hot tinkle of the piano in the drone of its spray. Dexter raising himself on his arms was aware of a figure standing at the wheel, of two dark eyes regarding him over the lengthening space of water—then the boat had gone by and was sweeping in an immense and purposeless circle of spray round and round in the middle of the lake. With equal eccentricity one of the circles flattened out and headed back toward the raft.

"Who's that?" she called, shutting off her motor. She was so near now that Dexter could see her bathing-suit, which consisted apparently of pink rompers.

The nose of the boat bumped the raft, and as the latter tilted rakishly he was precipitated toward her. With different degrees of interest they recognized each other.

"Aren't you one of those men we played through this afternoon?" she demanded.

He was.

"Well, do you know how to drive a motor-boat? Because if you do I wish you'd drive this one so I can ride on the surf-board behind. My name is Judy Jones"—she favored him with an absurd smirk—rather, what tried to be a smirk, for, twist her mouth as she might, it was not grotesque, it was merely beautiful—"and I live in a house over there on the Island, and in that house there is a man waiting for me. When he drove up at the door I drove out of the dock because he says I'm his ideal."

There was a fish jumping and a star shining and the lights around the lake were gleaming. Dexter sat beside Judy Jones and she explained how her boat was driven. Then she was in the water, swimming to the floating surf-board with a sinuous crawl. Watching her was without effort to the eye, watching a branch waving or a sea-gull flying. Her arms, burned to butternut, moved sinuously among the dull platinum ripples, elbow appearing first, casting the forearm back with a cadence of falling water, then reaching out and down, stabbing a path ahead.

They moved out into the lake; turning, Dexter saw that she was kneeling on the low rear of the now uptilted surf-board.

"Go faster," she called, "fast as it'll go."

Obediently he jammed the lever forward and the white spray mounted at the bow. When he looked around again the girl was standing up on the rushing board, her arms spread wide, her eyes lifted toward the moon.

"It's awful cold," she shouted. "What's your name?"

He told her.

"Well, why don't you come to dinner to-morrow night?"

His heart turned over like the fly-wheel of the boat, and, for the second time, her casual whim gave a new direction to his life.

### III

Next evening while he waited for her to come downstairs, Dexter peopled the soft deep summer room and the sun-porch that opened from it with the men who had already loved Judy Jones. He knew the sort of men they were— the men who when he first went to college had entered from the great prep schools with graceful clothes and the deep tan of healthy summers. He had seen that, in one sense, he was better than these men. He was newer and stronger. Yet in acknowledging to himself that he wished his children to be like them he was admitting that he was but the rough, strong stuff from which they eternally sprang.

When the time had come for him to wear good clothes, he had known who were the best tailors in America, and the best tailors in America had made him the suit he wore this evening. He had acquired that particular reserve peculiar to his university, that set it off from other universities. He recognized the value to him of such a mannerism and he had adopted it; he knew that to be careless in dress and manner required more confidence than to be careful. But carelessness was for his children. His mother's name had been Krimslich. She was a Bohemian of the peasant class and she had talked broken English to the end of her days. Her son must keep to the set patterns.

At a little after seven Judy Jones came down-stairs. She wore a blue silk afternoon dress, and he was disappointed at first that she had not put on something more elaborate. This feeling was accentuated when, after a brief greeting, she went to the door of a butler's pantry and pushing it open called: "You can serve dinner, Martha." He had rather expected that a butler would announce dinner, that there would be a cocktail. Then he put these thoughts behind him as they sat down side by side on a lounge and looked at each other.

"Father and mother won't be here," she said thoughtfully.

He remembered the last time he had seen her father, and he was glad the parents were not to be here to-night—they might wonder who he was. He had been born in Keeble, a Minnesota village fifty miles farther north, and he always gave Keeble as his home instead of Black Bear Village. Country towns were well enough to come from if they weren't inconveniently in sight and used as footstools by fashionable lakes.

They talked of his university, which she had visited frequently during the past two years, and of the near-by city which supplied Sherry Island with its patrons, and whither Dexter would return next day to his prospering laundries.

During dinner she slipped into a moody depression which gave Dexter a feeling of uneasiness. Whatever petulance she uttered in her throaty voice worried him. Whatever she smiled at—at him, at a chicken liver, at nothing —it disturbed him that her smile could have no root in mirth, or even in amusement. When the scarlet corners of her lips curved down, it was less a smile than an invitation to a kiss.

Then, after dinner, she led him out on the dark sun-porch and deliberately changed the atmosphere.

"Do you mind if I weep a little?" she said.

"I'm afraid I'm boring you," he responded quickly.

"You're not. I like you. But I've just had a terrible afternoon. There was a man I cared about, and this afternoon he told me out of a clear sky that he was poor as a church-mouse. He'd never even hinted it before. Does this sound horribly mundane?"

"Perhaps he was afraid to tell you."

"Suppose he was," she answered. "He didn't start right. You see, if I'd thought of him as poor—well, I've been mad about loads of poor men, and fully intended to marry them all. But in this case, I hadn't thought of him that way, and my interest in him wasn't strong enough to survive the shock. As if a girl calmly informed her fiancé that she was a widow. He might not object to widows, but——

"Let's start right," she interrupted herself suddenly. "Who are you, anyhow?"

For a moment Dexter hesitated. Then:

"I'm nobody," he announced. "My career is largely a matter of futures."

"Are you poor?"

"No," he said frankly, "I'm probably making more money than any man my age in the Northwest. I know that's an obnoxious remark, but you advised me to start right."

There was a pause. Then she smiled and the corners of her mouth drooped and an almost imperceptible sway brought her closer to him, looking up into his eyes. A lump rose in Dexter's throat, and he waited breathless for the experiment, facing the unpredictable compound that would form mysteriously from the elements of their lips. Then he saw—she communicated her excitement to him, lavishly, deeply, with kisses that were not a promise but a fulfilment. They aroused in him not hunger demanding renewal but surfeit that would demand more surfeit . . . kisses that were like charity, creating want by holding back nothing at all.

It did not take him many hours to decide that he had wanted Judy Jones ever since he was a proud, desirous little boy.

## IV

It began like that—and continued, with varying shades of intensity, on such a note right up to the dénouement. Dexter surrendered a part of himself to the most direct and unprincipled personality with which he had ever come in contact. Whatever Judy wanted, she went after with the full pressure of her charm. There was no divergence of method, no jockeying for position or premeditation of effects—there was a very little mental side to any of her affairs. She simply made men conscious to the highest degree of her physical loveliness. Dexter had no desire to change her. Her deficiencies were knit up with a passionate energy that transcended and justified them.

When, as Judy's head lay against his shoulder that first night, she whispered, "I don't know what's the matter with me. Last night I thought I was in love with a man and tonight I think I'm in love with you——" —it seemed to him a beautiful and romantic thing to say. It was the exquisite excitability that for the moment he controlled and owned. But a week later he was compelled to view this same quality in a different light. She took him in her roadster to a picnic supper, and after supper she disappeared, likewise in her roadster, with another man. Dexter became enormously upset and was scarcely able to be decently civil to the other people present. When she assured him that she had not kissed the other man, he knew she was lying—yet he was glad that she had taken the trouble to lie to him.

He was, as he found before the summer ended, one of a varying dozen who circulated about her. Each of them had at one time been favored above all others—about half of them still basked in the solace of occasional senti-mental revivals. Whenever one showed signs of dropping out through long neglect, she granted him a brief honeyed hour, which encouraged him to tag along for a year or so longer. Judy made these forays upon the helpless and defeated without malice, indeed half unconscious that there was any-thing mischievous in what she did.

When a new man came to town every one dropped out—dates were automatically cancelled.

The helpless part of trying to do anything about it was that she did it all herself. She was not a girl who could be "won" in the kinetic sense—she was proof against cleverness, she was proof against charm; if any of these assailed her too strongly she would immediately resolve the affair to a physical basis, and under the magic of her physical splendor the strong as well as the brilliant played her game and not their own. She was entertained only by the gratifi-cation of her desires and by the direct exercise of her own charm. Perhaps from so much youthful love, so many youthful lovers, she had come, in self-defense, to nourish herself wholly from within.

Succeeding Dexter's first exhilaration came restlessness and dissatisfaction. The helpless ecstasy of losing himself in her was opiate rather than tonic. It was fortunate for his work during the winter that those moments of ecstasy came infrequently. Early in their acquaintance it had seemed for a while that there was a deep and spontaneous mutual attraction—that first August, for example—three days of long evenings on her dusky veranda, of strange wan kisses through the late afternoon, in shadowy alcoves or behind the protecting trellises of the garden arbors, of mornings when she was fresh as a dream and almost shy at meeting him in the clarity of the rising day. There was all the ecstasy of an engagement about it, sharpened by his realization that there was no engagement. It was during those three days that, for the first time, he had asked her to marry him. She said "maybe some day," she said "kiss me," she said "I'd like to marry you," she said "I love you"—she said—nothing.

The three days were interrupted by the arrival of a New York man who visited at her house for half September. To Dexter's agony, rumor engaged them. The man was the son of the president of a great trust company. But at the end of a month it was reported that Judy was yawning. At a dance one night she sat all evening in a motor-boat with a local beau, while the New Yorker searched the club for her frantically. She told the local beau that she was bored with her visitor, and two days later he left. She was seen with him at the station, and it was reported that he looked very mournful indeed.

On this note the summer ended. Dexter was twenty-four, and he found himself increasingly in a position to do as he wished. He joined two clubs in the city and lived at one of them. Though he was by no means an integral part of the stag-lines at these clubs, he managed to be on hand at dances where Judy Jones was likely to appear. He could have gone out socially as much as he liked—he was an eligible young man, now, and popular with down-town fathers. His confessed devotion to Judy Jones had rather solidified his position. But he had no social aspirations and rather despised the dancing men who were always on tap for the Thursday or Saturday parties and who filled in at dinners with the younger married set. Already he was playing with the idea of going East to New York. He wanted to take Judy Jones with him. No disillusion as to the world in which she had grown up could cure his illusion as to her desirability.

Remember that—for only in the light of it can what he did for her be understood.

Eighteen months after he first met Judy Jones he became engaged to another girl. Her name was Irene Scheerer, and her father was one of the men who had always believed in Dexter. Irene was light-haired and sweet and honorable, and a little stout, and she had two suitors whom she pleasantly relinquished when Dexter formally asked her to marry him.

Summer, fall, winter, spring, another summer, another fall—so much he had given of his active life to the incorrigible lips of Judy Jones. She had treated him with interest, with encouragement, with malice, with indifference, with contempt. She had inflicted on him the innumerable little slights and in- dignities possible in such a case—as if in revenge for having ever cared for him at all. She had beckoned him and yawned at him and beckoned him again and he had responded often with bitterness and narrowed eyes. She had brought him ecstatic happiness and intolerable agony of spirit. She had caused him untold inconvenicence and not a little trouble. She had insulted him, and she had ridden over him, and she had played his interest in her against his interest in his work—for fun. She had done everything to him except to criticise him— this she had not done—it seemed to him only because it might have sullied the utter indifference she manifested and sincerely felt toward him.

When autumn had come and gone again it occurred to him that he could not have Judy Jones. He had to beat this into his mind but he convinced himself at last. He lay awake at night for a while and argued it over. He told himself the trouble and the pain she had caused him, he enumerated her glaring defi- ciencies as a wife. Then he said to himself that he loved her, and after a while he fell asleep. For a week, lest he imagined her husky voice over the telephone or her eyes opposite him at lunch, he worked hard and late, and at night he went to his office and plotted out his years.

At the end of the week he went to a dance and cut in on her once. For almost the first time since they had met he did not ask her to sit out with him or tell her that she was lovely. It hurt him that she did not miss these things—that was all. He was not jealous when he saw that there was a new man to-night. He had been hardened against jealousy long before.

He stayed late at the dance. He sat for an hour with Irene Scheerer and talked about books and about music. He knew very little about either. But he was beginning to be master of his own time now, and he had a rather priggish notion that he—the young and already fabulously successful Dexter Green—should know more about such things.

That was in October, when he was twenty-five. In January, Dexter and Irene became engaged. It was to be announced in June, and they were to be married three months later.

The Minnesota winter prolonged itself interminably, and it was almost May when the winds came soft and the snow ran down into Black Bear Lake at last. For the first time in over a year Dexter was enjoying a certain tranquillity of spirit. Judy Jones had been in Florida, and afterward in Hot Springs, and somewhere she had been engaged, and somewhere she had broken it off. At first, when Dexter had definitely given her up, it had made him sad that people still linked them together and asked for news of her, but when he began to be placed at dinner next to Irene Scheerer people didn't ask him about her any more—they told him about her. He ceased to be an authority on her.

May at last. Dexter walked the streets at night when the darkness was damp as rain, wondering that so soon, with so little done, so much of ecstasy had gone from him. May one year back had been marked by Judy's poignant, unforgivable, yet forgiven turbulence—it had been one of those rare times when he fancied she had grown to care for him. That old penny's worth of happiness he had spent for this bushel of content. He knew that Irene would be no more than a curtain spread behind him, a hand moving among gleaming tea-cups, a voice calling to children . . . fire and loveliness were gone, the magic of nights and the wonder of the varying hours and seasons . . . slender lips, down-turning, dropping to his lips and bearing him up into a heaven of eyes. . . . The thing was deep in him. He was too strong and alive for it to die lightly.

In the middle of May when the weather balanced for a few days on the thin bridge that led to deep summer he turned in one night at Irene's house. Their engagement was to be announced in a week now—no one would be surprised at it. And to-night they would sit together on the lounge at the University Club and look on for an hour at the dancers. It gave him a sense of solidity to go with her—she was so sturdily popular, so intensely "great."

He mounted the steps of the brownstone house and stepped inside.

"Irene," he called.

Mrs. Scheerer came out of the living-room to meet him.

"Dexter," she said, "Irene's gone up-stairs with a splitting headache. She wanted to go with you but I made her go to bed."

"Nothing serious, I——"

"Oh, no. She's going to play golf with you in the morning. You can spare her for just one night, can't you, Dexter?"

Her smile was kind. She and Dexter liked each other. In the living-room he talked for a moment before he said good-night.

Returning to the University Club, where he had rooms, he stood in the doorway for a moment and watched the dancers. He leaned against the door-post, nodded at a man or two—yawned.

"Hello, darling."

The familiar voice at his elbow startled him. Judy Jones had left a man and crossed the room to him—Judy Jones, a slender enamelled doll in cloth of gold: gold in a band at her head, gold in two slipper points at her dress's hem. The fragile glow of her face seemed to blossom as she smiled at him. A breeze of warmth and light blew through the room. His hands in the pockets of his dinner-jacket tightened spasmodically. He was filled with a sudden excitement.

"When did you get back?" he asked casually.

"Come here and I'll tell you about it."

She turned and he followed her. She had been away—he could have wept at the wonder of her return. She had passed through enchanted streets, doing things that were like provocative music. All mysterious happenings, all fresh and quickening hopes, had gone away with her, come back with her now.

She turned in the doorway.

"Have you a car here? If you haven't, I have."

"I have a coupé."

In then, with a rustle of golden cloth. He slammed the door. Into so many cars she had stepped—like this—like that—her back against the leather, so—her elbow resting on the door—waiting. She would have been soiled long since had there been anything to soil her—except herself—but this was her own self outpouring.

With an effort he forced himself to start the car and back into the street. This was nothing, he must remember. She had done this before, and he had put her behind him, as he would have crossed a bad account from his books.

He drove slowly down-town and, affecting abstraction, traversed the deserted streets of the business section, people here and there where a movie was giving out its crowd or where consumptive or pugillistic youth lounged in front of pool halls. The clink of glasses and the slap of hands on the bars issued from saloons, cloisters of glazed glass and dirty yellow light.

She was watching him closely and the silence was embarrassing, yet in this crisis he could find no casual word with which to profane the hour. At a convenient turning he began to zigzag back toward the University Club.

"Have you missed me?" she asked suddenly.

"Everybody missed you."

He wondered if she knew of Irene Scheerer. She had been back only a day—her absence had been almost contemporaneous with his engagement.

"What a remark!" Judy laughed sadly—without sadness. She looked at him searchingly. He became absorbed in the dashboard.

"You're handsomer than you used to be," she said thoughtfully. "Dexter, you have the most rememberable eyes."

He could have laughed at this, but he did not laugh. It was the sort of thing that was said to sophomores. Yet it stabbed at him.

"I'm awfully tired of everything, darling." She called every one darling, endowing the endearment with careless, individual camaraderie. "I wish you'd marry me."

The directness of this confused him. He should have told her now that he was going to marry another girl, but he could not tell her. He could as easily have sworn that he had never loved her.

"I think we'd get along," she continued, on the same note, "unless probably you've forgotten me and fallen in love with another girl."

Her confidence was obviously enormous. She had said, in effect, that she found such a thing impossible to believe, that if it were true he had merely committed a childish indiscretion—and probably to show off. She would forgive him, because it was not a matter of any moment but rather something to be brushed aside lightly.

"Of course you could never love anybody but me," she continued, "I like the way you love me. Oh, Dexter, have you forgotten last year?"

"No, I haven't forgotten."

"Neither have I!"

Was she sincerely moved—or was she carried along by the wave of her own acting?

"I wish we could be like that again," she said, and he forced himself to answer:

"I don't think we can."

"I suppose not. . . . I hear you're giving Irene Scheerer a violent rush."

There was not the faintest emphasis on the name, yet Dexter was suddenly ashamed.

"Oh, take me home," cried Judy suddenly; "I don't want to go back to that idiotic dance—with those children."

Then, as he turned up the street that led to the residence district, Judy began to cry quietly to herself. He had never seen her cry before.

The dark street lightened, the dwellings of the rich loomed up around them, he stopped his coupé in front of the great white bulk of the Mortimer Joneses' house, somnolent, gorgeous, drenched with the splendor of the damp moonlight. Its solidity startled him. The strong walls, the steel of the girders, the breadth and beam and pomp of it were there only to bring out the contrast with the young beauty beside him. It was sturdy to accentuate her slightness— as if to show what a breeze could be generated by a butterfly's wing.

He sat perfectly quiet, his nerves in wild clamor, afraid that if he moved he would find her irresistibly in his arms. Two tears had rolled down her wet face and trembled on her upper lip.

"I'm more beautiful than anybody else," she said brokenly, "why can't I be happy?" Her moist eyes tore at his stability—her mouth turned slowly downward with an exquisite sadness: "I'd like to marry you if you'll have me, Dexter. I suppose you think I'm not worth having, but I'll be so beautiful for you, Dexter."

A million phrases of anger, pride, passion, hatred, tenderness fought on his lips. Then a perfect wave of emotion washed over him, carrying off with it a sediment of wisdom, of convention, of doubt, of honor. This was his girl who was speaking, his own, his beautiful, his pride.

"Won't you come in?" He heard her draw in her breath sharply.

Waiting.

"All right," his voice was trembling, "I'll come in."

## V

It was strange that neither when it was over nor a long time afterward did he regret that night. Looking at it from the perspective of ten years, the fact that Judy's flare for him endured just one month seemed of little importance. Nor did it matter that by his yielding he subjected himself to a deeper agony in the end and gave serious hurt to Irene Scheerer and to Irene's parents, who had befriended him. There was nothing sufficiently pictorial about Irene's grief to stamp itself on his mind.

Dexter was at bottom hard-minded. The attitude of the city on his action was of no importance to him, not because he was going to leave the city, but because any outside attitude on the situation seemed superficial. He was completely indifferent to popular opinion. Nor, when he had seen that it was no use, that he did not possess in himself the power to move fundamentally or to hold Judy Jones, did he bear any malice toward her. He loved her, and he would love her until the day he was too old for loving—but he could not have her. So he tasted the deep pain that is reserved only for the strong, just as he had tasted for a little while the deep happiness.

Even the ultimate falsity of the grounds upon which Judy terminated the engagement that she did not want to "take him away" from Irene—Judy who had wanted nothing else—did not revolt him. He was beyond any revulsion or any amusement.

He went East in February with the intention of selling out his laundries and settling in New York—but the war came to America in March and changed his plans. He returned to the West, handed over the management of the business to his partner, and went into the first officers' training-camp in late April. He was one of those young thousands who greeted the war with a certain amount of relief, welcoming the liberation from webs of tangled emotion.

## VI

This story is not his biography, remember, although things creep into it which have nothing to do with those dreams he had when he was young. We are almost done with them and with him now. There is only one more incident to be related here, and it happens seven years farther on.

It took place in New York, where he had done well—so well that there were no barriers too high for him. He was thirty-two years old, and except for one flying trip immediately after the war, he had not been West in seven years.

A man named Devlin from Detroit came into his office to see him in a business way, and then and there this incident occurred, and closed out, so to speak, this particular side of his life.

"So you're from the Middle West," said the man Devlin with careless curiosity. "That's funny—I thought men like you were probably born and raised on Wall Street. You know—wife of one of my best friends in Detroit came from your city, I was an usher at the wedding."

Dexter waited with no apprehension of what was coming.

"Judy Simms," said Devlin with no particular interest; "Judy Jones she was once."

"Yes, I knew her." A dull impatience spread over him. He had heard, of course, that she was married—perhaps deliberately he had heard no more.

"Awfully nice girl," brooded Devlin meaninglessly, "I'm sort of sorry for her."

"Why?" Something in Dexter was alert, receptive, at once.

"Oh, Lud Simms has gone to pieces in a way. I don't mean he ill-uses her, but he drinks and runs around——"

"Doesn't she run around?"

"No. Stays at home with her kids."

"Oh."

"She's a little too old for him," said Devlin.

"Too old!" cried Dexter. "Why, man, she's only twenty-seven."

He was possessed with a wild notion of rushing out into the streets and taking a train to Detroit. He rose to his feet spasmodically.

"I guess you're busy," Devlin apologized quickly. "I didn't realize——"

"No, I'm not busy," said Dexter, steadying his voice. "I'm not busy at all. Not busy at all. Did you say she was—twenty-seven? No, I said she was twenty-seven."

"Yes, you did," agreed Devlin dryly.

"Go on, then. Go on."

"What do you mean?"

"About Judy Jones."

Devlin looked at him helplessly.

"Well, that's—I told you all there is to it. He treats her like the devil. Oh, they're not going to get divorced or anything. When he's particularly outrageous she forgives him. In fact, I'm inclined to think she loves him. She was a pretty girl when she first came to Detroit."

A pretty girl! The phrase struck Dexter as ludicrous.

"Isn't she—a pretty girl, any more?"

"Oh, she's all right."

"Look here," said Dexter, sitting down suddenly. "I don't understand. You say she was a 'pretty girl' and now you say she's "all right.' I don't understand what you mean—Judy Jones wasn't a pretty girl, at all. She was a great beauty. Why, I knew her, I knew her. She was——"

Devlin laughed pleasantly.

"I'm not trying to start a row," he said. "I think Judy's a nice girl and I like her. I can't understand how a man like Lud Simms could fall madly in love with her, but he did." Then he added: "Most of the women like her."

Dexter looked closely at Devlin, thinking wildly that there must be a reason for this, some insensitivity in the man or some private malice.

"Lots of women fade just like *that,*" Devlin snapped his fingers. "You must have seen it happen. Perhaps I've forgotten how pretty she was at her wedding. I've seen her so much since then, you see. She has nice eyes."

A sort of dullness settled down upon Dexter. For the first time in his life he felt like getting very drunk. He knew that he was laughing loudly at something Devlin had said, but he did not know what it was or why it was funny. When, in a few minutes, Devlin went he lay down on his lounge and looked out the window at the New York sky-line into which the sun was sinking in dull lovely shades of pink and gold.

He had thought that having nothing else to lose he was invulnerable at last—but he knew that he had just lost something more, as surely as if he had married Judy Jones and seen her fade away before his eyes.

The dream was gone. Something had been taken from him. In a sort of panic he pushed the palms of his hands into his eyes and tried to bring up a picture of the waters lapping on Sherry Island and the moonlit veranda, and gingham on the golf-links and the dry sun and the gold color of her neck's soft down. And her mouth damp to her kisses and her eyes plaintive with melancholy and her freshness like new fine linen in the morning. Why, these things were no longer in the world! They had existed and they existed no longer.

For the first time in years the tears were streaming down his face. But they were for himself now. He did not care about mouth and eyes and moving hands. He wanted to care, and he could not care. For he had gone away and he could never go back any more. The gates were closed, the sun was gone down, and there was no beauty but the gray beauty of steel that withstands all time. Even the grief he could have borne was left behind in the country of illusion, of youth, of the richness of life, where his winter dreams had flourished.

"Long ago," he said, "long ago, there was something in me, but now that thing is gone. Now that thing is gone, that thing is gone. I cannot cry. I cannot care. That thing will come back no more."

# The Benefits of American Life
## 1933

## James T. Farrell

*Ye orphan sons of Greece,*
*Scattered hither and beyond,*
*Persecuted and forlorn,*
*And by all nations beshun.*

(From a Greek poem translated by Paul Javaras)

Takiss Fillios was a strong shepherd boy whose home land was located just at the hollow valley of two mountains in Arcadia, Greece, in the central section of the Peloponnesus. He grew up on goat's milk and on pitch black bread whose cinders were not separated so as to produce more bread per pound. His hard-working mother sold a piece of land, which produced enough wheat to pull the family through the whole year, in order to pay his steerage fare to America. For in America the streets were paved with gold; the buildings were taller than mountains; the women all dressed like princesses and the men had their pockets lined with money; every boy had a bicycle; and every man and woman owned an automobile. At the age of thirteen, Takiss, large for his age, arrived in a paradise known as Chicago.

He was met at the railroad station, a scared and bewildered boy, by a relative who took him to a home on South Halsted Street. With voluble benefi-cence, the relative immediately employed Takiss, offering him a salary of fifteen dollars a month and the privilege of sleeping on marble slabs in his candy kitchen. He told Takiss that all successful Greek men started that way, and he showed the boy Greek newspapers with pictures of stern, mustachioed Greek restaurant owners and candy-store proprietors who recounted the story of their rise to fame and offered themselves as favorable candidates for marri-age. And as a final word of advice, the relative told Takiss that his mother was getting old now, and that he should send her some of his wages to help her out.

Takiss quickly discovered what it meant to live in paradise. It meant work-ing from six in the morning until six in the evening, and until even later on

week-ends. It meant sweeping out the store, washing dishes and windows, pol-
ishing, arranging, mopping, running errands. It meant attending night school to
learn English when he could scarcely keep his eyes open and where he was
frequently laughed at for his blundering efforts. It meant walking along, living
in the midst of dirty streets where coal dust, soot, smoke, and the poisonous
fumes of automobiles choked his nostrils and made him cough. It meant lonesome memories. For a long period, Takiss was a lonely boy remembering his
homeland and his Grecian mountain, remembering the long, slow days with the
sheep, remembering the games he had played with other boys, remembering the
smile and kiss of his old mother, remembering always.

And he was afraid of America, and of that tremendous paradise known
as Chicago. He worked doggedly day after day, earning fifteen dollars a month,
catching a cough from sleeping on marble slabs. He worked doggedly, and from
his wages he saved a pittance which he deposited in an immigrant's savings
bank. But he looked ahead to the day when he would be famous, with his picture in the Greek newspapers, a pride and an honor to his native Greece and to
the great tradition of the great Socrates about whom his relative so frequently
boasted. He dreamed of the time when he would become like Americans, talk
like them, wear their clothes, ride in automobiles just as they did, walk along the
streets with pretty American girls.

In time, Takiss learned things. He learned American words, but never
how to speak them like an American. He learned that he was considered a dirty
Greek greenhorn, and that many Americans would have been just as pleased if
he and many of his countrymen had never come to their land. And he learned
that American girls laughed sardonically at a young Greek greenhorn. Also,
he learned of a place owned by a cousin of his, where for a little money he could
go and find American girls who did not laugh at a Greek greenhorn, at least for
five or ten minutes. He learned how to buy American clothes on installments, to
wear a purple silk shirt, purple socks, and an orange tie. And he learned, also,
that in the store he could put some of the money received for sales into his pocket
instead of into the cash register.

Eventually, the cousin employing him discharged him in anger, branding
him a crook, a robber, a traitor. In the heated quarrel, Takiss asked him why,
if he wanted honesty, he paid only six dollars a week wages, when he made so
much money himself selling bad products and got his picture in the Greek newspapers as a successful pioneer in America.

Takiss was employed by other of his countrymen, in fruit stores, soda
parlors, at hot-dog stands, and in restaurants. He acquired additional American
knowledge, and more American words. And sometimes when he was dressed
up, wearing his purple silk shirt with socks to match, and the orange tie, he
would walk in the parks or along Halsted Street, seeing American girls, wishing
that he had one of his own, a blonde girl with a beautiful pink-white complexion.

Time slid from under Takiss, and he was a young man in his early twenties, with his first citizenship papers. He had worked like a dog, and he was still
slaving at the same jobs, performing the same tasks and chores as he had al-

ways done since he had come to America. He earned eight dollars a week and
was busy twelve hours a day in a candy store. He cleaned and he mopped; he
scrubbed; he polished; he washed; he waited on trade. And often when he was
alone in the store he pocketed money from the cash register. Every week he
deposited money in the bank, and almost nightly he looked in his bank book,
proud of his savings, thinking of how he was going to achieve fame in America.
But he was never able to save money, because he was always quitting or losing
jobs and having to use savings to support himself between jobs, as well as to send
money to his mother.

And he learned another thing . . . he learned how to dance like Americans. A Greek-American friend told him of a dancing school called a taxi-dance
hall on West Madison Street, and showed him an advertisement from the Greek-
American owner, Professor Christopolos, who stated in the ad that anyone
could be as graceful as he if they learned dancing from his beautiful girls at only
ten cents a dance. He paid a dollar and was given ten tickets and entered the
dimly lighted dancing school of Professor Christopolos on the fourth floor of a
dingy and decrepit building. Each ticket was good for one dance which lasted
from a minute to a minute and a half. Any girl in the place would dance with
him, because she received five cents for each dance. Takiss' tickets were
quickly used up, and he bought more. It did not matter if he danced woodenly
and clumsily, and the girls acted delighted to teach him. He went to this taxi-
dance hall regularly, spending three, four, and five dollars every visit, and once
in a while a girl would ask him if he wanted to take her home, and for a few
more dollars he could get other favors, too. After he started going to the taxi-
dance hall regularly he was able to save less money, and he sent little to his
mother.

Takiss then spent some of his savings for a suit with bell-bottom trousers.
He cultivated a mustache and long side-burns, greased his hair and parted it
in the middle with meticulous attention. He began to look like a sheik, and
listened to pick up all the words which the American-born sheiks used. He went
to public dance halls where there was only an admission fee and longer dances.
At these places, there were always swarms of girls, pretty American girls, some
of them tall and beautiful blondes with milky skins and red lips like cherries.
He would ask them to dance. Often they would dance with him, once. He
would talk, and they would catch his accent, and when he asked them for a
second dance they would thank him with great regret and exclaim that all
their other dances were taken. So he would quickly be driven to dancing with
the homely and ugly girls who were called wall-flowers. And then he would go
back to Professor Christopolos' dancing school, where all the girls would dance
with him for ten cents a dance.

One day, Takiss was twenty-five. His native Grecian mountains seemed
to have receded in time and he saw them only in painful mists of memory, re-
calling their details and contours with lessening concreteness. Greece to him was
a memory. He had been in America for twelve years, and he was working ten
hours a day in a hot-dog stand for ten dollars a week, and able to graft from

three to five dollars a week extra. He wanted to make money and to become famous like some of his Americanized countrymen. And when he was a rich man with a hot-dog stand or a restaurant of his own, he would return to Greece with an American wife and act like a millionaire. And he had thirty-five dollars in the bank as a start toward these riches. He wanted to get more money, but not by running a brothel as his fourth cousin George did, and not bootlegging as did George's friend, Mike. He remembered the things his mother, now dead, had told him, and he wanted to make his money and his fame in a way that his mother would have approved of. And then he would have his picture in a Greek-American newspaper.

And hard times came to America. Takiss was out of work in the winter, and again his savings melted. He was employed for ten dollars a week in a candy store, still working twelve hours a day, and in four months that job was gone. He worked for seven dollars a week washing dishes in a large restaurant, and then his pay was cut to five dollars, and he went home every night tired, with chafed hands and an aching back. He had less money, also, for taxi dances. And he lost that job.

He walked the streets looking for other work, and always he learned the same story . . . hard times. He ate very frugally, lived in a chilly, rat-infested room, and wished that he was back home again in his native Grecian mountains, or else that he was a rich and famous American Greek. Every day he went out looking for a job, and sometimes he· found work for a few days or a few weeks and was able to skim along while he tried again to find work.

One day he saw an advertisement with large letters at the top . . . DANCE MARATHON. The word Marathon struck him. Greek. He would win it and win another victory for his country as it had been done in ancient times. He would become a famous Greek athlete. He investigated, and learned that it was a contest in which everybody tried to dance longer than the others, and the winner received a five-hundred-dollar prize. And maybe if he won it, he would get a job in the moving pictures and become the idol of American girls, or go on the vaudeville stage, or be hired to dance in a cabaret. And while he was in the contest, he would be cared for, fed, and there would be no room rent to pay. He was strong and husky, even if he had been getting coughs in his chest for years ever since he had slept on those marble slabs. And he could dance. He was used to standing on his feet all day at work. And this was his chance to become rich. He would no longer have to tramp all over town to be told that there were no jobs because it was hard times. This was much better than saving up to own a candy store and grow fat like the American Greeks for whom he had worked. And after he won this contest, and became famous, he would go back to Greece with a trunk full of clothes and money, and maybe a rich American girl whose skin was like milk.

Takiss entered the dance marathon, and when the rules were explained to him, he only understood that he was to stay out on the floor and dance, and if he was able to do that longer than anyone else, he would get five hundred dollars. A number was pinned on his back, and he was assigned a partner named Marie Glenn, a beautiful blonde American girl of the type he had always dreamed of as a possible wife. At first, when she met him, she shuddered, and her face broke into an expression of disgust. But then she saw that he was strong and husky with broad shoulders, and she smiled, offering him a limp hand and sweetly telling him that she knew they were sure going to be the winners.

The dance marathon was conducted in a public dance hall on the south side of Chicago. A ring was placed in the center with an orchestra dais at one end. Aroung the ring there were box seats, and behind them, rising rows of bleacher benches. The opening was described, in advertisements, as gala. An announcer talked through a microphone, and the promoters and judges wearing tuxedoes also addressed a full house. The contestants were introduced and some of them, but not Takiss, spoke to the crowd and the large radio audience all over America. It was all a new and promising, if confusing, world to Takiss, and he walked around the floor, feeling as lost and as out of place as he had on those first days in America. But it was leading at last to paradise.

The contest swung into action. They danced for three minutes out of every ten, and walked around and around the floor for the remaining time; and they were given fifteen minutes rest out of every hour. There was glamor in being watched by so many people, in eating sandwiches and drinking coffee before them, in receiving attention from doctors and nurses, and meeting all the others who, like himself, saw at the end of this contest five hundred dollars and fame. As the contestants got to talking to each other, Takiss heard them using one word over and over again . . . celebrity. A celebrity was somebody who was important, like Jack Dempsey and movie stars and Mr. Delphos, the famous American-Greek who was wealthy and owned a large dance hall known as the Bourbon Palace. They all wanted to be celebrities. And Takiss, too, he determined that he was going to be a celebrity.

Takiss had not imagined that anyone could dance for more than a week like this, and that maybe after a sleepless and tiring week he would be the winner. In less than twenty-four hours he learned that it was a grind more gruelling than he had calculated, and while he doggedly gritted his teeth, he determined that he would not let himself drop out. Still, he wished that he had not entered it. He wished he were back working in fruit stores and ice cream parlors the way he had been before hard times had come. He wished that he were a shepherd back in the Grecian mountains.

When his partner was tired, she put her arms around his neck or hips, laid her head against him, and fell asleep while he dragged her heavily around the floor, and when he fell asleep she did the same with him. Again and again their bodies were jolted, shoved, pushed against each other, and he began wanting her so that her very nearness became excruciating. And he noticed that she, particularly in the early dog hours of the mornings when there were scarcely any spectators in the hall, began brushing herself against him at every opportunity, looking feverishly into his eyes and telling him smutty jokes. And the other dancers became the same way, and the fellows used to tell him how much they wanted one of these girls, any girl.

Day after day the marathon grind went on. His eyes grew heavy. His back ached. His feet became sore and raw, so that each step was pain and he felt as if he were walking on fire. The hall was almost continuously stale with cigarette smoke and foul with body odors. He felt constantly dirty, sweaty, itchy. Dust got into his nostrils and his eyes. He began to cough again. His muscles knotted. He became like a person who was always only half awake, and everything took on the semblance of being a semi-dream. Marie, also, changed. She began to swell around the buttocks. Deep circles grew under her eyes. She became haggard and blowsy and looked like a worn-out prostitute. She used more and more cosmetics, and her face became like a ghastly caricature of the pretty girl who had entered the contest.

In the beginning, particularly because of his accent and Greek heritage, Takiss became the butt of many jokes. Constantly, he would be asked why he wasn't running a restaurant, and he would be given orders for a piece zapple pie kid. He was nicknamed Restaurant, Fruit Store, Socrates, and Zapple Pie Kid. In time, this wore down and failed to anger or disturb him. The grind settled into habitual misery and torture. He, like the other contestants, would long for fresh air, and during rest periods, when they were not so tired that they would be dragged like walking somnambulists to the rest cots, they would enter the vile and filthy dressing rooms or the equally unsavory lavatory and jam their heads out of the windows to breathe fresh air and to look yearningly down at the street where people walked free to do what they wished, not tired, able to breathe fresh air, even the fresh air of a city street that was saturated with carbon monoxide fumes and sootiness.

Day after day dragged on. Sometimes Takiss, Marie, or the other contestants would live in stupors of six, twelve hours a day, even longer. As the time passed, the contestants would switch from affected and over-stimulated good spirits to nasty, fighting nervousness, and then into that glaze-eyed stupor. Particularly in those dog hours of the early morning, they would be raw, if awake, and fight and curse. Sex, too, became a growing obsession, and in time was almost madness. Living so near to one another, their bodies touching so frequently, they told smuttier and smuttier jokes. Perversities and desires or propositions for perversities sprang up among them. It became a relentless process of both physical and mental torture. Constipation, diarrhea, sudden inabilities to control their kidneys so that now and then a contestant would be walking around the floor, drugged in sleep, with wet lines down his trousers, or if a girl, down her beach pyjamas which most of them wore regularly. Broken blood vessels and swollen veins in the legs. Headaches, eye troubles, sore throats, fevers, colds. Periods of sweatiness, followed by shivers and chills. And always that returning stupor, caused by sleeplessness and fatigue, and by the dreams and fantasies which they entertained as relief from that endless procession around and around the floor. And at the end of it all, money, the chance to become a celebrity, sex, and clean white bed sheets and a soft, fresh bed.

Ways of making money from day to day quickly developed and were used to the utmost so that all of the contestants started bank accounts. Every one of them developed some trick or act, a song, a dance, a stunt of some kind, and after putting it on, they would be showered with money from the crowd. One of the contestants, a raw country youth of Lithuanian origin with a nasal twang to his voice, chewed razor blades as his stunt. Takiss learned a dance. Stores, theatres, and politicians also paid them fees to wear signs or sweaters and jerseys with advertising printed on the front or back. Money was sent to them, mash notes, written in as ignorant and as bad English as that which Takiss used and wrote in. The various spectators picked favorites, cheered for them, shouted encouragement.

And still the days stretched out, past the first month, with contestant after contestant dropping out, and the field narrowing down. One day there would be a birthday party. Another day there, was a floor wedding between two of the contestants who had met on the floor, and the wedding provided endless hours of raw jokes and humor about when they would have their wedding night, until, sex-crazed, both of the newlyweds went temporarily out of their heads and the girl screamed until she was dragged off the floor. Disqualified, they were out of the marathon, and a new note was introduced in the humor. Another day, a girl had an abscessed tooth extracted on the floor, and immediately afterward she rejoined the endless walking procession that tramped around and around in this ever dullening stupor. Another day, an Italian boy, who with his wife had entered the marathon because they were both unemployed and had been evicted, required crutches and ran a high fever. With his eyes intense from the fever, with suffering imprinted on his haggard face, he hobbled around and around. After twelve such hours he was forced out by the judges on the advice of a doctor.

Again and again Takiss wanted to quit and satisfy himself with the incidental money he had taken in, and as repeatedly he would go patiently on. Like the others, he would fall into that lumbrous sleep, and external means would be necessary to awaken him so that he might continue. The male nurses would slap him in the face with wet towels, put his shoes on the wrong feet, strap him into an electric vibrator machine, poke their fingers down his throat, tickle his calloused soles. During one period, his cough developed into a severe cold in the chest. For another period, he was not out of his stupor for three days. And Marie, his partner, experienced the same tortures. They went on. Days and nights, and days and nights, with the field narrowing to thirteen, ten, eight, five, finally two couples. Then Marie collapsed and was carried off the floor and shipped to a hospital, and Takiss was disqualified. They each collected the two hundred and fifty dollars second place money.

After recuperation, Takiss entered other dance marathons, and became a professional. He secured a copy of *Yes, We Have No Bananas* with a Greek translation, and this, with his dance stunt, became very popular. He was able, with both attractions and with a growing audience of fans, to earn from ten to fifteen dollars a day in extra money. Even when he was forced to retire from marathons or was disqualified, he departed with added money. Again the desire to return to his homeland like a rich American grew upon him, and now his bank account, with foreign exchange rates, would make him very rich in

Greece. He was something of a celebrity in this new world of his. His biography and picture appeared in Greek newspapers. A Greek merchant who sold a raisin beverage paid him and Marie each a hundred dollars to be photographed for a newspaper advertisement in which there was their signed testimony that they drank this beverage. He had a run of a week at a small theatre on South Halsted Street where there were many Greeks. Takiss became a famous American Greek.

In all, Takiss participated in sixteen dance marathons. In eight of them, he collected money and was the winner of a thousand-dollar super-marathon in which only finalists from other marathons were permitted to enter and in which there were no rest periods. He had money now, five thousand dollars. He returned to Greece. But the strain of the marathons had ruined his lungs and he had tuberculosis. Resorts for tuberculosis had been developed in his native mountains, and when he returned it was necessary for him to become a patient in one of them, and the money he had earned was paid out while he lived there with his lungs rotting away on him. Well could he recite his favorite Greek proverb:

*I ate practically the whole cow,*
*Why must I forget the tail?*

## Life in a Relocation Center
### 1944

### Carey McWilliams

No two impressions of life in a relocation center, from the evacuee's point of view, would be the same. The centers themselves differ each from the other. Minidoka in Idaho, Topaz in Utah, and Granada in Colorado—in the order named—are "the cream of the lot." Minidoka rates highest, on all counts, and there are at least a dozen explanations of the fact. The Minidoka evacuees are better adjusted; there has been virtually no trouble. One reason suggested is that most of the evacuees in Minidoka came from Portland where they were fairly well integrated in the community prior to evacuation. The theorizing about Minidoka is fancy and profuse. Topaz has its partisans and Granada insists that it is the best of all possible centers. It is difficult, therefore, to select, from the material I have collected, documents that might be said to be typical of the reaction of the evacuees to center life. I have, however, selected two. The first was written by a Caucasian observer about the Heart Mountain Relocation Center in Wyoming. It gives the "dark side" of the story. The other document was written by a Nisei friend of mine, S. J. Oki. It refers to the Topaz center, in Utah, and is the most objective document of the kind that I have seen. First, then, the story from Wyoming:—

As the first light breaks the darkness, the roosters of a concentration camp suddenly come to life. First one, then another, then a chorus of dishpans rattle and clatter the call to breakfast. It is partly clouded, and the deep pink in the Eastern sky suddenly gives way as the whole heavens blaze. The eyes are pulled up and up, above the drab barracks and the drab countryside, to this spectacle of the Great Plains. The color dies as quickly as it had lived. For a moment the whole world is gray, and then the sun catches the snow on the mountains to the southeast.

Inside the black barracks the people stir. Some groan and roll over. Others push back the covers and slip quickly into their clothes. Grabbing towel and toothbrush, they go outdoors where the bits of snow and ice crunch under their feet. "Cold," they say to one another, and hurry towards the warmth of the latrines. Soon they are lining up to get their breakfast: grapefruit, cold cereal, french toast, coffee.

As the sunlight reaches the camp, a bell on one of the barracks starts ringing and the kids come down to school. Lacking a schoolhouse, they sit in barracks all day, many on benches without backs, sharing textbooks because there aren't enough to go around. The teachers try to get along under the primitive conditions, finding their classes noisy because the partitions separating the rooms are flimsy and don't go up to the roof.

Over in the Administration Building the block administrators get together for their daily meeting. Appointed by the WRA, this group is all-Nisei. It carries out the minor functions of government, takes the complaints of the people to the Administration. Like any governing body that doesn't have much power, its members sit and smoke and appoint committees. The Issei, who are not eligible to be block administrators, serve on a block council. And the people laugh, and call the block administrators stooges and the block council blockheads, for they know who really runs the government.

Out in a corridor two Caucasian members of the Administration talk with each other about the colonists. Unlike the Army which ordered the evacuation, most of the WRA staff want to see the Japanese really relocated. One of these men is from Washington and tells how well former colonists who have gone out under student relocation have fared. He hopes the WRA will work on public opinion so that more and more colonists can go out. And the Administrators are tall, clean-cut, Caucasians who are rather embarrassed because they know as well as any one the difference between voluntary partnership and coercion.

And two of the people overhear a snatch of their conversation as they pass, and one mutters: "Colonists! Jesus Christ! I wonder if they call tigers pussy cats?"

As the morning goes on, the sun becomes warmer and now it falls full on the ground which forms the streets and the spaces between the barracks. The puddles of water which have been frozen hard all night long begin to melt. When a boot lands on them, they crack and break, and muddy water spurts up over the toe of the boot. Then the millions of little frozen water particles in the earth that had been holding the ground firm and hard, these too begin to melt, and the ground softens. As the sun continues to shine on it and the people to walk over it, it becomes muddy. The people's feet get wet and dirty whenever they step outside a building.

Two Nisei girls walking across the camp jump and slide in the mud, and try to keep in the shade of the barracks where the ground is still firm. They are social workers. Social workers in a place like this? What does a social worker do to prevent juvenile delinquency when kids are suddenly jerked from normal life to this? Recreation? When there's no item in the budget for recreational material and the recreation halls are even used as offices? Education? When they promise us school buildings and good equipment and we don't get them? Worthwhile work? When the majority of the jobs they give us are so meaningless that most of the kids act as if they were doing time?

How can you teach democracy in a concentration camp? Or praise American labor standards where people get $4 for a 44-hour week, and nothing for overtime? Or talk about racial equality when the Caucasians on the WRA staff are setting up a whole Jim Crow system of their own? Lookit these little boys. They used to worship football players. Remember when you were a little kid, how every little boy had a hero? Now they follow the toughest gang leaders, and the gangs get tougher and fight one another and steal lumber. New gangs are formed, and they look at the girls more often . . . lookit that girl, most gregarious damn person I ever saw. But even she needs to be off alone sometimes—but she never can. We're not individuals here, but cogs that eat and sleep and work and live all alike. Lookit that Mother—she used to be the core of her family, providing the meals, training her children, those little things that build a family unity. Now other people throw food at us, the kids no longer eat with the parents, but learn their manners from the roughnecks, run wild most of the time.

I read in a paper how a minister said we oughta be satisfied because we are being well-fed and housed and given a chance to work. Is that all living means to that guy? Is life just getting your belly filled and a hoe put in your hands? Betcha that same fellow talks a lot about liberty and spiritual values when he's thinking about Hitler. . . .

The people have learned to laugh at the things that hurt them most. Whenever anyone mentions that they may stay here permanently, "like Indians on a reservation," everyone always laughs. But they do not think the subject of Indian reservations is funny.

And they tell me about the two washrooms at the Pomona center. Over the big washroom was a sign which read: "Caucasian Administrative Staff Only" and over the little washroom, "Japanese Administrative Staff Only."

Then there's the story about the Caucasian history teacher who told her class: "Today we will study the Constitution." And the class laughed and tittered so that they never did.

And the people who have been hurt make cracks about the number of Jews on the WRA staff, and they say to one another: "Did you see the two new Hebes who are here?" And they make disparaging remarks about Negroes, and point to the economic degradation of the Mexicans.

In the afternoon many persons crowd into the "Courthouse" for a public forum. The Niseis who run it have hopefully hung a sign which proclaims Voltaire's famous statement about free speech. Toward the end of the speech a Caucasian walks in, and one woman whispers to another: "Here comes an administrative stooge. Now we can't say anything." But the other, sizing the newcomer up, disagrees: "Naw, he's only a kid high school teacher."

The discussion begins, and the chairman is nervous. He wants it to be a frank discussion to satisfy the people, but is scared of future censorship if it gets out of hand. A tall, lean fellow with a goatee rises again and again. "Are you going to participate in this camp government? Do you still think you're citizens of this country? Do you have the rights of citizens? Isn't the government just going to coddle you and make you into another bunch of people on an Indian reservation? Or will they ship you all back to Japan? What sort of jobs could you get if you could go outside? What are you, citizens or Japs? Or, are you donkeys?"

The fears that lurk in the people have been touched, and they stir nervously. The chairman raps for order. A block administrative officer jumps up: "I read in a novel once where Kathleen Norris or someone said a man and his wife with chickens could live on the prairie happily as in New York City. We've got plenty of prairie here. All we need is the chickens!"

The crowd roars, the chairman relaxes a little, the talk goes on and the Niseis ask each other about Nisei problems and discuss "Japanese-American Salvation" as if the Japanese-American problem was the only problem in an otherwise unimportant world.

It is Hallowe'en evening, and across the camp are many parties. In the mess-halls, gay streamers enliven the walls, and the people crowd together as the orchestra comes in. Ten Nisei boys, each wearing a red-and-black checked flannel shirt, and a girl at the piano, start to play remarkably good music. But no one dances. Finally a boy says to a girl: "Hell! Let's dance!" The ice is broken, and the floor is suddenly jammed with couples dancing or watching a hot jitterbug exhibition. People laugh and joke and a boy says to a girl he is dancing with: "I almost forgot where I am!" "I never do," the girl replies, as the smile goes from her face.

What will these camps produce? Out of them can come great leaders and prophets. Men and women of great faith and great patience, blazing new paths in overcoming racial prejudice. Will hardship burn and temper their faith and make it strong?

The people do not know. In one of the barracks, a late bull session is going on around the warm stove. "It's too easy," said one boy. "We get food, there's no rent to pay, the routine is deadening. Everything leads to a degenerative life instead of an invigorating one. Everyone is grabbing for himself. We grab the coal, grab bits of wood lying around, grab for clothing allotments, grab our food. No wonder the little kids are getting so that they do it too, and think only of themselves. No wonder we're apathetic and ingrown."

The people walk quickly home through the sharp cold of the night. The ground is hard under their feet along the brightly-lighted streets and alleys. From a thousand chimneys the harsh coal smoke tries to rise, curls under the weight of the cold air, and settles like a blanket close to the ground. A train whistle sounds in the darkness. Music comes from a guard tower where a bored soldier listens to the radio. From the floodlights an arc of light surrounds the camp.[1]

S. J. Oki, who wrote the following statement, is a "premature antifascist." I have known him for years, long prior to evacuation. A young man, he is at present serving in the language school at Boulder, Colorado. The following statement was written while he was at the Topaz Relocation Center. It is entitled "Notes on What They Think."

Objectively, and on the whole, life in a relocation center is not unbearable. There are dust-storms and mud. Housing is inadequate, with families of six living in single rooms in many cases. Food is below the standard set for prisoners of war. In some of the camps hospitals are at times understaffed and supplies meager, as in many ordinary communities. Yet while Mr. Ata, former San Francisco importer, complains of the low quality of the food, Mrs. Baito, widow of a San Joaquin farmer, is grateful for what the United States government is doing to make life as comfortable as possible for the evacuees. In short, no one is pampered and at the same time no one is starving or sick because of neglect on the part of the War Relocation Authority.

What is not so bearable lies much deeper than the physical make-up of a center. It is seen in the face of Mr. Yokida, 65, a Montebello farmer. It is seen in the face of Mrs. Wata, 50, a grocer's widow from Long Beach. It is seen in the face of little John Zendo, 9, son of an Oakland restaurant owner. It is seen in the face of Mary Uchido, former sophomore from UCLA and the daughter of a

---

[1] Note: This document is dated November 6, 1942.

Little Tokyo merchant. It is seen in the face of Sus Tana, young *kibei* who had been an employee in a vegetable stand in Hollywood.

Their faces look bewildered as they stare at the barbed-wire fences and sentry towers that surround the camp. Their eyes ask: Why? Why? What is all this?

Kats Ento, serious-looking ex-farmer from Norwalk, has made up his mind. He says: "I am an American citizen. I was born and brought up in California. I have never been outside the United States, and I don't know Japan or what Japan stands for. But because my parents weren't considerate enough to give me blue eyes, reddish hair, and a high nose, I am here, in camp, interned without the formality of a charge, to say nothing of a trial. Does the Constitution say that only white men are created equal? Put me down as disloyal, if you will, but I'm going where I won't have to live the rest of my life on the wrong side of the tracks just because my face is yellow. Keep me in camp for the duration. I will find my future in the Orient."

Mrs. Jones, elementary school teacher appointed by the WRA, sighs as she looks towards the little children in shabby but clean clothes. "To be frank with you, it embarrasses me to teach them the flag salute. *Is* our nation indivisible? Does it stand for justice for all? Those questions come up to my mind constantly."

Mr. Yokida, technically an enemy alien after forty years' continuous residence in California, appears tired. "For forty years I worked in central and southern California. I remember when Los Angeles was only a small town compared to San Francisco. This country never gave me citizenship, but I never went back to Japan and I have no interests there. The evacuation has worked a hardship on me and my family, but I suppose in time of war you have to stand for a lot of hardships. Don't ask me what I think of Japan or about the incident at Pearl Harbor. I don't know. What I know is that this is my country, and I have given my only son to its army. I wrote him just the other day, telling him to obey his commander-in-chief without reserve. I have worked as long as anyone and I am satisfied. The only thing I think about is my son. I hope that he will make good in the army. I hope that he will come back to me as a captain, at least."

"I have a son in the army too," says Mrs. Wata. "Besides, my daughter has volunteered to join the WAACS. I am an alien, and being an alien I have nothing to say about evacuation or about having to live in camp, although it would have been so nice to have spent the last winter in Long Beach. It was so cold here, and the stove in my apartment never gave out enough heat. I do wish, though, that they would let my children go back to California on furloughs. They have so many friends out there, and they miss them."

John Zendo, 9, is always talking about his friends, too, says his mother. "He was a pretty popular boy in the neighborhood," she smiles reminiscently as she speaks. "He talks about them all the time, and asks me when we can go back to them. When we were in Oakland, Johnny used to bring all his friends to our restaurant—Mexicans, Chinese, and white children—and my husband used to give each of them a dish of ice cream. Poor Johnny, he talks about such things every day."

"I keep on thinking about Los Angeles and the people I know," says Mary Uchido, an attractive girl of twenty. "My girl friend writes me and tells me all about the changes that have taken place since evacuation. How the Little Tokyo has been left unoccupied, how some of our Chinese and Korean friends are working in airplane factories, things like that. But I don't want to go back there any more, except perhaps for a visit. Yes, my father is in internment, but I don't think about him much. Maybe he will go to Japan the next time there is a boat, but I am going to stay here. We will try to relocate, of course. Maybe I will try to get a domestic job or something, because I can't possibly hope to continue my education. I would join the WAACS if they would put us in an ordinary unit instead of an all-Japanese unit."

Sus Tana, 32, is a volunteer for the special Japanese-American combat team. He smiles broadly and seems jolly, but his dark eyebrows betray an uneasiness which is concealed somewhat behind his sunburned forehead. "I am a kibei and a Young Democrat. I lived and worked in Los Angeles nine years after my return from Japan. I never made over a hundred dollars a month, mostly seventy-five to eighty, and I could never save enough money to buy any-thing. So when evacuation came, I had nothing to lose. I do miss my friends among the Young Democrats, though. They were such a fine bunch. You forgot you were a Jap when you were with them; you were just an American fighting for the President and the New Deal. I do wish I could be back there now. Maybe I could get a defense job and do what I can. But I am glad that we are going to have a combat unit. Maybe I can show the reactionaries in California that a Japanese-American can be just as good a soldier as any American—if not better."

Tana's best friend is Mr. Osaka, 40. He, too, is a kibei, but his English is good. They call him a Red, because he is an anti-fascist. He has been against Japanese imperialism for years, and for that reason he led a poverty-stricken life for twenty years among the Japanese-American communities in California where the Japanese consuls and fascist-minded officials of the Japanese chambers of commerce held a dominant position until the outbreak of the war. Osaka is a man of few words, except when he is aroused by a challenging topic. And now he speaks out: "They call me a Red, but I am only a democrat with a small *d*. In fact I am quite opposed to the way in which Communists seem to be doing things, and I have tried to make it clear a number of times. Yet there are peo-ple here, even people in administrative positions, who resort to name-calling in order to defend their 19th-century opinions against progressive ideas. While they denounce anti-Japanese racism, they themselves are anti-Semitic, anti-Ne-gro, and anti-Mexican. What do I think of evacuation? I don't believe there is a single right-minded Japanese-American who didn't feel the necessity of evac-uating some, though I personally think the government could have saved a tremendous sum of money and much manpower if they had tried selective evacua-tion. Post-war? If we can win the war for democracy, then we Japanese-Americans will be in a very fortunate and unique position of being able to choose one of the two courses for our future: remain in a fully democratized America or go to a defeated but popularly-controlled Japan to help construct a democratic Japan. There is no use talking about compensation. Wars require sacrifices. Draftees don't talk about the constitutionality of the draft act, and they don't complain when they are 'evacuated' from their homes into army camps. Everything must be concentrated on winning the war if we are to see the race-caste system destroyed in America as well as elsewhere."

Mr. Osaka smiles as he reads this passage from a pamphlet: "The color of one's skin is a permanent, immutable characteristic, while habits of dress, speech, or action can be modified and outgrown. An Americanized foreigner with an adopted name can pass completely into the dominant society as long as his skin is white and his features are not pronounced. An American of a different color is always apart. . . ."

Always apart?

"No, not always," says Mr. Osaka.

## How It Feels to Be Champ
### 1955

### Rocky Marciano (with W. C. Heinz)

At about eight thirty on the morning of September 24, 1952, I woke up in a hotel room in Philadelphia. You know how it is when you wake up in a strange place, and at first you don't know where you are. "Something nice happened to me," I thought to myself, and then I remembered. "That's right. Last night I won the heavyweight championship of the world."

When I tried to turn, it seemed like my whole body was sore. Over both eyes I had cuts that had been stitched and there was another cut on the top of my head, but I was as happy as I think anybody can be. Jersey Joe Walcott had given me the toughest fight I'd ever had, but I'd knocked him out in the thirteenth round, and I was heavyweight champion of the world.

I've had the title now for almost three years. In that time I've found out that in some ways it's everything you think it's going to be, and in other ways it's very different.

It's easy for me to remember what I thought it would be like to be champion, because I can remember the first night I ever thought I had a chance. On December 19, 1949, I had Phil Muscato down five times and knocked him out in five rounds in Providence. That was my twenty-fourth win without a loss as a pro and my twenty-second knockout, and after the fight I drove back to Brockton, like I always did after my Providence fights, with my pals Allie Colombo and Nicky Sylvester and Snap Tartarlia.

It was a nice night, clear and cold, but as soon as I got into the car I felt something was different. Usually on the way home after a fight we kidded a lot, but this night everybody was very serious.

"You know, Rock," one of the guys said after a while, "you haven't got very far to go now."

I said: "To go where?"

"For the title," one of the others said.

"Ah," I said. "Take it easy."

"No," somebody said. "Figure it out. About five good wins and you can be on top of the heap."

Then we started figuring who I'd have to get by—Roland La Starza, Rex Layne, Joe Louis, if he made a comeback. Jersey Joe Walcott and Ezzard Charles —and when they dropped me off at my house and I went to bed I couldn't sleep. I was a kid who never dreamed he could be heavyweight champion. I wanted to be a major-league catcher, but then I threw my arm out, and I started to fight to help support the family. Now I got to thinking what it would be like if I could be champion.

I remembered the night in 1933 when Primo Carnera won the title from Jack Sharkey. I was eight years old at the time, and in the Italian section of Brockton they had big bonfires burning and they sang and shouted around them almost all night long. I could remember those fires in the James Edgar playground right across the street from our house, and I figured: Gee, if I could win the title, I'd come back to Brockton and I'd throw a big party for the whole town and every kid would be invited and get an expensive gift.

Right after he won the title Carnera came to Brockton to referee at the old Arena that was across Centre Street from the Brockton Hospital. My uncle, John Piccento, took me that night to see him, and on the way out Carnera walked right by us and I reached out and I touched his arm.

"I saw Carnera and I touched him." I told my pop when I got home. "I really did."

"How big is he?" my pop asked me.

"Bigger than this ceiling," I said, "and you should see how big his hands are."

The year before I licked Muscato and was lying there thinking about what it might be like to be the champion of the world, I had shaken hands with Joe Louis for the first time. He was boxing an exhibition with Arturo Godoy in

Philadelphia, and I was fighting Gilley Ferron on the card. We were all in the dressing room when Joe came in.

"Say, Joe," my manager Al Weill said, "I want you to shake hands with my heavyweight."

Joe stuck out his hand and we shook. He looked like a mountain, and he had on a big, beautiful overcoat and a mohair hat, light brown with a nice feather in it. I figured that hat alone must have cost $50, and now I got to thinking about the money he must have made.

When Louis knocked out Max Schmeling in two minutes and four seconds in their second fight, Allie Colombo and I were talking about all that dough. We were just kids talking, but it said in the paper that, figuring the purse Louis got for the fight, he made over $150,000 a minute, which is more than the President of the United States gets paid a year.

Now, lying in bed after the Muscato fight, I got to imagining what it would mean to have money like that, not just for clothes but for security and for what I could do for my family and my friends and others. I thought: Boy when you're the heavyweight champion of the world it means you can lick any man in the world, and wherever you go in the world what an influence you must have.

There were a lot of things I didn't know then that I know now that I'm champion. I didn't know that my life would be threatened a couple of times. I didn't know that, although you do make a lot of money, it isn't as much as people think it is, expenses and taxes being what they are, and that you can't begin to do the things with it that you dreamed about. I didn't know that being champion is almost a full-time job, and that the influence you have on people is sometimes so strong that it worries you and can even bring tears to your eyes.

After I knocked out Joe Louis, for example, my mother got a letter saying that if I came home to Brockton for the celebration that was planned I'd be shot. Then, just before my first fight with Charles last June, my folks got another note from a man who said that if I beat Charles I'd be killed, because Charles is a gentleman and I'm a bully.

The Brockton police found the first letter was written by a thirteen-year-old girl. I don't know, or care, who wrote the second one, but although letters like that don't worry me, they worry my mother. After that first letter my sisters had to take her to Dr. Michael Del Colliano, in Brockton, and now every time I fight he picks her up at the house and drives her around all evening until the fight is over. I never imagined I'd put my family through anything like that, because I never realized how many people's lives are tied up in a fight.

I had a friend in Brockton named Miles Dempsey, and he was my first real fan. He used to go to all my amateur fights, and he was the first guy who asked me to arrange for him to buy good seats when I started to fight pro. During the excitement of the sixth round of that June fight with Charles he died at ringside of a heart attack. In my mind that is a part of that fight.

When you're the heavyweight champion the money, of course, is the big thing you're going for, because that's why you became a fighter in the first place. Before I started fighting, the most I ever made was $1.25 an hour as a manual laborer. When I retire, if I'm lucky, I should never have to worry about money again, but it isn't as much as you expect it to be, and your security is still a problem.

Last year, for example, I fought Charles twice. At the end of the year, after expenses and taxes, I came out with a lot less than $100,000. When I fight twice in a year I don't figure, with taxes, to net more than about $15,000 out of the second fight, and that's not a lot when you've got only four or five years of fighting and when, each time you go into the ring, you're risking the heavy-weight championship of the world.

I'm not complaining, because I couldn't make that kind of money doing any other thing, and when you come from a poor family you know it's a privilege to pay taxes. It's just that you feel other people don't understand.

I'll never, you see, be able to afford that big party for all the kids in Brockton. That's not important, just kind of a foolish dream, but the important thing is that you can't do all you want for charities and churches and just good people, and you have a feeling that they go away not liking you because of it. You want to be liked by everybody—not just for yourself, but because when you're heavyweight champion of the world you represent boxing and boxing did everything for you.

There'll be a church that needs $10,000 or a hospital that needs that much to help build a new ward. I'll get a letter from a woman I don't even know but she'll write that if I'd give her $1,500 her little boy could be made well again. How do you think I feel?

They run at you, too, with all kinds of business schemes, but that's only a nuisance. There are people who want me to sign notes for them, or lend them money or sponsor them in singing or acting careers. They've tried to sell me uranium and copper mines and oil wells and a dairy. Any salesman near Brockton, where I'm home only about two months a year, tries to get me to buy whatever he's handling, and it might be a carving machine or a salad mixer, books, a car or a horse.

Some of the things you do with your money don't pan out the way you dreamed, either. I always said that, if I became champion, one of the first things I'd do would be to send my mom and pop back to their home towns in Italy, and I used to think what a great time that would be for them.

I did it, right after the first Walcott fight. There were so many things pulling at me at the time, however, that I couldn't even see them off on the plane, and some of the pleasure was lost. Then instead of staying three months, they came back after one month, and they never did get to my mother's little town of San Bartolomeo, near Naples. They went only to my pop's town, Ripa Teatina, in Abruzzi, on the Adriatic coast, and it took a couple of months before my mother would tell me why.

"Too much sadness there," she said, and you should understand that my mother is the kind of a woman who can't stand to see suffering and wants to help everybody. "Every place we went they had nothing, and they looked to us and how much could we do? I did not want to go to my own town."

It took my mother that long to tell me about the trip because, when you become heavyweight champion, something comes between you and other people, even your family. Everybody stands back a little, not because of anything you do but because of what you are, even though you try so hard to prevent it. You end up a lonesome guy in a crowd.

"Rocco, there is something I would like to talk with you about," my mother said not long ago while we were at Grossinger's, in the Catskill Mountains of New York, where I always do my training and where I was getting ready for my San Francisco fight with Don Cockell on May 16th.

"Sure, Mom," I said. "I wish you'd talk to me any time you want."

"You are so important now," she said. "I don't like to bother you."

"I have been thinking," she said, and she had probably been carrying this around in her mind for a year or more, "that there is so much pleasure you miss. When your sister has a baby and when somebody gets married it is a beautiful thing. This is a happiness you should enjoy. The most wonderful things in life you cannot enjoy because you are so busy and a big man."

I knew this before she even said it, because it is part of being champion. My sister Concetta's baby is going on two years old now, and I didn't see her until she was almost six months old. When my old friend, Nicky Sylvester, got married I couldn't even get to the wedding. My own baby, Mary Anne, is two, and they tell me this is the time when it's the most fun to be with your child, that she's walking around the house now and that every day she's picking up a new word. Instead, I'm with my wife, Barbara, and the baby about four months a year.

When I get together with my old friends in Brockton it isn't the same, either. They never start a conversation. They answer my questions quickly, and I never do find out how they feel and what they're thinking, and we never have the laughs about the little things we used to have before. They no sooner get out to our house than they're starting for the door, because they're afraid they're bothering me, and I try to tell them they're not.

That's what it's like to be heavyweight champion, when you look at one side. But you have to give up something for everything you get, I guess, and when it gets me down and I lie in bed at night and feel a little depressed I think about all the good that there is in it, and it's more than you can imagine.

Take what it has meant to my pop. He's sixty-one years old now, and came to this country in 1917. He was gassed in World War I, fighting with the Second Marines at Château-Thierry, and he was never really well after that. For over 30 years he worked in the shoe shops in Brockton at a machine called a number 7 bed-laster, which is one of the tough ones. Four years ago I could see to it that he retired.

My mom was telling me that, when I was a kid, day after day would go by when Pop wouldn't say a word. With six kids to support on that little money at that tough job his life was a real drag. Just a few months ago Allie Colombo and

I were looking at some old pictures of Pop, and he was skin and bones. Now he's gained about ten pounds, and he has a great time in his quiet way, helping around the camp.

Outside of your own family, you can make the title mean so much for other people. One of my greatest pleasures is meeting some nice little guy, like my kind of people, and, when I can make it, going into town with him. This is a real honest, hard-working quiet little guy that nobody ever paid much attention to, and he takes me around and introduces me to everybody and this makes him important where he works and lives.

Once I made a speech at a dinner in Boston of the big shoe manufacturers. Everybody who spoke was telling jokes, and I'm not good at that, so I thought I'd try to make a point in a light way.

I told them that, if I was a good fighter, I thought they should take some of the credit for it. I said my pop worked in the shoe shops for thirty years and I used to carry his lunch to him and I saw how tough it was. I told them that sometimes I saw his pay and I saw how little he got. I said: "He used to tell me: 'I want you to stay out of the shoe shops.' So, to keep away from them, I became a fighter instead, and therefore I think you men had a part in making me a fighter."

I don't know if I got it across. I just thought it was worth a try.

The influence you have, that you can use for good without being a crusader, goes so far beyond what you think that sometimes it frightens you. After I won the title from Walcott, Al Weill, Charlie Goldman the trainer, two sparring partners—Bob Golden and Toxie Hall—and I made a five-week 30,000-mile exhibition tour of the Pacific, and when they say you're heavyweight champion of the whole world they mean it.

In Manila there were mobs wherever we went. Whenever I'd come out of the hotel for my walk there'd be 100 people waiting just to look at me. One day I went into a store to buy souvenirs, and there were 500 people watching for me outside. When I got in a cab, dozens of them ran after it.

Out there they don't look for autographs. All they want is to feel the muscles in your arms. One day I was walking along the street and a little guy stopped his car in the middle of heavy traffic, got out, ran up to me, felt my muscles and got back in his car and drove off.

I tell this to explain something else that happened. I was scheduled to box on a Thursday, but it rained that day and the next two days. Then the promoter suggested I box on Sunday.

"No," I said, "I'm a Roman Catholic, and I go to church on Sunday."

I didn't think anything of it, but it was a big front-page story in the newspapers. When I'm training for a fight I have to train on Sundays too, but I don't have to box exhibitions on Sunday, and a little later we went out to visit a leper colony, and a priest spoke to me. "Rocky," he said, "these people out here are great sports enthusiasts, and we try to get them to be better church people. You've done more for the Catholic religion in that one move than anyone has done here in my time."

That's what I mean when I say that sometimes it frightens you. You might, without realizing it, say a wrong thing. Allie Colombo and I have been taking long walks together since we were kids, and he still goes out on the road with me and many times when we're walking we work out what I'll say in a speech or if a certain question is asked.

Before we went to the leper colony we were a little nervous, because we didn't know what it would be like. There was a woman who explained that we couldn't contract the disease, and she told us how the poor people in the colony never see anyone important and have so little to look forward to.

There were, maybe, 1,200 people in the place, and when we got there they just moved back to make a path for us without anyone saying anything to them, and it was one of the saddest things I ever saw. I went up on a stage and they asked if they could see my muscles and how I train, so I took off my shirt and I shadow-boxed a couple of rounds.

Then we started out. Again they pulled away, to make that path, and they began to call to me.

"God bless you, Rocky," they were calling. "God bless you. May you reign long."

If you think that being heavyweight champion of the world is all happiness you're wrong. In Los Angeles, before we went to the Pacific, we visited the iron-lung patients in a hospital called Rancho Los Amigos, and maybe it was there more than any other place that I realized what being champion of the world means.

We went to the men's polio ward first and there was one kid lying there who knew everything about me, and we'd catch each other's eyes in his mirror while we talked. There was another guy who'd been a basketball player for Loyola, and when I looked in his mirror to talk with him I saw he had my picture pasted on it. They say I had guts in the Walcott fight, but this kid was telling me how he'd lick it and play basketball again.

After that we went to the women's ward, where there were a lot of fourteen- and fifteen-year-old kids, and the nurse told us that all that day they'd had all the nurses busy primping them because I was coming. With us was a friend of mine, Ernie Clivio, who has a dairy in Stoneham, Massachusetts, and when we got out we just looked at each other and I thought we might both cry.

Shortly after I won the title, Al Weill and I received a letter from the White House saying that the President doesn't get to see many sports events and so he was having a sports luncheon to meet some of the sports figures. They wanted to know if we'd be kind enough, if you can imagine, to attend.

I was more nervous than I've ever been going into a fight. Joe DiMaggio, Ty Cobb, Cy Young, Clark Griffith, Ben Hogan, Gene Sarazen, Florence Chadwick and about 40 others were there, and to begin with we were all formed in a semicircle in the White House when the President came in.

"So you're the heavyweight champion of the world," he said, when he came to me, and then he stepped back and looked at me and smiled.

"Yes, sir," I said.

"You know," he said, "somehow I thought you'd be bigger."

"No, sir," I said.

After the luncheon we posed on the White House steps, and one of the photographers who's a real fight fan took a picture of the President looking at my right fist.

Can you imagine me, Rocco Marchegiano, a shoe worker's son and a Pfc in the Army, posing with a five-star general who became the President of the United States?

Everybody, of course, isn't for you when you're champion. There are people who make remarks, and often you find that women don't understand.

"What makes you enjoy hurting people?" an elderly woman said to me one night at a dinner party in Milton, Massachusetts.

"I don't enjoy hurting them," I said.

"Then why do you do it?" she said. "Is it some sadistic impulse?"

I dropped it then, but I think it's important for people to understand what you feel about an opponent. I don't want them to think that the heavyweight champion of the world is just a pug.

When I train for a fight I devote 8 to 12 weeks getting ready to fight another man. The sports writers say I live a monk's life because I put all my thoughts and all my efforts into it, and all those around me devote themselves to the same thing.

There are a number of key people who are very important to a fighter getting ready for a fight. They are his wife and family, if he's married, his manager, his trainer and his best friend. In all of these I've been very lucky.

That's the usual thing to say, but I mean it. When a fighter goes into camps for those two or three months his mind should be free and no problems should move in on it. My wife, Barbara, and I find that even in the four months a year we have together we don't have the freedom we want, but she has yet to make one complaint. We talk on the phone regularly while I'm in camp, but two weeks before a fight she'll always say that I'm not to call her again until the fight is over, and my family is the same.

I couldn't have made it without Al Weill and Charlie Goldman, who trains me. On the way up Al got me opponents who, with only one exception and he got timid after I hit him a good punch, gave me a good fight for as long as it went.

"You see, you're learnin' while you're earnin'," Charlie used to tell me.

I'll never forget the first day seven years ago when I met Al and Charlie. Allie Colombo and I had bummed down from Brockton with our lunch in a paper bag, and I wanted Al to manage me and I was scared.

"If I manage you," he said, "you got to remember this. With me, I'm the boss. I do the managing and all you do is the fightin'. You don't ask me who you're fightin' or where you're fightin' or how much you're gettin'. When you go to the gym you do what Charlie tells you, and after the fight you get your share."

That's the way it should be with a fighter, really. I don't have any of the money worries, and I was a real crude kid as a young fighter and Charlie taught me everything I know.

Allie Colombo is a guy who thinks and feels just like I do. Camp could get pretty grim at the end if you didn't have somebody like that to talk with.

The last month before a fight I don't even write a letter. The last ten days I see no mail and get no telephone calls and meet no new acquaintances. The week before the fight I'm not allowed to shake hands or go for a ride in a car. Nobody can get into the kitchen, and no new foods are introduced. Even the conversation is watched.

By that I mean that the fellas keep it pleasant, with not too much fight talk. My opponent's name is never mentioned, and I don't read the write-ups because, as Charlie explained it, somebody might write one idea that might stick in my mind.

"Besides," he said, "think what fun it will be to read the clippings after the fight and see who was right and who was wrong."

For two or three months, then, every minute of my life is planned for one purpose. I don't even think about what I'm going to do the day after the fight, because that's going to be like an adventure, and exciting. Everything on my part and on the part of everybody else in camp is directed toward one goal—to lick the other man. I see him in front of me when I'm punching the bag. When I run on the road I've got him in mind, and always I'm working on certain moves that I hope will lick him.

Take the second Walcott fight. Willie Wilson, one of my sparring partners, had Walcott's moves down very good. He'd feint me and pull away or, after I'd hit him a punch, he'd pull down and try to tie me up. The big problem was to figure out what I was going to hit him with for a second punch, and one night Allie and I were talking about it, walking for about 45 minutes after dinner, and then we talked it over with Charlie and Al.

We decided to try right-hand uppercuts after a left hook, and I practiced it a lot on the big bag and then against Wilson. As it happened, the fight went less than a round, but the 3-D movies showed why very well. I hit him with a hook, but as he ducked to take it high on the head he moved right into the power of that uppercut, because, with an uppercut, the power is right after you start it.

When he went down I moved to a neutral corner, and when the count got to eight I said to myself: "You know, this fella isn't going to get up."

For the second La Starza fight—the one with my title on the line—we knew he carried his left high, and always brought it back high. I had to bring that hand down to get to his head, so I practiced throwing right hands to the heart. Finally, along around the tenth round, I got his arm down and I stopped him in the eleventh.

When you work and work like that with only one purpose in mind for weeks on end there's only one thing you want to do—and that's get out there and try it in a fight. Of course, to begin with, you enjoy the fight itself, or you wouldn't be a fighter.

What it comes down to in the ring is that it's the other guy or you. Anybody in there with me is there to get me and I'm in there to get him, but the one thing people don't seem to understand is that there's nothing personal about it and you don't carry it outside the ring. You get rid of it in there.

Walcott is an example. I never wanted to lick a man more, because I had to lick him to get his title. Coming up to the second fight his manager was complaining that I'm a dirty fighter and that I hit low and butted Joe in our first fight. One night on television in Chicago he even had a billygoat on with him to represent me, but you know that's only part of the publicity.

When I was training for La Starza, Walcott came up to see me work in the hangar where I train at the Grossinger airfield. After the photographers had finished posing us, Joe and I got to talking, with nobody listening, over behind the bags. "Joe," I said, "how's the motel going out there in Jersey?"

"Fine," he said. "Very good."

"I hope you make a lot of money with it," I said.

"Rock," he said, "I want to say this. I liked that title. I didn't want to lose it to anybody, but if I had to lose it, I'm glad I lost it to you. You're a good fighter and you're gonna be a great champ."

"I appreciate that, Joe," I said, "and I think you're a great guy."

This was a real warm thing, and why not? Walcott fought his greatest fight against me, and I fought my greatest against him. This is something that people are going to talk about for the rest of our lives, and we can be proud of it. It took two of us to do this together. One can't do it alone.

I have the same kind of fondness for other guys I fought. On the way up I knocked out Johnny Pretzie in five rounds, Gino Buonvino in ten rounds and then in two in a return, and Bernie Reynolds in three. After I became champ I wondered what they were doing and I wrote them post cards.

Reynolds didn't answer me, but I had a nice letter from Buonvino and his wife and one from Pretzie. Buonvino is a carpenter in New York now, and he and his wife sent me their best. Pretzie wrote me that he had a young fighter he was training, and he recalled our fight.

"But don't you think somebody might lick you?" I get asked. "Don't you ever worry about it?"

I don't want to seem like I'm bragging, but I don't think anybody in the world can lick me. I've never been defeated in 47 fights as a pro, and right now I hope maybe I can hold the title, if I'm lucky, four or five more years and retire undefeated. At the same time, once in a while, maybe seven or eight times when I'm building up to a fight, the thought comes to me on the road or while I'm resting: "Suppose this guy licks me? What will happen to all my plans?" That's as far as it gets. I never believe it can happen, really. It's just one of the things that come to your mind.

I can remember, though, the night that Joe Louis and Jersey Joe Walcott fought for the first time and Walcott had Louis down twice but didn't get the decision. I had had one pro fight 10 months before, and I was working for the

Brockton Gas Company and I was sitting on the bed at home listening to the fight.

It never occurred to me that I would be the guy to knock out Louis and retire him and then knock out Walcott and take the heavyweight championship of the world. Now that I'm champion I wonder, once in a while, if there is some other kid nobody ever heard of sitting someplace and listening to one of my fights, or watching it on television, who might, in a few years, do the same thing to me.

Out on the West Coast there's this big, young heavyweight named Charlie Powell. He put together a lot of knockouts last year, and they were touting him as a real good prospect. The night last fall when he fought Charley Norkus I watched on television, and when the fight got under way I could see that he was a big guy and boxed nice and could punch. "You know," I thought to myself, "this might be the guy."

Norkus finally knocked Powell out, but he's still a prospect. I'm heavy-weight champion of the world, but is there some young fighter somewhere who wants it as much as I did? The champion never knows.

---

## A Different Kind of Hell
### 1971

---

### Bill Libby

---

"In war," the war hero said, "we were so intent on death we forgot about life. Poverty and war robbed me of my youth. I never learned how to live. Life in Hollywood," the war hero turned actor said, "is not my idea of living, but it's become the only life I know. Sometimes I think it might have been easier on me if I'd of died back on one of those battlefields. I wouldn't of been unique. Lots of good boys died back there. I'm no better than they were. Who knows what they might of come to? A lot of 'em might of come to a lot more than me."

He had been in his time of heroism baby-faced, freckle-faced and hand-some. Now, nearly 25 years later, he remained boyish-looking, though his face had gotten fleshy and his small frame had filled out with a little fat. He was a partner in a production company financed by outsiders who were not Hollywood people, and his office was in the basement of a hotel on Franklin Street. He had made a low-budget film titled *A Time for Dying,* and he was struggling to arrange release for it from fellows who already had forgotten him.

He'd been on the phone all day seeking deals for money which might bail him out of debt. He was deep in debt. He owed money to many people and he owed back taxes to the government, which once had given him medals and now hounded him for money. And at night, when he went home, he did not go into the main house, as his neighbors assumed he did, but into the adjoining garage, which had been converted into living quarters for him, and where, separated from his second wife, he lived alone so he could be close to his two teen-age sons. Here, he had drifted through sleepless nights toward pills, which had addicted him and which he was resisting desperately.

"Where I've been was bad, but I wonder sometimes if where I'm heading isn't worse," he said. His pale eyes were clear, but seemed strangely cold. His empty hands fussed with papers on his desk that seemed unfamiliar to him. He said, "I've never found a place for myself. I'm here because it's where I have something I can do, but I don't do it well. The only thing I've ever found I was any good at was war, which is a terrible thing." He shook his head at the thought, depressed by it.

He said, "I used to think there could be nothing worse than war, than killing and maybe being killed and seeing your buddies killed. But in a way that was simple compared to live here in Hollywood. There, everyone understood the rules: You either killed or got killed. Here, the rules are much more complicated. A person gets mixed up in contracts and talent and no talent and big egos and phonies and it is hard to live, let alone have a decent marriage and raise a decent family.

"I have found there is nothing worse than owing people money and having them come after you about it all the time and not knowing how to make it and pay it back. Living like this is as bad as dying on a battlefield. After a while, you kid yourself that it's not real. By then you're losing your self-respect. Well, I'll tell you, I don't want that to happen. I'm strong. I'm too tough for this town. I won't let it break my heart. I won't let it break me. I'll fight it to the finish." He smiled a little then and shrugged and added, "I just wish it was a fight I knew how to fight."

This conversation took place some 18 months ago. Audie Murphy was having hard times, which did not ease with the passing of time. Last month, he had embarked on the last of several long-shot business ventures, which he hoped would save him from bankruptcy, when a private plane in which he was flying crashed in Virginia. In death he was remembered as a hero and given memorial services here and a burial with honors in Arlington, which his widow and his sons and many of his wartime buddies and some fans attended, but which former friends from Hollywood skipped.

He was the son of a poor Texas sharecropper, the product of a broken marriage and dirt poverty. He became famous and rich and admired, and he wound up going through two marriages, worrying about his own sons, poor again, and almost forgotten until the finish.

During the war, he killed or captured 240 men and was awarded 24 decorations. After the war, he made more than 40 movies and earned more than $2 million. He blew the money and wound up owing more than $1 million. He had written a book based on his battlefield experiences, *To Hell and Back,* which was successful, and he sold it for a film, and starred, himself, in it. The movie was successful, too, but he was not. He was our most decorated soldier and one of our least decorated actors. He fashioned for himself a new kind of hell there.

Murphy was born in June of 1924 in Farmersville, Texas, one of 11 children. His parents were poor tenant farmers. His father wearied of the struggle and deserted his family when Audie was a small boy. "I don't think about him any more. I stopped a long time ago," Murphy said. His mother struggled in the field to get by for her family, which never had much, and died when Audie was 16. "She worked herself to death. She died of despair," her son said. The younger children were placed in orphanages and the older ones worked to support themselves and each other. The family fell apart. "Some died. Some did other things. It's been hard to keep track of 'em, but few of 'em ever had the chance to do much."

Murphy made do with odd jobs in the fields and in town and had no idea what he would do with his life until World War II came along when he was 17. Then he had the war to do. He had often hunted for his food and like many farmboys he was good with a gun. And he was stirred by patriotism. He tried to enlist in the Marines and in the paratroops, but he was rejected because he was too small and underweight. Finally, he got into the Army, but after basic training he was made a clerk in a post exchange. He kept after his superiors until he got what he wanted—assignment to combat with the infantry.

He had never been more than 100 miles from his home when he was sent into combat in North Africa and wound up fighting on the beaches of Italy and France and in the invasion of Germany. At first, his fellows laughed at him because he looked too young and frail to wage war and endure its hardships. Their teasing tormented him. At first, he found he *was* afraid. He remembered vomiting in the dirt in the rain.

He remembered clearly the first deaths he saw: "One minute a man is sitting on a grassy slope talking about his family back home. In the distance, a gun slams. And in the next minute, the man is dead." He saw many men die. He remembers men with their faces blown away or half their bodies blasted off them. He said, "You never forget these things. They etch themselves in your brain and you keep seeing them in your mind. You try to put them aside, but they're always there. You're thinking of something else and the horror comes back to you."

It disgusted him and drove him to deeds of death of his own. "At first you're forced to fight because you have to and you're being pushed and don't want to be considered a coward, but then you want to because you want to kill those who are killing you, you want to save yourself and get even, because there's nothing else to do there but that, because killing and even dying loses its meaning in a place where there is so much killing and dying all the time," he said years later in that office of despair. He told this writer of fighting in scorching heat, sweaty and dirty, and in bitter cold, freezing and numb.

Once when a buddy was killed, he angrily moved out alone into the open with a machine gun on one hip and crossed a field mowing down Germans. Somehow, he was not hit. Another time, he jumped onto an abandoned tank, turned a machine gun on the enemy and single-handedly staved off a Nazi force of 250 men and six tanks. The tank was hit three times and he was blown off it, but he was not hurt.

He was not always so fortunate. He caught malaria. One shell injured one foot; another injured the other foot. This second shell landed near him and sprayed fragments around him like some deadly umbrella, killing men further away from it than he was.

A German soldier shot him in the hip, and Murphy turned around and shot the soldier dead. Gangrene developed in Murphy's wound, but treatment cleared it up. His injuries healed. Each time he voluntarily returned from treatment at hospitals to resume fighting at the front, alongside his buddies.

For a long time, he felt proud of himself. He felt like some noble killer. He described a rifle on his lap as "beautiful as a flower and more to be trusted than your best friend." For a long time he just accepted what he was supposed to do and he did it. "I always said you had to be young and ignorant to be a good foot soldier. I was both," he said in our conversation years later. "It helps if you think you're doing right. I thought so then. I'm not so sure now. In view of the fact that we've had so many wars and so much killing since, I'm not sure it was ever right. Even by the end of my war, I wasn't so sure. When we heard there was going to be peace, I stopped killing. I was supposed to go on. We were still fighting. But I began to miss. My desire had worn away. The heart for it had gone out of me."

He is credited with having killed more than 100 men, having captured more than 100 and having wounded close to 500. In that later time he shrugged and said, "I don't know how they know. Maybe the War Department kept count somehow. Maybe the officers sent in totals. I didn't keep count. I don't know how many. I don't want to know." For this, he won promotion from private to lieutenant in the field and was awarded, among many others, the Congressional Medal of Honor, the Distinguished Service Cross, the Legion of Merit, three Purple Hearts, two Silver Stars and a Bronze Star—more medals than any other soldier in World War II. He said, "Many never got medals they deserved. Many heroes were forgotten as they lay dead in the field."

When the war ended, this tiny, simple, shy Southwesterner was celebrated. He was the small-town boy who had made good. He did not even know he was the most decorated hero of the war until he returned home, not yet 21 and old enough to vote, and was told so at a victory banquet. Parades and receptions were staged in his honor. Famous men shook his hand, and women, like the kind he'd dreamed boyish fantasies about at the front, pursued him.

A publisher paid him to do his book and *Life* portrayed him on its cover. James Cagney studied the picture and read the story and suggested he come to Hollywood. "I had nothing better to do so I did," he explained later. "At home, some wanted to hire me because I was a famous killer, others wouldn't for the same reason. I couldn't get a job that left me any self-respect. I did like the idea of maybe making some money in movies."

He had no money to begin with and slept wherever he could find a bed for a while. At one time, his bed was the floor of a gymnasium which was deserted at night. Then a producer put him to work as a West Pointer in *Beyond Glory* and, after that, others jumped on the bandwagon, trying to cash in on Murphy's fame. He made such unmemorable movies as *Bad Boy, Ride Clear of Diablo* and *Guns at Fort Petticoat*. He was put into pictures in which he could hold a gun in his hand, shoot people and portray a hero. Most were westerns. He was typecast, but didn't look the type. You saw him in a sagebrush shootdown on the screen and thought, this is silly, this boy couldn't kill anyone—and then you remember that in real life he had killed a lot of people.

He had little acting ability and a pale personality, but he got by, getting a bit better as he went, and built a fair following, and, while there still was a market for B movies, he made as much as $125,000 a film. He was popular at parties, which he disliked. He wearied of being introduced around as "the boy who killed so many lousy krauts." He tried to fit in, to belong. Hangers-on attached themselves to him. He spent freely and was a soft touch for loans. Rather than annoy or offend anyone, he never pressed for repayment and never was repaid, even when he needed it.

He married Wanda Hendrix, an attractive actress, but the union lasted less than a year. He tried again, marrying Pamela Archer, an airline stewardess, and had two sons with her before this marriage, too, went bad. They had a fancy two-story English-style house with a pool in the Valley, which he managed to keep for his family. He also bought an 848-acre horse ranch about 60 miles from Hollywood, where he could hide out, and he loved this place more than any other, but he lost it.

As times altered in the late '50s, his acting career careened downhill. He was a freak and he began to flounder. He was a hero as we entered an era of antiheroes. The world was tired of war and violence. His fame had been eroded by time and poor pictures. He no longer seemed real. And as Hollywood was hit hard by television, his B movies no longer got made. Murphy began to be offered $20,000 for starring parts, then less for bits, finally nothing. In the early 1960s, he tried a TV series, *Whispering Smith,* which flopped. He refused offers to do commercials for beer and cigarette companies. He said, "How would it look: 'War Hero Drinks Booze'? I couldn't do that to the kids."

Then there were no more offers.

He had made some bad investments. Mainly, he sank $260,000 into an

Algerian oil venture which was wiped out in the six-day Arab-Israeli war. It was with some shock that he found himself not only going broke, but far behind in bills owed. He had to sell his beloved ranch to Bob Hope to keep going, but soon that money was gone, too. Money due him in residuals from showings of his old movies on TV were attached by the Internal Revenue Service, which began to press him for overdue past payments.

The '60s turned out to be a tough 10 years for Murphy, who tried it back in Texas for a while, failed there, too, and returned to Hollywood to be near his sons. He lived on hope, along with so many similarly hopeless souls here down on their luck and hustling after fortune in the shape of a movie or a business deal which will make it big and restore their status. He found he had few friends here and few elsewhere, and less hope.

A year and a half ago he sat in that basement office he had opened up and spoke of his life with a striking lack of pretense. He had the aura of a cardboard cutout character, but he was real and he was honest and he would not run from reality. "I had one hangup as an actor," he said, smiling. "I had no talent. I didn't hide that. I told directors that. They knew. I didn't have to tell them. They protected me. I made the same movie 20 times. It was easy. But it wasn't any good. I never got to be any good. No one helped me. No one cared if I got any good or not. They used me until I was used up.

"I only got to make three films with quality people and these were the only ones that got any quality acting out of me. They are the only things I've done in Hollywood I'm proud of. One was John Huston's *The Red Badge of Courage*. The critics liked it, but the public didn't. Another was *The Quiet American,* which had a chance until it was ruined in the cutting room, and then flopped. The last was my own *To Hell and Back,* which was my one big success. It's still playing around the world. It grossed more than $13 million and was the record money-maker for Universal-International at the time. I made $800,000 out of the book and the film. I have no idea where it went to."

Murphy had worn an expensive suit into his office. He sat at his desk in his shirtsleeves, his collar and tie loosened, but he seemed prosperous. His shoes were shined, his fingernails clean, his hair neatly trimmed. But, as he pointed out, appearances are deceiving. He said, "Money never meant much to me. I gave a lot away and lost a lot in investment. I hired agents and managers to take care of me, but some took care of themselves and took me, instead. Not all of them. Some of them. They were supposed to protect me financially. They were supposed to build their tax shelters for me. They took their 10 percent off the top, and sometimes much more, but they didn't protect me and anything I built up crumbled."

He shrugged and said, "I don't blame them. I blame me. I didn't know anything about business and money, but I should have made it my business to know. I left it up to others. But a man has to look out for himself. I didn't. No one does anything to you. You do it to yourself or let it be done to you. What the hell, it's an old story; I'm not unique."

Wistfully, he spoke of friends deserting him. "You can't call them friends," he said. "Hell, I don't think anyone has any friends in the industry anyway. Like ships that pass in the night, you make a picture with people, then go your separate ways. When you're hot, everyone wants a piece of you. When word gets around you're washed up, no one will touch you with a 10-foot pole. You take a little tumble and suddenly they can pass you in the street without seeing you. When you call, they're never in, and they never return your calls. They're afraid you'll ask them for a job. Or a loan. Or maybe repayment of an old debt. Even the hangers-on move on. People who used to invite you to parties stop inviting you. The good tables in the swank restaurants go to others. Soon you're lucky if you're eating."

He smiled a little and said, "Soon, you begin to feel like a prostitute who's over the hill." He swiveled around in his chair and leaned back and closed his eyes and looked up at his private thought for a few moments. Then he said, "I've left a couple of times to go home to Texas to look around. There was nothing for me to do there, except starve. When this Texan bit the dust, even his fellow Texans suffered paralysis of their trigger fingers. They'd fumble for their wallets and sneak out when my back was turned. So I came back here. I don't know how to do anything but act, and I don't know how to do that very well. I don't know any business except the movie business. I have learned that. I'm too old a dog to learn new tricks. I'm too old to try anything new. Hollywood is my home now. I have to make it here or nowhere."

He had found a couple of loyal friends outside of Hollywood who were interested in helping him here. These were Jerry Spellman, a tax attorney who lost a leg in the war, and Rich Clinton, an oilman and patriot. They had backed him in FIPCO Productions, named after Spellman's First Investment Planning Mortgage Company. Murphy didn't have unlimited backing, but he had something. He opened up this small office, hired a secretary and began to seek people who could make movies cheaply.

He found Budd Boetticher, another outcast, who'd once impressed many people in the industry by making good B westerns, but depressed others with his temperamental ways and has been in exile in Mexico for years. Boetticher had written a screenplay and Murphy hired him to direct it into a movie, *A Time for Dying*. They cast mostly unknowns but also such diverse performers as singer Beatrice Kay, stripper Betty Rowland and rodeo star Casey Tibbs. Murphy played a bit as a bearded Jesse James and even used his oldest son, Terry, in a part. It was brought in for $800,000 and now Murphy was trying to get distribution on it.

He said he had high hopes for it. He said he had other films planned, including a Mexican western in which his son would have another role. He said he wanted to make westerns because they were "surefire." He said he didn't want to make any war movies, "which glorify death," or political films, "which preach," or love stories, "which are nothing but sex orgies." He said he wanted to do some acting, but also wanted to do some directing. He said he figured he'd get three or four films out as fast as he could, "because the way business is, you never know, and if your first two or three are flops, you still may hit it big with your fourth."

His eyes brightened. He became animated and spoke with enthusiasm about the many promising projects that were going to put him back on top. He said he was planning a television series that would star his son as a kid who befriends a war dog in peacetime and which "just might make it, like *Lassie,* 'cause you never know." He said he'd written some poems ("Dusty Old Helmet" was one) and some songs and was going to launch a music publishing and recording firm. He also said he hoped to launch an investment service. "We have big dreams," he said.

He said his debts were down to $500,000 and his unpaid income taxes to $56,000, which he expected to pay off in a year or so. "The money wears on me some," he admitted. "Oh, you get used to being in debt in this town. Some say owing money is a sign of success. Actually, borrowing money is a sign of success, but I can't right now. Anyway, what the hell, a man knows what his obligations are. I'm not worried about getting rich. And I'm not worried about leaving a fortune to my sons. They can stand on their own feet. It's just that their old man wants to stand on his own feet, too."

An open man, Murphy was not secretive about his private life. He spoke freely of his marriages. He said, "Wanda and I were in love. It just didn't work. It would have worked, I think, if we hadn't been Hollywood stars. There's too much temptation when you're at the top here and she wanted to be big. She was ambitious and extroverted. She was fun-loving and liked parties. I wasn't ambitious. I was introverted. I didn't care about being a star. I didn't find parties fun. I wanted a home life, but we were never home. Our movies kept us apart. Finally, we came apart. We were divorced. She remarried. She's still acting some, seeking parts. She's a good girl. I have no hard feelings towards her."

He married again and there were two sons by this union. The second marriage, too, did not work out, but it wasn't dissolved. "I didn't want to leave my boys without a father while they were growing up," Murphy said. "So I had the garage fixed up and I moved in. It looks like part of the house. Somehow, I've held onto the house. We never told anyone. People didn't know I never got no further than that damn garage."

He hung his head a moment, his eyes averted. Then he smiled and looked up and said, "My sons are Terry and James and they're good boys and I'm deeply proud of them and I've tried to be a good father to them. I care, you see. Terry has acted some and he sings and plays the guitar, but he's not sure what he wants to be. Jim isn't sure what he wants to be. They're getting near draft age and one thing I don't want them to be is soldiers.

"I'm something of a super-patriot, but these aren't real wars we're fighting these days, except that boys really are being killed. These wars are morally wrong. It's not right to ask young men to risk their lives in wars they can't win. Anyway, war is a nasty business, to be avoided if possible and to be gotten over with as soon as possible. It's not the sort of job that a man should get a medal for. I'll tell you what bothers me. What if my sons try to live up to my image? What if people expect it of them?" His voice grew soft and sad. "I've talked to them about it. I want them to be whatever they are. I don't want them to try to be what I was. I don't want dead heroes for sons."

He was silent a few seconds, then said, "Anyway, God willing, they're about ready to lead their own lives. And I'm ready to begin leading my own life. During the war, the medics hooked me on pills. Remembering the war, I needed sleeping pills. For years, I couldn't sleep. Finally, I just threw away the pills. I pulled the monkey off my back and kicked the habit. Now I find I can sleep again. Now I want to begin sleeping in a decent bed again. I want to move out. I've been living this strange life, like a watchman, for a long time, but my boys don't need a watchman much longer. I want to find a decent place to live and do decent work and get decently out of debt and forget the war and the hero stuff and the past god-damn 10 years and make a new life for myself."

It was easier said than done. His production business and other projects didn't prosper. Many dreams did not materialize. He clung to his family and is said to have tried a reconciliation with his wife. Left with little more than his image, he seemed unable to discard it. He started acting tough. He had been appointed a special officer of the Port Hueneme police force and made some patrol-car rounds and offered help to the Los Angeles police in their efforts to combat the drug problem. Arrested on a charge of illegal possession of black-jacks, he was absolved because of his special status. Arrested on a charge of assault with attempt to commit murder when he backed up a bartender buddy in an argument over another man's treatment of a dog, he was exonerated. He did not seem to mind the publicity and television interviews, which gave him the first prominence he'd had in years.

Recently, he was working with D'Alton Smith, a former Teamsters' Union member convicted of federal securities violations in Texas, in an attempt to secure Teamster boss Jimmy Hoffa's release from federal prison. Murphy also was participating in patriotic causes with the likes of broadcaster George Put-nam, and the week he was killed he was scheduled to appear on Putnam's *Selling America* telecast. But on Memorial Day weekend, he was killed while on a trip to look over a Martinsville, Virginia, plant run by Modular Management, which produced factory-built homes and was interested in having the war hero as a front man.

In a thunderstorm, the plane carrying six, including officials of the firm, missed Martinsville and flew into the side of Birch Mountain in a fiery crash. Searchers picked up the remains out of the rugged woods and the charred wreckage and struggled up dirt roads with the bodies. Because Audie Murphy was one of the bodies, the crash made headlines. He was less than one month from his 47th birthday and more than 25 years from his greatest triumphs. War didn't kill him; peace did.

His body was flown back to Los Angeles, where funeral rites were con-ducted at the Church of the Hills at Forest Lawn Memorial Park in Hollywood. He was eulogized as "a quiet, unassuming, soft-spoken man." More than 600 listened. Many more who could not get into the chapel stood outside on the hills and terraces. But the only Hollywood personality noticed was Murphy's ex-wife Wanda Hendrix, who emerged weeping and said, "He was a great soldier. No one can ever take that away from him."

His body was then flown to Washington, D.C. The U.S. Army band played and a horse-drawn caisson carried him to his burial place in Arlington National Cemetery, in the shade of a black oak tree, near other former servicemen, near 250 other Medal of Honor winners, near The Tomb of the Unknowns.

Many of his former wartime buddies were there, reminiscing about his remarkable battle deeds. His former commanding officer, retired Colonel Kenneth Parter, was there; he said, "You can just say he was the best soldier there ever was." Army Chief of Staff William Westmoreland was there. Movie industry people were not there. Few from Texas were there and few from his adopted home town of Hollywood. No great crowd turned out; war heroes are not especially popular these days. But when the casket was lowered into the ground and the flag which had draped it was folded and presented to his widow, she held it in front of her proudly. She and her sons held their heads up proudly.

The last words this writer heard Audie Murphy speak were as follows: "In the war, we forgot how to live. Since the war, all these years in Hollywood, I've lived an unreal life. The war and the movies gave me a great deal, but they also took a great deal from me." The tense little man shook his head and said, "I've had tough times, but I found out I wasn't afraid of dying so why should I be afraid of living? I don't know how to be scared, do you know that? Since the war, nothing scares me and nothing excites me. What is there in this life that compares to a battle for excitement? What does money mean when a guy who can't act makes a hundred grand a film? Hell, someone could throw a million dollars in my lap today and I'd say, 'What the hell is this for?" His boyish face broke into a grin and he said, "Well, it was good for me being broke flat. It was good for me being hurt. It rekindled my spirit. It made me want to fight back. It made me want to begin living again," he said.

## To My White Working-Class Sisters
## 1970

## Debbie D'Amico

We are the invisible women, the faceless women, the nameless women . . . the female half of the silent majority, the female half of the ugly Americans, the smallest part of the "little people." No one photographs us, no one writes about us, no one puts us on T.V. No one says we are beautiful, no one says we are important, very few like to recognize that we are *here*. We are the poor and working-class white women of America, and we are cruelly and systematically ignored. All of our lives we have been told, sometimes subtly, sometimes not so subtly, that we are not worth very much. This message has been put across to me, a white working-class woman, all my life. I think the time has come to speak out against these insults, and so I have decided to write about parts of my life and my ideas. I am doing this for all my sisters who have been made to feel that they are not worth writing about, and for all those people who have to be convinced of poor white existence, those same people who told us that because we are all white our lives are the same as those of the middle and upper class.

When I was in the second grade, we were given a sample aptitude test to accustom us to the test-taking rut that would ultimately determine whether we would be programmed toward college or a dead-end job. After we had answered several multiple-choice questions, the teacher had us check our answers against the "right" ones. One of the questions pictured a man in a tuxedo, a man in a suit, and a man in overalls. The question read: "Which man is going to work?" The "correct" answer was: the man in the suit. I can still feel the shame that came with the realization that what went on in my home was marked "incorrect." I responded the way oppressed people often respond—by secretly hating myself and my family. I remember constantly begging my father to put on a suit—my father who worked an average of 65 to 80 hours a week driving trucks, checking out groceries in a supermarket, and doing any of the other deadening jobs which came his way. My mother didn't escape my judgments either. The unreal Dick, Jane, and Sally world our school books presented as the "right" way of life, reinforced by T.V. and middle-class school-

222

mates' homes, made me viciously attack her grammar whenever she spoke and ask her questions like: "How come *you* never wear dresses or get your hair done?" The world of my home gave me concrete answers: at the time my mother had three kids in diapers and another on the way, hardly a life style that called for a well-dressed mannequin. But the middle-class world of America was bigger than my home and I was overcome by its judgments.

As I went on through school, I continued to be taught about an America that had little to do with me. The picture of American life drawn in history books was almost always a comfortable one, with exceptions like wars and the Depression (hardships which the middle class participated in and thus wanted to talk about). Working-class sisters, wake up! Black people were not the only ones left out of history books. George Washington is no relative of yours; neither is Henry Ford, or Nixon or Agnew. While George Washington was relaxing at his Mt. Vernon estate, *your* ancestors may have been among the two-thirds majority of white settlers who served as indentured servants for Master George and others like him. They may have been servants who were kidnapped from the slums of England and Ireland and brought here in chains to be sold to the highest bidder. Your grandmother might have been one of the "huddled masses yearning to breathe free," who came to America and wound up in a tenement where free air never blew, working from can see to can't see, made to feel alien and ashamed of the Old World culture infinitely more alive and colorful than the drab, Puritan, "Mr. Clean" ways of America. I have listened to the old folks in my family talk about how they "came over," and how they survived, the first Italians in an all-Irish neighborhood. That is *my* history. While Mr. Pullman was amassing his fortune, our people were fighting and dying for the rights of working men and women, our people were being shot and beaten for what they believed. I was not taught this in school but learned it later on my own. In high school I continued to learn middle-class ways. I spent years learning to talk like them, eat like them, look like them. I learned a language that had little to do with the concrete terms of my life or the lives of my family and fellow workers.

At the same time that books were deluging me with middle-class culture, I began to feel the pinch of unworthiness in other ways. I attended a parochial high school for one year which was upper–middle-class dominated. If your family had no influential friends to take out $50 ads in the yearbook, you were punished—shame on you! they said, for your failure to measure up in America, shame on you because you haven't made it in the land of the free and the home of the brave.

During my high school years I entered the great rat race of women who were dedicated to snagging any and all men considered desirable. I was again led by middle-class values, and so I rejected the knit-shirted, "greasy"-haired, dark-skinned Italians I grew up with and made a mad dash for the Brylcreem man. All the while, of course, feeling I could never get him, because I wasn't the *girl* in the Brylcreem commercial. I read all the middle-class fashion and glamour magazines and tried to look like people who were able to look that way because of a life style that included a closet full of clothes I couldn't afford and a leisurely existence that allowed them to look cool and unruffled all the time. And there I was working in a luncheonette so shabby I never mentioned it to anyone for a lousy six dollars a Saturday that I immediately spent in vain efforts to make myself "acceptable" looking. During the day I gossiped condescendingly about the way people dressed, playing at being the glorious magazine girl, and at night I sulked off to the phone company to be bitten by cord lice and told all night that I was either very slow or innately stupid.

And people, in social and job situations, have been saying that ever since. In social situations it is said as I sit quietly by and watch well-dressed, slick, confident women of the upper classes, America's idea of beauty, steal the eyes, applause, and the image of woman from me. It is said in many ways on the job: at my last job I was mimeographer at a school, a "liberal progressive" school at that. I once spoke up at a staff meeting and the first remark to follow the stunned silence was, "Why doesn't someone put her on the faculty?" Yes, put me among the educated middle class because you absolutely can't deal with a worker who thinks and has ideas. After I mentioned this, I was told that it was a compliment and that I should be *grateful*. Grateful that they thought I was as good as them. At the same school I was once asked, "Are you the switchboard?" Naturally—since we are looked on as extensions of the machines we operate, not as human beings.

What all this has done to us is create a deep, deep sense of unworthiness, a sense so deep it dooms us. I have a thirteen-year-old friend who is well on the way to life either in prison or on heroin. We, *as a people,* have nothing that says to him, "You shouldn't ruin your life. You're a good, worthwhile person." If or when he does go to jail, there will be no Black Muslims to tell him he is a worthwhile person just because of what he is. No one will be there to give him the respect and support of an alternate culture that respects what he is. That is what the judgment of middle-class America has done to us.

Why has this happened to us? It has happened because we believed in the American dream, in the dream that *anyone* can be *anything* if he only tries, works hard, and if he doesn't make it it's only because something about *him* is rotten. Since we don't have much to begin with, we're made to feel we don't deserve much. And we believe it—even though the truth of our lives tells us that we have worked, and damned hard, but we still didn't have the kinds of lives we read about and saw on T.V. And America has kept us out of magazines and off T.V. *because* our faces and voices are full of this truth. We have hated black people, but we have hated ourselves more. By believing black people are inferior, we have kept the truth about ourselves from each other—that the people who have the power and money in America never intend to raise our incomes or those of black people, not because we aren't worthy, but because it would cut into their profits to do so. We believed black people were so inferior that they weren't supposed to make it—we believed we were superior and could make it—but we never did and we blame ourselves. As white people who haven't made it, we are the living proof of the American lie and we hate ourselves for it.

What can we do about all this? As poor and working-class women, we can *start* asking what is wrong with America and *stop* asking what is wrong with ourselves. In a culture where women are often judged by beauty alone, the standard of beauty does not fit us. We, as *ourselves,* as we go to work or wash dishes, we, *in our daily lives,* are never called beautiful. Black women have told themselves that they are beautiful in their natural lives, and we need to do the same for ourselves. We must begin to see ourselves as beautiful in our ability to work, to endure, in our plain honest lives, and we must stop aspiring to a false eyelash existence that is not and never has been for us. We are not the women in *Vogue, Glamour,* or *As The World Turns,* nor should we want to be. We are the women who have dealt all our lives with the truths and tragedies of real life, because we never had the option of the armchair-beautiful-people existence. We are the people who have no maids or therapists to dump our troubles on. We know what it is to work hard and we are not guilty of wearing silks while others wear rags. We should never admire the women in *Vogue,* because there is something undeniably ugly about women who wear minks while others can't afford shoes—and no amount of $20-an-ounce make-up can hide that brand of ugliness. We must start learning that other people have been victims of this middle-class culture aping the rich. Black and Puerto Rican, Mexican and Indian, Chinese and Japanese people have had their true history concealed and their faces scorned by T.V. and magazines. We must see that those who share the hardships we share are not the white middle and upper classes, but the black and brown people who work at our sides. As white working class and poor people we must begin to be proud of ourselves, our histories, and each other; we must unite and support ourselves as a people. Once we respect ourselves, we will find it necessary to struggle with a society and with jobs which tell us we are worthless. In that struggle we will learn that the anger of black and brown people which we have feared for so long has the same direction as our anger, that their enemies are our enemies, and their fight our fight.

# Part Three

---

## The Silent Generation: Growing Up
## in the 1950s

---

When they had won the war
And for the first time in history
Americans were the most important people—

When the leading citizens no longer lived in their shirt sleeves,
And their wives did not scratch in public;
Just when they'd stopped saying "Gosh!"—

When their daughters seemed as sensitive
As the tip of a fly rod,
And their sons were as smooth as a V-8 engine—

Priests, examining the entrails of birds,
Found the heart misplaced, and seeds
As black as death, emitting a strange odor.


Louis Simpson

*The Inner Part*


227

The particular political and cultural events of the 1950s helped to define the generation which now appears in most immediate contact with and contrast to today's students. When World War II ended, America, unlike the rest of the world, was powerful and secure, and the following years saw even greater economic success. The Korean War of the early 1950s never became as intrusive as the Vietnam War in the 1960s, nor was the country as obsessed with it. The great international struggle was seen as a "cold war" between capitalist and communist systems. "Cold," or "cool," an appropriate descriptive term here, also conveys the style of the times. The dominant personal mode was detachment, and many individuals followed basically selfish patterns of behavior; those who responded differently thought of themselves as alienated from the rest of society. Most Americans still pursued and almost worshiped achievement; yet the old sense of innovation and challenge which characterized the traditional myth had been replaced by ambitiousness on the one hand and passivity on the other. The successful recovery from the Depression and victory in World War II produced a generation which tended to believe that "truth will out," that "goodness can triumph." Men seemed more complacent than actively concerned about the general welfare of society.

This attitude was reflected in the political issues and personalities of the times: the Eisenhower Presidency from 1952–1960 produced no forceful programs and few forceful men. One of the most forceful, Senator Joseph McCarthy, was so in a dangerous and ultimately destructive way. His ambitious investigations as chairman of the Senate Permanent Investigations Subcommittee were a model for intimidation; they suggested, paradoxically, that silence and uninvolvement alone could insure freedom of action. There were few public protests against the committee's infringements on the rights of individuals, and whatever protest movements there were focused upon the larger, more general issues of nuclear disarmament. The possibility of an atomic war seemed very real because of the cold war atmosphere, perhaps more real because of memories of Hiroshima and Nagasaki. Awareness of imminent nuclear destruction, in turn, added to the sense of isolation and seemed to justify concern for one's own pleasure. The more serious side of this self-centeredness was manifested by an attraction to existential philosophy and literature. Camus' *The Stranger* and J. D. Salinger's *The Catcher in the Rye* were two of the most popular books of the time, because the young were able to identify with the protagonists and their dilemmas.

Like Salinger's Holden Caulfield, most youth responded to events of the time with silence and complacency. The personal philosophy of the Princeton student writing in "So Here I Am" derives from his particular past and the general atmosphere of society. While he thinks of himself as a "good Christian," his social consciousness extends no further than "sticking to professed principles." His goals are those of the fifties: competency, capability, achievement and above all security. If a child of this generation were to succeed, he would do so, like this young man, within the system, according to the values set by the majority of conforming Americans. His achievement, like that of an Alger hero, would be personal and his rewards, material; but unlike that of the mythical model, his success would be based not on private virtues but on his ability to work within a bureaucratic structure. Books like *The Organization Man* and *The Man in the Grey Flannel Suit* defined new stereotypes and new models which a young man could either deliberately emulate or consciously avoid.

As both W. H. Whyte, Jr. and Sloan Wilson suggest in these works, even those successful within the system were frequently dissatisfied; but when people from social or ethnic minorities could express their needs only in a framework of conformity and material rewards, the results were disillusioning and even destructive. It is interesting in this context to compare William Melvin Kelley, author of the essay "The Ivy League Negro," with Luther, the central character in Jay Neugeboren's short story. The former goes to Harvard, becomes involved in its traditions, even adopts the prejudices of white America. He recognizes, however, that by succeeding in an essentially white culture he has cut loose from and lost consciousnsss of his own race. Luther, vital and imaginative like his namesake, finds no sufficient help within the established educational system; and like the black children described in Herbert Kohl's *36 Children* and Jonathan Kozol's *Death at an Early Age,* he is almost destroyed by the schools. What saves him is a new religion completely of and for his own race, one destined to inspire fear and mistrust in the unbelievers of the sixties, but one which was able to provide him with an identity.

The energies which might have produced constructive or instructive changes either lay dormant, as the essay by Kelley suggests, or were dissipated because of lack of concern. On the most trivial level, they were directed into activities like phone-booth–stuffing contests. On a more serious level, Minnijean Brown describes how her attempts to enter Little Rock High School were frustrated by institutional inertia and a hostile southern society. Often discrimination turned youthful energies into negative, cynical or self-defeating channels. Piri Thomas' experience growing up in New York City's Spanish Harlem illustrates this; all his efforts were directed toward establishing his machismo, defending his reputation as a street fighter, and protecting the territory his gang had carved out of the public streets.

With few attractive models to emulate and little public recognition of large social issues it is not surprising that so few young Americans of the 1950s questioned their role in society or broke their silence at all. Paul Goodman, in his essay on "Patriotism" from *Growing Up Absurd,* makes the point that the atmosphere of this decade was not only comfort and conformity but also hypocrisy and meekness. For Goodman the great American Tragedy then was the loss of an honest, broad-based and humane patriotism in the young. The youth heard advertising men and politicians debase creativity, and they saw towns and cities become uglier and dirtier as they too grew without style.

Whatever illuminations brightened the general grayness of the times tended to be individual and more often than not were negative. Walter, in "Joe, the Vanishing American," is prepared to go to college, to accept his parents' notions of success. Unlike his counterpart of the 1930s, he can get a job, can earn money to help with his education. But his success at the automobile factory where he works is in discovering what is failing, what is vanishing in this affluent America. The illuminations of the protagonist in Leo Skir's "Other Chanukahs" are likewise negative: his parents are not what they profess to be; his religion is built on questioned facts; the culture in which he lives and the style in which he writes are changing and illusive.

The only movement opposing conventional values of the time was the Beat Generation, which John Clellon Holmes discusses; even they were silent in their opposition. They sought meaning and community among themselves, through paths which included drugs and cheap wine, jazz and poetry, promiscuity and wandering; but like the square society the beats sought to elude, they had no political commitment and no social program.

This generation, silent politically and socially, was ironically the last whose cultural orientation derived primarily from the written word. Although the fifties were called the "Golden Age" of television, the educational and cultural potentials of that medium went mostly unrealized. The more popular attractions were shows like "Howdy Doody" and "I Love Lucy"; there were situation comedies, westerns and quiz shows, but very little offering the controversial or the unusual. "You Asked for It," a program which guaranteed novelty, specialized merely in subjects like The World's Fattest Man and an oft-repeated fight between a cobra and a mongoose. The McCarthy hearings were televised, but more to warn Americans about threats to internal security than to illustrate the workings of government. For real information as well as entertainment, this generation still read books. Major publishers for the first time were producing inexpensive paperback libraries, reprinting important classical and modern works in literature, philosophy and the social sciences. The various schools of American criticism which began in the thirties and had little opportunity to flourish during the war became, in the fifties, a vital and important influence upon humanistic studies. As Renata Adler points out, most of her contemporaries who were students then and are writers now derived their influences and their models from literature, a practice which inevitably declined with the new role of television and other media in the sixties.

The silence of the fifties occurred because few voices were raised then against the complacency of the times; few people seemed to be sticking to their "professed principles"—most were too involved in pursuing phantoms of the American Dream, phantoms which from a later perspective seem unfortunate distortions of America's most cherished ideals.

# Luther
## 1965

## Jay Neugeboren

Luther arrived at Booker T. Washington Junior High School (Columbus Avenue and 107th Street, Manhattan) in September of 1955, six months before I did. I met him at the end of February, the third week I taught there, when one of the assistant principals asked me to cover the cafeteria during fifth period for a teacher who had to be at a conference. "Good luck with the animals," I remember him saying.

I was on my guard when I entered the cafeteria; perhaps even a trifle scared. The stories I had been hearing in the teachers' lounge had prepared me to expect anything. During the winter months the students were not allowed to leave the lunchroom and the results of keeping them penned in—the fights, the food-throwing, the high-pitched incessant chattering in Spanish, the way the Negro and Puerto Rican boys and girls chased each other around the tables—such things did, I had to admit, give the room a zoo-like quality.

The day I was assigned, however, was a Catholic holy day and many of the students were absent. Those who remained filled a little less than half of the large room and though they were noisy, it was relatively easy to keep them in order. Luther sat at a table by himself, near the exit to the food-line. Occasionally, I noticed, a few boys would come and sit next to him. The third time I patrolled his area, however, his table was empty and he stopped me.

"Hey, man," he said, poking me in the arm to get my attention, "you new here?"

He had a stack of about ten cookies in his other hand and he put one into his mouth as he waited for an answer. When I told him that I was not new, he nodded and looked at me. "You have any trouble yet?"

"No," I said, as sternly as possible. Despite my feelings of sympathy for the students, I knew that if I ever hoped to get anywhere with them, I had to appear tough and confident. "No," I repeated, almost, I recall, as if I were challenging him. "I haven't."

Luther cocked his head to one side then and smiled slowly. "You will," he said, and went back to his cookies.

231

In the teachers' lounge, the first time I told the story, somebody asked if the boy who had stopped me was a little Negro kid, very black, with a slight hunchback. I said he was. The teachers laughed. "That's Luther," one of them said.

"He's batty," said another. "Just leave him be."

I repeated the story endlessly. It was the first anecdote of my teaching experience that excited admiration and some sort of reaction from those I told it to, and this was important to me then. I had no more direct encounters with Luther that term, though I did see him in the halls, between classes. I always smiled at him and he would smile back—or at least I thought he did. I could never be sure. This bothered me, especially the first time it happened. Through my retelling of the story, I realized, he had become so real to me, so much a part of my life that I think I took it for granted that our encounter had assumed equal significance in his life. The possibility that he had not even repeated the story to a single one of his friends disturbed me.

Once or twice during the term I spotted him wandering around the halls while classes were in session, slouching down the corridor, his body pressed against the tile walls. When I asked the other teachers if he was known for cutting classes, they told me again to just leave him be—that the guidance counselor had suggested that the teachers let him do what he wanted to. He was harmless, they said, *if* you left him alone. Those teachers who had him in their classes agreed with the guidance counselor. Left alone, he didn't annoy them. When he wanted to, he worked feverishly—and did competent work; but when he did not want to work he would either sit and stare, or just get up, walk out of the room, and wander around the building. He was, they concluded, a mental case.

I returned to Booker T. Washington Junior High School the following September, and Luther turned up in one of my English classes. He had changed. He was no longer small, having grown a good five inches over the summer, and he was no longer quiet. When classwork bored him now he would stand up, and instead of leaving the room, would begin telling stories. Just like that. He had his favorite topics, too—his cousin Henry who had epilepsy, Willie Mays, what was on sale at the supermarket, the football team he played on, the stories in the latest *Blackhawk* comic book. When he ran out of stories, he would pull *The National Enquirer* out of his back pocket and begin reading from it, always starting with an item in the "Personals" columns that had caught his eye. I never knew what to do. When I would yell at him to sit down and be quiet, he would wave his hand at me, impatiently, and continue. Moreover, no expression on his face, nothing he ever said, indicated that he thought he was doing anything wrong. An hour after disrupting a class, if I would see him in the corridor, he would give me a big smile and a hello. After a while, of course, I gave up even trying to interrupt him. I listened with the other students—laughing, fascinated, amazed.

I tried to remember some of his stories, but when I retold them they never seemed interesting, and so I purposely gave Luther's class a lot of composition work, trying to make the topics as imaginative as possible—with the hope, of course, that he would use one of them to let loose. But all of the topics, he declared, were "stupid" and he refused to write on any of them. Then, when I least expected it, when I assigned the class a "How To—" composition, he handed one in. It was typewritten on a piece of lined notebook paper, single-spaced, beginning at the very top of the page and ending just at the first ruled line. It was titled: "How To Steal Some Fruits":

### How To Steal Some Fruits, by Luther

Go to a fruit store and when the fruitman isn't looking take some fruits. Then run. When the fruitman yells "Hey you stop taking those fruits" run harder. That is how to steal some fruits.

The next day he sat quietly in class. When I looked at him, he looked down at his desk. When I called on him to answer a question, he shrugged and looked away. At three o'clock, however, no more than five seconds after I had returned from escorting my official class downstairs, he bounded into my room, full of life, and propped himself up on the edge of my desk.

"Hey man," he said. "How'd you like my composition? It was deep, wasn't it?"

"Deep?"

"Deep, swift, *cool*—you know."

"I liked it fine," I said, laughing.

"Ah, don't put me on, man—how *was* it?"

"I liked it," I repeated, my hands clasped in front of me. "I mean it."

His face lit up. "You mean it? I worked hard on it, Mister Carter. I swear to God I did." It was the first time, I remember, that he had ever addressed me by my name. He stopped and wiped his mouth. "How'd you like the typing? Pretty good, huh?"

"It was fine."

"Christ, man," he said, stepping down from my desk and moving to the blackboard. He picked up a piece of chalk and wrote his name, printing it in capital letters. "How come you so tight? Why don't you loosen up? I ain't gonna do nothing. I just want to know about my composition. That's all."

I felt I could reach him, talk to him. I wanted to—had wanted to for some time, I realized, but he was right. I was tight, uncomfortable, embarrassed. "Where'd you get a typewriter?" I offered.

He smiled. "Where I get fruits," he replied, then laughed and clapped his hands. I must have appeared shocked, for before I could say anything, he was shaking his head back and forth. "Oh, man," he said. "You are really deep. I swear. You really are." He climbed onto my desk again. "You mind talking?"

"No," I said.

"Good. Let me ask you something—you married?"

"No," I said. "Do you think I should be married?"

"It beats stealing fruits," he said, and laughed again. His laugh was loud and harsh and at first it annoyed me, but then his body began rocking back and

forth as if his comment had set off a chain of jokes that he was telling himself
silently, and before I knew it I was laughing with him.

"I really liked the composition," I said. "In fact, I hope you don't mind,
but I've already read it to some of the other teachers."

"No shit."

"They thought it was superb."

"It's superb," he said, shaking his head in agreement. "Oh, it's superb,
man," he said, getting up again and walking away. His arms and legs moved
in different directions and he seemed so loose that when he turned his back to
me and I noticed the way his dirty flannel shirt was stretched tightly over his
misshapen back, I was surprised—as if I'd noticed it for the first time. He
walked around the room, muttering to himself, tapping on desks with his fingertips, and then he headed for the door. "I'm superb," he said. "So I be rolling on
my superb way home—."

"Stay," I said.

He threw his arms apart. "You win!" he declared. "I'll stay." He came
back to my desk, looked at me directly, then rolled his eyes and smiled. "People
been telling stories to you about me?"

"No."

"None?" he questioned, coming closer.

"All right," I said. "Some—."

"That's all right," he said, shrugging it off. He played with the binding of
a book that was on my desk. Then he reached across and took my grade book.
I snatched it away from him and he laughed again. "Oh man," he exclaimed.
"I am just so restless!—You know what I mean?"

He didn't wait for an answer, but started around the room again. The
pockets of his pants were stuffed and bulging, the cuffs frayed. The corner
of a red and white workman's handkerchief hung out of a back pocket. He
stopped in the back of the room, gazed into the glass bookcase, and then turned
to me and leaned back. "You said to stay—what you got to say?"

The question was in my mind, and impulsively I asked it: "Just curious—
do you remember me from last year?"

"Sure," he said, and turned his back to me again. He looked in the bookcase, whirled around and walked to the side of the room, opening a window.
He leaned out and just as I was about to say something to him about it, he
closed it and came back to the front of the room. "Man," he exclaimed, sitting
on my desk again. "Were you ever scared that day! If I'd set off a cherry bomb
you'd have gone through the fan." He put his face closer to mine. "Man, you
were scared green!"

"Was I scared of you, Luther?" I asked, looking straight into his eyes.

"Me? Nah. Nothing to be scared of." He hopped off the desk and wiped
his name off the blackboard with the palm of his hand; then he started laughing
to himself. He looked at me, over his shoulder. "Bet I know what you're thinking now," he said.

"Go ahead—."

"You're thinking you'd like to *help* a boy like me. Right? You're getting this big speech ready in your head about—."

"No," I interrupted. "I wasn't."

He eyed me suspiciously. "You sure?"

"I'm sure."

"Not even with compositions? Oh man, if you'd help me with compositions, before we'd be through with me, I'd be typing like a whiz." He banged on a desk with his palms, and then his fingers danced furiously on the wood as he made clicking noises inside his mouth. "Ding!" he said, swinging the carriage across. "Ain't it fun to type!"

"Okay," I said. "Okay. Maybe I was thinking that I would like to help you."

"I knew it, man," he said, to himself. "I just knew it."

"You have a good mind, Luther—much better than you let on."

"I do, I do," he muttered, chuckling. I stood up and went to the closet to get my coat. "Okay. What do I get if I work for you?" he asked.

I shrugged. "Nothing, maybe. I can't promise anything."

"I *like* that, man," he said.

"Could you call me Mister Carter?" I asked, somewhat irritably. "I don't call you, 'hey, you'—."

"Okay, Mister Carter," he said. He took my coat sleeve. "Let me help you on with your coat, Mister Carter."

We walked out of the room and I locked the door. "You ain't a *real* social worker like the others," he commented as we started down the stairs. He held the door open for me. "I do like that."

I nodded.

"Playing it close to the vest again, huh? Tight-mouthed."

"Just thinking," I said.

When we were outside he asked me what he had to do.

"For what?" I asked.

"To get you to help me to be somebody, to educate myself—all that stuff."

"Do what you want to do," I said. "Though you might start by doing your homework. Then we'll see—."

"I know," he said, cocking his head to one side again. "If I play ball with you you'll play ball with me. Right? Okay, okay. I know."

Then he was gone, running down the street, his arms spread wide as if he were an airplane, a loud siren-like noise rising and falling from him as he disappeared from view.

The next few months were without doubt the most satisfying to me of any during the eight years I've been a teacher. Luther worked like a fiend. He was bright, learned quickly, and was not really that far behind. He did his homework, he paid attention in class, he studied for tests, and he read books. That was most important. On every book he read I asked him to write a book report: setting, plot, theme, characters, and his opinion of the book—and once

a week, on Thursday afternoons, we would get together in my room for a discussion. During the remainder of the term he must have gone through at least
forty to fifty books. Most of them had to do with sports, airplanes, and insects.
For some reason he loved books about insects. All the reports came to me typed,
and on some he drew pictures—"illustrations" he called them, which, he
claimed, would be a help to me in case I had not read the book.

When we would finish talking about books, I would help him with his
other subjects, and his improvement was spectacular. I looked forward to my
sessions with him, to his reports, to just seeing him—yet from day to day, from
moment to moment, I always expected him to bolt from me, and this pleased
me. Every time he came to me for a talk I was truly surprised.

When the term ended he asked if I would continue to help him. I said I
would. He was not programmed for any of my English classes during the spring
term, but we kept up with our weekly discussions. As the weather improved,
however, he read less and less; I didn't want him to feel as if he *had* to come
see me every Thursday, and so, about a week before the opening of the baseball
season, I told him that I thought he had reached the point where he could go it
alone. "When you feel like talking, just come knocking—" I said. "We don't
need a schedule." He seemed relieved, I thought, and I was proud that I had
had the sense to release him from any obligation he might have felt.

Then, suddenly, I didn't see him anywhere for three weeks. I asked his
home-room teacher about him and she said she hadn't seen him either; she had
sent him a few postcards, but had received no reply. That very night—it was
almost as if he had been there listening, I thought—he telephoned me at home.

"Is this Mister Carter? This is Luther here."

"Hi, Luther," I said.

"I looked you up in the telephone book. You mind me calling you at
home?"

"No, no. I don't mind."

"Okay," he said, breathing hard. "I just wanted to let you know not to
worry about me because I'm not in school. Okay?"

"Sure," I said. "Sure."

"I had some things to take care of—you know?"

"Sure," I said.

"Man, you *know* you're itching to ask me *what?*" He laughed. "You are
deep. I'll be back Monday."

That was all. On Monday, as he had promised, he returned to school
and came to visit me in my room at three o'clock. We talked for a while about
the way the pennant race was going, and then he said, "Okay, let's cut the jazz,
man. I got something to say to you." He seemed very intense about it and I told
him that I was listening carefully. He pointed a finger at me. "Now, we stopped
our sessions, right?"

"Right," I said.

"And the day after we stopped, I began to play the hook for three straight
weeks, right?"

"Right."

"Okay. Now you can tell me it ain't so, but I'll bet you'll be thinking it was your fault. It ain't. If you want the truth, I ain't done a stick of work all term for *any* teacher—so don't go thinking that I stopped being a good student cause we stopped our meetings."

He let out a long breath. "I'm glad you told me," I said.

"Shit, man," he said, getting up and going to the door. "Don't *say* anything, huh? Why you got to *say* something all the time?" He came toward me. *"Why?"* He was almost screaming and I slid my chair back from the desk. He shook his head frantically. "Why, man?" he said. He reached into his side-pocket and I started to stand up. Abruptly, he broke into laughter. "Oh man, you are deep! You are just so deep!" He clapped his hands and laughed at me some more. "Ra-ta-tat-tat!" he said as he banged on a desk. "You're real sweet, man! Just so sweet! Ra-ta-tat-tat! Comin' down the street!" He sat down in one of the seats. "But don't you worry none. I got seven liberry cards now and books growing out the ceiling. I got a liberry card for Luther King and one for Luther Queen and one for Luther Prince and one for Luther Jones and one for Luther Smith and one for Luther Mays and one for Luther B. Carter." He banged on the top of the desk with his fist, then drummed with his fingers again. "But don't you worry none—ra-ta-tat-tat—just don't you worry—."

"I'm not," I said.

"That's all," he said, and dashed out of the room.

He attended classes regularly for about two weeks and then disappeared again for a week. He returned for a few days, stayed away, returned. The pattern continued. In the halls when we saw each other he would always smile and ask if I was worrying and I would tell him I wasn't. Once or twice, when he was absent, he telephoned me at home and asked me what was new at school. He got a big charge out of this. Then another time, I remember, he came riding through the schoolyard on a bicycle during sixth period, when I was on patrol. "Don't report me, man!" he yelled and rode right back out, waving and shouting something in Spanish that made everybody laugh.

Near the end of May, the assistant principal in charge of the eighth grade called me into his office. He knew I was friendly with Luther, he said, and he thought that I might talk to the boy. For the past six or seven months, he told me, Luther had been in and out of juvenile court. "Petty thefts," the assistant principal explained. I wasn't surprised; Luther had hinted at this many times. I had never pressed him about it, however, not wanting to destroy our relationship by lecturing him. The assistant principal said he didn't care whether I said anything to Luther or not. In fact, he added, he would have been just as happy to get rid of him—but that before he was shipped off to a 600-school or put away somewhere else, he wanted to give me an opportunity to do what I could. More for me, he said, than for Luther.

About a week after this, on a Friday, Luther telephoned me.

"How've you been?" I asked.

"Superb, man," he said. "Hey listen—we ain't been seeing much of each other lately, have we?"

"No—."

"No. Okay. Listen—I got two tickets to see the Giants play tomorrow. You want to come?" I didn't answer immediately. "Come on—yes or no—tickets are going fast—."

"I'd like to," I said. "Yes. Only—only I was wondering where you got the money for the tickets?" I breathed out, glad I had said it.

Luther just laughed. "Oh, man, you're not gonna be like that, are you? You been listening to too many stories again. That judge from the court must of been gassing with you. Tell you what—you come to the game and I'll tell you where I got the tickets. A deal?"

"A deal."

"Meet you in front of the school at eleven o'clock—I like to get there early to see Willie go through batting practice. Batting practice—that's more fun than the game, sometimes. You know?"

He was waiting for me when I got there a few minutes before eleven the following day. "Let's go," he said, flourishing the tickets. "But don't ask me now, man—let's enjoy the game first. Okay?"

I did enjoy the game. The Giants were playing the Cardinals and to Luther's delight, Willie Mays had one of his better days, going three-for-four at bat, and making several brilliant plays in the field. For most of the game, I was truly relaxed. Along about the eighth inning, however, I began to think about the question again—to wonder when would be the best time to ask it. Luther, it seemed, had forgotten all about it. The Giants were winning 5–2.

"Oh man," he said. "If only that Musial don't do something, we're home free. Look at Willie!" he exclaimed. "Ain't he the greatest that ever lived. He is just so graceful! You know? How you like to see a team of Willie Mayses out there? Wow!" Wes Westrum, the Giant catcher, grounded out, short to first, and the eighth inning was over. "One to go, one to go," Luther said. Then he jabbed me in the arm with his finger. "Hey, listen—I been thinking. Instead of an All-Star game every year between the leagues, what they ought to do one year is have the white guys against our guys. What you think?"

I shrugged. "I don't know," I said.

"Sure," he said. "Listen—we got Willie in center. Then we put Aaron in right and Doby in left. He's got the raw power. Some outfield, huh? Then we got Campy catching and Newcombe pitching. You can't beat that. That Newcombe —he's a mean son of a bitch, but he throws. Okay. I been thinking about this a long time—." He used his fingers to enumerate. He was excited, happy. "At first base we put Luke Easter, at second—Junior Gilliam, at short—Ernie Banks, and at third base we bring in old Jackie Robinson just to give the team a little class —you know what I mean? Man, what a line-up! Who could you match it with?"

When I said I didn't know, Luther eyed me suspiciously. "C'mon—Musial, Mantle, Williams, Spahn—you name 'em and I'll match 'em, man for man, your guys against ours." He stopped and cheered as a Cardinal popped out to

Whitey Lockman at first. "What's the matter—don't you like the idea? Ha! Face it, man, we'd wipe up the field with you. Swish! Swish!" He laughed and slapped me on the knee. "Hey, I know what's bugging you, I bet—." He leaned toward me, cupping his hand over his mouth, and whispered in my ear. "Tell the truth now, would you have ever offered to help me if I wasn't colored?"

"Would I—?" I stopped. "Sure," I said. Of course I would. Of course—."

Luther smiled; triumphantly, dubiously. "Look," I said. "As long as we're asking questions, let me ask you something."

"About the tickets, right?"

"No," I said. "Forget the tickets. No long lectures, either. Just a question. Just one: how come you steal?"

"Oh man," he said, laughing. "That's an easy one!—Because I'm not getting what I want and when you don't get what you want, man, you got to take. Don't you know that?"

I stared at him, not sure I had heard right. He winked at me. "Enjoy the ballgame, man! Say hey, Willie!" he shouted, as Mays caught a fly ball, breadbasket style, for the second out. "Ain't he the sweetest!"

A minute later the game was over and the players were racing across the field toward the clubhouse in center field, trying to escape the fans who scrambled after them. "They won't get Willie," Luther said. "He's too swift, too swift."

When we were outside I thanked Luther and told him how much I had enjoyed the game. "How about a Coke or something?" I offered.

"Nah," he said. "I got things to do." He extended his hand quickly and I shook it, the first time we had ever done that. "Okay. You go get spiffed up and get a wife. Time you were married." He tossed his head back and laughed. "Ain't you married yet? No, no. *Smile,* man—how you gonna get a wife, never smiling." He started away, through the crowd. "Stay loose," he called back.

"Don't steal no fruits."

I never questioned him again about stealing, but even if I had wanted to, I wouldn't have had much opportunity. He did not come to see me very often the rest of that year. When he returned to school in September of 1958 for his last year of junior high school, he had grown again. But not up. He never did go higher than the five-five or five-six he had reached by that time. He had taken up weightlifting over the summer, however, and his chest, his neck, his arms—they had all broadened incredibly. Instead of the dirty cotton and flannel shirts he had worn the two previous years, he now walked through the halls in laundry-white T-shirts, the sleeves rolled up to the shoulder, his powerful muscles exposed. There were always a half-dozen Negro boys following him around now also and they all dressed the way he did—white T-shirts, black chino pants, leather wrist straps, and—hanging from their necks on pieces of string— miniature black skulls.

The guidance counselor for the ninth grade came to me one day early in the term and asked me if I could give him any evidence against Luther. He claimed that Luther and his gang were going around the school, beating and torturing those students who refused to "loan" them money. All of the students, he said, were afraid to name Luther. "The kid's a born sadist," he added. I told him I didn't know anything.

The term progressed and the stories and rumors increased. I was told that the police in Luther's neighborhood were convinced that he and his gang were responsible for a series of muggings that had occurred. I tried not to believe it, but Luther all but gave me conclusive proof one afternoon, right before Christmas. He came into my room at three o'clock, alone, and said he had something for me. He said he trusted me not to tell anybody about it or show it to anyone. I said I wouldn't.

"Okay, man—here it is—." His eyes leapt around the room, frenzied, delirious. He took a little card from his wallet. "You might need this sometime —but don't ask me no questions. Ha! And don't you worry none. I'm doing okay. Expanding all the time. Don't you worry." I took the card from him. "See you now, Mister Carter. See you, see you."

He left and I looked at the card. Across the top was printed: THE BLACK AVENGERS, and below it was written: "Don't touch this white man. He's okay." It was signed by Luther and under his name he had drawn a skull and cross-bones. I put the card in my wallet.

In January, to no one's great surprise, Luther was sent away to reform school in upstate New York. I was never exactly clear about the precise event that had led to it—the policeman assigned to our school said it had to do with brutally beating an old man; Luther's friends said it had to do with getting caught in a gang war. They claimed the fight was clean but that the cops had framed Luther. There was nothing in the papers, Luther had not contacted me, and I did not find out about it all until he had already been shipped off.

I received a postcard from him that summer. It was brief.

I hate it here. I can't say anymore or they'll beat shit out of me. I hate it. I'm reading some. I'll visit you when I get out and we'll have a session.

I answered the card with a letter. I told him I was sorry about where he was and that I'd be glad to talk to him whenever he wanted. I gave him some news of the school and included some current baseball clippings. I asked him if there was anything he needed and if there was anybody in his family he wanted me to get in touch with. I told him that in return for the time he'd taken me to the baseball game I had ordered a subscription to *Sport* magazine for him.

He replied with another post card.

Visiting day this summer is August 21. I'd like for you to come.

When I arrived, he seemed glad to see me, but I remember that he was more polite than he had ever been before, and more subdued. I wondered, at the time, if they were giving him tranquillizers. I was only allowed an hour with him and we spent most of that time just walking around the grounds—the school was a work-farm reformatory—not saying anything.

The visit, I could tell, was a disappointment to him. I don't know what he expected of me, but whatever it was, I didn't provide it. I wrote him a letter when I got home, telling him I had enjoyed seeing him and that I'd be glad to come again if he wanted me to. He didn't answer it, and I heard no more from him for a year and a half.

Then one day in the spring of 1961, just about the time of the Bay of Pigs invasion of Cuba, I remember, he popped into my room at school. He looked horrible. His face was unshaven, his clothes were filthy and ragged, his eyes were glazed. Underneath his clothes, his body had become flabby and he bent over noticeably when he walked. At first I didn't recognize him.

When I did, I was so glad to see him, I didn't know what to do. "Luther —for crying out loud!" I said, standing up and shaking his hand. "How the hell are you?"

He smiled at me. "I'm superb, man—can't you tell from looking at me?" He laughed then, and I laughed with him.

"You've gotten older," I said.

"Past sixteen," he said. "That means I don't got to go to school no more—"

He waited, but I didn't offer an opinion. "How about going down with me and having a cup of coffee? I'm finished here for the day—just getting through with mid-terms."

"Nah," he said, looking down and playing with his hands. "I gotta meet somebody. I'm late already. But I was in the neighborhood so I thought I'd come let you know I was still alive." He came to my desk and looked down. He shook his head as if something were wrong.

"What's the matter?" I asked.

"Don't see no wedding ring on your finger yet." He looked straight into my face. "Hey, man—you ain't a fag, are you?"

"No," I said, laughing. "Not that I know of—."

He laughed, his mouth opening wide. "Okay. That's all the gas for today. I'll see you, man."

During the next few months he visited me several times. Sometimes he looked good, sometimes bad—but I never could find out what he was doing with his days. He never gave a straight answer to my questions. More and more, I felt that he was asking me for some kind of help, but when I would touch on anything personal or even hint that I wanted to do something for him, with him, he would become defensive.

I didn't see him over the summer, but the following fall he came by periodically. He seemed to be getting a hold on himself, and sometimes he would talk about going to night school. Nothing came of the talk, though. In November he was arrested and sent to Riker's Island—to P.S. 616, the combination prison-school for boys between the ages of sixteen and twenty. His sentence was for eighteen months and during the first three months I visited him twice. Both times all he wanted to do was to talk about the English class we had had, and the stories and compositions he had made up. He said he was trying to remember some of them for the English teacher he had there, but couldn't do it all the time. He seemed to be in terrible shape, and I didn't have much hope for him.

So I was surprised when I began getting postcards from him again. "I am studying hard," the first one said. "There is a Negro who comes here to help me. I like him. I will be a new man when I come out. Yours sincerely, Luther." It was neatly and carefully written. The ones that followed were the same and they came at regular intervals of about five weeks. He told me about books he was reading, most of them having to do with Negro history, and about how he was changing. "Improving" was the word he used most.

I answered his cards as best I could, and offered to come see him again, but he never took up any of my offers. When his eighteen months were up, I expected a visit from him. He never came. Sometimes I wondered what had become of him, but after the first few months passed and I didn't hear from him, I thought about him less and less. A year passed—two since we had last seen each other at Riker's Island—and then we met again.

I spotted him first. It was a beautiful summer night and I had gone up to Lewisohn Stadium for a concert. It had been good, I was relaxed and happy as I walked out of the stadium. Luther was standing at the corner of Amsterdam Avenue and 138th Street. He was wearing a dark blue suit, a white shirt and a tie. He was clean shaven, his hair was cut short and he looked healthy and bright. He was stopping people and trying to sell them newspapers.

"How are you, Mister Carter?" he asked, when I walked up to him. His eyes were clear and he seemed very happy to see me. "Interested in buying a newspaper to help the colored people? Only a dime—."

"No thanks," I said. The paper he was selling, as I had expected, was *Muhammad Speaks,* the newspaper of the Black Muslims. "You look fine," I added.

"Thanks—excuse me a second." He turned and sold a copy to somebody. People snubbed him but this didn't stop him from smiling or trying. I waited. When the crowd had gone, he asked me where I was going. "Home," I said. "Cup of coffee first?"

"No thanks," he said. "Thanks, but no thanks."

"When did all this start?" I asked, motioning to the newspapers.

"At Riker's Island," he said. He put up a hand, as if to stop my thoughts from becoming words. "I know what you're thinking, what you hear on TV and read in the newspapers about us—but don't believe everything. We're essentially a religious organization, as you may or may not know."

"I know," I said.

"And it's meant a lot to me—I couldn't have made it without their help. They—they taught me to *believe* in myself." His eyes glowed as he twisted his body toward me. "Can you understand that?" It seemed very important to him that I believe him. *"Can* you?" He relaxed momentarily and shrugged.

"I don't believe everything they teach, of course, but I follow their precepts: I don't smoke, I don't drink, I don't curse, I don't go out with women who aren't Muslims—I feel good *inside,* Mister Carter. Things are straightening themselves out." He paused. "It hasn't been easy."

"I know," I said, and smiled.

He nodded, embarrassed, I thought. "I'm going back to school also—."

"I'm glad."

"Even my body feels good! I'm lifting weights again, too." he said. Then he laughed and the sound tore through the warm night. His eyes were flashing with delight. "Oh man—someday I'll be the head of a whole damned army! Me and my old hunchback." He laughed again, pleased with himself. Then his laughter subsided and he patted me on the shoulder. "Oh man, you are still so deep, so deep. Don't worry none, Mister Carter. I don't go around advocating no violence." He chuckled. "I've got to go," he said, extending a hand. "It's been good seeing you again. Sure you don't want to buy a copy?"

"I'm sure," I said, shaking his hand. "Good luck to you, Luther. I'm glad to see you the way you are now—."

"Thanks." We looked at each other for a minute and he smiled warmly at me. Then I started toward the subway station. When I had crossed the street he called to me.

"Hey—Mister Carter—!"

I turned.

"Let me ask you something—do you still have that card I gave you?" He howled at this remark. "Oh man, I'd save that card if I were you! I'd do that. You never know when you might need it. You never know—."

I started back across the street, toward him. He tossed his head back and roared with laughter. "You never know, you never know," he repeated, and hurried away from me, laughing wildly. I stared at him until he disappeared in the darkness. Then I just stood there, dazed, unable to move—I don't know for how long. Finally I made myself turn around, and as I walked slowly toward the lights of Broadway all I could feel was the presence of his muscular body, powerful, gleaming, waiting under his white shirt, his clean suit.

# What They Did to Me in Little Rock
## 1958

### Minnijean Brown (and J. Robert Moskin)

I'm never sorry that I'm a Negro. I've heard it said that every Negro child has times when he wishes he was white, but I've never had times like that.

While I was growing up, I never ran into that deep prejudice when someone pushes you in the street or says something to you. But I do remember reading about someone who was lynched and asking my mother what that meant.

The first time I realized that life could be different for a Negro was when a girl from Syracuse, New York, came to visit good friends of mine. At the station, she started to enter the white waiting room, and my friends had to grab her. In her home town, this girl could go into any waiting room or restaurant or school.

When my tenth-grade teacher in our Negro school said there was a possibility of integration in Little Rock, I signed up. We all felt good. We knew of so many kids who had been graduated from Negro schools and couldn't get jobs. We knew that Central High School had many more courses, and dramatics and speech and tennis courts and a big, beautiful stadium.

I was one of the kids "approved" by the school officials. We were told we would have to take a lot and were warned not to fight back if anything happened. But when we went to the school, Governor Faubus's National Guard troops turned us away. Two weeks later, when the court ordered the Guard withdrawn, the police took the nine of us going to Central in very quietly by a side door. We were in school.

One girl ran up to me and said, "I'm so glad you're here. Won't you go to lunch with me today?" I never saw her again.

We were taken to the principal's office and had a discussion about books and courses. Just like anyone might who's going to a new school. I didn't even know there was a mob outside until I heard noise and clapping and saw them out of a window.

We walked to class on the third floor. There was just one of us in a classroom. Never more. Chemistry was in session. A boy let me use his book. He was never friendly again either. Then we went to English class on the first floor and then to glee club. That day, everybody was so nice. We all sat together. I tried out for the chorus to find my voice range. I'm a first soprano and love to sing. After I tried out, some of the kids said, "Oh, you're so good." I was just like anybody else.

Fifteen minutes before the period was over, Mrs. Huckaby, the girl's vice-principal, came and got me. The officials feared the mob might try to get in the school and we had to get out.

We didn't go back until the Army troops arrived and took us to school in an Army station wagon, guarded by a jeep front and back. That was a wonderful feeling, knowing that no mob would have the nerve to come through the Army troops.

My first real trouble came in French class: a boy put his feet on the seat across the aisle. I asked if I might go by very politely. He said, "Nigger, if you want to go by me, you'll have to kill me or walk around the room." Then he told me to walk over his legs, and when I did, he kicked at me. In stepping over him, I touched his foot: he was ready to beat me up. I called my guard (each of us had a soldier who met us at the school door, walked behind us and stood outside our classroom). The teacher told the guard to leave the room. She said she would keep order in her classroom.

One day, a boy whose locker was near mine said, "Don't touch my locker, nigger, or I'll kick the —— out of you." I was mad and answered him back. He reported it, and it went on my record as using unladylike language. My guard heard the whole thing and reported my side of the story, but it didn't help.

I never had a temper before; I was a very happy person. I suppose I never had to take this sort of thing. But when I was called on to recite in French class, some kid would say out loud, "Jees, look at the nigger reciting." I changed, I grew up a great deal. Not a day went by that I wasn't called something dreadful.

The day the 101st was taken off duty inside the school, the kids "massacred" us. We went to General Clinger and said we would have to go home, because the white kids didn't respect the National Guard. The officers didn't want us to leave; they put two guards with each of us. The guards acted real unhappy about their job. The next day, the 101st was brought back inside the building.

While the 101st was there, we had an abundance of friends, but after they left, I had only one. She made me realize that everyone didn't hate me. But most of the time it was lonely. When the teacher said we could talk in class, I'd be sitting there with no one to talk to.

We could tell when the "incidents" would get worse. It was always when Governor Faubus or Amis Guthridge, attorney for the White Citizens' Council,

or the leaders of the Central High Mother League made a statement. We'd kid
about it, and say we'd go and buy knee pads because we knew we were going
to get it.

I know how I got to be the most hated girl in Little Rock. The glee
club at Central decided to have a special Christmas program. We had already
had a program in class, and I sang in it. A girl played *Chances Are* for me. I
was so nervous. After hating you for just sitting there, what must they think
of you up there singing? If you are lower than they are, they can love you,
but just don't be equal.

Everyone had to try out for the Christmas program. They needed three
sopranos, and I made it. Mother was going to make me a white dress for the
performance, but she warned me I would never be allowed to sing. She was
right. One day, the teacher said that Mr. Matthews, the principal, didn't know
if it would be best if I was on the program. I asked to talk to him. He said
he feared the kids would walk out or throw things or riot. Anyway, I was
never allowed to sing in the auditorium at Central.

After that, the kids picked me out more and more. One white girl told
a reporter, "I hate Minnijean. She thinks she is as good as we are."

One day in the cafeteria, I tried to walk in the narrow aisle between the
tables, holding my tray high as we always had to do. Five boys in a row
pushed their chairs back to block me. I stepped back. They moved their
chairs in. The one boy pushed his chair out again. I spilled my bowl of chili
over two of the boys.

A National Guardsman took me to the principal's office. Mr. Matthews
became very upset. He called the superintendent, and I was suspended for 10
school days. Later, Mr. Blossom, the superintendent, asked me if I did it on
purpose. I said I didn't really know. He said I made more trouble than anyone,
so I must have invited trouble. He even complained to me that he was getting
threatened. I suggested that he was older, and he ought to be able to take it as
well as I could. He complained that they called him a "nigger lover." That he
certainly was not. Nothing was done to the boys.

I walked home. I didn't want to go home. I felt I had failed someone and
made a flop of the whole thing. I wished a car would run over me. I held
off crying until I got home.

After the Christmas holiday, I was allowed to go back to school. I
promised to say nothing to anyone—not to fight back. The kids would boo
me down the hall, and they told the other eight Negro kids that if they had
anything to do with me, they would get it. They said they were getting it
anyway, so it didn't make any difference.

When I was back four days, I was paid back for the chili. A boy, David
Sontag, spilled soup on me. He walked behind me and stood there. Then tilted
the tray and dropped the bowl on my head. It hurt so bad, but I couldn't cry.
The kids gave the boy 15 rahs. He was a hero.

A guardsman took me to the principal's office. I put on a smile. Mr.

Matthews asked what happened, and I said they paid me back. He just said, "Too bad!" But he suspended the boy.

Gym was the most heartbreaking class. Girls can be cruel. They would stand around and dance what they said were Ubangi dances. Basketballs and deck-tennis rings would fly at your head. The girls would ask, "Is your mother black?" They'd draw pictures and say that's how your mother looks. That is the kind of thing you want to choke people for. It hurt so.

Elizabeth Eckford was with me in gym class: we were put together for partner games. Elizabeth and I would think of Jackie Robinson. We said if somebody else could do it, we could do it too. We were kicked often. If something happened to me, they'd laugh so hard, and they'd clap when I did something wrong. When I got real mad, I'd just go over in a corner by myself until I got over it. Once I was so mad, I sat in the dressing room a long time, and when I came out, they hissed—almost all of the 70 girls.

When the hate started to creep in, I'd just sit there and convince myself that I didn't hate them. I just had to. I'd have to pick out one person to hate most of all and make allowances for the rest. If you hated them all, you couldn't walk through the halls. I decided not to hate the kids, so I hated someone I didn't see every day—the school officials.

I had a very wonderful Sunday school teacher. One time, I asked her if you can pray to make someone like you. She said, "No." You pray every night at bedtime and in the mornings before I would go to school, and all nine of us went to chapel in the school until they started getting us there too.

We Negro kids had a ritual. After school, Melba, Thelma and I would mark the day off on Melba's calendar. One more day finished. And we would bow our heads. Then we'd laugh and clap to sort of break the tension.

There was more and more violence. We had a lot of bomb scares at Central, and once they found some dynamite in the school. After the Army was gone, I felt that those kids would do anything. Boys would come up behind me and kick me; you can't get much lower. I had to wear special clothes for soup days, and they would squirt ink at us from their pens. Sammie Dean Parker, who was expelled and later reinstated, was called the "Queen of the Segregationists." Kids like her would wear little cards on their sweaters saying things like "Brotherhood by Bayonet" and one with a little black man saying, "I come here to integrate for the NAACP."

There was one boy I was especially scared of—Richard Boehler. The day he was suspended for poor schoolwork, I was walking to the car after classes when he kicked me hard. I cried that time. I couldn't help it. Mother saw him do it. She asked a guard if he saw it. He didn't even answer her. This time, mother took me to the prosecuting attorney. He said they would look into it, but, so far as I know, nothing ever came of it.

The last day, I went to school in a happy mood. When I would walk into the building, I used to get that "here we go again" feeling.

At my locker, there was a blonde, Frankie Gregg. She would follow me up to the third floor every morning saying, "Nigger, nigger, nigger," all the way. This morning, I didn't think anything about it when she and some other kids did the same thing. But this time, she even stepped on my heels and ran right into me. Then she said if I did that again, she'd beat me up. I didn't answer her even then.

When I went into my home room, she kept yelling from the door. Finally, I turned to the girl and said, "Don't say anything more to me, white trash."

Then I walked to my seat. Frankie got so mad she started screaming at me. She threw her pocketbook and hit me in the back of the head. My first impulse was to beat her with it, but I just picked it up and threw it down again and walked to the office. Frankie and the guard came into the office too.

Frankie said, "Minnijean called me white trash." I said, "Frankie has been calling me 'nigger' for a week and threw her pocketbook at me after I called her 'white trash.' " Frankie refused to apologize. I said I would if she would. I guess I was supposed to apologize whether she did or not.

When I went back to class, everyone was saying, "Did you hear that Minnijean called Frankie 'white trash'? We'll have to do something about her." In glee club, I had to sit in a row by myself. This time, all the bad ones got behind me and said things. I told the teacher I wanted to go home. I couldn't take any more.

I tried to phone mother, but three boys wouldn't let me in the phone booth. I telephoned from the office, but mother wasn't home. At lunch, a boy threw hot soup on me. They gave him 15 rahs too. When I finally went home, I cried for hours.

That night, the radio said I had been suspended. At 11:30 mother called the superintendent. She was pretty angry. She said I'd be in school the next day. In the morning, Mr. Matthews phoned to say officially that I was suspended. Several days later, the school board expelled me for the rest of the term. I haven't been back to Central High since.

Mrs. Daisy Bates of the NAACP said not to worry. I could go to school in New York. I just didn't believe anything that good could happen. Then Mrs. [Kenneth B.] Clark wrote a letter inviting me to live with them, and Dr. John L. Brooks sent a wire inviting me to go to the New Lincoln School.

I've heard that the incidents at Central kept on after I left. The segregationists next picked out Ernest Green and tried to stop him from graduating. They kept throwing rotten eggs and tomatoes and water. White kids spit on Elizabeth and Thelma. One boy started to spit on me once, and I said I'd hit him with my book, and he didn't do it.

When we first started, I felt I was breaking new ground for Negroes. But after the 101st left and nobody who was causing trouble was caught, I got to feel it wasn't doing any good. Mother would say it does help, and, even though he lost his business and has to work nights as a bartender, daddy still said education is the most important thing you can have in your life. But I never had any hope for the next day.

Still, I know it can work. In Van Buren, Arkansas, a friend of mine has gotten along very well in an integrated school. The police chief there said this was not going to be a Little Rock. My friend was called a "nigger" just once, and the boy who said it was suspended.

In Little Rock, the whole thing would have been different if Governor Faubus hadn't called out the Guard, and if General Clinger's Arkansas troops had protected us better. And if people like Mr. Blossom—I'm sure he really was not in favor of integration—had done more.

The Bill of Rights seemed to be a joke in Little Rock, like it was planned for white people, and they didn't expect us to get in on it.

Maybe you have to start this when kids are young—before they have all this hate. But people fear that if you start them in school together in the first grade, they'll end up marrying each other. I don't know anyone whose big idea is to marry a white person. But at least, if they start school together when they are young, little children won't be hurt. Teen-agers get hurt easily and know how to hurt each other.

It's not all that much pleasure to sit next to someone white in a class-room, but you want the same education and chance in life as they have. I'm going to try to go back to Central next fall. This summer, I'll ask the super-intendent to get reinstated. I'm so happy in New York, but I have eight friends in Little Rock. One thing I know: It's hard not to fight back.

# If You Ain't Got Heart, You Ain't Got Nada
## 1967

### Piri Thomas

We were moving—our new pad was back in Spanish Harlem—to 104th Street between Lex and Park Avenue.

Moving into a new block is a big jump for a Harlem kid. You're torn up from your hard-won turf and brought into an "I don't know you" block where every kid is some kind of enemy. Even when the block belongs to your own people, you are still an outsider who has to prove himself a down stud with heart.

As the moving van rolled to a stop in front of our new building, number 109, we were all standing there, waiting for it—Momma, Poppa, Sis, Paulie, James, José, and myself. I made out like I didn't notice the cats looking us over, especially me—I was gang age. I read their faces and found no trust, plenty of suspicion, and a glint of rising hate. I said to myself, *These cats don't mean nothin'. They're just nosy.* But I remembered what had happened to me in my old block, and that it had ended with me in the hospital.

This was a tough-looking block. That was good, that was cool; but my old turf had been tough, too. *I'm tough,* a voice within said. *I hope I'm tough enough. I am tough enough. I've got* mucho corazón, *I'm king wherever I go. I'm a killer to my heart. I not only* can *live, I* will *live, no punk out, no die out, walk bad; be down, cool breeze, smooth.* My mind raced, and thoughts crashed against each other, trying to reassemble themselves into a pattern of rep. I turned slowly and with eyelids half-closed I looked at the rulers of this new world and with a cool shrug of my shoulders I followed the movers into the hallway of number 109 and dismissed the coming war from my mind.

The next morning I went to my new school, called Patrick Henry, and strange, mean eyes followed me.

"Say, pops," said a voice belonging to a guy I later came to know as Waneko, "where's your territory?"

In the same tone of voice Waneko had used, I answered, "I'm on it, dad, what's shaking?"

"Bad, huh?" He half-smiled.

"No, not all the way. Good when I'm cool breeze and bad when I'm down."

"What's your name, kid?"

"That depends. 'Piri' when I'm smooth and 'Johnny Gringo' when stomping time's around."

"What's your name now?" he pushed.

"You name me, man," I answered, playing my role like a champ.

He looked around, and with no kind of words, his boys cruised in. Guys I would come to know, to fight, to hate, to love, to take care of. Little Red, Waneko, Little Louie, Indio, Carlito, Alfredo, Crip, and plenty more. I stiffened and said to myself, *Stomping time, Piri boy, go with heart.*

I fingered the garbage-can handle in my pocket—my home-made brass knuckles. They were great for breaking down large odds into small, chopped-up ones.

Waneko, secure in his grandstand, said, "We'll name you later, *panín.*"

I didn't answer. Scared, yeah, but wooden-faced to the end, I thought, *Chevere, panín.*

It wasn't long in coming. Three days later, at about 6 P.M., Waneko and his boys were sitting around the stoop at number 115. I was cut off from my number 109. For an instant I thought, *Make a break for it down the basement steps and through the back yards—get away in one piece!* Then I thought, *Caramba! Live punk, dead hero. I'm no punk kid. I'm not copping any pleas.* I kept walking, hell's a-burning, hell's a-churning, rolling with cheer. *Walk on, baby man, roll on without fear. What's he going to call?*

"Whatta ya say, Mr. Johnny Gringo?" drawled Waneko.

*Think, man,* I told myself, *think your way out of a stomping. Make it good.* "I hear you 104th Street coolies are supposed to have heart," I said. "I don't know this for sure. You know there's a lot of streets where a whole 'click' is made out of punks who can't fight one guy unless they all jump him for the stomp." I hoped this would push Waneko into giving me a fair one. His expression didn't change.

"Maybe we don't look at it that way."

*Crazy, man. I cheer inwardly, the* cabrón *is falling into my setup. We'll see who gets messed up first, baby!* "I wasn't talking to you," I said. "Where I come from the pres is president 'cause he got heart when it comes to dealing."

Waneko was starting to look uneasy. He had bit on my worm and felt like a sucker fish. His boys were now light on me. They were no longer so much interested in stomping me as in seeing the outcome between Waneko and me. "Yeah," was his reply.

I smiled at him. "You trying to dig where I'm at and now you got me interested in you. I'd like to see where you're at."

Waneko hesitated a tiny little second before replying, "Yeah."

I knew I'd won. Sure, I'd have to fight; but one guy, not ten or fifteen. If

I lost I might still get stomped, and if I won I might get stomped. I took care of this with my next sentence. "I don't know you or your boys," I said, "but they look cool to me. They don't feature as punks."

I had left him out purposely when I said "they." Now his boys were in a separate class. I had cut him off. He would have to fight me on his own, to prove his heart to himself, to his boys, and most important, to his turf. He got away from the stoop and asked, "Fair one, Gringo?"

"Uh-uh," I said, "roll all the way—anything goes." I thought, *I've got to beat him bad and yet not bad enough to take his prestige all away.* He had *corazón.* He came on me. *Let him draw first blood,* I thought, *it's his block.* Smish, my nose began to bleed. His boys cheered, his heart cheered, his turf cheered. "Waste this chump," somebody shouted.

*Okay, baby, now it's my turn.* He swung. I grabbed innocently, and my forehead smashed into his nose. His eyes crossed. His fingernails went for my eye and landed in my mouth—crunch, I bit hard. I punched him in the mouth as he pulled away from me, and he slammed his foot into my chest.

We broke, my nose running red, my chest throbbing, his finger—well, that was his worry. I tied him up with body punching and slugging. We rolled onto the street. I wrestled for acceptance, he for rejection or, worse yet, acceptance on his terms. It was time to start peace talks. I smiled at him. "You got heart, baby," I said.

He answered with a punch to my head. I grunted and hit back, harder now. I had to back up my overtures of peace with strength. I hit him in the ribs, I rubbed my knuckles in his ear as we clinched. I tried again, "You deal good," I said.

"You too," he muttered, pressuring out. And just like that, the fight was over. No more words. We just separated, hands half up, half-down. My heart pumped out, *You've established your rep. Move over, 104th Street. Lift your wings, I'm one of your baby chicks now.*

Five seconds later my spurs were given to me in the form of introductions to streetdom's elite. There were no looks of blankness now; I was accepted by heart.

"What's your other name, Johnny Gringo?"

"Piri."

"Okay, Pete, you wanna join my fellows?"

"Sure, why not?"

But I knew I had first joined their gang when I cool-looked them on moving day. *I was cool, man,* I thought. *I could've wasted Waneko any time. I'm good, I'm damned good, pure* corazón. *Viva me!* Shit, I had been scared, but that was over. I was in; it was *my* block now.

Not that I could relax. In Harlem you always lived on the edge of losing rep. All it takes is a one-time loss of heart.

Sometimes, the shit ran smooth until something just had to happen. Then we busted out. Like the time I was leaning against the banister of my stoop, together with Little Louie, Waneko, Indio, and the rest of the guys, and little Crip, small, dark and crippled from birth, came tearing down the block. Crip

never ran if he could walk, so we knew there was some kind of trouble. We
had been bragging about our greatness in rumbles and love, half truths, half
lies. We stopped short and waited cool-like for little Crip to set us straight on
what was happening.

"Oh, them lousy motherfuckers, they almost keeled me," he whined.

"Cool it, man," Waneko said, "what happened?"

"I wasn't doin' nothing, just walking through the fuckin' Jolly Rogers'
territory," Crip said. "I met a couple of their broads, so friendly-like, I felt
one's *culo* and asked, 'How about a lay?' Imagine, just for that she started
yelling for her boys." Crip acted out his narrow escape. We nodded in un-
impressed sympathy because there wasn't a mark on him. A stomping don't
leave you in walking condition, much less able to run. But he was one of our
boys and hadda be backed up. We all looked to Waneko, who was our president.
"How about it, war counselor?" he asked me.

We were ready to fight. "We're down," I said softly, "an' the shit's on."

That night we set a meet with the Jolly Rogers. We put on our jackets
with our club name, "TNT's." Waneko and I met Picao, Macho, and Cuchee
of the Jolly Rogers under the Park Avenue bridge at 104th Street. This was
the line between their block and ours. They were Puerto 'Ricans just like we
were, but this didn't mean shit, under our need to keep our reps.

"How's it going to be?" I asked Macho.

Picao, who I dug as no heart, squawked out, "Sticks, shanks, zips—you
call it."

I looked at him shittily and said, "Yeah, like I figured, you ain't got no
heart for dealing on fists alone."

Macho, their president, jumped stink and said, "Time man, we got heart,
we deal with our *manos*. Wanna meet here at ten tomorrow night?"

"Ten guys each is okay?"

"That's cool," Macho said and turned away with his boys. The next night
we got our boys together. They were all there with one exception—Crip. He
sent word that he couldn't make our little 10 P.M. get-together. His sister,
skinny Lena, was having a birthday party. We took turns sounding his mother
for giving birth to a *maricón* like him.

Our strategy was simple. We'd meet in the Park Avenue tunnel and each
gang would fight with its back to its own block to kill any chance of getting
sapped from behind. Our debs sat on the stoops watching for the fuzz or for
any wrong shit from the Jolly Rogers.

It got to 10 P.M. and we dug the Jolly Rogers coming under the Park
Avenue tunnel. We walked that way too. Macho had heart; he didn't wait for
us in the tunnel; he came with his boys right into our block. My guts got tight,
as always before a rumble, and I felt my breath come in short spurts. I had
wrapped handkerchiefs around each hand to keep my knuckles from getting
cut on any Jolly Roger's teeth. We began to pair off. I saw Giant, a big, ugly
Jolly Roger, looking me over.

"Deal, motherfucker," I screamed at him.

He was willing like mad. I felt his fist fuck up my shoulder. I was glad 'cause it cooled away my tight guts. I side-slipped and banged my fist in his guts and missed getting my jaw busted by an inch. I came back with two shots to his guts and got shook up by a blast on the side of my head that set my eyeballs afire. I closed on him and held on, hearing the noise of pains and punches. Some sounded like slaps, others hurt dully. I pushed my head into Giant's jaw. He blinked and swung hard, catching my nose. I felt it running. I didn't have a cold, so it had to be blood. I sniffed back hard and drove rights and lefts and busted Giant's lip open. Now he was bleeding too. *Chevere.*

Everybody was dealing hard. Somebody got in between me and Giant. It was Waneko, and he began dealing with Giant. I took over with the Jolly Roger he'd been punching it out with. It was Picao. He had been fighting all along—not too hard, I suspected. I got most happy. I'd been aching to chill that *maricón.* He didn't back down and we just stood there and threw punches at each other. I felt hurt a couple of times, but I wanted to put him out so bad, I didn't give a fuck about getting hurt. And then it happened—I caught Picao on his chin with an uppercut and he went sliding on his ass and just lay there.

I felt king-shit high and I wanted to fight anybody. I had the fever. I started for Giant, who was getting wasted by Waneko, when one of our debs opened up her mouth like an air-raid siren. "Look out, ya gonna get japped," she shouted.

We saw more Rogers coming from Madison Avenue. They were yelling their asses off and waving stickball bats.

"Make it," Waneko shouted. "Them *cabrones* wanna make a massacre!"

Everybody stopped fighting and both gangs looked at that wasting party tearing up the street toward us. We started cutting out and some of the Rogers tried grabbing on to some of us. Waneko pulled out a blade and started slashing out at any J.R. he could get to. I tore my hand into my back pocket and came out with my garbage-can-handle brass knucks and hit out at a cat who was holding on to one of my boys. He grabbed at a broken nose and went wailing through the tunnel.

We split, everybody making it up some building. I felt bad those *cabrones* had made us split, but I kept running. I made it to number 109 and loped up the stairs. *"Adiós,* motherfuckers," I yelled over my shoulder. "You *cabrones* ain't got no heart!" I crashed through my apartment door with thanks that Momma had left it open, 'cause two or three Jolly Rogers were beating the air inches behind me with stickball bats.

*"Qué pasa?"* yelled Momma.

The Jolly Rogers outside were beating their stickball bats on the door for me to come out if I had any heart. I hollered to them, "I'm coming out right now, you motherfuckers, with my fucking piece!" I didn't have one, but I felt good-o satisfaction at hearing the cattle stampede down the stairs.

"What happened, *muchacho?*" Momma asked, in a shook-up voice.

I laughed. "Nothing, Moms, we was just playing ring-a-livio."

"What about your nose, it got blood on it," said Sis.

I looked bad at her. "Bumped it," I said, then turning to Momma, I asked, "Say, Moms, what's for dinner? Je-sus, I'm starvin'."

# Joe, The Vanishing American
## 1957

## Harvey Swados

If Walter had not been so desperately anxious to go away to college he might never have been able to stick it out those first few weeks at the factory. His father, once district sales manager for a bankrupt sewing-machine concern, had come down in the world and was now a continually uneasy clerk in the branch office of a usury outfit called the Friendly Finance Corporation; his mother, who had borne Walter late in life, clung jealously to the fading prestige conferred on her by her many beneficences on behalf of the Ladies' Guild.

Walter had never done anything harder than shovel the neighbors' snowy driveways and sell magazines to reluctant relatives. But the night of his graduation from high school his father grunted in a choked voice that there was no money to send him to college. Walter swore to himself that he would get a college education if he had to rob a bank. At the commencement exercise a classmate had told him that you could get a job at the new auto assembly plant if you said on your application that you had worked as a garage mechanic. While his parents rocked creakily, proud but miserable, on the porch glider, Walter mounted the narrow steps to his little room and sat down at his desk. If he could work steadily at the plant for a year he ought to be able to save several thousand dollars even after contributing his share of the household expenses. Without saying a word to his parents, he went to the plant the following morning and filled out an application blank. Three days later he received a telegram asking him to report for work at 6:30 A.M.

When he returned, grey and exhausted, from his first long day in the body shop to which he had been assigned, Walter found his mother sitting in the parlor and sobbing into a handkerchief. She raised her eyes at the slamming of the door and stared at him in horror.

"Look at you!" she cried, and immediately Walter knew that her first shock was at the way he *looked*, not at how he must have *felt*. Nevertheless Walter felt it his filial duty to explain that he would not have to march past the neighbors in greasy coveralls, but could wear sport clothes to work and change

255

at the plant; furthermore, he hinted, when his mother was preparing his sandwiches for the next day's lunch, he could just as easily carry them in a little paper sack as in a metal lunchbox.

His father, keeping them company in the kitchen, took a different tack, and even blustered a little about the advantages of working for a huge corporation.

"I don't see why Walter couldn't have started with something more pleasant," his mother said plaintively, smoothing mayonnaise across white bread. "In an office he could at least use his brains."

"Don't kid yourself," her husband replied. "There's no shame attached to factory work any more. Besides, Walter has a darned good chance to advance if he shows them the stuff he's got."

Implicit in all this was his parents' fear that Walter had started down a dead-end street, and their own shame at not having been able to send him away to college. Anxious not to inflame their feelings, Walter refrained from defending his decision; even if he were only to point out that he would be making big money, it would be a direct insult to his father, who at fifty-nine was making only five dollars a week more than his son. So he put the case negatively.

"There's just no place else around," he said, "that would pay me anything like what I'm going to be making at the auto plant."

"The boy is right, Mother," his father said decisively, much to Walter's satisfaction. "You're doing the smart thing, Walter."

Thus challenged at home, Walter had no alternative but to grit his teeth and swear to himself that nothing would make him quit until he had reached his goal. Like a groggy but game boxer, he measured out his future not with the end of the fight in view, for that would have been too far away, but rather in terms of more immediate accomplishments: his first automatic nickel raise at the end of four weeks, his second automatic nickel raise at the end of eight weeks, his acceptance as a permanent employee at the end of ninety days, and most of all his listing as a metal-finisher, which would mean that he would be in the highest-paid group in the plant and that he would be recognized as a skilled worker, a man who had made the grade.

His surroundings meant nothing to Walter, who had not expected that the factory would look like an art gallery; but the work, and the conditions under which he had to do it, were a nightmare of endless horror from which Walter sometimes thought, stumbling wearily out of the plant after ten hours of unremitting anguish, he would one day awaken with a scream. It was not simply that the idea of working on an endless succession of auto bodies as they came slowly but ineluctably rolling down the assembly line like so many faceless steel robots was both monotonous and stupefying, or that the heavy work of finding bumps and dents in them, knocking them out and filing them down, was in itself too exhausting.

No, it was the strain of having to work both fast and accurately, with the foreman standing over him and glaring through his thick-lensed glasses, that made Walter dread the beginning of each day. Under the best of conditions, he figured, he had three and a half minutes to complete his metal-finishing work from the time he started a job on his line to the time it reached the platform and was swung off on hooks toward the bonderizing booth. If he began at the very beginning, as soon as the inspector had indicated bad spots with a stump of chalk, circling hollows and x-ing high spots, he could finish before the job reached the final inspector at the far end of the line—unless the dents were too deep or too numerous, in which case he was still madly pounding and filing, squatting and straining with the sweat running down his temples and his cheekbones while the solder-flower worked next to him in a tangle of rubber hose, melting lead and a blazing gun with a flame so hot that it scorched dry the running sweat on his face, and the final inspector stood over him, imperturbably chalking newly discovered hollows and pimples in the infuriating metal. Then he would straighten up from his hopeless effort and with a despairing glance at the impassive pickup man, who had to finish what he had left undone, he would hurry back down the line, praying to dear God that the next car—he did every third one—would be in fairly decent condition.

Worst of all were the times when he would hear a piercing whistle and would look up from the damnable dent at which he had been rapping blindly with the point of his file to see Buster the foreman all the way past the platform, waving angrily with his cigar. Hurrying from his unfinished work to his punishment, Walter would try to steel himself against what he knew was coming, but it was no use.

"You call yourself a metal man?" Buster would ask, stuffing the cigar between his teeth with an angry snap. "You want to get metal-finisher's pay and you let a job like that go through?" His eyes glinting with rage behind his thick spectacles, Buster would gesticulate at one of Walter's cars, freshly speckled with chalk marks as it swung in the air. "Get going on it!"

And Walter would hurl himself at the job, dashing the sweat from his brow with the back of his gloved hand and filing away in a clumsy fury.

By the time he had somehow or other repaired what he had left undone, he would find on hastening back to the line that he was far behind once again in his regular work, so far behind that it might take him the better part of an hour to gradually work his way back on the line to where he really belonged, safe for the moment from shouted complaints.

Inevitably the men around him had suggestions as to how Walter might better his condition. Of the two other metal-finishers who worked on the line with him, one was a dour, fattish man, a leader in the opposition of the local union and disgusted because it did nothing to provide security for probationary employees like Walter.

"I'll tell you something else. There's countries where a bright young hard-working fellow like you, that wants to go to college, doesn't have to waste the best years of his life in factory work just to save the money for college fees. He gets sent right through school and the government foots the bills. All he has to do is show that he's got the stuff and his future is secure."

Walter allowed that this sounded fine, although "having the stuff" sounded uncomfortably like his father's eulogies of life in America, but he could not see what practical good it did him here and now—unless he was supposed to get satisfaction from the bitterness of knowing that in mysterious other countries his opposite numbers were better off than he.

The third metal-finisher, a lean efficient sardonic man, had been listening silently to this talk of free college careers. He put his wiry hand inside his open-necked khaki shirt, scratched the coarse curling hair below his throat, and laughed aloud.

"What's the matter?" asked his fattish colleague suspiciously.

"You think your propaganda's going to change this boy's ideas about the other side of the world when everything here tells him he's got it so good?" He tapped the fat man on the shoulder with the butt end of his file as patronizingly as if he were patting him on the head. "Even if he has to suffer for his education in a way that shouldn't be necessary, he's free. He can blunder around and maybe even learn something that isn't listed in the college catalogues. Those poor kids you want him to envy, they may be getting their college for nothing, but they're paying a higher price for it than this fellow ever will. And the sad part is that most of them probably don't even know what the price is." And he turned back to his work without giving the fat man a chance to reply.

Fortunately for the three of them, the fat metal-finisher was transferred. He was only replaced, however, by an intense worker with two vertical wrinkles between his brows, who watched Walter's ineffectual work with growing impatience. At last he could stand it no more.

"In this game, kid, the knack of it is in the speed. The speed," he said fiercely, "and the way you concentrate on the job. If you're going to fumble around and just bitch about your mistakes, you'll be a long time getting straightened out." He greeted his own badly dented job, rolling toward them, with a smile of genuine pleasure. "Size it up quick, pick out the worst dents, and get going on them right away. Leave the high spots for last—the pickup men don't mind doing them."

The third man, the grey-haired cynic whom everyone liked but no one seemed to know, had been listening quietly, with a strange, mild grin on his long and youthful face. He put a stick of chewing gum in his mouth, ruminated for a moment, and said: "What you really want is for him to enjoy his work, Orrin. Might be more practical if you'd get down and actually show him how to do it. Here, hold on a minute, Walter."

Walter had been squatting on his haunches before the wheel-housing of his job, blindly pounding with a hammer at his hidden screwdriver, trying hopelessly to punch a hole underneath so that with the screwdriver he could dig out a deep dent as the others did, trying so hopelessly that as he smashed the hammer against his left hand, missing the butt end of the screwdriver, he had to squeeze his eyes to keep the tears from starting forth.

"Give me that screwdriver."

Handing up the tool to the laconic man, Walter noticed for the first time that he bore an unusual tattoo, faded like an old flag, on his right forearm: an American eagle, claws gripping his wrist, beak opened triumphantly at the elbow—you could almost hear it screaming. Without a word the man took the screwdriver and swiftly pressed it to a grinding wheel, fashioning a beveled point.

"Try it now."

Walter stuck the screwdriver under the car, rapped at it smartly several times—*bang!* it was through and resting against the outer skin of the car, just at the very dent. Gratefully, he turned to the grey-haired man, but he was gone, like a mirage.

There was something miragelike about him, anyway. He drove to and from work alone, he never engaged in small talk, he never hung around with a group at lunch hour or before work, he kept a paper book in the hip pocket of his khaki trousers, and always when he was not concentrating on his own work, when he was watching Walter or listening to the others handing him advice, he had that mocking irreligious smile on his long narrow youthful face. What was more, his cold blue eye seemed always to be on Walter, sizing him up, watching not so much his work, as everyone else did, but his temperament and his personality. It made him uncomfortable.

Gradually Walter began to sort out the other men around him, the ones who had more common reality in their talk and their tastes. Most companionable of them all was Kevin, the former rural school teacher, now an immigrant hook-man. His accent was so delightful, his turns of speech so happy, that Walter engaged the towering redhead in conversation at every opportunity.

"Hey, Kevin," he shouted at him one day, "how old were those kids you taught in County Kerry?"

"Ah, Walter," Kevin sighed, showing his long white teeth as he spoke, "they weren't *all* such children. If you were to see some of the older girls— quite well developed, they were. Oh, how shameful if they had known what was passing through their schoolmaster's mind!"

Kevin laughed at the memory, Walter at the picture the big fellow conjured up of countryside lust; he turned around and there was the grey-haired metal-finisher, smiling too, but so coldly you would have thought him a scientist observing a successful experiment. It was chilling, and yet not wholly unpleasant. In a way that he could not define, Walter felt that he was being judged and approved.

This third man, reserved and anonymous as ever, continued to observe him as Walter chatted not only with Kevin and the second metal-finisher, but with all of the other men on their line. Conversation was necessarily shouted and fragmentary, but Walter was astonished at how intimacies could be revealed in the course of a few phrases:

"A man's a fool to get married."

"Grab the overtime while you can. In the auto industry you never know when you'll be laid off."

"Happiest time of my life was when I was in the army."

"Only reason I'm here is because I was too stupid to learn a trade."

"I came here out of curiosity, but my curiosity's all used up."

"My wife says if I quit I'll have a better chance to line up a construction job."

"Walter, don't turn out like those college men who can tell you how to do everything but can't do a damn thing themselves."

The only one to rebuff Walter's friendly overtures was Pop, the seamy-faced little inspector with a rooster's ruff of yellowing white hair that rose and tumbled down over his forehead, and sunken old lips from which depended miraculously a heavy, unlit cigar. Wizened, pale and bloodless, he regarded Walter, for no apparent reason, with bottomless contempt. With a little cap perched sideways on his Niagara of a head like a precarious canoe, and a soft brown cloth knotted about the hand with which he probed Walter's work for defects and omissions, he seemed to Walter like some strange and hateful gnome.

"Kids like you," he said in a dry and rusty monotone, "they come and go. Twenty-three years I'm here, and I seen a million like you. Not steady, not reliable, don't want to learn, just out for fun. You'll never make a metal man."

I don't want to be a metal man, Walter wanted to reply; I just want to make my money and get out of here. But this was, he knew, just what Pop was goading him to say, so he held his tongue. A moment later he was glad that he had, for he was startled to hear the third metal-finisher address him.

"Pop is an exception," he said, bending over Walter's car and scrubbing at it with his sandpaper as he spoke. "By and large there is a democracy of age in the factory. Men who have been here since before you were born fought for a union contract guaranteeing equal treatment for you. Ninety days after you start you get the same wage as a worker who's been on the job nineteen years. A man twice your age will treat you as a working partner and an adult. Where else is that true?"

"Yes," Walter replied angrily, "but Pop—"

"He's got reason to be bitter. Some day I'll tell you why."

He straightened up abruptly and walked away to his own job. But the words he had used reverberated in Walter's mind. Who was he, with his young-old face and his expressions like "democracy of age"? Walter asked, but no one seemed to know. Some said he was a seaman and adventurer, and his big tattoo was pointed to as proof, for he had been heard to state himself that he had acquired it in Lourenço Marques; but others, who had themselves come to the assembly line from rural homesteads, were positive from clues he had let fall that he had formerly been an itinerant farm laborer; and there were even those who swore that he was really an educated man, a kind of college professor amusing himself by slumming among them.

Whoever he was, for the time he had nothing more to say. But Walter felt his presence, for he was always ready to lend a hand, always laconically helpful, always silently observing and listening.

One day the younger inspector at the beginning of the line, blowing genial clouds of illegal pipe smoke, gave Walter some frank and cynical advice.

"Been listening to the bosses talking about you, buddy." He took the pipe from his mouth and formed a fat smoke ring. "Want to know what's wrong with what you're doing?"

"I guess so," said Walter dully.

"You try too hard. You're trying to do a good job—that's the worst thing you can do."

Walter stared in bewilderment at the inspector. "But why?"

"They're interested in pulling production. If you're going to be running up and down the line all day trying to make every job perfect, you're just going to get in people's way. What the bosses will do is, they'll look for an excuse to fire you before your probationary period is up, or else they'll stick you in a routine lower-paying job."

"Then . . ."

"I've been here ten years. Believe me," he drew on his pipe once again and smiled disarmingly, "they're not interested in making good cars, they're interested in making cars. You know what production means? Volume. And you know what they hired you for? To camouflage, not to get rid of every flaw. Hide them so they don't show up after the car's been through paint, so the customer doesn't see them at the dealer's, and you'll get along great."

"Camouflage them how?"

"With your sandpaper. With the grinding wheel. If you hit them up and down and then across, final inspection will never know what's underneath. Make it look good, and confusing. Be a camouflage artist and the bosses'll very seldom bother you."

Walter could not help laughing. "Listen, how could you stand it here for ten years? Every day I think maybe I ought to get out and look for something else."

"For six years," the inspector said pleasantly, "I was like you. This was going to be just temporary until I found something with a real future. It took me six years to realize that I was going to be spending the rest of my life here—it's like breaking in a wild horse, only with a human being it takes longer. I got married, had three kids, now I'm building a home near the plant. So I make the best of it, I take it easy, and I have as much fun as I can, and I hate to see a guy like you breaking his back all for nothing."

Bending over his work, Walter raised his file and heard the inspector's final shot, lightly enough intended but bearing its own weight of bitterness and resignation: "You'd be surprised how many fellows I've heard talking just like you, couldn't stand the work, going to quit any day, and now they're five- and ten-year men, starting to think about retirement benefits."

Walter could not clarify in his own mind what it was about the inspector's attitude that increased his desperation, not until his silent partner eased up to him from nowhere and said quietly, "Kind of terrified you, didn't he?"

"Not exactly terrified."

"Just the same, it's no fun to be doing time and to be told that your sentence just might turn out to be indefinite. Then if you've got a good imagination you can see yourself gradually getting used to it, even getting to like the routine, so that one day follows another and the first thing you know the wrinkles are there and the kids are grown up and you don't know where it's all gone to, your life."

Walter felt himself shuddering. Was it from the blower overhead that he felt his hot sweat turning cold and drying on his face? He said, "I suppose you have to be cynical if you're going to stay here."

"Day after day your life becomes a joke without any point, a trick that you play on yourselve from punching in to punching out."

"But that's only if you're an imaginative or a sensitive person."

For the first time, the man's angular face hardened. "Don't you think somebody like that inspector had his ambitions? Don't you think he still has his man's pride? Did you ever figure the cost of the job in terms of what it does to the personality of a clever intelligent fellow like him? He says if you're going to be trapped you might as well make the best of it, and by his lights he may be right. Anyway don't be too quick to blame him—he probably never had the opportunity to save money and go off to college."

No one had ever, not ever in eighteen years, talked to Walter in such a way. He would never again be able to look at a man like the inspector without compassion. Even at home in the evening with his father, whom he could no longer talk to about anything but baseball or the weather (although they both tried clumsily to broach other more serious topics), Walter found that he was viewing this desolate man not just as his father but as a man who had his own miseries; and this, he knew, was a part of growing up that could not have come about as it had without the influence of his strange friend in the factory.

More and more as the weeks passed and exhaustion was gradually overcome by vitality, only to be transformed into monotony, Walter came to feel that only this man could explain the real meaning of the assembly line. But he remained aloof, insubstantial as a ghost. The more he held to himself, the more Walter was piqued, and determined to make the ghost speak.

At last one day he ventured to demand: "Say, what does that tattoo of yours stand for, that big bird?"

The man smiled with one side of his mouth. "That old bird is the American eagle." He raised his arm briefly, flexed it, and let it fall to his side. "It's screaming with rage at what's happened to the republic."

"What *has* happened?"

"Where are the guts? Where's the drive? In a place like this a man's life goes down the drain like scummy water."

"But you're working here too," Walter said boldly.

The man shook his head slowly, with such finality that there was something elemental about the gesture. "I'm not a settled-down man, I'm just passing through."

Walter cleared his throat. "I don't even know your name."

"Why should you? Instead of learning names, we refer to the fellow with the bad teeth, or the guy with the blue coveralls. When I work next to a man for months and learn that his wife is being operated on for cancer of the breast and still don't know his name, it tells me something not just about him and me, but about the half-connections that are all the factory allows you in the way of friendships."

"The old-timers are clubby enough, but everybody else claims they're here for a limited time. The place is so big and everything seems so temporary that I suppose we don't feel the need of introducing ourselves."

The older man looked at Walter somberly. "No one who comes here wants to admit that the place has any real connection with his real life. He has to say that he is just putting in his time here, and so no matter how friendly he is by nature he has to think of the people around him as essentially strangers, men whom he can't even trouble to say goodbye to when he quits or gets laid off."

"But *your* name—"

"Call me Joe."

Walter pursued him: "Every third guy on the line must be named Joe. Joe what?"

He smiled again, his long Yankee countenance creasing in a cold grin. "Joe, the vanishing American." And he turned his back on Walter and bent to his work as the line resumed its endless progress.

But he was a curious man, a nosy man, and he was there, listening and leering, when Walter found a minute to respond without cursing to a bitter remark of Pop's. Walter turned on him with the anger he had managed to suppress when speaking to the old inspector.

"It's easy for you to stand there and laugh. You think you're better than anybody else in the shop."

Joe hitched up his khaki trousers and replied with deliberate anger, "I never claimed that. I just read a little more and ponder a little more than the average fellow. That's why I don't laugh at them, I feel sorry for them. If I'm a little freer, I've had to make sacrifices for it—no dependents, no ties." He added cryptically, "They punish you one way or they punish you another way."

Walter did not quite understand, but it struck him that these remarks were a prelude to farewell. He asked uneasily, "You're not going to quit?"

"One of these days. Maybe the weather will turn, or I'll hear of something else, or I'll have words with Buster . . ." He added with somewhat more warmth, "But I'll be back—if not here, some place like here. You won't though. That's why I hope you won't forget what it was like for the people who made the things you'll be buying."

Walter cried indignantly: "How could I? How could I ever forget?" It seemed to him that the thick scurf of silver through which he shuffled as he worked, the glittering waste of lead filings and melted sticks, were so many needles, each carrying its stinging injection of memory—of sweat, exhaustion, harrying, feverish haste, and stupid boredom.

"You forget worse things, don't you? Pain, and even death? You'll think back on the days when you were slaving away to save money for college, and they'll strike you as comical, maybe even romantic."

"God forbid!" Walter laughed. And yet he had suddenly a shivery foretaste of a future beyond the one of which he daydreamed as he worked.

When the siren screamed the end of their nine and a half hours Walter hurled his file and apron into his toolbox and trotted down the aisle toward the time clock. Turning the corner of the body shop office just as its lights were extinguished, he ran headlong into the iron antennae of a fork truck and cried aloud with pain as the metal plate struck his shinbone. Tottering backwards, Walter was suddenly gripped by the forearm and pulled erect. He turned gratefully and found himself staring into the eyes of Joe.

Smarting with soreness and embarrassment, Walter demanded aggressively, "I suppose that's what you want me to remember!"

A faint stubble glinted along Joe's narrow cheeks. Greying like his iron hair, it aged him as it grew. He scraped his hand across it wearily and replied quietly, "Never mind the machinery. Remember the men. The men make the machines, and they make their own tragedies too. Once your own life gets easier, you'll take it for granted not only that theirs must be easier too, but that they deserve what they get anyway, that some law of natural selection has put you up where you are and them down where they are."

They had reached the clock bay where they took their place meekly in line, waiting to punch out, shuffling forward every few seconds while they spoke in low voices. Around them a swarm of men surged toward freedom— noisy boys with laughter to spare for the evening, haggard weary men in their forties, surly powerful black men in stained coveralls and scrawny brown men chattering in Spanish, vacant-faced fools with slack jaws and dangling hands, shrewd-eyed men fingering their union contract books, composing their campaign leaflets, and computing their chances of election to positions that would lift them out of the work routine.

"Why do they stay?"

"They're trapped, that's why. They say everybody's supposed to be, one way or another, but it's worse to be stuck here. Spending your life on the production line means counting out the minutes, being grateful that Mondays go fast because you're rested, and hating Tuesdays because the week is so long. It means that you're paying off forever on all the things you've been pressured into buying by getting up every day in order to do something you'd never, never think of doing if it was a matter of choice. It means never having anything to look forward to in all of your working life." Joe took his card from the rack, clicked it in the time clock, and with a wave of his hand was gone.

What was happening, as Walter woke daily to the dawn's dull alarm and went from the still house through the newly washed streets to the waiting assembly line, was that his self-pity, so strong that the page blurred before him when he lay in bed reading himself to sleep, was altering into a maturer concern with the fate of others who could not, like himself, set a term to their labor.

He began to question the men on the line with him, one after another, to find out how many of them felt as he did about what they were doing for a living. More sure of himself with every passing hour, he moved up and down the line, demanding, whenever there was a moment, an answer to his insistent question: "Do you think anybody likes coming in here to work?"

"Everybody does one day a week—payday," said the solder-flower.

"Not even the bosses," said the deck-fitter. "Do you think anybody with sense would knock himself out in this dirt and noise if it wasn't for the money?"

And the door-fitter said wryly, "Do you know what this kind of work is? It's colored man's work. Why, even the colored men are smartening up—they turn up their noses at it too, unless they get strapped."

Saddened and bewildered by this last comment, Walter turned away from the man who had made it, and who had punctuated his bitter remark with a series of thunderous blows on a door that he was fitting. Only Orrin, the second metal-finisher, grudgingly admitted that the work was a challenge to him, that the pay was fair, and that there were worse jobs. Behind them all, long-jawed Joe, caught up with his work as usual, stood casually beveling his screwdriver.

"I hear you've been taking a little poll," he said to Walter.

"What's it to you?" Walter asked truculently. He was in no mood to be mocked.

With apparent irrelevance, Joe replied by demanding, "How come you fixed on being an engineer?"

Walter was taken aback. "Why, that's where everybody says the future is."

"That's not reason enough for a fellow to struggle and sweat to get to college. Damn it, doesn't anybody go out and do what he wants to any more? I'm not saying you wouldn't make a good engineer, or that it wouldn't be fine for a change to have some engineers who care as much about people as they do about gadgets. But supposing you find out after you get to college that you want to spend your time learning something useless—are you going to leave yourself open for it?"

"Boy, you sure are free with advice."

Joe looked at him gravely. His long sad jaw had the hint of a smile. "The men on the line like you, Walter. They don't think you're just nosy when you ask questions. They think you're one of them, and in a good way you are. Maybe that's why I've got hopes for you."

Walter fought hard against the influence of the older man, whose crabbed and subversive outlook was so foreign to everything Walter had been taught, but he was forced to admit to himself that more and more he was seeing the factory through Joe's cold discerning eyes; and he began to fear that if Joe were ever to leave, the plant would have no real existence other than as a money-producing nightmare. Not only was there no one else really to talk to about it, but Joe had forced Walter to try to formulate his emerging ideas in an adult and comprehensible way.

"The worst thing about the assembly line is what it does to your self-respect," he said to Joe early one morning as they squatted on their haunches, waiting for the starting siren. "It's hard to keep from feeling like a fool when you know that everybody looks down on what you're doing, even the men who are doing it themselves."

Joe hung his hammer and metal spoon from the brass hook at his belt. "The big pitch has always been that we're a practical people, that we've proved to all the impractical European dreamers that production can serve people. But instead people are serving production. Look how frightened, how hysterical the bosses get when the line stops—they can't afford to figure what it costs *you* to keep it moving—they only know they've got a production quota. Of course when sales resistance starts building up and they put the cork back in themselves, they give you just the opposite story. Who can blame the poor slob in the middle for suspecting that the whole setup is really as nutty as a fruitcake, and for feeling ashamed of himself for being caught up in it?"

"All right," Walter challenged him. "Who's crazy? You, me, the guys around us, or the board of directors?"

"Anybody who gets suckered into believing that there's anything real behind the billboards they put up to get the show on the road, so that he commits himself to buying the billboard pictures by selling his life on the installment plan. I sympathize with any joker who begins to suspect that the whole world is against him, that he's the victim of a huge conspiracy organized to make his car fall apart before it's been paid off. Doesn't life in the factory seem to be deliberately designed to lower your own self-esteem? What happens when you're knocking down a dent? If you rap it too hard from the inside, you have to file it down that much more, and you hate yourself for it. If you don't rap it hard enough you only find out after it's moved on down the line, and then you have to hurry up and wallop it again. In either case you hate yourself instead of hating the car, or the invisible man that started up the line." He laughed briefly in anticipation of what he was about to add. "It's like the man that hits his thumb with a hammer while he's hanging a picture—only here he keeps hitting his thumb because they're moving the wall as fast as the union will let them. Who does he yell at every time that ball peen comes down on his nail? Himself."

"I wonder," Walter said slowly, "how many people actually feel that way."

"More than you can count. It's always safe to figure that if you feel something, the world must be full of people who feel the same way. Every sensible man realizes as he gets older that his feeling aren't unique. After all, that's the basis of the best art: the fact that you recognize yourself in it, and all those inner experiences that you'd thought no one else but you could know."

Walter was willing to recognize that he was not the only one to cringe when Buster called him back on a badly done job, to swear at himself for the mistakes that made him fall behind, to realize how he was being trapped into swearing at himself and deflecting his anger from what he did to the way he did it. But it was hard for him to believe that there were others who felt as intensely as he did, who beat their heads against the bars as he did, who dreamed of sunlight and freedom as he did, even though Joe tried to persuade him that the difference was often one of degree, or of his being able to express his feelings in a way that others couldn't. This was one of the questions that Walter was eager to argue with Joe, who moved from one extreme position to another, always mocking, always challenging him to learn what he stood for and to defend it like a man.

"You know something," Walter burst out impetuously one day, "I don't know what I would have done here without you."

Instead of laughing, or belittling this praise, Joe's face darkened. The next morning he was not on the line.

By the third day of his absence Walter was beginning to feel as though it had all been a dream, as though he were slipping once again into the awful pit of loneliness, exhaustion and self-doubting despair. As a last resort he sought out the men on the line to learn what they thought of Joe.

"He's irresponsible," said Pop.

"He's the kind of guy that just don't care," said the younger inspector. "No wife, no kids, no wonder he can take off three days without worrying about getting a reprimand or getting fired."

"He knows his work," said Orrin grudgingly. "I don't know where he learned it, but he did. Just the same, he takes off. You can't *afford* to take off like that nowadays, not if you want to hold down a job."

On the fourth day he came back. He told no one where he had been. "Am I glad to see you!" Walter exclaimed—but Joe merely indicated, with a cold grin and a turn of his tattooed arm, that from time to time things came up that were more important than the making of automobiles. He did not set to work, but almost immediately was engaged in serious talk with Buster the foreman and with the union shop steward. The two were arguing vigorously, but suddenly Joe cut them off simply by lifting his hand. He said something very briefly, shoved his hands into his pockets, and the discussion was finished.

To Walter's amazement, he came back to the line, picked up his toolbox, and nodded casually to him.

"I just quit, Walter," he said. "Going to hit the road."

"But—"

"You'll make out all right, no matter what you do. I don't even have to wish you good luck."

Then he was off down the aisle, on his way to the tool crib and the plant police and the parking lot and God alone knew where after that, without so much as a handshake or an inclination of his lean frame. Suddenly Walter remembered something: "Hey!" he shouted. But Joe—if he heard him—did not turn around and soon was out of sight.

You never told me about Pop, he wanted to tell Joe, you never answered all the questions I was going to ask you—but even if Joe had not gone for good, Walter would not have known how to say to him all the things that should have been said, the words of gratitude and self-confidence.

When the relief man came a few minutes later to give him a twelve-minute break, he hurried to the bathroom. There, just beyond the big circular sink that could accommodate half a dozen men, he could see out the tilted window to the vast parking lot.

The dull winter light was gloomy and deceptive, and so vague was the air that the dark ranks of massed automobiles were no more than darker blurs against the background of the grey metal fencing and the lowering sky. One of the cars moved, or was it his imagination? But no, the red tail-light dimmed, glowed, dimmed. Joe, the vanishing American, was swinging out of the lot and away from the production line, out of Walter's life and into someone else's, out of the present and into what lay beyond the gate. He was leaving the future to Walter, who now at last could wave his farewell, with his face pressed to the cool window as he watched the little light disappearing from view.

Then he washed the sweat from his face and returned to his work.

## So Here I Am
## 1958

## A Princeton Student

Before I tell you about myself, I think I'll introduce you to my family. That way, maybe you'll understand me a bit better. My father—my real father, that is—was in his late fifties when he married my mother. She was just out of high school and off my grandfather's little farm in East Texas. Why she married him I'll never understand. He had already lived a full life; she still had hers to live. But she did, and so here I am.

Dad was quite a character. He was born in one of the Dakotas—which one I don't think even he knew. While he was still a kid, his father died. Because he was the oldest, and his mother couldn't support all three of her children, he was sent out to earn his keep. He had a hard time of it—he even got buggy-whipped a few times—and he built up some real hate. I gather he ran away, because at the next stage of his life I know of he was riding the ranges in Kansas, I think. This was a rather colorful period—at least once he even got himself shot at. (He was fooling with another man's girl, just because the other fellow had told him not to.) Next, he served an apprenticeship as a watchmaker and then set himself up as a watchmaker and jeweler in a Southern coastal city. He was an excellent watchmaker. He probably forgot more than most watchmakers today know (if I may use an old cliché). He apparently developed a fairly good business. He married, had one daughter, whom he sent to a good Southern girls' school, and built himself a fine house. However, some time in the late Twenties, his business failed. For a while, too, his family life had not been satisfactory. So he and his wife were divorced, and he left with effectively nothing. He teamed up with a friend of his, leasing land in East Texas, in the hope that oil would be found on it. The other man supplied the capital, and Dad did the leg work. It was at this time that he met my mother.

Mother was the third of eight children. Her family lived on a small East Texas farm. And believe me, they lived hard. To eke a living out of that damn clay, every one of them had to pitch in. Mother went to grade school in a little one-room schoolhouse near the farm. A pretty rural place, I gather. And later, when she went to town to high school, she was treated as one of the country hicks. Apparently she was, too. The five miles into town by wagon and team was quite a distance. And that's how she remembers travelling it. The town and country were really separate. I think the way Mother was treated in high school has a lot to do with her marrying Dad. When she finished high school, she continued living in town with some relatives, and took a job as an elevator operator. It was on this job that she met Dad. She was apparently quite impressed with his showing any interest in her. So against her family's wishes, she married him. I consider this to be the greatest mistake she ever made in her life. But I suppose I shouldn't condemn it too much as, without it, I wouldn't be.

Before I was old enough really to be aware of much, we moved far from East Texas to another little town. The reason for the move was Dad's poor health. And this other town was where I grew up. We had a little house not too far from the school, and a nice lawn where I could play. Things seemed really rosy to me. But they weren't. Until recently I never knew it, but we were really quite poor. All we had was the small income from the oil-land leases Dad had worked out, plus what Mother made as a waitress. Dad could have found himself a job as a jeweler, but because he wanted to maintain the façade that he was a "retired" man, he just puttered around in his garden.

Mother and Dad didn't have a stable marriage. It seems obvious to me now that they never could have had one. When I was eight, they were divorced. Mother told the court that she did not want custody of me. What the court didn't know was that Dad had told her that if she tried to take me, he'd kill us both. And he probably would have. A few days after Mother left, she married another man, whom she'd met working as a waitress. I can't blame her for leaving. Dad made life pretty tough for her. But I can't help feeling cheated. I lost a mother when I needed one most, and I completely lack the sense of security and companionship which people have who have had a real family. And I can never really know or love my mother as I could if I had had her in those years.

Dad never forgave Mother for leaving him. And he figured the best way to get back at her was through me. He began almost immediately from the time she left to indoctrinate me against her. Seven years later, when he died, I had been thoroughly "brainwashed." At that time I would not have gone to live with my mother under any circumstances.

Dad loved me a great deal and was very good to me. While he disciplined me severely and had many chores for me, he gave me everything he could. I loved him a great deal, too. And I respected him. Besides instilling in me the desire "to get ahead," he drilled into me principles of honesty and ethical behavior. Unfortunately, as I know now, he didn't always obey these rules himself. I will always love him, but I can never have the respect for him I once had.

Dad's death brought many complications. I was firmly decided not to go to live with my mother. Now in order to assure that Mother would never get me, Dad had had my half sister adopt me. So on his death, she and her worthless (in my opinion) husband came out, I think, to see what they could get. What they found were a lot of debts, and very little else. Anyway, I had no intention of leaving the little town where I had grown up. I hadn't bothered to figure out how I was going to manage this, but I knew I was. At this time, in what was really the darkest moment, help came from an unexpected quarter. The Edwards family offered me a home. So I was adopted by the Edwardses and went to live with them.

The Edwards family is completely different from anything else in my background. They really were a family unit. And they were well educated. Mr. Edwards is a Princeton man, and Mrs. Edwards, in addition to having graduated from the best college in the state, is a prodigious reader. Besides Mr. and Mrs. Edwards, whom I now call Dad and Mother, there was a boy, Bill, who was one year ahead of me, and a girl, Ann, two years behind me. The emphasis in this family was much different from that in my previous "family." My real father had stressed making more money than anyone else, and showing it. What mattered most with the Edwards family was people— living with them and helping them. What they did for me is a good example. And there was something else that the Edwardses stressed—superior performance on the job. While we kids were in high school, where good marks came easily, this expectation never showed up. Once we got to college we could feel it unmistakably.

Mr. Edwards is one of the finest men I have ever known. He's a successful businessman, and very competent in his work. But what I find really outstanding about him is the way he helps people all around him. Ever since I have known him he has been supporting, at least partially, one family or more in addition to his own. In a way, I look at him as a giant, carrying everyone else along on his coattails. This is not to say that I think he is without faults; I just find his faults trivial.

Mrs. Edwards I idealize a little less. She's a fine, educated woman, and has very friendly manners. But she tends to be domineering. (She was especially so towards us children.) She can be very stubborn, sarcastic, and even condescending. These qualities, combined with her keen intelligence, can be incredibly cutting. And she had a fabulous temper. No sane man would stand in her way when she is angry. Still, it is primarily because of her that the Edwards family has the orientation towards other people that it does. She is a devout Catholic, who will have both strong Faith and many Works on her record when she knocks at the Gate. She built up the local library practically singlehanded. And she is the driving force that keeps it going. Yet she's never been paid a cent for it. I should point out that, even though I may realize her shortcomings, just as I saw those of my real father, I know that I am very much in debt to this second mother of mine—and I do love her.

Bill Edwards was a boy whom I knew well long before I became his foster brother. He's quite intelligent, and just a shade conceited. But he has plenty to be conceited about. Besides being president and valedictorian of his class, he was the school photographer, a first-rate debater, and the best trumpet player the school ever had. In short, he had a really great high-school record— a record which is based entirely on his own competence and which he built up in spite of the fact that he has a rather cold personality. Until I got to college Bill Edwards was my ideal. Because I admired his intelligence and abilities so much, I found myself imitating not only his hobbies but even his reserved personality.

Ann is just the opposite. She's bright, too. But where Bill is a worker, she's lazy. Consequently, she never built up the spectacular record that Bill did. However, as long as she doesn't overeat (as she likes to), she is and will stay a very pretty girl. And pretty girls, I guess, don't need a record of special achievement.

The years I spent with the Edwardses I look on as the happiest of my life. And they have been among the most important, too, certainly as far as my intellectual development has been concerned. And of course, if it hadn't been for Mr. Edwards, I would never have applied to a first-class college—if I'd gone to college at all. It was through him, and through him alone, that I became interested in Princeton.

These, briefly, have been the major characters in my life. Now let me see what I can tell you about myself.

Physically, I'm a little, nervous, thin fellow. I look much younger than I am. (People often take me for a freshman or a high-school student.) I feel sure that I'm intelligent—or else I wouldn't be at Princeton. I'm not poised at all. So among people whom I don't know very well I'm usually rather quiet.

This gives the impression that I'm shy. Actually, I don't think I'm shy. I just can't think of anything worth saying—so I don't say anything. I have a tremendous drive (to do just what, I'm not sure) which enables me to work very hard and a great deal. During my four years at Princeton I have probably had an average work week of about seventy hours. This, combined with the fact that my department marks high, will enable me to graduate in the upper quarter of my class.

I don't know exactly where this is leading me. Originally I thought I wanted to get rich. But now I find myself more interested in science. If I go into science, I know that I'll never be lacking a comfortable living, but I also know that I will never have a great deal of wealth. The fact is that I'm not quite sure just what I want from life. Actually, now I tend to consider more what I'm capable of *doing* rather than what I *want*. I would like to have enough money to be comfortable and somewhat well-to-do. Beyond that it doesn't make any difference. I'd only give it away, anyway, either before or after I die—probably before, so that I could enjoy doing it. What else is it good for?

But I do want something out of life which I can consider as evidence that I am better than average—an ego booster, if you please. When I say "better," I don't mean in the social sense, or on account of my family, or anything like that. "Better" to me means more competent, more capable. The best man, to me, is the one who does the job best, regardless of who his family is or whom he knows. I want to be more capable than the mediocre masses, whom I despise because of their apathy and mediocrity. This is why I work as I do. To ensure that I will never fall into those masses.

In life the thing I value most is happiness, which to me is roughly material comfort. I not only want this for myself, but also for the rest of the world. This is one of the reasons I am a scientist—so I can chip in my two bits' worth towards the well-being of the rest of the world. If during my lifetime I make the rest of humanity, or humanity to come, just one iota more comfortable, then I will be content.

From a purely personal point of view, what I want is a position where I do the kind of work I'm interested in. I want a comfortable, friendly home where I can hang my hat, with a wife I can love, and be loved by, a couple of kids, and a dog whose ears I can scratch. Home to me will be a place I can come to tired, and where I can be at peace with the world.

And where, I've sometimes been asked, does God fit into this scheme of mine? The truth is that religion has become a very touchy subject with me. When I look at the world around me, I find it difficult to conceive of an omnipotent, all-good, fatherlike deity. Such a deity wouldn't permit the pain and suffering that exists. It seems to me that deity can be all-good and father-like only if he is infinite. But if he is really infinite, he must be very sadistic to allow the things he does. The argument that God tortures us to test our faith is so much bull to me, because if he's truly infinite, he *knows* how we will react. He doesn't need to test the faith of tiny infants in India by letting them starve to death! I prefer to believe in no god at all rather than in this kind of a god. And any finite god that exists seems to be quite inert, at least to me. The universe seems pretty well to function regularly, in the manner which science has described. Maybe God just triggered everything, and then sat back on his haunches to watch. I figure I can be indifferent to an indifferent god.

There are other aspects of the concept of deity that disturb me. Where did he come from? Wouldn't one have to consider an omnipotent deity morally responsible for all the evil in the world, since he has the power to prevent, and foresees it? If I know a dog is vicious, and I release him from a chain, I'm held responsible for the damage he does. Aren't people who cause damage in our world analogous to the dog, since omnipotent deity could restrain them? All these things bothered me long before I came to Princeton. I used to sit in church and worry about them. In high school I attended church quite regularly —twice every Sunday, plus Sunday school. I wanted to believe. I wanted to believe very much. I used to pray—just pray for an answer, a sign that I could have faith in, or for faith itself. That's all over now. Before I finished high school I was aware of the logical paradoxes which riddle the Christian religion, and I was nearly saturated with doubt about the existence of God. I still don't know, but now I've decided that I can't wait for the answer. There may be a God, and there may not. I'm inclined to say there isn't. But rather than worry about this, the practical problem before me is to work out a way of life—a *modus vivendi* of some sort with the world. So far as religion goes, what I want now is to be left alone.

It seems to me a bit ironic that even with such mixed-up religious views, I find myself living by stronger, harder principles than most of the faithful Christians I know. I accepted a job offer in my junior year, and then received another offer with a considerably higher salary from another company. Several good Christian friends suggested I take the second offer and dump the first company. The idea horrified me, and still does. I think a man's word should be as good as his signature on a legal contract. I like to be able to trust people, and I like to be trusted. If the so-called Christians around me would stick to their professed principles, then I *would* trust them. But they don't. Christians often seem to ignore the Golden Rule unless they know the other person to some degree, and even then they don't rigorously stick to it. Their sexual morality is a farce; and business ethics, except in one or two closely knit professions, have to be codified into law. If people would stick to their professed principles, *this* world could be a much better one. And it is *this* world, not the next one, that I'm concerned with.

Go ahead! Call me a blind, foolish idealist. I am. I know that I am. If I weren't, I wouldn't adhere to the things I think are right, without even hope of reward after death, and the certainty of no reward in this world. Perhaps I'm just inhibited. Perhaps going to church so long brainwashed me. This is probably the case. Consequently I would like to marry a girl who really is a Christian—who really sticks to her principles—and to send my children to church, just as I went. Then maybe they'll be brainwashed, too.

Supposedly, any frank autobiography, in order to be complete, must contain a vivid description of one's sex life. So I suppose I ought to give it at least a line or two. I can count the number of times in my life that I have "necked" with a girl on my fingers (of one hand, if you please). I have never had intercourse, and I don't intend to until I am married. I feel that it's wrong. Furthermore, I want to marry a girl who is a virgin, and I think that it would be grossly unfair of me to demand that she be something that I am not. While I find that most of the striving of women for "equality" is actually a disguised effort to expand their already preferential status, I think that in this respect they're not getting a fair deal. The double standard just isn't right. It's got to be everybody either on one standard or the other, but not some on one, and some on the other. I'm for chastity, myself.

Closely analagous are my feelings concerning treatment of the Negroes. I don't think they're getting a fair break, especially from an economic stand-point, and I think they should. Equal schools are essential for this. It is evident that the South will never make them really equal. So I think integration is the only answer. I do, however, object to the Supreme Court's *telling* us we must integrate. I'd rather see the states themselves do it, but, of course, that would probably never happen. While I want to see the Negroes have an equal opportunity for economic and academic achievement and the like, I don't give a hang what happens to them socially (just as I don't care what happens to any-one else socially). I'm totally indifferent to whether or not there happens to be a Negro at the party I go to. I'm not going out of my way to get one there. He'll have to bring himself. On the other hand, like a true Southerner, my dander rises over intermarriage. This I oppose violently for purely emotional reasons. And I'd pull the whole works down to prevent it.

When I come right down to it, I think I have two conflicting goals in life —achievement and security. I'm ambitious in that I want respect for the work that I do. I want to rise in status as far as my abilities will carry me. But I'm a coward when it comes to taking a chance. I don't want to gamble. What I want is a stable order of things in which I can work without exposing myself to ruin.

Princeton has given me one such order. There are only two factors in academic achievement—intelligence and hard work. Since nearly everyone at Princeton has exceptional intelligence, work is the primary means of differentiation between students here. There are only a few people here who are so much smarter than the rest of us that they can make top grades with little work. Hard work is something I do well.

Because I need a stable order in which to operate, I dislike people who break the rules of the order. Because I am a worker, I dislike the loafers who do not produce to the maximum of their ability. There are a number of such people at Princeton. I call them "hackers." They are the people who do a minimum of work and who simply pursue their own enjoyment—often recklessly and at the expense of others. They are the students who get drunk and smash windows, destroy the janitors' tools, and throw beer cans down the stairs. (Have you ever tried to concentrate with beer cans clattering down the stairs outside your door?) And whom do these people blame when they're punished for what they do? It's all the fault of the fellow who reported them or of the Dean who is obviously biased and doesn't understand their side. With these people I have no sympathy. If they don't want to stick to the system, then I favor getting rid of them. Fortunately at Princeton they are a small minority.

Many people claim to be entirely self-made. I would like to be able to claim this, but it simply is not so. I have already had at least two major breaks in my life. Harsh as it may seem to say it, the first of these was my real father's death, which threw me into the Edwards family. This made possible the second—my admission to Princeton. This in turn now leads on to greater possibilities—to graduate studies and a Ph.D., and from there probably to another "secure order" in a company hierarchy, the draft board willing. Princeton has given me just what I came here to get—a good, solid education.

Well, maybe now you understand a little bit about me, and what makes me tick. There's really nothing extraordinary to me except for a mixed-up family background, and unorthodox religious views. In a roomful of people you'd never notice me. But it takes just plain people to keep the world going.

## What Really Matters
### 1964

### Malcolm Wood

I ask myself, will I be living in a place like home, with Formica and chromium in the kitchen? Or will the drainboard be made of little, six-sided tiles like the Kirkbroads' had? Aurelia Kirkbroad would say, "Dope, it really doesn't matter."

The tiles were white, with an occasional blue one. Frank Farrell says those tiles were in style about fifty years ago. According to Farrell, the experts believe that practically everything stays in your mind, and you can fish it up if circumstances are right. It can work the other way, too. Important things can be pushed way to the *back* of your mind. I once overheard Doctor Kirkbroad say I was a "cool customer" and "very sharp." He said some other things. His remarks pushed me toward this joint, in a way, though it's more complicated than that. But until recently I never let myself think about that period at the Kirkbroads.

You can see why I like talking to Frank Farrell. He's the librarian here at the Correction Center. You can mention a little thing to him, like these six-sided tiles, and it may lead to something interesting. Farrell is about forty, with a red moustache that wiggles when he talks.

It was the fifteenth of September, three years ago, that I pulled my Olds 88 alongside the hitching post in front of the Kirkbroads' house. That hitching post's an antique. The whole house is an antique—a three-story, shingled place with stained glass above the front door and sleeping porches out back like the older farmhouses out home. The carriage house had been converted into a garage, with overhead doors and a concrete apron. Whenever Eric Kirkbroad came home from Yale it was a three-car family—four, counting mine. It was a quiet neighborhood because after school most of the kids were away taking music lessons, or French lessons, or exercising their horses—not that the Kirkbroads had horses. They went in for sailboats.

I'd come into the city to start junior college, and I'd been invited to live with the Kirkbroads. I went up and used the door knocker. Nothing happened. I knocked harder. There was a scraping sound above, then a clatter like a Great Dane charging downstairs and a bang against the door. The door was thrown open and a frail, white-faced girl frowned at me. This was my cousin, Aurelia Kirkbroad. At the time she was seventeen, a year younger than myself. Her eyes were large and her eyebrows pinched together in a scowl. She seemed to be thinking hard all the time.

"I'm Ken Sprague," I said.

Aurelia kept frowning.

"You don't remember me. I just came in from Mesaville——"

"Hey, of course!" Aurelia's face changed for a moment as if someone had pulled on a bulb. "I'm Aurelia. Do you remember the time I visited?"

I nodded. "You played at helping me with the chores, and they paid you for it. It made me sore."

Aurelia grinned swiftly, then looked out at my Olds. "That your heap?"

"Yeah."

She frowned at the Olds. "We were expecting you," she said. "Come on, I'll help you bring in your stuff."

She carried in some cartons and she got interested in my record collection. "Gosh," she said, "I never heard of these people. Who's Eldred Haines?"

"Just a band leader. He was popular a couple years ago."

"Can we listen to some of these after dinner?"

"Listen to them now."

She shook her head. "I've got to study and do some practicing. That's why I can't entertain you or anything. Is that all right? Just poke around on your own. You're practically part of the family. The others will be home in a while."

I wasn't exactly worried about meeting the family, or how to act at dinner. I'd lettered in basketball at Mesaville and I was secretary of the Corinthian Club, and the group of guys I went with were the elite. Still, there had been an attitude around home that the Kirkbroads were above us. Long before, when Aunt Eliza first married Kirkbroad and ran off to England, he was a broke, unsuccessful actor. But somehow Kirkbroad had become a Doctor of Philosophy, and a college professor, and he wrote books.

I think I expected that every night the Kirkbroads' dinners would be like my stepmother's dinners when she invited in company to show off something new. After we moved from the ranch into Mesaville, my stepmother was always remodeling, and buying new drapes, and getting more appliances. We had a refrigerator and freezer, naturally. And an electric stove, an electric rotisserie, a garbage disposal, a dishwasher, a washer-dryer, an ironer and mangle, a humidifier, and all sorts of little things like a waffle iron and a sandwich grill and an electric skillet. We had three TV's. I guess we lived about as well as anyone around Mesaville.

Aunt Eliza came home in her station wagon, and she reminded me so much of Dad that I felt comfortable. Same bushy eyebrows and square jaw. Even her small wrists and knotty forearms were like Dad's. I suppose those arm muscles came from squeezing the clay around on her potter's wheel.

Gail, three years older than Aurelia and two years older than me, came in next from the university with her arms full of books. Classes at the university had already begun. Gail had a beat-up Volkswagen of her own. She was short, with a good figure—kind of dumpy, though—and cool, gray eyes. We shook hands and she said, "Say, you're *handsome,* Kenneth. You could be a bobby-sox idol. That wave of blond hair is quite a touch." She winked. She wasn't being unfriendly, and certainly not flirtatious. I was a lot taller than she was, naturally, but she made me feel like a kid.

Gail disappeared and a door right near us in the hall opened suddenly. Kirkbroad was standing there. Apparently he'd been in his study all afternoon, ignoring everything that went on. "What time is it, Liz? My watch stopped," he said to Aunt Eliza. He was a small, bald-headed guy with rimless glasses and a bent-down pipe in the side of his mouth. He wore old moccasins, baggy pants that were riddled with holes from pipe embers, and one of those button sweaters that baggage agents wear. "I thought I heard a strange voice," he said. His eyes looked at me like a couple of gun barrels.

"This is Kenneth, Alex," said Aunt Eliza.

"Kenneth? Let's see, whose nephew are you?"

"Yours," said Aunt Eliza.

"Never mind, Liz. I mean, which side of the family?"

"He's Holman's boy," said Aunt Eliza.

"Ah! From out on the ranch."

"Well—"

"Kenneth, don't be offended," said Aunt Eliza. "Alex has five nephews and nieces on his own side of the family, and seven on mine."

"What time is it?" asked Kirkbroad again.

I said that it was six-thirty. I wondered if we were ever going to have dinner.

"Go up and pour the sherry," said Aunt Eliza to Kirkbroad. To me she said, "We have dinner at seven-fifteen."

Kirkbroad climbed the stairs. I looked through magazines in the living room. I could hear the skinny sound of Aurelia practicing the oboe. Aunt Eliza went out in the kitchen and then followed Kirkbroad upstairs. I learned later that one of the porches on the third floor looked over the trees and across the bay toward some mountains. Aunt Eliza and Kirkbroad had fixed up the porch with greenery and comfortable chairs, and just the two of them drank sherry wine up there before dinner every night.

Every single night the Kirkbroads had table wine with dinner. Also different kinds of bread, undercooked vegetables, and meat that was practically raw. The salad was a main course. They never had a regular dessert—just cheese and fruit. After dinner they always brought out an Italian machine and made bitter coffee right at the table.

That first night I told them the latest about home. They didn't realize that Dad had acquired more acreage and hired a full-time dairy manager, or that we'd moved into Mesaville. I explained that Dad spends his time now on beef brokerage. I described our new house casually, and let them know we have a Chrysler Imperial. "Heck, Kenneth," said Aurelia. "I thought you'd be able to teach me where to find eggs, and how to skin a frog. You don't sound like a farm boy at all anymore."

"The country has caught up with the city," I said. "Everybody has television now. Most of my friends have their own cars. My best friend has a new Thunderbird."

I didn't suspect that all this bragging was backfiring. With me the Kirkbroads were already covering up, as if they were wearing masks. But with themselves they were fantastically outspoken. That first night, out of a clear sky, Gail said, "I forgot to tell you, Mother. Last weekend Max and I stayed at the cabin."

Aurelia jerked her head and stared at Gail. Aunt Eliza went on serving up beets, very cool. Kirkbroad was pouring himself wine, and he paused for an instant and looked at Gail with raised eyebrows.

"What happened to the original plan?" asked Aunt Eliza.

"Florence and I were supposed to stay at the cabin, and Max was going to sleep on the boat. But when Florence called home, her mother said she had to come right back, her father was in the hospital."

"What's the matter with him?"

"Ulcers, I guess. Florence took the bus."

"I'm a little surprised at Max," said Kirkbroad.

"It was *my* idea," said Gail. "I insisted. I didn't want to stay in the cabin alone. The papers have been full of stories about rural punks breaking into summer places and terrorizing people. Max was against staying, but I made him."

"It might have been better to come home," said Aunt Eliza.

Gail looked grim. Aurelia said, "Don't be paleolithic, Mother. Let's face it. Any boy and girl can do anything practically anytime they want." Aunt Eliza winced. "All they have to do is go somewhere and park."

"Perhaps you had better stay out of this," said Kirkbroad.

"The subject interests me deeply," said Aurelia.

Everyone smiled.

"We *couldn't* come back," said Gail. "We had to gather our sea urchins on the low tide in the morning."

There was a silence. The older Kirkbroads seemed to be considering whether to probe this delicate matter further, and Gail seemed to be defying them quietly. It was Aurelia who said, "Max *could* have slept on the boat and left you at the motel in Vista Del Mar."

"I suppose we could have done that," said Gail. She darted an icy look at Aurelia, then looked steadily at her father.

Kirkbroad studied the lamb roast. Then he said, "Hereafter, that would be a better way, Gail."

Gail made no reply. It was clear she had deliberately not said a word about whether she and this Max had slept together or separately.

Everybody ate the rare lamb and Kirkbroad offered wine again. Aurelia and I took a little. Then Aurelia said in her grown-up way, "I raised an issue that nobody has acknowledged." (Aurelia talked this way. She was a senior at a girl's prep school where all the kids took Latin and two other languages, and extra math. She liked it.) "Isn't the business of chaperones completely obsolete? I don't date much, but even *I've* had a dozen opportunities to do anything I wanted. I'm talking about parking somewhere in a car. Aren't you just trying to avoid seeing the problem? Or are you worried about *your* reputation if someone sees your daughter and a man coming out of your summer cabin some morning?"

Kirkbroad said, "Aurelia, your mother and I simply want to discourage thoughtless behavior."

Aunt Eliza said in a calm, definite voice, "Making love in an automobile must be a furtive, awkward business—for the girl especially. I should think it would be humiliating. Perhaps it takes place, but this doesn't mean you, or any other young girls, should therefore feel perfectly free to spend whole weekends in summer cabins with men."

"In other words," said Aurelia, "you don't care what happens as long as it's not satisfying, and you don't know about it."

This set Aunt Eliza back, but only for a moment. "Aurelia," she snapped, "I'll be perfectly glad to hear about any humiliating and sordid experiences you may have."

Everyone laughed. Kirkbroad said, "You know by now that we want you girls to enjoy the pleasures of sex *after* you're married. Quite apart from pregnancy and disease, sexual experiments probably damage a person's capacity for a satisfying sexual partnership when the person does marry. I suspect many divorces are caused by the young people's confusion about sex . . . from too much *bad* experience before marriage."

"Authority!" snorted Aurelia. She turned to me. "You see, Kenneth? Around here issues aren't settled by the Bible, or tradition, or science. All issues are settled by Alexander S. Kirkbroad, Ph.D."

"I haven't settled the issue," said Kirkbroad. "You and Gail will have to resolve it for yourselves. In the meantime, don't take your boyfriends to the cabin for any more weekends. We can't control everything you do, but we can discourage certain patterns and encourage others."

Aurelia sipped her wine and muttered into the glass, "Hypocritical, bourgeois tyrant." She winked at me.

During dessert the Kirkbroads got into a terrible argument over whether Bobby Kennedy had been pro-McCarthy. At one point Aurelia got up from the table in a fury and hurled her napkin on the floor. Even Aunt Eliza got mad enough to swear. Later I realized that they enjoyed arguments, and that it was usually matters of "principle"—often politics—that got them worked up.

Upstairs in my room Gail said, "Gosh Kenneth, where did you get all the clothes?" We put on some records and they immediately got interested in my Latin Rhythm albums. For the next hour I actually had some fun. I taught both Gail and Aurelia the Cha-cha, the mambo, and the samba. They didn't know any real dances, but they had plenty of rhythm. We opened the door into the hall and I'd dance with one sister until she was exhausted, and then I'd take on the other. I was more used to it. Finally Gail sprawled out on the bed on top of my sport coats and said, "I'm pooped." Aurelia was leaning against the wall. She let her feet slide out until she'd slipped to a sitting position on the floor. She looked around again at my stuff and said, "Criminee, Kenneth. Don't you have *any* books?"

I made some excuse about not having any books, and Aurelia and Gail went back to their rooms. I felt like watching TV, but I hadn't seen a set in the house. I went out and cruised around in my car for a while. I dragged a '57 Plymouth and took him easy. I found a drive-in and had a milk shake and fries. Then I went back to the Kirkbroads. Aunt Eliza told me to help myself from the refrigerator and I found a cold chicken leg and ate it. Up in the hall I could hear violin music coming from Aurelia's radio and no sound from Gail's room. I went in my room and turned out the light and listened to ROKC, which was the station I and this redhead I'd been going with always listened to. I thought about her. I was lonesome already. Later I heard that right after I left Mesaville she started going with some older guy who had an Impala convertible.

During those weeks, miserable as I was, I had respect for the Kirkbroads. Of course it's natural to respect people who have money, but it wasn't just the money. They always tried to cut me in on things—parties, and plays, and eating out at restaurants sometimes. But it wasn't just their hospitality, either. They all lived with the gas pedal right on the floor. They worked like maniacs, and they had fun—their kind of fun, at least. On a Friday night they might all go to a Chinese restaurant and then to a play or a concert. Afterward they'd sit in a coffeehouse listening to folk music and arguing about the play, or about some book, until one-thirty or two o'clock. Did they ever sleep late in the morning? Never. They'd be off to the library, or a biology field trip, or a Young People's Symphony rehearsal, which Aurelia played in. Aunt Eliza would start thumping on her pottery right after breakfast, if it was Sunday, no matter how late they'd been up the night before, Kirkbroad and Aurelia would leave the house at eight o'clock for a sailboat race.

They had their problems. Gail had migraine headaches, and I got the impression she'd had some sort of breakdown once. Aunt Eliza was a chain smoker, so you can figure she was under plenty of strain. Kirkbroad could be sarcastic, really cruel. When they had their terrible arguments over some "principle," you could tell they were sore at each other underneath. And Aurelia talked about her "depressions." I think she was serious one night in the kitchen when she said to Gail, "Do you ever get the rotten feeling that deep down you're superficial?" That broke everyone up. You should have seen the grin come over Aurelia's face when she realized she'd said something really funny.

In many ways I admired the Kirkbroads, yes. But I didn't like them. How could I? Aurelia once told me I was a lousy driver. For once she leveled with me. I was furious. I could drive better than that whole family put together. And I found out that this boyfriend of Gail's, Max, was a Jew. His name was Fishbein or something like that. He was a skinny little guy with a big Adam's apple and glasses. I didn't get it. Gail was a good-looking chick. Naturally he was smart, and he had a sense of humor, but I never felt he had much use for me.

Max was a Jew, and Aurelia's best girlfriend at school was Negro, which reminds me of something else. I made one friend at the junior college, a guy named Tom who was in two of my classes. All he had was a '52 Plymouth, but he was saving for a Corvette. He was good-looking—tall and blond, kind of like Paul Newman. One Saturday night Aurelia and Gail were showing far-out movies in the big room in the basement, and having a kind of party. They asked me to bring my records in case people wanted to dance afterward. They said I could invite some friends. I invited a girl I'd gotten to know in geology that was good enough looking and stacked. She had fun at the party, all right. She made it plain that it was my cousins and their friends that she thought were so terrific. But I had fun myself. When we came in, Aurelia announced to the whole crowd, "Here's my favorite cousin, Kenneth!" I was grinning. "Isn't that the greatest grin you ever saw?" said Aurelia, and Gail said, "Every night at dinner, Kenneth's smile makes me feel better."

Anyway, this Tom came to the party. He didn't bring a girl, and Aurelia's best friend Melanie, the Negro girl, had come by herself. So Tom stuck close to her. Maybe I'd given him the wrong impression of the Kirkbroads by telling him how they talked about sex and the kind of plays they went to. During the evening he whispered to me that this chick Melanie reminded him of Lena Horne, and maybe she would change his luck. I don't know exactly what happened. He took her home. The next afternoon Aurelia said to me, "Where in hell did you find that boy Tom?"

"He's just a guy from school," I said. "What happened?"

"Never mind. But I'd rather you didn't bring *him* around again."

I asked again what had happened.

"I said never mind. It was pretty traumatic for Melanie, that's all. He isn't very bright."

I must have looked worried, because Aurelia said, "Don't sulk, Kenneth. It wasn't your fault." Whatever it was, I figured Aurelia and Gail really did blame me.

Tom and I both had trouble with the same English instructor. That was another thing. I was doing well in geology, only fair in world history, and poorly in French and especially in English. The first composition was supposed to be about something you knew. I wrote on "What To Do If Your Car Burns Oil." I got an A for content, and a D for grammar and spelling. After that we worked on business letters and I got C's. Then we read this play, *Death of a Salesman,* and had to write about it. I really worked on that paper, looking up all the spelling in the dictionary. This time I got a C on grammar and spelling and an F for content. The instructor wrote on the front, "Incredibly superficial. Are you naïve or callous?" This seemed pretty snotty to me. I didn't understand what he meant, but I wasn't going to ask *him.* I showed the paper to Aurelia.

She read it and a pained expression came over her face. She tried not to show it. When she'd finished reading she looked out the window. She was only seventeen, but believe me, she was smart. Finally she said, "Somehow you missed the point, Kenneth. You're supposed to *like* Willy Loman, and sympathize with him in spite of his faults. Arthur Miller would blame Willy's phony dream, not Willy."

"How can you like a liar?" I asked. "He was weak, and a failure, and he wouldn't admit it. He ruined his two boys."

We had a long argument. Since then I've read *Death of a Salesman* again, and a lot of other books besides. Frank Farrell has a record of the actual play in the Correction Center library and I listened to that with earphones. I guess I *was* pretty naïve. I have different ideas about a lot of things now. But it's funny: When you get to telling things that happened, you feel the way you felt back *then,* even if you've changed since. I can still get mad at that snotty English instructor. And I remember that in some ways I enjoyed that argument with Aurelia. It was the first time I ever got worked up about a book. But when it was all over, I felt ignorant, and a little as if I'd been kicked in the belly.

I started playing things super-cool. I made it a point not to start a conversation, never to say anything enthusiastic and definite, because if it turned out stupid, I'd be stuck. "Don't act, *re*act," was my rule. When I was sure of my ground, I'd make some comment that was funny. But I couldn't blast around, saying and doing anything that popped into my head like the Kirkbroads did. For kicks I hung around with Tom at the Broadway Bowl. We'd both practically quit studying. Sometimes on Friday night we picked up quail at the roller rink. Naturally I said nothing about this at the Kirkbroads.

Everything came to a head down at the vacation place. The Kirkbroads called it a "cabin." What a laugh. It was on a hill above the ocean and had enough room to sleep twenty people. Besides a couple of bedrooms and two big dormitory sleeping rooms (one for boys, one for girls) there was a new kitchen, a deck, and a living room with a fireplace.

I agreed to go because, as usual, the Kirkbroads urged me as if they meant it. Aurelia and Gail were inviting friends I hadn't met, as well as out-of-towners that would be there for the sailboat race on Saturday. You always figure there may be one new chick that will go for you. I day-dreamed about a brunette who would like my dancing, and be interested in basketball, and may-be have a sports car of her own. Does a person ever get daydreams out of his head?

First of all, nobody would ride down with me. They all had explanations: Gail was going with Max in his brand new M.G.; Aurelia had to take food and extra bedding in the station wagon; Melanie and Aurelia's other friends had their own cars, or wanted to go in the station wagon to sing; and they all objected that my Olds didn't have any seat belts. That whole bunch was fanatic about seat belts. They probably all believed Aurelia's line about me driving too fast. I could have ridden in the station wagon myself, but I knew I'd feel kind of helpless down there without my own car.

When I arrived at Vista Del Mar it was a bright blue day with a hard wind blowing. The surf was huge. Offshore there were millions of white-caps. I located the "cabin," but nobody was there—just cars and boat trailers. On the door was a note.

> Kenneth:
> Come down to the harbor before 1:15. Urgent!
> Aurelia

Aurelia and Melanie were alongside the dock in a little sailboat that wasn't as long as my car. The sails looked tremendous and were making a terrific noise flapping in the wind. Other little boats were bobbing around and banging against the floats, and several were already flying across the harbor practically tipped over.

Aurelia hollered at me, "Can you swim?" I nodded. "I need a heavy crew," she said.

I looked at all the ropes going this way and that, none of which I understood. I looked out at the water. The waves were about six feet high, even inside the breakwater. None of the little boats had capsized—yet. Aurelia said, "Don't come unless you *want* to, Kenneth. Melanie will come."

"Can't three of us go?"

"The rules only allow two."

There was Aurelia in her yellow oil-skins, no bigger than a minute, with her little pinched girl's face. She was raring to get out there. I couldn't chicken.

Melanie's slicker was too small, and Aurelia warned I'd get soaked and frozen. She urged me again to back out if I wanted. I climbed into the boat, and just my weight made it sink way down on one side. Aurelia showed me where to sit. "You'll have to do everything I tell you, Kenneth, and don't do *anything* I don't tell you. Here, put this on." When I'd buckled the life jacket, Melanie shoved us off. Aurelia tightened some ropes and shouted. "Wahoo!" The sails stopped flapping. In the sudden silence the boat leaned way over and began streaking across the water. The first big wave we came to we went *through*. Water crashed over me like I'd dived through a surf.

I sat up on the high side and leaned back over the water like Aurelia told me. I guess my weight did help hold the boat down. Then we'd change course, and I'd have to scramble over to the other side, scraping myself, cracking my shins, getting fouled up in the ropes. Aurelia would holler, "Take up on the jib sheet! Slack off the centerboard pennant!" "Whataya mean?" I'd holler. Then she'd translate into English. There was a terrific mess, with all the boats running toward each other, and then the starting gun went off.

Let's not talk about the next hour. I guess we were out in front right from the first. We ploughed one direction and then another, working toward markers I couldn't even see, me scrambling and ducking the boom. Waves kept breaking over us. I was scared. The cold made me shake as if I were having a fit. Aurelia kept looking back at the other boats and grinning like a fiend. Looking at me once, she whopped, "Poor Kenneth! You're really out of your element. But I love you. You're so *heavy!*"

So we won the race. I shivered for hours. Everyone kept congratulating Aurelia, and I realized that we were mostly racing against men, not just kids and girls. You had to admire her. Someday I might try sailing myself if there wasn't so much complicated stuff to learn. Aurelia kept saying, "Congratulate *Kenneth!* He was a terrific crew, and he'd never been out before."

"How do you like sailing?" the person would ask. "I was frozen and scared to death," I would say, which usually got a laugh. I can see that sailing is a great sport, but for me at the time, the whole thing was a drag. Among other things I ruined a good pair of slacks.

It was a mixed party. Aurelia's friends were mostly seventeen and eighteen. Gail's and Max's friends were in their early twenties. Then there was an uncle and his wife. He was a dentist, and they were about fifty. Then there was a biologist friend of Max's and his wife, who were about thirty-five. They had two tiny kids. It was a complete hodgepodge, and everyone still had fun. Now take my own family, and people out in Mesaville. I've thought about it. Nobody out there thinks of having fun except with people their own age. It's because they're always hiding things from each other. The kids cover up what they really do and think; the parents hide everything important from the kids;

and parents *and* kids hide things from the grandparents. With the Kirkbroads nobody covered up anything. Since everyone's so relaxed, they can have fun without thinking anything about it.

I didn't have any fun. Before dinner everyone drank wine and beer and got a little high. Then they had an enormous mess of spaghetti. Afterward hardly anyone thought of drinking, which might have made them want to dance. (I'd brought my records.) Instead they built a fire and began singing. There were two guitar players, and everyone kept singing one song after another— folk songs, foreign songs, old pop songs. Not all of them knew all the songs, but most of them knew most of them. I watched their lips. I hardly knew any of those songs.

Then they got excited about "The Game," they called it. They chose up two teams and wrote the names of books on scraps of paper. Then a member of one team had to act out the title so that his own team (they hadn't seen the scrap of paper) could guess what the book was. They timed how long it took. The whole game was invented for the know-it-alls to show off. There was one redheaded friend of Max's who drove me crazy. He was *always* guessing, and about half the time he was right. When it was his turn to act, he just held up three fingers. "Three words?" asked Aurelia. He nods, and holds up three fingers again. "Third word?" asked Melanie. He nodded. Then he acted like he was shooting a gun. Aurelia said instantly, *"The Great Gatsby!"*

"Right."

"Eleven seconds!" says the dentist, who had been keeping time. Everyone laughed and clapped.

I never made one single guess. When it was my turn to act, my face and arms and legs felt like they were made of cement. I picked out a piece of paper and it said *"Oedipus Rex."* At that time I'd never heard of it. I went over to the other team and asked them to whisper how to pronounce it. This redheaded guy made a kind of concealed sneer. But it was Melanie, Aurelia's friend, who said, "Books aren't Kenneth's strong point. He thought *Death of a Salesman* was just about a slob who didn't know how to sell."

Everybody gets a big belly laugh. I was too paralyzed to act out anything. I could have killed Aurelia. After about a minute of agony I gave the piece of paper back and sat down. I kept my eyes on my shoes. When the rest of them decided to take a midnight swim (they were crazy: it was almost November and the water was freezing), I put my suitcase in the Olds and took off.

I did one stupid thing. I came to a back road called Eucalyptus Cañon Road and I remembered Max saying his new M.G. had broken down and he and Gail had walked the last two miles to the cabin. I went up that way and sure enough, I found the M.G. parked on a shoulder. I hated Max for having that car. It was a bright red. He didn't appreciate it. He was a graduate student and made good money working in some laboratory. He just went down and bought the car one day like he was buying razor blades.

I removed the fancy FM radio and locked it in my trunk. The road was completely deserted. Then I took my pocket-knife and ripped the top a couple times. Then I got in my car and worked over the left side of that M.G. with the end of my bumper. This made a racket and brought me to my senses. I decided I'd better go back to the cabin and cover up.

They were all coming up from the beach, whopping and hollering. Even the dentist. I realized they'd gone in nude, but nothing wild or sexy. Now they were going to make popcorn and coffee and all that wholesome jazz. I kidded around a little and acted natural. I stayed away from Aurelia because she had that apologizing look in her eye. Then I took a long shower and went to bed early. I didn't sleep much. At daybreak I got up and left a note on the kitchen table saying I'd promised to visit Tom, who'd gone home for the weekend to a nearby town.

I never found Tom because his last name was Johnson, and there were about forty Johnsons in the book. So I drove fifty miles to another town that has Sunday drag races, but there weren't any that Sunday. I bought some steel wool and rubbed the red paint off my bumper and I threw the radio into a ditch. I began just cruising around, all the time thinking about things. That valley country was depressing. The squash and cabbage had just been harvested and the fields looked like they'd been blasted in a war. At one point I considered going down the highway at ninety miles an hour until I hit something. I was still way out in the country when my fuel pump conked.

By the time I hitched back to the Kirkbroads it was after three A.M., and I slept through until the middle of Monday afternoon. Aunt Eliza was in the kitchen when I got up. She fixed me a sandwich and some broth, and I told her my car was broken down. She said the station wagon was broken too, that something was dragging on the street. I said I'd look at it.

First I went downtown and bought a rebuilt fuel pump. Then I crawled under the station wagon, and sure enough, a muffler bracket was rusted out. All it needed was a little wire. I was still under there, wiring it up, when Gail's VW rolled into the garage. You'd think they would have noticed me under the station wagon: I guess my own car not being parked out front fooled them.

Old man Kirkbroad was driving. As soon as he turned off the VW ignition I could hear him perfectly. They all just sat there finishing the conversation, the way people do before they get out of a car.

"Quit condemning yourself, Aurelia," Kirkbroad was saying. "You and Gail did your best. Anyway, I suspect you're exaggerating."

"He was about to crack, I tell you. . . ." It was Aurelia's voice from the back seat of the VW. "You should have seen his eyes. I tried to talk to him but he kept slipping away. Melanie feels terrible. The minute she said it, she wanted to cut her tongue out."

"You don't *know* it was Kenneth that wrecked Max's car," said Kirkbroad. "Even if we knew, we wouldn't do anything. It's pretty understandable. I tried to warn you girls that first week. It has nothing to do with Kenneth's I.Q., or his other natural gifts. I suspect he's a cool customer, and very sharp. But here's a kid who has been something of a big shot in a small town. He comes to live with us, and what does he find? He doesn't know anything about books, he doesn't know anything about real music, or tide zone animals, or international affairs, or sailboats, or politics—or anything else we care about. No matter what goes on around here, Kenneth comes in last. He's about nineteen years behind. The things he does know about we look down on."

"That's an awfully depressing analysis," said Gail.

"Perhaps. But it's an enormous gulf."

"I thought about buying a Model A," said Aurelia, "and having Kenneth soup it up for me. Then he'd be an expert on something. But I don't really want a Model A anymore. I got over that."

A door opened and Kirkbroad got out. His crummy moccasins were about four feet from my head. He went out of the garage. I could see the girl's feet as they got out on the other side. Aurelia said, "Keys, Gail. I've got to pick up Mother's groceries."

"Use the station wagon. I'm going back to the campus," said Gail.

"I can't. There's supposed to be something loose underneath."

Aurelia's beat-up sneakers came around to the side of the station wagon. Suddenly she kneeled down. There she was, looking right in my face. She gave a big gasp, naturally. After she'd stood up again she said, "Come out from there, Kenneth. Really! I don't think that was very fair. . . ."

I didn't get into any conversations. I just gathered all my stuff together and called a cab. Forty-five minutes later I checked in at the Y.M.C.A. That was the last I saw, probably ever will see, of the Kirkbroads.

I turned out to be very sharp, all right. I went to another city and got a job helping a guy with a used-car lot. I washed cars, answered the phone, made small repairs. After a while he let me sell. He reamed me on commissions, but I made pretty good dough. Eventually I realized twenty percent of his cars were hot—faked motor numbers, forged registrations, payoffs at the vehicle bureau. I dropped a hint to the kid who was delivering this stuff from out of state, and eventually a guy named Ludwig Bohm offered me a deal. "We have an organization," he says. "You got to start at the bottom."

I started at the bottom, and I was picked up on my first run. Bohm hadn't told me the trunk was full of arts and crafts—license plates made from welding together phony numbers from stolen plates that had been cut up.

They sent me here, which hasn't been bad. For a while I was in a daze. But I got to reading more and more books. First I just read mysteries and science fiction. But in the library I'd recognize authors and books from hearing the Kirkbroads argue. One book would lead to another. I read a book by Steinbeck I liked, so then I read all of Steinbeck's books. Same thing with Dostoevski. The more I read, the more I talked about books with Frank Farrell. He's the librarian with the red handlebar moustache. Farrell is definitely not a phony. He helped me file my parole application and he has actually lined up a job for me. I'm going to work for a friend of his who has a book store in Kansas City, Missouri.

The main thing Farrell did was to make me think about what kind of kid I'd been and what kind of life to try for outside. Farrell is a lot like old man

Kirkbroad. He sees things very clear and he calls a spade just that. After I trusted Farrell, he questioned me about everything before I was convicted. For a long time I hadn't thought about the Kirkbroads, for instance, but when I finally started, I remembered plenty, as you can see.

A thing that hit me hardest was that Kirkbroad was mostly right. That guy was deep. I thought he wasn't noticing me at all.

It's funny how I've built up the Kirkbroads in my mind. I'll never see them again, but if I did go back there, they'd probably accept me. They're like Frank Farrell. They could believe that an ex-con still has a chance. But out home in Mesaville? I'm finished out there.

Naturally I realize I'll never be in the Kirkbroads' league. Kirkbroad would say I'm twenty-two years behind now. But I'm not so sure. I mentioned wondering about Formica or old tiles on the drainboard after I get out, remember? Actually I'll rent a furnished room and cook on a hot plate. I may not even own a car. I may save my money and go back to college eventually. Some people say that nobody ever really changes, but I am personally convinced that that's baloney.

## Other Chanukahs
## 1965

## Leo Skir

It was the first night of Chanukah. I had been working in the Columbia Library that day, on a paper for my History of the English Language class, which paper was to be on a line of Chaucer, chosen by the student. The line was to be translated into modern English, a phonetic transcription to be given of both lines, and the history of each word-change was to be given. For my line I had chosen:

"I have, God woot, a large feeld to ere."

Being a Columbia alumnus, I have the privilege of a stack card, which means that I cannot take the books home. That day, as always, I found reading in the stacks a suffocating experience. The pronunciation guide to Chaucer had been printed, oddly enough, in Stockholm.

I was to meet Ariela at eight down in Washington Square Park before the session of the Country Folk Dance Society. It was our last session before she would leave for her winter vacation in Palm Beach.

Before going home for supper and a shave and shower (Ariela is very particular about those things), I called my parents to wish them a happy Chanukah.

"Where are you phoning from?" my mother said. She always asks this. I always phone from outside my apartment so she won't know I have the phone connected.

"From the library," I said.

"It doesn't sound like a library to me," she said.

"The phones are in a hallway," I said. "Sometimes when people want to get out of studying for a little while they come into the hallway and smoke and laugh."

"Are you in a bar?" she said.

"No," I said, "a library."

"What are you doing tonight?" my mother said.

"Studying," I said.

I have real paranoid feelings about my mother's being able to tell where I really am at any time, her apparent stupidity being, to my deranged senses, only the fumbling put on by a professional blind man.

"Why don't you come to the house tonight?" Mother said. "Daddy's expecting you." (The reader will note that this was the first indication I had that I was either invited or expected.)

"I'm sorry Mother," I said. "I can't."

"If you can't, you can't," mother said, with the air of Hagar being driven into the desert. "I was just thinking tonight how nice it would be to have the whole family together for Chanukah."

"Well, I'm really sorry," I said (what wonderful villainous hypocrisy! Where did I learn it! Probably Ariela, she is an accomplished liar).

"Do you think you can come Friday night," she said, "and spend *Shabbos* with us? You could put on your little pee-jays and we'd open up the couch and you could sleep over."

"I'd love to," I said, "but I can't. Look, I have to get out of the phone booth. Goodbye."

Now, the reader, reading this, has come to an immediate misunderstanding of the situation. He sees me as the younger iconoclastic son, having no respect or love for the ancient ceremonies.

Nothing could be further from the truth. I am exceedingly fond of holidays of any sort, and had, as a matter of fact, been reading about just that period of Jewish history in Tcherikover's *Hellenistic Civilization and the Jews,* which had recently come out in English. (It was originally published in Hebrew.)

Let us suppose that I had accepted my mother's invitation.

For the sake of those readers who are not quite sure just what Chanukah is, and what happens during it, I will explain. Chanukah is the celebration of the successful revolt of the Jews against the Syrian-Hellenistic overlordship of Antiochus IV. The rebels were able to chase the Syrians out of the country and they restored the Temple, which had been converted to paganism, to its purity. They were called the Maccabees, after Judah, the leader of the band of brothers who led the rebellion. They were in time to establish the Hasmonean dynasty, whose fate is detailed in Moshe Shamir's *The King of Flesh and Blood* (wonderful novel!).

The central miracle (the only one) of Chanukah is the following. When the Temple was recaptured, they put holy oil in the lamp. But it was only enough for one day. It would be eight days before the new batch of pure oil could be produced. But during those eight days the oil, which was only enough for *one* day, continued to burn. To celebrate this miracle, the holiday of Chanukah lasts eight days, and during each day a larger number of candles is lit, one the first day, two the second, three the third, etc. Gifts of money and candy are given out, and games are to be played. The holiday food is potato *latkes* (pancakes). Often, in the Temples in a neighborhood, Chanukah plays are given.

Now:

I come into the house, having brought along the Tcherikover book to show my father. The Tcherikover version of the Maccabee revolution is quite a different story from that told in the Bible in Maccabees I. Tcherikover, in a very clever reconstruction, based only on internal contradictions in that text, suspects that the Hellenistic rulers had not originally violated the people's religious principles, but their later harshness, essentially not religious but political, had been brought about by the need to curb a fanatical high-orthodox Jewish group which had rebelled against the Syrian rule.

Well, of course I am never going to be able to say anything like this to my father, it being impossible in my parents' house to say five continuous sentences on any general subject.

Let us make the attempt:

*I:* "I've been reading an interesting book about the Hasmonean period."

*Dad:* "It looks very good. I'd like to read it sometime." My father's spastic experience is such that he has been unable to read any prolonged prose narrative for many years now, his diet being only the New York *Times*. It is his peculiar illusion that he has a great interest in and appetite for history, and that if he had the time he would devote himself to reading history books. The reading of the *Times* he takes as a sign of his vital interest in current history.

I say, "Tcherikover thinks that the Jews brought their troubles on themselves, that the rule of the Hellenistic rulers was, in all probability, lenient, at least in regard to religion."

*Dad:* "Let me look at it." He takes the book and looks at it.

*Dad*: "It's got nice print. How much did you pay for it?"

*I:* "It's only $2.50. It was one of my yearly selections from the Jewish Publication Society."

*Dad:* "Only two-fifty? I can't afford to get a book for two-fifty. Mother and I don't go around buying books."

This is true. The only books they have bought recently have been paperback editions of —*Lolita* and *Lady Chatterley's Lover:* both of which my father said were "full of street language." Why he and my mother, who disapprove of "filth" in literature, had selected, during an entire year, only two books, both suspected of obscenity, I leave as a question for cultural historians.

Dad has handed the Tcherikover book back to me. The reader will note that the discussion has left the Hasmonean period and Hellenism completely and has evolved into that operation for which my father and mother were ordained, namely the remedial treatment of pathological features in my makeup.

"Don't you buy a lot of throw-away books and magazines?" Dad asks.

"What's a throw-away book?" I ask.

"Oh you know what I mean," he says, "those paperbacks!"

"Yes, I buy them," I say, "but I don't buy them to throw away. I buy them to read."

"Couldn't you get them out of the library?" he says.

Like all people who have never had a desire to read a specific book, he is absolutely certain that any book one might wish to read is immediately obtainable in the local library. For some reason I have never told him that this is not so.

He has returned the book to me, and I, distracted by his discourse, which had, as was inevitable, become trained on me, like the rays from a cathode tube upon a patient, have made the mistake of putting the book on the coffee table instead of in my lap, as is my custom.

No sooner have I put it on the coffee table than Mother comes in with a cocktail glass full of tomato juice and puts the glass on the book. Mother regards any horizontal book as either a coaster or a hot-plate.

"Mother," I say, "please take the tomato juice off my book."

"Oh," Mother says, "is that your book? I thought it was one of ours. The juice is for you. I don't want you to get too hungry before dinner. Wait, I'll get a coaster."

The coaster turns out to be a napkin with the words *Aincha Glad You Came?* printed on it.

"How do you like these napkins?" Mother asks.

"They're wonderful," I say.

"I bought them in a store," she says, "I thought they'd be nice if you have guests and you want to give them cocktails before dinner."

Now, there is not in the house any gin, vermouth, shaker, cherries, onions, olives, or any of the possible ingredients of a cocktail, nor does my mother know how to make a cocktail, nor has she ever served cocktails.

"That's a good idea," I say.

Now we go into supper. The reader will remember that the holiday is celebrated by the lighting of the Chanukah lights. Three blessings are said on this first night:

Blessed art thou, O Lord, our God, Ruler of the world who hast sanctified us by Thy commandments and hast bidden us to kindle the Chanukah lights.

Blessed art Thou, O Lord, our God, Ruler of the world, who didst wondrous things for our fathers, at this season in those days.

Blessed art Thou, O Lord, our God, Ruler of the world, who hast granted us life and hast sustained us to celebrate this joyous festival.

The dinner is a perfectly ordinary dinner, ordinary, that is, qua Mother. If it were anyone else, one might find it curiously deficient. My mother is unable to prepare and serve an entire meal of soup, salad, meat, vegetables, and dessert. I must admit that I sympathize with her, that to prepare all these foods and use all those dishes and silverware, which must be washed afterward, *is* an ordeal, and I can imagine many possible alternatives. To mention only two: having foods which do not need to be cooked, such as cold sliced meats, which can be served in sandwiches, and even to have paper plates—or again, to go out to a restaurant.

But, of course, a restaurant is *not,* as my mother has pointed out, one's own home, and of course, as she adds, "You never know what you're getting in a restaurant."

"Do you like chicken?" Mother says. "I bought it in the store. It's as soft as butter. You could cut it with a butter knife. Here! I want you to have a piece of my breast. It's as soft as butter."

A piece of chicken is deposited in my plate.

"Did you light the lamp?" I ask Mother.

"I went to the store today," she says, "and they were all out of candles. But I took out the lamp. I know you like the lamp."

(These are all imaginings since I did not go to my parents' house on that night, or on any of the eight nights of Chanukah.)

"Wasn't there any store in the neighborhood that had candles?" I ask.

Of course there would be. Rockaway in this section is almost all Jewish, and even if she could not have gotten them, I could have bought some in Manhattan. There are also no potato pancakes.

"Are there any *latkes?*" I ask Mother.

"I know you like them," Mother says, "but it's silly making them for only three people. It's so much trouble cutting up the potatoes, and my hands are bad."

What could I possibly say? That I wanted her to spend time scraping her fingers in a grater so that I could have the pleasure of eating potato *latkes* for a minute or so?

I guess Mother is the other side of the miracle. Instead of the oil which burnt for eight days rather than one, we have the woman who goes to the store and finds that there aren't any candles in stock, and instead of Hannah

and her seven sons (all of them, even the youngest, he a tiny child, faced martyrdom and horrible tortures rather than bow to pagan idols), we have Mother
who finds that a company of three is under the Critical Mass for which the
*latkes* can be prepared.

After supper my father reads the New York *Times* and watches the news
on television. Then he falls asleep. Before I leave they give me some *Chanukah*
gelt, Chanukah money, which has always been given in the same way, my
mother suggesting it and then, in front of me, discussing the amount with Dad,
this conversation being held in Yiddish. It was the only time that Yiddish was
spoken, since I did not understand Yiddish.

So it can be seen that when Mother invited me to supper on Chanukah, it
was not because she was desirous of my participation in any particular feast or
ceremony, or even that she wanted to see me.

What was it that she wanted?

Her speech is not to be compared with communication but more to be
likened to the gasping of a fish out of water, and with her I always felt
that same pity one would feel for the fish, the desire to put it in water. *But*—
(how many times I have asked myself this question) *Where Was That Element
Where She Would Be At Home?* Neither at Chanukah nor Christmas, Passover
nor Easter! She, who had served as homemaker and as nurse for my father in
his office, which was in our home, had never been either. If she dies before me
and I call to mind her image, it will always be as the composite of these two
occupations, she in her white nurse's uniform in the kitchen, carefully turning over the lamb chops in the broiler, or opening the refrigerator to get out the
cole slaw, each operation being in some way pitifully clumsy, and I, watching
her, knowing that the cooking smells would reach the waiting room, feeling
shame for her clumsiness and her lack of professionalism in her nurse's capacity, and also—shame (which I feel now in writing this) for my contempt for
her—but having before me my father's example, feeling somehow that the acceptance of these faults of hers, even the passive toleration of them, was dangerous, and that their quantity being legion and they, the faults themselves,
being as it were, united, one would find oneself their subject.

But still, as I on this first night of Chanukah went down in the subway
train to meet Ariela (who would be standing near the statue of Garibaldi in
Washington Square Park), I felt bad—that I had deserted her—as if somehow, I
possessed the key, or enchantment, and could, with some word of action, wake
her up and take her—where? Some place where Chanukah was celebrated! In
Israel, during the Mandate, on Chanukah, a series of relay racers carried a
torch from Modein (where the revolt of the Macabees had started) to Jerusa-
lem.

When I was eight years old, in 1941, and they were putting on a Chanukah play at the Shaari Zedek in my neighborhood, I had gone to the casting
session and told them that I wanted to be Judah Maccabee. But I was too
young, it seemed, and was offered only the part of one of the fiddlers of King

Antiochus, which I refused. I didn't know how to play the fiddle, I told them.

They had explained to me that these were toy fiddles and it didn't matter.

And *I* said, that repulsive as the idea of real fiddling was to me, fake fiddling seemed even worse. I would not be a fake fiddler.

I was finally offered what the director said was a part in the chorus. There was, in effect, no chorus. The entire cast lined up was a chorus, and the show consisted simply of each member stepping forward in turn, explaining in a short, sung quatrain, who he was (or in the case of the king's three musicians, who they were) and having their lines repeated by the rest. I was the only one who was not someone.

"You have the biggest part," the director explained to me, "You sing everything."

I stared at her wondering, first, if she believed what she was saying, and then, after dismissing this as impossible, whether this lie was one she found acceptable to all eight-year-olds and whether I, in not accepting it, would prove some sort of maverick.

I said nothing and stayed through the rehearsal that Sunday afternoon, walking home moodily through the dirty slush-snow afterward, wondering how I could tell my parents of my defeat. Of course, when I did tell them, they saw nothing wrong with being in the chorus.

But the next Sunday, when the play was given, I did not go to Sunday school. I had a cold, one of the many which filled each winter of my childhood, and I told my parents I had to stay home.

I sat there and thought about the play, hating the play, hating the director. The play was a *comedy* and anyone in his right mind could see that the story of the Maccabees was not a comedy! One of the Maccabees had been killed, crushed underneath an elephant! What a silly play! How glad I was that I had not dignified it with my presence!

And then Dad had come back.

He had gone to the Temple and sat through the entire play! And when it was finished, he had gone backstage where the father of one of the boys who had been in the play was distributing gifts to all the members of the cast. To the boys he gave Indian headdresses, a paper strip in which colored chicken feathers had been inserted. My father had told him that his son had been in the play but had not been able to come, and the man had given Dad an Indian headdress to give me.

Which headdress he now held in his hand.

The wind whistled in the tree outside my window. Few Brooklyn homes had trees outside their windows. I lived opposite a small park which even had a real hillock on which children could sled in winter. That hillock was to be leveled the following winter and the tree outside my window was to fall during the 1941 hurricane.

Now, the eight-year-old Leo only felt discomfort at the coldness of the winter room and also—how odd—at the fact that his father had exposed him. He, Leo, had absented himself from the play, dismissed it entirely, and his father, possessed, had attended the play.

My father had, has, the most genial of open-faced, childlike smiles, which smile he now presented along with the paper Indian headdress. I stared at him, wondering why he was not indignant at the childishness of the play, or bored at being distracted from his own, more vital concerns, and was pleased by this absurd headdress, which was, so obviously, not the proper gift for Chanukah.

"How is it that they let you backstage when you weren't in the play?" I said, staring at the red cherry-flavored cough medicine in the bottle beside my bed.

This recollection of the eight-year-old Leo was the first Leo story.

I have never felt the shames of childhood less valid than those which follow later. Often myself a victim of shames and regrets, I would find it salutary to remember these former occasions in order to show myself that my present worries would in time appear in a similar diminutive form.

At fourteen I was attending a private school in Brooklyn. It was called Olympus. At one time it had been restricted, but it had let in Jews during the Depression, and now the Children of Israel had conquered it, and although there was still Chapel each Monday, during which we sang "Holy, Holy, Holy," the institution was as much a part of Judah as the threshing floor of the Jebusite.

Now:

On a September morning of 1946, the fourteen-year-old Leo was sitting on a swinging couch on the roof garden of his apartment house. He had brought up his biology textbook and also a small notebook and a pencil.

His mother (I will now switch to the first person to preserve the illusion of veracity), my mother had told me to sit in the sun and I had at first obediently done so, but I found that it was simply quite impossible to read in the sun and had transferred myself to the other side of the roof, which was shaded by an awning. This side was a bit chilly but much more comfortable. Sitting there I had the oddest feeling that my mother would be coming up to the roof and would question me as to why, having taken the trouble to get up there, I now was sitting in the shade, and this thought—that I was disobedient—took away the pleasure I would have felt at the peace of being on the roof and in an environment that I liked. It almost seemed to work itself out into a chemicphysical equation:

$$\text{Too much sun} + \text{approval} = \text{Coolness} - \text{approval}.$$

My general conclusion was that Life, as far as I had seen it, seemed to consist of imbalance and discomfort. I wondered on this conclusion for a while and also questioned whether I, knowing only one life, my own, could say that life was happy or unhappy. How could I, being unable, by definition, to be someone else, know if the life of anyone was happier or sadder, or more or less comfortable than mine? I thought on this matter for a while, but, as always with myself, felt my logic was inferior to my intuition. I also thought that there was certainly, for me, the criteria of my life prior to these moments.

It was then that my non-performance of the role of Judah Maccabee came to me, and, sitting on the swinging couch on that Brooklyn rooftop, I wrote the story in my notebook and then looked at it, wondering if the words—which resembled, of course, the ordinary words of notes taken in biology classes and letters and such—were really that magic thing called a story, the sort of thing that (magic possibility!) could appear in print.

When I came downstairs at noon, my parents were getting ready to go to the Bronx to visit our relatives. My brother, Stanley, couldn't go because he was meeting the boys for baseball practice. After our lunch, which was fishcakes and spaghetti, we went outside, and it was then, unable to contain myself, that I told my parents about the story I had written.

They were very angry.

By now we were outside the house, the black-painted, cast-iron, quatrefoil doors had closed behind us, and we were going toward the Pontiac.

"You must be crazy, mister," my father said, his angry face, red with anger, being almost, it would seem, the counterpart of the happy smiling face he had presented the day he returned with the chicken-feather Chanukah headdress. "Are you planning to hand that into school?"

"Yes," I said, "for the school magazine."

"Give it to me!" he said.

"No," I said.

"You heard me," he said. "Give it to me!"

"Why?" I said.

"Are you going to give it to me?" he said, "Or am I going to have to make you?"

"Please Abe," my mother said. "Not in the street. You can get it from him in the car. Leo, let's go to the car."

My father placed his fists on his hips. He is a short man and it was only at such times as these, when he felt that he had to assert his authority, that he looked ridiculous and ineffectual. I think, at that moment, and often later, I would give it to him, not out of fear of his countenance, but out of the desire to sustain his illusion of power.

"Are you going to give it to me *now?*" he said.

"Please Abe—" said my mother, "you'll get it from him in the car. Leo, darling, get in the back of the car."

"No!" my father said. "Now!"

"Here," I said.

I handed him the notebook and he tore out the two pages with the story. Standing there in the street, his legs separated like those of the Colossus of Rhodes (Richard Halliburton says they were not separated, this being, *bien entendu,* too undignified a posture for a statue), he tore the sheets into pieces, and then, being neat, went to the sewer grating at the corner and threw them in.

He had not read the story.

"What's wrong?" I said.

"You're asking me what's wrong!" my father said. "You don't see anything crazy in that?"

"No," I said.

"It's a Jewish thing," my father said. "They wouldn't be interested in a thing like that. You start talking about Chanukah to them and they'll think you're crazy."

"Most of the kids in the school are Jewish," I said, "and the Gentile kids might possibly be interested in a Jewish holiday. Catholics write books about Catholic holidays and Jews read them!"

"No, silly!" my father said. "It's a Christian country and you're going to a Christian school. If you want to write about Chanukah, you write for a Jewish magazine in a Jewish school."

"We should have sent him to a yeshiva," my mother said, and turned her head around to the back to face me, "Would you like that? to go to a yeshiva and wear a skullcap? Would you like that? We'll send you to the yeshiva on Eastern Parkway and you wear a skullcap!"

She turned around again.

The car went through the Bedford-Stuyvesant district, which I had been seeing that morning from the rooftop, and onto the Williamsburg Bridge.

My parents were during this time repeating their complaints about my behavior. It is apparently the nature of those complaints that, since they follow irremediable wrongs, which cannot be caught up and righted, they, the complaints, must have circular and eternal paths like those of the sinners in Dante's hell driven forever by their passions. But whereas my faults were evident to me only in their consequences, the complaints, which kept at their heels, were all too audible. They would only cease when I was outside their orbit which, at that time, in the back seat of the Pontiac, was not possible.

To distract myself I looked out the window and down below. Through the grating which made the road surface of the bridge, the waters of the East River appeared far below.

*The Parable of the Fishes.**

The Romans had decreed that the people of Israel should no longer occupy themselves with Torah.

And during that time Pappos ben Judah came and found Rabbi Akiba holding great assemblies and studying Torah.

Ben Judah said to Akiba:

"Akiba, are you not afraid of the Roman government?"

To which Akiba replied:

"I will tell you a parable. A fox was walking along the bank of a stream, and saw some fishes gathering together to move from one place to another. He said to them, 'From what are you fleeing?' They answered: 'From nets which men set for us.' And the fox said: 'Why not come on the dry land?' To which the fish replied: 'And they say you are the wisest of animals! If we are afraid in our life-element, how much more so in our death-element?'

"So also it is with us: If now while we sit and study Torah, in which it is

* Adapted from Montefiore's *A Rabbinic Anthology.*

written, 'For that is thy life, and the length of thy days' (Deut. XXX, 20), we
are in such a plight, how much more so if we neglect it."

Some time after he said this, the Rabbi was arrested by the Romans. He
died a horrible death, skinned alive, his flesh torn off with hot metal combs.

The Williamsburg Bridge on the Manhattan side ends at Delancey Street.
Dad stopped at a traffic light outside Ratner's.

"Would you like to live here?" my father said. "If you live here you could
go to a yeshiva and wear *pais*. Is that the way you'd like to live? Huh?"

"Please, Abe," my mother said, "think about your heart. You can't kill
yourself over him."

My father turned around (he was still stopped at the red light so that
the car was not moving), and said, "When you're in Rome, you do what the
Romans do!"

The fourteen-year-old Leo had cringed in the back of the car, tears starting to his eyes. . . .

"What are you looking at?" said Ariela.

We had been walking along Greenwich Avenue to the dance meeting,
and I had stopped outside the window of an antique shop, staring at two metal
combs which were beside a set of glass beads. They were curling iron combs,
with insulated handles. In the parking lot beside the shop stood an old abandoned Pontiac, battered as if someone had beaten it. The rear window facing
me was broken. I would have been afraid to look inside the car.

# The Ivy League Negro
## 1963

## William Melvin Kelley

If I have seen one, I have seen at least ten movies about an immigrant father (named Mendelberg, MacNabb, Martinez or Mazoni—take your pick) who saves his pennies to send his boy, John, to college. There is usually a scene in which the father stands before a group of well-wishers and, in broken English, toasts his son: "I didn't mind working hard because I know it is my son, Johnny, that I am breaking my back—for Johnny to take and go to the college and come back a great man."

The next important scene is John's homecoming. He looks at the cheap furniture, the doilies covering everything, and feels shame and disgust for it all. His world is bigger and newer now and he is uncomfortable in the old house. He sees his father (it is his father because the Oedipal conflict has to appear sooner or later) as an antiquated old tyrant. He and his father argue and John walks out, slamming the door.

Finally, after he has amassed a fortune in some business of which his father does not approve, John gets an urgent three-in-the-morning phone call from Mama: "Johnny, come quick. Papa's had a stroke." John, turning to his blonde, blue-eyed wife, who is in the other twin bed, says, "It's Papa. He's going fast. I must get to him."

John jumps into his Ferrari (a concession to the Old World) and drives to the local slum. He and his father have a death-bed reunion. His father gasps that he knows in some ways John was right; the world is moving forward. John reciprocates by saying he now realizes that some of the old ways are better; Madison Avenue is not all they say it is. The old man dies happy. John drives back to his mansion and his wife meets him at the door with a plate of bacon and eggs and a Martini.

I must admit in all fairness that this movie has been made so many times probably because it contains good doses of truth. The cultural differences between the immigrant father and his American son are vast. Ironically, the father brought his son to America to secure for him an education and better opportunities.

It has been different for the American Negro. Here at least is one stereotype with which, until recently, he has not been connected. The reasons are well-known: the Negro did not come here looking for broader opportunities; he was brought by force. Even after slavery was abolished, horizons did not widen. It took the European immigrant one generation to be accepted in America's mainstream; after six or more generations, the African "immigrant" remains one.

Now, finally, the brown Johnny is beginning to march home from college to argue with his father. But when he denounces the old man and stomps out, slamming the door, he finds that in most cases there is no place for him to go.

The last is perhaps an oversimplification, as are most statements about The Problem. But there is some truth in it. A lot depends on the individual Negro and what his life has been, on what he wants and why. Even to understand such a simple statement you will have to know what it is like for a Negro to grow up in America, whether it be in Mississippi, in Harlem, or as I did, in the Bronx.

There is a time in the childhood of every Negro when he realizes he's different. I am not talking now about his awareness that prejudice and inequality exist in America, nor about the bitterness, resentment and hatred that may or may not grow in his heart with the awareness of his being different; I am talking merely of the realization he is different.

As I said, I was raised not in a ghetto, but in the north Bronx, the only Negro boy on a predominantly Italian-American block. Knowing this, you must not immediately assume I was always unhappy; you must not assume I was always fighting my way to school; this was not at all the case. On the contrary, being the only Negro gave me a wonderful advantage; I was always a very important part of the games my white friends and I played. When we played The Lone Ranger, I was always Tonto. When we fought the Japs, I was always the Friendly Native. This is because I was not so much "colored" as brown, and too good a friend to be one of the outlaws or Japanese.

Being the Friendly Native is perhaps more important than you may realize for the way we played it, the Friendly Native was second only to General MacArthur, and since the good general was continually being captured, drugged, wounded, beaten or shot, it was the Friendly Native who took over command of Allied Operations in the Pacific Theater.

If it is important for a child to be part of the group of boys his age in his neighborhood, then I was content and secure. I remained so until the day I took my first good look at my grandmother.

My grandmother was white; at least she looked white, like an old Italian woman who sat, on spring and summer afternoons, in a red beach chair on the sidewalk across the street. My grandmother had long, soft, straight white hair, which she bunned at the back of her head. Her nose was not flat like mine and her lips were thin. This did not bother me at all, but it was certainly interesting, and so one day I asked her about it. Why did she look white when I looked Negro?

She told me it was a long story. And it was too. I cannot remember how much of it she told me at the time, for later she told it all, but she did say, in passing, that her grandfather had been a general in the Confederate Army. (Actually he was a colonel, but to me any soldier who was not a private, sergeant or captain was a general.) I was not even interested in which war he fought; being related to a general was all I needed to know.

At this time, around 1944, everybody on the block under ten was actively engaged in fighting the Japanese in the vacant lot next to my house, and so I ran outside that day, bursting with news of the general in my family. I expected my friends to be impressed to their very sneakers. Instead, they did not at all believe me. "That's a lie. And, besides, who ever heard of a colored general?"

"But he wasn't colored. He was white."

"Then how can he be your relative? You're colored."

I am sure that no unkindness was meant; theirs was simply the viewpoint of our age. Negroes were Negroes; whites were whites. But still I could not answer the question. I only knew something had happened a long time before that had returned to make me seem a ridiculous liar to my friends. For me, it never really went any further than that and I must consider myself lucky. To other Negro children, growing up in other places, the awareness of difference grows into bitterness and hatred—or resignation and despair.

Not too long after he learns he is different, the Negro child discovers how ambiguous is his position in this country. He learns that being colored is not a matter of actual color, not a fact of description—dandelions are yellow, Negroes are gold ochre—but something else and he does not know what.

The plight of the Negro in America is not that he is different, rather that he spends so much time in painful contemplation on the meaning of the difference. He realizes the white man, and most other Negroes, have attached a value to the difference, and that the value is usually a negative one. He can discover no basis in fact for the negative value, but since everyone else seems to accept it, he becomes convinced that his own judgment is faulty. At this point he is close to convincing himself or has already convinced himself of his own inferiority. Further, since his belief in his own inferiority is an irrational one, it does not help him to define himself, to gain self-knowledge. He is not better off than when he started, in fact, a good deal worse.

This is not true of any other minority in this country, or perhaps in the world. A Chinese in America has a language, a food, a way of life. As a child, his father can tell him all manner of things about the meaning of being Chinese. He may later decide the Chinese way of doing things is inferior to the American way. In this case, however, it will be a real decision, based on real alternatives. This is true, in varying degrees, of all religious, racial and national groups in America. But the Negro was so completely cut loose from Africa that next to nothing is left of it in his culture. He is more completely American than anyone else in this country, not because, as some say, he has been here so long, but because the American culture is the only culture he knows.

You may say the Negro developed the spirituals and jazz. And perhaps because Negroes did these things, the entire race can be proud. But being Italian is not only knowing that Leonardo da Vinci was Italian. It is knowing too an Italian way of doing everything from cooking food to raising children. And in these terms, the Negro way is the American way. To a Negro, a beautiful Negro girl is one who looks most white, because the standards of beauty of white America are the only ones a Negro knows. If this girl is almost white, if she has light skin, straight hair, thin lips, blue eyes and a sharp nose—what is the meaning of the adjective *Negro?* The Negro does not know, but still it is his name.

To be a Negro is to be a man waking up in a hospital bed with amnesia. He asks the doctor who he is, what is his name. The doctor tells him, but the name means nothing to the man. He will take the name anyway, simply because it is better to have a name, even one which holds no meaning, than to have no name at all.

In the same way the Negro takes his name, trying to find personal value in the value others give it. By the time any Negro reaches his late teens, no matter what his life may have been, whether he grew up in the South, in Harlem or in private school, as I did, he has seen a bewildering number of reactions to his "name," to his skin color. More mystical Negroes will tell him he is a "brother," that his skin knows innately things the white man will never know, that it has natural rhythm, the natural talents of dancing, singing and athletics, that he is innately "soulful" and in the next breath will condemn the white man for believing in the stereotypes of natural athletic and show-business talent. White bigots will tell him that he is lazy, shiftless, dull-witted and jovial, and that he is also sullen, conniving, and has enough energy to pursue, catch and rape any white woman within a hundred miles. Professional liberals will treat him as a cause, will tell him he should get the same treatment as any other human being, but will forgive him the most vulgar behavior as if he were some big, dumb animal. He will have been told all manner of things about himself, and chances are he will be able to see none of these things in himself.

And so he comes to an Ivy League school—to Harvard (for Harvard is the Ivy League school I know best)—and whether or not he knows it, he will be hoping to find himself, not only in the same way that all young men hope to find themselves in exotic places—in Paris, Tahiti or Cambridge, Massachusetts —but also as a Negro; he will want to discover finally and forever the importance to him of the one-sixteenth of an inch of brown skin which covers his body.

I first entered Harvard Yard one afternoon in late September. I walked through the gate leading past Lehman Hall. On my left was Matthews Hall, built in the Victorian era, and covered with the black spidery fire escapes and grotesque stonework of that period. On my right was Grays Hall, built a few years earlier and somewhat plainer. I stopped between them, as the empty Yard opened up in front of me. The leaves on the trees were dark green;

the grass too was green and I remember thinking that it looked like the view in an Easter Egg. A lone student, pale from a summer in Widenner Library, appeared and walked along one of the crisscrossing black asphalt paths. "This is the place," I whispered to myself. "This is the place I've been looking for."

It was, but not exactly in the way I thought it would be.

An academic community, especially one like Harvard, attaching so much importance to intellectuality that it sometimes seems the ideal situation would be one in which only disembodied ideas and minds went to class, is a place where a Negro can forget almost entirely about his skin, his Negro consciousness. Negro consciousness has been discussed fully by others; I need not go into it except to say, for those who have never heard of it, the Negro consciousness is the part of a Negro's mind that functions not for him as an individual human being, but for him as a Negro, for his race. It is the part of his conscience which asks him, before he commits any act, "Is it good for the Negro race?"

At Harvard, this part of his mind is soon lulled to sleep. He does not need it. He only has time enough to think of himself as an individual student, going to class, studying for examinations, waiting for his marks. Furthermore, among Harvard Negroes, race pride, as it would be known in Harlem ("If a Negro does it, it's good") is something like patriotism, in a flag-waving sense—antiquated, shallow-minded and conformist. Everything at Harvard is geared to make a man think for himself, to formulate his own ideas. Blind devotion to race does not stand up against analysis, so as often for college students a belief in God does not. To believe in God, Old Glory or the Marines, and finally the mystical power of a sixteenth of an inch of brown skin takes faith. Harvard is a pragmatic and empirical place.

So at Harvard, a Negro will gain an awareness of himself as a single human being, an awareness of his apartness from any group of human beings, and further, if he has never had one before, chances are he will make one good white friend. They may even room together. They will go to movies, get drunk, study and eat together; across the darkness, they will listen to each other snore.

He will then have found something in common with a white man, on a human level. This takes away a big piece of his Negro consciousness. In order to be a Negro, truly and completely, to believe in a mystical racial unity, a Negro must hate all whites. But having formed an attachment to a white man, a Negro can never again believe in the single and complete attachment of race, can never again believe, if he did before, that all white men are the devil incarnate.

Some do keep their Negro consciousness intact. They are in a minority, and are usually from the South; their wounds are too deep; their scar tissue is too tough. A fellow in my class believed without reservation that the white man was born hating Negroes. Nothing could shake his belief in this principle. He finally became a Socialist, deciding that capitalism bred racial prejudice. Nothing short of a Socialist revolution in this country would change the situation.

For most, constant awareness of their skin color fell away. They did remember from time to time, but remembered it as a nightmare they had dreamed once outside the walls of Harvard Yard.

At Harvard, and at any other Ivy League school, the Negro not only loses his Negro consciousness or at least the sore edge of it, but perhaps will acquire something else: the opportunity to develop a certain aristocratic attitude even toward the white man. Not that he is boorish and goes around telling non-Harvard people they are beneath him. It is rather that he comes to believe, in a quiet way, that Harvard is the best school in the country and therefore that he is one of the select. Yale Negroes feel the same about Yale; Dartmouth Negroes the same about Dartmouth and so on.

One summer, I worked as a plasterer's helper, and having only my lunch hour to do it, I ventured into a bank to open a savings account. I was wearing my work clothes, plaster-covered dungarees and a dirt-encrusted sweat shirt. I asked the teller to instruct me. He eyed me up and down—wondering, I suppose, if I had stolen the money I was about to deposit.

"Step this way." I could hear distaste in his voice.

We walked across the marble floor to a desk, behind which sat a man of forty or so, who had the distinguished look which can only be acquired by working in close proximity to huge sums of money. He, too, looked at me with distaste, but coolly gracious, gave me the forms to fill out. He deposited my money for me, and returned with the cashier's receipt.

I got up to leave, moving just fast enough to cover his glass-top desk with a film of plaster dust. Then I remembered I would be returning to school in a few weeks and decided to register the change of address with him now. I came back to his desk. He looked up, annoyed: "Yes?"

"I'll be going back to school the last week in September and I want to give you that address."

"All right." He rattled through some things on his desk, and came up with a blank slip of paper. "What's the address?"

By this time I was self-conscious at having come into a bank dressed as I was and stammered, "Adams House A-24, Harvard Coll——"

I stopped as he looked up surprised. There was a new expression on his face, something close to stunned respect. "Harvard?"

I nodded.

"Well." His tone changed immediately, became more friendly. "Harvard. Why don't you sit down, Mr. Kelley."

I did. We discussed Ivy League sports. He knew far more about them than I did. He asked me what my major was; I told him. His had been the same. "But," he was timid and almost ashamed, "I only went to Columbia myself."

Graciously I replied: "I'm sure you got a good education at Columbia." (As they used to say in nineteenth-century novels I blush to admit I actually said that.)

His reply was as self-depreciating as mine had been condescending: "But, Mr. Kelley, not as good as at Harvard."

From time to time at Harvard, I had conversations with both Negroes and whites which centered around the magical power of the name—Harvard. And I feel sure the power applies to the names Brown, Columbia, Cornell, Dartmouth, Princeton and Yale, along with Williams, Amherst and a good many other Eastern colleges. But as his self-esteem grows, the Ivy League Negro sometimes fails to realize that in order for the spell to be invoked, the magic word must be said aloud. In other words, to my bank executive, I would have remained a dirty, irreverent Negro if I had not told him my college address. There have been times when, because I said nothing of my education, I was guest to the same scorn and discrimination that any Negro faces. I have also run across people who have considered me no more than an educated savage, thus leaving their racial prejudice wholly intact. At such times, I was treated ambiguously, with respect for the school I attended, but with none for me as a human being.

I have not meant to give the impression that Harvard is an oasis for the Negro; as free from prejudice as the academic community can be, in that a Negro can gain respect and stature because of intellectual achievement—and even though, to an instructor, grader or professor, a Negro is an albino, without color—when it comes to socializing and dating, his sixteenth of an inch of brown skin-still serves to inhibit and exclude him.

Very few white girls at Radcliffe and fewer at Wellesley would date a Negro. If a white boy and a Negro boy roomed together, they might go on double dates, but probably this would be the exception.

Because of the shortage of Negro girls at Radcliffe—in my class, I think there were two out of three hundred—the Negro at Harvard goes for his social life across the river to Boston, and especially to Boston University, which is called jokingly, "The Howard University of the North," because so many Negroes attend and because, in comparison to Harvard, they seem to party so much. The city of Boston also has chapters of the three major Negro fraternities: Alpha Phi Alpha, Kappa Alpha Psi and Omega Psi Phi. Most Negroes at Harvard join one of these and get their cans fanned and heads shaved before Initiation finishes. The fraternities give parties and dances, and each has a traditional connection with one or another Negro sorority.

In my class at Harvard, out of a thousand boys, there were ten Negroes. By the end of the first three weeks of the term, I had met them all. A Negro in a new situation will look, either consciously or unconsciously, for the other Negroes. He will not feel really at home until he knows how many there are, their names and where they came from. I always compare it to two spies in enemy territory dropping notes scribbled on matchbook covers as they pass one another in the street.

If you had taken the ten in my class and the two girls at Radcliffe and added to these twelve all the Negroes in the entire Ivy League and the women's colleges of similar stature (Smith, Vassar, Wellesley and so on) and tossed all of us into one room, each of us would know at least ten others.

This is because, among other reasons, richer people send their children to better schools. There are few enough rich Negroes for all of them to have met at least once, and thus their children know one another. Also the names of these rich Negroes appear quite often in the social columns of the Negro press and magazines and are well-known. Further, college boys are always looking for attractive, datable girls.

By the end of October, a Negro at Harvard who really cares will know at least the names of all the attractive Negro girls at all the women's Ivy League colleges. An example: my wife went to Sarah Lawrence. I had heard of her at least three years before I finally met her.

Although these students do not make up a tightly-knit social group, they will often turn up at the same parties in New York, Boston, Washington and Philadelphia where, in April each year, are held the Penn Relays. For more than one obvious reason, when spring vacation arrives, Negro students cannot go to Florida or Bermuda. It has become traditional for not only Ivy League but most Negro college students (from as far west as Chicago, as far south as Tennessee or Louisiana) to go to Philadelphia in the spring, to view the Relays through a drunken haze, to party throughout a sleepless weekend.

The Ivy League Negro, and in general, most educated or upper-class Negroes, have an ambiguous attitude toward the uneducated, lower-class Negro. There is, at the same time, disdain and deep love for the "diddy-bop" and the "jungle-bunny"—that is, the lower-class Negro man and woman. With one breath, the Ivy League Negro will ridicule him for his lack of taste, the flashy and revealing clothes of his women, his "dese, deys, dem and doses," and with his next breath he will envy him for his apparent love of life, his women's Africanesque or exotic beauty, and, believe it or not, his rough-and-ready sexuality.

In short, I am saying that in an unconscious effort to become completely integrated into American life, the Ivy League Negro sometimes adopts and accepts the stereotypes and the prejudices of mainstream America—including color prejudice.

Well, not completely. As the Ivy League Negro becomes more learned, more refined, he develops certain feelings of superiority toward all uneducated people, white and Negro. By his new standards, or perhaps by those he brought with him to college, the diddy-bop's tastes are crude and gaudy, his language is crude.

It is not so much real prejudice as it is that he has come to feel himself closer to the educated white man than to the uneducated Negro. This has nothing to do with pomposity or snobbishness. It is that his interests are different.

The upper-class and educated white man can view, without guilt, the lower-class white man with a certain distaste and contempt. But an educated Negro who holds the same attitude toward uneducated Negroes carries on his back huge bundles of guilt. His Negro consciousness begins to work. He feels he has betrayed his race. It is hard for him to separate acceptance of the prejudices of the American mainstream from justified feelings of apartness from the uneducated Negro, from justified pride in his accomplishments.

This ambiguity of feelings is more or less general to every Negro. It is one ramification of the conflict between the Negro consciousness and the individual personality. If a drunken white man boards a subway, stretches out on a seat and goes to sleep, the other whites on the subway will react to him only in individual ways, but they will not feel he has brought shame on the entire white race.

However, should a drunken Negro board a subway, each Negro present will be attacked by a confusing variety of emotions, all descending on him at about the same instant. He will feel his individual attitude toward drunks, ranging from sympathy to disgust, depending on who and what he is. He will hate and be ashamed of the drunk because he is undermining the image of dignity the race is trying to present in its struggle for equal rights (as if a human being must be dignified to be treated as a human being). He will hate the white man because he is sometimes so shallow as to see the entire composition of a race in one drunken member, and also because given the choice between a drunken Negro and a sober Negro, he will choose to think the worst. And finally, he will feel love and sympathy for the drunk because he knows it is the white man's shallow and prejudiced attitude which has helped to drive this Negro, not only to the bar or the bottle, but also to the dope pusher, the phony religious leader, the fortune-teller and the palm reader, and more recently, to the Black Muslims, who have not only supplied escape, as do the others, but also the taste of victory and power; who teach that rather than feeling downcast because of his rejection and exclusion from American life, the Negro should not desire to enter in the first place to contaminate his divine blood by mixing it with the blood of the white devil; who have turned the American Nightmare of irrational prejudice on its head and made it a Faith.

An ambiguity of feeling, then, is not confined to the educated Negro, but it probably takes a greater toll on him, simply because education has never seemed to make things clearer and more absolute, but more shadowy and many-sided. They say usually that the more questions a person asks, the more answers he receives. It is also quite true that the more questions a person asks, the more questions that are left unanswered.

The uneducated Negro growing up in a ghetto learns different things. As far as he is concerned, his experiences boil down to one absolute principle: the white man hates him. He is certain without doubt the white man will hire him last, fire him first, that the white man will exploit him in his own neighborhood in any way he can, that the white man will send his police to brutalize him. He knows all this and carries his defenses high. He finally reaches the point when he believes that even a genuinely kind act hides a savage blow. The white man has always, and will always hate him. For his own good, he must always hate the white man.

It is in the nature of man, I think, to search constantly for an absolute truth in which he can believe, be it God, Jesus, the Blessed Virgin, Allah, Art, Country, Home, Mother or Race. It does not seem to matter that his search turns up chaos under apparent order; man searches for his absolute anyway. If you can accept this, you can see that the uneducated Negro comes closer to having found his Truth—the white man hates him—and the educated Negro, the Ivy League Negro is far from finding his.

At the very beginning, I said that when the brown Johnny denounces his father and storms out of the house, he finds he has no place to go. That may not only be an oversimplification, but an exaggeration. It is rather that if the entire Negro race is caught between an Africa to which it can never return and an America in which it has so far been denied the right to participate completely, then the educated Negro is further caught between a race he feels he has grown away from and a class which will not fully accept him. The only way out is for an educated Negro to work for the betterment of his race. Since very few human beings have the reformer's zeal, very few educated Negroes find fulfillment in the cause for Negro rights. Those who do have found a way to resolve the conflict between Negro consciousness and individual personality.

A friend of mine, a recent graduate from quite a good Eastern college, decided not to take a safe, well-paying job in New York, but went to Georgia to help in registering Negroes to vote.

Recently, I met a mutual friend of ours, an Ivy League Negro. He was working in some not very important job in some not very important agency. I asked him if he had heard about our friend in Georgia.

He said he had. "I got a letter from him. He said he'd been spit at a couple of times. Someone told me he'd been shot at. I don't know if that's true."

"That takes guts," I said.

"Yeah, but you have to be a little nuts too. Going down there, getting spit on by those ignorant bastards, maybe even shot at, and working with a lot of dumb colored people." He looked a trifle sad. Then he chuckled. "I guess I'm just too  .  .  .  refined for that kind of crap."

That about sums it up.

## This Is the Beat Generation

## 1952

### John Clellon Holmes

Several months ago, a national magazine ran a story under the heading "Youth" and the subhead "Mother Is Bugged At Me." It concerned an eighteen-year-old California girl who had been picked up for smoking marijuana and wanted to talk about it. While a reporter took down her ideas in the uptempo language of "tea," someone snapped a picture. In view of her contention that she was part of a whole new culture where one out of every five people you meet is a user, it was an arresting photograph. In the pale, attentive face, with its soft eyes and intelligent mouth, there was no hint of corruption. It was a face which could only be deemed criminal through an enormous effort of righteousness. Its only complaint seemed to be: "Why don't people leave us alone?" It was the face of a Beat Generation.

That clean young face has been making the newspapers steadily since the war. Standing before a judge in a Bronx courthouse, being arraigned for stealing a car, it looked up into the camera with curious laughter and no guilt. The same face, with a more serious bent, stared from the pages of *Life* Magazine, representing a graduating class of ex-GI's, and said that as it believed small business to be dead, it intended to become a comfortable cog in the largest corporation it could find. A little younger, a little more bewildered, it was this same face that the photographers caught in Illinois when the first non-virgin club was uncovered. The young copywriter, leaning down the bar on Third Avenue, quietly drinking himself into relaxation, and the energetic hotrod driver of Los Angeles, who plays Russian roulette with a jalopy, are separated only by a continent and a few years. They are the extremes. In between them fall the secretaries wondering whether to sleep with their boy friends now or wait; the mechanic beering up with the guys and driving off to Detroit on a whim; the models studiously name-dropping at a cocktail party. But the face is the same. Bright, level, realistic, challenging.

Any attempt to label an entire generation is unrewarding, and yet the generation which went through the last war, or at least could get a drink

309

easily once it was over, seems to possess a uniform, general quality which demands an adjective. . . . The origins of the word "beat" are obscure, but the meaning is only too clear to most Americans. More than mere weariness, it implies the feeling of having been used, of being raw. It involves a sort of nakedness of mind, and ultimately, of soul; a feeling of being reduced to the bedrock of consciousness. In short, it means being undramatically pushed up against the wall of oneself. A man is beat whenever he goes for broke and wagers the sum of his resources on a single number; and the young generation has done that continually from early youth.

Its members have an instinctive individuality, needing no bohemianism or imposed eccentricity to express it. Brought up during the collective bad circumstances of a dreary depression, weaned during the collective uprooting of a global war, they distrust collectivity. But they have never been able to keep the world out of their dreams. The fancies of their childhood inhabited the half-light of Munich, the Nazi-Soviet pact and the eventual blackout. Their adolescence was spent in a topsy-turvy world of war bonds, swing shifts and troop movements. They grew to independent minds on beachheads, in gin mills and USO's, in past-midnight arrivals and pre-dawn departures. Their brothers, husbands, fathers or boy friends turned up dead one day at the other end of a telegram. At the four trembling corners of the world, or in the home town invaded by factories or lonely servicemen, they had intimate experience with the nadir and the zenith of human conduct, and little time for much that came between. The peace they inherited was only as secure as the next headline. It was a cold peace. Their own lust for freedom, and the ability to live at a pace that kills (to which the war had adjusted them), led to black markets, bebop, narcotics, sexual promiscuity, hucksterism and Jean-Paul Sartre. The beatness set in later.

It is a postwar generation, and, in a world which seems to mark it cycles by its wars, it is already being compared to that other postwar generation, which dubbed itself "lost." The Roaring Twenties, and the generation that made them roar, are going through a sentimental revival, and the comparison is valuable. The Lost Generation was discovered in a roadster, laughing hysterically because nothing meant anything any more. It migrated to Europe, unsure whether it was looking for the "orgiastic future" or escaping from the "puritanical past." Its symbols were the flapper, the flask of bootleg whiskey, and an attitude of desperate frivolity best expressed by the line: "Tennis, anyone?" It was caught up in the romance of disillusionment, until even that became an illusion. Every act in its drama of lostness was a tragic or ironic third act, and T. S. Eliot's *The Wasteland* was more than the dead-end statement of a perceptive poet. The pervading atmosphere of that poem was an almost objectless sense of loss, through which the reader felt immediately that the cohesion of things had disappeared. It was, for an entire generation, an image which expressed, with dreadful accuracy, its own spiritual condition.

But the wild boys of today are not lost. Their flushed, often scoffing, always intent faces elude the word, and it would sound phony to them. For this generation conspicuously lacks that eloquent air of bereavement which made so many of the exploits of the Lost Generation symbolic actions. Furthermore, the repeated inventory of shattered ideals, and the laments about the mud in moral currents, which so obsessed the Lost Generation, do not concern young people today. They take these things frighteningly for granted. They were brought up in these ruins and no longer notice them. They drink to "come down" or to "get high," not to illustrate anything. Their excursions into drugs or promiscuity come out of curiosity, not disillusionment.

Only the most bitter among them would call their reality a nightmare and protest that they have indeed lost something, the future. For ever since they were old enough to imagine one, that has been in jeopardy anyway. The absence of personal and social values is to them, not a revelation shaking the ground beneath them, but a problem demanding a day-to-day solution. *How* to live seems to them much more crucial than *why*. And it is precisely at this point that the copywriter and the hotrod driver meet and their identical beatness becomes significant, for, unlike the Lost Generation, which was occupied with the loss of faith, the Beat Generation is becoming more and more occupied with the need for it. As such, it is a disturbing illustration of Voltaire's reliable old joke: "If there were no God, it would be necessary to invent him." Not content to bemoan His absence, they are busily and haphazardly inventing totems for Him on all sides.

For the giggling nihilist, eating up the highway at ninety miles an hour and steering with his feet, is no Harry Crosby, the poet of the Lost Generation who planned to fly his plane into the sun one day because he could no longer accept the modern world. On the contrary, the hotrod driver invites death only to outwit it. He is affirming the life within him in the only way he knows how, at the extreme. The eager-faced girl, picked up on a dope charge, is not one of those "women and girls carried screaming with drink or drugs from public places," of whom Fitzgerald wrote. Instead, with persuasive seriousness, she describes the sense of community she has found in marijuana, which society never gave her. The copywriter, just as drunk by midnight as his Lost Generation counterpart, probably reads *God and Man at Yale* during his Sunday afternoon hangover. The difference is this almost exaggerated will to believe in something, if only in themselves. It is a *will* to believe, even in the face of an inability to do so in conventional terms. And that is bound to lead to excesses in one direction or another.

The shock that older people feel at the sight of this Beat Generation is, at its deepest level, not so much repugnance at the facts, as it is distress at the attitudes which move it. Though worried by this distress, they most often argue or legislate in terms of the facts rather than the attitudes. The newspaper reader, studying the eyes of young dope addicts, can only find an outlet for his horror and bewilderment in demands that passers be given the electric chair. Sociologists, with a more academic concern, are just as troubled by the legions of young men whose topmost ambition seems to be to find a secure berth in a monolithic corporation. Contemporary historians express mild surprise at the lack of organized movements, political, religious, or otherwise, among the young. The articles they write remind us that being one's own boss and being a natural joiner are two of our most cherished national traits. Everywhere people with tidy moralities shake their heads and wonder what is happening to the younger generation.

Perhaps they have not noticed that, behind the excess on the one hand, and the conformity on the other, lies that wait-and-see detachment that results from having to fall back for support more on one's capacity for human endurance than on one's philosophy of life. Not that the Beat Generation is immune to ideas; they fascinate it. Its wars, both past and future, were and will be wars of ideas. It knows, however, that in the final, private moment of conflict a man is really fighting another man, and not an idea. And that the same goes for love. So it is a generation with a greater facility for entertaining ideas than for believing in them. But it is also the first generation in several centuries for which the act of faith has been an obsessive problem, quite aside from the reasons for having a particular faith or not having it. It exhibits on every side, and in a bewildering number of facets, a perfect craving to believe.

Though it is certainly a generation of extremes, including both the hipster and the "radical" young Republican in its ranks, it renders unto Caesar (i.e., society) what is Caesar's, and unto God what is God's. For in the wildest hipster, making a mystique of bop, drugs and the night life, there is no desire to shatter the "square" society in which he lives, only to elude it. To get on a soapbox or write a manifesto would seem to him absurd. Looking at the normal world, where most everything is a "drag" for him, he nevertheless says: "Well, that's the Forest of Arden after all. And even *it* jumps if you look at it right." Equally, the young Republican, though often seeming to hold up Babbitt as his culture hero, is neither vulgar nor materialistic, as Babbitt was. He conforms because he believes it is socially practical, not necessarily virtuous. Both positions, however, are the result of more or less the same conviction— namely that the valueless abyss of modern life is unbearable.

For beneath the excess and the conformity, there is something other than detachment. There are the stirrings of a quest. What the hipster is looking for in his "coolness" (withdrawal) or "flipness" (ecstasy) is, after all, a feeling of somewhereness, not just another diversion. The young Republican feels that there is a point beyond which change becomes chaos, and what he wants is not simply privilege or wealth, but a stable position from which to operate. Both have had enough of homelessness, valuelessness, faithlessness.

The variety and the extremity of their solutions are only a final indication that for today's young people there is not as yet a single external pivot around which they can, as a generation, group their observations and their aspirations. There is no single philosophy, no single party, no single attitude. The failure of most orthodox moral and social concepts to reflect fully the life they have known is probably the reason for this, but because of it each person becomes a walking, self-contained unit, compelled to meet the problem of being young in a seemingly helpless world in his own way, or at least endure.

More than anything else, this is what is responsible for this generation's reluctance to name itself, its reluctance to discuss itself as a group, sometimes its reluctance to be itself. For invented gods invariably disappoint those who worship them. Only the need for them goes on, and it is this need, exhausting one object after another, which projects the Beat Generation forward into the future and will one day deprive it of its beatness.

Dostoyevski wrote in the early 1880's that "Young Russia is talking of nothing but the eternal questions now." With appropriate changes, something very like this is beginning to happen in America, in an American way; a re-evaluation of which the exploits and attitudes of this generation are only symptoms. No single comparison of one generation against another can accurately measure effects, but it seems obvious that a Lost Generation, occupied with disillusionment and trying to keep busy among the broken stones, is poetically moving, but not very dangerous. But a Beat Generation, driven by a desperate craving for belief and as yet unable to accept the moderations which are offered it, is quite another matter. Thirty years later, after all, the generation of which Dostoyevski wrote was meeting in cellars and making bombs.

This generation may make no bombs; it will probably be asked to drop some, and have some dropped on it, however, and this fact is never far from its mind. It is one of the pressures which created it and will play a large part in what will happen to it. There are those who believe that in generations such as this there is always the constant possibility of a great new moral idea, conceived in desperation, coming to life. Others note the self-indulgence, the waste, the apparent social irresponsibility, and disagree.

But its ability to keep its eyes open, and yet avoid cynicism; its ever-increasing conviction that the problem of modern life is essentially a spiritual problem; and that capacity for sudden wisdom which people who live hard and go far, possess, are assets and bear watching. And, anyway, the clear, challenging faces are worth it.

# Patriotism
## 1960

## Paul Goodman

### 1

In 1783 Washington sent a circular letter to the States, describing the situation of the new nation as he saw it. "We have equal occasion to felicitate ourselves," he said, "on the lot which Providence has assigned to us, whether we view it in a natural, a political, or moral point of light." He pointed to the natural resources of the new nation, its independence and freedom, the Age of Reason during which it had come of age, an age of "the free cultivation of letters, the unbounded extension of commerce, the progressive refinement of manners, the growing liberality of sentiment, and above all the pure and benign light of Revelation. . . . If these citizens," he concluded, "should not be completely free and happy, the fault will be certainly their own. Such is our situation and such are our prospects."

It is hard to read these sentences without agitation and tears, for they are simply true and simply patriotic.

In the next generations, almost to our own times, patriotic rhetoric did not cease to sound, more pompously and falsely, but never without a core of truth. There was always something special in the American destiny to be proud of. In 1825 it was the broad democracy. In 1850 it was the magnificent spread and settlement from coast to coast. In 1875, the material progress, the cable and the Pacific railroad, the building of modern industrialism. In 1900, America was the melting pot, the asylum of the poor and the oppressed.

In our century, the patriotic rhetoric began to be unbelievable—not by accident, for foreign wars (1898 and 1917) are incompatible with reasonable rhetoric. In recent decades there has been almost a surcease of such speech. Even references to the American Way, free enterprise, high production, and the economy of abundance have finally died out, because they call up the idea of tail fins and TV commercials. Highbrow journalists mention the American Way with scorn.

Our case is astounding. For the first time in recorded history, the mention of country, community, place has lost its power to animate. Nobody but a scoundrel even tries it. Our rejection of false patriotism is, of course, itself a badge of honor. But the positive loss is tragic and I cannot resign myself to it. A man has only one life and if during it he has no great environment, no community, he has been irreparably robbed of a human right. This loss is damaging especially in growing up, for it deprives outgoing growth, which begins with weaning from Mother and walking out of the house, of the chance of entering upon a great and honorable scene to develop in.

Culture is, first of all, city and patriotic culture. I shall try to show that patriotism is the culture of childhood and adolescence. Without this first culture, we come with a fatal emptiness to the humane culture of science, art, humanity and God; and this emptiness results in the best people *not* turning back, like Plato's philosopher who has emerged from the cave, to serve their country. Many of the best Americans have a strong philanthropic and local-community zeal, yet it would seem odd for somebody nowadays to put himself to a big and hard task just to serve his country, to make her better, and be proud of that. Young people aspire mightily to appearances on television and other kinds of notoriety, but I doubt that many now think of being honored by a statue in the park and winning "immortal" fame, the fame of big culture.

Let me make the same point by analyzing a remarkable proposition of Otto Jespersen, the grammarian. He shows that, contrary to expectation, a child does not learn his mother tongue at home from his mother and immediate family, he does not pick up their accent. The accent, vocabulary, syntax, and style that form his speech are learned from his first peer groups, outside the home. Jespersen does not explain it, but the psychology seems evident. Speech occurs at the stage of the developing of the "I," it is a forming of the image of the self, it is a self-appointment to one's ideal and putting on its uniform. Changes occur as we appoint ourselves to one peer group after another. At a certain stage a lad appoints himself or commits himself to a band of friends and puts on its jargon, jacket, tattoo, and masculine ring on the fourth finger of the left hand. If he is insecure and disturbed, this conformity is a cowering protection and the band is a delinquent gang, but in every case it is also, we see by the blazon, an achievement. And one way in which the Governor of New York does not take the juveniles seriously, when he speaks of giving them a sense of belonging, is that he does not offer an ideal that promises equal manliness. He has none to offer.

It is tragic when there is no great adult peer group to meet growth. Consider the case of an artist, my own case. To have simple and sounding language, rather than merely the lovely colloquialism of Sherwood Anderson or William Carlos Williams, it is necessary to believe in the great national culture of one's people. Our popular culture does not warrant the belief, even to make the sacrifice that Virgil made when he sadly gave up his best vision because strife-torn Rome needed a national poet. True, an artist can then jump to the international and universal, for mankind and God do not let him down (mankind is the fellow on one's own block), but this is at the loss of pomp and glitter, of the glancing present. Without a patriotic peer group, it is impossible to have the brilliance of Handel, the material grandeur of Venice. With us the style of the big bright sensation belongs to cheap musical dramas on Broadway.

2

The area of patriotism is intermediate between childhood and adulthood. We must delimit it carefully or we play into the hands of fools and rogues who have done our country plenty of damage.

To what can we correctly attach the adjective "American"? There is no "American" animal, sexual, or primary family life. The idea of American child-rearing or American medicine is idiotic, and the thought of an "American family" is abominable. At the further extreme, there is no "American" university, "American" science, religion, or peace. In only an equivocal sense is there an "American" art: the subject matter may be American, but the art is international and the aim is universal.

In between, however, there *is* an American landscape, an American primary and secondary education, an American classlessness, an American Constitution, an Anglo-American language, and an American kind of enterprising. That is, just where a child ventures from home and grows up through adolescence, the great environment becomes his scene, and this is American, a characteristic geography and history, place and community. It is just in growing up, which is the subject of this book, that a patriotic opportunity is essential. It is just this opportunity that, for ingenuous youth, is corrupted. And so it is hard to grow up.

Let us be quite clear what this American landscape and community is. I quote from a recent issue of *Life:*

> [Teen-agers] own 10 million phonographs, over a million TV sets, 13 million cameras. Counting only what is spent to satisfy their special teen-age demands, the youngsters and their parents will shell out about $10 billion this year, a billion more than the total sales of GM. Until recently businessmen have largely ignored the teen-age market. But now they are spending millions on advertising and razzle-dazzle promotional stunts. If parents have any idea of organized revolt, it is already too late. Teen-age spending is so important that such action would send quivers through the entire national economy.

This is a description of the landscape, and the prose of *Life* is part of the landscape.

3

Equal to our businessmen, our government and public spokesmen have a knack for debasing the noble and making the excellent trivial. The current disease is to make Cold War capital out of everything, no matter what. We cannot dedicate a building of Frank Lloyd Wright's in New York without our Ambassador to the United Nations pointing out that such an architect could not have flourished in Russia. This is tasteless; the matter becomes serious when our freedoms are involved.

Not long ago there was a great to-do about the Russian censorship of Pasternak's *Dr. Zhivago*. The editorials and the rhetoric of organized friends of culture kept repeating freedom of speech, freedom of culture. (You would think that we did not have our own means of censoring, by commercial selection and by swamping.) But the outcry about Pasternak was not sincere, it was propaganda in the Cold War. In the same year, for instance, the Archbishop of Dublin effectually banned the spring theater festival because of plays of O'Casey and Joyce. (He refused to say the festival Mass if those plays were to be given. The director then canceled the plays. But the actors manfully struck and would not play at all, and this resulted in an important loss of tourist revenue. Such admirable behavior is inconceivable in my country.) On this theme, the *New York Times* ran no editorials, no, nor the New York *Herald Tribune*. For we are not at cold war with the Catholic hierarchy. (I wrote a letter to the *Times* asking that this and *Zhivago* be coupled for mention, but no one was interested.) But such behavior is patriotically disastrous; it teaches that our spokesmen are not earnest; they pick and choose when to stand up for freedom of thought. How then can a boy be proud? (But to be sure, we have little such freedom, compared with the British, for our *mass* media are not, like theirs, open to fundamental controversy. It is not surprising, therefore, that for English Angry Young Men an important topic is their outraged patriotism, whereas our Beats do not care about that.)

4

Consider the behavior of our professors and universities during the Dies, McCarthy and Feinberg Law investigations. It is hard to say which set the worse example to the students during those hearings: the Communist professors fearful for their jobs, or the colleges that—with magnificent exceptions, like Harvard—supinely received the investigators. A monumental blunder was being made—which did us desperate damage among thoughtful Europeans —and our professors shivered in their boots and our "radicals" hid like roaches. The important thing is not which group betrays the ideal in any particular case, but that young people become cynical about political action and resigned about the possibility of making a change. Following a party line, Communist teachers, e.g., at New York's City College, denied their membership. This was a disastrous betrayal of the students. Not that it is wrong to avoid insolent force with fraud, but that young students can grow only by politically affirming themselves. With the young, honor is more important than tactics or even than prudence. Leaders of youth must be knightly—a grisly identity, but there it is.

We have now passed through a decade in which the students in our colleges showed a political apathy probably unexampled in student history. Several causes have conspired to it. First, simple shell shock: the war and the atom bomb aroused such deep anxiety that the only defense against it was conventionality. (I remember lecturing on Kafka in 1948 to a hall of collegians consisting largely of veterans on the G.I. bill, and they frantically protested that Kafka was psychotic and should be paid no attention, he had no relation to reality—they who had lived through some of the Trial and were even then roaming under the Castle!)

Secondly, the students have been seduced by business firms, which tempt and reward them for conformity; but as W. H. Whyte, Jr. points out, they are eager to conform even before they are paid. Correspondingly, in its appeal to lower-class boys, the Army has found it wise to accept the stirring slogan, "Retire at 37." If you question a boy draftee who has re-enlisted, he will explain that it is a "good deal." That is, the Army has become the IBM of the poor boy.

But finally, is there any doubt that an important cause of the present political apathy of the young is the dishonorable radical leadership that they had in the Thirties and Forties? They now believe that *all* political thinking is a sell—just as those bright Catholic lads who stop believing the superstitions of scholasticism now believe that all philosophy is an intricate fraud, including the truths of scholasticism.

This hipster skepticism is pervasive. It is partly, of course, resignation that a revolution has failed and the way is too thorny; but students are usually more resilient. I think that a more important factor is disgust that the radicals were not bona fide; the students were had. But also, I fear, it is cynical superiority, an identification with either the fraudulent or the powerful.

I referred above to the similarity between some of the Communists and young Organization Men today, in their lust for control apart from any objective good and, more deeply, in their use of an organized power-system in order to make the ingenuous and worthy not exist. In the Thirties it came about that Communists had high status in Hollywood and somewhat in publishing, so the two kinds of organized systems worked in the same offices— nor do I doubt that many of the refinements of present-day organization life were learned during this cohabitation. But it has remained for our own decade to enjoy the brutal comedy of McCarthy and the FBI investigating the Communists in Hollywood, so we had on one stage the three most cynical tribes in the country.

But let us go back to more simple ignobility.

## 5

Certainly the most thrilling and romantic happening of these years is the adventure in space, surpassing in promise the voyages of the fifteenth and sixteenth centuries. This adventure makes life worth the trouble again. When the Russians beat us out, we are miffed but we can be proud that these exploits have been performed by men and man is great; Copernicus was a Pole, Galileo an Italian, Kepler a German, Newton an Englishman—and the rockets were Chinese; and we hope that we shall win the next round, for it belongs to America to achieve first in this kind of enterprise. The experiments are expensive, but it seems mean-spirited to question the appropriations and few have done so. So far, grand. But now we have corrupted even the exploration of space into the Cold War. Against an agreement of the International Geophysical Year, we, like the Russians, withheld the wave length of a satellite for strategic reasons. (I was ashamed and again I wrote dutifully to the *New York Times,* but they again had no space for such an odd way of viewing the news.) Next, we carried out a secret nuclear experiment in the ionosphere, and this one was kept secret not from the Russians for military reasons, but from the American people, because of possible objections to the fall-out. The *Times* kept the secret till the Russians were about to publish it, explaining (March 19, 1959), that "it had learned of the plans for Project Argus last summer, some weeks before it took place. Nevertheless, scientists associated with the government said they feared that prior announcement of the experiment might lead to protests that would force its cancellation." A. J. Muste, an editor of *Liberation* magazine, asked them for an apology for this unexampled betrayal of journalistic responsibility, and got the astounding reply:

> It seems to me that you are suggesting that the *Times* enter the propaganda field and, in effect, set its judgment above that of military men and scientists as to what can be published. . . . After all, the *Times* is a responsible newspaper. [!!] [Robert Garst, Assistant Managing Editor. In *Liberation,* May, 1959.]

But what is the effect on our people when we are told that our chief newspaper does not print the news? Constitutionally, for instance, *how in a democracy do they then deserve their mailing privileges, to circulate their official press releases and advertisements for department stores?* [The purpose of second-class mail is to circulate information.] When Muste wrote a letter for publication about the *Times'* handling of the story, the *Times* found no space for that letter.

But to my mind, even more important is the effect of cutting people off from the adventure of science, no matter what the risks. What an illiberal and dishonorable policy to pursue! Our government cannot see that noble things must not be made base, romance must not be turned into disillusion, or what will become of the young people? Take another example. This glorious enterprise of space! And now we have chosen seven astronauts for special training. But the nemesis of the organized system haunts us. All prove to be white Protestant, in their early or middle thirties, married, with small children, and coming from small towns—in brief, models of salesmen or junior executives for International Business Machines. And these seven have now made a solemn pact, reported in the press, that whichever one goes aloft will split evenly with the others his take from syndicated stories and TV appearances. Concerning them, Dr. George Ruff, the Air Force psychiatrist who tested them, has explained, "Knowing the qualities that made them this way, and working hard at applying those qualities in your daily life, can help you [too] to come closer to achieving what they have become: comfortable, mature, and well-integrated individuals. It's a worth-while goal."

Of course, by this writing (June 1960), it is commonly accepted that our new Midas satellite has the *function* of espionage. But it has remained for a proper scientist to hit the bottom: the professor who has advised us *not* to reply to any signals we might receive from outer space, because the astral beings are likely to be technically more advanced than we and they will come down and eat us up. This projection of the Cold War into the starry vault was favorably reported by the science editor of the *Herald Tribune*.

6

In the time of Washington, the public men—Adams, Jefferson, Madison, Marshall, Henry, Franklin, Hamilton, Jay—were a fair sampling of the good spirits in the country, humane, literate, brave, not self-seeking. (There is a remarkable letter of Jefferson's to David Rittenhouse, urging him to waste no more time in mere politics, for the world needed him more in his capacity as a scientist.) By and large, it could not be said of our presidents and governors at present, the symbols of the country, that they are a fair sampling of the best of us. It would not be difficult to make a list of a hundred, or two hundred, who are superior to them in every relevant way, in whom a boy could feel pride and trust.

Of course this is not a new trouble among us. Just as the European writers of the eighteenth century idolized our statesmen as if they were demigods, so in the nineteenth they spoke of their inferiority. This is the consequence of another missed revolution, the democratic revolution. A man of sense obviously cannot waste his life learning to sue to an ignorant electorate and coming up through political ranks in which disinterestedness and pure convictions are not the most handy virtues. Yet the fault is not with democracy, but that we have failed to have enough of it. For instance, if our emphasis had been on perfecting the town meeting and the neighborhood commune, there would not be ignorant electors and they would choose great officers. If people had the opportunity to initiate community actions, they would be political; they would know that finally the way to accomplish something great is to get together with the like-minded and directly do it.

But the men in power do not think politically either. For instance, this year we have had the usual spectacle of politicians going about the country looking for nominators for the Presidency, presumably (why else?) because they have important new programs to offer. But as soon as it becomes clear that the county leaders of the party do not want them, they retire from the race and rally to elect whomever. What becomes of the programs? Since this is what political responsibility means to a politician, why should the electorate respect politics, and how could an honest boy be inspired to enter on such a career?

In a recent essay, the historian Henry Steele Commager asks how it is possible that we have an absolute dearth of statesmen at present in America (he cannot think of one). Characteristically, we have an immense amount of formal training in flourishing institutes for public administration at Harvard, Princeton, Syracuse, Tufts, etc., as if we could get the thing by learning the role. Commager sensibly concludes that that training does not begin early enough and it lacks the content of actual experience. The environment does not encourage public service, it does not esteem public goods. Few fathers give much thought to the distant generations of posterity, and children do not take fire in reading about the great men of history and thinking "Why not I?" as a plausible purpose. And finally, says Commager, the narrow chauvinism and energetic hostility to subversive ideas that are now the test of our politicians are precisely disastrous to patriotism, for that must be spacious, disinterested, and broad-based, otherwise it is intolerable foolishness. Let me quote a fine passage:

> The men who won our independence and laid the foundations of the American nation were devoted patriots but they were, too, men of the world. They were children of the enlightenment. Reason taught them that all men were brothers, that purely national distinctions were artificial, that there existed a great community of arts and letters and philosophy and science cutting across and transcending mere national boundaries. . . . The nationalism of the eighteenth century did not rest on a narrow base but on a broad one. It did not find nourishment in fear and suspicion but in faith and confidence. Perhaps one reason for the decline in statesmanship is that we have hemmed our potential statesmen in, we have denied them tolerant and spacious ideas.

As it is, what must be the effect on a boy when he comes to realize that the public spokesman up there is not even speaking his own words, but repeating, like a performer, something written for him by a staff from Madison Avenue? The boy must learn to shout, "Shame! make your own speech at least!"

Our present President (Mr. Eisenhower) is an unusually uncultivated man. It is said that he has invited no real writer, no artist, no philosopher to the White House. Presumably he has no intellectual friends; that is his privilege. But recently he invited the chief of the Russian government to a banquet and musicale. And the formal music of that musicale was provided by a Fred Waring band playing "Oh, What a Beautiful Morning" and such other numbers. This is disgraceful.

7

The American landscape has been badly corrupted. European writers no longer even notice the natural wonder of it, they are so put off by the ugliness and conformity of the towns. But worse than the ugliness and conformity is the neglect that baffles pride of place. Our poets try to move themselves by nostalgically repeating the names of towns: "Biloxi and Natchez, Pascagoula and Opelousas"—but beware of paying a visit.

The Americans disesteem public goods, and improving the landscape is a big expense. Historically, the neglect of appearance and plan of our scores of thousands of villages and small towns, especially in the Middle West and South—the diner, the Woolworth's, and two filling stations—can be analogized to the neglect of the present-day poor. In the tide of expansion, appearance was disregarded as not essential; later, the matter would be mopped up. But the neglect rigidifies, it is a hard core not easy to change.

Instead, the present tendency is to impose on the countryside a new corporation style altogether, in the form of shopping centers (= national chain supermarkets) on the highway. This works out disastrously for the communities, for these "centers" are not centers of villages, and there cease to be villages at all, simply scattered family houses. This is the end of a long process of disruption, for in any case the industry is gone, the men work in plants thirty miles away. It is possible to travel many miles even in New England and not see a single activity a man could make a living at, except automobile agencies and filling stations; not even a food store. The schools too are large and centralized. The families tend to move away frequently, but even while they are put, they are driving around. This does not make much community to grow up in.

In more primitive societies, a chief community activity is working together, thatching a roof, net fishing. But with us, precisely this co-operative labor, for instance the work in a factory, is removed from its community setting and emptied, by the relations of production, of any community spirit.

Places that have no shape have no face-to-face functioning, for the shape *is* the functioning community. The loveliness of so many hamlets in Europe is that they have shape and are built of local materials by local craft. Perhaps the people had to cluster to attend early masses. In Ireland, where they farm out the back door, the rows of thatched houses line both sides of a little street. In France, where men go off to their farms, there may be a square. In our own early New England villages, where congregational and political spirit was strong, there was a common green with public buildings, though the families lived scattered on the farms they worked. There was the shape of a community, with its economy, its crafts, and its ideas. The advantage of growing up in such a community in one's early years is evident. It is not family supervision, on which the physicians of juvenile delinquency are now laying such stress; quite the contrary! it is that the family does *not* have to bear the burden of teaching the culture. In a community, everybody knows the child face to face. There is an easy grading of overlapping ages, right up to the adults who are going about their business in a going concern, and not paying too much attention to children. A good city neighborhood works in the same way.

From this point of view, the swarm of kids in a city housing project form a better community than present-day country boys or the kids on Park Avenue. *Therefore* they have more local patriotism. The bother with this community chain, however, is that it terminates abruptly before it reaches the adults, who belong to a different world; so the kids are a gang and the local community spirit turns into loyalty to a Code; it does not eventuate in anything socially cohesive and culturally worth while. And such a gang is prone to be delinquent because, as we shall see, in such conditions it is the forbidden that best cements loyalty.

Politically, a delinquent gang is not lawless and not in the state of nature. Balked in its growth, the local loyalty turns on itself and simply reinvents the feud-code of Alfred the Great, marking out safe territories and making provision for special classes of revenge. On this view, if one teen-age gang, pursuing its vendetta, falls on another and murders a kid, it would not be our business to interfere in the law of that differently constituted society. Also, like Danes or Vikings of Alfred's time, they regard our larger society merely as a field of sport and plunder; they have not yet reinvented International Law. But we, of course, cannot view it so, for we live in an advanced state of politics and law: they are members of our community. We are not children but more experienced and somewhat wiser, and therefore responsible, so we cannot simply annihilate them like pirates (they are small in size, few in numbers, and armed with primitive weapons); and we cannot let them hurt themselves.

(I think it is wise sometimes to regard disaffected groups as if there *were* plausibly these two viewpoints, rival patriotisms. It is better humanity and it might make better law. The advantage is that it takes the disaffected seriously as disaffected, rather than merely pathological; it keeps in the foreground the question of allegiance. We must *deserve* allegiance.)

## 8

But they are children. Let us consider rather the peculiar patriotic problem of an older disaffected group, the Beat young men, for then we can see that it *is* a patriotic problem.

Here too, I think, there has often been a strong community influence of growing up together. For instance, fellows who went to Black Mountain College, which was oriented to community and creative arts—a powerful, and powerfully disaffecting, combination—are pillars of Beat society. Other fellows were buddies in the armed services. However it was, as Beat their community spirit is strong. They barge in to sleep, they share property, they share a culture. Now think of this community, disaffected from America, as engaged in a pathetic quest for some other big patriotism, an adult peer group.

We saw how, appointing themselves outcast, they affirm the accidental symbols of other outcast groups: Negro, Puerto Rican, and criminal. But this is pretty thin gruel for intellectual young men, many of whom have been to college. On the other hand, they are unable to make the jump to the great international humanist community because, simply, they don't know anything, neither literature nor politics. (I once taught at Black Mountain College, and to my astonishment I found that the students had never read the Bible, Milton, Dryden, Gibbon, etc., etc., nor did they feel—as a lack—that such things existed. But they knew odd facts about Mayan hieroglyphics which their teacher had been interested in.)

What then? Since it is necessary for grown fellows to have some major allegiance or other, they have latched on to the dead Japanese masters of Zen Buddhism. (This is a late effect of the early-century discovery of Japan by Fenollosa, Frank Lloyd Wright, the Misses Lowell and Ayscough, and Ezra Pound, suddenly reinforced by the postwar occupation under General MacArthur.) Now, as we shall see, Zen is *not* irrelevant to these young men's needs, for it is a theology and style of immediate experience. But the pathos is that Zen was the flower of an intensely loyal feudal system that fed, protected, and honored its masters, and to which the Zen masters in turn had fealty. For example, it is said that the haiku was invented by a poet as a public service when he was suicidally despondent because his Emperor had died. But Zen without farmers and servants is an airy business; and the young men, as we have seen, are betrayed into dubious devices to keep body and soul together, nor do they have a flag to salute.

9

I have tried broadly to paint some of the background conditions that discourage patriotism: the lack of bona fides about our liberties, the dishonorable politics in the universities, the irresponsible press, the disillusioning handling of the adventure in space, the inferior and place-seeking high officers of the State, the shameful neglect of our landscape and the disregard of community; later I shall speak of our trivial leisure which has no community meaning. But besides these not usually mentioned background conditions, there are of course the persistent immediate uglinesses that everybody talks about and every child sees: the cases of graft, social injustice, stupid law, and injustice to persons. Yet in an important sense, these scandals do not discourage patriotism, so long as there is the feeling of a persistent effort against them. My guess is that more pride of country is engendered by one good decision, or even a good powerful dissenting opinion, of the at least traditional Supreme Court, than by billions of repetitions of the pledge of allegiance.

Racial segregation and prejudice destroy community by definition, and we need not discuss them. Here again the revolution commenced in Jefferson's time and recommenced by the abolitionists, went unfinished; and we have inherited the consequences.

But it is perhaps useful to point out again that, when there is prejudice, the community of the dominant class is equally destroyed. The whites in the South, for instance, used to talk a blatant patriotism and a specious regionalism grounded in nothing but keeping the blacks under. The result is that flag and cross have become contemptible in their own eyes. (Real regionalism, that finds its culture and satisfaction in its own geography and economy and can withstand the temptations of the national cash-nexus, has long ago succumbed to Madison Avenue, Hollywood, and Wall Street.) Now that law and religion side against them, the Southerners are maniac with wounded conceit and sexual fear; their behavior on integration should be referred not to the Attorney General but to the Public Health Service. All this has come banging down on the children as the battleground. Yet, paradoxically, among all young people it is perhaps just the young people in the South, whites and Negroes both, who most find life worth living these days, because something real is happening. During the Montgomery bus boycott against Jim Crow, there was little delinquency among the Negro boys.

(In Northern cities and towns, also, the children are thrown into a central position in the community crisis of exclusion and prejudice, but sometimes as peacemakers. Let me give an interesting architectural example. It has become common to use the new centralized school building as the community building for meetings and recreation. One reason is economy. But another reason that is given is that the school is the one community function that brings together the otherwise discordant elements in the neighborhood, so maybe the adults can get together in the school. It is a curious situation when the grownups have to rely on the children to make sense for them, and when the school building is the chief community building. But it is better than nothing.)

## 10

Deep in the organized system itself there has been an important new effort toward community. The postwar boom in young marriages and the sensational rise in the urban birth rate that for the first time promises to surpass the rural birth rate, have been accompanied by the moving of affluent workmen to suburban projects and of the middle status to ranch houses. These new settlements devote time and energy to common interests. Do they do anything for local patriotism?

They are communities for small children, one to five, and for women as the mothers of small children. These are the groups in society unequivocally benefited by high production, full employment, and the high standard of living. They thrive on animal security. Labor-saving devices make the world of the infants much pleasanter. Morally and vocationally, there is no question that having and caring for the children is justified work for the mothers, necessary, honored, and using good human capacities. Nearly forty years ago, H. L. Mencken pointed out in his book on women that women had real jobs, whereas men were likely to be certified public accountants or politicians. Today, when so many work in the Rat Race, few would deny that he was right.

So now men too try earnestly to devote themselves to the small ones as a secondary but real career. This is called the New Fatherhood.

The child world, in the suburbs and surrounding country, and somewhat less in the city, is the best that small children have had in modern times. The new psychology of belonging is feeble stuff, but the new psychology of infant care has been radical: no toilet training, permissive thumb sucking and pre-genital sexuality, free crying and movement, exposure to the grownups' naked-ness, honest answers to questions. The new medicine gets them quickly over the usual diseases (though there is debate about the later consequences). The school system as a whole is poor, but the nursery schools are often first-rate, progressive, and have intelligent and dedicated young teachers. It is said that children's toys and games are excellent, practical and imaginative, up to the age of six, when the commercial criteria of the eleven-billion-dollar market begin to operate.

For the adults, the improvement of this child's world results in genuine community participation, committee meetings and lectures on psychology, concern for traffic and zoning, and even extension courses in cultural subjects to create the proper atmosphere for growing up. It seems astonishing, given so much active participation, that these community activities have not much de-veloped into other important political and social action. But courage gives out at the political issues relevant to age six. The sponsorship and control of the organized system are everywhere apparent.

(For instance, in a recent agitation that has prevented Negroes from moving into Deerfield, a suburb of Chicago—average income $9,000–10,000— an "attractive young married couple" explained that most of their friends had most of their money tied up in their houses: "We don't expect to live in them very long. Some of the junior execs expect to become seniors and move to the real North Shore, and a lot of us will be transferred all over the United States. When this happens, we want to be sure our houses have resale value." [Reported in the *New York Times,* April 17, 1960.] The spiritedness of this speaks for itself.)

Unfortunately, when the adults devote themselves thus to the child's world, there isn't much world for the child to grow up into in the next stage. For Father to guide his growing son, it is necessary for him to have a community of his own and be more of a man. In the circumstances this is difficult. But if there is no big environment, there are no grounds for patriotism.

The corporations, however, have now entered into this arena too, to organize the next stage of growing up. This is the meaning, surely, of the publicity that has been trumped up for the Little League, the baseball teams of subteen-agers sponsored and underwritten by various business firms. What value the Little League has as play, I don't know, I haven't watched games. The high-pressure advertising has been violently denounced by the older sports writers as giving kids an unsportsmanlike taste for publicity. As a school of rule making, responsibility, and impersonality, the Little League certainly cannot compare with the free games of the street, but we saw that these have been passing away. Economically, however, the function of the Little League is clear-cut: it is child labor, analogous to ten-year-olds picking hemp in the factory a century ago: it keeps idle hands out of mischief; it is not profitable as production, but it provides valuable training in attitude and work habits.

Viewed so, the suburban and exurban trends are the formation of a new proletariat, producers of offspring.

## 11

Naturally the Public Relations have been unable to restrain themselves from invading the public schools. The classes are flooded with pamphlets and documentary films on electronics and the introduction of cows into New Zealand, put out by Consolidated Edison, Ford, Shell, Westinghouse, the National Dairy Council, Union Carbide, Bell, etc., and even Merrill Lynch. These proclaim their sponsorship with more or less discreet plugs.

In the ninth grade, however, at a New York City school I know well, they have spent class time with an item called *The Educational ABC's of Industry,* a collection of advertisements interlarded with reading matter; and the class was actually required, by a teacher distracted by overwork, to copy out jingles in which C stands for Orange-*Crush,* "taste it and see," and F for the *Ford* Motor Company, "where the first car grew." I would gladly share this literature with the reader, but its publisher has not given me permission.

## Radicalism and the Skipped Generation
## 1969

**Renata Adler**

In May, 1969, as I was watching *Another World,* Lee Randolph died. I had bought my television set more than two years before, after going to California to do a piece about the Sunset Strip. Buying the set had nothing to do with the piece at all, or any piece. But on assignment, in the sunny upper rooms of the Chateau Marmont in Los Angeles, I had had a case of laryngitis so extreme that I couldn't speak, even whisper on the telephone, and when I was not following the flower children of the Strip about, I stayed in my room watching daytime television—the soap operas, and when they were not on, the quiz programs. I became seriously preoccupied by them. The NBC peacock, with the announcement "the following program is brought to you in living color," was frustrating, even reproachful on a hotel room's black and white. When I got home, I bought a color set, my first TV, a Zenith Space Command with remote control, which I could operate from my bed.

For two and a half years—until now, in fact—I watched *Another World, The Doctors, Love of Life, Search for Tomorrow, Days of Our Lives,* and later *Hidden Faces* (I have never cared for *Secret Storm* or *Edge of Night*) whenever I could, and nearly always when I thought I should be doing other things. They had their tired stretches. I missed some crucial episodes. But when Lee Randolph died, a suicide who had lingered on for weeks, I watched her face being covered by a sheet, and I was ridden by the event for weeks. I suppose the script for Lee had run out, or that the actress had found another part. But it was not at all like losing a character in fiction of any other kind—not just an event in a two or ten hour imaginative experience, and then in memory. The soap operas ran along beside life five days out of seven. I saw the characters in them more often than my friends, knew their relationships, the towns. It had a continuity stronger even than the news, where stories and characters submerge and reappear—or don't—depending on where the limelight is. I know of no more constant, undisjunct narrative than the soap operas. Perhaps they are what personal life was like, before the violent, flash discontinuities of media news and personal air travel came along.

I had thought of my soap hours as a total waste of time, not a joke, not camp, not for a piece, not critically, a serious waste of time. But when the loss of Lee became such an important thing, I found that those two-and-a-half-year, open-ended narrative experiences define a lot of what I am and what I think, what I would like to write, what I think America, particularly a certain age and voice group, is, and what I think the American radical and intellectual communities are not. I guess I am part of an age group that, through being skipped, through never having had a generational voice, was forced into the broadest possible America. Even now (and we are in our thirties), we have no journals we publish, no exile we share, no brawls, no anecdotes, no war, no solidarity, no mark. In college, under Eisenhower, we were known for nothing, or for our apathy. A center of action seemed to have broken down in us. Lacking precisely the generational tie (through the media, mainly, kids now know about other kids) and just after the family unit began to dissolve, we knew what there was of our alienation privately, and not yet as a claim or a group experience. We now have vertical ties, loves, friendships, loyalties to people older, younger, other than ourselves. We are unnoticed even as we spread clear across what people call, without taking account of us, the generation gap.

I think that is our special note—we cut across. Across ages, idioms, stresses, cultural values, memories. At a moment of polarization, and other clichés that drain the language of meaning, the continuity of the American story seems to rest just now in us. The first age group to experience in its youth a murderous overvalue on precocity (which leads now to an idiot generational impasse), we held back. We grew up separately, without a rhetoric, drawing our ideas from age and cultural groups already formed, as we were not. The idiom of *Another World* is no more foreign to us than *The Green Hornet*, Joseph Conrad, *The New York Review of Books*, bourbon no more or less our own than marijuana is. Unaware of each other until now, we are in it all. Some of us have dropped a generation back, to lead a student movement that belies everything we are. Others have taken their positions quietly, in society as it was before we came and as, in the years of its most annihilating smugness, it nearly killed us off. But most of us, I think, were formed and remain one by one—formed by books and by the media, but, through the accident of our span of history, formed alone. And now I think we are a force.

In a way, in culture and in politics, we are the last custodians of language —because of the books we read and because history, in our time, has wrung so many changes on the meaning of terms and we, having never generationally perpetrated anything, have no commitment to any distortion of them. Lacking slogans, we still have the private ear for distinctions, for words. I happen to know no one who regularly watches *Another World* (although millions of Americans clearly do), or who would watch it—except to do a piece of materialism, escapism, pop culture or something. But that is the point. I know of no one whose cultural and political experience I completely share. And yet there are elements of my soap hours that seem common to a particular, still unaccounted-for sort of activist in early middle years: on the set, a sense of the human condition and the rhythm of life, with endless recapitulations for those who have not been watching, going forward; in ourselves, the bouts of muteness, watching and inertia, the sense of work one ought to do in what is going on, the patience with continuity, even the nostalgia for a kind of corniness. And always a characteristic quality of attention, at a certain humorous remove from our own experience. Lacking an idiom entirely our own, we cannot adopt any single voice without a note of irony. (I can't write about the soap operas, or anything that does not make specific, human claims for action on my part, with perfect seriousness.) A suspicion of glibness or fluency has made the generation immediately after us value the rhetorical and inarticulate. Not us. We all seem to view the world still in words, as writers, arguers, archivists—even, perhaps even especially, those who do not write. In strange times, we have kept our language, energies and heads. (It is no surprise that the disturbances at San Francisco State dissolved under police called in by one—albeit aging and not very profound—semanticist.) And we are here.

I think the historical bridge and the moral limits of our experience—mine anyway—were defined in World War II, which most of us still remember as The War. Totalitarianism, freedom, genocide, courage, passion, gentleness, a community of decent men, most of my conceptions of idealism, the monstrous and the public world date from that war, in which we were too young to have a part. And the bland repressions and unacknowledged disillusion of the succeeding years. Everyone looked alike or tried to, every sort of maverick was cut off and lost. Art was the province of ladies' painting and lecture clubs; intelligence was subsumed in the grand idea of American know how. The schools were levellers for the general mediocrity; unions, parodying their origins and aims, were becoming entrenched forces for corruption and reaction. Odd cliffs were papered over. When, on his birthday in 1956, Adam Clayton Powell announced his support for Dwight David Eisenhower for president, the Republican candidate sent a birthday present to the people of Harlem—white trucks full of black cupcakes—and the present was graciously received. The dream everywhere was going flat. Teachers, who had begun in the Depression when, on the basis of their regular salaries, they could afford maids and were considered rich, were now poorer, embittered and threatened by any sort of difference. In small towns, in a travesty of the New Deal dream of education, teachers had risen above their own class to the extent that their brothers and their colleagues' brothers—contractors and factory workers—were no longer good enough for them. They seldom married. They subscribed to the Book of the Month Club and *Reader's Digest* and shared the general passion for the ordinary. Our rebellions then, in the years when the sum of hope was to be adjusted and popular, when boys still broke themselves at team sports on a military model, which would never be of use to them again (when, in fact, people still spoke of the Army for anybody as making a man of him), were separate and one by one, and threw us back, unknowing, on the past. Some of us cut school and invented juvenile delinquency, others read.

What I am trying to say is that if there is any age group that should loathe what is called the System in its bones that group is us. We had it, in spite of Korea, at its height—the years when society was going, to its own satisfaction, so extremely well; when telephones, neon signs, subways, Western Union worked, as they haven't since; and when, through and after Senator Joseph McCarthy, the spirit of the redneck, the junior college and the drum majorette had spread so deep into the land. I think the first post-war jolt the System had in its complacency, in our time, was not social or humanitarian, but technological: in 1957, when Sputnik went up. After that, there began to be a little room for change and mavericks, who, when there is not a desperate community lie at the heart of things, are the rule. But in the interim, before the general boredom had begun to lift, we, one by one, had made some beginnings, some progress on all the public and private fronts that now exist—frontiers that polarization, paradoxically, obscures and language has to be hard won and individual to approach at all.

Accessible, almost by generational default, to all the idioms of America, we also went overseas. We were the first non-military age group to travel internationally on an almost national scale. We knew, since we had been at the mercy of institutions so utterly, what institutions were like at home, and what American tourists were like, and were treated like, abroad. But there is a particular totalitarian lie at the heart of political cliché too, and the simplicities of "imperialism," "genocide," "materialism," "police brutality," "military-industrial complex," "racism," tossed about as though they were interchangeable, and as though they applied equally to anything with which one is out of temper, are not for us. Neither are the simplicities of anti-Communism, free world, "violence," and "radicalism" itself. We observed in The War the literal extreme of violence that men have done so far. Since then, bombs dropping on villages, cops beating kids on the head, kids throwing bottles at cops, the violence to the spirit of the McCarthy years, the violation of human dignity in exclusion and poverty—there is a degree of violence in them all, but a difference of degree, an extent of metaphor, and we still distinguish among literalisms, metaphors, questions of degree. Or radicalism. A radicalism that draws its terms from the System's violence in Vietnam, then claims to be driven to revolutionary violence of its own, and, as an act of revolution, turns upon the liberal universities has an inauthentic ring, a ring of sublimation, theater. If revolutionary outrage over Vietnam had had a substantive thrust of Guevara courage on the line, there would have been American brigades fighting for Hanoi—a disaster for the country, surely, but a disaster in authentic terms. (The white revolutionary movement certainly left the American South, where the physical risk was high, fast enough.) There is an authentic radicalism in this country now, but it does not abuse the metaphor of revolution. It is not the radicalism of rhetoric, theater, mannerism, psychodrama, air. And it is not paralyzed in its own unconsummated moral impulses by viewing every human problem at a single level of atrocity.

I think what has muddled terms, what has emptied vocabularies into rhetorics and made generations out of what are only persons after all, is, in the end, a major implication of The War. Ours was the first age group to experience the end of the Just War as a romantic possibility. There are no justifications for group violence in this country any more—no outlets for aggressive physical courage, irrational fervors, the fraternity of the barricades and the decent human war. And there aren't likely to be any. Technology has made the stakes too high. We knew that separately, saw the last great romantic group fight to the death, and knew we could never have one of our own. That sounds like a blessing, and perhaps historically it is, but it puts a tremendous strain on any generation of young. From now on, it is all patient effort, un-simple victories. In this, the Vietnam War was a hiatus in normal terms. The System lifted the vocabulary of the just war, in the name of the free world, to Vietnam, and found it did not work. Radicalism lifted essentially the same vocabulary and turned it, in the name of revolution, against the System, where it does not work either. The very fact that radicalism leans so comfortably, half-consciously, upon the System and its laws, goes on almost risk-free, beside *Another World,* confirms that the System's thrust is still, on an unprecedented scale, democratic and benign. No famous or privileged white revolutionaries have gone to jail for long just yet. But obscure and black radicals have, in numbers—which raises questions, I think, not so much of politics as of fame, privilege and the inauthentic revolutionary.

What these pieces, looking back, are about, if anything, is true radicalism as opposed to what I would call the mere mentality of the apocalypse. The apocalyptic vision has never been true to the America we know. By some accident of our size, our mix, our resources and the perfectibility of our laws, brinks vanish here and become frontiers, immense real tensions are resolved in a paradigm of the modern world, material resources make it possible to pose moral and social questions which have never been approached on such a scale before. I think that is where we are—we who have lived from The War till now—not too old or tired to give the whole thing up, not too young to remember a time when things were worse. And, through the accident of our span of years, not too simple in the quality of our experience to know that things get better (The War's end) and worse (the succeeding years) and better again (the great movement of nonviolence sweeping out of the South to move the country briefly forward a bit) and, of course, worse. But when a term like violence undergoes, in less than thirty years, a declension from Auschwitz to the Democratic convention in Chicago, from A-bombing even to napalm, the System has improved. Terribly and with stumbling, but improved. And there are characters in these pieces—mocked for their tokenism when they succeeded, claimed as radical martyrs when they failed or died—who burned themselves out over an inch of that improvement. Which is how the human condition, in its historical continuity, or real radicalism, in its social framework, works at all.

But with the closing of The War option, with the loss of final and romantic victories, there is a tendency, particularly among intellectuals and the young, and oddly accelerated by an obscene confluence of psychoanalysis and the media, to think in terms of final solutions anyway. To use the vocabulary of total violence, with less and less consciousness of its ingredient of metaphor, to cultivate scorched earth madness as a form of consciousness (of courage, even), to call history mad, and to dismiss every growing, improving human enterprise as a form of tokenism, an irrelevance in which one has no obligation to take part. The System drew back from its apocalypse in Vietnam—always draws backs from brinks so far—restrained, in spite of everything, the full force of its technology. But the scorched earth psychology remains, particularly on the Left. I happened to encounter that psychology, long before Vietnam, first in the arts, when I was reviewing books. The professional alienist in fiction, the group polemicist in criticism, the unearned nihilist and overeasy break-through artist in mixed media, the blown mind vanguardist in the audience. Then (except for a few reviews of what I considered genuine, private innovators: "Conversations," "Instruments") I found I was doing a lot of overeasy polemic of my own, and I gave it up—except for one last piece on the breakthrough artists: "Selling an Enraged Bread Pudding."

Reporting was better, but somehow the apocalyptic sensibility had moved into politics too, into every part of life. Its earmarks were clenched teeth, personal agonies, rhetoric, the single plane of atrocity view of Western man, above all, a psychoanalytic concept of moral responsibility—based, not on conscience, which is exercised in substantive action, but on guilt, which is appeased in confession, sublimation, symbolic purge. Confessions were every-where. The guilt became retroactive, vicarious, unappeasable: a country, in-curably genocidal, and founded on a genocide; white Western man, blood insatiable, leaving nothing but war, exploitation and pollution in his wake. No matter that none of us (and few of our isolated, refugee fathers either) were here a hundred years ago to kill an Indian, that countless nations—India, for one—were founded by invasions that exterminated aborigines, that there have always been wars, within the limits of available technology, wherever man is (notably tribal slaughters in Africa, and in Vietnam ever since the Annamites), that Western powers have been the first to try to come to terms with an international responsibility for social, medical meliorism and military restraint. (With, of course, grotesque lapses. The question is whose mistakes there is time to be patient with.) Guilt, atrocity, the luxurious mystique of the everybody else, which liberates from responsibility for one's own time and place. There was a special radical infatuation with religions of the Orient, notably Hinduism and Zen—which produced, as it happens, some of the most repellent, anti-humanist, repressive and belligerent social systems in man's history. A let-them-starve-on-earth-Nirvana sensibility caught on among a Third World-infatuated contingent of radicals.

There was nothing to show for the apocalyptic sensibility on any front— not in art, not in politics, not in mind expansion (a ghastly misnomer), not even in the apocalyptic-pornographic view of sex—no breakthroughs, only gesture, celebrity quietism, rage, symptom, backlash. Not Rimbaud and Baudelaire, child mutations of John Dewey and Freud. Symptoms do have their real effects on the status quo (even *Another World* has its impact on the world out here), but the effects were mindless, random, dumb, a non-negotiable demand to dismantle the human experiment and begin again. A view of evil as banal was distorted into a view of banality as evil, and of all meliorism as boring and banal. Intellectual cartwheels, bad art, spite politics (I gave up reporting that after "Radicalism in Debacle" at the Palmer House), and a happy collusion, by default, with the worst elements of the System: pure huckster fashion and the red-neck Right. (It is not unthinkable that, except for the broader evolution of America, we should all be called one day before an investigating committee composed of Strom Thurmond, Tom Hayden and some suitable representative of pop art and café society.) And fame: the cry of alienation made good fellows and good copy. The gesture and rhetoric of revolution were well suited to that natural creator of discontinuous, lunatic constituencies, the media.

I think radicalism's flirtation with the media, its overvalue on personal image, personal sensibility, pure air, was nurtured by the spirit of the Kennedys. Their beauty, promise, absolute lack of delivery, and their power—a power which found its major application, in the end, only in controlling the image that the country was to have of them. I don't mean anything about the sincerity of the men themselves; I mean what they came to represent. The notion that you can love glamour and be concerned with grit, that you can promise in prose and never quite deliver in fact, that as long as power is wrested into the right hands (one's own) good will follow in time, the gap between image and substance, impulse and legislation—the country was simultaneously over-stimulated and corrupted by these princelings of the air. Working for Senator Joseph McCarthy, silent in the censure vote, wiretapping, Mayor Daley, segregationist judges in the South, the logic of the Bay of Pigs and Vietnam (if Cuban exiles couldn't do it, American counterinsurgents could: win an easy, a "little war"), losing cufflinks simultaneously to blacks with hopes and white auto workers armed against the possibility that a black should ever live in peace beside them—none of it fit. It generated unreason and violence. All these disparities could be considered part of a personal process of education, or seem to be reconciled on some higher symbolic plane, but they were not true to the country, to the real balance and struggle of huge forces that is here. President Johnson, I think, delivered substantively on all that promise: the social legislation and, alas, the war. But Kennedyism, cut off en route, stayed in the air, style, media power, personal packaging. Suddenly there were too many stars, too many artists, too many who thought the world well lost for their own image and sensibilities. The new enemy was boredom, in the sense of lack of drama. The new currency was fame. With special implications for the intellectuals. Ours has not been a great thirty years for intellectuals. We saw, and survived, anti-intellectualism in this country, but we also saw a generation of intellectuals—Stalinist at the time of Stalin, quiescent in the McCarthy years, mesmerized by the power and beauty of the Kennedys, nerveless in the face of the radical redneck young—always weak, always somehow lifeless and wavering in the face of force and violence. But through it all, we saw something infinitely fragile and viable in the System, in its accommodations with radicals, rednecks, soldiers, blacks, thinkers, visionaries, lunatics, the ordinary, getting better.

I guess a radical middle, in age and in politics, acts out of a consciousness of how much has been gained, how far there is to go, and what there is to lose. It is content to be obscure—to measure and implement accommodations with the System: how many blacks and former poor in jobs, unions, polling booths, public office, neighborhoods, even in soap operas, how many soldiers withdrawn, how many arms unmade, how many material, aesthetic and technological advances applied to ameliorating the human condition, how to divorce liberalism from arrogance and violence. Not many advances, but some. Enough to stay aboard and to maintain distinctions on every side: to get the unpolarized student to his class without having him clubbed or teargassed by a cop—who is not too good at making distinctions either.

We have lived after all through two sunny periods of lies, and seen some of the truth in both of them: the Eisenhower lie that the noble American experiment was complete, that all was well, that there was no need to move; and the Kennedy era lie that with glamour, image and the instantaneous application of power you can gratify immediately, totally, those human concerns that are, in reality, met by inches, by years of work and suffering. I believe that the generation gap is in part an almost meterological collision of those airs, the two lies of those years. Some have moved and see no reason why anyone else should rock the boat: others, impatient with the slowness of motion, see no reason to move at all until the coming of the Word. We are between. Our heroes, I suppose, mine anyway, are both famous and obscure: Martin Luther King, Bob Moses, Charles Evers, Alvin Poussaint of the Medical Committee on Human Rights, John Doar, others. Our thinkers—Hannah Arendt, Richard Rovere, Bayard Rustin, Harold Rosenberg, Daniel P. Moynihan, others—write from an awareness of precedent, of what has already been said and done and what can still be said and done, without mixing artistic and political metaphor. (Everything that has been said has, after all, been said many times.) In this collection, even in the dated or term-paper influenced pieces, there ought to be a sense of tendency, despite a suspicion of groups, of that emergent "we." We are not in the world for therapy. We are non-violent. Our values are corny ones, reason, decency, prosperity, human dignity, contact, the finest, broadest possible America. Some of us have despaired and, in the only indisputably sincere expression of the apocalyptic vision, immolated themselves. But somewhere there is a reconciliation of that auto worker and that black, not on a symbolic plane, but because history is irreversible and there is a real common interest in the rich, mixed quality of life. And three of us have just come back (substantively and yet with drama), from the way to perhaps other populations, outer limits, from the moon.

# Part Four

An American is unique among peoples.
He looks and acts like a boyman.
He never looks cruel in uniform.
He is rednecked portly rich and jolly.
White-haired serious Harvard, kind and wry.
A convention man a family man a rotary man & practical joker.
He is moonfaced cunning well-meaning & righteously mean.
He is Madison Avenue, handsome, in-the-know, and
    superstitious.
He is odd, happy, quicker than light, shameless, and heroic
Great yawn of youth!
The young don't seem *interested* in politics anymore.
Politics has lost its romance!
The "bloody kitchen" has drowned!
And all that is left are those granite
façades of Pentagon, Justice, and Department—
Politicians do not know youth!
They depend on the old
and the old depend on them
and lo! this has given youth a chance
to think of heaven in their independence.
No need to give them liberty or freedom
where they're at—

Gregory Corso

"America Politica Historia, In Spontaneity"

337

Although the general trend of the 1950s had been to deny and ignore the problems of American society, two developments made it inevitable that the following generation would have to come to terms with all aspects of American life. One was the 1954 Supreme Court decision to outlaw segregation in public schools; the other was the spread of television into most American homes. In 1950 there had been ten million television sets in the United States; by 1962 there were almost sixty million. Although it might have been possible in the fifties to disregard the Court decision or to believe it had solved the problem of segregation, the publicity through television meant that people could no longer pretend that equality had been achieved.

The 1960s began optimistically. With the inauguration of John F. Kennedy, a new spirit, a new vitality seemed to insure the realization of a New Frontier promising equal justice to all. If part of Kennedy's successful campaign derived from his attractive television personality, much of the effect of his programs depended upon constant exposure by the media. More people watched and listened to America's highest officials repeating its oldest promises, and more began to take direct, peaceful action aimed at producing social changes. The Student Nonviolent Coordinating Committee was formed to organize civil rights activities in the South, attracting dedicated young people like Jean Smith. After the first sit-ins to integrate white lunch counters, young men and women from all parts of the country came to join Freedom Rides designed to end segregation in public transportation facilities. These activities in turn awakened more citizens so that from these initial stirrings a movement grew which was able to gather over 200,000 people in Washington in August 1963, for the cause of civil rights. Young Amercians joined the Peace Corps and VISTA (Volunteers in Service to America); encouraged by new Supreme Court rulings and President Kennedy's civil rights legislation, they were determined to rid American life of segregation, poverty and misery.

But in November 1963, President Kennedy was shot. The nation watched the assassination on television, as it soon would watch scenes of rioting, burning and looting in ghettos; police clubbing, gassing and shooting demonstrators; and increasingly militant campus protests. The shock of Kennedy's death was to reverberate for years, and the country was never to recover the optimism of the early sixties. President Johnson with his plans for a "Great Society" might have been able to accomplish more than Kennedy, but he stimulated and inspired less. There were, however, more basic reasons for the change of atmosphere in America. Our military involvement in Vietnam intensified until the term "escalation" lost all meaning. Finances needed for domestic programs were diverted to the war, and among the young, concern about the nation's priorities sharpened to a growing and active resistance. A number of college and university students, who early in the sixties had learned to apply the civil rights techniques of peaceful demonstration to internal problems on their own campuses, began to focus their attention outside their own environment to the ghettos and to the war in Vietnam; and their methods of protesting changed accordingly. Like some members of the civil rights movement, they became frustrated and impatient when nonviolence brought only slow progress or none at all; they felt that most Americans could be moved by nothing but more militant behavior. The noblesse oblige of the southern mother in Flannery O'Connor's *Everything That Rises Must Converge* no longer was silently ignored by the rest of the country; and the kind of integration that William Melvin Kelley achieved at Harvard in the fifties was no longer acceptable for a concerned Black. For many Blacks in and out of college, self-definition and self-respect had to be found within their own communities; by the summer of 1965 the entire country was forced to acknowledge the problems of poverty and hatred exploding the urban ghettos. The first riot occurred in Watts; in the summers following there were more in Detroit, Newark and throughout the United States.

There were, however, other developments during the sixties which brought other kinds of hope. A revolution in cybernetics, along with technological developments surpassing those of any other nation, seemed to be making possible one dream of maximum industrial production with minimum human labor. The increased leisure and material wealth produced by these advances stimulated changes in styles of culture, such as those Barry Schwartz describes in "Youth in the Technological Era." Although the traditional American attitudes, behavior and dress remained, groups like the flower children and hippies, with long hair, beads, colors and textures never before seen in America, were the sign of the new age. Like the Beats, they were often dropouts from society and were attracted to communal living. As Ralph Gleason suggests and as the interview with Chris documents, they were alienated and dissatisfied by established patterns of living and sought with the help of mind-altering drugs to experience cosmic consciousness and to discover a more meaningful existence. Theoretically, they embodied that part of the American Dream money could not buy: freedom, self-expression and happiness. Practically, they were still disparaged by the majority of "straight" Americans who nevertheless picked up, popularized and exploited aspects of the new youth culture as they never had that of the Beats. Their dress was imitated on Main Street, the contemplative Eastern religions they followed were studied in suburbia, their music became fashionable among those who were once only metaphorically known as "long hairs," and their spokesmen attacked Establishment values on popular Establishment television shows.

For some youths rejection of conventional society meant more than stylistic and cultural changes. Members of groups like the Youth International Party (Yippies) were conscious that their defiance of traditional behavior had political implications. As the war in Vietnam continued, and public protests increased and intensified, socially concerned young people with no group identity felt the need to disassociate themselves from the forces they held responsible for destruction and death.

The events accompanying the 1968 Democratic Convention seemed to bring all the opposing forces in American society into open conflict for the first time. Along with the small number of Yippies who came to Chicago to nominate Pigasus the pig as their Presidential candidate were thousands who wanted to register their peaceful protest against the priorities and policies of the Democratic Party. Their presence was seen by many older, more conservative Americans as a threat to established processes and to "Law and Order"; when the confrontations between police and demonstrators took place, this group justified the police tactics and argued that even the bystanders who were gassed and beaten received no less than they deserved. For those, however, who participated in or supported the protests, the compulsion for order shown in Chicago seemed to destroy the possibility as well as the hopes for future nonviolent demonstrations. Jim Gardiner, a politically aware high school student, describes how his experience with the ineffectuality of conventional protest completed his disenchantment with America. In his radical analysis of society, the revolution is inevitable.

In the conspiracy trial of the Chicago Eight, which grew out of the convention disorders, many claimed that at last the worst aspects of America were emerging: repression and punishment of minorities, of youth and of all those deviating from the safe behavior characteristic of the 1950s. The extreme responses to this realization were with violence on the one hand and disinterest on the other. Because of constant personal and political frustration, a few small groups concluded that conventional protest was no longer valid; often influenced by foreign revolutionary models, they turned to acts of terrorism and destruction. A much larger group ignored politics completely. The phenomenon of Woodstock, during which three to four hundred thousand youths peacefully assembled to hear rock music, despite rain, mud and numerous other inconveniences, represented the highpoint of this kind of response. When popularized by the film industry, the media which has most captured the energies and imagination of the contemporary generation, this alternate "nation" of youth became for many the hope and promise of our country's security and creativity.

Although the majority of young Americans belonged to neither of these extreme categories, nevertheless they demonstrated, as their predecessors did not, a willingness to act for social causes. More healthy, more wealthy, more educated and also more aware of the injustices in America than any previous generation, they now confronted a dilemma more profound. Chastised in the 1950s by intellectuals for their lack of social concern, the young were now being criticized by middle America for their manners and mannerisms and in some cases punished in the streets and the courts for attempting to demonstrate their conviction and for acting upon social issues. Once again the paradox of the American myth was manifest, but now the conflict was between generations. When the young Indian girl Peter Collier discusses sought aid from older and more established members of the Bureau of Indian Affairs, she was ill-advised and almost destroyed; but by viewing her own difficulties in the context of more general racial problems and joining with other young Indian activists, she experienced for the first time a sense of purpose and accomplishment. It is this necessity to accomplish something that underlies Connell Persico's defense of student activities; a comparison between his arguments and those of Russell Kirk against the New Left further illustrates the gap between generations—a gap that has now become ideological as well as psychological.

At the end of the 1960s, however, both young and old were becoming increasingly aware of the growing threats to man's physical survival on earth: overpopulation, overconsumption and overpollution. These environmental problems were now added to the long list of causes. Space flights made man vividly aware of the unity of "this spaceship Earth"; by just looking at television, Americans could see the whole earth in perspective and were made to realize how interdependent their lives were with all other life on the planet. The ecologists' predictions became frighteningly immediate; neither America nor any other nation could afford actions which would continue to deny the promises of life to any person or country.

As the experience of America has demonstrated, the desire for an ideal society, even accompanied by the awareness of problems, is in itself no guarantee that such a society can be created. But the crises and shocks of the decade have at least awakened the consciousness of many and forced responsibility on all—whether or not they will now respond.

# Chris
## 1970

### Roderick Thorp

Chris is sixteen years old and is a sophomore in a suburban New Jersey high school. His family lives in a house appraised at $57,000, surrounded by an acre of lawn. He has used marijuana and hashish more than one hundred and fifty times. Chris knew he was talking for a tape recorder. He talked about himself, his parents, his girl, his friends, drugs, religion, school, the local police, his own future. He is a neat, clean youngster, blond, blue-eyed. His family is upper middle class. He has all the material advantages that American society takes pride in offering its young. Next year he will have a car.

There are a lot of things that I don't know about my parents. My father goes out on the road. He never talks about what he does, but I have to wonder sometimes. My parents fight. My mother wants to know if he has something going on out there. Then they fight all night. The first time I had sex—you know, intercourse—with my girlfriend, I wanted to talk to him about it. But he turned me off. I was really climbing the walls, but I couldn't talk to him. He's somebody who goes out and supports me, works like a dog, but I don't know him. I guess in his own way he thinks he loves us.

I just don't know how it is between my parents. I figure I have something better with my girl. My father comes home from being on the road, and they have some stupid fight. If I'm in the room, I just walk out and go upstairs. I can hear them screaming at each other. Then he'll sleep in the bed and she'll sleep in the family room. She'll just fall asleep in front of the TV. I come in and it's twelve o'clock and I say, "Are you going to bed now, Ma? You'd better go to bed now." And she goes, "Yeah, yeah." And I turn out the lights and I wake up in the morning and she's still sleeping there, in a chair. It happens two, three times a week.

There are things she never does when he's home. She never works late. "I've got to work until eight o'clock"—she does that when he's away. I don't know what she's doing, but I do have these thoughts.

It took me years to figure it out, but it's simple: they owe too much money. We have this big house and a pool and two cars, but the furniture is shit, all coming apart, and we eat hamburger more times in a week than I care to tell you. There just isn't any money. I had five hundred and fifty dollars saved up, but she—my mother—took it. I don't know what she used it for. She didn't even tell me she took it; one day it was just gone. It was money I earned.

The outside of our house is always neat, the lawn always cut—I should know, I'm the one who cuts it—but the inside is always a mess. No amount of cleaning is going to make a house look nice if the stuffing's coming out of the chairs. There's always dirty dishes in the sink. With all that food lying around, you're bound to attract bugs.

Let me tell you about Christmas. We've never had a Christmas like you see on television or in the magazines. One year I got three pairs of socks, three undershirts, a book, and a football game. How much is that? Why do we have a pool? There's a public pool in town. Status—keeping up. There are people on my block with three, four cars. Well, I suppose it's all right if you have a driver for every one, because you have to have a car out here. For a while my father had this Jaguar fantasy, so he bought a Jaguar. It never ran, but it was a cool car, I'll give you that. He had to give it up after six months. They fought about it—I don't remember exactly what the fighting was about, but he gave it up.

I suppose it is kind of schmucky of me to want to get married after what I've seen at home, but I have a better thing with my girl, and I can do a better job. She hasn't said that I have to give up doing grass for her, but she doesn't know half the things I've done.

Our bedroom is next to theirs and we can hear them. They fight about little things, but they scream and yell—not very often, but when they have fights, they're loud. We go on vacation together and it's a real mess, all of us piled in the station wagon together. We go up to Maine or out to Illinois. The little ones get cranky. It used to be worse when Cathy lived at home. Cathy's my older sister, she's at nursing school. My parents went together for three years before they got married, and then they had all of us children, bang, bang, bang. I asked my mother about that, and she said she never went to bed with anyone before she got married, and she doesn't expect me to, either. I guess that's why she figured I asked. Well, Joanne's already gone and done that. Joanne's my younger sister. My mother couldn't know about that from the way she sounded. Sometimes I don't know what she thinks. The other weekend she had a call from someone who said that my kid brother was saying that he was getting grass from Joanne and me. He doesn't blow grass—at least, I don't think so; he's just a snotty little kid—and, anyway, we wouldn't give him any. So she asked us if we were giving him grass, and we said no, and that was the end of it. She didn't ask us if we were using it. We both use it, but she didn't ask. Maybe she's afraid to find out.

It was a dinner party. They all got there at six-thirty. I was busy mixing whiskey sours. On the whole they were drinking three or four an hour. You know, I would go out to the kitchen, get the glasses, you know, mix the drinks, back to the living room, give them the drinks, pick up more glasses, you know, whiskey sours, martinis, everything. I learned how to mix drinks out of a book.

Finally the lady of the family who was throwing the party comes over and she goes, "Well, my husband will take over the drinks now; you go out and get lasagna out of the garage." Well, here are these two big plates of lasagna, I mean twelve pounds apiece and frozen. So I stick them in the oven. The guests have been boozing for about two hours. Some of them were getting very sloppy. One of them was cool and he came out to the kitchen and talked with me awhile, and he said, "Isn't it against the law for you to mix drinks here?" And I said it's not against the law, it's a private party and their daughter could mix them if she wanted to, but he was the only guy there to say anything.

They were all quite loud by this time. Ah, yeah, quite loud. The children come over and go, "Oh, why do they throw these parties all the time?" You know, they're down on it. They don't really dig it at all, 'cause there are all these raving maniac drunks around. What's funny is that they all sit around the table while they're consuming their liquor and this guy who wasn't drinking was a doctor, and he would just sit around and listen to this bullshit. Like they would all have cigarettes in their hands, smoking like a pack an hour— tobacco, not grass, although you never can tell. No, I don't think any of them were heads. Anyway, they're all sitting there, drinking, and they'd ask the doctor things, you know, and they'd say, "My doctor says it's not good for me to drink," sip, sip, sip. And you know, higher, and higher, and higher, or lower, whichever way they'd go. And they're all smoking and one says, "My brother's got cancer and the doctor told him to stop smoking or he'll get it again, and he still goes out and sneaks a smoke once in a while, and I'm afraid of this," and all that crap.

I don't have any thoughts about these people. This is what they got their own selves into. I don't think they enjoy going to these stinking parties when all they do is sit around the table and talk about why they shouldn't drink and smoke while they're doing it.

So it just got louder and louder. Nobody got out of hand during it all. Nobody grabbed anybody and I didn't hear any of the women let out that noise you hear at parties that's bad news. You know, they get a couple of drinks into them and they start whooping and if you're sober it's really pretty embarrassing, but it's not serious. But then there's that other noise, it has a different pitch, you know, it means trouble. It usually means somebody is going to get knocked down, and the condition they're in, somebody could hit his head on the corner of a table. You can see the wives suffering, man, it's really bad, trying to get these guys out the door. So my job was to bring the cars around in front—they had this long, curving drive, and the cars are halfway down the street. I don't have a driver's license, but anybody can drive automatic cars, so I'm bringing them around front. This one guy was in real bad shape and he needs help getting out to the car. So the hostess and the guy's wife load him onto me and I help him out to the car. He's going to drive and he's raving, mumbling about something or other. At the door of the car he pulls some money out of his pocket and pushes a twenty at me. I say, "No, thank you, I'm being paid," because he's drunk, and he takes a swing at me. I duck back just in time—it just brushes the end of my nose.

I really do not like to read for school. I like to think of a book when I read it, what I get out of it myself is my own thing. But in school, say you go into an English class and you've got your own ideas about what you've read and try to get these ideas out and here's this dumb ass up front of the class who says, "Yeah, yeah, O.K., but this is the way I think and this is the way you have to write it down on the test." So I read books that don't have anything to do with school, science fiction and such. . . .

I really know that I'm not going to college. I realize that I just couldn't take it, if it's anything like high school, I just don't like to study. I don't like to pay attention in school or anything.

I could probably be getting average grades if I studied three hours a night and paid attention in school. But I just can't. I fall asleep.

I'm pretty good in biology. And I used to be good in English, but this year I'm not doing good in that. Really, what it comes down to is I know I shouldn't go to college because it would be a waste.

I try not to worry. When I go to sleep I try to think of the things I like, but sometimes you can't help what you think. Like death. I was raised a Catholic and went to Catholic schools when I was little, so I was taught to believe in God and Christ and Mary. All I heard was that there is a God and you have to believe. But I don't know what to believe—the world is so mixed up. People are always getting killed.

It was a Friday night. We had nothing to do and one of the guys had some tabs. I don't know why I did it. All the time I had thought, I am never going to do acid. But the first time I had the chance, I popped for it.

It was so freaking small. I did half of the tab. It was so small and I was expecting to sit down and just be stoned, you know, like grass. I didn't have any idea what was going to happen to me. Well, so I'm sitting down for a half hour. All the guys were there, and two girls, I think. This was in the house of the guy who had the acid. They were smoking pot. They had done acid the night before.

They were all there, doing grass, and I started to get removed all of a sudden. There was one girl, and the other girl, who came in while I was starting to soar. I tuned in on her, I mean I got into her head.

She didn't get into mine. I got into hers. I was like on the same beam. I looked into her eyes and she was staring at the other girl, who, when I looked at her, I thought she's fucked up, you know? A mess. And she was thinking, this is one thing I never want to be. And I said to her, "I agree with you." She started to cry. She knew what I was talking about, and she was clean. She was clean.

So things started to happen to me, I was sitting down and I started to get the first vibrations, and at first I thought they were it, you know, like I had these green glasses on, you know, and the whole room, which was very small, just became huge. And I could see everybody, everybody doing everything. I had these green glasses on and I stared down at my arm, and every muscle, every vein, and every pore turned red and moving and then I got the message that something was going to happen to me that I never believed was going to happen, and so I started to get scared. I *was* scared.

I wasn't out of control. I realized that I was in trouble for the next ten or twelve hours, so I thought, I have to protect myself, I have to fight back.

So the phone rang. It was the kid's parents. They were coming home. They thought he was just having a party, and they didn't want to walk in on that. So we all had to get out—I mean, some of the kids were pretty wrecked on grass. But there was no panic, except for me. I had gone there just to drink. Anyway, I started to get very paranoid and I ran from room to room, yelling, "I've got to get out of here." All the while I was thinking, I want one of them to help me. My head was going through so many changes and they couldn't keep up. I mean, only about a minute had passed.

Now I was flying on acid, it was just the beginning, I hadn't reached the height, it was three hours after this that I started to level off. This is no good, I have got to get out, because I could not begin to know what would happen if I faced anybody, you know?

So we went over to another guy's house. I had this lump in my stomach. I was very scared, and I was starting to hallucinate. This guy's brother who's straight was feeling sorry for me. Everybody in this group felt sorry, twelve people including me, because it's deeply getting to me. So we go up to his room and they're all around and they're all talking to me. Like I would go off into a stupor and then I'd wake up, you know, and I'd gasp. I'd have these two things, you know, they were people, and they said, "We're still here, we're still talking to you." This is the love that's generated and I'm having a bad time. It wasn't a bad trip, you're just—it was a paranoiac thing because people were coming. So they're telling me, "It was better that you got out, because you can't face anybody while doing this." And they're saying, "Everything will be all right," and I know that everything isn't. I was thinking how this was going to change my life and how this was going to screw me up for the whole run of things. Finally I stopped worrying because I know that I've done the right thing, done the wrong thing by dropping it, but I've done the right thing now that I'm in the situation, by getting out. So I've done the right thing and I'm there and I'm not going to worry about it. That's the only way, because it could have gotten worse, you know, if I hadn't gotten off that stupor.

So they're all there and they start to smoke again. And now, things begin to happen, the whole screen is just, you know, vaguely outlined by pipes, you know, colored pipes, and it's just like a web, like you're really up close, and this is fantastic and scary because I can't think. It went on like this for hours; not in my head, either. Real hours.

I finished out the night walking around. It was four, four-thirty when I finally stopped hallucinating. I was really wrecked, and I couldn't go to sleep.

I ended up going around to my girl's house. I was going to wake her and tell her. She doesn't smoke—do grass or hash—or anything, but she knows that I do. She doesn't like it and keeps telling me to quit. I wanted to tell what I did and I wanted to go to her for that one reason. I wanted to tell her—and I tried.

I saw lights on—they always leave some lights on. I was knocking around and I thought, I had this whole feeling of everybody locking their doors towards me—a paranoiac reaction because I know that that household is open to me.

And then I thought, well, like if they ever found out it would wash me up completely, and so then I went home and I tried every door and now it was getting really bad because I don't have any connection there. I mean, I felt like I didn't belong there, either.

I actually did get to my girl's window. I knocked, but she didn't hear me. That was very bad. You see, I was getting into this thing. I was knocking very lightly and praying that—to God that she would wake up, you know, and that didn't work. I was afraid that she did hear me and was not opening the door. I had to have somebody that I could talk to. I ended up staying out until the sun rose. And at sunrise, right outside my house, looking up, you know, I got a very good feeling, watching the sun come up. Not staring, just watching the whole thing. That was very good. Ducks would fly over and I would blink and there would be millions of ducks flying over, and there was an inch of snow on the ground and I imagine I was freezing but I couldn't feel it, so I went up on the porch and I could see New York City and that was great, you know. In fact, you really can't see New York City from the porch, so it was a hallucination, but it was still great.

I walked along the porch, creaking boards, they were so loud, and I thought I guess they're not loud because I'm just doing this thing. So I went around the side of the house, crawled in a basement window—I was wondering why I didn't think of it earlier—and got to my room and into bed. I slept until three in the afternoon. When I got up my mother wanted to know what happened to me, and I told her I had been drinking beer at the party.

My girl still doesn't know I dropped acid—I decided not to tell her after all.

It [Chris's first experience with drugs] was after school, about a year and a half ago. One of the guys had some grass. He said, "Do you want to try some?" I said, "Sure." We passed it around and I took a couple of tokes, and nothing. Nothing happened. The next time, which was the next week, I believe, what a *blast!* Rockets, Cape Kennedy. One long BOOOOOM, straight up—I remember thinking, this is like my first ejaculation, only I wasn't scared.

So that weekend, or maybe the weekend after, but it was very soon after the first time I went up, I went to a party. I didn't know the guy who gave it; he was a senior in my school at the time. By the time I got there it didn't matter whether he knew me or not. Everybody, but everybody was wrecked. There were couples in the bedroom and quite a few people were parading around in the nude. They were all high-school age, and maybe were a couple of years older, but no one was over twenty. So my friend and I went downstairs to the playroom and did a couple of joints and got wrecked ourselves. I've hallucinated on grass, but not that night. The screen came down. That's happened to me a lot since.

It's a whole thing by itself. Once a joke is cracked while I'm stoned, it's very funny and I start laughing and then this screen just comes down. I can just look back and the whole thing is in focus, the whole picture.

Usually I'm with the guys I know. One time I was up at this guy's house, and there were, oh, ten or eleven of us. One girl. Not my girl, another girl. I told you my girl won't touch the stuff.

Well, we're smoking away and there it goes, the screen comes down. And now I'm gone. Nothing's going on at this party. The whole idea about it is kids would get together and smoke, and there's none of this sex. The guy who had that party is all fucked up. He's an orgiast. Most of the people I know steer clear of that stuff.

So here's this one girl and you know, everybody is giving her a good time, talking to her a lot because she feels out of place. She's a girl among eleven guys, and they're all blowing grass and everybody's just sitting around taking it all in and talking and beautiful things are being said. A guy would come out with a poem, just right off the top of his head, say about Viet Nam or parents. What I do remember is the old man downstairs, the kid's father. One kid said, "Your old man is coming up." He wanted to know what was going on. The scene is that there's smoke in the room, you can't even see your hand, a couple of guys are giggling. You just have to breathe deep and you're going. So the father comes up the stairs, and the kid goes to the door and says, "What do you want, Dad?"

He says, "What are you doing, having a party up there?" And the kid says, "Yeah, can you go downstairs? We're having a nice time." So his old man goes downstairs again.

I find it very hard to believe that the old man didn't know what was going on. There was the smoke and all. And the giggling. It was very weird.

I don't see how they can stop grass now. I can get all I want in five minutes. Really. There hasn't been any time in the past year when I haven't been able to make a buy.

Sometimes I think things happen just to drum up business, the kids have so much stuff. The other week—it was a Thursday—the word went out that there were narcos in the area, so everybody dumped his stuff—threw it in the woods, flushed it down the toilet. The next day, the scare was over. Don't ask me how or why. The kids who deal were in school with attaché cases full of stuff. They were dealing in the halls between classes. I would guess that three thousand dollars' worth of stuff changed hands that day.

It doesn't matter whether they make it legal or not. The first party I told about happened over a year ago. The kids who were at it were mostly seniors and juniors. Some kids were older, but I was the youngest, I know that. Now the freshmen are smoking—and worse. That's really scary stuff. They're experimenting. A lot of the grammar-school kids are sniffing airplane glue, but there's a couple who are sniffing Carbona, the rug cleaner, and there's one kid—he's in my school—who's been shooting white wine. I asked him about it. He says that he does a hypodermic-full and he's stoned before he can get the needle out of his arm.

I can't tell you any more about it than that. Sometimes you set out to do one thing, you wind up doing another. Like the time I dropped acid. I wasn't going to go that far. Everything in my head had been against it. One night we went bowling—that's what we were going to do. Then this gone guy—his boss was having a party, so we went there. There were just the two of us—I kept him company.

It was a bunch of old people, so we had a couple of beers. That's when we decided to go out and smoke some, but we were quite drunk, we had about seven beers apiece, so maybe that explains it.

We went back to the car. We got the grass and the pipe, and then we walked behind school and down across the football field and into the woods. We lit up a pipe. When we finished we couldn't walk, from being drunk and stoned, stoned drunk.

Finally we got back onto the football field and it was really cool; we were very small particles on this huge football field, like in the Beatle movie, *A Hard Day's Night*. This is what brought it back actually. We started running around, jumping and doing head stands and hand stands. We were screaming and yelling and everything, and then a cop comes out of the dark and stops us. I was going to tell him a story when the other guy opened his mouth, so I let him go. He said, "We went to visit our friend." And the cop said, "What's your name, what's your address? What's your cock size? What kind of feet do you have? What color are your eyes? What are you doing here? Why were you running and jumping and screaming?" And my friend said—he did a very bad thing— he said, "Well, why are you talking to us like this?" So then we started walking back to the police car, of course, with all this dope on us. This was very scary and we were quite stoned, which was scary, too.

The cop flashed the light and said, "Hold it a minute." So I'm like stretching my eyes, because they're super bloodshot. He said, "What's this car doing here?" My friend says, well my girl's baby-sitting, right? And the parents didn't want any cars in front of the house and all that stuff. So the cop goes, "Oh, it's an orgy, huh?" Then my friend goes, "No, it's a boy," which is really stupid, but it turned the cop off. It shut him right up. So finally we drove off. We were really lucky.

Another time six of us got wrecked and drove around—maybe there were seven. I don't remember, but we went to the Dairy Queen. There was one girl, going with one of the guys. We got some hamburgers and that kind of stuff. I had a chocolate malt. We were really in bad shape, but we ate and then we just sat in the car, doing nothing. Another carload pulled in, and they're all wrecked, too, so we started talking with them. We decided to shuffle ourselves up, just to see what would happen. I was supposed to go back to the first car. The girl and the guy she was going with had never gotten out. One of the other guys came running back. "She's got no clothes on," he says. So I said a very stupid thing. "You mean she doesn't mind?" He says, "Oh hell no, what the fuck." You know, so we walked over there. I got into the front seat. She was in the back. I was sitting there really stoned. I didn't give a shit what the hell was going on. They were making it in the back seat. I'm in the front seat stoned, on the partition between the two front seats. She's got her legs around him, and they're still working at it. They're screwing and three of us in the front are having a normal conversation, like, "What are we going to do tonight?" They're screwing, and we're just la la la and blah blah blah. One was tripping at the time and another was messing with mescalin. And the two in the back were just fucking. They were on fucking, that's what they were doing. They had just had a couple of tokes, so they couldn't have been more than mildly high.

The driver felt very depressed, I guess because they were screwing in the back of his car and he wasn't getting any screwing, so he said, "Well, I want to get really stoned tonight." So he rolls a joint in the Dairy Queen, I couldn't give a damn, so nobody else could either—all of us were just gone. And he rolls a joint and he starts to smoke it, you know. After that, where did we go? I don't know. I think we went home.

There was another night, but that was all day. In the morning I was going to cut school and go shopping with my friend, you know, in the city. We weren't going to do anything. We were going to buy some clothes.

That didn't work out because he decided at the last minute not to do it. And I decided I didn't really want to do it anyway. I don't like to cut school. So we went over to pick up another guy and somebody said something about turning on then, before we went to school. We were laughing and kidding around, you know.

So this is funny, about this. The other guy goes back in his house for some dope. A second later he comes back with three nickels. A big one, a medium size one, and I guess take your choice, so of course we took the biggest one. Then we drove to school, rolling joints. The question was, where to do it? One of the guys said, "We'll do it in the school parking lot." I said, "I don't like that idea, you know." So he said, "We've been doing it at the Dairy Queen, why not the school parking lot?" I said, "Well I'm not stoned now, you see, and I think it's not good." So we parked in the school parking lot and did it anyway. We walked into school quite stoned. That was the first of the day. It was a long day. I asked my friend if he'd pick me up at two-thirty, so we could go smoke some more. So he did and we went over to his house and we smoked about the rest of the nickel bag. When you got it, flaunt it. So then we went over to my house and I got hold of *Cheap Thrills,* the album, and we listened to that, which was neat. Then another guy came over and he had thirty dollars' worth of hash that he wanted to get rid of. So we bought that.

I think he had a thousand dollars' worth, all told. He wanted to get rid of it, so he walks in and he goes, "You want to buy some hash?" So we said, "O.K., how much you got?" He said, "I got a thousand dollars' worth." We said, "Well, we'll take about thirty." We got a good deal because he had so much. We smoked about a dime and a half, and man, by this time, we were quite enthusiastically stoned, and we could not move. I mean, total immovability and we were both hallucinating from all the shit we took in. And then, you know, it's like the beginning of a trip, you know, when first you drop acid, you get just one rush and it all goes blooie. It was like that first rush, you know. We were moving and things like that. And when I shut my eyes I would see little blue people running around. They were cartoon figures. No inner meaning and all that crap. We were just stoned and digging it, you know. And my friend's face would go blah, and turn green.

So he left, and he left all the stuff with me because he had to go pick up his father at the airport. And he was seeing little blue people. So I called some other guys, and they wanted to get stoned. Two guys, so the three of us got together down in the basement and I guess we did a lot of hash. I ground it up and shoved it into a cigarette, and we put some on the cigarette and smoked it. We tried all the strokes for all the different folks. One of the guys was a second-timer and he really was digging it. The only thing I heard from him was, "Oh, man, am I stoned." And when I'd look at him, I'd see this kind of big grin that people get when they're stoned. It's like their whole face is that big grin.

O.K., we finished that. Then the kid who dealt us the hash comes back, and he says, "Listen, I've got some grass I got to get rid of." And I go, "Where'd you get this?" He says, "Well I just came by it." He probably traded for it. So we bought that—he gave us credit.

And so there I am with about one hundred and fifty dollars' worth of dope in my house, in my drawer. Everything is cool. We're all stoned. We went up and listened to my records and stuff, and then one guy had to leave. The two of us left smoked another joint because he wanted to see what it was like to get more stoned. He was the second-timer, of course. And I was glad to oblige because I wanted to see what it was like to get more stoned, and after that I settled down and didn't have anything for about the next three hours. But I was walking around in a daze. Then the other guy got back from the airport—it was about seven o'clock, I had rolled a huge hash joint. I had put a half cigarette of grass in and I put about a dime of hash in over the grass. That was dynamite. We went over and picked up another guy and we smoked our boomer on the way. I was gone. That did it. I wasn't there any more and they were talking to me, and I was saying, "What? What did you say?" I couldn't smoke any more. I just couldn't even hold the freaking joint up to my mouth any more. *Space Odyssey* was playing at the drive-in so we went on in there.

We got there right when the monkey was crashing down the bone. We stayed for a little while, until I could roll a joint. It took about an hour, I was so disabled. Totally impossible to do anything. So then we all rolled a joint apiece. I scratched up the last of the hash we had with us and dumped it in one of the joints.

In about a half hour's time we had, I think, about twelve joints. And the one with the hash—that was the surprise.

We passed them around and I do believe that I reached the peak of the tops stoned, because after I started smoking nothing was happening to me. I was just staying on the same level. I couldn't get any higher. It wasn't intense, it was like a trip, very intense in your body, but one level below. That was it. Somehow, sometime, I went home. I don't remember—I can't remember.

The next day, someone offered me a can of beer and like a fool I took it. I was wrecked all over again. I even saw the little blue men. I know, you don't have to tell me. I have to be careful.

## The Power of Non-Politics or the Death of the Square Left

### 1967

### Ralph J. Gleason

Joe MacDonald is a folk singer, a guitar player and a political activist. Or he was.

He used to get his songs published in *Broadside,* the magazine of protest songwriters; and when they wanted musicians to play along the line of march of the Vietnam Day Parade to Oakland they called in Joe MacDonald.

Now Joe MacDonald has long hair, wears beads and sometimes war paint, plays an electric guitar, and leads a rock group called Country Joe & the Fish who record for Vanguard.

Late last spring, Joe went to a meeting in Palo Alto, the creamy rich suburb and intellectual elephant graveyard of the San Francisco Bay Area. The meeting was political and the people at it wanted to talk to someone from the New Youth, the Love Generation—a Hippie.

"No one wants to listen to speeches," Joe MacDonald told the stiff politicos. "We had the groovy anti-war march and then the speakers rapped away with the same old political bullshit. The revolution is now. It's happening on the streets."

"Politics and social activity have to be entertaining, rather than boring," MacDondald said later. "When the left wing does things, there's no energy. But when the hippies do something, there's energy and the radicals are beginning to realize this."

It's not "flower power" to Joe. That's just a slogan on a button and no more to be taken seriously than "Make Me High" or "If It Moves, Fondle It" or any number of other silly slogans the button entrepreneurs are marketing.

"What Joe told them," says Saul Landau, co-author with Paul Jacobs of *The New Radicals,* a friend and associate of C. Wright Mills, and a veteran politico himself, "is that if they want to make politics, make it groovy. When one of them asked him what his political program was, Joe thought for a moment and answered: 'Free music in the park.' 'What about the social organization of the society?' another one asked him, and Joe snapped back 'Fuck it!' "

The trouble is that radical politics in the United States has demonstrated its bankruptcy too openly now to have any real attraction for youth anymore. If you postulate—and no one operates on any other basis—that armed revolution in this country is an impossibility, then there is no hope in radicalization of politics. Without guns the radicals are powerless to make any fundamental changes because politics does not now and never really has made the machinery go in the U.S. of A. What runs this country is money, as the steel companies demonstrated when they socked it to LBJ and told him where to go.

The increasing attraction of the long-haired Haight-Ashbury hippies is in the obvious fact that what they do generate is power. You may call them flower children, call them The Love Generation, call them mindless LSD idiots, call them anything you please, they are the most powerful single social movement in the country amongst Caucasians. They generate psychic force; they accomplish things and they have created a community that is effectively functioning, surviving the guerrilla attacks made upon it by the Establishment, and within the ordinary society. And, as the hard reality of white politics is revealed to youth—the Free Speech Movement never had a chance and its leaders are in jail this minute, not for revolting against the stodgy University of California administration, but for trespassing; i.e., threatening property—more and more of them are simply turning away from the traditional forms of dissent because they find dissent meaningless.

"Turn on, tune in and drop out" is widely read as meaning drop out completely from society, which is what the beatniks did. This is not at all what is going on with the hippies. Thy are doing something else, much more constructive and much more meaningful and infinitely creative. They are, in effect, the first creative social movement in decades among white people in the U.S.

The hippies are dropping out of the Madison Avenue, LBJ society in which a Hubert Humphrey can publicly put his arm around Lester Maddox and say there's room for him in the Democratic Party. They are dropping out of a society which condones napalm (and from the radical intellectual society which condones it in one country and condemns it in another).

But they are not just dropping out into Limbo or Nirvana. They are building a new set of values, a new structure, a new society, if you will, horizontal to the old but in it.

Plato said that forms and rhythms in music are never changed without producing changes in the most important political forms and ways. One recent night outside The Matrix, a San Francisco rock 'n' roll club which is non-alcoholic (more on that in a moment) the lead guitarists from two groups featured that night found out they both had been in the Sproul Hall FSM sit-in at Berkeley and that the drummer in one of the groups was also involved. None had known of the others' background until that moment.

Thus old politicos. From the FSM to rock 'n' roll. And, as the Supreme Court appeal was refused and the jail sentences loomed a couple of weeks away (the University of California and most of the rest of the educational establishment has been talking about educational reform for two years now, thanks to Mario Savio—and Clark Kerr is a martyr for being fired and Mario is in jail), one defendant said: "Man, I got to get that bread! I can't afford the fine, but I really can't spend two months in jail now. The group needs me. We're just getting going."

Now the point of that is that the rock groups and the Diggers represent communal, low-pressure-on-the-individual organizations in which the whole of the Haight-Ashbury hippie world operates, as opposed to plastic uptight America.

Communes, handcrafts, survival in the wilderness, farming, and other similar activities are a part and parcel of the movement. Maybe the Luddites did have a bad press, as E. J. Hobsbawm has suggested, and we may have to go back to them or even before, to take up the thread of history and straighten things out.

But the fact of the matter is that these people are trying, by demonstration, to show the world *how* to live now.

In a communiqué distributed on Haight Street this spring by a group of Diggers, the statement is printed: "Enlightenment, described in many tongues and in many ways, teaches, among other truths, that truly to feel the unity of all men that is love requires the giving up of the illusion of game-playing abstractions. A perfection of inner self, sometimes attainable through LSD-25 or other psychedelics, reveals the failure of all political games . . . the failure to LET IT GO. Do you want to SHOW people a groovy way of life, or do you want to TELL THEM HOW TO LIVE, and back it up with bottles, bricks, boards and even bullets?"

This is where the hippies are at.

That all this should gestate in the San Francisco Bay Area is no accident— the anti HUAC demonstrations and the spectacle of the San Francisco police hosing the non-violent students took place here. So did the Chessman vigils, the Palace Hotel sit-ins, the FSM, the Vietnam teach-ins, and the troop-train demonstrations.

And the same freedom to dissent, which allowed all those movements to rise and to evolve (the existence of the anti-McCarthy newspaper, *The Chronicle;* the free-speech non-commercial FM station, KPFA; Harry Bridges' radical-turned-respectable union, the ILWU), allowed the hippies to turn on, tune in (on life), and drop out of the games.

It's no accident that *Ramparts,* the muckraker of the Square Left, was born in San Francisco's foggy climate, even though its existence was made possible by the abandonment of their responsibilities by the mass media, from the *Times* through TV to *Time.* But *Ramparts* is only the white hope of the Square Left, just as its managing editor, Bob Scheer, became the white hope of radical politics. He polled forty-five per cent of the Berkeley vote in a race with Democrat Jeffrey Cohelan for Congress last fall.

But congressmen don't run the country, and it made no difference whether or not Scheer—who soft-pedalled his legalization-of-marijuana plank, trimmed his beard, got married and began to wear a tie, button-down collar, and a vest when he became a serious candidate—was or was not elected. If Wayne Morse can't do anything, what can a congressman do?

This is what the hippies understand. And this is what the Square Left can't dig in any way. And this is what Stokely Carmichael knows, too. The kinds of change that need to be made in this society cannot be made by electing congressmen. Short of guns, they can only be made by changing the heads of man, and the hippies are quite openly and definitely and consistently going about just that.

Not everything they do is laudable; not everyone who looks like a hippie is one. "Long hair doth not a hippie make, nor scraggy beard a knave," says an Ancient Irish Proverb (invented by me to illustrate a point). This generation of cultural dropouts has invented its own Bohemia. It is not the old Greenwich Village or North Beach, the Greenwich Village of San Francisco. They went out and found a new place. And, intuitively or, as is the case of the Diggers, intellectually, they realized the truth of the *Catch*-22ish idea that any attempt to deal with the system makes you a victim of it.

A word on the Diggers. This is a loose group within the hippie society which takes its name from the seventeenth-century British communal group which took possession of land after the Civil War, tilled it in the name of the people, and gave the food away. The Diggers abolished money a year ago. They have been feeding anyone who shows up every afternoon at four at Oak and Ashbury in the Panhandle of Golden Gate Park with a perpetual picnic. "Take it, it's yours, it's free," they say.

There are no Digger leaders. Only spokesmen. "I may be a spokesman tonight and somebody else is a spokesman tomorrow," says Emmett Grogan, who is, if not a leader, one of the principal figures within the group. But think of that fact. There are no leaders ("don't follow leaders, watch your parkin' meters," I seem to hear Louis Simpson's favorite poet singing). And the fact is that there *are* no leaders either of the Diggers or the hippies. They read Alan Watts, they read Allen Ginsberg. They dig Michael McClure and Tim Leary and Ken Kesey. But they don't follow them and when any one of them makes the mistake, as some have done, of telling the hippies what to do, it just doesn't get done.

The Diggers are the monks of the Haight/Ashbury, some observers say. They are certainly the self-appointed conscience of the community. And they are attacking the very basic principle upon which this society is built: It is more sacred to make money than to be a good man. The Diggers began during the week last summer when a San Francisco policeman shot and killed a young Negro who was running away from an auto the cop suspected had been stolen, property being more valuable than human life. The Diggers refuse money. You can give them food and you can do things for them, but they will burn your ten dollar bill if you offer it. Their philosophy, Grogan once said, is accepting the futility of either fighting or joining the system.

In planning how to keep the people off Haight Street and thus avoid confrontations with the police, Digger elements and other interested hippies such as a group called The Summer of Love, organized or rather prepared the way for a series of free afternoon concerts in the Panhandle with rock bands.

"We have discovered the power of music, when played for free, to remove the hostilities of crowds," says Peter Cohan, another Digger. At the Great Be-In in Golden Gate Park last January 20,000 people, at least, gathered and spent the afternoon listening to music, digging themselves and one another, and there were only two cops in evidence.

The Digger *modus operandi* is "do your thing." A University of California professor, a good and honest and gentle and liberal man, genuinely concerned about the necessity of providing food and housing for the summer invasion of flower children, came to a meeting and asked "for an inventory of your needs." A Digger told him, "No, man, you know what we need. You see something we need and you get it. Do your thing, man. That's all. We need whatever you think we need."

"I don't care too much for money, money can't buy me love," The Beatles sing and Bob Dylan says, "Money doesn't talk, it swears." Roy Ballard, another Digger, observes that maybe these artists don't even know how seriously the youth is taking what they say. But the point is that youth *is* taking it seriously.

The experimental colleges, the Free Universities which have sprung up all over the U.S. in the past two years, were born in the corridors of Sproul Hall that grim December night when the students felt the armed might of the State risen in the defense of property. The Diggers' free food and abolishment of money has spawned other organizations in New York, in Los Angeles, in Berkeley, and even in Cleveland. One can, with logic (but aren't we all in some sense the prisoners of logic, as Malvina Reynolds points out?), say that one swallow doesn't make a summer and that the Diggers won't change the world. But there remains something strongly attractive to the idea of money being no good. Free food has come to the Diggers from as far away as Texas and New York.

Maybe the Diggers won't change the world. But they have certainly changed the heads of those they have touched. What other cauldron has so altered the young in this society as to cause any of them to abandon money?

"The Haight is a subsistence community, living on a fringe of surplus never before present . . . in this or any country and creating a new culture based on a radically different sense of human and social priorities," observes Michael Rossman, one of the FSM leaders (currently in jail) and now a close student of the hippie culture.

"Just do your thing, man, it'll be all right." Hang loose. "It's all right ma, I got nuthin' to live up to." We have raised this generation in an emotional pressure cooker and they are saying to us, hey there, you with those achievement stripes, that logic in your head, those meetings and those plans and those proposals. IT ISN'T WORKING.

And we know it. That's what has frightened the daylights out of all the older generation faced with the long hair. The youth looks peaceful and content and at ease. It has dignity. It is not hustling and it is not, so very obviously not, striving for the same values its parents strove for.

Cleanliness is no longer next to Godliness and logic is not sacred. It is all right to have fun and the human body is not a thing to be ashamed of ("if the merchandise is offensive, complain to the manufacturer," Lenny Bruce used to say).

It is perfectly okay to smoke pot. Everyone who really knew anything at all about it, in contrast to the professional, Parkinson's-law narcotic fuzz and the bluenoses, always knew this but didn't expect to operate on it. Liquor is the real enemy. An outstanding characteristic of the be-ins, the dances, the other happenings in San Francisco ever since the hippies began to congregate there is the absence of drunks. There are no fights at the dances. None at all. And no booze. Beer sales are off in some territories, including Northern California, and the night-club business, which depends on hard liquor for its real profits, is in deep trouble. Is it true that Schenley and a tobacco company have merged and does it mean what the hippies think it means?

If we can accept the idea that black pride is not racist, then white pride is not racist either, and a characteristic of this Bohemian group is that they are not ashamed of being white. A SNCC worker, a young man who was arrested in the Oakland *Tribune* picketing, a young veteran of civil rights, saw no evil in the dance poster from the Avalon Ballroom which showed, in full blazing color, a very black, very old woman with a red bandana wrapped around her gray and grizzled head. "We've got to get past the old images. If it's a groovy picture, it's a groovy picture."

The Beatnik world of the fifties was an interracial world first and foremost. But an interracial world based on a white assumption of innate black superiority. The hippies' world is quite different. The stereotype black stud from *The Dutchman* is discovering that the hippie chicks don't get uptight when he tells them "you won't make it with me because you're prejudiced." This, too, is changing.

Hippie groups, including the Diggers, recently put on a two-day free festival with free food and music and balloons and sundry goodies in the *Black Orpheus*-style ghetto of Hunter's Point and they called it a Muhammad Ali Festival in honor of Muhammad Ali's stand on the draft. There are no leaders in the Haight, just people who do things, one of them said. And they just went ahead and organized this event.

The hippies simply disregard laws that they do not approve of, most of the time. They now hitch-hike with one foot usually on the curb to keep from getting busted on a state law, but they blow pot when and where they feel like it in blissful disregard of the reality of the law. And many don't register for the draft or report for induction.

"We know something has got to be changed about the draft law," said a parole officer who visited me on a case where I was listed as a reference. "We can't put them all in jail. The law is inflexible and unjust and inadequate."

When the Bob Dylan film *Don't Look Back* was shown in San Francisco this summer, the hippie audience applauded the line "I don't read *Time* or *Newsweek* to find out what's going on." They know the truth of that. They *do* read the underground press. Some magazines. A few people. But basically the radio is the communications medium because it is instant. In the Haight, the society is back to the broadside. Sheets appear on the street three, four, and sometimes more times a day in runs of five hundred to get the message out to the people on the street.

The hippies, represented by various groups including the Diggers and The Summer of Love people, had been bugging the city authorities all spring about making plans to feed and house the summer invasion.

"They're begging the city, they're dropout middle-class kids and they're asking for things the Negro kids would never ask for, because they've had things given them all their lives," a critic said. That is quite true. But the point is that they know that what they need is possible to get and that the State is there to serve the people and a public servant is a servant of the public. So they step up and they say it, loud and clear. And this causes the city and the authorities to explain and explain but it also makes everyone, old and young, re-evaluate the concepts. When the San Francisco City Board of Supervisors adopted a resolution that said, in effect, we don't want the hippies here (which is what it *did* say, later denials to the contrary), even the *Chronicle* had to speak out against it. Willie Brown, the Negro member of the State Assembly from San Francisco, pointed out in a public statement to the Supervisors (one of whom is Terry Francois, a long-time leading Negro civil-rights leader) that discrimination against one minority opens the door to discrimination against others.

The hippie culture is a drug culture, too. I suppose one has to say that. But in saying it, it should be pointed out that the entire American culture is a drug culture. "Mother's little helpers," the Rolling Stones sang, and Grace Slick of the Jefferson Airplane in "White Rabbit" sings of the pills that make you tall and the pills that make you small "and the ones that mother gives you don't do anything at all."

Between the use of tranquilizers, alcohol, and other drugs (even excluding tobacco) the majority of the people in this country are on one thing or another. LBJ has been on tranquilizers since 1955, James Reston reveals.

So what is pot? So what is LSD? They may freak out those unfamiliar with them and, surely, the society has made official LSD research all but impossible and you are punished more severely for possessing marijuana than for drunken driving. Who's worse off, the alcoholic or the guy on a bum trip?

Something is wrong here. Psychiatrists don't know how to handle LSD bum trips, but the hippies know, and the first thing they do is to keep the guy on a bum trip out of the hands of the cops and the psychiatrists.

"What should we do when a kid makes his defense on a marijuana charge temporary insanity and we know he is really sane?" a reputable psychiatrist asked me.

"Lie to the cops, if you're trying to save people rather than be Adolph Eichmann," I told him and he gasped, "It's against my code of professional conduct!"

Like the hippies, I fail to see the distinction between that and hedging on your income tax report or telling a traffic cop you were only doing thirty mph when you know you were doing forty.

The sacredness of authority. The sacredness of logic. The sacredness of money. In fact, almost all of what our history has been built on is being questioned.

And why the hell not? Look where it all has got us in 1967.

That these kids are operating from a childhood spent gazing at TV Westerns in which right is right and wrong is wrong may put them on a TV Western trip in buckskins and beads, but Executive Suite, Adlai Stevenson, John Kennedy, and Hubert Humphrey got us backing General Ky in Vietnam.

"For the reality of politics, we must go to the poets not the politicians," Norman O. Brown says. And the truth of the matter is that Allen Ginsberg has more illuminating things to say about the American condition in his *Wichita Vortex Sutra* than all the SDS literature of the past four years.

The youth is having none of the ideology of its parents. The radical line that folk music and Woody Guthrie were where it really was at makes no more sense than anything else the Square Left has said.

"We have the chance to change the world," one of The Byrds said on TV recently. And I was reminded of the night that Kennedy instituted the blockade of Cuba. I was in the audience at a Nelson Algren talk at the University of California in Berkeley. He was speaking on Hemingway and he interrupted himself to look out at the audience and said: "I would regard a United States invasion of Cuba as a violation of everything I have been taught as an American."

Later, at a party, a member of a well-known folk-singing group, himself a radical of lifelong standing, said, "What courage that took! We never can say *anything* when we have 5,000 people out there!" And Algren smiled and quietly said it didn't take courage at all.

And that's the way the hippies are going to change this society. It doesn't take the kind of courage we have been taught to believe it does. What it takes is men like the Diggers and the rock musicians and the rest "doing their thing."

We may not live to see the complete change. We may be blown to bits in the meantime. It may well be too late. But precinct politics are not going to stop that, if the anti-war demonstrations don't mean anything we are truly helpless.

Money is losing its power to buy and thus its power to corrupt. Conformity is being lost in the Dylan ethic of "Dig yourself" and the Digger ethic of "Do your thing."

The revolution, as Country Joe MacDonald says, is already happening in the street. Radicals had better get with it if they can (most of them probably can't unless their kids can blow their minds, somehow, possibly with pot).

Everyone remembers the feeling of mutual understanding and love and the blessing of a common cause, from everything from the Free French to the Stevenson campaign. The hippies have it all the time. "I came here because of the psychic energy. I get recharged," said Arthur Lisch, a painter who is now a full-time active Digger.

And the release of that psychic energy is what will change the form of American life. The beginning has already been made.

---

## Growing Up Radical

### 1970

---

### Jim Gardiner

---

I live at 121st Street and Amsterdam Avenue in Manhattan, four blocks from both Harlem and Columbia University. Here I have lived since I was eight, in the summer of 1964—through riots, droughts, boycotts, strikes, snowstorms; through long, hot years and short, cool ones.

The immediate neighborhood is a pattern of small grocery stores, bookstores, and bars. Morningside Heights, as the area is known, is torn between the two extremes of America: the affluent and the poor, the cultured and the deprived, the overeducated and the subliterate. Each new construction seems to push it one way or the other, but every June the students leave and Harlem is victorious. Harlem, it seems, will always be victorious, for it is a huge black constant, unchanging, eternal. It has survived the promises of liberals and conservatives alike, the rampages of police, and the actions of radicals, wars and peace. It bears silent testimony to the guilt of the white man.

Just up the street from my home is the Riverside Church. Riverside is a Protestant, non-sectarian, largely white church. Here Martin Luther King spoke, and here James Forman delivered his Manifesto. There aren't many black people among the congregation. Sundays, they are to be found at the local Baptist, Methodist, and Lutheran churches. The community meets under these circumstances for catharsis and to retain hope.

Religion is an integral part of Harlem, as it is of most black ghettoes. For many years the black clergyman has had a strong influence on his parish, been ignored by the white Establishment, and must now be reckoned with. I spent three years at Public School 125, which is still 15 percent white, 50 percent black, and 35 percent Puerto Rican. To be white in a black school would be frightening to many, I suppose, but I was not frightened. At eight, I entered the fourth grade of P.S. 125. That was in the fall of '64, immediately after the first major ghetto riot in decades, in Harlem. Nearly all of the faculty was white, largely Jewish, and in most cases scared.

Even at that early stage in urban education, racism had been perpetuated. Tests had been given determining which students would be placed in the ostensibly smarter classes and given the benefit of the best teachers in the school, and which students would be placed in the inferior classes, consigned from the first to an educational career doomed to repeated failure, frustration, and a future as black as their skin. Typically, these tests concentrated on reading comprehension, vocabulary, and word usage. The wording of the selections and problems was directed solely to pupils with the background of a middle-class white, leaving blacks and Puerto Ricans, culturally deprived by White America, in a position of apparent ignorance. How can a child to whom words like "banker," "phonograph," "painting," or "airline" are mere imaginings possibly contend with children whose parents can spare the time to help educate them?

My black classmates exhibited no prejudice toward me, nor do I feel that the teachers favored me visibly because of my race. Rather, the length of my hair (very long for that period) caused me to be hounded and teased incessantly. The faculty, good Americans all, seized upon every opportunity available to insult, embarrass, and downgrade me on the basis of my "haircut." This placed me in a situation similar, if more individualistic, to that of the black kids. My well-being was handled with the same disinterest, my education treated with the same lack of care, my future plotted with the same boredom.

To my eternal discredit, I contradicted the carefully formulated plans of the system for me by exhibiting signs of intelligence, that most dangerous of diseases among the masses. I remember commenting in fourth grade that the stories in our *Dick and Jane* reading book, a never-ending saga of a WASP family growing up straight, conservative, and thoroughly indoctrinated, were propaganda. This being true, and incontestably so, the teacher intimated that it was good propaganda, designed benevolently to instruct us gradually. Bullshit, I proclaimed then; and, five years later, bullshit I proclaim still.

In those days, the formative years of decentralization, one of the first battles for community control took place. During the 1966–1967 term, the Parent's Association of the elementary school, having broken off negotiations with the Board of Education, declared a boycott of all grades until the Board, as repeatedly promised, would allow the community to choose four candidates for principal, with the superintendent of schools retaining the final decision. One-third of the faculty and eighteen hundred of the school's two thousand pupils participated in the boycott, and many of them attended the Liberation School set up at the Riverside Church. I dug the free spirit of learning that was the medium of expression there. When both teacher and student are involved in a common protest, the gap between them is easier to bridge; and simply by virtue of our presence we all had made a commitment to ourselves and to our community.

Liberation School was taught by many of the regular teachers, sympathetic Columbia and Barnard students, and by parents. The community was very much into this scene; food was provided cheaply, gym facilities offered, materials donated, and people involved.

Eventually, the boycott was successful, and we went back. Reluctantly, I returned to a world where knowledge was a lifeless, stagnant mass of impersonal data, where human students are mere receptacles for the prejudices of whomever has been selected to instruct them.

The community of Harlem, or more specifically, Manhattanville, is extremely difficult to become familiar with. I have lived for five years within it, spent three full terms at one of its elementary schools, played in its playgrounds, and shopped in its stores. The people there are those one reads about in Riot Commission reports, front page stories in newspapers, third-rate novels, and books by urban sociologists. We are bombarded by a stream of misinformation and analysis; the words of men who have forgotten what it means to live in a ghetto, or in the shadow of one.

Our cities are dying, New York is crumbling; yet Harlem is not unlike a dormant volcano, which erupts as soon as his flame is forgotten, his rage ignored, his torment unlessened. Rats and cockroaches don't please suburban Americans, so they change the channel when the conditions in the ghettoes come up; when reports are given of children who cannot learn because their teachers are on strike, not teaching, and not interested; when pictures of looting, rioting, burning, and the rubble are shown. They change the channel because Harlem, Watts, Roxbury, Detroit, Cleveland, Miami, Flint, Bedford-Stuyvesant, and Ocean Hill–Brownsville are America's asshole. White America brought the black man in chains from Africa, subjected him to 250 years of slavery, preyed upon his illiteracy, terrorized him in his so-called freedom, denied him his manhood, refused him his rights, and sentenced him to virtual economic slavery.

Every American President until Lincoln owned slaves, and every one since has played politics with the rights of black people. Less than twenty years ago the U.S. government sanctioned by its silence (and until 1954 used none of the institutions at its command to condemn) the open, public, and state-empowered discrimination against and segregation of blacks in the deep South.

Racism in our institutions, no matter how deeply it runs, can and must be uprooted—even if the institutions must be uprooted with it. Black people will have their rights, or we shall level the earth in our attempts to get them.

Not quite three blocks from Union Square in Manhattan, there is a squat, four-story building, looking as if it didn't have the money to retire in Florida and is therefore condemned to the fortunes of summer, rain, and snow on a New York City sidestreet. Every four months or so, its environs are breached by a horde of students, radicals, revolutionaries, G.I.'s, and perennial volunteers. On the third floor is the office of the Fifth Avenue Peace Parade Committee.

Sometime in the early spring of 1969, perhaps in that very office, the Peace Parade Committee decided that it was time to remind Nixon of his extensive promises of peace in Vietnam, and to remind the American public that despite soothing words from the President and his Cabinet, talks in Paris, and a lull in the fighting, Vietnam had recently exceeded the War of Independence and become the longest continuously-fought war in the nation's history, and that 33,000 U.S soldiers had died and were continuing to die at the rate of 150 and 200 a week. April 5 was appointed the date of the demonstration, and permits for a march up Sixth Avenue and a rally in Central Park were obtained.

At about 9:00 A.M. on a Saturday morning at the end of the third week in March, I walked out of the Union Square subway station to the Committee's headquarters. Mark, a coordinator of volunteer activity, put me to work as soon as I had stashed my jacket and made some coffee. I was assigned to a folding machine: feeding leaflets in, stacking them as they came out folded in half, and placing the stacks in boxes. The next day, there was more work—stuffing, sealing, and stamping envelopes.

It is my experience that a successful march is made not by the publicity it is given, but by the people working it and shaping it, by their activism and their attitude. A march or a demonstration is a beautiful, esthetic entity: it can be a fair, fickle woman, lovely in expectation, orgastic at its frenzied peak, and feminine in its acceptance of failure. It is a thing of beauty for a single instant.

With vivid memory I recall that spring of '69, memory mixed fondly with nostalgia. Then, like the Movement, I was at a political crossroad: poised uncertainly at a point somewhere between liberalism and radicalism, wary of either course; almost afraid, whether of a wrong decision or of my very indecision in the face of what I was sure must be an obvious choice, I know not.

Working, and working hard, as I did, precluded active pursuit of this eventual choice. Morally committed to efficient performance of my functions as a marshal, I found a substitute for ideological dogmatism in blind faith. Faith, that is, not in some forgery of duly constituted authority, but rather in those who labored for my own ideals with a positive sense of conviction in their tactics.

It was not quite early spring. Eating, sleeping, laughing, working—somehow each of these acts fit in with the March we were shaping—as if creating a painting on a blank canvas. Our canvas was a shameful awareness within America, the solemn knowledge of Vietnam. By exhortation, publication, education, and constant reminder, we must extract the painful guilt of America-Vietnam.

April 5 at 5:00 A.M. I awoke, dressed, and left, as dawn rose over Harlem outside my window. Walking through Union Square at six, tired and cold, past the sleeping statues, the weary buildings, I thought, finally, of myself. Of the six years I had before I came of draft age, of the war, and of peace.

The Central Park bandshell, under a drizzle, echoed with the sounds of the first few marshals rigging sound systems, pinning on the yellow armbands that were our only identification, ignoring the many uniformed policemen and the few undercover detectives, briefing each other on assignments, contingents, and responsibilities, and eating quietly. We ate matzoh and drank a good deal of coffee, joked a little bit, and replied with the laughs of guerrillas before an action. The park filled up slowly, until there were one hundred of us, carefully hoisting speakers to the tops of telephone poles, inflating huge balloons, unloading microphones, placards, and bullhorns from the van containing the borrowed equipment.

My group commander assigned me to Contingent G, which formed in Forty-third Street at Sixth Avenue. After about an hour and a half of waiting for the other groups to go by, we moved out. As I walked, keeping the pace orderly and uniform, watching out for attacks by right-wing fascists, doing the countless things a good marshal must do simultaneously, I was aware of the political decision facing me being made, almost on a subconscious level, by an entity which was not quite me.

Here were thousands of people with a massive potential for revolutionary action passively marching in docile submission to the limitations set by the power structure. Rather than offer violent resistance to the fascist, imperialist pigs whose malevolent acts perpetrated poverty, fear, and death on masses of oppressed people, they marched pointlessly past scores of policemen bordering their path. Yet I was one of them; I presumed to lead them. The total futility of mere nonviolent demonstration became clear. The rain came down, baptizing me. I was a radical.

Those of us within the public schools of large cities such as New York who are radically inclined have often encountered some form of obstruction and administrative interference, be it over matters of hair-length, attire, publicly expressed opinions, leaflets, petitions, or injustice. We strain to move aside the dead weight of authority blocking our path, but are either overcome by the bureaucracy, or are forced to use violent means.

When I was eleven, I entered the first half of a two-year Special Progress program at Intermediate School 44, Manhattan. Since I had just come out of the sixth grade at P.S. 125, the prospect of entering tenth grade in two years— provided I passed both terms—was an entertaining one; at the time I was sold on intellectualism as the ultimate trip. I.S. 44 was a cool school from this standpoint; it had a few excellent teachers, whom the office naturally assigned to the smartest, furthest advanced, S.P. classes. These Special Progress classes were almost completely white, the system having done its job of segregation well. The school had five different levels, or "tracks," ranging from the S.P. X track down through A, B, C, and D. Predictably, the lower the track, the higher the proportion of non-white students. Apathy dominated the scene, along with the burgeoning social awareness of adolescence.

The teacher strike of Fall 1968, affected us in a weird way. About half of the faculty stayed out, and the rest attempted a reasonable facsimile of normal operation. Not many students showed up, but this lack was more advantageous than detrimental, for in effect it served to weed out the motivated pupils from those who came simply because it was required of them.

Emotion over the strike ran high; animosity between the union teachers and the "strike-breakers" was continual. This polarization left its scars on the rest of the year; when an extended session was proclaimed by the Board of Education, a number of faculty members refused to participate in it on the ground that they had put in the required extra time during the two-month strike. The racial connotations of a work stoppage called by a primarily white, Jewish union against a black and Puerto Rican community are strong, so that it was a tense, uneasy peace which overhung 44.

During the 1968–1969 term, I became engaged in an effort to obtain administrative permission for the student body to exercise a basic right: leaving the physical school grounds during lunch. We also requested amnesty for five students who had done so contrary to official policy and had been threatened with suspension when caught. We formed an ad hoc Action Committee, printed and circulated leaflets, set up a meeting with the principal, and drew up a petition which was signed by one hundred members of the eighth grade. A nucleus of natural, unappointed leaders coalesced—which sounds very romantic, almost divinely inspired, until one considers that no one else gave a damn enough to lead what was mostly a group of uninterested faddists.

Our little quintet of leaders met briefly with the principal, and we were unenthusiastically told off. The threats of suspension were silently dropped, and another meeting scheduled; the Lone Ranger had ridden again. No mention was made of our grievances, nor of the possibility of instituting a non-captive lunch, a promise which had been made and broken on many occasions in the past.

I recall a very good friend of mine, a Mr. D—— of the Social Studies Department, voicing, among his praise and approval of our actions, an emotion which neighbored on awe but retained a degree of wariness. He is ideologically from that portion of his generation which has, after the diversion, patronizations, and eventual failure of the New Frontier crusades, at last yielded in principle to the ruling powers. Their philosophy died in Mississippi with Evers, in Dallas with Kennedy, in Nashville with King, and in L.A. with Bobby. They are morally afraid to become radical, too young to be conservative, and too "progressive" to be liberal. The immediate successes of radical youth in provoking change and drawing attention to its causes alienate these people and make them unpleasantly aware of their ages. These are the people who will be forced to stand with or against the oppressed masses when the revolution comes.

For the second time, we met with representatives of the administration in a vain attempt to persuade them that our program was a valid one. They gave us one week to design a foolproof, inexpensive plan for the entry and exit of students under a non-captive lunch, one in which they might go home for the meal or remain at school. With late hours, a lot of sweat, and help from parents, we fulfilled this requirement. Then the administrative office insisted that assurances of police protection of pupils at large in the neighborhood be gotten from the precinct. The leadership made four separate visits to the police station —a place where we were unlikely to be found voluntarily. When at last we spoke with the commanding officer, he said that his men would cooperate with I.S. 44 on the program. Our beloved warden, that is, principal, was undaunted by our success; she responded by telling us that the recommendations could not be acted upon unless fifteen parents could be enlisted to act as assistants to the teachers who would be responsible for the operation. Most of the families of the students were poor, many fatherless and on welfare, and there were very few in which the parent(s) did not work. It was impossible for fifteen of these adults to spend an hour a day working in the school as volunteers.

We had asked for nothing more than a basic student right. We had outlined a simple, cheap method to operate our plan effectively. Our efforts had wound through the bureaucratic maze and resulted in police support. We had the backing of faculty, parents, and one hundred members of the Senior class. Had we taken violent action to achieve our aim, tactically impossible because of lack of sufficient numbers, we would have been justified.

The United States enslaves, oppresses, silences, and murders to extend the scope of its power, its empire. It is often an ogre, a horrific beast who will suffer not the slightest defiance, the merest of disobediences. Nowhere is this attitude more evident than in the classrooms of the nation. Colleges, universities, and public school systems are jails. The educational Establishment has the arbitrary power to fail, suspend, and expel any student with the merest of justifications.

We are segregated, forced to pray to an All-American corporate-blessing God, denied knowledge of sex and evolution, restricted in our "inalienable rights" of free speech, petition, and protest, made to conform to puritanical standards of attire and appearance, and used as pawns in petty, racist power plays. If we dare to question, or worse, to protest, our leaders are squashed and our causes banned. No longer.

The big power structure is going up against the wall. At Berkeley, Columbia, San Francisco State, Cornell, Wisconsin, Harvard, the battle lines are being drawn. We shall be free.

The Radical-Hippie-Yippie-Black Panther-Militant-Anarchistic-Subversive-Anti-American-Ultrafanatic-New Left-Communist Infiltrated-Moscow-Peking Controlled-Drugridden-Takeover-Conspiracy-Plot, in short, the revolution, is misreported, distorted, disregarded, underestimated, and INEVITABLE.

# Everything That Rises Must Converge

## 1965

---

## Flannery O'Connor

---

His doctor had told Julian's mother that she must lose twenty pounds on account of her blood pressure, so on Wednesday nights Julian had to take her downtown on the bus for a reducing class at the Y. The reducing class was designed for working girls over fifty, who weighed from 165 to 200 pounds. His mother was one of the slimmer ones, but she said ladies did not tell their age or weight. She would not ride on the buses by herself at night since they had been integrated, and because the reducing class was one of her few pleasures, necessary for her health, and *free,* she said Julian could at least put himself out to take her, considering all she did for him. Julian did not like to consider all she did for him, but every Wednesday night he braced himself and took her.

She was almost ready to go, standing before the hall mirror, putting on her hat, while he, his hands behind him, appeared pinned to the door frame, waiting like Saint Sebastian for the arrows to begin piercing him. The hat was new and had cost her seven dollars and a half. She kept saying, "Maybe I shouldn't have paid that for it. No, I shouldn't have. I'll take it off and return it tomorrow. I shouldn't have bought it."

Julian raised his eyes to heaven. "Yes, you should have bought it," he said. "Put it on and let's go." It was a hideous hat. A purple velvet flap came down on one side of it and stood up on the other; the rest of it was green and looked like a cushion with the stuffing out. He decided it was less comical than jaunty and pathetic. Everything that gave her pleasure was small and depressed him.

She lifted the hat one more time and set it down slowly on top of her head. Two wings of gray hair protruded on either side of her florid face, but her eyes, sky-blue, were as innocent and untouched by experience as they must have been when she was ten. Were it not that she was a widow who had struggled fiercely to feed and clothe and put him through school and who was supporting him still, "until he got on his feet," she might have been a little girl that he had to take to town.

"It's all right, it's all right," he said. "Let's go." He opened the door himself and started down the walk to get her going. The sky was a dying violet and the houses stood out darkly against it, bulbous liver-colored monstrosities of a uniform ugliness though no two were alike. Since this had been a fashionable neighborhood forty years ago, his mother persisted in thinking they did well to have an apartment in it. Each house had a narrow collar of dirt around it in which sat, usually, a grubby child. Julian walked with his hands in his pockets, his head down and thrust forward and his eyes glazed with the determination to make himself completely numb during the time he would be sacrificed to her pleasure.

The door closed and he turned to find the dumpy figure, surmounted by the atrocious hat, coming toward him. "Well," she said, "you only live once and paying a little more for it, I at least won't meet myself coming and going."

"Some day I'll start making money," Julian said gloomily—he knew he never would—"and you can have one of those jokes whenever you take the fit." But first they would move. He visualized a place where the nearest neighbor would be three miles away on either side.

"I think you're doing fine," she said, drawing on her gloves. "You've only been out of school a year. Rome wasn't built in a day."

She was one of the few members of the Y reducing class who arrived in hat and gloves and who had a son who had been to college. "It takes time," she said, "and the world is in such a mess. This hat looked better on me than any of the others, though when she brought it out I said, 'Take that thing back. I wouldn't have it on my head,' and she said, 'Now wait till you see it on,' and when she put it on me, I said, 'We-ull,' and she said, 'If you ask me, that hat does something for you and you do something for the hat, and besides,' she said, 'with that hat, you won't meet yourself coming and going.'"

Julian thought he could have stood his lot better if she had been selfish, if she had been an old hag who drank and screamed at him. He walked along, saturated in depression, as if in the midst of his martyrdom he had lost his faith. Catching sight of his long, hopeless, irritated face, she stopped suddenly with a grief-stricken look, and pulled back on his arm. "Wait on me," she said. "I'm going back to the house and take this thing off and tomorrow I'm going to return it. I was out of my head. I can pay the gas bill with that seven-fifty."

He caught her arm in a vicious grip. "You are not going to take it back," he said. "I like it."

"Well," she said. "I don't think I ought . . ."

"Shut up and enjoy it," he muttered, more depressed than ever.

"With the world in the mess it's in," she said, "it's a wonder we can enjoy anything. I tell you, the bottom rail is on the top."

Julian sighed.

"Of course," she said, "if you know who you are, you can go anywhere." She said this every time he took her to the reducing class. "Most of them in it are not our kind of people," she said, "but I can be gracious to anybody. I know who I am."

"They don't give a damn for your graciousness," Julian said savagely. "Knowing who you are is good for one generation only. You haven't the foggiest idea where you stand now or who you are."

She stopped and allowed her eyes to flash at him. "I most certainly do know who I am," she said, "and if you don't know who you are, I'm ashamed of you."

"Oh hell," Julian said.

"Your great-grandfather was a former governor of this state," she said. "Your grandfather was a prosperous landowner. Your grandmother was a Godhigh."

"Will you look around you," he said tensely, "and see where you are now?" and he swept his arm jerkily out to indicate the neighborhood, which the growing darkness at least made less dingy.

"You remain what you are," she said. "Your great-grandfather had a plantation and two hundred slaves."

"There are no more slaves," he said irritably.

"They were better off when they were," she said. He groaned to see that she was off on that topic. She rolled onto it every few days like a train on an open track. He knew every stop, every junction, every swamp along the way, and knew the exact point at which her conclusion would roll majestically into the station: "It's ridiculous. It's simply not realistic. They should rise, yes, but on their own side of the fence."

"Let's skip it," Julian said.

"The ones I feel sorry for," she said, "are the ones that are half white. They're tragic."

"Will you skip it?"

"Suppose we were half white. We would certainly have mixed feelings."

"I have mixed feelings now," he groaned.

"Well, let's talk about something pleasant," she said. "I remember going to Grandpa's when I was a little girl. Then the house had double stairways that went up to what was really the second floor—all the cooking was done on the first. I used to like to stay down in the kitchen on account of the way the walls smelled. I would sit with my nose pressed against the plaster and take deep breaths. Actually the place belonged to the Godhighs but your grandfather Chestny paid the mortgage and saved it for them. They were in reduced circumstances," she said, "but reduced or not, they never forgot who they were."

"Doubtless that decayed mansion reminded them," Julian muttered. He never spoke of it without contempt or thought of it without longing. He had seen it once when he was a child before it had been sold. The double stairways had rotted and been torn down. Negroes were living in it. But it remained in his mind as his mother had known it. It appeared in his dreams regularly. He would stand on the wide porch, listening to the rustle of oak leaves, then wander through the high-ceilinged hall into the parlor that opened onto it and gaze at the worn rugs and faded draperies. It occurred to him that it was he, not she, who could have appreciated it. He preferred its threadbare elegance to anything he could name and it was because of it that all the neighborhoods they had lived in had been a torment to him—whereas she had hardly known the difference. She called her insensitivity "being adjustable."

"And I remember the old darky who was my nurse, Caroline. There was no better person in the world. I've always had a great respect for my colored friends," she said. "I'd do anything in the world for them and they'd . . ."

"Will you for God's sake get off that subject?" Julian said. When he got on a bus by himself, he made it a point to sit down beside a Negro, in reparation as it were for his mother's sins.

"You're mighty touchy tonight," she said. "Do you feel all right?"

"Yes I feel all right," he said. "Now lay off."

She pursed her lips. "Well, you certainly are in a vile humor," she observed. "I just won't speak to you at all."

They had reached the bus stop. There was no bus in sight and Julian, his hands still jammed in his pockets and his head thrust forward, scowled down the empty street. The frustration of having to wait on the bus as well as ride on it began to creep up his neck like a hot hand. The presence of his mother was borne in upon him as she gave a pained sigh. He looked at her bleakly. She was holding herself very erect under the preposterous hat, wearing it like a banner of her imaginary dignity. There was in him an evil urge to break her spirit. He suddenly unloosened his tie and pulled it off and put it in his pocket.

She stiffened. "Why must you look like *that* when you take me to town?" she said. "Why must you deliberately embarrass me?"

"If you'll never learn where you are," he said, "you can at least learn where I am."

"You look like a—thug," she said.

"Then I must be one," he murmured.

"I'll just go home," she said. "I will not bother you. If you can't do a little thing like that for me . . ."

Rolling his eyes upward, he put his tie back on. "Restored to my class," he muttered. He thrust his face toward her and hissed, "True culture is in the mind, the *mind*," he said, and tapped his head, "the mind."

"It's in the heart," she said, "and in how you do things and how you do things is because of who you *are*."

"Nobody in the damn bus cares who you are."

"I care who I am," she said icily.

The lighted bus appeared on top of the next hill and as it approached, they moved out into the street to meet it. He put his hand under her elbow and hoisted her up on the creaking step. She entered with a little smile, as if she were going into a drawing room where everyone had been waiting for her. While he put in the tokens, she sat down on one of the broad front seats for three which faced the aisle. A thin woman with protruding teeth and long yellow hair was sitting on the end of it. His mother moved up beside her and left room for Julian beside herself. He sat down and looked at the floor across the aisle where a pair of thin feet in red and white canvas sandals were planted.

His mother immediately began a general conversation meant to attract anyone who felt like talking. "Can it get any hotter?" she said and removed from her purse a folding fan, black with a Japanese scene on it, which she began to flutter before her.

"I reckon it might could," the woman with the protruding teeth said, "but I know for a fact my apartment couldn't get no hotter."

"It must get the afternoon sun," his mother said. She sat forward and looked up and down the bus. It was half filled. Everybody was white. "I see we have the bus to ourselves," she said. Julian cringed.

"For a change," said the woman across the aisle, the owner of the red and white canvas sandals. "I come on one the other day and they were thick as fleas—up front and all through."

"The world is in a mess everywhere," his mother said. "I don't know how we've let it get in this fix."

"What gets my goat is all those boys from good families stealing automobile tires," the woman with the protruding teeth said. "I told my boy, I said you may not be rich but you been raised right and if I ever catch you in any such mess, they can send you on to the reformatory. Be exactly where you belong."

"Training tells," his mother said. "Is your boy in high school?"

"Ninth grade," the woman said.

"My son just finished college last year. He wants to write but he's selling typewriters until he gets started," his mother said.

The woman leaned forward and peered at Julian. He threw her such a malevolent look that she subsided against the seat. On the floor across the aisle there was an abandoned newspaper. He got up and got it and opened it out in front of him. His mother discreetly continued the conversation in a lower tone but the woman across the aisle said in a loud voice, "Well that's nice. Selling typewriters is close to writing. He can go right from one to the other."

"I tell him," his mother said, "that Rome wasn't built in a day."

Behind the newspaper Julian was withdrawing into the inner compartment of his mind where he spent most of his time. This was a kind of mental bubble in which he established himself when he could not bear to be a part of what was going on around him. From it he could see out and judge but in it he was safe from any kind of penetration from without. It was the only place where he felt free of the general idiocy of his fellows. His mother had never entered it but from it he could see her with absolute clarity.

The old lady was clever enough and he thought that if she had started from any of the right premises, more might have been expected of her. She lived according to the laws of her own fantasy world, outside of which he had never seen her set foot. The law of it was to sacrifice herself for him after she had first created the necessity to do so by making a mess of things. If he had permitted her sacrifices, it was only because her lack of foresight had made them necessary. All of her life had been a struggle to act like a Chestny without the Chestny goods, and to give him everything she thought a Chestny ought to have; but since, said she, it was fun to struggle, why complain? And when you had won, as she had won, what fun to look back on the hard times! He could not forgive her that she had enjoyed the struggle and that she thought *she* had won.

What she meant when she said she had won was that she had brought him up successfully and had sent him to college and that he had turned out so well—good looking (her teeth had gone unfilled so that his could be straightened), intelligent (he realized he was too intelligent to be a success), and with a future ahead of him (there was of course no future ahead of him). She excused his gloominess on the grounds that he was still growing up and his radical ideas on his lack of practical experience. She said he didn't yet know a thing about "life," that he hadn't even entered the real world—when already he was as disenchanted with it as a man of fifty.

The further irony of all this was that in spite of her, he had turned out so well. In spite of going to only a third-rate college, he had, on his own initiative, come out with a first-rate education; in spite of growing up dominated by a small mind, he had ended up with a large one; in spite of all her foolish views, he was free of prejudice and unafraid to face facts. Most miraculous of all, instead of being blinded by love for her as she was for him, he had cut himself emotionally free of her and could see her with complete objectivity. He was not dominated by mother.

The bus stopped with a sudden jerk and shook him from his meditation. A woman from the back lurched forward with little steps and barely escaped falling in his newspaper as she righted herself. She got off and a large Negro got on. Julian kept his paper lowered to watch. It gave him a certain satisfaction to see injustice in daily operation. It confirmed his view that with a few exceptions there was no one worth knowing within a radius of three hundred miles. The Negro was well dressed and carried a briefcase. He looked around and then sat down on the other end of the seat where the woman with the red and white canvas sandals was sitting. He immediately unfolded a newspaper and obscured himself behind it. Julian's mother's elbow at once prodded insistently into his ribs. "Now you see why I won't ride on these buses by myself," she whispered.

The woman with the red and white canvas sandals had risen at the same time the Negro sat down and had gone further back in the bus and taken the seat of the woman who had got off. His mother leaned forward and cast her an approving look.

Julian rose, crossed the aisle, and sat down in the place of the woman with the canvas sandals. From this position, he looked serenely across at his mother. Her face had turned an angry red. He stared at her, making his eyes the eyes of a stranger. He felt his tension suddenly lift as if he had openly declared war on her.

He would have liked to get in conversation with the Negro and to talk with him about art or politics or any subject that would be above the comprehension of those around them, but the man remained entrenched behind his paper. He was either ignoring the change of seating or had never noticed it. There was no way for Julian to convey his sympathy.

His mother kept her eyes fixed reproachfully on his face. The woman with the protruding teeth was looking at him avidly as if he were a type of monster new to her.

"Do you have a light?" he asked the Negro.

Without looking away from his paper, the man reached in his pocket and handed him a packet of matches.

"Thanks," Julian said. For a moment he held the matches foolishly. A No Smoking sign looked down upon him from over the door. This alone would not have deterred him; he had no cigarettes. He had quit smoking some months before because he could not afford it. "Sorry," he muttered and handed back the matches. The Negro lowered the paper and gave him an annoyed look. He took the matches and raised the paper again.

His mother continued to gaze at him but she did not take advantage of his momentary discomfort. Her eyes retained their battered look. Her face seemed to be unnaturally red, as if her blood pressure had risen. Julian allowed no glimmer of sympathy to show on his face. Having got the advantage, he wanted desperately to keep it and carry it through. He would have liked to teach her a lesson that would last her a while, but there seemed no way to continue the point. The Negro refused to come out from behind his paper.

Julian folded his arms and looked stolidly before him, facing her but as if he did not see her, as if he had ceased to recognize her existence. He visualized a scene in which, the bus having reached their stop, he would remain in his seat and when she said, "Aren't you going to get off?" he would look at her as at a stranger who had rashly addressed him. The corner they got off on was usually deserted, but it was well lighted and it would not hurt her to walk by herself the four blocks to the Y. He decided to wait until the time came and then decide whether or not he would let her get off by herself. He would have to be at the Y at ten to bring her back, but he could leave her wondering if he was going to show up. There was no reason for her to think she could always depend on him.

He retired again into the high-ceilinged room sparsely settled with large pieces of antique furniture. His soul expanded momentarily but then he became aware of his mother across from him and the vision shriveled. He studied her coldly. Her feet in little pumps dangled like a child's and did not quite reach the floor. She was training on him an exaggerated look of reproach. He felt completely detached from her. At that moment he could with pleasure have slapped her as he would have slapped a particularly obnoxious child in his charge.

He began to imagine various unlikely ways by which he could teach her a lesson. He might make friends with some distinguished Negro professor or lawyer and bring him home to spend the evening. He would be entirely justified but her blood pressure would rise to 300. He could not push her to the extent of making her have a stroke, and moreover, he had never been successful at making any Negro friends. He had tried to strike up an acquaintance on the bus with some of the better types, with ones that looked like professors or ministers or lawyers. One morning he had sat down next to a distinguished-looking dark brown man who had answered his questions with a sonorous solemnity but who had turned out to be an undertaker. Another day he had sat down beside a cigar-smoking Negro with a diamond ring on his finger, but after a few stilted pleasantries, the Negro had rung the buzzer and risen, slipping two lottery tickets into Julian's hand as he climbed over him to leave.

He imagined his mother lying desperately ill and his being able to secure only a Negro doctor for her. He toyed with that idea for a few minutes and then dropped it for a momentary vision of himself participating as a sympathizer in a sit-in demonstration. This was possible but he did not linger with it. Instead, he approached the ultimate horror. He brought home a beautiful suspiciously Negroid woman. Prepare yourself, he said. There is nothing you can do about it. This is the woman I've chosen. She's intelligent, dignified, even good, and she's suffered and she hasn't thought it *fun*. Now persecute us, go ahead and persecute us. Drive her out of here, but remember, you're driving me too. His eyes were narrowed and through the indignation he had generated, he saw his mother across the aisle, purple-faced, shrunken to the dwarflike proportions of her moral nature, sitting like a mummy beneath the ridiculous banner of her hat.

He was tilted out of his fantasy again as the bus stopped. The door opened with a sucking hiss and out of the dark a large, gaily dressed, sullen-looking colored woman got on with a little boy. The child, who might have been four, had on a short plaid suit and a Tyrolean hat with a blue feather in it. Julian hoped that he would sit down beside him and that the woman would push in beside his mother. He could think of no better arrangement.

As she waited for her tokens, the woman was surveying the seating possibilities—he hoped with the idea of sitting where she was least wanted. There was something familiar-looking about her but Julian could not place what it was. She was a giant of a woman. Her face was set not only to meet opposition but to seek it out. The downward tilt of her large lower lip was like a warning sign: DON'T TAMPER WITH ME. Her bulging figure was encased in a green crepe dress and her feet overflowed in red shoes. She had on a hideous hat. A purple velvet flap came down on one side of it and stood up on the other; the rest of it was green and looked like a cushion with the stuffing out. She carried a mammoth red pocketbook that bulged throughout as if it were stuffed with rocks.

To Julian's disappointment, the little boy climbed up on the empty seat beside his mother. His mother lumped all children, black and white, into the common category, "Cute," and she thought little Negroes were on the whole cuter than little white children. She smiled at the little boy as he climbed on the seat.

Meanwhile the woman was bearing down upon the empty seat beside Julian. To his annoyance, she squeezed herself into it. He saw his mother's face change as the woman settled herself next to him and he realized with satisfaction that this was more objectionable to her than it was to him. Her face seemed almost gray and there was a look of dull recognition in her eyes, as if suddenly she had sickened at some awful confrontation. Julian saw that it was because she and the woman had, in a sense, swapped sons. Though his mother would not realize the symbolic significance of this, she would feel it. His amusement showed plainly on his face.

The woman next to him muttered something unintelligible to herself. He was conscious of a kind of bristling next to him, a muted growling like that of an angry cat. He could not see anything but the red pocketbook upright on the bulging green thighs. He visualized the woman as she had stood waiting for her tokens—the ponderous figure, rising from the red shoes upward over the solid hips, the mammoth bosom, the haughty face, to the green and purple hat.

His eyes widened.

The vision of the two hats, identical, broke upon him with the radiance of a brilliant sunrise. His face was suddenly lit with joy. He could not believe that Fate had thrust upon his mother such a lesson. He gave a loud chuckle so that she would look at him and see that he saw. She turned her eyes on him slowly. The blue in them seemed to have turned a bruised purple. For a moment he had an uncomfortable sense of her innocence, but it lasted only a second before principle rescued him. Justice entitled him to laugh. His grin hardened until it said to her as plainly as if he were saying aloud: Your punishment exactly fits your pettiness. This should teach you a permanent lesson.

Her eyes shifted to the woman. She seemed unable to bear looking at him and to find the woman preferable. He became conscious again of the bristling presence at his side. The woman was rumbling like a volcano about to become active. His mother's mouth began to twitch slightly at one corner. With a sinking heart, he saw incipient signs of recovery on her face and realized that this was going to strike her suddenly as funny and was going to be no lesson at all. She kept her eyes on the woman and an amused smile came over her face as if the woman were a monkey that had stolen her hat. The little Negro was looking up at her with large fascinated eyes. He had been trying to attract her attention for some time.

"Carver!" the woman said suddenly. "Come heah!"

When he saw that the spotlight was on him at last, Carver drew his feet up and turned himself toward Julian's mother and giggled.

"Carver!" the woman said. "You heah me? Come heah!"

Carver slid down from the seat but remained squatting with his back against the base of it, his head turned slyly around toward Julian's mother, who was smiling at him. The woman reached a hand across the aisle and snatched him to her. He righted himself and hung backwards on her knees, grinning at Julian's mother. "Isn't he cute?" Julian's mother said to the woman with the protruding teeth.

"I reckon he is," the woman said without conviction.

The Negress yanked him upright but he eased out of her grip and shot across the aisle and scrambled, giggling wildly, onto the seat beside his love.

"I think he likes me," Julian's mother said, and smiled at the woman. It was the smile she used when she was being particularly gracious to an inferior. Julian saw everything lost. The lesson had rolled off her like rain on a roof.

The woman stood up and yanked the little boy off the seat as if she were snatching him from contagion. Julian could feel the rage in her at having no weapon like his mother's smile. She gave the child a sharp slap across his leg. He howled once and then thrust his head into her stomach and kicked his feet against her shins. "Be-have," she said vehemently.

The bus stopped and the Negro who had been reading the newspaper got off. The woman moved over and set the little boy down with a thump between herself and Julian. She held him firmly by the knee. In a moment he put his hands in front of his face and peeped at Julian's mother through his fingers.

"I see yooooooooo!" she said and put her hands in front of her face and peeped at him.

The woman slapped his hand down. "Quit yo' foolishness," she said, "before I knock the living Jesus out of you!"

Julian was thankful that the next stop was theirs. He reached up and pulled the cord. The woman reached up and pulled it at the same time. Oh my God, he thought. He had the terrible intuition that when they got off the bus together, his mother would open her purse and give the little boy a nickel. The gesture would be as natural to her as breathing. The bus stopped and the woman got up and lunged to the front, dragging the child, who wished to stay on, after her. Julian and his mother got up and followed. As they neared the door, Julian tried to relieve her of her pocket-book.

"No," she murmured, "I want to give the little boy a nickel."

"No!" Julian hissed. "No!"

She smiled down at the child and opened her bag. The bus door opened and the woman picked him up by the arm and descended with him, hanging at her hip. Once in the street she set him down and shook him.

Julian's mother had to close her purse while she got down the bus step but as soon as her feet were on the ground, she opened it again and began to rummage inside. "I can't find but a penny," she whispered, "but it looks like a new one."

"Don't do it!" Julian said fiercely between his teeth. There was a street-light on the corner and she hurried to get under it so that she could better see into her pocketbook. The woman was heading off rapidly down the street with the child still hanging backward on her hand.

"Oh little boy!" Julian's mother called and took a few quick steps and caught up with them just beyond the lamppost. "Here's a bright new penny for you," and she held out the coin, which shone bronze in the dim light.

The huge woman turned and for a moment stood, her shoulders lifted and her face frozen with frustrated rage, and stared at Julian's mother. Then all at once she seemed to explode like a piece of machinery that had been given one ounce of pressure too much. Julian saw the black fist swing out with the red pocketbook. He shut his eyes and cringed as he heard the woman shout, "He don't take nobody's pennies!" When he opened his eyes, the woman was disappearing down the street with the little boy staring wide-eyed over her shoulder. Julian's mother was sitting on the sidewalk.

"I told you not to do that," Julian said angrily. "I told you not to do that!"

He stood over her for a minute, gritting his teeth. Her legs were stretched out in front of her and her hat was on her lap. He squatted down and looked her in the face. It was totally expressionless. "You got exactly what you deserved," he said. "Now get up."

He picked up her pocketbook and put what had fallen out back in it. He picked the hat up off her lap. The penny caught his eye on the sidewalk and he picked that up and let it drop before her eyes into the purse. Then he stood up and leaned over and held his hand out to pull her up. She remained immobile. He sighed. Rising above them on either side were black apartment buildings, marked with irregular rectangles of light. At the end of the block a man came out of a door and walked off in the opposite direction. "All right," he said, "suppose somebody happens by and wants to know why you're sitting on the sidewalk?"

She took the hand and, breathing hard, pulled heavily up on it and then stood for a moment, swaying slightly as if the spots of light in the darkness were circling around her. Her eyes, shadowed and confused, finally settled on his face. He did not try to conceal his irritation. "I hope this teaches you a lesson," he said. She leaned forward and her eyes raked his face. She seemed trying to determine his identity. Then, as if she found nothing familiar about him, she started off with a headlong movement in the wrong direction.

"Aren't you going on to the Y?" he asked.

"Home," she muttered.

"Well, are we walking?"

For answer she kept going. Julian followed along, his hands behind him. He saw no reason to let the lesson she had had got without backing it up with an explanation of its meaning. She might as well be made to understand what had happened to her. "Don't think that was just an uppity Negro woman," he said. "That was the whole colored race which will no longer take your condescending pennies. That was your black double. She can wear the same hat as you, and to be sure," he added gratuitously (because he thought it was funny), "it looked better on her than it did on you. What all this means," he said, "is that the old world is gone. The old manners are obsolete and your graciousness is not worth a damn." He thought bitterly of the house that had been lost for him. "You aren't who you think you are," he said.

She continued to plow ahead, paying no attention to him. Her hair had come undone on one side. She dropped her pocketbook and took no notice. He stooped and picked it up and handed it to her but she did not take it.

"You needn't act as if the world has come to an end," he said, "because it hasn't. From now on you've got to live in a new world and face a few realities for a change. Buck up," he said, "it won't kill you."

She was breathing fast.

"Let's wait on the bus," he said.

"Home," she said thickly.

"I hate to see you behave like this," he said. "Just like a child. I should be able to expect more of you." He decided to stop where he was and make her stop and wait for the bus. "I'm not going any farther," he said, stopping. "We're going on the bus."

She continued to go on as if she had not heard him. He took a few steps and caught her arm and stopped her. He looked into her face and caught his breath. He was looking into a face he had never seen before. "Tell Grandpapa to come get me," she said.

He stared, stricken.

"Tell Caroline to come get me," she said.

Stunned, he let her go and she lurched forward again, walking as if one leg were shorter than the other. A tide of darkness seemed to be sweeping her from him. "Mother!" he cried. "Darling, sweetheart, wait!" Crumpling, she fell to the pavement. He dashed forward and fell at her side, crying, "Mamma, Mamma!" He turned her over. Her face was fiercely distorted. One eye, large and staring, moved slightly to the left as if it had become unmoored. The other remained fixed on him, raked his face again, found nothing and closed.

"Wait here, wait here!" he cried and jumped up and began to run for help toward a cluster of lights he saw in the distance ahead of him. "Help, help!" he shouted, but his voice was thin, scarcely a thread of sound. The lights drifted farther away the faster he ran and his feet moved numbly as if they carried him nowhere. The tide of darkness seemed to sweep him back to her, postponing from moment to moment his entry into the world of guilt and sorrow.

# The Red Man's Burden
## 1970

### Peter Collier

When fourteen Indian college students invaded Alcatraz on a cold, foggy morning in the first part of November—claiming ownership "by right of discovery," and citing an 1868 treaty allowing the Sioux possession of unused federal lands—they seemed in a light-hearted mood. After establishing their beachhead, they told the press that they had come there because Alcatraz already had all the necessary features of a reservation: dangerously uninhabitable buildings; no fresh water; inadequate sanitation; and the certainty of total unemployment. They said they were planning to make the five full-time caretakers wards of a Bureau of Caucasian Affairs, and offered to take this troublesome real estate off the white man's hands for $24, payment to be made in glass beads. The newspapers played it up big, calling the Indians a "raiding party." When, after a 19-hour stay, the Indians were persuaded to leave the island, everyone agreed that it had been a good publicity stunt.

If the Indians had ever been joking about Alcatraz, however, it was with the bitter irony that fills colonial subjects' discourse with the mother-country. When they returned to the mainland, they didn't fall back into the cigar-store stoicism that is supposedly the red man's prime virtue. In fact, their first invasion ignited a series of meetings and strategy-sessions; two weeks later they returned to the rock, this time with a force of nearly 100 persons, a supply network, and the clear intention of staying. What had begun as a way of drawing attention to the position of the contemporary Indian, developed into a plan for doing something about it. And when the government, acting through the General Services Administration, gave them a deadline for leaving, the Indians replied with demands of their own: Alcatraz was theirs, they said, and it would take U.S. Marshals to remove them and their families; they planned to turn the island into a major cultural center and research facility; they would negotiate only the mechanics of deeding over the land, and that only with Interior Secretary Walter Hickel during a face to face meeting. The Secretary never showed up, but the government's deadlines were withdrawn.

*"On this island, I saw not whether the people had personal property, for it seemed to me that whatever one had, they all took share of, especially of eatable things."*—CHRISTOPER COLUMBUS

Alcatraz is Indian Territory: The old warning to "Keep Off U.S. Property" now reads "Keep off Indian Property;" security guards with red armbands stand near the docks to make sure it is obeyed. Women tend fires beneath huge iron cauldrons filled with food, while their kids play frisbee in what was once a convict's exercise yard. Some of the men work on the prison's wiring system or try to get more cellblocks cleared out for the Indian people who are arriving daily from all over the country; others sit fishing on the wharf with hand-lines, watching quietly as the rip-tides churn in the Bay. During the day, rock music plays over portable radios and a series of soap operas flit across a TV; at night, the prison is filled with the soft sounds of ceremonial drums and eerie songs in Sioux, Kiowa and Navajo.

In the few weeks of its occupation, Alcatraz has become a mecca, a sort of red man's Selma. Indian people come, stay a few days, and then leave, taking with them a sense of wonderment that it has happened. Middle-aged "establishment" Indians are there. They mix with younger insurgents like Lehman Brightman (the militant Sioux who heads a red power organizations called the United Native Americans), Mad-Bear Anderson (the Iroquois traditionalist from upstate New York who fought to get the United Nations to stop the U.S. Army Corps of Engineers' flooding of precious Seneca Indian lands), Sid Mills (the young Yakima who demanded a discharge from the Army after returning from Viet-Nam so that he could fight his real war— against the state of Washington's denial of his people's fishing rights), and Al Bridges (one of the leaders of the first Washington fish-ins in 1964, who now faces a possible ten-year prison sentence for defying the state Fish and Game Commission). The composition of the ad hoc Indian community changes constantly, but the purpose remains the same: to make Alcatraz a powerful symbol of liberation springing out of the long American imprisonment.

The people enjoy themselves, spending a lot of time sitting around the campfire talking and gossiping. But there is a sense of urgency beneath the apparent lassitude. Richard Oakes, a 27-year-old Mohawk who worked in high steel construction before coming West to go to college, is one of the elected spokesmen. Sitting at a desk in the old Warden's Office, he talks about the hope of beginning a new organization, the Confederacy of American Indian Nations, to weld Indian groups all over the country into one body capable of taking power away from the white bureaucracy. He acknowledges that the pan-Indian movements which have sprung up before have always been crushed. "But time is running out for us," he says. "We have everything at stake. And if we don't make it now, then we'll get trapped at the bottom of that white world out there, and wind up as some kind of Jack Jones with a social security number and that's all. Not just on Alcatraz, but every place else, the Indian is in his last stand for cultural survival."

This sentiment is reflected in the slogans lettered on walls all over the prison, the red paint bleeding down onto the concrete. One of them declares: "Better Red than Dead."

*"I also heard of numerous instances in which our men had cut out the private parts of females and wore them in their hats while riding in the ranks."*—A U.S. ARMY LIEUTENANT, TESTIFYING ABOUT THE SAND CREEK MASSACRE OF 1864

The Alcatraz occupation is still popularly regarded as the engaging fun and games of Indian college kids. In its new coverage of the U.S. Coast Guard's feeble attempt to blockade ships running supplies to the island, one local television station found amusement in showing their films to the musical accompaniment of U.S. cavalry bugle calls. It was not so amusing to the occupiers, however. The California Indians now on the Rock know that their people were decimated from a population of 100,000 in 1850 when the gold rush settlers arrived, to about 15,000 thirty years later, and that whole tribes, languages and cultures were erased from the face of the earth. There are South Dakota Indians there whose grandparents were alive in 1890 when several hundred Sioux, mostly women and children leaving the reservation to find food, were caught at Wounded Knee, killed, and buried in a common grave—the old daguerreotypes still showing heavily-mustachioed soldiers standing stiffly over the frozen bodies like hunters with their trophies. Cowboys and Indians is not a pleasant game for the Alcatraz Indians and some must wonder whether, in another 150 years, German children will be gaily playing Nazis and Jews.

But the past is not really at issue. What is at stake today, as Richard Oakes says, is cultural survival. Some of the occupiers have known Indian culture all their lives; some have been partially assimilated away from it and are now trying to return. All understand that it is in jeopardy, and they want some assurance that Indian-ness will be available to their children. It sounds like a fair request, but fairness has never ruled the destiny of the Indian in America. In fighting for survival, the Indians of Alcatraz are challenging the lies perpetuated by anthropologists and bureaucrats alike, who insist that the red man is two things: an incompetent "ward" addicted to the paternalism of government, and an anachronism whose past is imprisoned in white history and whose only future is as an invisible swimmer in the American mainstream. The people on Alcatraz have entered a struggle on a large scale that parallels the smaller, individual struggles for survival that many of them have known themselves; it is the will to exist as individuals that brought them together in determination to exist as a people.

*"When Robert Kennedy came, that was the only day they ever showed any respect for the Indian, just on that one day, and after that, they could care less."*
—A FRESHMAN STUDENT AT BLACKFOOT, IDAHO, HIGH SCHOOL

One of the original 14 on Alcatraz was a pretty 22-year-old Shoshone-Bannock girl named La Nada Means. Her hair is long and reddish-black; her nose arches slightly and prominent cheekbones square out her face. Her walk is slightly pidgeon-toed, the result of a childhood disease for which she never received treatment. If you tell her that she looks very Indian, she will thank you, but with a searching look that suggests she had heard the same comment before, and not as a compliment.

"When I was little," she says, "I remember my family as being very poor. There were 12 of us kids, and we were always hungry. I remember sometimes getting to the point where I'd eat anything I could get my hands on—leaves, small pieces of wood, anything. The other thing I remember is the meanness of the small towns around the reservation. Blackfoot, Pocatello—they all had signs in the store windows to keep Indians out. One of them I'll never forget; it said, 'No Indians or Dogs Allowed.' There were Indian stalls in the public bathrooms; Indians weren't served in a lot of the restaurants; and we just naturally all sat in the balcony of the theaters. You learn early what all that means. It becomes part of the way you look at yourself."

She grew up on the Fort Hall reservation in southern Idaho. The Jim Crow atmosphere of the surrounding small towns has lessened somewhat with the passage of time and the coming of the civil-rights bills, but it is still very much present in the attitude of white townsfolk towards Indians. And while there are no longer the small outbreaks of famine that occurred on the reservation when La Nada was growing up in the '50s, Fort Hall is still one of the bleakest areas in the country, and the people there are among the poorest.

Like most Indian children of her generation (and like a great many today), La Nada Means was sent away to school. Her youth became a series of separations from home and family, each more traumatic than the one before. The first school she attended was St. Mary's School for Indian Girls in Springfield, South Dakota. "I took a lot of classes in subjects like 'Laundry,' " she remembers, "where the classwork was washing the headmaster's clothes. All Indian people are supposed to be good with their hands, you know, and also hard workers, so we didn't do too much regular schoolwork at St. Mary's. They also had what they called a Summer Home Program where you're sent out during the summer break to live with a white family. It was supposed to teach you white etiquette and things like that, and make you forget your savage Indian ways. When I was 13, I was sent up to Minnesota where I became a sort of housekeeper for the summer. I don't remember too much about it, except that the wages I got, about $5 a week, were sent back to St. Mary's and I never saw them. After being at that school a little while, I got all upset. They said I was 'too outspoken,' and expelled me. After I got back to Fort Hall, I had my first breakdown."

For awhile she attended public school in Blackfoot, the small town bordering the reservation. She was suspended because she objected to the racial slurs against Indians which were built into the curriculum. She was 15 when the Bureau of Indian Affairs (BIA) sent her to its boarding school in Chilocco,

Oklahoma. On her first day there, the matrons ordered her to lower the hems on the two dresses she owned. She refused and was immediately classified as a troublemaker. "At Chilocco, you're either a 'good girl' or a 'bad girl,' " she says. "They put me in the bad girls' dormitory right away with Indians mainly from the Northwest. The Oklahoma Indians were in the good girls' dorm, and the matrons constantly tried to keep us agitated by setting the tribes to fighting with each other. Everything was like the Army. There were bells, drills and set hours for everything. The food was called 'GI Chow.' There was a lot of brutality, but it was used mainly on the boys, who lived in another wing. Occasionally they'd let the boys and girls get together. You all stood in this big square; you could hold hands, but if the matrons saw you getting too close, they'd blow a whistle and then you'd have to march back to the dorm."

La Nada made the honor roll, but was expelled from Chilocco after a two-month stay for being involved in a fight. "The matrons just had it in for me, I guess. They got about 100 other Indian girls against me and a few other 'bad girls.' They put us in a small room and when the fight was ready to begin, they turned out the lights and walked out, locking the doors behind them. We had a "riot," and I got beat up. The next day, the head of the school called me into his office and said that I didn't fit in."

She was sent off with one dollar, a sack lunch, and a one-way bus ticket from Chilocco back to Idaho. She lived with her family for a few months, helping her father collect data about conditions at Fort Hall, and then was sent by the BIA to another of its boarding schools, Stewart Institute, in Carson City, Nevada. Her reputation as a "difficult Indian" followed her, and she was again sent home after being at Stewart for less than a day. The BIA threatened to send her to "reform" school; then it forgot about her. "I stayed around the reservation for awhile," she says, "and when I got to be 17, I took GED [high school equivalent] exams. I only had about nine real years of schooling, but I scored pretty well and got into Idaho State College. I lasted there for a semester, and then quit. I didn't really know what to do. At Fort Hall, you either work in some kind of menial job with the BIA agency there, or you go off the reservation to find a job in one of the towns. If you choose the BIA, you know that they'll try to drill a subservient mentality into you; and in the towns, the discrimination is pretty bad."

La Nada again spent time working with her father, a former tribal chairman. They sent out letters to congressmen and senators describing conditions on the reservations, and tired to get the Bureau of Indian Affairs office to respond. As a result, her father was harassed by local law enforcement officials. La Nada drifted for a time and then asked the BIA for "relocation" off the reservation. Many of the Fort Hall Indians have taken this route and 80 per cent of them return to the reservation, because, as La Nada says, "things in the slums where you wind up are even worse than on the reservation, and you don't have your people to support you."

The BIA gave her a one-way ticket to San Francisco, one of eight major relocation centers in the country. When she first arrived, she sat in the local

BIA office from 8 to 5 for a few days, waiting for them to help her find a job. They didn't, and she found a series of temporary clerk jobs by herself. As soon as she found work, the BIA cut off her $140 a month relocation payment. She wound up spending a lot of time in the "Indian bars" which are found in San Francisco and every other relocation town. She worked as a housekeeper in the private home for Indian girls where the BIA had first sent her, and as a barmaid in a beer parlor. She was "drunk most of the time," and she became pregnant. She was 17 years old.

"After I had the baby," she says, "my mother came out from the reservation and got him. She said they'd take care of him back home until I got on my feet. I really didn't know what to do. The only programs the BIA has are vocational training for menial jobs, and I didn't especially want to be a beautician. Actually, I wanted to try college again, but when I told this to a BIA counselor, he said they didn't have any money for that and told me I was being 'irrational and unrealistic.'

"All types of problems develop when you're on relocation. The Indian who has come to the city is like a man without a country. Whose jurisdiction are you under, the BIA's or the state's? You go to a county hospital when you're sick and they say, 'Aren't you taken care of by the Indian Affairs people?' It's very confusing. You hang around with other Indians, but they are as bad off as you are. Anyway, I started sinking lower and lower. I married this Sioux and lived with his family awhile. I got pregnant again. But things didn't work out in the marriage, and I left. After I had the baby, I ended up in the San Francisco General psychiatric ward for a few weeks. I was at the bottom, really at the bottom. Indian people get to this point all the time, especially when they're relocated into the big city and are living in the slums. At that point, you've got two choices: either kill yourself and get it all over with—a lot of Indians do this—or try to go all the way up, and this is almost impossible."

As she looks at it now, La Nada feels she was "lucky." She tried to get admitted to the local colleges, but was refused because of her school record. Finally, because the University of California "needed a token Indian in its Economic Opportunity Program for minority students," she was admitted in the fall of 1968. She did well in her classes and became increasingly active, helping to found the United Native Americans organization and working to get more Indian students admitted into the EOP program. "After my first year there," she says, "everything was going along all right. I liked school and everything, and I felt I was doing some good. But I felt myself getting swallowed up by something that was bigger than me. The thing was that I didn't want to stop being an Indian, and there were all these pressures, very hidden ones, that were trying to make me white." At the summer break she went back to the reservation and spent some time with her family. The next quarter she became involved in the Third World Liberation Front strike at Berkeley, fighting for a school of Ethnic Studies, including a Native American program. She was suspended by the University.

La Nada's experiences, far from being extreme cases, are like those of most young Indians. If she is unique at all, it is because she learned the value of fighting back.

*"We need fewer and fewer 'experts' on Indians. What we need is a cultural leave-us-alone agreement, in spirit and in fact."*—VINE DELORIA, JR.

Each generation of Americans rediscovers for itself what is fashionably called the "plight" of the Indian. The American Indian today has a life expectancy of approximately 44 years, more than 25 years below the national average. He has the highest infant mortality rate in the country (among the more than 50,000 Alaskan natives, one of every four babies dies before reaching his first birthday). He suffers from epidemics of diseases which were supposed to have disappeared from America long ago.

A recent Department of Public Health report states that among California Indians, "water from contaminated sources is used in 38 to 42 per cent of the homes, and water must be hauled under unsanitary conditions by 40 to 50 per cent of all Indian families." Conditions are similar in other states. A high proportion of reservation housing throughout the country is officially classified as "substandard," an antiseptic term which fails to conjure up a tiny, two-room log cabin holding a family of 13 at Fort Hall; a crumbling Navajo hogan surrounded by broken plumbing fixtures hauled in to serve as woodbins; or a gutted automobile body in which a Pine Ridge Sioux family huddles against the South Dakota winter.

On most reservations, a 50 per cent unemployment rate is not considered high. Income per family among Indian people is just over $1500 per year—the lowest of any group in the country. But this, like the other figures, is deceptive. It does not suggest, for instance, the quality of the daily life of families on the Navajo reservation who live on $600 per year (exchanging sheep's wool and hand-woven rugs with white traders for beans and flour), who never have real money and who are perpetually sinking a little further into credit debt.

To most Americans, the conditions under which the Indian is forced to live are a perennial revelation. On one level, the symptoms are always being tinkered with half-heartedly and the causes ignored; on another level, the whole thrust of the Government's Indian policy appears calculated to perpetuate the Indians' "plight." This is why La Nada Means and the other Indians have joined what Janet McCloud, a leader of the Washington fishing protests, calls "the last, continuing Indian War." The enemies are legion, and they press in from every side: the studiously ignorant politicians, the continuously negligent Department of the Interior, and the white business interests who are allowed to prey upon the reservations' manpower and resources. But as the Indian has struggled to free himself from the suffocating embrace of white history, no enemy has held the death grip more tightly than has his supposed guardian, in effect his "keeper": the Bureau of Indian Affairs.

The Bureau came into being in 1824 as a division of the War Department.

Fifteen years later it was shifted to the Department of the Interior, the transition symbolizing the fact that the Indian was beginning to be seen not as a member of a sovereign, independent nation, but as a "ward," his land and life requiring constant management. This is the view that has informed the BIA for over a century. With its 16,000 employees and its outposts all over the country, the Bureau has become what Cherokee anthropologist Robert Thomas calls "the most complete colonial system in the world."

It is also a classic bureaucratic miasma. A recent book on Indian Affairs, *Our Brother's Keeper,* notes that on the large Pine Ridge reservation, "$8040 a year is spent per family to help the Oglala Sioux Indians out of poverty. Yet median income among these Indians is $1910 per family. At last count there was nearly one bureaucrat for each and every family on the reservation."

The paternalism of the BIA, endless and debilitating, is calculated to keep the Indian in a state of perpetual juvenilization, without rights, dependent upon the meagre and capricious beneficence of power. The Bureau's power over its "wards," whom it defines and treats as children, seems limitless. The BIA takes care of the Indian's money, doling it out to him when it considers his requests worthy; it determines the use of the Indian's land; it is in charge of the development of his natural resources; it relocates him from the reservation to the big city ghetto; it educates his children. It relinquishes its hold over him only reluctantly, even deciding whether or not his will is valid after he dies.

This bureaucratic paternalism hems the Indian in with an incomprehensible maze of procedures and regulations, never allowing him to know quite where he stands or what he can demand and how. Over 5000 laws, statutes and court decisions apply to the Indians alone. As one Indian student says, "Our people have to go to law school just to live a daily life."

The BIA is the Indian's point of contact with the white world, the concrete expression of this society's attitude towards him. The BIA manifests both stupidity and malice; but it is purely neither. It is guided by something more elusive, a whole world view regarding the Indian and what is good for him. Thus the BIA's overseership of human devastation begins by teaching bright-eyed youngsters the first formative lessons in what it is to be an Indian.

*"It is unnecessary to mention the power which schools would have over the rising generation of Indians. Next to teaching them to work, the most important thing is to teach them the English language. Into their own language there is woven so much mythology and sorcery that a new one is needed in order to aid them in advancing beyond their baneful superstitions."*—JOHN WESLEY POWELL

The Darwinian educational system which La Nada Means endured is not a thing of the past. Last spring, for instance, the BIA's own Educational Division studied Chilocco and came to the following conclusions: "There is evidence of criminal malpractice, not to mention physical and mental perversion, by certain staff members." The report went on to outline the disastrous conditions at the school, noting among other things that "youngsters reported they were handcuffed for as long as 18 hours in the dormitory . . . or chained to a basement pillar or from a suspended pipe. One team member . . . verified a youngster's hurt arms, the deformed hands of another boy, and an obviously broken rib of another. . . ."

The BIA responded to this report by suppressing it and transferring the investigators who submitted it. The principal of Chilocco was fired, but more as punishment for letting such things be discovered than for the conditions themselves. The same story is repeated at other BIA boarding schools. At the Intermountain Indian School in Utah, Indian children suspected of drinking have their heads ducked into filthy toilets by school disciplinarians. At Sherman Institute in Riverside, California, students of high school age are fed on a budget of 76 cents a day.

But there is a far more damaging and subtle kind of violence at work in the school as well. It is, in the jargon of educational psychology, the initiation of a "failure-orientation," and it derives from the fact that the children and their culture are held in such obviously low regard. Twenty-five per cent of all BIA teachers admit that they would rather be teaching whites; up to 70 per cent leave the BIA schools after one year. If a teacher has any knowledge at all of his student's needs and backgrounds, he gets it from a two-week non-compulsory course offered at the beginning of the year. One teacher, a former Peace Corps volunteer who returned to teach at the Navajo reservation, told the Senate Subcommittee on Indian Education that the principal of her BIA school habitually made statements such as "All Navajos are brain-damaged," and "Navajo culture belongs in a museum."

The results of the Indian's education, whether it be supervised by the BIA or by the public school system, indicates how greatly the system fails him. Twenty per cent of all Indian men have less than five years of schooling. According to a recent report to the Carnegie Foundation, there is a 60 per cent drop-out rate among Indian children as a whole, and those who do manage to stay in school fall further behind the longer they attend. A study of the Stewart Institute in Carson City, Nevada, for instance, shows that Indian sixth graders score 5.2 on the California Achievement Test. Six years later, at graduation, their achievement level is 8.4.

In a strange sense, the Indian student's education does prepare him for what lies ahead. What it teaches him is that he is powerless and inferior, and that he was destined to be so when he was born an Indian. Having spent his youth being managed and manhandled, the Indian is accustomed to the notion that his business must be taken care of for him. He is thus ideally equipped to stand by and watch the BIA collect mortgages on his future.

> *"We should test our thinking against the thinking of the wisest Indians and their friends, [but] this does not mean that we are going to let, as someone put it, Indian people themselves decide what the policy should be."*—STUART UDALL

The Indians of California have more than their share of troubles—in part because they never received an adequate land base by government treaty.

They are scattered up and down the state on reservations which are rarely larger than 10,000 acres and on rancherias as small as one acre. It takes a special determination to find these Indians, for most of them live in backwoods shacks, hidden from view as well as from water and electricity.

They have to struggle for every bit of federal service they get; disservice, however, comes easy. In 1969 the only irrigation money the BIA spent in all of Southern California, where water is an especially precious commodity to the Indians, was not for an Indian at all, but for a white farmer who had bought an Indian's land on the Pala reservation. The BIA spent $2500—of money appropriated by Congress for the Indians—to run a 900-foot pipeline to this white man's land. The Indians at Pala have been asking for irrigation lines for years, but less than one-half of their lands have them.

At the Resighini rancheria, a 228-acre reservation in Northern California, the Simpson Timber Company had been paying the Indians 25 cents per 1000 feet for the lumber it transported across their land. The total paid to the Indians in 1964 was $4725, and the right of way was increasing in value every year. Then the BIA, acting without warning, sold the right of way outright to Simpson Timber Company for $2500, or something less than one-half its yearly value.

The tiny Agua Caliente band of Indians sits on top of some of the most valuable land in the country: over 600 acres in the heart of Palm Springs. In the late '50s, the BIA, reacting to pressure from developers, obligingly transferred its jurisdiction over the Agua Caliente to a judge of the State Superior Court in the Palm Springs area who appointed "conservators" and "guardians" to make sure that the Indians would not be swindled as development took place. Ten years later, in 1967, a Riverside Press Enterprise reporter wrote a devastating series of articles showing the incredible fees collected for "protecting" the Agua Calientes. One conservator collected a fee of $9000 from his Indian's $9170 bank account; an Indian minor wound up with $3000 out of a $23,000 income, his guardian taking the rest. The "abdication of responsibility" with which the BIA was charged is surely a mild description of what happened to the Agua Calientes, who are supposedly the "richest Indians in the world" living on what is regarded as "an ermine-lined reservation."

The Indian Claims Commission was set up in the 1940's to compensate tribes for the lands stolen during the period of white conquest. In the California claims award of 1964, the Indians were given 47 cents an acre, based on the land's fair market value in 1851. The total sum, $29 million, less "offsets" for the BIA's services over the years, still has not been distributed. When it is, the per capita payout will come to about $600, and the poorest Indians in the state, will have to go off welfare to spend it. The BIA opposed an amendment to the Claims Award which would have exempted this money in determining welfare eligibility. The BIA testified that such an amendment constituted preferential treatment, and that it had been struggling for years to get *equal* treatment for the Indian. The amendment failed, and California's Indians will have to pay for a few months bread and rent with the money they are getting in return for the land that was taken from them.

Cases such as these exist in every state where Indian people live. If the Indian is the Vanishing American, it is the BIA's magic which makes him so. California Indians are fortunate only in one respect: they have an OEO-funded legal rights organization, the California Indian Legal Services, which attempts to minimize the depredations. Most Indians have no one to protect them from the agency which is supposed to be their advocate.

> *"Once we were happy in our own country and we were seldom hungry, for then the two-leggeds and the four-leggeds lived together like relatives, and there was plenty for them and for us. But the Wasichus [white men] came, and they have made little islands for us . . . and always these islands are becoming smaller, for around them surges the gnawing flood of the Wasichu; and it is dirty with lies and greed. . . ."*—BLACK ELK, AN OGLALA HOLY MAN

At the entrance to the Fort Hall reservation, where La Nada Means grew up, there is a plaque which commemorates the appearance in 1834 of the first white traders and indicates that the Hudson Bay Company later acquired the Fort and made it into an important stopover on the Oregon Trail. But other aspects of the history of Fort Hall are left unmentioned. It is not noted, for instance, that by the time a formal treaty was signed with the Bannock and Northern Shoshone in 1868, the whites who settled this part of Southern Idaho were paying between $25 and $100 for a good Indian scalp.

Today, the approximately 2800 Shoshone-Bannocks live on the 520,000-acre reservation, all that remains of the 1.8 million acres of their land which the treaty originally set aside for their ancestors to keep. The largest single reduction came in 1900, when the government took over 416,000 acres, paying the Indians a little more than $1 an acre for the land. As late as the beginning of World War II, the government took over another 3000 acres to make an airfield. It paid the Indians $10 an acre; after the war, it deeded the land to the city of Pocatello for $1 an acre, for use as a municipal airport. Each acre is now worth $500.

But the big problem on the Fort Hall reservation today is not the loss of large sections of land; rather it is the slow and steady attrition of Indian holdings and their absolute powerlessness to do anything about it. In 1887, the Dawes Allotment Act was passed as a major piece of "progressive" Indian legislation, providing for the break-up of community held reservation land so that each individual Indian would receive his plot of irrigable farming land and some grazing land. The federal government would still hold the land in trust, so it could be sold only with BIA approval, the assumption being that an individual holding would give the Indian incentive to be a farmer and thus ease him into American agricultural patterns. Fort Hall shows that the law had quite different effects.

Today, some of these original allotments are owned by anywhere from two to 40 heirs. Because of the complexity of kinship relationships, some Indian people own fractional interests in several of these "heirship lands" but have no ground that is all their own. These lands are one of the symbols of the ambiguity and inertia that rule at Fort Hall. As Edward Boyer, a former chairman of the tribal council, says, "Some of the people, they might want to exchange interests in the land or buy some of the other heirs out so they can have a piece of ground to build a house on and do some farming. Also, a lot of us would like the tribe to buy these lands up and then assign them to the young people who don't have any place of their own. But the BIA has this policy of leasing out these lands to the white farmers. A lot of the time the owners don't even know about it."

The BIA at Fort Hall doesn't like the idea of any Indian lands laying idle. And the land is rich, some of the best potato-growing land there is. Its value and its yield are increasing every year. Driving through the reservation, you can't avoid being struck by the green symmetry of the long cultivated rows and by the efficiency of the army of men and machinery working them. The only trouble is that the men are white, and the profits from Fort Hall's rich land all flow out of the Indian community. The BIA is like any technocracy: it is more interested in "efficient" use than in proper use. The most "efficient" way for Fort Hall's lands to be used is by white industrialist-farmers with capital. Thus the pattern has been established: white lessees using Indian land, irrigating with Indian water, and then harvesting with bracero workers.

All leases must be approved by the BIA Superintendent's office; they may be and are given without the consent of the Indians who own the land. The BIA has also allowed white lessees to seek "consents" from the Indians, which in effect provide for blank leases, the specific terms to be filled in later on. The BIA authorizes extremely long leases of the land. This leads to what a recent field study of Fort Hall, conducted by the Senate Subcommittee on Indian Education, calls "small fortunes" for white developers: "One non-Indian in 1964 leased a large tract of Indian land for 13 years at $.30-$.50/acre/year. While the lease did stipulate that once the lessee installed sprinkler irrigation the annual rent would rise to $1.50-$2.00/acre, Indians in 1968 could have demanded $20-$30 for such land. Meanwhile, the dependent University Agriculture Extension Service estimates that such potato operations bring the non-Indian lessee an annual *net* profit of $200 per acre." In addition, these leases are usually given by the BIA on a non-competitive, non-bidding basis to assure "the good will of the surrounding community." Fort Hall has rich and loamy land, but Indian people now work less than 17 per cent of it themselves and the figure is declining.

The power of white farmer-developers and businessmen within the local Bureau of Indian Affairs office is a sore point with most people at Fort Hall. They have rich lands, but theirs is one of the poorest reservations. They are told that much revenue comes both to the tribe and to individuals as a result of the BIA farm and mine leasing program, yet they know that if all the revenues were divided up the yield would be about $300 per capita a year. But for some of them, men like Joseph "Frank" Thorpe, Jr., the question of farming and mining leases is academic. Thorpe was a successful cattleman until BIA policies cut down the herds; now he is in the business of letting other people's cattle graze on his land.

Livestock are something of a fixation with Thorpe. He comes from a people who were proud horsemen, and he owns an Apaloosa mare and a couple of other horses. As he drives over the reservation, he often stops to look at others' cattle. In the basement of his home are several scrapbooks filled with documents tracing the destruction of the cattle business at Fort Hall. There is a yellowing clipping from the Salt Lake City Tribune of November 4, 1950, which says: "Fort Hall Indians have been more successful in cattle raising than any other activity. Theirs is the oldest Indian Cattleman's Association in the country. Association members raise more than 10,000 head of purebred herefords, and plan gradually to increase the herd. . . ." That was how it was 20 years ago. Thorpe, just back from war-time duty with the Marines, worked his herd and provided jobs for many of his kinsmen; the future was promising. Yet by 1958, there were only 3000 head of Indian owned cattle left, and today there are only ten families still involved in full-time cattle operation.

"Around the early '50s," Thorpe says, "the BIA decided that the Indians who'd been using tribal grazing lands without paying a grazing fee were going to be charged. The BIA also made us cattle people set up a sinking fund to pay grazing fees in advance. The bills just got higher and higher, and pretty soon we found we had to start selling off our seed stock to pay them."

Less than 30 per cent of all Fort Hall Indians are permanently employed today. Men like Frank Thorpe once had a going business that harked back to the old times and also provided jobs on the reservation. The BIA had decided that the best use for Fort Hall land was farming; it removed the Indians' cattle from trust status, which meant they could be sold, and began the accelerated program of leasing Indian lands to whites that is still in effect today.

Thorpe spends a good deal of time driving his dust-covered station wagon along the reservation's unpaved roads. A former tribal chairman, he spends much time checking up on the BIA and trying to function as a sort of ombudsman. He drives slowly down the dirt highways where magpies pick at the remains of rabbits slaughtered by cars. He points out where white farmers have begun to crop-dust their leased fields from airplanes. "The game, rabbits and pheasants and all, is disappearing," he says. "Our Indian people here rely on them for food, but the animals are dying out because of the sprays. And sometimes our kids get real sick. These sprays, they drift over and get in the swimming holes. The kids get real bad coughs and sometimes rashes all over their bodies."

Near the BIA agency office on the reservation sits a squat, weathered concrete building. "That's the old blouse factory," he says. "The BIA cooked up this deal where some outfit from Salt Lake City came in here to start a garment plant. The tribe put up the money for the factory, about $30,000, and in return the Salt Lake people were going to hire Indians and train them to sew. It lasted for about a year, and now we've still got the building. The last few years, they've used it to store the government surplus food that a lot of Indians get."

The old blouse factory is one symbol of the despair that has seized Fort Hall. Thorpe points out another one nearby. It is known as a "holding center," and it is a place for Fort Hall Indians who are suspected of being suicidal. The reservation has one of the highest suicide rates in the nation. Last year there were 35 attempts, mostly among the 18–25 age group. Many of them occurred in the nearby Blackfoot City Jail.

Blackfoot town authorities, embarrassed by the number of Indian suicides which have occurred in their jail, now use the holding facility at Fort Hall. It is headed by John Bopp, a former Navy man who is the public health officer on the reservation. "I guess kids here just feel that their future is cut off," he says. "A lot of them are dropouts and rejects from schools. They look around and see their elders pretty downtrodden. They get angry, but the only thing they can do is take it out on themselves. From reading some of their suicide notes, I'd say that they see it as an honorable way out of a bad situation."

"The young people," says Thorpe, "they're our only hope. They've got to clean things up here. But a lot of our young guys, they've just given up." The human resources at Fort Hall, like the land, seem to be slipping away. The best interpretation that could be placed on the BIA's role in it all is to use the words of a teacher at nearby Idaho State College who says that they are "guardians of the poorhouse."

## I Learned to Feel Black
### 1967

### Jean Smith

I think that once you knew me. It was a time not long past, about four years ago. I was the bright, well-mannered girl who lived down the street from you. My grandmother was always stopping you on your way to the grocery store; she would call you to the door to show you, proudly, college-newspaper clippings about her granddaughter's winning a scholarship or achieving a place on the dean's list.

Or possibly you remember me from church. I was the girl who helped sustain the small, overambitious choir by appearing faithfully every Sunday to sing the praises of the Lord in songs that often were too difficult or out of my range. Sometimes you would stop and offer me a few words of encouragement because, you said, you liked my spirit.

Or you may remember me as the girl in the neighborhood who went off to join the civil rights movement or the Peace Corps. You might even have been among those who tried to persuade me not to waste my talents on those other people when there was so much work to be done at home. I could build a fine professional career, you told me; I could make a starting salary of $7,000.

I'm sure you knew me once. At least you knew a something in me, something that continued to grasp at the reality of the American image of the full person, blessed by our society with the resources and opportunities to be whatever he wants to be. I kept trying to be that full person, to use the talents I had toward widening opportunities for other people so that they also could make the most of their lives.

And so I tried to know everything and to be the best at everything I tried. I wanted to learn all about science, art, music, Greek mythology, Oriental philosophy. I wanted to learn the newest theories, study the most difficult courses and sing the hardest songs. It all would be useful in the refinement of this society where every man could be his best.

Thus I studied chemistry at college and planned to go to medical school, because I felt that I could be most useful in this way. And I had to join the civil rights movement because I saw in it a basic method of making our society stand completely behind its image of the full person and of every man's right to be a full person. I felt sure that once the country was made aware that some of its Negro citizens were being deprived of very basic rights and was brought face to face with the contradiction between its image and what was happening to the Negro people, then our society would necessarily correct the oppressed condition of the Negro people.

Yes, I'm certain that you knew, if only superficially, that *something* in me which reached toward the American image.

What was the source of my belief? It was based on my assurance that in this country there was room for everybody, that for every man there was, or soon would be, some place where he could be free to explore and employ the creative potential within him. So that my job was simply to develop the skills I possessed and then to fit my abilities into the massive machinery that, I trusted, was working day and night to create for every person a place of comfort and freedom. In short, I believed in guaranteeing everyone freedom, equality and democracy as the means of living full lives, and I thought that the rest of the country believed in these things too.

I had good reason to believe all this. My family was sort of upper lower class. There were just four of us, my mother, my two sisters and I. (My father, a pilot in the Army Air Force, was killed in World War II.) My mother worked as a practical nurse in Detroit, Michigan, when we were young, and she managed to get two of us through college. She herself graduated from college at the age of 40 and has just embarked on a new career, teaching deaf children. My youngest sister is in college now. All of us have or can get any *thing* we really want (a house, a car, a trip to Europe).

Thus my early personal experiences suggested that there was room for everybody. After all, I was nobody special and yet I was doing quite well. In fact, it was a long time before I became conscious that being a Negro made me different. I thought I was like everybody else.

It was in the context of my belief in our society's potential for making good on its promise of full men through freedom and democracy that I responded to the urgings of some of my classmates at Howard University. They were members of the Students' Nonviolent Coordinating Committee (or SNCC, pronounced "Snick") and I joined the Movement. I truly felt, and I think that many SNCC workers then felt similarly, that most Americans believed in these principles, and that when confronted with our documentation that they were being violated in the South, Americans would move to support the rights of Negro citizens.

When I left Washington, D.C., in 1963 to go South with SNCC, you knew me. Now, four years later, I am a different person.

Essentially the difference is that I became consciously black. I came to understand that there wasn't room enough in the society for the mass of black people, that the majority of Americans are acting either in unbearably bad faith or in tragic ignorance when they project to their children the image of an American society where all men are free and equal.

Since, in a way, I was once a friend of yours, perhaps you'll invest a little time and emotional energy in trying to understand what happened.

I went South after the sit-ins that were aimed at desegregating eating places. In the summer of '63 I went to Georgia and then to Mississippi as a SNNC field worker. The focus of SNCC's activity in the Deep South then was voter registration. The logic of it seemed very clear to me. Negroes had a right to vote, to participate in our democracy. In fact, our society wanted everyone's participation. Because of some curious isolation from the rest of the country, the white Southerners had managed to deprive Negroes of this right. But the South was still part of the United States. What we had to do was to show the rest of the United States that democratic participation was being denied our people. Then the rest of the country would insist that the South allow Negroes to vote.

I saw the relationship between political representation and economic and social development: If Negroes could get the vote, then we could use it to attack the poverty and misery which plagued the Negro community. If we could vote, we would be well on our way to full economic and social participation in the larger society. And so I worked with the other SNCC staff people to show the rest of the country that Negroes in the South wanted to vote and couldn't.

We got our people to go down to the courthouse to try to register to vote. After they were turned away from the courthouse or were not allowed to "pass" the test of eligibility for voting or were intimidated by threats of violence from whites, we appealed to the Justice Department, documenting carefully the instances of refusal and intimidation. Next we organized picket lines and marches to the courthouse to demonstrate to the rest of the country that Negroes *did* want to vote. The marches often ended in mass arrests and in violence, but they were reported in the newspapers and on television and the Movement's case was made clear to the public. After there had been much marching and many protests, Congress passed the 1965 Voting Rights Act, which assured Negroes the right to vote.

It would seem that this was a great victory. It was certainly a goal into whose attainment I had put my heart. I worked every available minute at reaching it. I used to walk through the whole town every day, canvassing neighborhoods to tell people about voting. I canvassed until evening; I took part in the mass meetings that were held every two or three nights. Then I went back to the office to work until one or two o'clock in the morning to establish files on potential voters and help organize our new library.

When finally I went home it was to a deep, satisfying sleep. I would be ready to go again at six the next morning, awakened by my eagerness to start a new day of efforts to secure the rights of my people to vote and be represented. We all worked so hard. And Negroes did get the right to vote.

We found it was a shallow victory. After the earlier sit-ins, the civil rights movement had had to stop and ask: "What have we gained by winning the right to a cup of coffee downtown?" In the same way, we who had worked for voting rights now had to ask ourselves what we had gained. In both cases the answer was the same: Negroes were in fact not basically better off with this new right than they had been before; they were still poor and without the power to direct their own lives.

It is a subtle problem to acknowledge that there was some value in having achieved these rights and yet to understand that there was no basic gain. The value was in the way Negroes could feel like real men and women as they broke old traditions about "staying in their place" and went up to the courthouse to vote. The value was in the solidification of the Negro community, in our recognition of the possibility that we could work together to build decent lives. But you must see that there was no basic change. I personally resisted seeing this for a long time. I had invested so much of myself in the fight that I didn't want to admit that it came to so little.

The best way to understand is to look at what the Negro people who cast their lot with the Movement believed. They believed, I think, that their participation in the drive for voting rights would ultimately result in the relief of their poverty and hopelessness. They thought that with the right to vote they could end the exploitation of their labor by the plantation owners. They thought they could get better schools for their children; they could get sewers dug and sidewalks paved. They thought they could get adequate public-health facilities for their communities. And of course they got none of these.

The crux of the matter is that they believed there was a link between representation in government and making that government work for you. What they—and I—discovered was that for some people, this link does not exist. For most black people, voting has not much more benefit than the exercise of walking to the polls. Why is this the case? Because the link between voting and partaking of the benefits of society exists at the pleasure of society. The society must be willing to respond to the legitimate needs of the people; only then can the channels for the expression of these needs, such channels as voting, be meaningfully employed.

A dramatic example is glaringly visible today on the national scene. In January of 1967, when Adam Clayton Powell was barred from his seat in the House of Representatives, he was prevented from acting for his Harlem constituents, the people of the 18th Congressional District of the State of New York, who had elected him. When he was stripped of his chairmanship of the House Education and Labor Committee, which shaped and handled most of the antipoverty legislation, he was stripped of his power effectively to represent the Negro people, a power it had taken him 22 years to build. He was prevented from representing these people because the majority of Congress, which in this instance speaks for the larger society, does not want him to. It is as simple as that.

Our effort in the South to enter the society through the use of the vote came to an anticlimax because we had been lied to. We had worked feverishly to qualify under objective standards for our rights, only to learn that these rights are arbitrarily conferred by those in power. In the end we learned that there are a thousand ways for a people who are weaker than the rest to be "kept in their place," appeals to good conscience notwithstanding. There are simple mechanisms, like last-minute changes in election laws and altering the boundaries of election districts. And there are subtler means, such as making bank loans to the "leaders" of a poverty-striken community so that they can never afford to disagree with you; such as busing newly eligible voters off to Florida to pick fruit.

It was through my efforts as a SNCC worker to bring my people into the larger society through the channel of voting that I first gained insight into the fact that there was not room in American society for most black people.

In August of 1964 the Mississippi Freedom Democratic Party (MFDP) went to the Democratic National Convention in Atlantic City. The MFDP went to challenge the right of the white Mississippi delegation to represent Mississippi at the convention where the Democratic candidate for President of the United States would be chosen. I helped to organize the challenge.

Our argument was that the regular white delegation had been chosen by a process from which Negroes had been excluded, and consequently that the delegation did not represent the total population. It certainly did not represent the 43 per cent of the state's population that was black. We knew it did not and we could prove it did not.

Negroes first tried to attend the series of meetings that were held by the Mississippi Democratic Party on the precinct, county and district levels to elect the delegation to the national convention. Most of these meetings were inaccessible to us. Only people who had registered to vote could participate in them, and it was not until a year later, under the 1965 Voting Rights Act, that our people were even *promised* the right to vote. In many cases, when our people arrived at the place and time appointed for a precinct meeting, there was no meeting. In many other instances, we were simply refused admission to the meetings.

After we had been refused participation in the precinct and county meetings from which the regular Democratic party delegates to the convention were ultimately chosen, we set out to hold our own meetings. The MFDP organized precinct, county, district and state meetings open to everybody, meetings from which the MFDP elected a sixty-eight man delegation to the Democratic National Convention. The delegation, primarily black but including those few whites who were willing to stand with us, was to ask the national convention for seats as the Democratic delegation from Mississippi.

There was real fire in the civil rights workers as we organized the MFDP and held precinct, county and district meetings all over the state. We thought that this time we would surely make a breakthrough. As I helped to run educational workshops preparatory to the formal precinct meetings I thought, Yes, this is what democracy is all about.

But the delegation that could have represented us never got the chance to speak. Mississippi Negroes were never allowed to participate in the choice of the Presidential candidate. Although the rules of the convention provided that a delegation could be challenged as not representative of the constituency that it claimed to represent, our challenge was never heard by the convention. Our challenge was heard by the Credentials Committee preceding the convention.

We had worked for almost a year to substantiate our legal case that the only reason we were not represented in the regular Mississippi delegation was that the white Democrats in Mississippi had not allowed us to be: they hadn't allowed us to register to vote and they hadn't allowed us to participate in the process by which the delegation was selected.

After our case was heard by the Credentials Committee, the committee voted not to seat the MFDP delegation at the convention; it offered to seat two of our sixty-eight man delegation, members whom it would specify, whom we would not even be permitted to choose. We rejected this offer. The only concrete gain we could show for all our work, for all our documentation and the eloquence of our members' testimony before the committee, was a promise that the delegation to the next convention would be integrated.

In retrospect, I think that in our hearts we knew our flawless arguments would fall on deaf ears. We were aware, at least subconsciously, that no group of white people was going to send some of its own packing in order to make room for us. No matter that that group had said to the world that it regarded all people as equals and no matter that we had a right to representation in that group. It took a few more turns at knocking our heads against stone walls (walls that, according to our society, did not exist) before we became fully conscious that this was the case.

In this experience can be seen one of the origins of the call for black power, which I consider the other side of the coin of black consciousness. One cannot exist without the other. Imagine the MFDP's 1964 experience repeated hundreds of times in hundreds of conventions and back-room meetings. Imagine that in every corner of the United States black people are coming face to face with the fact, never before so widely or so publicly acknowledged, that it is through this exercise of power that decisions are made, and that those decisions have little or nothing to do with morality. The next logical step is the call for black power.

I think for many Negroes it was our experience with the poverty program that finally crystallized our consciousness of how black we really were. It was through the poverty program that we were forced to admit that the society apparently had no use for us and that assurances to the contrary were, unfortunately, instances of white deception.

Along with several other civil rights people, I worked with the Child Development Group of Mississippi when it was first established in the summer of 1965. CDGM is a Head Start program in Mississippi, with funds from the Office of Economic Opportunity. We worked with CDGM because we thought this would be a chance to put thousands of poor people in command of one small sector of their lives, the preschool education of their children. It was a chance to have a several-million-dollar program actually run by poor Negroes. OEO's expression for this was "maximum feasible participation of the poor." The theory was that programs for helping the poor were best run when poor people, who best know their own problems, are given the power to solve them. For a while CDGM was actually allowed to be this sort of program. In each community poor people were running their own centers and hiring their own people to work in the centers.

All this lasted until white Mississippians began to realize that Negroes were benefiting from a program that white people did not control. The program was then attacked, primarily on the grounds that it was hiring civil rights workers and mismanaging funds. (Dispute still rages as this is written over how much money was "mismanaged" out of a total of $7,100,000. The amount ranges from the $1,100,000 charged by Mississippi Senator John Stenis down to the $65,653 that a national firm of accountants reported may have been spent in "technical violation" of regulations. Meanwhile, according to one estimate, investigations of CDGM have cost about $300,000.)

But think for a moment about the accusations. Why shouldn't the program hire civil rights workers, people who had proved their interest in and ability to work with the poor? Consider too that most of the Negro people involved in the program traditionally had been excluded from handling any money at all. How could they develop a perfect fiscal system in so short a time? Yet Negroes must have the experience of handling money if they are ever to participate in the economic life of the country.

It is impossible to trace here the complications of the CDGM fight. Through attacks and counterattacks, appeals and counterappeals, through periods when the program was held together completely by volunteer labor and donated funds, CDGM managed to keep its Head Start program going. OEO was sufficiently satisfied with CDGM's responses to its accusers that it provided funds for the program several times. The current grant is for more than $5 million over a twelve-month period.

But the re-funding has been at great cost to the character of the program. Because of the jeopardy in which the charges of mismanagement placed CDGM, Negroes themselves, fearing to lose the program entirely along with the benefits it brought to their children, did not insist that they continue to have a large part in running it. Its working area in the state is being decreased continually, and an effort is now under way to replace CDGM with a group more politically acceptable. In another year it is very possible that there will be no more CDGM; the whole program will be run by the public-school system without even token participation by the poor.

It amounts to a paradox: The poverty program says it wants "maximum feasible participation of the poor" but it *doesn't* want the poor to participate. For me it was a devastating paradox. It required me to abandon my last hope that American society would willingly make room for us. When I surrendered this last hope I had also to surrender my belief that American society was honestly trying to create conditions where, through promised freedom, equality and democracy, men could be their best. I felt the great loss of this belief on two levels.

On one level I was damaged as a member of a race of people who could no longer look to society for the means of relief from their poverty and from their condition of powerlessness over their own lives. The depth of this damage was crystallized for me one evening in Washington, D.C., in the park that faces the White House. I had come to Washington with a group of ninety people who sought funds from OEO to build houses with their own hands in Mississippi to replace the shacks and tents in which they lived. When after several days of meetings with OEO officials we had no positive response, we set up tents in Lafayette Square Park to demonstrate to the President and to the country that our people were in desperate need of decent places to live. This happened last year, at Eastertime.

On the second evening of sleeping in the tents there was a light rain, which continued for several hours. The rain curtained the trees of the park, reflecting the light of the street lamps and casting a wonderful warm glow over everything.

Because I felt too damp and cold to sleep, I got up and walked among the newly blooming tulips. I became aware that others who were awake were staring through the mist at the White House. They watched the beautiful, glowing White House from their tents. They watched and waited for some sign that they could abandon their hand-to-mouth existence and take up tools to build homes from which they could begin new, fruitful lives. And I was hurt for them because by then I knew their hopes were unfounded. There was nothing for them there. They would have to go back to their tents and shacks, back to hustling for $2 to pay a gas bill or 20 cents to buy a bag of pinto beans.

On another level, the loss of my belief was damaging to me as an individual. I had been stripped of a principle around which my life had been organized. No more could I seriously think that I was helping to build this country by making it stand behind its promises to all its people. I could no longer work at helping to build a society of full, free men. The image of that society was a joke. When considered in this light my work became meaningless. In existentialist terms, I was reduced to absurdity.

For me and many other black people the only allowable conclusion from these experiences has been that Negroes must turn away from the preachings, assertions and principles of the larger white society and must turn inward to find the means whereby black people can lead full, meaningful lives. We must become conscious that our blackness calls for another set of principles, principles on whose validity we can depend because they come from our own experiences.

We have to build a broad-based black consciousness so that we can begin to depend on one another for economic, political and social support. We have to build our own businesses to put money into the development of the Negro community, businesses to establish foundations to support our own new educational and social ventures. We have to make our politicians responsible to us so that either they improve our communities or they go. Living, growing communities must be built to replace our strife-ridden ghettos. The problems of illiteracy and the inability to communicate must be tackled.

Can we do all this by ourselves? Probably not. Obviously we need access to the capital and to the intellectual resources of the larger society. We need to know how to build lathes and how to market products. We need to learn the ins and outs of prevailing political forms and to have access to the body of scientific knowledge and cultural tradition. We need those few white people who are genuinely interested in helping.

It's not that we have to do it by ourselves. Rather it is that we have to reorient our efforts and to train ourselves, black people, to build for us. Our immediate objective must be the strengthening of the black community instead of the apparently unattainable goal of diffusion of all black people into the main stream of American life. We have to become strong so that we can depend on one another to meet our needs and so that we'll be able to deal with white people as we choose to, not as we are obliged to.

I realize that we are only ten per cent of the population and that in the end we may well need the large-scale assistance of the larger society. But I also realize that except on the level of tokenism, we can't win the fight for meaningful integration any time soon. (Soon, for me, means in my lifetime.)

I think the fight for integration must continue because we derive some benefits from it. It means better living conditions for a few of us, a few more low-cost housing units, a few more yearly incomes above the poverty level. It means that we can feel more like men and women because we've insisted on the rights that society says are ours. And we gain valuable knowledge and experience by being the only Negro architect in the firm or by being one of three Negro judges in the city or by being the agency's only black model.

Clearly there's much to be learned in the outside world. But basically I think we must have before us the objective of building strong black communities on which we and our children can depend and in which we can lead full, rich lives. I think that after the black community has become strong enough, the rules of the game may change; society may decide that it can live with us on equal terms. It may even decide to join hands with us to build a country where all of us, white and black, can live.

The call for black consciousness is at first painfully hard to answer. It's hard to start all over again and establish new principles and modes of operation. For we have struggled vainly for so long, trying to approximate white culture! Our artists, our scientists, our leaders, have been respected by us only after they have been "legitimatized" by the white world. For so long, events have not occurred unless they were recorded in the white press; world issues have not existed unless the President made a speech about them. The extent of our reality has been the width of our TV screens. We face a prodigious task. We've danced to the tune so long; and now it becomes necessary to stop and gather our senses, to stop and listen to the tune and decide which of its elements warrant our response.

Sometimes I am nostalgic for the days when you knew me. Sometimes

I miss the clarity of those days, the assurance that what I was doing was right because it was helping to make a better country and, in turn, a better world. The black self that I am now has a difficult time, having to start all over again and discover the best ways to work in this new, black world. And yet, after a searching and painful evaluation of the last years' experiences, it is the only self that I can honestly allow.

---

**Live and Let Live**

**1967**

---

**Connell Persico**

---

For some time students have been working in slums, marching in demonstrations, sitting-in, burning draft cards and going on hunger strikes. A great deal has been written about them. Their actions have contributed to the passing of considerable legislation. And they have been called a great many names. If the pursuit of a vision born in this country almost two hundred years ago is to continue, it is necessary to take a look at these young people who have been so active in the 1960s and to develop an understanding among all generations of Americans.

Some say this student awakening began as a movement with the first lunch counter sit-in in the South in early 1960. Others date it from the City Hall anti-HUAC[1] demonstration in San Francisco in May of 1960. Some even believe it started as a reaction against the so-called silent generation. How strange today sounds the statement written in 1959 by Clark Kerr, President of the University of California: "The employers will love this generation; they are not going to press many grievances. . . . They are going to be easy to handle. There aren't going to be any riots."[2] This able scholar was apparently looking at the fifties just ending, rather than at the new decade about to take shape.

---

[1] House Un-American Activities Committee of the United States Congress.
[2] Quoted in Jack Newfield, "Revolt Without Dogma," *Motive*, Vol. XXVI No. 1, October 1965, p. 21.

Like so many other experts, he was wrong. When 1960 rolled around, the quiet was broken by a thundering wave of young people trying to find themselves in their society.

Much confusion reigned over this new activity. Some people felt it necessary to find names for us. And, of course, the usual ones came first: rebels, radicals, subversives and Communists. The names soon became more refined and positive: New Moralists, New Anarchists, the Committed Genera- tion, and so on. We don't want those names under which we've been grouped. They imply that there is something strange about us, different from other people. They create a chasm between us and other people. And it's not true that all of us distrust everyone over thirty! Why can't you see us for what we are? We are your own sons and daughters, not someone far away to be read about in a newspaper.

Human beings are what we are—flesh, blood, conscience, emotions, intellect. Like everybody else, we, too, worry about the mystery known as life. We're unfulfilled lovers trying to introduce compassion as the means and ends of international relations. We're amateur artists painting a landscape of blending whites, reds, browns, blacks and yellows. We're stumbling poets creating an ode to the beauty of all men everywhere. We're simply human beings trying to maintain our integrity.

So we have been marching, sitting-in, getting arrested, and going to jail over free speech, civil rights, and Vietnam. The FBI attributes our actions to Communist influence. Others attempt to find some other external force that is supposed to be pressuring us into direct action. Each time a demonstration takes place, people look past the demonstrators for an explanation. They ought to look into the eyes of the people who are marching. They would find that every pair of eyes tells a different story. Every one of the thousands who has become involved in this revolution has his own particular motives and reasons. There are Stalinists, Trotskyites and Maoists; there are Republicans and Democrats; there are opportunists and know-nothings; there are people who can't tell you why they are participating—they just feel that they have to do *something*. There are the nonviolent people and the egg-throwers; there are people with nothing but questions; and others with all the answers. Yet for all of our differences, we come together and pursue a common interest. We feel compelled to work for a life that is worth living.

How I wish I could explain the joy, the beauty, the warmth that emanate from the camaraderie we have. It's not the blind discipline of any dogma or ideology that brings us together. We're all searching for answers to the same age-old questions: Who am I? Why am I here? As people of the mid-twentieth century, we feel that cooperation among humans is the only road to survival. We've wrapped up our freedom with the freedom of all men; our personal peace with the peace of the world. We enjoy being together because the spirit unleashed frees us to be fully human. We come together, live together, rarely condemning, always trying to understand, and always attempting to relate to each other and the world with compassion and respect. The ideals that bring us together are peace, equality, freedom and justice. These are also the concrete realities that we work for. They are our common bond. It's not our victories nor the publicity we gain that give us our strength and keep us together. It's our sense of community, our being human. For we have seen how difficult it is to live a full life alone. We separate sadly, for alone we stumble and fall, and our vision becomes hazy.

We've all of us in one way or another been afraid: afraid to come of age in the America of the sixties; afraid of its complacency and apathy; afraid of its affluence. We had thought life would be the way we were taught it would be, and yet we saw something different in the way adult Americans actually live. So we set out to create a better world based on our country's traditions and heritage, a world we had thought already existed. We were not going to let the "affluent society" dictate how we should act, so we developed our own concepts of morality and integrity. We've found a way of living that we feel presents more hope for mankind as a whole and individually. Our motto could be "Live and let live," for among us no one tells anyone else how to live, or how to be accepted, or how to become a success; everyone is left on their own, to develop their own ideas of life and love.

As for myself, I was afraid even of my peers and their lives, for I couldn't kick some of the morality I'd learned that kept me from living the way they did. For a while, I existed in both worlds, the world of the "middle class" and the world of the "new breed." I felt I couldn't be comfortable living totally in either. But after a long struggle with my fears, after facing up to myself, I am coming to understand that I have no one else to answer to for my life, that I can live as I want to, as a unique individual. And there are thousands of us, rebuking affluence and so-called middle-class values. We're trying out a whole range of values and ideas in order to find our own ways of being individuals in this modern American society. This may involve seeking acceptance, for who wants to be alone, to have no one to share dreams, feelings and thoughts with? It may even involve hating you and all we see you as standing for. But most of all, it's a grand experiment in living as total human beings. And isn't it only natural to identify this individual struggle for freedom with all who are oppressed everywhere? Doesn't that help to create a base of understanding among us? And doesn't it show that all of us, no matter what age or outlook, are really allies and friends?

So next time we are marching for civil rights or to protest the Vietnam war, don't condemn us as unpatriotic or subversive. Understand that we are people like you trying to create a better world for all, people trying to figure out what's happening in the world, what its possibilities are, and how we can honestly relate to them. We don't ask that you accept our tactics. (Many of us wish there were other ways.) We don't even ask that you approve of us as people. All we ask is that you try to understand why we are there, why we are concerned, why we are giving up the guaranteed material security of a college degree for the sake of problems that seemingly are not even ours. Why do we worry about freedom, equality, and peace, when we could be so

comfortable if we would only forget about them? Why are we willing to experience mental and physical pain over a woman burned by napalm in a
Vietnamese village, when we could be soaking up sun on a beach?

I was born eighteen months before the destruction of Hiroshima and
Nagasaki. I grew up in the Eisenhower era. The most vivid experience of my
early life was McCarthyism. My mother apparently couldn't get it into her
head that at the time you either had to give up your beliefs or remain silent.
So she went on writing and talking about the injustices she saw. And she took
me to meetings where people were talking about the Rosenbergs and Alger
Hiss. I remember her being branded a Communist because she was teaching the
Declaration of Independence and the Bill of Rights, along with how important
it is to stick to your beliefs. At one point I remember being sent off to another
school because someone had written in my brother's religion book, "Your
mother is a Red." Most of the time I played baseball and rode my bike—that
other stuff was for grownups. But I listened and learned. Then, after a while,
I started reading on my own—the Hardy Boys series, Thomas Paine, Jefferson,
Thoreau, and other Americana. And by 1956 I knew enough about American
politics to understand why my first hero, Adlai Stevenson, lost the presidential
election.

These early educational experiences were supplemented by the fact that
I've attended a total of thirteen different schools. This not only helped me to
develop means of survival without a group of friends but also tended to build
up a strong sense of insecurity. As a result, though I learned to do things on
my own—mainly reading about American politics, culture and social problems
—I grew up lacking yet always desiring the warmth and fun of true friends.
Many other events have gone into making me what I am—accidents, prolonged
illnesses, deaths in my family, people I've met, and probably a lot of things I
don't even remember.

My thirteenth school was San Francisco State College. It was there that I
began developing my own view of the world. This college first provided me
with the freedom, encouragement and intellectual tools to begin finding myself
and my place in this society that seemed too big and frightening. When I
entered State in 1961, we had just been through an anti-HUAC demonstration
and the trials that followed and needed to talk about the whys and wherefores
of our actions, what had happened, and where we were going from there. We
wanted to talk about how we were and what we could do in this world. So we
set up a makeshift platform and began speaking about civil rights. We collected
money and distributed literature. And it all happened without a Free Speech
Movement, thanks to an alert and progressive administration. No college
official ever told us to be quiet. Instead, they sat down, drew up and got
approval for a statement of philosophy that recognized students as adults and
guaranteed for them all the rights and responsibilities of full citizens.

Is this any way to run a college? You bet it is! People can become
educated only if they can ask those "controversial" questions that shake the
base of our system, those questions that are necessary to understand the

paradoxes of our society. How can people find out what they can do about injustice, if they can't get together with other people who feel the same way?

With no battle to wage against a college administration denying our rights, we could concentrate on the important issues of peace, freedom and equality. We marched through San Francisco in protest against the Birmingham bombings, we sat-in at the Sheraton Palace Hotel on behalf of nondiscriminatory employment, we got arrested on Automobile Row for the same struggle, and we supported our breathren over at Berkeley when they began insisting on the same freedom we had already had for three years. Through it all, San Francisco State College provided a forum where we could not only decide what to do in each situation that came up, but also discuss the results. The pros and cons of any action would be discussed freely and openly and each person would be made aware not only of his responsibilities but also of the possible consequences of his behavior. Ah, what beautiful agony we often went through as we struggled with the question of personal participation and all the moral and practical considerations it seemed to involve!

Then in March, 1965, a group of us became so disturbed by the events in Selma, Alabama, that we decided to leave school for a couple of weeks and travel there to do what we could. I'll never forget walking round the campus the Sunday before we left. An eighteen-year-old friend and I struggled with the whys of the situation, eyes filled with tears, hearts filled with fear, minds filled with doubt. He couldn't understand why he had to become a man at eighteen, why there weren't enough adults fighting against injustice so that he could stay home, why it was his responsibility to bring about civil rights for others. We never did resolve these dilemmas, but as we left we received a note from a friend: "We sometimes must do what we have to do, rather than what we want to do."

We arrived in Selma a few days later—tired, hungry, scared, wanting to do something, anything. We marched; we sang; we went to jail; we listened; and we learned. The evening before we went out marching, we practiced how to fall. When it came time to march into the aroused white community's home ground, six of us stood in the street asking one another, "Is it worth it?" "Do you think we'll be beaten or killed?" "Can you stand the pain?" And then we marched. When the verse of "We Shall Overcome" which begins "We are not afraid" came around, we sang loud enough for the whole United States to hear us. For the fact was that we were afraid. But we knew that by concerted action, by many acting as one, we *would* overcome.

We were Americans at last; we weren't really afraid—shaking and defecating in our pants, yes, but afraid, no; we were in the field, working for the ideals that were all we knew as great in America: equality, justice, freedom. And we were side by side with other Americans: all those beautiful black people who had faced fear and through it had become strong. They imbued us with a new patriotism, a new vision of the American dream. And they made me recognize my prejudices; I came face to face with my feelings for the Negro, and they weren't ideal. But one field worker said, "Me too, baby, I don't like you white men either, but we can work it out." And so we marched together and bridged the gap that misunderstanding and separation had created. For it had been fear that we had feared, and once having overcome that fear, we marched almost serenely, even knowing that we might be killed. As other men had faced death on various foreign battlefields for what they believed America represented, so we were willing to die right here at home. Heroic? No. Martyrs? No. Just young people trying to relate themselves to their society, trying to create a world with which they could in good conscience identify. When we left Selma we knew the world hadn't changed very much, if at all, but each of us had a new understanding of the Southern dilemma, and each of us had a new vision of brotherhood, community, and America's potential. All of us came back a little more human, a little less afraid to live as we are.

If it hadn't been for the free, inquiring kind of education I enjoyed at San Francisco State College, I probably wouldn't have been there. If I hadn't had the opportunity to open my mind and to develop a feeling for the world as adults and humans, I could not have ever understood the great meanings of Selma. I had that opportunity because my alma mater offers those who attend it a chance to participate in the educational process as policy-makers and educators. It acknowledges the right of students to a full voice in the kind of education they are to receive. The results are exciting. Thanks to the efforts of the last four student governments, and a gentle nudge by the F.S.M., students now participate in every decision affecting the campus. They have a seat and vote on all faculty and administrative boards and committees. They have initiated a new, student-organized program in General Education, with its own specially designed courses and hand-picked professors. Working together with members of the faculty and administration, they have established an "experimental college"—an informal, educational focus within the college as a whole and intended to explore politically and humanly relevant topics that the regular curriculum passes over, among them the topic of "Nonviolence in a Violent World." And the whole operation has been student-led the whole way. It has been possible only because of the mutual trust among all campus elements— students, faculty and administration alike. As a result, there's been no energy wasted on internal feuds. Instead, there's a concerted effort on the part of all concerned to make the education offered at the College the very best in the country. And if present trends continue, it will be education for the full development of total human beings—people who will be informed, capable of thinking and creating, and sensitive to the issues of our times.

Isn't that what education should be? Why study only how things have been, or how they are right now? Isn't that only background preparation? Isn't the most urgent question of all the challenge of how to develop a world in which one can live peacefully, ethically, honestly, and in a way to help people work out their individual and collective problems? Isn't that what the curriculum should be most concerned about? If this concern for humanity and personal growth is the real business of education, the present grading system is a hindrance and an anachronism. If education is to be a humanizing process, an occasion to help young people to find themselves and develop their own unique relationship to their society, how can such an experience be graded? What can a grade of average, above average, or excellent mean? There is no need for competitiveness in education conceived in this manner. It can do no good, only a lot of harm. There is need only for freedom of exploration and understanding, and for respect and personal encouragement. The object must be to help each person to confront himself, to find his own meanings and purposes, and to overcome his fears of living, loving, and being himself. For while there is always someone to tell us what is good and bad for us and how we ought to live, only the individual can know what is really best for himself. Education should provide the means for each person to find this out. Its job isn't done by merely offering courses of study in specific fields. These are important. But the student is only secondarily a student. He is first and last a human being. And his education has to be attuned to him as such.

Contemporary formal education makes one serious mistake. Too great a portion of the energies of colleges and universities is still devoted to the expansion of the intellect, at the expense of the emotions. Since education should be the means of developing the total person, much greater emphasis should be devoted to the exploration and understanding of emotions. Everywhere I look I see people of all age levels and groups being afraid of their feelings, of love, of their common humanity. I know how afraid of these dimensions of my life I have been myself; it finally took help through counseling to break down those fears. For I am looking for people, a community, and I rarely find them through discussions of political science or any other exclusively analytical discipline. I find them through struggling with people about the questions of love, what it means to be alive, and what life's purposes can and ought to be.

It is not only for our individual sakes that we must overcome the fear of our emotions. It is also for our life as a society. For when we are captives of fear, we become manipulatable by anyone who understands how to trigger and direct our fears. In this way fear weakens our ability to be ethical people. It was this, I think, that Franklin D. Roosevelt was getting at in his speech of March 4, 1933, when he said, "So first of all, let me assert my firm belief that the only thing we have to fear is fear itself—nameless, unjustified terror which paralyzes needed efforts to convert retreat into advance." [3] These words, it seems to me, get to the heart of the problem of all mankind. They apply not only to our lives and relations as individuals but to human dealings within and among nations. The evidence is all around us that people are afraid. They are afraid to become involved with anyone or anything that may affect their material security. They are afraid to risk their paycheck to speak out against discrimination or government policy. They are afraid to risk being rejected or ridiculed for

[3] Ben D. Zevin, ed., *Nothing to Fear,* New York, Popular Library, 1961, p. 26.

questioning generally accepted beliefs. No, I don't condemn them. But I do say that people are afraid and that it undermines their moral capabilities and that the time comes when we have to overcome these fears and take our stand. It's a great feeling to be able to stand in front of one's mirror and look oneself in the eyes! But first one has to recognize that one has been afraid.

The same thing applies to our government, with its priceless heritage. It pays lip service to America's high ideals, and then does the opposite. It also seems afraid of being its real self. Engaged in a war that everyone knows is a mistake, our government refuses to withdraw or negotiate with the "enemy" for fear of loss of face. It too is afraid. And it would rather risk destruction than admit its mistake. How ignoble, how unmanly, how fearful! Our government is afraid of America and would rather shatter the mirror than look in it. And yet how else to become strong and healthy again except to confront its fears?

But our country has so many riches and gadgets and busy-nesses that keep it from facing up to its real feelings, needs and opportunities. I was for a long time distracted by these things myself. As far as material things go, America has provided me with a comfortable existence. Rarely have I gone without food, clothing, or other necessities. In fact, I've rarely gone without a good many luxuries. I've traveled throughout the United States and was able to spend one summer in Europe. I've had a good education at minimal cost, and after graduation I'll have the potential to earn more money than is necessary to exist. I have the world by the tail because I am an American, and yet I'm not content, for all around me I see people denied what I have and can have. I've worked in a tutorial program in one of San Francisco's "poverty pockets" and have seen the vicious circle that prohibits the people living there from escaping. I'm powerless to do anything about it, and yet I know this country has the resources and the ability to help these people help themselves. What keeps our government from taking rapid, radical steps to alleviate these problems? The War on Poverty has so far proved mainly a farce and has effected little change. There have to be jobs, education and reeducation, an eradication of slums, and a direct encounter with discrimination. Our government makes halfhearted stabs at these problems but fails to meet them head on. Why? Is it late middle age that keeps our country from experimenting? The willingness to see ever new challenges in life has been the source of our unique strength. Have we now grown altogether afraid of risks? Are we on the decline, a stagnant society content to revel in its past glories and eventually to die with nothing but a whimper? Or can we become visionaries again, casting away our fears and plunging headlong, with national pride and integrity, into the battle for equality at home and a fuller life for all men everywhere?

America has not only provided me with the material necessities and an education for which I am thankful. She has also bred me on the finest ideals any nation ever espoused. Take the Declaration of Independence: "We hold these truths to be self-evident, that all men are created equal, that they are endowed by their Creator with certain unalienable Rights, that among these are Life, Liberty and the pursuit of Happiness." Take our Bill of Rights, with which we are

all familiar. Take Woodrow Wilson's moving statement in *The New Freedom:*
"How always have men's hearts beat as they saw the coast of America rise to
their view! How it has always seemed to them that the dweller there would be
rid of kings, of privileged classes, and of all those bonds which had kept men
depressed and helpless, and would there realize the full fruition of his sense of
honest manhood, would there be one of a great body of brothers, not seeking
to defraud and deceive one another, but seeking to accomplish the general
good." [4] This is what America has always meant to me. Weren't you too once
caught up with a dream that America was the land of equality, and opportunity,
an enormous community where each person would help his neighbor, where
all would work together for the common good? And yet look around us.

In the midst of our riches, there are millions who remain poor, ignorant
and neglected. And all our government's much-publicized efforts to help them
are in effect mere political gestures insufficient even to keep up with the rate
of human deterioration involved. The rest of us are wallowing in consumer
goods, most of which by now we could live without, and to pay for which we
remain ever in debt and harnessed to jobs that mean little to us but money. So
absorbed in the high-priced prosperity have we become that we have lost our
capacity for human adventure. As our late President, John F. Kennedy, said,
"It is a harsh fact that we have tended in recent times to neglect [the] deeper
values in favor of our material strength. We have travelled in 100 years from
the age of the pioneer to the age of payola." [5]

What has happened to us? Have we given up our old values because we
are afraid of involvement with the problems of others? Do we keep our eyes,
minds and hearts shut because we feel impotent in a mass society, afraid that if
we speak out against injustice we'll be misunderstood and called "kooks"? But
isn't that what being a patriotic American really consists of—speaking the truth
even when the vogue is untruth, refusing to compromise even when the pressures
of the consensus are against us? And aren't these qualities more needed than
ever—in the light of the problems we face both here at home and throughout
the world?

How come America is no longer a model for other peoples, an inspiration
for the world? How come other countries are looking elsewhere for understanding and moral leadership? Let's face it, folks, when our actions are in so
many ways the opposite of our pious speeches, people are bound to regard us
as liars and devious cheats. So when we speak of peace in Vietnam and yet
refuse to look into an offer of negotiations because of an impending election,
people think twice about our sincerity. When we talk about helping the people
of Vietnam and then haphazardly burn rice and strew the countryside with
bombs, the rest of the world laughs through their tears. How much longer can
we refuse to become outraged by the slaughter of innocent people? What has

---

[4] Finley Foster and Homer Watt, eds., *Voices of Liberty,* New York, Macmillan,
1941, p. 207.
[5] Gerald Gardner, ed., *The Quotable Mr. Kennedy,* Popular Library, 1961, p. 10.

happened to our much-touted morality, our national ideals, and our religious commitments? I refuse to believe that there are no more Americans left. I can't believe that the honest concern for human worth is gone forever as a part of the American character. Am I wrong? Have we all become so callous that even the sight of a pregnant woman burned by napalm doesn't cause us pain and make us want to put an end to war?

My dad died a year and a half ago. The agony and pain of his death for those of us close to him were difficult to bear, and I wish that no one would have to experience that sorrow unnecessarily. He was only one, yet so many people suffer because he is gone. War kills many unreasonably and the suffering is multiplied numerically and also because of the futility of it all. My whole being rebels against lifting a weapon to inflict that agony on another. I don't understand how anyone who has personally witnessed death could possibly want to make anyone else experience that distress. Can't we sincerely look upon all the peoples of the world as our brothers, and attempt to work out our problems without resorting to military power? That would be in keeping with another set of ideals that are supposedly basic to America; peace, honor and justice, with the use of force only as a last resort.

Yet how far we have moved from that ideal of a peaceful world! It seems that we as a nation have lost confidence in our way of life and so must resort to military power whenever we feel even slightly threatened. So when our government suspects that Communists (only fifty-five of them) are involved in a revolt in the Dominican Republic, we openly and with great pride send in thousands of troops to squelch an honest attempt to attain decent government. And look at Vietnam! As far as I am concerned the United States years ago assumed the role of an aggressor nation interfering in the internal affairs of another country which has been attempting to achieve unity and peace after decades of war. So now, even all the declarations stating that we would never initiate aggressive military action are proven false.

Are we going to accept these new redefinitions of what America is? Are we so afraid of what we are supposed to be? Are we so weak as a nation that we are no longer willing to take chances on our version of truth and perfection? Are we no longer going to be an example to the rest of the world of how people from all nations with different outlooks on life can live together harmoniously? If America is afraid to maintain its pioneer spirit, its lust for experimentation, its recognition of equality of all peoples, then she shall fail. We shall have proven that government of the people, by the people, for the people cannot survive.

And I, as an American, refuse to let that happen! I refuse to see an ideal that holds so much promise for mankind become shattered. I refuse to see a country that has offered so much to so many fade away into oblivion. No, America means too much to me to let a government destroy it. There is a difference between society and government. As Thomas Paine wrote in *Common Sense,* "Society is produced by our wants, and government by our wickedness; the former promotes our happiness positively by uniting our affections, the latter negatively by restraining our vices." [6] It is to that American society that I owe my allegiance, just as I am more personally concerned with what I am than with what someone tells me I am. I shall continue to pursue the dream, America, rather than follow the dictates of a government that is more concerned with short-range electoral gain or personal aggrandizement.

I hope that this view of America helps a little at least to explain the youth of today: those kids who took too seriously all that they were taught America was; those kids who saw parallels between their quest to become human, and the plight of their country and the world; those kids who are willing to go to jail for their belief in a world of equality and peace; those kids who seek understanding but can do without it.

For we are not afraid of our world, our government, abuse, or prison. We are pioneers again. We have a mission. We have a mission finally to make America the bastion of freedom, the arsenal of democracy, to make the world a place of brotherhood and peace. So we will continue to demonstrate against the war in Vietnam, in support of civil rights, in defense of freedom of speech. We will continue to discuss with anyone who will talk to us our government's policies and our own actions. Though we know that we were put on this earth for no reason but to live, we have made ethical human choices to involve ourselves in the affairs of the world. We have chosen not to be afraid to regard the people of Vietnam as our brothers. And we have seen that people in Selma are no different than we are and should have the same opportunities for fulfillment as we.

Some of us have stopped marching and are looking for other ways to be effective in moving the world one step further toward a utopia envisioned by our forefathers almost two hundred years ago. What those ways will be we are still struggling with, for trying to find an individual way of coping with the world is difficult. But we will never turn back. We have seen what we can do, what ordinary human beings, no different than you who read or hear this, can do. Yes, we are not afraid, for we know that we have nothing to fear but fear itself.

So this is what I wanted to get off my chest. Yet I cannot conclude without issuing an invitation. I hope that I will have contributed at least a little to a deepening of understanding among the different generation of Americans, and that this will have been only a beginning. Let us start a national dialogue about the meaning of life. Let us talk together to try to bridge the remaining gaps between us, to help one another to overcome our respective fears. For only by doing so can we develop a united community that is committed to peace and progress. Through the understanding we could gain by such an open and mutually respecting encounter we all could then truly live and let live.

---

[6] *Writing of Thomas Paine*, New York, Carlton House, p. 1.

# I Am Staying Where I Am

## 1970

### John Clayton

After my divorce I was out in California visiting friends; and so I dropped in to see Paul Kagan, who'd been my student when I taught there last summer. I'd parked my beat-up Mercedes out front and was upstairs—his apartment was empty and open—sipping some wine, sitting on my suitcase by the window— when craziness started happening down on the street.

"Get your fucking head in!" A cop below pointed a shotgun at my window. I ducked and pulled the shade, waited a couple of seconds, then looked out again. The cop was down the block. Four or five other cops at arms distance moved heavily down the street. I sat on the windowsill, watching. Then three young guys slipped along the row of shops across the street. They reached into a doorway. Now each had a bottle with a lit fuse. I didn't call out. The bottles arched end-over-end, burning past the street lamp. I watched them flash; the cops scattered, one cop screamed curses. All of them turned and let go a shot-gun blast, but the guys were gone.

"Holy shit!" I pulled back from the window. Police sirens—a line of cops on motorcycles with sidecars—exploded through the street. Then the door to the apartment burst open and Paul flung himself through the room to the bath-room and retched over the toilet. Susan sat down dazed, went off to wash when Paul came back.

I asked, "What's going on?"

Susan was laughing as she came from the bathroom. "Hi, John. I'm stoned from the tear gas, John. Isn't that freaky, isn't that freaky?" Gas had crystallized on her clothes; as she walked, she sprayed the room. My eyes began to run, my throat burned.

Paul shook his head. "What fucking pigs. We're running down a side street, okay? They get another load of pigs up the other end of the street popping gas. Then the TPF comes in by bus. No one was really mad till then: The TPF, fucking pigs, man, scared the shit out of us, come in with clubs. We made it

413

down an alley. Lots of kids *didn't*. This city belongs to the pigs. It's their city."
A cherry bomb went off down in the street. I clenched my eyes shut.

The bomb / exploded for me again, now, where I am sitting quiet in a
farmhouse / Western Massachusetts. I am on sabbatical. I am in retreat. Mist
is just lifting from these hills. There is sun on the jack-in-the-pulpits along the
rock wall. Mr. Swenson plants them and is angry when someone picks them,
they are like his fishing reels and rifles. When my six-year-old daughter comes
to visit weekends we walk by the rock wall to a forest path, then traverse a
hill of slippery moss to a pine needle carpet under a stand of tall trees.
    Jackboots at the edge of the city / edge of my mind. I am staying where I
am. Last weekend my daughter and I were taken by surprise by a forestry truck.
There was no machinegun mounted on the rear. I think a lot about Paul. Last
week I ripped a WANTED BY FBI handbill off a country postoffice wall. It
said *Wanted in San Francisco for Unlawful Interstate Flight to Avoid Prosecution for Unlawful Possession of Explosives*. It wasn't Paul.

Paul is hidden away in a cheap apartment behind my eyes. The stereo
blasts rock all night. Paul, Susan and I are drinking wine. Her jeans are stained
with oil from the street. She changes to a yellow print dress, and the room becomes a party. Then Paul's friend Tony Garcia comes in and asks where I am.
    "I'm going to spend next year, maybe the next couple of years, in Europe
or at my place in Massachusetts," I told them.
    Paul was annoyed. "You're still the same. Listen, man, you're like a fuck-
ing tourist here."
    I sat back with a pipeful of grass and got ready for his speech about
American napalm and foreign investments. And I knew it was true. In Vietnam
heat-sensitive receptors plugged into Saigon computers are calling down heli-
copter gunships in strikes on any living beings. Our policy is genocide. Back home
we're more selective: 28 Panthers were murdered last year. It's going to take
more sacrifices and more blood to keep the god comfortable. I am staying where
I am.
    Paul talked about the seven interlocking banks and corporations that con-
trolled this city and the university. He talked about the Defense Department's
*Project Themis* that was spreading millions of dollars around universities for
defense research. "That's what got us started here last week at the physics lab,"
Paul said. "Here—we had these leaflets printed up. Tony and me and a few
others wrote it. It'll explain things. Why don't you distribute leaflets with us
tomorrow?"
    "Maybe." I put a leaflet in my jacket pocket.
    Paul turned down the music. "We're going to sleep, teacher. I don't feel
like talking; my throat is sore."
    I am staying where I am. But voices brood like mists in the lower pasture.
Paul screaming YOU FUCKING PIGS! from a rooftop. My grandfather sits
wrapped in his tallis in a cold synagogue in Rochester, New York. He is mourn-

ing his life. The old men wait on the sea bottom, nodding. Their beards pulse, seaweed in the tide. Seamen, semen, drowned, nodding. Have you any hands? The old Jews nodding prayers wait with sad eyes.

The street is quiet, rain starts to fall in the tear-gassed city streets. Tony has gone home. I am outside their bedroom imagining Paul kissing Susan, imagining / *I love you*. She has long bright hair gold smoke and her breasts are slack, soft under the Indian shift. Maybe Chagall's fiddler is perching on the headboard of their bed. Rain falls washing away tear gas stink. Cops relax and I relax in this farm kitchen: I am not fighting anyone.

Paul and Susan turn out the ceiling light and light a candle. They hold each other a long time feeling for the special places like a contour map of each other.

He lies next to her and the soldiers stop stomping faces. I love you Susan. He kisses her breasts and the quiet inside of her thigh, reverently. The cops are asleep. His body opens to her like a woman letting tears fall. They are sharing a ritual, he lifts down the silver cup of fire. Nodding some kind of agreement, they lie on their sides and begin to move very slowly, touching each other's faces with an acknowledgment of a sadness. Why? The broken toys can't be fixed. The fish are dying in the polluted river. This is where we are. When we move it opens up deeper and rivers layers of my body. It begins in my cock but moves out until my thighs and my back are just as alive. Touch my thighs. Hold my ass with the tips of your fingers. Me too my breasts I love you my neck so strange. You're with me. Isn't any giant. Lie with me. Lie with me. The queen and prince of the blood dance in the golden room upstairs. They aren't going to disturb us. The castle is full of velvets that lie smooth over your hands. Your hands so soft. I . . . Paul. It's so deep. Oh, it's so deep. Baby it's so / there's still more. Baby there's more. The soldiers are exploding in the back of the brain, it's all you can do to stay love and keep firing. Bitch, bitch love. Hurt, steal me away my blood from my body, kill me. Who are you? I'm nobody, I'm here. Bodies smooth with sweat and caresses. The Led Zepplin pounds heavy blues rock on the stereo next to me in the living room. Next to Paul and Susan the telephone rings, it rings, they lie side by side not answering.

These are pleasant dreams. Putting two and two together. I remember my aunt in New York, the nurse props her up in bed she opens her paralyzed right hand with her left. They are enemies. She has no pity for her hand. Her breasts hang like tears she is always crying.

It was like that with you I couldn't make it. You paralyzed my body. I was trapped in the bed. My eyes are lenses screwed into sockets. My skin a uniform. To stop being a hard-on would mean go limp and get carried away by the cops. I will never be carried away. I keep you off with words.

My belly. Let your belly swell, open up, you said. I thought about Buddhas and tigers I am neither. I am ashamed. If my belly is open I will cry, and also you will laugh at my body. *Your* body makes *me* cry. It's foolish, gross. Your belly scarred from operations and our children, earth after battle. What am I supposed? Your body makes me cry. It has something to do with loving. If it were a plastic television body I could buy it or haggle over the price.

It's not worth purchase. If I have to love it I may die, it scares me. I open my belly to breathe. What kind of a bargain would you be getting? A smile and a hard belly afraid to give birth: holding onto my life as if it mattered.

The city is under attack. William Blake shakes the bloody walls. The houses are falling down and killing thousands of rats. The city is straining under two hundred years of siege. It is going up in smoke. I run my finger along the windowsill. Legislative committees have been sent out to investigate. They pin the blame on an increase in marijuana smoking. The city, nevertheless. The city, still. Is filled with smoke. Marchers carrying signs through the clogged streets / can't be seen. Now the ghettos are on fire. The landlords of course blame the heat of protest. My body is politic. But the fever is catching, it is hard to breathe. Stagnation and pollution of the blood / my blood flows with bric-a-brac of 19th Century industrial parlors, the lymph system conducts guided tours for cancer cells. This is the heart. This is the brain. Hidden in the cells are CIA operatives. Please destroy me, the city says. The web of lines in high tension. The city wants to die / fucked up the ass by a stick of dynamite. We are out of our minds. The city is built on a black mirror.

By the time I woke up next morning, Paul's apartment, close to the action on Fiske, began to fill with street people. They put their sleeping bags against the walls and got ready for the evening: another march at curfew. While Tony Garcia and Paul composed letters for the Coalition to the newspapers and the administration, a team was preparing face masks and first aid kits: vaseline, Murine, wash-and-dries. Three collie pups played tag through the apartment; Susan washed the tear gas out of her hair then dried her hair in front of the oven. I played blues on somebody's guitar.

We got to the demonstration early and set up loudspeakers. A block behind us a lot of guys were building barricades out of old crates, cardboard boxes, tires from a gas station dump. The police established a line 100 yards down the street; they wore helmets; their plastic visors were down, ready. A few leaders spoke.

Paul climbed up on a station wagon roof. "Cannot take *any* more ideological shit, brothers and sisters. Polemics. If you want to argue, there's a lot of empty halls just ignore the stink of tear gas. I don't want no more. The pig is no paper tiger. But the power back of the pig is a paper tiger. It can stand only so much defection, so much disruption. It's going to take a year or five, ten years, we're going to pull it all down. Tonight, we get busted as a group, we break into two's and three's and rip this city down. They maybe killed Jimmy Maslow yesterday. Dig it. They blinded Carol Wright and let the mace eat her eyes away while she begged for a doctor. I say we hit them tonight. We take back our city."

Tony climbed onto the car; he stood with raised fist and waited for silence. He spoke quietly. "The brother is right to be angry. But he's fucked up in how he's using that anger. We've got to unravel a social structure in which we ourselves, we ourselves are utterly implicated. Our anger should make us see our oppressors and ourselves more clearly. It's going to be a long struggle. Tonight we've got to demonstrate, but that's not where the struggle is: it's day after day. It's learning from and teaching each other and people who aren't with us yet. It's day after day."

"You should have been a priest," Paul laughed as Tony stepped down. Tony blessed him with the fist of revolution.

Sirens blew. The police line started advancing. Then the cries came! GAS! GAS! And the crowd gave. The cannisters flew high and exploded. A rain. Pop, pop, pop. Susan and Paul, me and Tony, checked for one another; we tied our face masks tight. WALK! WALK! WALK! the crowds chanted. A few yelled and pushed, some on the sides were running. But most of us gave ground slowly. From the middle of the crowd bricks and bottles were tossed out at the line of cops pressing forward with black gas masks. Street people picked up cannisters and tossed them back. Some of us were leaping up and down yelling and some tossed ash cans into the street. Up the block the crowd was forming again behind barricades of cardboard boxes, ash cans, a Chevy station wagon pushed into the middle of the street.

The cops marched slowly towards us, fifteen abreast. Paul shouted, "Light up your barricades!" and he split. The gasoline exploded across the barricade. In the hot red light a circle of demonstrators rocked the station wagon like a ritual lamb and screamed as it hit the fire. Everybody ran. Tear gas shells exploded and spun along the ground. Someone picked up a brick left over from last night and heaved it at the plate glass of a department store. Black spider glass in the flame light. My face / I wanted to tear at the smarting flesh / I held a wet handerchief over my mouth / we ran. Someone was shooting. *What the fuck am I doing here?*

The street was rocking with music. A fantastic second-floor stereo blasted out. The cops were marching two-step and the street-fighting men were dancing to the Stones—darting in with a cherry bomb or a Molotov cocktail, running back; the rooftops, the stairwells, clubs and gas and the street lamps' weird light / a light show. The cops were shadowed on the wall by their own searchlights and the wastebasket fires. I remember Nancy, a girl I taught last summer, running down a side street—a carload of cops jammed her against a wall and cracked her in the face and snapped an arm, someone shoved her to the pavement. I remember standing on a rooftop later on with a bucket of shit we collected that day. Country Joe playing nice. As the line of TPF converged on about twenty street people, somebody let the shit fly. And a few bricks. The street people made it around the corner.

After about an hour most of us were back at the apartment. A boy named Jimmy took a walk down the corner; he said, "The fuzz is there in two, three cars."

"Play some music."

Playing blues harp and acoustic guitar.

*Swear it's all all right*
*No strings attached*
*Don't get uptight*
*Baby flip down the latch. . . .*


It was a good sound. Then somebody came in with a gallon of wine out of a liquor store window. We drank and smoked some until Jimmy shouted, "Paul's back—busted up, a lot of blood, man," and Paul came in and put down maybe half a quart of cheap wine before he'd say anything.

He was caught in a coffee shop—he'd ducked in off the street. They came in and beat on everyone who looked like a street person. Pulled him outside and beat on him.

"Fucking pigs, man. Just too much. Too much."

He had bandages wrapped around his temples like an Indian headband. "Just too much. . . ." Tony and Susan made him lie down on the couch; they changed his dressings and gave him some codeine.

"Can I get you anything?" I asked.

"How did you feel out in the street, John?"

"I don't know. Times I wanted to kill someone; or sometimes it was like war games. *All* the time I kept looking at myself and laughing, 'You crazy ass-hole what are you doing here?' What good was it, Paul?"

Paul was getting sleepy. Speech took a long time. He examined me through deep water. "What the fuck good is it to stand outside yourself?"

"It's good. Hey, I'm not a kid. I'll be thirty next month. Jessica is six years old."

"Sure. And you've got a career to protect, right?"

Tony sat next to me on the floor. He grinned. "John has got a social disease, nothing personal. We all sit in separate offices and stay safe, and the safer we are the more uneasy about giving ourselves up to anything."

"Anything useless," I said. "I don't want my head busted for nothing, Tony."

"To *any*thing. Listen, we know what it is we're up against. What power. We're dwarfed by the city. It's their city. And our training has taught us to take only individual action. Which *is* useless. So we sit in our separate offices and feel shitty. Then we turn our defeat into a victory by boxing it up in an ironic vision."

In the other room Ed-with-crazy-eyes pounded his fist like an oil rig down and down, reciting the catechism of the police-in-his head, the beating last night on the cement floor of the jail. Like Don Quixote his paranoia becoming realistic. "Gonna get me a pig, man. Get me a pig. . . ."


Who are you come snooping? Say you dig inside one of my eye sockets. My eye is sperm jelly, jellied gasoline nitroglycerine, *watch out*. The caves are where I keep my supplies. Old bearded men on bicycles are laughing. The river is sheened with oil. Perch get trapped in the muck at the edge of the Charles in Cambridge. I sat with my wife watching the fish and feeling together. We weren't. We won't give ourselves up: the sacrificer may turn out to be a butcher. The fish / I could have picked them up out of the polluted water, river where MIT and Harvard radiation labs drain, river of industrial chemicals and sewage. Forty million fish floated belly up in the lower Rhine, watch out. I see the painting by Thomas Eakins the one-man scull on the Charles. Sculls still race. The crews race long, elegant sculls like fish / knife through slime. My body is polluted. I found an inch worm in my bed tonight, woke me up, I checked out my asshole. My cells are infiltrated. My cells fight to remain pure and walled-in / old Jews the community in England which refused to convert: the rabbi ordered all the men to kill the women and children, cut the throats of the men himself, and at last his own throat. The cell was pure. No spy, no agent provocateur. Our cells are in constant touch, too much contact dangerous. My sperm came out tonight in a guilty pink from the dye the doctor gave me to clean out my urinary system. The river is unclean, we need to call in experts. The river is brown, it must run red blood, clean out the city. The graceful arched footbridge near Harvard will topple. Industry will be tamped off with the wastes of industry. I see empty turnpike / all day stuck horn a diesel will wail in front of the public library. No good! No good! Paul's grandfather shakes his head. And my own grandfather, once a landowner in Kishnieff.

Blood is thicker than water.

You asked for it.

Nail him to the cross.

Paul, wearing a bloody headband. Like Tony, who got his head cracked open in Paris, spring 1968. But Tony speaks about it happily: "We were pushing them back for five hours. State power was in question that night. I fought alongside some Algerian workers. They were tough motherfuckers, I'll tell you. We wound up 4 A.M. after deGaulle had made his deal with the army, wound up on the bank of Ile de la Cité drinking out of a wineskin and singing the *Internationale* and crying. John, I'm gonna sleep one night on the floor of the White House Ball Room. And ball all night. Ball all night."

Me, I have no heart left. I stay pure and walled in.

> *The longing to be pure*
> *the weight*
> > *a band around*
> *my forehead a*
> *hippie headband many colors*
> *cigar store Indian*
> *fake wood*
> *no blood*
> *no brave*
> *sham tomahawk no fight left the land is dust*
> *and sagebrush*
> > *a frieze*
> *in sandstone I can't help you*
> *Leather thongs wrapped wet around the skull to dry:*

stake out the white-man skull cracks your pain is mine. The rocks are a band of spirits watching. Eyes like stones, I am stoned, a circle of stonefaces. Pointing.

I wear phylacteries around my temple. Prayer shawl to keep out the cold. I insulate my house.

Paul squatted next to Tony and me on the carpet of the Freedom Church basement. I talked with Tony about tactics. He wasn't tuned in to the arguments between splinter groups up at the front of the room. He told me about his father, who'd been a traveller for the CP until the purge trials and then a CIO organizer. Tony believed in the "industrial proletariat" and was active in organizing a workers-students community union. I thought that was a lot of crap; which was cool with him. His quiet was strange to me. He made notes on scrap paper. From time to time he watched Paul squirm.

Paul groaned: "Fuck these hassles over ideology, the Continental Congress now in session. Ben Franklin, hanging by his rod, continues to extort the troops. . . ." He got up. "Let's split." We went with Tony out the side door and drove downtown in my car. "There are two dead street people now, Tony. I won't sit still for parliamentary ego-games." Tony put his arm around Paul's shoulder until Paul relaxed.

We played pool; Tony shooting steady, setting himself up for easy shots, while Paul went after the tough ones. As for me—I'm no pool player. Paul calmed down. We shared a joint on the way back to the university district.

Tony Garcia: wears mustachios and a suede vest over a flowered shirt. His boot heels click hard on the concrete. Six-guns do *not* hang low from an ammunition belt and his eyes are wrinkled at the corners from good humor, not sun. (Broad street of Guatemalan village, a chicken squawks, a 1935 Pontiac swerves out of its way, a cluster of men stare and pass a bottle. Tony pops out of the bottle in joyful laughter and blesses them. He waves his guns in the air and returns them to his belt. To the estate of the landowner! The wine is left in the shadow of the stucco wall. Machine gun bullets spike pockmarks in the wall. Wine spatters the dust. A stage manager shouts STRIKE THE SET— they do. Fire hydrant, First National Bank window and aluminum wall. Some of the wine has splattered through to this set. I have bad eyes. Have to go up close to read the wall. It says, WATCH OUT: THIS WALL LIABLE TO CRUM- PLE AND CRUMBLE).

Paul and me and Tony walk by the bank. Paul is laughing now. "Gonna bang my way to freedom tonight, Tony." All of us a little stoned. Paul looks up at the bank windows; the spider cracks from last night's fight are lit up by the street lamp. A cop stands by the front door with a rifle. "Tony, I'm going to get some plastique," Paul said.

"You're fucking crazy," Tony told him. "You're crazy. You haven't learned what it is to think as a revolutionary."

We didn't talk about it anymore.

Paul examined maps of the city. His desk was piled with books. He pulled at his sideburns. (I think of pale cheeks of yeshiva bokher. But he refused to be stamped kosher by dead ancestors.)

Susan watched him as she and Tony composed another leaflet. She was very afraid. Without words he was telling her, Susan, you hold onto me sometimes, I want to break out of your city. You nestle me beyond the sirens. Then the door will bang open, they will bargain for my hair. Already I want to cut it off to please you.

Sirens. Sirens. And I remember most of all the terrible helicopters always overheard, ready to discharge their gas on us. Tony told me how when the copters had begun spraying gas last year, people had cheered—thinking that somebody had shot it down, it was smoking. Fists went up. Then they knew and the cheering stopped.

Air raid. I remember school corridor, we sat on the floor in line, hands covering our heads against glass splinters when the bombs would explode. I tried to sing. And I think now about another line of children marching across a half-demolished bridge, singing. Another cry—take cover! They run to the other side. Some of them make the ditch before the line of small bombs starts to burst in the rice field. Somebody is screaming, screaming. A little girl is dancing, dancing on the road, screaming / an older girl starts up after her but someone pulls her back to the ditch. Then the secondary explosions start: whistling "anti-personnel" fragments of jagged steel spin a foot above the ground. The girl crumples like a rag doll between the ditches.

The apple trees in my pasture: bear no fruit. At the top of my hill the trees are turning. Burn and defoliate. The banks of Massachusetts bulldoze the land and us. Burn and defoliate. The leaves shiver a secret telegraph of the rebel wind. Who negotiates with the jungles of Vietnam? I am disgusted by the smell of burning skin. LAMPSHADES, a woman named Koch made lampshades.

Paul is on the street before the sirens fade, running in sneakers, the crowd cheering track star, fathers in open white shirts eating their hearts out in the stands and the emperor raises his hands to cheers as the lions enter the arena. My grandfather sits taking notes for the Nurenberg Trials. Paul passes a kosher delicatessen with a special on, warning fingers between smoked white fish and roast beef. He sees himself served up as roast beef to a Lion's Club banquet in honor of Alameda County sheriff. Once a month in fury Paul's father used to balance his checkbook. Paul balances at the end of a warning finger. On up-lifted fuck-you finger Paul balances on his asshole where the sheriff tells him he belongs, patting him on the rump with a wishbone. I remember Eric told me he lay on his back in a prison courtyard, Alameda County. Seven hours. Peed in his pants, not allowed to go to the john. Couldn't turn his head. Ex-Marine just back from Vietnam rifle butt a foot over Eric's groin whispered, "You just want to suck my Blue Meanie dick. . . ."

Paul ducks into a doorway for a package, turns up the alley, over a loose-board fence and up to a wire gate behind the police station. He takes wire cutters from his jeans and snips through a dozen links to make a doorway a cat could just about get through. From cellar steps in the tenement behind him, he lets the cat out of the bag; attaches wires to plastique and makeshift plunger. (Flash to floor plan, police station arsenal in the rear basement—that tiny wired window.) The emperor counts his ammunition in the counting house. Paul ties the plastique to a child's roller skate and rolls it through the tiny doorway toward the arsenal window, easing it into position with the wires.

He ducks back into the basement doorway of the tenement behind the police station, peeling wire like fishing line. And steps behind the furnace and squeezes down on the handle / Warden pushes electrocution switch / crowd watches knife upraised over the netted slave: the emperor holds his thumb poised. Arthur Campbell has me on my knees, I am going to *come* in tears, I am trying to hold off ejaculation, arm twisted up behind my back waiting to hear the crack / his money sticks out of every pocket like fish. My bones, snap, go all the jivey fingers of all the cats on the school staircase. The crack of bamboo, Marine boot kicks in a door, flames up hot wind of napalm fire, cracks across a forest. I am going to hide away in the cool of the woods, my cock will root and turn tree, spray silver leaves, and there won't anymore be me.

In the cellar where Paul stands even the furnace rocks and shivers as the arsenal blows. (We were all on our feet and moving heads so high, heads *so* high, the drums exploding heavy organ bass on full amps. Bull-horn voice of thick-throated cop last summer at the rally before they came on with gas and shotguns. Nixon at his press conference. I hold an upraised fist. The emperor shoves down his thumb, small countries on a wet clay globe squash into the Pacific / tiny people under giant's thumb. The great black iron ball slams the tenement (Welcome to Springfield: a Mass Mutual Property) it crumbles bedroom where people are undressing for love the woman covers herself with a towel, the man picks up a newspaper and rolls it into a club. There are small girl children with crying pigtails / one sucks her thumb. Rag doll falls. Hundreds of gawkers crowd around to see the walls crumble and dust rise up flour in the kitchen, the woman's loaves. The project of middle-income housing rises on banknotes. My grandfathers sit shiva for the dead. That's not enough. Not enough.

The moon wears pants. I have a penny in my sight. There are only slaves and barnacles. Tonight the sun is dark. Clouds from the dark tower dirty him. I want to explain and justify. It is not my fault. The sun's face is evil energy turned inwards. I hide behind a rock. In case the earth tilts, the rock will hold me.

I ache to walk out onto the plains. Gorse, scrub grasses, moss. To spread out my arms. I will breathe and be warm, nothing else to do. But the mesa is an altar. I haven't written any script for the ritual. I see placentas empty sacks of skin like cast-off clothes.

Penny, penny. Copper skin, copper rock, no human land. I want to become elementary. I know what the sky can do. My skin is soft / peel it away! To organs and skeleton, skeleton-dance to organ music.

> *Iguana:*
>     *so much itself not*
> *to be fucked over*
> *no human animal*
>         *dog mouse wolf*
>         *of human meanings*
> *The most old. At home*
>     *in no-home.*

I make words. I spin out Paul like a spider or a fly cast into the stream. The old men at the bottom disapprove, but they can't drag me down.

I imagine a trucker offering Paul a stick of gum. The big red cab: control panel chrome and glass dials like on a jet. The trucker's partner asleep in the rear bunk. The trucker is heavy-set and dull-eyes the way Paul expects. But he is gentle, almost effeminate. At first Paul thought the guy was putting him on. They stop twice in Colorado. He buys Paul coffee and a hamburger, tells him to hold on to his money. The second stop he accepts a cup of coffee. (WHAT do I know about this country? I'm a foreigner here.) Down U.S. 40, past heavy sandstone buttes. They gas up before heading through Rabbits Ears Pass. The other trucker stays asleep. Paul feels his clean shaven face and brush cut. He sleeps a lot and dreams of the road. As I dream in front of my wood stove in this kitchen. I dream and remember the shell of a spine fish on the beach near Marseilles. Remember the snails: we turned a flashlight on them out of their shells, searching water at the Tierenia campeggio. House trailers crawl over the Colorado Rockies. Night crawlers.

We are all hitch hiking to New York. Or away. The minyan in the synagogue shake their beards in warning. Paul hunches his pack to his back.

Paul hitching in Nebraska. Not knowing himself now in gas station mirrors his short hair and deep tan. Flat land under the bowl of sky, you *know* it's sky, nothing holds it up, breaks into it, except jets from Colorado Springs or commercial planes or a bank / of rich clouds. Cobalt blue fading at the horizons. In all directions. You have to be the man on the cross, the man at the crossroads killing his father / cut off for good from his own willed future. There's nothing to do then but go on, to let it happen. Fanon says that the revolutionary is free of the expectation that he will live. That's a humility like Oedipus at Colonus, once he knew where he was. Just going on, not in his own hands. So Paul finds himself heading towards New York. And I am looking at a topographical contour map of Shutesbury, Massachusetts. I am thinking about my grandmother and grandfather. My grandmother gave up her Russian passport to a woman too old to walk. They slipped into Roumania along ridge trails of forest paths, afraid of roads except at night. Then their trip across Roumania, Austria, into Italy to get a ship to America, money sewed into dresses and shoes.

On top of a slight rise Paul sits by the road, eats a chunk of salami and a tomato and drinks wine out of the canteen he picked up in Denver. It's growing hot. In all directions the heat makes the horizon quiver, the weeds and earth are throwing up a rich smell. No ties, now. But he knows he is going on, somewhere. He stands 100 feet above himself and smiles down at the young man believing he can make a decision. He is going where he is going, like a figure in someone else's dream. He is curious about it, but there is no decision to be made, he is not attached. So he drinks and eats like the cows in the pasture behind the fence or the corn across the road. It's nice. He remembers Susan. Wishes he could make love, spend the day, but he can't make that happen or anything. He lets his mind balloon into the sky. But now, with the wine and knowing he's not in charge, there's no terror in floating.

After half an hour his legs and hands push at the ground, some weeds snap and as he gets up his nose has to screw up against the ache of odor. It makes him laugh. The cows don't look up. He hoists his pack and hurries down to the road to thumb a farmer's truck: shiny new Ford pickup with home-made side rails that wobble. The driver waves but goes on, and Paul shrugs his pack into position on his back and follows down the road.

Lake of green corn along the highway. The surgeon who picks up Paul, his collie barks at cows and horses, never sheep, it's funny. Paul dozes, doesn't want to answer questions. There's a peeling Eugene McCarthy sticker on the surgeon's back window. Paul tells him he's not into politics. They share the driving. Lakes of corn. (The smoke hangs in an even layer over the police station. Mushroom cloud / napalm cloud / three men injured in the explosion. The guerrilla band in the city, Che says, takes its orders from the countryside. Terrorism to be used selectively against the recognized enemies of the people.) Like a fish in water, the Volvo slips between the lakes of corn / a knife between the ribs. "I'm concerned," Paul says, "with ecological imbalance. . . ." The smoke a pall over the city. Appalls. Orders from no cell. Revolt of the body.

I live by myself in the house my grandfather bought. Old Russian Jew who owned land and sheep in the Pale, although Jews were not permitted to own land. Just before he died he bought this late Colonial farmhouse, he became a Yankee and died where there was no minyan to say prayers for him. My father was in the middle of a business deal that morning; so the old man's housekeeper had to arrange for a funeral home in Amherst to ship the body to New York. I live alone, except on weekends, when my daughter comes to visit, or when a woman friend comes to see me for a few days.

I was alone when Paul, Susan, and Tony came up to see me last week. We ate brown rice and took long walks. Somewhere in a deserted apple orchard, deep in the woods, we found a 1926 Ford truck buried in leaves. We played New England farmers taking produce to market and Bonnie and Clyde getaway. Later we carried home rusted pieces of the truck to hang up in the kitchen.

Paul had a new name. After dinner Tony handed him a pewter dish with a forged social security card and draft card. We toasted the birth.

"What does it mean to blow up a police station?" I asked Paul.

"It means he got very, very angry," Tony said. "This guy being born tonight won't blow up police stations. He'll learn."

"You're all alone," I said to Paul. "You've stepped outside the world into space. Outside every definition. You scare the shit out of me how alone you are." But even then I knew I was more alone.

Somewhere now there is a clock on a mantel. Paul looks up from his book: the clock strikes him between the eyes a notch of worry. Susan is practicing a new bass run on guitar. She laughs at him that he has to keep his hair cut short and wear a suit. He's gone underground, somewhere, waiting. I don't know for what.

I'm standing by a clear stream in Shutesbury, Massachusetts, fishing with Mr. Swenson. The air is clean. Mr. Swenson is teaching me how to use my wrist on a cast. I don't believe there are real fish underneath, but it doesn't matter. The leaves are quietly turning. The land is gentle to me. My car is covered with red and gold. So that at last what will we know about the black kids locked up in their Boston schools or political prisoners in detention camps? Our woods will flame up with foliage. But in Vietnam the trees are burning. I am in America in the eye of the firestorm, spreading mortar on brick, rebuilding my chimney. The fire rises to unify itself with the sun, its father, its source. Fire has no mother, it can't cry. My eyes tear as I put log on log over the coals in my stove. The leaves are piled and burned or banked against the house over tar paper tacked to the lowest clapboards to keep out weather. The leaves cruble dead brown and the snows will drift against the house, begin to rot them into mulch. (A man is burned, he is buried, and others share the weight of his ammunition and supplies. They go on. In the forest under the smoke the leaves are quietly turning.)

I have no doctors for this pain. It is a certified operation, a life. I give it up to the Yiddish raconteurs and bushwack salesmen. The entrepreneurs of existence. As for me there are no cures I can speak. No tears bottled and sold as brine, no brine as tears. The sea has its own business. It's not there to rock me. We meet half way. I am besieged by creditors but will finally pay all debts. There are no alternatives. Whosoever believeth in Me shall not die. I can appreciate his case. It's not the run of the mill. A useful set of apprehensions. Can you believe in swans? I sing sorrow, sing sorrow. The politics of silence.

# Youth in the Technological Era
## 1969

## Barry N. Schwartz

The unique characteristic of the generation now passing through adolescence in America is that it is the first to have been born into a thoroughly technological society, where instantaneous data processing, telstar, atomic energy, moon exploration, push-button warfare, "the pill," and LSD are regarded as environmental facts and not startling innovations. The young are the first generation to experience pervasive technology and affluence as if no other human condition had ever existed. The Depression usually means nothing beyond two pages of a glossy new high school text which will be phased out in two years. Gone is the legendary craftsmanship which produced the enduring appliances their parents so often mourn. Theirs is the world of planned obsolescence and unrelenting change. Because the technological era in which we now live is the only world the young have known, their values, their sensibilities and their aspirations are distinctly different from those of their parents. Today many of our youth have only to be alive to be a radical conflict with, and alienated by, the ideas and values of an adult society which prides itself on its luxury and consumes gluttonously.

The parental generation matured in an industrial society striving for the fixed goal of a "higher standard of living," a goal which demanded nose-to-the-grindstone rigidity and strict adherence to prescribed social postures. Our young are growing up in a technological society, soon to become cybernated, which creates ever greater abundance, is conducive to spontaneity, and frees individuals for new ways of thinking and behaving. Consequently, our young live within a different reality from their elders. They sincerely do not feel the sense of the "practical" which characterizes the adult world. Ironically, the drives and personal values of parents who survived a depression and a climb to prosperity are made untenable by their achievement of abundance. The belief that the worth of an individual is determined by his work function and his productivity motivated industrial society toward the present day. But in our affluent age, in which machines will soon produce goods endlessly, such motivations are obsolete.

Non-agrarian economic systems move toward maximizing profit, and to-day the great obstacle to profit is labor. The cost of raw materials is generally stable; the price of machinery defined and easily absorbed in time; but the cost of labor is an ever-increasing, constantly frustrating, and often unpredictable economic variable. To attain higher profits and greater efficiency, corporations have machines assume the tasks of men. With automation freeing men from their work functions, and with greater quantities of goods available, the value relevant to increasing numbers of young people is not what a man earns by his work, but how satisfying his work is. The current interest is nonspecialized edu-cation, the creation of interdisciplinary and general "humanities" programs, and the fact that only twelve per cent of last year's college graduates chose business careers, all reflect a shift in values. Our young constitute the first gen-eration in history to be confronted in the mass by the problem of leisure, and they in turn are challenging society's definition of work.

In the older industrial society objects are the goal of production, a produc-tion made possible largely by the expenditure of man's labor. The universal value which necessarily gains ascendancy in such an environment is possession. In the technological era machine-produced objects are abundant and easily re-placed, and man is freed from the necessity of laboring to produce in order to consume. As machines assume more of men's productive functions a value based on use rather than possession emerges.

The incentive implicit in the economic system of industrial capitalism is ownership. For the great mass, work is performed in exchange for purchasing power. The young, however, relate to objects as they contribute to individual extension, since most young people are consumers long before they are pres-sured to become wage earners. These different attitudes and values cause con-siderable conflict. Many urban adults, for example, take great pleasure in owning a car despite the fact that it may sit idle six days a week. As a possession it is valuable because it symbolizes status and an object achieved. The young are interested in an object as it extends the individual's powers; a car is to go, to be used, and when it is idle it has little importance. Consequently the young use objects in ways adults view as reckless or irresponsible. Because it is important that something be in use, the young often own and use objects communally. In the adult world, where individual possession is a prime value, this kind of mul-tiple extension is not possible.

This difference in values explains why adults collect junk while the young throw things away or "lose" them. Many adults store old or broken objects to be fixed "someday when they may be needed," even though re-placement parts may by then be unobtainable. The young discard an unusable object immediately or create a new use for it, perhaps as an art object, in which case it is hung on the wall for display.

This discrepancy between the values of possession and extension also accounts for the change in social relationships. When the adult male was young, he probably valued a woman for her purity. If she was of good repu-tation, and virgin, the male who won her acquired a possession that was unmarked by previous ownership; she was not "second-hand." If the woman was dull and failed to contribute to the growth of the man, at least she was *his* woman. After marriage he expected fidelity, which affirmed possession. Today among many young men we find that if a woman extends a man, leads him to new experiences, helps him to grow, he is willing to be patient with occasional infidelities or at worst an erratic or difficult relationship. Young women tend to feel similarly.

The sexual mores of the adult world are grounded in a capitalist framework of values which supported the industrial society. Sex is a woman's resource, her labor value, which she invests in amounts sufficient to lead to the desired result—marriage. The idea that she herself could experience pleasure from sex, or even desire this pleasure as an end in itself, threatened the ethical dictates of the adult world. In the past, as theologian Myron Bloy, Jr., suggests, parents used the triple threat of infection, conception, and detection to insure that human relationships arrived at their socially programmed conclusions. But in the technological era the youth have penicillin, contraception, and candor. The life style now emerging among our youth demands that the moment be satisfying, and sex provides a very satisfying moment. The meaning of sex becomes redefined as technology makes it possible as an experience of intrinsic worth.

An industrial society reinforces the very old notion of distinction between the sexes: the man goes to work and is the provider; the woman stays home and cares for the objects and the offspring. The major role relationships between men and women are based on their different work functions. But technological society is breaking down these differing roles. Traditional masculine work is passed on to machines; women's work is greatly reduced by household "labor-saving" machines, nursery schools, and service industries. The qualities usually assigned to men—involvement, logic, imaginative thinking—and to women—sensitivity, perception, warmth, emotion—are now desired in both sexes. The young of both sexes go to school together, work together, and live together. Clothes traditionally assigned exclusively to one sex only are now worn by both, and certain hair styles signify the diminishing of visible difference between them. We can anticipate in the cybernated era that there will be even fewer role distinctions.

Another inherent value of the capitalist system is belief in investment. The adult world encourages the sacrifice of the individual's time and aspiration if it promises future success, where success is usually measured in improved consumer status. In this view man is a means and objects are the end. A man will work thirty-five hours a week for his paycheck. While adult wage earners do what they must, the young, in large part, enjoy the privileges of a leisure class. Millions of them sit in high school and college classrooms getting involved with ideas, activities that after age sixteen would have been inconceivable to any but the sons of the rich only two generations ago. As society achieves greater prosperity, the young enter the work market later and later in life. Consequently, many of the young respond to the values of leisure, not to those of work. Among many, the idea of investing oneself in an uncertain and abstract future has little currency. Indeed, many "dropouts" find it difficult to spend years of their lives in an educational system which values the degree or diploma over the act of learning. Ironically, the result of the older generation's investment makes the principle of investment untenable for its children. The new value, one made wholly practical by a technological era, is that the process itself must satisfy.

Evidence of this emergent value can be seen in the political attitudes of the young. What adult analysts have classified as mere youthful idealism, perhaps in an attempt to dismiss the activist politics of the young altogether, actually represents a philosophical view which sees all men's well-being as the measure. In the politics of the adult world what counts is the result of human activity, a result which may be achieved by lying, by hypocrisy, and by the sacrifice of personal ideals. The investment made is meaningful solely in terms of the success achieved. This concept, root and branch of a capitalist system of economics and morality, defines anything done successfully as inherently good. The politics of youth rejects the idea of investment and demands that the particular act be meaningful. The political process is validated not by the nobility of its ends, but by the authenticity of its means. This is why youthful politics usually are nonideological. Whereas both the Protestant Ethic and Marxism assume that the individual should be subservient to some abstract and overriding end, arguing over which end is just, youth increasingly rejects the adult-projected future along with the past. The present is the only time which can satisfy. This contemporaneity seems reprehensible to those who see history as a continuum.

As I am writing, an important political activity of the young is opposition to the war in Vietnam. Yet rarely does one encounter an individual who believes that he or his group can actually do anything about the war. All the evidence unmistakably indicates that the adult world, the generation in control, is not listening to the protesting young, referred to *en masse* as "prophets of doom." How can one explain the gathering of energies for a cause which its supporters believe cannot succeed? The answer, again, is not youthful idealism, but the fact that the political activity of the young is based less on predictions of success or profit than on a belief that activity itself is affirmative and fulfilling. Protesting a social or political evil, whether the denial of civil rights, war, or illegitimate authority, justifies itself, even if it accomplishes nothing.

This belief in the "rightness" of the act, the demand that the activity itself be fulfilling, leads inevitably to violation of the law. The forms of illegality may be as political as draft-card burning, draft evasion, or disruption of traffic; or as social as underage drinking and the use of drugs; or as private as abortion and sexual deviation. In all cases the law is seen as the coercive arm of the adult world, an aspect of its malignant self-righteousness. Thousands, probably millions, of young people today smoke marijuana in direct violation of laws passed by elders who exist comfortably with abundant alcohol and pep and sedative pills. As many young people feel that before the law is to be respected it must make sense, the unjustified rules that the adult world imposes are flouted with mass irreverence, a social phenomenon for which there can be no effective reprisals. Widespread illegality is but another example that the youth born into a technological society are not compromising with the old industrial society's system. They either confront it openly or subvert it privately, but they seem genuinely unable to accept it.

The dissent of the very young appears in their music. The sounds and lyrics they produce and consume feature improvisation and word combinations nearly unintelligible to adult ears, for the young dislike order and distrust words. Words are the manipulative tools used by Mom and Dad, the System, the Establishment, to herd them into the fold. The new attitudes toward time and activity account for the increasing involvement of youth in the many forms of art. Since the young demand that the moment fulfill, and that the process rather than the result be meaningful, it is inevitable that art is an important part of their life choices. Art, it must be remembered, is that area of human activity in which the values emerging from the youth have been historically significant. Art-as-act is the essence of the artistic experience, one which places the emphasis on creating rather than on what is gained by the activity. Young people will tend to make heroes of artists and emphasize the arts as the technological era makes material existence comfortable and the subjective enjoyment of life viable.

The previous generation, which wished to provide its children with everything they themselves never had, has acclimated the young to plenitude. In the material Eden they have inherited, the young are accustomed to choose what suits them and "turn off" what does not. But it is hard to turn off one's parents. The young and their elders live in the tension created by a vast difference in value systems which has never in history existed between two successive generations in the same society, and the resultant conflict has reached explosive proportions. While the adults seem severe in their judgment and their condemnation, many of the young exhibit a real sense of toleration. While the adult world respects structure, seeing form as all, the young favor content and seek to live in what adults call anarchy. While the adult world finds security in sameness, the young are fascinated with the unusual. While repetitive and familiar experiences usually mark the scope of adult behavior, the young explore the unknown. While most elders want security, most young people are willing to risk. While the elders see virtue in moderation, the young see moderation as inhibiting. While the adults are concerned with the "should," the young are motivated by the "want to." While the older generation assumes an aggressive posture toward different systems and ideas, the young are less willing to leave the conference table for the battlefield.

When young people enter the institutions of the adult world they find that they must conform in order to succeed; their assumption of choice is antithetical to their chances of survival. Some succumb, some rebel. But institutions do not allow dissention. The power which lies in the hands of the older generation coerces obedience with subtle efficiency. The young are often expelled when they demand "relevant" education, outlawed for their private satisfactions, too frequently beaten and jailed for publicly supporting their convictions, and given the option of war, exile, or five years of hard labor if they are unable to avoid the draft. The encounter with the adult world is so frequent, so often severe in its consequences and hopeless in its outcome, that youth is plunged into a daily deepening crisis. Given the fact that half the population of the United States is now under twenty-six, this cleavage between the generations would be the most significant internal confrontation in this country were it not for a more overt racial conflict.

For the young, as for all human beings in crisis, there are four possibilities: suicide, escape, rebellion, and submission. It is predicted that five thousand college students will have committed suicide in 1968. But suicide is less desirable in the technological era because another possibility, escape, has become so easy. Geographic escape and mental illness are choices made by many of the young, as the stepped-up exodus to Canada and statistics on adolescent mental disorders indicate. The elaborate psychological services on the campus, the number of "freakouts," the psychological distortions of ghetto youth, all attest to a mode of escape which undeniably signifies damaged personalities. But by far the most popular way of removing oneself from the necessity of responding to an intolerable situation is the drug experience, that inexpensive and not irrevocable transformation of an ugly world into one far more congenial. While drugs do make an oppressive social situation less oppressive, they do not, and cannot, lead to social confrontation, only to social evasion. They are strictly a personal solution. Submission was thoroughly explored by the Silent Generation of the 1950's. The "Now" Generation of the 1960's has chosen action over passivity, protest over silence.

The question of how many young people actually constitute the "young" under discussion might fairly be raised. The polarizations and generalities presented here indicate patterns and are not, of course, definitive. These patterns may describe a minority or majority of young people; but that is a moot question. The significant point is that the more vocal and active youth present overtly feelings apparently shared throughout the younger generation. It is certain that the pressures on the young—the draft, institutional authority, manipulation—affect *all* the young. The response to this pressure varies from radical rejection to comfortable acceptance, although Bob Dylan's assertion that "the times, they are a-changing" as manifest in social attitudes, mores, politics, clothing and song, indicates that the latter choice does not essentially represent the way most young people behave. Nor is the adult world properly characterized by a homogenous attitude, although the behavior of those adults in positions of power and influence betrays apparent similarities of view.

A committed life, and a life which makes little concession to the "practicalities," is possible today without subsequent material hardship. The young can choose for creation, for synthesis of knowledge and experience, and for communication if they are willing to struggle with their parents and the institutions of society; or they can stand passively aside in the belief the old system will destroy itself. Fortunately the technological era is not conducive to passivity. Increasing pressure from above inspires reciprocation from below, and the lines of stress are extending further across existing society.

The young are already the main drive in our society for social change, for equality, and for democracy. It is the young who envigorate the civil rights movement, who demand educational relevance, who serve in the Peace Corps, and who provide the bodies for radical politics. Yet it is problematic whether the young will find the mechanism for directly influencing the direction of our society.

What that influence may mean is the decentralization of massive power, new and meaningful uses of leisure time, education more concerned with understanding and relevance than with sorting and selecting corporate personnel, the revitalization of our cities, a concern for our natural resources, racial integration, human ways of helping the unfortunate, and the search for our society's lost identity and purpose.

The young will either confront society in the hope of changing it, or they will individually and in communities live apart from it. If Marshal McLuhan's predicted humanistic tribalization of society is to occur, it will not happen because the young sit mesmerized before a televised stream of trivia, but because dedicated and intelligent young men and women, using the tools of the technological era, will attempt to refashion society. For this to happen the new values not exhibited negatively as dissent must be transformed into positive realizations. One dissents *from,* but rebels *for*. Whatever their decision, it will indelibly alter the fate of our world.

# You Can't Trust Perpetual Adolescents

## 1969

## Russell Kirk

Early in 1966, in the pages of a women's magazine, Mr. Edward Keating, editor of the radical journal *Ramparts,* proclaimed that today's youth knows that you can't trust anyone over thirty. Reading farther in this essay, however, one discovered that you can't trust many people under thirty, either, by Mr. Keating's admission. Indeed, Keating soon was taught that you can't trust even radicals under thirty: for he was expelled by conspiring young associates from control of the magazine he had founded, edited, and heavily subsidized.

The only trustworthy folk, Keating believed before his juniors heaped indignities upon him, are such of the rising generation as follow the *Ramparts* line—or some line farther to the left—grow beards (if masculine), and parade in the streets their own moral superiority to those dreary dogs who enforce the laws, defend the republic, and turn the great wheel of circulation.

What a happy, just, peaceful world would be ours if only these youthful fantastics were endowed with total authority! Or so Mr. Keating believed.

But I am unable to agree, even though this nation urgently needs responsible criticism in addition to moral imagination. In the groups which Keating admires, I find little except the attitudes of prolonged adolescence—though I have talked with the "New Left" enthusiasts on dozens of campuses, and have seen them at their demonstrations.

To pose as a virtuous young rebel seems pleasant—for a while. How boring it is to turn from slogans and demonstrations to the painful labor of practical accomplishment in this imperfect world! Shouting about other people's alleged injustices is more fun than trying to establish tolerable order in one's own soul and community; demanding immediate universal peace is less risky than personally repelling aggression.

Yet the young Pharisee, declaring himself holier than his misguided elders, may be frozen into an attitude of perpetual adolescent rebelliousness. Few human types are more repellent than the smug radical who declines to assume responsibilities—who, hurling abuse at anyone stodgy enough to perform regular duties, nevertheless lives in comfort and safety provided by the very institutions and men he denounces.

Haven't we been through all this before? I remember with clarity the cult of youth which enjoyed considerable influence in the early thirties. Those were the years of "strength through joy" and "youth solidarity" in various forms: Communist youth movements, Socialist youth movements, pacifist youth movements, Fascist youth movements. One such association of young zealots attained power, for a time—a group called Hitler Youth, headed by an idealistic social revolutionary now serving a sentence in Spandau prison.

In any age, there exists much against which intelligent and conscientious young people ought to protest. But reckless protest for the sake of protest, like revolution for the sake of revolution, can convert a fairly tolerable society into general misery. Revolutions do not remain peaceful, and they devour their own children.

How genuinely serious and imaginative are the youth movements which Keating applauded? Against what evils do they contend? In Keating's eyes, the young radicals are alarmed primarily by the Bomb. They recognize, however, that general peace cannot be achieved until justice becomes concrete. Then Keating and his young friends fall into bathos. Youth must protest, according to Keating, for the sake of "the starving child in India, the Negro who needs dignified employment, the mother smothered in napalm in some Vietnam village."

Well! More food in India, better employment for American Negroes, and security for civilians in Vietnam are earnestly to be desired. These things are as much sought by people over thirty as by those under thirty, and as much advocated by the young "conservators," whom Keating denounces, as they are by the young bearded demonstrators whom he idealizes.

Yet precisely how are these goals to be achieved by sit-ins, teach-ins, street demonstrations, burning of draft cards, or even loose rhetoric? India will obtain more food only by a massive improvement of Indian agriculture— certainly not by breast-beating in Berkeley, Washington, and New York. The Negro will obtain a better job only by a complex process of improved education and training, responsible and tolerant conduct on the part of both white and colored people, and restoration of community and family life among the Negroes who have poured abruptly into the big cities. The Vietnamese mother will be saved only by military and diplomatic policies which teach the Communists of the North that their game is not worth the candle.

What are Keating's humanitarian radicals under thirty doing to insure the improvement of Indian agriculture? How are they bringing about better understanding between whites and Negroes, healing old wounds, helping the Negroes settle down to practical improvement? What do they propose, after their allegedly "nonviolent" fashion, for southeastern Asia?

Far from recommending practical alternatives to present policies, the under-thirty set commended by Keating seems more interested in the ego-gratifying defiance of the malcontent adolescent. Denounce whatever exists.

Blame Daddy. Be a rebel, on any pretext. Form a gang, and give it a name, and adopt a gang-costume. But never condescend to look critically at your own actions, or to propose any rational alternative to the ways and institutions you denounce. And sedulously avoid any strenuous personal involvement—except in mass demonstrations.

The young radicals, according to Keating, regard the medical and legal professions as "petty ambitions." Through the law, practical justice is obtained. Through medical science, suffering is alleviated. But how much more dramatic to man the barricades! Thought and self-discipline always are exacting. Instead, sprawl on the floor, listening to Pete Seeger records; sing along with Pete: don't think—just drift with the rhythm. When you're in the mood, simply act—nonviolently, of course.

What are these youth groups that Keating trusts so unreservedly? What way are they drifting? Why, they have the approbation of Gus Hall, chief spokesman for the Communist party in America. In the summer of 1965, Hall declared publicly that "Fronts are a thing of the past. We don't need them. We've got the W. E. B. DuBois Clubs, the Student Nonviolent Coordinating Committee, and Students for a Democratic Society going for us, but they're not 'fronts' in the usual sense of the word. They're just part of the 'responsible Left'—that portion of American youth that realizes society is sick."

Consider one of these organizations, Students for a Democratic Society. I have encountered many members of SDS, from coast to coast. They are sentimental, bearded, earnest, and muddled. In the beginning, SDS members spoke of the Communists contemptuously, as old fuddy-duddies, not sufficiently radical. The society professed to be free from any rigorous ideology; it was merely seeking avenues to radical reform. In the beginning, SDS refused to admit Communists to membership.

But since then, the society has decided that its anti-Communist stand was "irrelevant"; anyone can join now. And anyone does. Once it became clear that such loose-knit protest clubs could be used to denounce American policy in Asia and elsewhere, Communist infiltration commenced—a fact remarked by the United States Attorney General, by the director of the Federal Bureau of Investigation, and by the Internal Security Subcommittee of the Senate.

Nowadays it is somewhat painful to observe the evasions and contortions of an SDS activist when he is questioned about the presence of Communists in his organization. I wish these people would read Lionel Trilling's novel *The Middle of the Journey,* because they are involved in the grim process described by Trilling—passing through stages of self-deception and willful blindness which must lead them to totalist ideology and intellectual servitude, if not to extreme violence.

So I distrust the vagueness of these "under-thirty" organizations, easily subjugated by fanatics. I distrust, too, in many instances, their professions of nonviolence on principle.

Take the Student Nonviolent Coordinating Committee, so active at

Selma, and since then given to chanting hymns about killing Whitey. Rabbi Richard L. Rubenstein, chaplain to Jewish students at Pittsburgh universities and colleges, led some 135 students from Pittsburgh to the Alabama demonstrations. He found himself aghast at the character and tactics of the "activists and revolutionaries" who form the Student Nonviolent Coordinating Committee. The SNCC zealots, Rabbi Rubenstein declared upon his return to Pittsburgh, deliberately tried to push demonstrators into trouble—so that "martyrs" might be created and violence provoked. SNCC fanatics repeatedly lied to the Pittsburgh students in order to incite incidents with the police, illegally invaded a high school to recruit children for demonstrations, and broke through police lines. "They wanted dead bodies—our bodies," Rabbi Rubenstein said.

To put it mildly, we cannot entrust our civil social order, so laboriously developed through many centuries of trial, error, and discovery, to the mercies of people with the mentality and the temperament of adolescents. Bearded or shaven, the new radical youth seems altogether incompetent to renew the vitality of our civilization. The youthful neurotic is a symptom of our personal and social disorders, but scarcely the physician we need.

Yet I do not despair of the rising generation. The little groups of extremists are few in number, really, and generally ineffectual, obtaining far more attention in the press than their influence justifies. The political understanding of many Americans under thirty is sounder than were the opinions of most young people a generation ago. The abler students and other people under thirty are beginning to think; and reflection, not frantic action, is what our time needs. The recovery of order in the soul and order in society is the first necessity of this century. By a mere prolonged teen-age rebelliousness, a doctrinaire detestation of all authority, the world is plunged deeper into confusion and injustice.

Of this hard truth, the present excitement over the war in Vietnam is sufficient illustration. American diplomatic and military policies in southeastern Asia should be scrutinized closely—and improved. People under thirty should have a part in this scrutiny. But an hysterical "mass protest," sloganizing and almost mindless, cannot bring justice or peace to Vietnam. Flight before Communist terrorism does not abolish the Bomb. Yet such silliness can provoke a public reaction which would make more difficult any prudent criticism of foreign policy.

Edward Keating wishes youth to recast this world nearer to his heart's desire. How? Why, "just capture the feel of the music," says Keating. Like the intemperate young fantastics whom he praises, Keating reduces politics to a mood, or to a pastiche of vague humanitarian sentiments. Get into the rhythm, you glorious youths: swing it. "Trust in the music," Keating tells us, benignly.

But what if the progressive orchestra is playing a *danse macabre?* What if the music is Wagnerian? What, after all, if politics is more than a game of musical chairs? *Who* shall overcome what? Is Pete Seeger, the Marx of folksong, a messiah who shall usher us into the Earthly Paradise to the twang of a guitar?

Defy convention: grow a beard. There's the profundity of the under-thirty radicalism. I have no objection to young beards, having sported one myself when I was a graduate student. But beard-wearing is a perilous measure of the wisdom of people under thirty. Hell's Angels, those kindly motorcyclists who are continually being involved in altercations with the police, wear beards quite as impressive as the whiskers displayed by Students for a Democratic Society. Once *youth* and *rhythm* are made the criteria for social leadership, it becomes difficult to discriminate among beards and guitars.

The appeal to emotionalism, the unqualified praise of Youth in the abstract, the contempt for old political forms, the sneering at our ancestors' wisdom, the exhortation to lose ourselves in movement, rhythm, the feel of things, confidence in a revolutionary future—some of us have encountered these notions before. German youth heard them, a generation gone—and acted upon them. When idealized youth is told repeatedly that youth must be served, theories of non-violence do not endure long.

Youthful ignorance and inexperience work much more harm than do the alleged apathy and complacency of older minds. I do not intend to entrust my dearest interests to persons suffering from senility; but I do not mean, either, to entrust them to persons still afflicted by the psychological disturbances of adolescence. Although not enamored of Mr. Lyndon Johnson, I had rather have him keep the Bomb than place our national security in the hands of the young freaks of the May 2nd Movement.

Age does not necessarily make a man clean, brave, and wise; but neither does youth. The unlikeliest person to trust, in private concerns or in public, is "the humanitarian with the guillotine," the enthusiast confident that the world lay in darkness until he, in his moral perfection, burst upon mankind. You do not have to be elderly to become a destructive fool. All you require is sufficient arrogance—and to "trust in the music," the unreasoning rhythm, of perpetual adolescence.

## To the American People
## and Recommendations
## September 26, 1970

---

## President's Commission on Campus Unrest

---

The crisis on American campuses has no parallel in the history of the nation. This crisis has roots in divisions of American society as deep as any since the Civil War. The divisions are reflected in violent acts and harsh rhetoric, and in the enmity of those Americans who see themselves as occupying opposing camps. Campus unrest reflects and increases a more profound crisis in the nation as a whole.

This crisis has two components: a crisis of violence and a crisis of understanding. We fear new violence and growing enmity.

On the nation's campuses, and in their neighboring communities, the level of violence has been steadily rising. Students have been killed and injured; civil authorities have been killed and injured; bystanders have been killed and injured. Valuable public and private property and scholarly products have been burned.

Too many Americans have begun to justify violence as a means of effecting change or safeguarding traditions. Too many have forgotten the values and sense of shared humanity that unite us. Campus violence reflects this national condition.

Much of the nation is so polarized that on many campuses a major domestic conflict or an unpopular initiative in foreign policy could trigger further violence protest and, in its wake, counter-violence and repression.

The Constitution protects the freedom of all citizens to dissent and to engage in nonviolent protest. Dissent is a healthy sign of freedom and a protection against stagnation. But the right to dissent is not the right to resort to violence.

Equally, to respond to peaceful protest with repression and brutal tactics is dangerously unwise. It makes extremists of moderates, deepens the divisions in the nation, and increases the chances that future protest will be violent.

We believe it urgent that Americans of all convictions draw back from the brink. We must recognize even our bitter opponents as fellow Americans with rights upon which we cannot morally or legally encroach and as fellow human beings whom we must not club, stone, shoot, or bomb.

We utterly condemn violence. Students who bomb and burn are criminals. Police and National Guardsmen who needlessly shoot or assault students are criminals. All who applaud these criminal acts share in their evil. We must declare a national cease-fire.

There can be no more "trashing," no more rock-throwing, no more arson, no more bombing by protesters. No grievance, philosophy, or political idea can justify the destruction and killing we have witnessed. There can be no sanctuary or immunity from prosecution on the campus. If our society is to survive, criminal acts by students must be treated as such wherever they occur and whatever their purpose.

Crimes committed by one do not justify crimes committed by another. We condemn brutality and excessive force by officers and troops called to maintain order. The use of force by police is sometimes necessary and legal, but every unnecessary resort to violence is wrong, criminal, and feeds the hostility of the disaffected.

Our universities as centers of free inquiry are particularly vulnerable to violence. We condemn those groups which are openly seeking to destroy them.

We especially condemn bombing and politician terrorism. The full resources of society must be employed to bring to justice those who commit terroristic acts. Anyone who aids or protects terrorists, on or off campus, must share the moral and legal responsibilities for the crimes they commit.

We find ominous and shocking reports that students are laying in supplies of weapons, and that others are preparing to take the law into their hands against protesters and minorities they dislike. There can be no place in our society for vigilantes, night-riders, or militants who would bring destruction and death upon their opponents. No one serves the law by breaking it.

Violence must stop because it is wrong. It destroys human life and the product of human effort. It undermines the foundations of a just social order. No progress is possible in a society where lawlessness prevails.

Violence must stop because the sounds of violence drown out all words of reason. When students and officials resort to force and violence, no one can hear and the nation is denied a vital call to conscience. It must stop because no nation will long tolerate violence without repression. History offers grim proof that repression once started is almost impossible to contain.

Campus protest has been focused on three major questions: racial injustice, war, and the university itself.

The first issue is the unfilled promise of full justice and dignity for blacks and other minorities. Blacks, like many others of different races and ethnic origins, are demanding today that the pledges of the Declaration of Independence and the Emancipation Proclamation be fulfilled now. Full social justice and dignity—an end to racism in all its human, social and cultural forms—is a central demand of today's students—black, brown and white.

A great majority of students and a majority of their elders oppose the Indochina war. Many believe it entirely immoral. And if the war is wrong, students insist, then so are all policies and practices that support it, from the draft to military research, from ROTC to recruiting for defense industry. This opposition has led to an ever-widening wave of student protests.

The shortcomings of the American university are the third target of student protest. The goals, values, administration, and curriculum of the modern university have been sharply criticized by many students. Students complain that their studies are irrelevant to the social problems that concern them. They want to shape their own personal and common lives, but find the university restrictive. They seek a community of companions and scholars, but find an impersonal multiversity. And they denounce the university's relationship to the war and to discriminatory racial practices.

Behind the student protest on these issues and the crisis of violence to which they have contributed lies the more basic crisis of understanding.

Americans have never shared a single culture, a single philosophy, or a single religion. But in most periods in our history, we have shared many common values, common sympathies, and a common dedication to a system of government which protects our diversity.

We are now in grave danger of losing what is common among us through growing intolerance of opposing views on issues and of diversity itself.

A "new" culture is emerging primarily among students. Membership is often manifested by differences in dress and life style. Most of its members have high ideals and great fears. They stress the need for humanity, equality, and the sacredness of life. They fear that nuclear war will make them the last generation in history. They see their elders as entrapped by materialism and competition, and as prisoners of outdated social forms. They believe their own country has lost its sense of human purpose. They see the Indochina war as an onslaught by a technological giant upon the peasant people of a small, harmless, and backward nation. The war is seen as draining resources from the urgent needs of social and racial justice. They argue that we are the first nation with sufficient resources to create not only decent lives for some, but a decent society for all, and that we are failing to do so. They feel they must remake America in its own image.

But among the members of this new student culture, there is a growing lack of tolerance, a growing insistence that their own views must govern, an impatience with the slow procedures of liberal democracy, a growing denial of the humanity and goodwill of those who urge patience and restraint, and particularly of those whose duty it is to enforce the law. A small number of students have turned to violence; an increasing number, not terrorists themselves, would not turn even arsonists and bombers over to law enforcement officials.

At the same time, many Americans have reacted to this emerging culture with an intolerance of their own. They reject not only that which is impatient, unrestrained, and intolerant in the new culture of the young, but even that which is good. Worse, they reject the individual members of the student culture themselves. Distinctive dress alone is enough to draw insult and abuse. Increasing numbers of citizens believe that students who dissent or protest—even those who protest peacefully—deserve to be treated harshly. Some even say that when dissenters are killed, they have brought death upon themselves. Less and less do students and the larger community seek to understand or respect the viewpoint and motivations of the other.

If this trend continues, if this crisis of understanding endures, the very survival of the nation will be threatened. A nation driven to use the weapons of war upon its youth is a nation on the edge of chaos. A nation that has lost the allegiance of part of its youth is a nation that has lost part of its future. A nation whose young have become intolerant of diversity, intolerant of the rest of its citizenry, and intolerant of all traditional values simply because they are traditional has no generation worthy or capable of assuming leadership in the years to come.

*　　*　　*　　*　　*

We urgently call for reconciliation. Tolerance and understanding on all sides must reemerge from the fundamental decency of Americans, from our shared aspirations as Americans, from our traditional tolerance of diversity, and from our common humanity. We must regain our compassion for one another and our mutual respect.

There is a deep continuity between all Americans, young and old, a continuity that is being obscured in our growing polarization. Most dissenting youth are striving toward the ultimate values and dreams of their elders and their forefathers. In all Americans there has always been latent respect for the idealism of the young. The whole object of a free government is to allow the nation to redefine its purposes in the light of new needs without sacrificing the accumulated wisdom of its living traditions. We cannot do this without each other.

Despite the differences among us, powerful values and sympathies unite us. The very motto of our nation calls for both unity and diversity: from many, one. Out of our divisions, we must now recreate understanding and respect for those different from ourselves.

Violence must end.

Understanding must be renewed.

All Americans must come to see each other not as symbols or stereotypes but as human beings.

Reconciliation must begin.

We share the impatience of those who call for change.

We believe there is still time and opportunity to achieve change. We believe we can still fulfill our shared national commitment to peace, justice, decency, equality and the celebration of human life.

We must start. All of us.

Our recommendations are directed toward this end.

### Recommendations

Far more important than the particular recommendations of this Commission are the underlying themes that are common to all:

¶Most student protesters are neither violent nor extremist. But a small minority of politically extreme students and faculty members and a small group of dedicated agitators are bent on destruction of the university through violence in order to gain their own political ends. Perpetrators of violence must be identified, removed from the university as swiftly as possible, and prosecuted vigorously by the appropriate agencies of law enforcement.

¶Dissent and peaceful protest are a valued part of this nation's way of governing itself. Violence and disorder are the antithesis of democratic processes and cannot be tolerated either on the nation's campuses or anywhere else.

¶The roots of student activism lie in unresolved conflicts in our national life, but the many defects of the universities have also fueled campus unrest.

Universities have not adequately prepared themselves to respond to disruption. They have been without suitable plans, rules, or sanctions. Some administrators and faculty members have responded irresolutely. Frequently, announced sanctions have not been applied. Even more frequently, the lack of appropriate organization within the university has rendered its response ineffective. The university's own house must be placed in order.

¶Too many students have acted irresponsibly and even dangerously in pursuing their stated goals and expressing their dissent. Too many law enforcement officers have responded with unwarranted harshness and force in seeking to control disorder.

¶Action—inactions—of government at all levels have contributed to campus unrest. The words of some political leaders have helped to inflame it. Law enforcement officers have too often reacted ineptly or overreacted. At times, their response has degenerated into uncontrolled violence.

¶The nation has been slow to resolve the issues of war and race, which exacerbate divisions within American society and which have contributed to the escalation of student protest and disorder.

¶All of us must act to prevent violence, to create understanding, and to reduce the bitterness and hostility that divide both the campus and the country. We must establish respect for the processes of law and tolerance for the exercise of dissent on our campus and in the nation.

We advance our recommendations not as cure-alls but as rational and responsive steps that should be taken. We summarize here our major recommendations, addressed to those who have the power to carry them out.


### For the President

We urge that the President exercise his reconciling moral leadership as the first step to prevent violence and create understanding. It is imperative that the President bring us together before more lives are lost and more property destroyed and more universities disrupted.

We recommend that the President seek to convince public officials and protesters alike that divisive and insulting rhetoric is dangerous. In the current political campaign and throughout the years ahead, the President should insist that no one play irresponsible politics with the issue of "campus unrest."

We recommend that the President take the lead in explaining to the American people the underlying causes of campus unrest and the urgency of our present situation. We recommend that he articulate and emphasize those values all Americans hold in common. At the same time we urge him to point out the importance of diversity and coexistence to the nation's health.

To this end, nothing is more important than an end to the war in Indochina. Disaffected students see the war as a symbol of moral crisis in the nation which, in their eyes, deprives even law of its legitimacy. Their dramatic reaction to the Cambodian invasion was a measure of the intensity of their moral recoil.

We urge the President to renew the national commitment to full social justice, and to be aware of increasing charges of repression. We recommend that he take steps to see to it that the words and deeds of Government do not encourage belief in those charges.

We recommend that the President lend his personal support and assistance to American universities to accomplish the changes and reforms suggested in this report.

We recommend that the President take steps to assure that he is continuously informed of the views of students and Blacks, important constituencies in this nation.

We recommend that the President call a series of national meetings designed to foster understanding among those who are now divided. He should meet with the governors of the states, with university leaders, with law enforcement officers, and with black and student leaders. Each participant in these meetings should be urged to bring with him practical suggestions for restoring trust and responsibility among those whom he represents, and commit himself to continue this process of national reconciliation in frequent meetings throughout the school year.

### For Government

We strongly urge public officials at all levels of government to recognize that their public statements can either heal or divide. Harsh and bitter rhetoric can set citizen against citizen, exacerbate tension and encourage violence. Just as the President must offer reconciling leadership to reunite the nation, so all government officials—at all levels—must work to bring our hostile factions together.

Like the President, the governors of the states should hold meetings and develop contacts throughout the school year to further the cause of reconciliation. Like the President, other federal, state and local officials must be sensitive to the charge of repression and fashion their words and deeds in a manner designed to refute it.

We urge state and local officials to make plans for handling campus disorders in full cooperation with one another and with the universities. We urge the states to establish guidelines setting forth more precisely the circumstances that justify ordering the Guard to intervene in a campus disorder.

We recommend that the federal government review all its current policies affecting students and universities to assure that neither the policies nor administration of them threatens the independence or quality of American higher education. At the same time government should increase its financial support of higher education.

We urge public officials to reject demands that entire universities be punished because of the ideas or excesses of some members and to honor their responsibility to help preserve academic freedom.

We recommend that the Department of Defense establish alternatives to ROTC so that officer education is available to students whose universities choose to terminate on-campus ROTC programs.

We recommend greatly increased financial aid for Black colleges and universities. All agencies of government that support such institutions should massively increase their grants to enable these colleges to overcome past shortcomings.

We support the continuing efforts of formerly all-white universities to recruit Black, Mexican-American, Puerto Rican, and other minority students, and we urge that adequate government-sponsored student aid be made available to them. We recommend that in the process of becoming more representative of the society at large, universities make the adjustments necessary to permit those from minority backgrounds to take maximum advantage of their university experience.

Bombing and arson pose an increasing threat to lives and property on campus. We urge prompt enactment of strict controls over the sale, transfer and possession of explosive materials. Such statutes are needed at both the Federal and state levels.

### For Law Enforcement

We have deep sympathy for peace officers—local and state police, National Guardsmen, and campus security officers—who must deal with all types of campus disorder. Much depends on their judgment, courage and professionalism.

We commend those thousands of law enforcement officers who have endured taunts and assaults without reacting violently and whose careful conduct has prevented violence and saved lives.

At the same time, we recognize that there have been dangerous and sometimes fatal instances of unnecessary harshness and illegal violence by law enforcement officers.

We therefore urge that peace officers be trained and equipped to deal with campus disorders firmly, justly, and humanely. They must avoid both uncontrolled and excessive response.

Too frequently, local police forces have been undermanned, improperly equipped, poorly trained, and unprepared for campus disturbances. We therefore urge police forces, especially those in smaller communities, to improve their capacity to respond to civil disorders.

We recommend the development of joint contingency plans among law enforcement agencies. They should specify which law enforcement official is to be in command when several forces are operating together.

Sending civil authorities to a college campus armed as if for war—armed only to kill—has brought tragedy in the past. If this practice is not changed, tragedy will come again. Shoulder weapons (except for tear gas launchers) are very rarely needed on the college campus; they should not be used except as emergency equipment in the face of sniper fire or armed resistance.

We recommend that National Guardsmen receive much more training in controlling civil disturbances. During the last three years, the Guard has played almost no role in Southeast Asia but has been called to intervene in civil disorders at home more than 200 times.

We urge that the National Guard be issued special protection equipment appropriate for use in controlling civil disorders. We urge that it have sufficient tactical capability and nonlethal weaponry so that it will use deadly force only as the absolute last resort.

*For the University*

Every university must improve its capability for responding effectively to disorder. Students, faculty, and trustees must support these efforts. Universities must pull themselves together.

The university should be an open forum where speakers of every point of view can be heard. The area of permitted speech and conduct should be at least as broad as that protected by the First Amendment.

The university should promulgate a code making clear the limits of permissible conduct and announce in advance what measures it is willing to employ in response to impermissible conduct. It should strengthen its disciplinary process. It should assess the capabilities of its security force and determine what role, if any, that force should play in responding to disorder.

When criminal violence occurs on the campus, university officials should promptly call for the assistance of law enforcement agencies.

When faced with disruptive but nonviolent conduct, the university should be prepared to respond initially with internal measures. It must clearly understand the options available to it and be prepared to move from one to another if it is reasonably obvious that an earlier tactic has failed.

Faculty members who engage in or lead disruptive conduct have no place in the university community.

The university, and particularly the faculty, must recognize that the expansion of higher education and the emergence of the new youth culture have changed the makeup and concerns of today's student population. The university should adapt itself to these new conditions. We urge that the university make its teaching programs, degree structure, and transfer and leave policies more flexible and more varied in order to enhance the quality and voluntariness of university study.

We call upon all members of the university to reaffirm that the proper functions of the university are teaching and learning, research and scholarship. An academic community best serves itself, the country, and every principle to which it is devoted by concentrating on these tasks.

Academic institutions must be free—from outside interference, and free from internal intimidation. Far too many people who should know better—both within university communities and outside them—have forgotten this first principle of academic freedom. The pursuit of knowledge cannot continue without the free exchange of ideas.

Obviously, all members of the academic community, as individuals, should be free to participate actively in whatever campaigns or causes they choose. But universities as institutions must remain politically neutral except in those rare cases in which their own integrity, educational purpose, or preservation are at stake.

One of the most valid criticisms of many universities is that their faculties have become so involved in outside research that their commitment to teaching seems compromised. We urge universities and faculty members to reduce their outside service commitments. We recognize that alternative sources of university funding will have to be developed to take the place of the money attached to these outside commitments. Realistically, this will mean more unrestricted government aid to higher education.

Large universities should take steps to decentralize or reorganize to make possible a more human scale.

University governance systems should be reformed to increase participation of students and faculty in the formulation of university policies that affect them. But universities cannot be run on a one-man, one-vote basis with participation of all members on all issues.

Universities must become true communities whose members share a sense of respect, tolerance, and responsibility for one another.

### For Students

Students must accept the responsibility of presenting their ideas in a reasonable and persuasive manner. They must recognize that they are citizens of a nation which was founded on tolerance and diversity, and they must become more understanding of those with whom they differ.

Students must protect the right of all speakers to be heard even when they disagree with the point of view expressed. Heckling speakers is not only bad manners but is inimical to all the values that a university stands for.

Students must face the fact that giving moral support to those who are planning violent action is morally despicable.

Students should be reminded that language that offends will seldom persuade. Their words have sometimes been as offensive to many Americans as the words of some public officials have been to them.

Students should not expect their own views, even if held with great moral intensity, automatically and immediately to determine national policy. The rhetorical commitment to democracy by students must be matched by an awareness of the central role of majority rule in a democratic society and by an equal commitment to techniques of persuasion within the political process.

The Commission has been impressed and moved by the idealism and commitment of American youth. But this extraordinary commitment brings with it extraordinary obligations: to learn from our nation's past experience, to recognize the humanity of those with whom they disagree, and to maintain their respect for the rule of law. The fight for change and justice is the good fight; to drop out or strike out at the first sign of failure is to insure that change will never come.

This Commission is only too aware of America's shortcomings. Yet we are also a nation of enduring strength. Millions of Americans—generations past and present—have given their vision, their energy, and their patient labor to make us a more just nation and a more humane people. We who seek to change America today build on their accomplishments and enjoy the freedoms they won for us. It is a considerable inheritance; we must not squander or destroy it.

# Author Biographies

RENATA ADLER (1938–) was born in Milan, Italy, and educated at Bryn Mawr college, Harvard University, and the Sorbonne. She has been a writer for the *New Yorker* magazine since 1962 and film critic for the *New York Times*. "Radicalism and the Skipped Generation" is the preface from *Towards a Radical Middle,* a collection of essays and film reviews.

HORATIO ALGER, JR. (1834–1899), after a strict childhood and a brief career as a minister, became the most famous author of his time. He wrote about 130 novels for boys, in series of eight or ten novels, all of which expressed themes similar to those in the story presented in this book.

SHERWOOD ANDERSON (1876–1941) grew up in Ohio, became well known as an author with his third book, *Winesburg, Ohio,* published in 1919. Numerous volumes of short stories followed. His best novels are *Poor White* (1920) and *Dark Laughter* (1924); he also published an autobiographical narrative, *A Short Story Teller's Story* (1924).

MILLEN BRAND (1906–) grew up on a farm, attended Columbia University, worked for the New York telephone company for eight years until publication of *The Outward Room,* a novel, in 1937. Most of his works concern working people.

ELBRIDGE STREETER BROOKS (1846–1902) worked for publishing houses, newspapers, and juvenile magazines, and wrote over forty books, all of them historical or biographical, for young people.

MINNIJEAN BROWN was sixteen when the incident she writes about took place in 1957; subsequently she accepted a scholarship offer from the New Lincoln School, an integrated, private institution in New York City.

JOHN J. CLAYTON teaches contemporary literature and creative writing at the University of Massachusetts. He has written a critical book, *Saul Bellow: In Defense of Man.* A companion story to "I Am Staying Where I Am" appeared in the summer 1969 issue of the *Massachusetts Review*.

PETER COLLIER is one of the editors of *Ramparts* magazine.

FREDERICK DOUGLASS (1817–1895), born a slave, was the son of a slave, escaped to New York in 1838, worked for the Massachusetts Anti-Slavery Society, and was widely known as an orator active in the anti-slavery and woman's suffrage movements. His works include his autobiography, *The Narrative of the Life of Frederick Douglass: An American Slave* (1845), *My Bondage and My Freedom* (1855), and *Life and Times of Frederick Douglass* (1881).

JOHN FANTE (1911–) was born in Denver, came to California in 1930, wrote for *American Mercury, Atlantic Monthly,* published two novels, a collection of short stories, and has worked in motion pictures.

JAMES THOMAS FARRELL (1904–) was born and educated in Chicago, received a Guggenheim fellowship for creative writing in 1936, has written many short stories and novels; *Studs Lonigan* (1932–1935) is his most famous work.

FRANCIS SCOTT KEY FITZGERALD (1896–1940) came from a middle-class family in St. Paul, Minnesota, left Princeton University to join the army, in New York sold stories to *Smart Set,* and became the representative novelist of the "jazz age" with *This Side of Paradise* (1920) and *The Great Gatsby* (1925). He wrote numerous short stories and one unsuccessful play.

BENJAMIN FRANKLIN (1706–1790) was a printer, the author of *Poor Richard's Almanack* (1732), the founder of hospitals, libraries, educational institutions, and fire companies, an inventor and a scientist, a diplomat in London and Paris, and one of the framers of the Declaration of Independence.

CLAUDE M. FUESS was headmaster of Andover Academy for forty years. He has written biographies of Daniel Webster and Calvin Coolidge; "The Schoolboy's Code" is from his autobiography *Independent Schoolmaster.*

JIM GARDINER was a thirteen-year-old sophomore at New York City's Bronx High School of Science when his article was published in 1970. He has been active in political demonstrations since he was eight.

RALPH J. GLEASON (1917–) has been the jazz and popular music critic for the *San Francisco Chronicle* since 1950 and now has a daily column. He has written extensively and lectured widely on both jazz and rock music.

PAUL GOODMAN (1911–) has taught in many colleges and universities, and practiced as a lay psychotherapist; he has written numerous works of poetry, drama, and fiction (both short stories and novels), as well as essays on art, society, and education. "Patriotism" is from *Growing Up Absurd* (1960).

BEATRICE GRIFFITH received a Literary Fellowship Award for *American Me,* published in 1948. She has worked for the State Relief Administration and the National Youth Administration.

WILFRED CHARLES HEINZ (1915–) has written numerous books, articles, and short stories about sports.

M. CARL HOLMAN (1919–), born in Mississippi, is a black poet and writer. He has worked as Information Officer for the U.S. Commission on Civil Rights.

JOHN CLELLON HOLMES (1926–) has published poetry, numerous articles on the beat generation, and three novels: *Go* (1952), *The Horn* (1958), and *Get Home Free* (1964).

ALFRED KAZIN (1915–) has been an editor for *New Republic* and *Fortune.* He has taught at C.C.N.Y., Smith College, Amherst College, and Princeton, and is presently teaching at the State University of New York at Stony Brook. He has written numerous studies about American authors.

WILLIAM MELVIN KELLEY (1938–) grew up in New York City, attended Fieldston School and Harvard University, has written essays, short stories, and two novels—*A Different Drummer,* which won the Rosenthal Foundation Award in 1963, and *Dunfords Travels Everywheres.*

JOHN FITZGERALD KENNEDY (1917–1963) served in Congress as representative and senator from Massachusetts before becoming President of the United States in 1960.

RUSSELL AMOS KIRK (1918–) is an author and lecturer on conservative thought, educational theory, and literary topics. He has written numerous books, including *The Conservative Mind* (1953) and *A Program for Conservatives* (1954), and more than 400 essays and stories.

EMMA LAZARUS (1849–1887) wrote eight books of poetry, verse drama, and translations—including one volume of poems written when she was fourteen to sixteen years old.

JACK LONDON (1876–1916) grew up in poverty, left home at fifteen to become a tramp, went to the Klondike when gold was discovered in 1896, and wrote fifty books of fiction, both novels and short stories, many based on his experiences in Alaska.

MALCOLM X (1925–1965), born Malcolm Little, took the name Al Hajj Malik Shabazz when he joined the Black Muslims; he formed his own Organization for Afro-American Unity after he resigned from the Muslims in 1964; he was shot at a rally in New York City on February 21, 1965. His autobiography, published in 1964, was a best seller.

ROCKY MARCIANO (1924–1969) became world heavyweight boxing champion in September 1952 by defeating Jersey Joe Walcott; he retired undefeated. He died in a plane crash in the summer of 1969.

CAREY MC WILLIAMS (1905–) was a lawyer before becoming an editor of *The Nation;* he has written works about farm workers, prejudice, immigrants, and California.

JOHN ROBERT MOSKIN (1923–) has been a newspaper reporter and an editor for *Woman's Home Companion, Collier's,* and *Look;* he has written several books as well as articles for national magazines.

AMADO MURO was born in Mexico, now lives and works in El Paso; his stories have appeared in *Arizona Quarterly* and *New Mexico Quarterly*.

JAY NEUGEBOREN (1938–) has contributed articles and short stories to *New Republic, Commonweal, Commentary,* and *Transatlantic Review;* his novel *Big Man* was published in 1966.

FLANNERY O'CONNOR (1924–1964) won numerous awards for her writing, which included two novels, *Wise Blood* (1952) and *The Violent Bear It Away* (1960), and two collections of stories, *A Good Man Is Hard to Find* (1955) and *Everything That Rises Must Converge* (1965).

CONNELL PERSICO was twenty-two, a senior majoring in political science at San Francisco State College, when he wrote his article. He plans to become a writer and a college professor.

NORMAN PODHORETZ (1930–) is editor of *Commentary* and a contributor to *Commentary, Partisan Review, New Yorker, Show, Esquire, Harper's* and *New Republic*.

PRESIDENT'S COMMISSION ON CAMPUS UNREST, reporting September 26, 1970: William W. Scranton, chairman, 52, former Governor of Pennsylvania; James Ahern, 38, police chief of New Haven; Erwin D. Canham, 66, editor in chief,

*Christian Science Monitor;* James E. Cheek, 37, president of Howard University; Benjamin O. Davis, 57, Director of Civil Aviation Security, Department of Transportation; Martha A. Derthick, associate professor of political science, Boston College; Bayles Maning, 47, dean of Stanford Law School; Revius O. Ortique, Jr., 46, a New Orleans lawyer; Joseph Rhodes, Jr., 22, a Junior Fellow at Harvard University.

BARRY N. SCHWARTZ is an instructor in humanities at Pratt Institute, Brooklyn, New York, where he also lectures in the Art School and the Social Science Department. He has worked as an educational consultant, conducted a radio program, edited the magazine *Readers and Writers,* and written poetry and books on psychedelic art and white racism.

JEAN SHEPHERD (1921–) grew up in Chicago's South Side; in 1942 he went into the Army Signal Corps and became involved with radio. Since 1956 he has had a late night show on WOR radio in New York City, composed largely of his reminiscences of boyhood and Army experiences. His stories and articles have appeared in *Esquire* and *Playboy.*

HENRY A. SHUTE (1856–1943), a judge in Exeter, New Hampshire, for forty-three years, found the diary of his childhood days in Exeter while rummaging in his father's house in the winter of 1901–1902.

LEO SKIR (1932–) was born in Brooklyn and received degrees from Columbia University and New York University. "Other Chanukahs" is part of a novel, *Boychick.*

JEAN SMITH worked for SNCC after graduating Phi Beta Kappa from Howard University. Subsequently she and her husband set up a foundation to aid black families in the Mississippi delta area.

HARVEY SWADOS (1920–) has taught writing at the State University of Iowa, New York University, and San Francisco State College. He has published novels, three collections of short stories, and a collection of essays, and has won many awards for his work. His most recent novel is *Standing Fast.*

GENEVIEVE TAGGARD (1894–1948) worked in publishing and editing; taught at Mt. Holyoke College, Bennington College, and Sarah Lawrence College; and has written stories, articles, and book reviews as well as poetry.

PIRI THOMAS (1928–) is presently a staff associate at the Center for Urban Education. The selection included is from *Down These Mean Streets,* about his childhood in Manhattan.

RODERICK THORP, along with Robert Blake, edited *The Music of Their Laughter: An American Album,* published in 1970.

BOOKER TALIAFERRO WASHINGTON (1859–1915) was educated at the Hampton Institute of Virginia, was a teacher there, then head of Tuskegee Institute. He wrote extensively and traveled widely to speak about racial and educational subjects.

MALCOLM WOOD (1924–) was born in Denver, has degrees from Harvard University and the University of California. He teaches humanities at the California College of Arts and Crafts in Oakland. His short stories have been published in many magazines.

# Alternate Contents

The selections in *Growing Up American* are intended to be read for their individual merit as well as for their contribution to the major theme of the book. In choosing material we were also concerned that a variety of attitudes, forms, styles, and manners of presentation were represented, so that the anthology would be useful as an aid to beginning writers and critics and as a text for students of American culture. To these ends we suggest the following approaches to the material, in addition to the basically chronological organization of the Contents. Our selection of topics and illustrative examples is merely suggestive and not meant to be exhaustive. Selections are referred to by author, within each section of the Contents.

I. Organization by Theme

    A. Stages of Growing Up

        1. *Childhood.* Part I: Elbridge S. Brooks; Part II: Jacob Riis.

        2. *Adolescence.* Part I: Boy Scout Oath, Boy Scout Law, Benjamin Franklin, Booker T. Washington, Henry A. Shute, Horatio Alger, Jr., Alfred Kazin; Part II: Frederick Douglass, Millen Brand, Jean Shepherd, Sherwood Anderson, Norman Podhoretz, John Fante.

        3. *Teen-age.* Part II: Malcolm X, M. Carl Holman, Jack London, Amado Muro, Beatrice Griffith, James T. Farrell; Part III: Jay Neugeboren, Harvey Swados, Minnijean Brown, Piri Thomas; Part IV: Roderick Thorp.

        4. *College and After.* Part II: F. Scott Fitzgerald, Rocky Marciano, Bill Libby; Part III: ". . . So Here I Am," Leo Skir, Malcolm Wood, William Melvin Kelley; Part IV: Flannery O'Connor, Peter Collier, Connell Persico, John J. Clayton, Russell A. Kirk, "To the American People."

    B. Attitudes and Ideals

        1. *Morality and Moral Choice.* Part I: Boy Scout Oath, Boy Scout Law, Elbridge S. Brooks, Benjamin Franklin, Booker T. Washington, Horatio Alger, Jr., Claude M. Fuess; Part II: Millen Brand; Part III: Jay Neugeboren, "So Here I Am," John Clellon Holmes, Paul Goodman; Part IV: Roderick Thorp, Ralph J. Gleason, Connell Persico.

        2. *Work and the Work Ethic.* Part I: Benjamin Franklin, Booker T. Washington; Part II: Sherwood Anderson, Malcolm X, Jack London, F. Scott Fitzgerald, James T. Farrell, Debbie D'Amico; Part III: Harvey Swados, "So Here I Am"; Part IV: Barry N. Schwartz.

3. *War and Militancy,*   Part II: Carey McWilliams, Bill Libby; Part III: Renata Adler; Part IV: Jim Gardiner, Connell Persico, John J. Clayton, Russell A. Kirk, "To the American People."

4. *The Hero*

   a. *American Manhood.*   Part I: Boy Scout Oath, Boy Scout Law, Elbridge S. Brooks, Horatio Alger, Jr.; Part II: Jack London, James T. Farrell, Rocky Marciano, Bill Libby; Part III: Jay Neugeboren, Piri Thomas, Harvey Swados; Part IV: John J. Clayton.

   b. *American Womanhood.*   Part II: Amado Muro, F. Scott Fitzgerald, Debbie D'Amico.

5. *Culture and History.*   Part I: Alfred Kazin, John F. Kennedy; Part II: M. Carl Holman, Debbie D'Amico; Part III: Malcolm Wood, William Melvin Kelley, Renata Adler; Part IV: Ralph J. Gleason, Russell A. Kirk.

C.  Relationships and Conflicts

   1. *Child and Peers*

      a. *Innocence.*   Part I: Henry A. Shute; Part II: Jean Shepherd; Part III: Harvey Swados.

      b. *Racial Awareness.*   Part II: Norman Podhoretz, Amado Muro, Beatrice Griffith, John Fante; Part III: Minnijean Brown.

      c. *Gangs.*   Part I: Henry Shute; Part III: Piri Thomas.

      d. *Acceptance.*   Part II: Norman Podhoretz, Malcolm X, M. Carl Holman, Amado Muro, Beatrice Griffith, John Fante, Debbie D'Amico; Part III: Minnijean Brown, William Melvin Kelley.

   2. *Child and the Family.*   Part II: Millen Brand, Sherwood Anderson; Part III. "So Here I Am," Malcolm Wood, Leo Skir; Part IV: Roderick Thorp, Flannery O'Connor.

   3. *Child and Education*

      a. *Self-Education.*   Part I: Benjamin Franklin; Part II: Frederick Douglass.

      b. *Institutional Education.*   Part I: Booker T. Washington, Alfred Kazin, Claude M. Fuess; Part II: Malcolm X, M. Carl Holman; Part III: Jay Neugeboren, Minnijean Brown, William Melvin Kelley.

   4. *Child and Society*

      a. *The Neighborhood.*   Part I: Alfred Kazin; Part II: Norman Podhoretz; Part III: Piri Thomas; Part IV: Roderick Thorp.

      b. *The World Outside.*   Part II: Jacob Riis; Part III: Harvey Swados; Part IV: Ralph J. Gleason, Peter Collier, Barry N. Schwartz.

      c. *Political Commitment.*   Part II: Debbie D'Amico; Part III: Paul Goodman; Part IV: Ralph J. Gleason, Jim Gardiner, Connell Persico, John J. Clayton, Russell A. Kirk, "To the American People."

II.  Organization by Geographical Divisions

A.  *The South.*  Part I: Booker T. Washington. Part II: Frederick Douglass; Part III: Minnijean Brown; Part IV: Flannery O'Connor.

B.  *The Urban East.*  Part I: Alfred Kazin; Part II: Jacob Riis, Millen Brand, Norman Podhoretz, Malcolm X; Part III: Jay Neugeboren, Piri Thomas, Leo Skir, William Melvin Kelley; Part IV: Roderick Thorp, Jim Gardiner.

C.  *The Midwest.*  Part II: Jean Shepherd, Sherwood Anderson, M. Carl Holman, F. Scott Fitzgerald, James T. Farrell.

D.  *The West.*  Part II: Amado Muro, Beatrice Griffith, John Fante, Carey McWilliams; Part IV: Ralph J. Gleason, Peter Collier, John J. Clayton.

III.  Organization by Structure and Genre

A.  Subjective Modes

1.  *Autobiographical Diary.*  Part I: Henry A. Shute.

2.  *Autobiographical Journal.*  Part I: Benjamin Franklin.

3.  *Impressionistic Essay.*  Part II: Debbie D'Amico.

4.  *Autobiographical Essay.*  Part I: Alfred Kazin, Booker T. Washington, Claude M. Fuess; Part II: Frederick Douglass, Norman Podhoretz, Malcolm X, M. Carl Holman, Jack London, John Fante, Rocky Marciano; Part III: Minnijean Brown, Piri Thomas, "So Here I Am," William Melvin Kelley; Part IV: Jim Gardiner, Connell Persico.

5.  *Autobiographical Fiction.*  Part II: Jean Shepherd; Part III: Leo Skir.

B.  Objective Modes

1.  *Interview.*  Part IV: Roderick Thorp.

2.  *Portrait.*  Part II: Bill Libby; Part IV: Peter Collier.

3.  *Analytical Essay.*  Part III: Paul Goodman, Renata Adler; Part IV: Barry N. Schwartz, Russell A. Kirk.

4.  *Report.*  Part IV: "To the American People."

5.  *Formal Document or Address.*  Part I: Declaration of Independence, John F. Kennedy.

6.  *Fiction.*  Part I: Horatio Alger, Jr.; Part II: Millen Brand, Sherwood Anderson, Amado Muro, Beatrice Griffith, F. Scott Fitzgerald, James T. Farrell; Part III: Jay Neugeboren, Harvey Swados, Malcolm Wood; Part IV: Flannery O'Connor, John J. Clayton.

IV.  Organization by Rhetorical Principles

A.  *Exposition*

1.  *Identification.*  Part I: Benjamin Franklin.

2.  *Definition.*  Part II: Rocky Marciano; Part III: William Melvin Kelley, John Clellon Holmes, Paul Goodman, Renata Adler.

3.  *Classification.*  Part IV: Connell Persico.

4.  *Illustration.*  Part I: Alfred Kazin; Part II: Jacob Riis; Part IV: Russell A. Kirk.